A HISTORY OF THE ENGLISH PEOPLE
IN THE NINETEENTH CENTURY

A HISTORY OF THE ENGLISH PEOPLE IN THE NINETEENTH CENTURY

A HISTORY OF THE ENGLISH PEOPLE
IN THE NINETEENTH CENTURY — IV

VICTORIAN YEARS

1841—1895

by

ELIE HALEVY

With a Supplementary Section by
R. B. McCALLUM

Incorporating 'The Age of Peel and Cobden'
Translated from the French by
E. I. WATKIN

LONDON · ERNEST BENN LIMITED
NEW YORK · BARNES & NOBLE INC.

The Age of Peel and Cobden
first published in French 1946
first published in English 1948
by Ernest Benn Limited
Bouverie House, Fleet Street, London, EC4
and Barnes & Noble Inc.
105 *Fifth Avenue, New York,* 10003

Victorian Years
first published 1951
second impression 1962
first Paperback Edition 1961
third impression 1970

© *Ernest Benn Limited* 1962
Printed in Great Britain
510–27061–1
Paperback 510–27071–9

Publisher's Foreword

ELIE HALEVY did not write his History of the English People in the Nineteenth Century in chronological sequence nor did he live to complete it. Having dealt with the period from 1815 to 1841 in three volumes, he turned to his epilogue, covering in two further books the years from 1895 to 1915.

In what proved to be his last work, *The Age of Peel and Cobden* (published posthumously in French in 1946, in English in 1948), Halévy had begun to bridge the gap; and his English publishers, in presenting a new edition of the entire history, invited Mr. R. B. McCallum to contribute a supplementary essay to link this volume with the concluding ones.

The present book, therefore, contains in Part I a reprint of *The Age of Peel and Cobden* and in Part II Mr. R. B. McCallum's essay and chronological table, the whole appearing under the title *Victorian Years, 1841-1895.*

Contents

PART I
THE AGE OF PEEL AND COBDEN
(1841—1852)

Editor's Preface

MONSIEUR HALEVY'S French friends entrusted me with the task of assisting Madame Halévy to prepare Part I of the present volume for publication. My master and friend, who visited London every year to work, was unable to finish it. But these new chapters of his monumental History, a work of such great and permanent value to historians, could not be left unpublished. In the execution of my work I asked and received the generous help of many of M. Halévy's English friends, Dr. Gooch, Dr. and Mrs. Hammond, Professor Barker, Mr. H. L. Beales, and Professor Power, who kindly read the manuscript in its entirety or in part, and gladly gave me the benefit of their advice.

M. Halévy had completed the first and third chapters. The second was still unwritten, no doubt because he had not finished his study of Peel's financial policy. For chapters four, five, and six there was only a preliminary draft; nevertheless in my opinion his work had been carried far enough to make publication possible and desirable. Moreover, the text was accompanied by notes and detailed plans. When the latter made clear beyond possible doubt the order and the main lines of the treatment he had in mind, it seemed advisable to compose a summary statement of what he would have said, every care being taken not to introduce any opinion not sanctioned by something he had left in writing. To distinguish these passages from M. Halévy's manuscript, they are indented in the present volume. These additions will be found chiefly in chapter six.

I have not dealt with Foreign Policy after 1848 for the notes on that subject were not sufficiently detailed, but to relate the economic and domestic policy of England during the same period I have attempted to link up the fragments M. Halévy had left. Not only was this linking up indispensable to render his account intelligible; it was clear that M. Halévy attached great importance to carrying his narrative down to 1852, to the return of the Peelites to office, with which he intended to conclude the volume. It was also necessary if the significance of the picture of England which follows was to be fully grasped. This picture forms chapter seven of the present volume.

3

M. Halévy's original intention had been to choose the year 1860 for his picture. For the works of the writers most representative of British thought at that epoch had been published around that year. But he finally decided to choose an earlier date, for the revolution effected by the adoption of free trade might be considered as complete by 1852. The picture was to have consisted of three parts devoted respectively to the growth of the national wealth, the social classes, and the state of religion. Of these M. Halévy was able to write only the third, which he regarded as the most important. When read in connection with the sections of the preceding book which treat of political economy, it makes clear his view of the problem which interested him more than any other, the relative importance of the parts played by material and spiritual forces in shaping British society. He left only a few notes giving his sources, but it was possible to discover most of these from his papers and thus to complete the documentation of this volume in correspondence with that of previous volumes.

. . . It is fortunate that he decided to publish in advance Volumes V and VI in which he tells how the nineteenth century on its death-bed witnessed the Imperialists in power and prepared the future triumph of democracy. He had related the close of the Victorian era and thus given his work its final conclusion. But the present volume, the story of the years when that era reached its zenith, covers a decisive period of his great History.

PAUL VAUCHER.

Paris, 1946.

CHAPTER I

Difficult Years (1841–1843)

I THE EARLY DAYS OF PEEL'S ADMINISTRATION

I

WHEN the Whigs resigned office Sir Robert Peel had no difficulty in forming a government. With a few unimportant changes his Cabinet was identical with that of 1834. Since, however, he considered the work of a Prime Minister too important to be combined with that of any other department, he was content with the titular office of First Lord of the Treasury and left the care of the national finances to his subordinate, Goulburn, at the Exchequer. Wellington was replaced at the Foreign Office by Lord Aberdeen and became a minister without portfolio. The Home and the Colonial Offices, which were thus left vacant, were given to two former Whigs; Graham took the Home, Stanley the Colonial Office.

Peel made a gesture to the extreme protectionists of the agricultural interest by giving the Privy Seal to the Duke of Buckingham.[1] The young and ambitious Gladstone became Vice-President of the Board of Trade under the President, Lord Ripon. He consoled himself for his failure to enter the Cabinet—after all he was only thirty-two—by the reflection that since his chief was a peer it was he who would represent his department in the Commons. Though in some quarters surprise was expressed that commerce should be entrusted to the philosopher of High Toryism, a man almost more of a theologian than a politician, events would very soon prove that Sir Robert had not been mistaken when he saw behind the pupil of Oxford the son of a Liverpool merchant. Disraeli would gladly have been invited to join the administration. Indeed, he complained to Peel of his exclusion. But it was intentional and for definite reasons.[2]

[1] *Greville Memoirs*, November 19, 1841. 'If Peel proposed Liberal measures and can prevail on Buckingham to go along with him, his task will be much easier. If he is obstinate, and they turn him out, it will tell well with the country. I never contemplate the other alternative of Peel's succumbing to the Duke of Buckingham and the Corn Law monopolists.'

[2] See in C. S. Parker's *Sir Robert Peel*, vol. ii, p. 486, the correspondence exchanged between Peel and Disraeli. If we can credit W. F. Monypenny (*The Life of Disraeli*, vol. i, pp. 121-2), Peel wanted to give Disraeli a post, but was dissuaded by his friends, and in particular by Lord Stanley. For Gladstone, see F. E. Hyde, *Mr. Gladstone at the Board of Trade*, 1934.

When Parliament reassembled on September 16 the violent debates made it immediately clear that the contest at the polls between the two historic parties was not the key to the political situation. The real struggle throughout the country had been fought by the two powerful groups which by writing in the Press and speaking at public meetings had competed for the favour of the masses, the Chartist Association on the one hand and the Anti-Corn-Law League on the other.

2

During the past year Chartism had recovered from its defeat in 1839. The imprisoned agitators had one after another regained their liberty, and as each emerged from gaol he was greeted by a popular demonstration staged to prove to the nation that the movement had lost nothing of its vigour. Between the opening of the summer of 1840 and the end of the following winter an important achievement had been successfully carried through; the union of all the local groups which hitherto had refused to unite lest they should incur the penalties of the Act of 1799 which made any association of political societies illegal. The National Charter Association of Great Britain evaded the law by setting up a General Council composed of the local officials and the central executive committee. Since it was thus a single body it was not technically an association. The subscriptions, twopence a quarter, paid the salary of the general secretary, two pounds a week, and the other officers, and supported an organized propaganda by paid 'Missionaries'. The foundation of this organization consisted of 'Classes' of ten under the guidance of 'Leaders' appointed by the executive committee. Classes, leaders, and missions were designations borrowed from the Wesleyan body. The programme was the Six Points of the Charter. The weapon which no doubt they already proposed to employ was not violence, but a petition to be presented to the new Parliament which would be returned at the General Election, universally recognized to be imminent. As regards the part they would play in the election the Association, it seems, approved O'Brien's tactics, a revival of those adopted in 1817 and 1819. In each constituency the Chartists would take part in the nomination when candidates were designated by a show of hands. It would be an easy matter in many cases to secure a majority for the Chartist candidate. They would have nothing to do with the remainder of the election, leaving a servile and corrupt electorate to return the candidate of its choice. They would then declare that the sole legitimate representatives of the country were the Chartist candidates originally chosen by a genuine popular majority. The latter would meet and constitute the true Parliament. On the eve of the election, however, Feargus O'Connor, who was still in prison, as was also Bronterre O'Brien, decided in favour of different tactics. He had always hated the Whig aristocracy, and the recent adoption of free trade by Lord Melbourne's Cabinet was not calculated to win his sympathies. He ordered his followers everywhere to vote for the Tory candidate. His order was widely obeyed and explains many victories won by the Tories in popular constituencies. One of the two seats for Knaresborough, which the Whigs regarded as a fief of theirs, was won from them by Busfield Ferrand. For the first time for many years the two West Riding seats went to two Tories. John Stuart Wortley and Edmund Denison defeated the two Whig candidates Lord Morpeth and Lord Milton, who were devoted to the cause of the people and convinced that their popularity with the electors was unshakable. The campaign was fought by Tory and Chartist to the slogan 'No Bastilles', the name given to the workhouses built in accordance with the provisions of the New Poor Law. There were, in fact, few candidates, were they Radicals, Liberals, Whigs or Tories, who did not promise the voters some alleviation of the Poor Law. But it was easier for Tory candidates to denounce a measure which had been the work of a Whig Government and inspired by the Radical Utilitarians, and by so doing win Chartist votes.[1]

The opponents of the Poor Law in the new Parliament claimed the Conservative victory as their own. Ferrand, member for

---

[1] For the attitude of the Chartists, see M. Hovell, *The Chartist Movement*, 1925, pp. 197 sqq. and 237 sqq.; R. C. Gammage, *History of the Chartist Movement*, ed. 1894, pp. 192 sqq.; H. of C., September 27, 1841, C. Wood's speech (*Parliamentary Debates*, 3rd Ser., vol. lix, p. 906): 'It could not be forgotten that the war-cry of one party during the last elections was "No Bastilles".' J. L. and B. Hammond, *Lord Shaftesbury*, ed. 1923, p. 59: 'We have triumphed in the West Riding: this is indeed a marvellous work, and calls aloud for our humblest and heartiest thanks.' Gammage, op. cit., p. 194: 'Harney and Pitkeithly contested at the hustings with Lords Morpeth and Milton the West Riding of Yorkshire, where they carried public opinion in favour of the Charter.' For the election of 1841, see *Quarterly Review*, No. 136, art. viii, 'The Old and New Ministries' (vol. lxviii, p. 494), and *Edinburgh Review*, Oct. 1842 (art. viii, 'The Late Session').

Knaresborough, made a violent attack on the Poor Law and the factory system in general in a speech which was well received and, printed as a pamphlet, circulated widely.[1] The powers conferred on the three Commissioners, which the Parliament of 1840 had refused to renew for more than a year, were on the verge of expiring. There were still districts, Lancashire, for example, where the Poor Law had not been put into operation. The formation of new unions to cover these districts should, many members urged, be forbidden. The Commissioners should no longer be empowered to refuse outdoor relief. An appeal was made to the pity of the House by telling the story of a weaver found dead of hunger at his loom for lack of public assistance. The Government was compelled to promise an inquiry. It was, in fact, in an extremely awkward position. For though Peel and his immediate circle approved the stern provisions of the new law he had, nevertheless, given, if not his explicit approval, at least the consent of silence to the alliance at the polls between the Tories and Chartists. All the new Home Secretary, Sir James Graham, could do was to plead extenuating circumstances in the Commissioners' defence. Since their powers were discretionary they could temper, when they thought fit, the severity of the statute. Many exceptions were, in fact, permitted by the general order prohibiting outdoor relief. And Sir Robert had to be content with asking Parliament to prolong the Commissioners' powers for a further six months. Before that period had elapsed Parliament would meet in the ordinary course, and there would be an opportunity to examine the entire question thoroughly.[2]

3

But though O'Connor's electoral tactics had been accepted by the majority of his supporters, and he might fairly regard the proceedings in Parliament during the extraordinary session of 1841 as their justification, they had by no means secured the unanimous approval of the party. They found an inflexible adversary in O'Brien who was flatly opposed to any coalition whether with the Whigs or the Tories. A certain indecision was manifest in the

---

[1] *The Speech of W. Busfield Ferrand, Esq., in the House of Commons*, Tuesday, September 28, 1841, on 'The New Poor Law'.

[2] H. of C. Speeches by Sir James Graham and S. Wortley, September 27, 1841 (*Parliamentary Debates*, 3rd Ser., vol. lix, pp. 883 sqq.).

Chartist ranks. There were revolts against O'Connor's dictator-ship. William Lovett had worked out in prison a comprehensive plan for reforming the Chartist organization, which he published as soon as he regained his liberty. He proposed to transform the movement into a vast system of democratic and free education supported by voluntary subscriptions. To spread his views he launched a National Association whose founders included out-standing leaders of middle-class Radicalism: Hume, John Stuart Mill, Grote, and Brougham. Henry Vincent, released from prison a little later, combining zeal for social justice with hatred of alcohol, founded a Temperance Chartist Association. In Scotland the Chartists erected Christian Chartist churches where political sermons were preached every Sunday.[1] O'Connor was suspicious of these fantastic developments and denounced what he called Knowledge Chartism, Teetotal Chartism and Christian Chartism. And he was undoubtedly right in seeing in these separatist move-ments evidence of a trend which constituted a more dangerous threat to his authority than O'Brien's intransigent Radicalism, a tendency among the Chartists to join forces with the Radical free traders.[2]

Nothing could be more distasteful to O'Connor, a native of rural Ireland, than this Anglo-Saxon and industrial type of demo-cracy. Nevertheless, during the election he had surrendered to the pressure of the left wing among his followers and advised his friends to vote for the extreme Radical Wakley and the Radical Roebuck.[3]

Brotherton's return for Salford was as significant as Ferrand's for Knaresborough.[4] Employed in a cotton mill from the age of nine, he rose in the social scale until he became a wealthy manu-facturer. He was returned on a programme of a radical reform of the franchise, an amelioration of the Poor Law and free trade.

Results such as these were the fruit of a campaign which dated from the beginning of 1841. To distinguish themselves from the Chartist revolutionaries the Parliamentary Radicals had adopted the programme of household suffrage, by which the vote would

[1] The movement spread later to England. See J. L. and B. Hammond, *The Age of the Chartists* (pp. 251-2).
[2] For these movements, see Julius West, *History of the Chartist Movement*, 1920, pp. 150 sqq., and Gammage, op. cit., p. 196.
[3] R. G. Gammage, *History of the Chartist Movement*, p. 193.
[4] For Brotherton, see *Annual Register*, 1847, p. 115.

9

be given not to all males, but only to those who were directly taxed. A large meeting was held on January 21 in the new factory of the wholesale draper Marshall, under the auspices of the Leeds Reform Association to pass a resolution demanding household suffrage. But the huge hall was invaded by the Chartists, and the committee adopted a resolution couched in vague terms so as to be acceptable to both parties, the advocates of household and of universal suffrage.[1]

It should be possible surely to give a more definite form to the pact of alliance between these two rival groups which had been thus concluded under the pressure of circumstances. To this task a new periodical, *The Nonconformist*, founded at this juncture by Miall, addressed itself, and between October 13 and December 1 published a series of articles demanding under the name of complete suffrage, chosen to avoid the compromising Chartist associations attached to the term universal suffrage, something which bore a close resemblance to the latter from which it differed only by disfranchising those in receipt of poor relief and requiring six months' residence to qualify for a vote. The articles were collected and published in book form with a preface by a wealthy Birmingham Quaker, Joseph Sturge, who became the outstanding figure of this new agitation. The title chosen for the volume was *Reconciliation between the Middle and the Labouring Class*, in other words between the Anti-Corn-Law League and the Chartists.[2]

4

O'Connor viewed with little favour this 'reconciliation' with men for whom he had no liking. But his contribution to the victory of the Tories had not strengthened his hold over the masses, the less indeed since it soon became evident that, even as regards the Poor Law, they would not honour the pledges given during the election to their Chartist allies. He, therefore, accepted

---

[1] *Leeds Mercury*, January 23, 1841. Gammage, op. cit., pp. 190 sqq. He gives the text of the resolution adopted: 'That the great experiment made by means of the Reform Bill to improve the condition of the country hath failed to attain the end desired by the people, and a further reform having therefore become necessary, it is the opinion of this meeting, that the united efforts of all reformers ought to be directed to obtain such a further enlargement of the franchise as should make the interests of the representatives identical with those of the whole country, and by this means secure a just government for all classes of the people.'

[2] *Reconciliation between the Middle and the Labouring Class*, reprinted from *The Nonconformist*, Manchester, 1842.

the reconciliation though never ceasing to protest against it. Richard Cobden, no democrat, had no great affection for a movement which compromised the purity of his economic programme. But he was widely blamed by free traders for having been too conciliatory in accepting, as a provisional measure at least, the Whig proposal of a fixed and moderate tariff. And what had he gained by these tactics? He had not even secured a Whig victory at the polls as O'Connor had obtained a Tory success.[1] Nor could he overlook the fact that nine-tenths of his followers had given their support to Sturge's programme of complete suffrage.[2]

Like O'Connor he protested and acquiesced. He was not, in fact, it would seem, unaware that this fusion between Chartism already past its prime and his own movement in the fullness of youthful vitality was more advantageous to the latter than the former. The fact that he had compromised himself with the Whigs, and was associated with their defeat, does not appear to have been so detrimental to the propaganda of his League as O'Connor's share in the Tory victory had proved damaging to his agitation. For the Whig defeat had been due, not to their partial adoption of free trade, but to the fact that no one took seriously a death-bed conversion, obviously dictated by electioneering motives. The members of the League, who had no respect for these noble Whig politicians, no love for this aristocracy of great landlords, were delighted to have forced upon them this initial capitulation. But it was only in the expectation of a more complete surrender. And in the north, above all in Lancashire, they had secured the return, in face of the opposition of Whigs and Tories alike, of uncompromising leaguers who were not prepared to accept the substitution of a fixed tariff for the sliding scale, but demanded the complete abolition of duties on corn. All the honours of the extraordinary session were won not by the advocates of a reformed franchise,[3] but by Cobden who

[1] See in The Nonconformist, October 6, 1841, the controversy between Cobden and Joseph Sturge. For Cobden's return at Stockport, see Morley, Life of Richard Cobden, p. 22.

[2] Speech delivered on August 1, at a meeting held in London by the Anti-Corn-Law League. (Anti-Bread Tax Circular, August 11, 1842.)

[3] The Radical member, Sharman Crawford, proposed an amendment to the address which declared that the true cause of the people's sufferings was the faulty representation of the masses. He was heard with little attention, and secured only thirty-nine votes. H. of C., August 25, 1841 (Parliamentary Debates, 3rd Ser., vol. lix, pp. 231-3). He returned to the charge on April 21, 1842 (ibid., 3rd Ser., vol. lxii, pp. 909 sqq.), when he

opened his career as a parliamentary orator—and his performance had been awaited with no little curiosity—by three impressive speeches which attracted wide attention. He made the Tories, who wished to shirk the issue, and the Whigs, whom he suspected of the same intention, understand that the conflict between the two parties was a farce in which the country was no longer interested, and that one question overshadowed all others which were raised only to distract public opinion, the question of the Corn Law and the people's food.[1]

At this critical moment it is important not to misconceive the character of the campaign which for the last three years Cobden had been conducting in the country, and which he would now conduct on two fronts, in the House as well as in the country. The League and the Chartist agitation are often contrasted as representing respectively the sober wisdom of the middle classes and the fanaticism of the proletariat. In fact, there was the same fanaticism in both camps. Both agitations appealed to the passions of the populace. In this respect there was nothing to choose between Cobden and his supporters and Oastler, Stephens, and O'Connor. The latter denounced the factory owners, whom they portrayed as murderers who deliberately starved their mill hands. Cobden and his friends used the same language of the landowners. They were a selfish class who, to secure their rents, were bent on destroying the manufactures which were England's legitimate pride and her true wealth, were determined to ruin the manufacturers and reduce the workers to penury. They hoped, in fact, to compel them to emigrate on a large scale, which would amount to deporting them, or return as a body to the land to endure the yoke of a revived feudalism. When O'Connell drew applause at Manchester by declaring that 'the landlords' venison was sweetened with widows' tears and their claret dyed with orphans' blood',[2] the English leaders of the Anti-Corn-Law League could not fairly be held responsible for this Irish extravagance. But Cobden in the Commons denounced the Corn Law as 'a law that had been baptised in blood, begotten in violence and injustice,

pointed out that a hundred and seven members owed their election to the irresistible influence of a patron and two hundred and twenty-six others to the influence of the landed gentry.

[1] H. of C., August 25, September 17 and 24, 1841. Three speeches by Cobden (*Parliamentary Debates*, 3rd Ser., vol. lix, pp. 233, 576, and 791).

[2] The speech is reported by Ferrand in his speech in Parliament on September 23, 1841 (ibid., 3rd Ser., vol. lix, p. 940).

perpetuated at the expense of the tears and groans of the people'.[1] The weekly organ of the League termed the sliding scale a consummate system of legalised theft and murder, and an infernal machine worse than Fieschi's. For the latter had made only fifteen victims, the scale had condemned hundreds of thousands of Englishmen to the slow tortures of famine. And these passionate denunciations of the crimes committed by the enemy were followed by appeals to revolt.

Speaking in the Commons[2] Cobden predicted riots in Manchester during the following winter, and condemned the irresponsibility of men who expected Englishmen to stand by with arms folded while their children died of hunger before their eyes. A speaker on a free trade platform prophesied a revolution in the following summer comparable to the French revolution on those three July days ten years earlier.[3] Another threatened the young Queen with the fate of Louis XVI if, like that monarch, she followed the advice of a selfish class.[4] And the important Liberal organ, the *Morning Chronicle*, welcomed and spread wild rumours. The London office of the League, it was reported, was snowed under with letters whose writers urged that a financial crisis should be produced by withdrawing bank deposits or refusing to pay taxes. In the north leading manufacturers were said to have stated that it was in their power, if they thought fit, to put an end to the Corn Law at one blow. Since the landlords were bent on destroying industry, the owners would anticipate their wishes. They would close all the factories, and thus compel the entire population they maintained to return to the rural parishes from which they had come. The aristocracy would thus be compelled to feed them in the workhouses, because they had so obstinately refused to enable the industrial section of the community to support them.[5]

---

[1] H. of C., September 17, 1841, Cobden's speech (*Parliamentary Debates*, 3rd Ser., vol. lix, p. 582). It was his peroration.

[2] H. of C., September 17, 1841 (ibid., 3rd Ser., vol. lix, p. 581).

[3] *Manchester Guardian*, September 22, 1841, quoted in the *Quarterly Review* for December 1842, vol. lxxi, p. 258.

[4] *Anti-Bread-Tax Circular*, No. 69, August 12, 1841, p. 51.

[5] *Morning Chronicle*, October 20, 1841: 'The business committee of the Metropolitan Anti-Corn-Law Association was literally inundated with letters, some anonymous, others signed, detailing well-arranged and gravely considered plans for bringing on a political crisis. . . . The contemplation of such measures is not confined to the poorer classes.' The last-mentioned plan of campaign had been suggested as early as the beginning of 1839 by the *Sunday Times*, August 28, 1842.

5

In this way the popular agitation conducted by the free traders reinforced the popular agitation of the Chartists. This double agitation possessed very dangerous possibilities had it issued in civil war. Thanks, however, to the wisdom, not of the agitators, but of the British public it was not destined to produce civil strife. And that being the case its effect on the country was beneficial. Chartists and members of the League vied in eloquent descriptions, supported by abundant evidence, of the squalid destitution in which the poor of the large manufacturing towns were plunged. They differed only in the remedies they respectively advocated. The emissaries of the League looked in a direction from which the Chartists, whose leader was a reactionary agriculturalist, averted their gaze, and deplored the hard lot of the farmers, crushed by the rise in rents, and the agricultural labourers who lived in conditions more bestial even than those of the urban factory hands. And while the Chartists and their Tory allies commiserated with the factory workers on the long hours of toil they and even their little children had to endure in the mills, the free traders waxed indignant at the exploitation of the miners, their wives and children in mines which, as a general rule, were the property of the landed aristocracy. At this very time the Poor Law Commissioners were making use of their powers to conduct an inquiry into the sanitary conditions of the working class and the crying scandal of the slums.

The immediate effect of this spate of speeches and reports, and above all, of novels and poems inspired by the former was to discredit England on the Continent. She was now regarded as a country of organized selfishness and callous indifference to the sufferings of the poor, disguised by a mask of Liberalism. All this output of literature proved on the contrary that, if the gigantic strides made by industry had overwhelmed British philanthropy with the host of problems raised by the new order, England was also the country most concerned with the welfare of its workers. The true significance of the election of 1841, and the seeming victory of the Tories, was the disgust created by six years of Whig rule with a policy of talk and face-saving, and the general desire that the chief topic of debate in Parliament and the primary consideration determining the Government's programme of legislation should be to improve what was called the condition of the people.[1]

6

If theie was a statesman in whose mind problems of political economy took precedence of purely political questions, who cared little for his reputation and whose chief preoccupation was the material conditions in which the people lived, he was Sir Robert Peel, and everyone knew it. Moreover, if he must choose between the Chartist creed and that of the League, leaving out of account the oratorical excesses of both parties, which were equally distasteful to him, he would certainly prefer the League. For he was in a sense a Manchester man by origin, and was universally regarded as such. But unlike the Leaguers there was nothing of the doctrinaire about him. He had always been an opportunist who took his often energetic decisions with an eye to the wishes of the country and the needs of the moment. This was still understood and appreciated.

The Prime Minister allowed it to be given out by his entourage that in the main the election had not been fought on the issue of free trade. Nor was this wholly untrue. Though the manœuvre performed at the last moment by Melbourne's Cabinet had compelled him to declare more categorically for protection than he would have desired, and to permit too many of his candidates to accept the assistance of the Chartists against the free traders, the fact remained that the electorate had voted for Peel himself and his supporters because it was weary of Whig arrogance and nepotism, of Melbourne's indolence, Lord John Russell's blunders, Baring's financial vacillations and even, a year after his Syrian victory, of Palmerston's whimsies at the Foreign Office. The nation wanted ministers who took their work seriously, were capable and hardworking. And Peel was a model of these virtues.

Two or three Radicals deserted the Whig Government even before it resigned,[2] explaining that, since the choice lay between Melbourne and Peel, they preferred Peel. The former ministers disclaimed any intention of making difficulties for their succes-

[1] See the first chapter of Carlyle's *Chartism* entitled 'Condition-of-England Question'.
[2] They abstained from voting on the Address. See the statements made by Ward and Roebuck on August 28 (*Parliamentary Debates*, 3rd Ser., vol. lix, pp. 163 sqq.).

sors.[1] They were obviously delighted to pass on to others the responsibility for the serious decisions which seemed inevitable if the country were to be rescued from the grave economic difficulties with which it was grappling so desperately. Cobden, who, however, counted on mob violence to intimidate the new Prime Minister, expressed his conviction that the 'present government will do something'.[2] Peel kept silence. As soon as he had secured the credits necessary to meet current expenditure he asked for an adjournment of three months in which to work out the definitive policy which he would put before the House when it met in January. A new doctor had been called to the patient's bedside and could prescribe nothing until he had completed his examination. He was granted the adjournment for which he asked. 'The aristocracy and the people', Cobden wrote, 'are gaping at him, wondering what he is going to do.'[3]

II THE REFORMS OF 1842

I

The speech from the throne on February 3, 1842, did not break the reserve. It was content to draw the attention of Parliament to 'the state of the finances and of the expenditure of the country', and the fact that in time of peace 'for several years past the annual income has been inadequate to bear the Public Charges', and on the other hand to 'the state of the laws which affect the import of corn, and of other articles, the produce of foreign countries'.[4] But the public did not have to wait a week to learn the intentions of the Government. On February 9 Peel introduced in an important

[1] Lord John Russell's address to his constituents (The City), July 19, 1841: 'In this altered position [resignation in consequence of a hostile vote in the Commons] it would be inconsistent with my notions of public duty to harass the government of the day by vexatious opposition, still less to deny to the Crown the means of maintaining the reputation of the country abroad and internal quiet at home. But when the great principles of religious, civil and commercial liberty come into question, those principles must be firmly and fearlessly supported. Whatever party may be in power, they are so inseparably connected with the progress of society, that although the country may doubt, may pause, may ponder, it will examine, discuss, and finally adopt them.' But *The Nonconformist*, August 25, 1841, expressed its regret that Peel was content to be a party leader.
[2] Letter to G. Wilson, October 12, 1841, in Morley, *Life of Richard Cobden*, ed. 1881, vol. i, p. 209.
[3] Letter to his brother, September 1841, ibid., vol. i, p. 181.
[4] *Parliamentary Debates*, 3rd Ser., vol. lx, pp. 2 sqq.

speech a Bill to alter the system by which duties were levied on cereals.

That system was the sliding scale of 1828,[1] which, when passed by a Tory Cabinet, had been presented as a modification of the prohibitions enacted in 1815. Its object, which can hardly be said to have been achieved, had been to keep the cost of a quarter of wheat at 60 shillings more or less. The opponents of the sliding scale pointed out that during the fourteen years it had been in operation it had in fact aggravated the fluctuation of prices it was intended to obviate. It favoured speculation. When prices were approaching the figure of 73 shillings, at which cereals could be imported for all practical purposes without payment of duty, it was in the interest of those who held imported wheat in bond to do everything in their power to force prices up that they might reap in the shortest possible time a double profit, from the higher price of corn and the all but complete removal of the duty. They could do this by falsifying the averages which must be fixed before the sliding scale could be adjusted. The imposition of a fixed tariff of 8 shillings, an amount which would just balance the burden of taxation on landed property, was the new system which for the past year Lord John Russell had put forward as the official Whig policy. It would, he maintained, stop this fraudulent speculation. If, however, the price of wheat rose above 73 shillings the effect of Lord John's fixed tariff would be more protective than that of Wellington's sliding scale. And if the Government were empowered to remit the duty, in that event there would be an abrupt fall of 8 shillings—a fall not like those under the sliding scale of 1828, an automatic adjustment—and this would give fresh scope to the malpractices of the speculator.

Peel proposed to remedy the evils of the sliding scale not by abandoning but by reforming it. In the first place the average price of cereals would be determined by a new and stricter method. In the second place the scale of tariffs set up in 1828 would be modified so as to keep the price of wheat at a rough level not of 60 but 54 shillings. In the third place the variations in the scale would be made more continuous, less abrupt. When the price of wheat was 50 shillings the duty under the existing tariff was 36s. 8d., rising

[1] 9 Geo. iv, c. 60. See my *History of the English People*, vol. ii, p. 291. The duty payable was 20 shillings when the quarter cost 54, and was lowered as the price rose. When it had reached 73 corn was imported free of duty.

if the price fell below 50 shillings. Peel proposed a duty of 20 shillings which would not be altered if prices fell. If the price rose above 50 shillings the duty would be lowered at the regular rate of a shilling for every increase of a shilling in the price of wheat, with two 'rests' between 52 and 55 shillings and between 66 and 69 shillings, during which the duty would remain at the same level. A duty of 10 shillings, not as at present 23s. 8d., would be reached when the price was 63 shillings. From this point instead of the rapid fall prescribed by the Act of 1828 it would suffice to continue the regular reduction of a shilling for every increase of a shilling in price, and as hitherto when the price rose to 73 shillings imported corn would be subject to the trifling duty of a shilling a quarter.[1]

The debate was lifeless. A hundred Tories protested that to alter the scale of 1828 would be an initial surrender to the free traders' attack, and were confident that an amendment would be passed hostile to the new scale. On the other hand, a hundred members of the Radical Opposition supported Villiers's amendment in favour of a total abolition of the duties. The uncompromising free traders, however, were aware that both the Government and the Opposition recognized that their position was impregnable. The only argument put forward by Lord John against total abolition was the necessity to take account of the special taxation to which, according to him, landed property was subject. The only argument put forward by Peel in defence of a special tariff on cereals was not economic but political. The landed gentry on whom the traditional working of British institutions reposed must not be destroyed. The country must be self-supporting in the event of war, and the people's food must not be at the mercy of a foreign foe. In short, the Bill which was finally passed was among those measures which intended to please everybody,

[1] H. of C., February 9, 1842, Peel's speech (*Parliamentary Debates*, 3rd Ser., vol. lx, p. 201). J. R. M'Culloch, *Statements Illustrative of the Policy and Probable Consequences of the Proposed Repeal of the Existing Corn Laws* (1841, 2nd ed., postscript, pp. 35-6): 'We have already seen that there can be nothing steady or continuous under a fluctuating scale . . . that it every now and then forces importation far beyond the quantity really required by the wants of the country; and that by preventing anything like a regular trade in corn, it obliges the imports to be paid principally in bullion, and thus periodically lays the Bank of England and the commercial classes under the greatest possible difficulties. . . . The first really bad harvest that occurs under the existing Corn Laws will certainly make an end of them. But the probability unhappily is, that it will, at the same time, reduce the Bank of England to the greatest straits and spread bankruptcy and ruin throughout the country.'

satisfy nobody. The speeches delivered by Peel to explain and defend it were pronounced feeble.[1]

From the eminent physician called to England's sick-bed, bolder and more novel measures had been expected, the more so that the Duke of Buckingham's resignation a few days before Parliament met had led the Liberals and free traders to expect a decisive rupture with the agricultural interest. It was believed in these circles that Peel had been prepared to go further, but had been checked by the fear of splitting his party immediately.[2] To-day we know that this was not the case.[3]

Peel, it seems, wanted to postpone the question of the tariff on corn till the next session or the close of the present. Some of his colleagues, however, who advocated an immediate relaxation of the existing tariff insisted that it should be dealt with at once. Among them was Sir James Graham, a deserter from the Whigs who already enjoyed the prestige of an old and experienced parliamentarian. In the secret discussions of the Cabinet he took the lead, though the Liberal Opposition showed him no gratitude for it, in pushing his chief along the path of commercial Liberalism. Another member of the group was the youthful Gladstone, alarmed at first by the novel problems he was called upon to face, but converted immediately to free trade by his permanent officials. When after much bargaining the Cabinet agreed on the figures of the new sliding scale his zeal for free trade was so ardent, and the Bill in his opinion so plainly unsatisfactory, that it required Peel's utmost efforts to prevent him from beginning his career as

[1] *Greville Memoirs*, February 11, 1842. Miss Martineau, *History of the Thirty Years' Peace*, vol. iv, p. 171. R. Cobden to his brother, February 28, 1842 (John Morley, *Life of Richard Cobden*, 1902, p. 31): 'The Tories have not liked the debate. Peel feels that he has not come out of it well. He looks dissatisfied with himself.'

[2] *Edinburgh Review*, vol. lxxvi (October 1842): 'Indeed, it is obvious that in the principles he laid down and the admissions he made, he has prepared the way with great adroitness, but with much caution for the final abandonment of all protection whatever. His two "Rests", at a duty of 6s. and 17s., are his preparations for a fixed duty; a fixed duty on his part will lead him further still.'

[3] Francis E. Hyde, *Mr. Gladstone at the Board of Trade*, 1934, pp. 42, 45, and 49—Tooke, *History of Prices*, vol. v, pp. 427-9. Gladstone to his father, June 30, 1849: 'As respects my "having made Peel a free trader", I had never seen that idea expressed anywhere, and I think it is one that does great injustice to the character and power of his mind. In every case, however, the head of a Government may be influenced more or less in the affairs of each department of state by the person in charge of that department. If then, therefore, there was any influence at all upon Peel's mind proceeding from me between 1841 and 1845, I have no doubt it may have tended, on the whole, towards free trade' (John Morley, *Life of W. E. Gladstone*, vol. i, pp. 283-4). For the part played by MacGregor at the Board of Trade, see *Greville Memoirs*, November 19, 1841, and Cobden to his brother, June 22, 1842 (John Morley, *Life of Richard Cobden*, p. 29).

a statesman by the sensational step of resigning eight days before the Duke of Buckingham. Peel, who no doubt thought no better than Gladstone of the Bill he was to sponsor in the House, may well have regretted his failure to postpone this awkward problem of the Corn Law. And no doubt he regretted it even more when on March 11 his first Budget achieved a brilliant success. Why could it not have been his first measure?

2

The financial position was extremely serious. On this everyone was agreed and in the conviction that urgent and drastic measures were necessary to deal with it. Whig finance had always been bad, but it became disastrous when years of economic prosperity were followed by years of crisis and distress, and it was no longer a question of abolishing at haphazard all taxes unpopular with particular sections of the community, but of raising as soon as possible and indiscriminately the yield of all the existing taxes or borrowing. The result of their hand-to-mouth finance was that the financial year, ending in April 1842, showed a deficit of £2,334,000. For the financial year for which he was budgeting, Peel expected a revenue of £48,350,000, an expenditure of £50,819,000, that is to say a deficit of £2,469,000.

To make it up Peel proposed to revive the income tax imposed during the Napoleonic war.[1] It had been abolished immediately on the return of peace. He excused the innovation by pointing out that owing to the mistakes of the Whig Government the country was not altogether at peace, but waging war in India and China. It was the more sensational because during the past twelve years Peel had often declared himself opposed to a tax on income. In this matter also he had no doubt been influenced privately by Sir James Graham, who had been a member of the Whig Cabinet of 1830, and, in opposition to his more timid colleagues, had been its avowed advocate.[2] The new tax would be levied on every species of income without exception, rent, profits from farming, interest on investments in public funds, all income from whatever

[1] H. of C., March 11, Peel's speech (*Parliamentary Debates*, 3rd Ser., vol. lxi, pp. 429 sqq.).
[2] MacCullagh Torrens, *The Life and Times of the Rt. Hon. James R. G. Graham*, 1863, vol. ii, p. 206. For Peel's conversion to an income tax, see, on the other hand, the letters published by Parker, op. cit., vol. ii, pp. 490 sqq.

source which did not fall under these categories, in particular income from investments or professional earnings, salaries and pensions. Incomes below £150 a year would be exempt. The amount of the tax would be 7d. in the pound, that is to say a little less than 3 per cent. Moreover, it was to be a temporary impost, to be continued for not more than five years. And Parliament could abolish it, if the revenue were sufficient to justify the step, at the end of three years. For this improvement in the revenue Peel did not rely exclusively on an automatic recovery of trade. He sought to assist that recovery by another fiscal measure as bold as the revival of the income tax, a general reduction of imposts or rather of a particular form of impost. The experiment could be made the more safely in view of the fact that from the income tax, together with some other taxes imposed to compensate for the exemption of Ireland from the income tax, he estimated a revenue of more than four millions. Since without the income tax the deficit would be less than two and a half millions, he would have a surplus of a million and a half.

3

It was to a revision of the tariff that Peel looked for that rapid improvement of the country's economic position which would increase the revenue. His calculations were inspired by the principles of free trade. By lowering tariffs he expected to increase their yield. The Committee appointed in 1840 to study the question of Import Duties[1] had condemned not only protection, but the inextricable labyrinth of the English Tariff. Eight hundred and seventy-two articles were dutiable, and of these seventeen provided almost 95 per cent of the total revenue. This profusion of unproductive duties served no purpose. At a stroke Peel effected a thorough, indeed a dramatic, revision of this tariff.[2]

He removed the ban on the importation of any article. He reduced all duties on raw materials, none of which might in future exceed 5 per cent, on all articles partly manufactured, none

---

[1] *Report from the Select Committee appointed to Enquire into the Several Duties Levied on Imports into the United Kingdom.* 1840 (601), V. 99.

[2] John Morley, *Life of Richard Cobden*, 1902, p. 33: 'The labour of preparation was enormous. Mr. Gladstone, who was then at the Board of Trade, and on whom much of the labour fell, said many years afterwards, that he had been concerned in four revisions of the Tariff, namely, in 1842, in 1845, in 1854 and in 1860; and he told Cobden that the first cost six times as much trouble as all the others together. There was an abatement of duty on seven hundred and fifty articles.'

of which might exceed 12 per cent, and on articles completely manufactured, none of which might exceed 20 per cent. To compensate for a loss of no more than £270,000 he counted on an increase in output sufficient to balance the Budget within five, possibly three, years and make the income tax no longer necessary.[1]

The magnitude of the reform, whose principles Peel developed in his exposition, left his audience at the outset speechless.[2] But they soon recovered from their amazement, and the new tariff and the income tax were the subject of a furious battle on the floor of the House.

4

The first criticism of the Government's financial measures put forward by the Opposition was that they had been stolen from the Whig programme, and a Conservative ministry was not playing fair when it sought popularity by pursuing a Liberal policy. The complaint was no more than a half truth. It was true, indeed, that the Budget of 1842 was substantially a faithful application of the principles laid down in 1830 by Sir Henry Parnell, and that at the time they were expected to shape the financial policy of the Liberal party if it were returned to power. But the event proved that the Liberals, who came into power sooner, and whose hold of office was firmer than Sir Henry had anticipated, had no desire to apply his principles. It was not Peel's fault that the Whigs had been untrue to that portion of their programme which was most conservative in the sense he attached to the term, namely the programme least threatening to the country's political institutions and religious traditions. It required the election of 1841, ostensibly a Tory success, to inaugurate the era of the great Liberal budgets of modern England.[3]

[1] *Annual Register*, 1843, p. 47. At the same time, the Government adopted a measure which was scarcely consistent with its general policy, by re-imposing the duty on exported coal abolished in 1831. The step was taken to assuage the fears of those who predicted the exhaustion of the country's mineral wealth. See Sp. Walpole, *History of England*, vol. v, pp 14-15.

[2] *Greville Memoirs*, March 13, 1842. 'Only a few weeks ago I heard from my Whig friends of nothing but his (Peel's) weakness and embarrassments . . . but now they have not a word to say, and one of them, who had been loudest in that strain, brought to the Travellers', where I was dining, an account of Peel's speech, and said, "One felt all the time he was speaking: Thank God, Peel is Minister." There can be no doubt that he is now a very great man.'

[3] H. of C., March 18, 1842. Labouchere's speech (*Parliamentary Debates*, 3rd Ser., vol. lxi, pp. 917 sqq.), March 21, 1842; C. Wood's speech (ibid., p. 989), May 10, 1842; Gladstone's speech (ibid., 3rd Ser., vol. lxiii, pp. 394-5).

The Whigs had a stronger case when they complained that Peel had presented the House with a project of financial reform less thoroughgoing than their own proposals of the previous winter. They had not claimed to deal with every problem at once, but they had done what he had not dared to do, attacked the three great monopolies, the London grain monopoly, the Canadian timber monopoly, the West Indian sugar monopoly. But the ministers could point out in reply that the criticism was but partly justified. They had proposed a better solution of the timber question than that put forward by the Whigs. For instead of raising simultaneously the duties on timber from the Baltic and Canada they had lowered them both, so that the British consumer would benefit as well as the Canadian producer. As regards cereals they were obviously faced with the difficulties we have already pointed out. As for sugar, the sugar interest was undoubtedly too powerful to be safely defied. Moreover, the Prime Minister and his supporters did not consider that their newborn commercial liberalism obliged them to abandon entirely a system of colonial preference. On the contrary, it seems clear that the men who worked out the financial measures of 1842 never lost sight of it.[1]

A further criticism was urged against Peel—like the last justified only in part. He preferred, his critics complained, to satisfy the manufacturers, consumers of raw materials, rather than the workers, consumers of foodstuffs. As we have just said, this complaint was not wholly true. If the duties on sugar were left untouched, the duties on coffee did not escape. If grain received special treatment, all other agricultural products were affected by the lowered duties of the new tariff, and the Corn Importation Bill, inadequate though it might be, set up a sliding scale which did not keep out imported corn to the same extent as the former. When, however, these qualifications have been made, there was substance in the criticism. Cobden's plan of campaign was to shelve provisionally the question of industrial protection and concentrate the entire attention of the public on the undernourishment of the lower classes, for which the landed interest was held responsible. Peel countered these tactics by leaving in the shade the question of cereals, which, in view of the composition of his party, he knew he could not solve at the moment, and fixing

[1] Henry George Grey, *Review of the Colonial Policy of Lord John Russell's Administration,* 1869, vol. i, pp. 7-9.

public attention on the other question, different though not unconnected, of industrial protection.

Yet another criticism was made which must also be regarded as justified from the standpoint of what would later be the accepted orthodoxy of free trade. Sir Robert explained that of the twelve hundred items of the existing tariff, four hundred and fifty had been left untouched. The reason was that commercial treaties were being negotiated with several nations, and if Britain were to secure reduced tariffs from foreign Powers she must have something to bargain with.

This was the case with the duties on imported wines, duties, moreover, which were not protective. With an intransigence which amused those who recollected his Budget of 1840, Baring protested against a procedure which would make the adoption of free trade depend upon the good will of foreign nations. Peel, however, did not subscribe to the creed of unqualified free trade. The head of a Conservative administration, he was deliberately following the tradition of a qualified free trade to be realized progressively by means of bilaterial treaties of commerce, the policy, in fact, which Huskisson had advocated before his advent to power. He might have added that this was the traditional Tory policy, whereas in the eighteenth century the Whigs had been the party of protection. Disraeli, in fact, who though disgruntled at his exclusion from the Government had not yet broken with it, made this observation.[1]

The battle, however, did not turn on any of these issues. It was the revival of the income tax which drew the concentrated fire of Peel's opponents. Twenty-five years had not elapsed since a Tory government had been compelled by an outbreak of public hostility to abandon in haste the war-time income tax. On that occasion the attack in the Commons had been led by Brougham, then a young Radical barrister. Now as Lord Brougham in the House of Lords he once more led the opposition to the tax.[2]

Was it not, in fact, imprudent if the Government wished to keep the good will of the electorate to propose a tax which voters only would have to pay, those without a vote being exempt? Cobden's hostility to Peel could not let slip this opportunity to

---

[1] In a speech delivered on July 21, 1842 (Monypenny, *Life of Disraeli*, vol. ii, p. 133).
[2] H. of L., March 14 and 17, Lord Brougham's speech (*Parliamentary Debates*, 3rd Ser., vol. lxi, pp. 507 and 723).

compass his defeat. After hesitating a few hours or days at most the official Opposition joined an attack which threatened to endanger the Government. Nevertheless, it failed. Peel was rewarded for the courage he had shown in challenging so many selfish interests.[1]

The landed interest had, indeed, good cause for alarm. Land was hit most immediately by a direct tax which was less easily evaded than in the case of other property. But the country gentlemen reflected that after all the amount of the tax was slight, only 7d. instead of the heavy war-time income tax,[2] that it was a temporary measure, that abatements in favour of agriculture were granted, and that they must trust the daring pilot who had steered them into power. The manufacturers were warned against a tax which, if levied on their profits, must constitute an inquisition into their private concerns. But would it necessarily be levied in this inquisitorial fashion? If not, their profits would enjoy greater immunity than any other form of wealth. Moreover, they also took account of the fact that the tax was light, temporary and introduced to compensate the Treasury for a reduction of the tariff pre-eminently favourable to their interest. Petitions in support of the tax were received from the manufacturers of the Midlands and the North. On this point Cobden, it would seem, had been deserted by his followers. Many Radicals, moreover, were in favour of the tax. To retain their support the opponents of the tax were obliged to qualify their opposition to it and be content to demand not its withdrawal, but simply its amendment, that it should be levied on a sliding scale or, and, this was their most pressing demand, that a distinction should be made between earned and unearned income, and the former exempted so that the income tax would be, in fact, a property tax. But was it worth the labour and time necessary to set up the complicated machinery for effecting this distinction? And surely the simplest form of levy was the best for a tax which was very light and intended to be a temporary measure. In any case, it was no longer possible in 1841 as it had been in 1816 to rouse the country against the tax. There was no prospect of huge open-air meetings of protesting Chartists like the meetings called by the Radicals at

---

[1] Cobden, letter to his brother, March 22 (John Morley, *Life of Richard Cobden*, p. 241).

[2] Above £150 the tax, as first imposed in 1803, was 5 per cent; Pitt raised it, in 1805, to 6¼ per cent; Lord Henry Petty, in 1806, to 10 per cent (*History of the English People*, vol. i, pp. 374-6).

the earlier date. Then the agitation to abolish a tax which had been essentially a war tax had been a demonstration against war which sought to deprive of revenue an administration unpopular because of its association with war. This was no longer the case. These motives had ceased to operate. And if the Chartists did not actively support an income tax they were indifferent to an issue with which they had no concern.

The new financial policy destined, as the future would prove, to mark an epoch in English history was an indisputable victory for the principle of free trade, though it did not take the form or direction desired by those responsible for the policy of the Anti-Corn-Law League. And during the course of the same session what may be called the Chartist creed also suffered marked reverses, though in this connection we must understand Chartism in a wide sense, as a movement not so much to enlarge the franchise as such as to extend by this or any other appropriate device the competence of the State to protect the weak against the strong.

III SOCIAL PROBLEMS

I

In view of the display of public feeling the previous summer, and the pledges given by so many members sitting on the Government benches, it would have seemed inevitable that an attempt should be made to mitigate in one way or another the harsh application of the Poor Law. It was plain, however, even before the new session opened that the system of Commissioners would not be touched. For when one of the places on the Commission became vacant it was filled immediately, in accordance, moreover, with the admirable precedent established by the late Government, without regard to party. A Liberal was appointed. The Government, indeed, promised a Bill. But as it would not be introduced till after the Easter recess and the powers of the Commissioners expired on July 1 very little time was left to debate such an important measure. In fact, the reform of the Poor Law was finally postponed till the following year. Meanwhile, the Commissioners' powers were extended with a few unimportant alterations of procedure for another five years. This defeat of a campaign conducted with such bitterness only a year earlier seems to have had no repercussions in the country.[1]

A Royal Commission had been appointed in 1840 to enquire into the conditions of child labour in the mines. Its report was published at the beginning of 1842. It was appalling.[2] It depicted these children, these youngsters of both sexes, almost naked, harnessed to trucks loaded with coal which they drew on all fours, a chain between their legs, for fifteen hours a day along galleries only three feet high, often even lower. The abuse was not indeed universal. In the larger mines conditions were better, and in uncivilized Ireland no women or children worked in the mines. But it was sufficiently widespread to shock the public conscience, which, indeed, was offended by the immorality even more than by the cruelty of the system. Lord Ashley secured the passage of a Bill by the Commons forbidding the employment in the mines of women or children under thirteen. It also made it illegal to put minors in charge of machines, and abolished the system of apprenticeship by which workhouses provided for the maintenance of pauper children by sending them to unpaid labour in mines. No restriction, however, was placed on the hours of labour. For it was thought impracticable to secure the enforcement of such a provision in the depths of a mine, and inspectors might well have to suffer at the hands of the adult miners, only too pleased to exploit child labour. An attempt was, however, made to get round this difficulty by permitting children to work only one in every two days.

The House of Lords made several amendments which the Commons accepted. The age below which child labour was prohibited was lowered from thirteen to ten. The employment of workhouse apprentices between the ages of ten and eighteen and of women above ground was permitted. The age at which a youth might take charge of a machine was lowered to fifteen. And the provision by which children might work only one day in two was dropped. But the substance of the Bill survived. For the first time women were excluded by law from a particular kind of labour.[3] Another significant fact deserves remark. The free

[1] *Annual Register*, 1842, pp. 212-13. *Greville Memoirs*, November 30, 1841.

[2] *First Report of Commissioners for Enquiring into the Employment and Conditions of Children in Mines and Manufactories*, 1842 (380), xv, 1.

[3] 6 & 7 Vict. Cap. 99. An Act to prohibit the Employment of Women and Girls in Mines and Collieries, to regulate the Employment of Boys and to make other provisions relating to Persons working therein.

traders gave the Bill an enthusiastic welcome. Cobden crossed the floor of the House to shake hands dramatically with Lord Ashley.[1] We have seen how anxious the League was at this juncture in its campaign to win the sympathy of the working class. Its members were delighted to denounce the abuses of capitalism when the exploiters were not Lancashire millowners, but for the most part Tories and Protectionists.

'If the Bill passed in that shape', was, however, the warning of one of the few members of the House of Commons who dared oppose it, 'hundreds of children would be thrown out of employment and hundreds of families would be driven into workhouses. . . . Such a Bill if passed would very likely introduce discontent and political agitation where they were unknown before. The colliers would repeal an Act of Parliament much sooner than the House of Commons. . . . As a county magistrate he could not be responsible for the public peace if the Bill were carried into effect in its present shape.'[2] His prophecy was fulfilled without delay. Even before the passage of the Bill the mineowners seemed determined to provoke a revolt of the miners by deciding at the very moment, when the prohibition of child labour would in effect reduce the parents' earnings, upon a general lowering of wages. In South Staffordshire and Lancashire the men met this reduction by declaring a strike which in August spread to all the mines and factories in north-western England. This widespread revolt of labour is usually treated as the second phase of the Chartist agitation. But in our opinion its causes and character cannot be correctly understood if its connection with the agitation against the Corn Law is lost sight of.[3]

2

On the day in February fixed for the introduction of the Government's Bill dealing with the import of corn, five hundred

[1] E. Hodder, *The Life and Works of the Seventh Earl of Shaftesbury*, p. 227: 'June 7, 1842. The most striking tribute came from Cobden, who crossed the floor of the House to wring him warmly by the hand: "You know how opposed I have been to your views; but I don't think I have ever been put into such a frame of mind, in the whole course of my life, as I have been by your speech." '

[2] H. of C., July 5, 1842, Ainsworth's speech (*Parliamentary Debates*, 3rd Ser., vol. lxiv, p. 1001; also *Annual Register*, 1842, p. 172).

[3] For this revolutionary agitation by the free traders, about which the panegyrists of Liberalism on the one hand, and many Socialist historians of Chartism on the other,

manufacturers in obedience to the instructions of the League assembled in London. Four abreast they marched from the City to Westminster, where they attempted to enter the House and were driven off by the police. Shouting 'Down with tyranny' they forced their way to the entrance of the Houses of Parliament and greeted members as they arrived with cries of 'Down with the sliding scale,' 'Down with the Corn Laws.'[1] When the text of the Bill was published the free traders saw that more effective methods of intimidation were required. Peace with the Government was henceforth impossible.

The agitation which Sturge had organized the previous autumn now assumed its full proportions. 'The forced maintenance of the Corn Laws', Villiers declared in the Commons, 'was making all men in the country politicians and driving the middle and working classes to think they were misrepresented.'[2]

On February 15 a number of meetings held in Lancashire passed resolutions in favour of a combined programme, the abolition of the Corn Laws and 'complete suffrage'.[3] And when on April 5

are completely silent, see *Quarterly Review*, December 1842, art. vii, 'Anti-Corn-Law Agitation' (vol. lxxi, pp. 244 sqq.). It is amply documented and has never been refuted. See also Friedrich Engels, *Die Lage der Arbeitenden Klassen in England*, 1933, vol. ii, pp. 168 sqq. Engels's account has obviously been inspired by the article in the *Quarterly*. But the fact that he was an eye-witness of the troubles gives weight to his endorsement of the conclusions reached by the latter. See also E. Dolléans, *Le Chartisme*, vol. ii, pp. 210 sqq.

[1] A. Prentice, *History of the Anti-Corn-Law League*, vol. i, pp. 309 sqq. R. A. J. Walling, *The Diaries of John Bright*, p. 63.

[2] H. of C., February 18. 1842, Villiers's speech. *Annual Register*, 1842, p. 44. [Not in Hansard's report. From which I quote the following: 'In his opinion, the people of this country . . . a sufficiently large number of persons of all classes to justify him in using that title, had determined that "the Corn Law" should not continue. He believed that the mind of the great majority of the people was made up on the subject, and that they would use every means in their power, . . . to emancipate the industry and commerce of the country from this law' (*Parliamentary Debates*, 3rd Ser., vol. lx, pp. 651 sqq.)—Trs. Note.]

[3] The above-mentioned article, in the *Quarterly Review* (December 1842, vol. lxxi, pp. 244 sqq.), gives a detailed account of this agitation. On January 1 an Operative Corn Law Association held its first meeting at Manchester (see *Morning Chronicle*, January 3). At the London meeting, on February 11, Cobden delivered a violent speech: 'Why would they submit to be starved and put upon short allowances by thirty or forty thousand men? He was sure that if they knew how insignificant, both morally and physically, those thirty or forty thousand aristocrats and squires were, they would not fear them.' On February 15 a meeting of reconciliation was held at Manchester by the Chartists and Free Traders, and addressed by W. R. Greg. John Bright addressed a meeting at Manchester on March 1. See the reports in the *Stockport Chronicle*, February 18 and March 18: 'Let not squeamish individuals shrink from the course he pointed out, from any false notion of its apparent harshness. The people sent to their settlements must not go crawling like ordinary paupers; they must go as if they were *marching to battle with their oppressors*, to take possession of magazines of plunder—to storm the fortress of oppression—and to quarter upon a deadly enemy' (*Quart. Rev.*, art. cit., pp. 259-75).

the first meeting of the group founded by Sturge was held in Birmingham, the entire programme of the Charter was adopted with his more or less willing assent.[1]

But it cannot be said that the Chartist extremists were converted to the moderation of the League, or, on the other hand, that the moderate Leaguers were converted to Chartist extremism. For if among the Chartists who accepted the alliance Lovett represented the moderate section, this was not the case with Vincent, or O'Brien. And, on the other hand, the Leaguers had no claim whatever to be called moderate. The truth is that the free trade extremists had concluded an alliance with the Chartist extremists. This was evident when on May 2 the Chartists presented Parliament, in the dramatic setting devised in 1839, a petition in support of their programme, a monster petition bearing, they claimed, more than three million signatures. Macaulay warned the House that universal suffrage meant the abolition of property, and, in consequence, the end of civilization. The petition included an express condemnation of the Poor Law and demanded legislation restricting hours of work in the factories. Notwithstanding, Bowring, on behalf of the free traders, spoke in support of it. And Bowring, Villiers, and Cobden together with Fielden, Wakley, and Duncombe, were among the minority of fifty-one who voted in favour of taking it into consideration.[2]

The advocates of free trade dwelt on the fearful suffering endured by the factory workers; destitution, unemployment, and the urgent threat of famine. A violent revolution was declared imminent. And the free traders were delighted to believe it. For nothing short of a revolution would bring about the repeal of the Corn Laws and restore prosperity. Since they desired a crisis they sought for the most effective means to produce it. At this moment, projects already in November the subject of rumour were put forward openly. Cobden advised the taxpayers to strike and refuse to pay their taxes. A young Quaker manufacturer of Oldham, John Bright, whom Cobden had won for the League, and whose eloquence stirred the masses, called for a lockout. The

---

[1] For the Birmingham meeting, see the *Anti-Bread-Tax Circular* of April 11—M. Hovell, *The Chartist Movement*, p. 247.

[2] R. G. Gammage, *History of the Chartist Movement*, p. 209. M. Hovell, *The Chartist Movement*, pp. 254 sqq. H. of C., May 2, 1842 (*Parliamentary Debates*, 3rd Ser., vol. lxiii, pp. 13 sqq.).

millowners should all close their mills and throw the entire body of workers on the street.[1]

The great criminal, the man who was starving the British people, was Peel. In several provincial towns he was burned in effigy.[2] A poster, printed at the cost of certain members of the League and stuck to walls in Manchester, pronounced him 'responsible' for all the evils under which the country was suffering.[3] 'Responsible' was, in fact, the refrain of the Radical press.[4] What did they mean by it? When a meeting of free traders was held in London in July, similar to that held in February, to support the representatives of their cause in the House, extremely violent language was used. Not only did the mayors of the large towns of the north rise in turn to state that if riots broke out they would not allow the military to fire on the crowd, but a speaker who called for the formation in London of a Committee of Public

[1] At Manchester thirty thousand put their signatures to a manifesto calling for the refusal of taxes (*Morning Chronicle*, July 18, 1842). For both these plans, see the account given by Acland, one of the League's lecturers, of an interview with O'Connor: 'On the probability of the Chartists succeeding in their object at an earlier period than the League could hope to succeed in theirs, O'Connor enquired, "Will the League stop all the mills?" I replied, "That would give you the Charter in three weeks, which you can hardly expect from longheaded men who are not Chartists." O'Connor then remarked, "The middle classes have no other practical measures by which to obtain their ends." I replied, "By the non-payment of taxes they could procure the repeal of the Corn Laws in three months"' (*Morning Chronicle*, August 26, 1842). R. Cobden to G. Wilson, February 27, 1842: 'I feel some little difficulty in offering my advice as to the course which the League should henceforth pursue. That course depends very much upon the spirit of the people who are acting with us. If they were all of my temper in the matter, we would soon bring it to an issue. I presume, however, that your friends are not up to the mark for a general *fiscal revolt*, and I know of no other plan of peaceful resistance. . . . After all, I hardly entertain a hope that we shall effect our object by old and regular methods; accidents may aid us, but I do not see my way, in the ordinary course of things, to beating down the power of aristocracy' (John Morley, *Life of Richard Cobden*, p. 31). R. Cobden to F. Cobden, June 22, 1842: '. . . The Government are at their wits' end about the state of the country. The Devonshire House Whigs are beginning to talk of the necessity of supporting the Government in case of any serious troubles, which means a virtual coalition; a point they are evidently being driven to by the force of events. Peel will throw overboard the bigots of his party, if he has the chance. But the real difficulty is the present state of the country. The accounts from every part are equally bad, and Chadwick says that the poor rates in the agricultural districts are rising rapidly. A great deal of land has been offered for sale during the last three months, and everything seems working beautifully for a cure in the only possible way, viz. distress, suffering, and want of money' (Morley, op. cit., pp. 33–4). H. S. Leach, *Public Letters of Mr. Bright*, p. 68, *The Nonconformist*, August 17, 1842.

[2] *Annual Register*, 1842, p. 53.

[3] H. of C., June 3, 1842. Ferrand's speech (*Parliamentary Debates*, 3rd Ser., vol. lxiii, p. 1154; *The Nonconformist*, July 27, 1842).

[4] *Morning Chronicle*, July 12, 1842: 'The anxiety and trepidation observed in the Prime Minister of this great nation comport well with the fearful responsibilities which he has brought on his own head. . . . He is responsible. . . . He is responsible. . . . He is responsible. . . . On his head be the consequences of which he has had earnest and solemn warning.'

Safety to rouse the metropolis from its apathy informed his audience that a friend of his, a *gentleman*, had informed him that he was prepared, if the order were given, to assassinate Peel. Though he could not approve this suggestion of murder, he could not refrain from observing that on the day of Peel's funeral very few tears would be shed.[1] It is not, therefore, surprising that when Cobden, addressing the House two days later, pictured in dramatic language the 'anarchy' impending in the manufacturing districts of the north his disclaimer of any intention to utter threats was greeted with ironic cheers.[2]

3

It was in this month of July that the crisis reached its culminating point. The protracted debates on the Income Tax Bill and the New Tariff Bill aggravated the general disquiet by the prolonged uncertainty what imposts producers would have to pay.[3] The price of corn rose. Wheat which at the end of April cost less than 59 shillings a quarters rose above 60 by the end of May, and by the end of June exceeded 62. The Government took alarm and hurried through Parliament a Bill permitting the sale of wheat in bond free of duty.[4]

The League was delighted by what it regarded as the first step to surrender.[5]

In spite of the measure the price of wheat continued to rise and before the close of July had passed the figure of 64 shillings.[6]

There could not have been a more unpropitious moment to lower wages. And in the coalmines above all, where the Act restricting child labour which would shortly be debated would in any case have reduced the family earnings. The step was taken, nevertheless, by the Staffordshire coalowners. The miners replied by organizing, under Chartist leadership it would seem, a general strike.[7] The entire industry of the Potteries was brought to a stand-

---

[1] *Morning Chronicle*, July 5, 1842; *Morning Herald*, July 15, 1842; *Anti-Bread-Tax Circular*, August 11, 1842.

[2] H. of C., July 8, 1842 (*Parliamentary Debates*, 3rd Ser., vol. lxiv, p. 1217).

[3] *Edinburgh Review*, October 1842 (vol. lxxvi, p. 267). See also Gladstone's observations on February 13, 1843 (*Parl. Deb.*, 3rd Ser., vol. lxvi, pp. 479 sqq.).

[4] 5 & 6 Vict. Cap., 92. See H. of C., July 7, 1842 (*Parl. Deb.*, 3rd Ser., vol. lxiv, pp. 1133 sqq.).

[5] *Anti-Bread-Tax Circular*, June 30, 1842.

[6] Tooke, *History of Prices*, vol. iv, pp. 9 sqq.

[7] For these troubles, see R. G. Gammage, *History of the Chartist Movement*, ed. 1894, pp. 217 sqq.; E. Dolléans, *Le Chartisme*, 1830–48, 1913, vol. ii, pp. 189 sqq.; M. Beer,

still for lack of coal. What course of action would the free-trade manufacturers of Lancashire adopt? They had no love for the coalowners. At Westminster they were voting or getting their friends to vote for the Act protecting the miners' children against their exploitation. Nevertheless, the order was given not to condemn the wage reductions. The coalowners and colliers were depicted as victims of the same evil, ruined alike by the detestable Corn Law. Not only did they refuse to blame the coalowners, they decided to follow their example. Though they did not adopt Bright's advice and with a frank callousness close their factories, they decided to give notice of a reduction in wages, encourage the men to strike and thus confront the Government with a movement amounting almost to an insurrection affecting not only Staffordshire, but the entire industrial north.[1]

Geschichte Des Sozialismus in England, 1913, p. 387; Mark Hovell, *The Chartist Movement*, 1925, pp. 259 sqq.; Slosson (Preston William), *The Decline of the Chartist Movement*, 1916, pp. 60 sqq.; Julius West, *A History of the Chartist Movement*, 1920, pp. 171 sqq. Further information of interest may be found in Sir A. Alison, *Autobiography*, 1883, vol. i, pp. 486 sqq.; Absalom Watkin, *Extracts from His Journal*, ed. A. E. Watkin, 1920, pp. 215 sqq.; Alexander Somerville, *The Autobiography of a Working Man by 'One who has Whistled at the Plough'*, 1848, pp. 424 sqq. (on the Chartist agitators); Thomas Cooper, *The Life of . . . Written by Himself*, 1872, chap. xvii, and the following, ed. 2, pp. 177 sqq. For the impression produced by these troubles in France, see *Le National* for August 22: 'We can see no issue to the industrial and social crisis from which England is suffering at the present moment. She needs a thorough and radical reform; in fact, a revolution which will completely change the conditions of industry and the rights of property. How will this revolution which the entanglements of British foreign policy are promoting and making more urgently necessary be brought about? That none of us is in a position to say. For it would be rash for Frenchmen with our ways of thought and behaviour to pronounce on what is happening among a people so near to us in geographical situation, mentally and morally so remote.'

[1] Extract from the author's earlier draft: The disturbances for which the way had been paved by many meetings of the men seem to have begun in Scotland, in Lanarkshire, in the mining district round Airdrie. Twenty thousand miners went on strike, and to obtain food without wages organized nocturnal forays throughout the entire county (*The Times*, August 5, 1842). Almost simultaneously disturbances broke out in the manufacturing district of Lancashire. On the ninth of August strikers to the number of several thousand marched on Manchester and, without encountering the least resistance, split up into small groups which visited one factory after another, enforcing an immediate stoppage of work and putting the machinery out of action, and going from shop to shop compelled the terrified shopkeepers to supply them with the food and money necessary for their subsistence. The strike movement spread to Glasgow, Tyneside, the mines of the pottery district and South Staffordshire, and even reached South Wales. . . . Was this outbreak of strikes then, the spontaneous reaction of the workers as a body? When the employers gave notice of wage reductions and fixed their approximate amount were they submitting to the inevitable? When the men replied by striking to the slogan, 'A fair day's wages for a fair day's work', were they guilty of imprudence, and, if the strike caused the employers no alarm, was it because they saw in it a golden opportunity to get rid of superfluous stocks while saving the unpaid wages? Before accepting this view of the matter, we should observe that in early August, at the very time the disturbances broke out, the uncertainty into which the country had been plunged by the pro-

They achieved their object. The strike spread to the entire cotton industry, also to the coalmines of Lancashire and South Wales. The strikers' slogan was in truth neither that of the Anti-Corn-Law League nor that of the Chartists. They demanded that the wages paid in 1840 should be restored or 'A fair day's wages for a fair day's work'. The strike was accompanied by the acts of violence normal in all such movements. Those who deserted their fellows and persisted in working were attacked. And to make this blackleg labour impossible the strikers hit upon the plan of removing certain plugs without which the machines could not be operated. Hence the name given to the Lancashire strike, the plug plot. In other places the weavers wrecked the machines. Farms and bakeries were pillaged, country houses set on fire. A mechanic who left the train at Manchester reported that as he passed through Drayton he had seen Sir Robert's mansion going up in flames.[1] This false rumour reached London, where for some hours it spread panic.

The movement seemed on the point of spreading to the West Riding. Would it take hold of that district as it had taken hold of Lancashire? Would it reach the Midlands, even perhaps the capital, and produce one of those popular risings of the Parisian type of which since 1815 the ruling class had been unreasonably afraid?[2]

Such was the situation about August 20. Was the movement Chartist? Or was it a campaign for free trade? If we consider the movement in itself we must reply that it was neither. It was simply a movement of despair, a revolt of hunger. If, however, we take account of the agitators who worked upon the despair to exploit it for their profit, the answer must be that it was both. For as we have shown when speaking of the previous spring, there was a close alliance between the Chartists and the free

tracted discussion of Peel's financial measures came to an end. They were on the verge of being passed. Business, it was generally agreed, was improving. A bumper harvest was in sight, and the Cabinet was counting upon this combination of favourable circumstances to secure their economic policy a good reception by the country. The fact that the discontent of the masses, caused by three years of bitter hardship, had remained passive so long, and had at last taken an active form when the workers had reason to hope for better days, can be explained only by the fact that it had been fanned, roused, and guided by agitators working for the new policy of alliance with the Anti-Corn-Law League. No alliance, it is true, existed between the executive committee of the National Charter Association and the committee which decided the official policy of the League. It was individuals from both camps who fraternized. But they were important individuals, Bright among the members of the League, Vincent and O'Brien in the Chartist ranks.

[1] *Morning Chronicle*, August 20, 1842.
[2] *The Times*, August 25; Graham to Peel, August 16, in Parker, op. cit., vol. ii, p. 540.

traders.[1] The alliance, however, as we have seen aroused distrust and evoked formal protests on both sides. And the cleavage would develop in the course of events.

O'Connor had always refused to associate himself with the movement inaugurated by Joseph Sturge. Deserted first by Vincent, then by O'Brien, he retained an energetic lieutenant in the person of Thomas Cooper, a former shoemaker who had given himself a thorough education. He was a good speaker and a good writer. He had collected a body of followers on whom he had bestowed the quaint designation, 'The Shakespearean Association of Leicester Chartists',[2] and their 'Shakespearean General' was always at O'Connor's orders for breaking up meetings of the League. Nevertheless, the movement of reconciliation was so powerful that O'Connor often exerted himself to prevent the dissension on this issue becoming an open conflict. The circumstances of his last intervention were dramatic. John Walter, the

[1] For the part played in these strikes by the Anti-Corn-Law League, see *The Times* of August 12, 1842, and the reply of *The Nonconformist*, August 17, 1842; also the *Manchester Courier* quoted by the *Morning Post* of August 16. The *Sunday Times* of August 14 categorically designates the League as the source of the movement. A fortnight later, however, it withdrew the allegation. The *Anti-Bread-Tax Circular* of August 15 was content with calling attention to the fact that the movement had begun, not at Bailey's factory at Staleybridge, but in the colliery of a Conservative in Staffordshire. For the Staffordshire strikes, see the *Manchester Guardian* of August 3, 1842. Replying to the charges made in the *Quarterly Review*, the *Anti-Bread-Tax Circular*, in its issue of January 3, 1843, published the following passage, which has the air of a confession: 'If we have made many bad moves and are yet winning the game, either we have made more good moves than bad, or our cause is so good that even when we ourselves cannot destroy it. That we are winning the game is clear from the ill-temper of our opponents.' Manufacturers of free trade views presided at the meetings which arranged Ashton's march on Staleybridge to enforce the stoppage of work in every mill and the march on Manchester of which we spoke above. It is significant that nowhere did the manufacturers oppose the least opposition to this revolt of the workers. Only a single millowner, Bailey, resisted the strikers at the risk of his life. On August 11 a number of the *Anti-Bread-Tax Circular* appeared containing a report of the proceedings at the seditious meeting in London (see above, p. 35). The same day, the Council of the League published a manifesto declaring that the country was on the verge of revolution and Parliament was powerless. In these circumstances it was just, necessary, and opportune that the machinery of government should be immediately brought to a standstill. The extent to which the two agitations, the Chartist and the free trading, were confused at this moment is shown by an incident debated this August in the Commons. The Rev. Thomas Spencer, a member of the Anti-Corn-Law League, who had also taken part in founding the Complete Suffrage Union, delivered, on July 21, a speech on the free trade platform condemning the corruption of the Government and the base conduct of those who, as soldiers, policemen, or jurors, were accomplices of its wrongdoing. He was denounced as a Chartist, and the Home Secretary opened an enquiry into the matter (H. of C., August 12, T. S. F. Duncombe's speech and Sir James Graham's reply, *Parliamentary Debates*, 3rd Ser., vol. lxv, pp. 1306 sqq.).

[2] 'As we now held our meetings in its Shakespearean Room, we styled ourselves "The Shakespearean Association of Leicester Chartists" ' (Thomas Cooper, *Life of* . . , 2nd ed., chap. xv, p. 163).

editor of *The Times*, who had been returned at Nottingham in the spring of 1841 on a Tory programme with Chartist support, had lost his seat at the General Election. It was now once more vacant, and he came forward as a candidate at a by-election held on August 4 at the very moment when the Lancashire strikes broke out. In the circumstances there could be no question of O'Connor supporting a Tory candidate. Walter's opponent was Joseph Sturge. The *Northern Star* conducted a campaign on behalf of the paladin of 'complete suffrage', and in consequence of O'Connor's support Sturge came within an ace of winning the seat. Eighteen hundred votes were cast and his opponent was returned by a majority no larger than eighty.[1] But at the same time, when the Plug Plot broke out, O'Connor passionately denounced the strike. The workers, he argued, should hold aloof from a movement which aggravated their poverty and induced them to commit acts of violence at the instigation of middle-class

[1] See the *Northern Star*, August 1, 1842. At Nottingham, Sturge's candidature was identified with the cause of O'Connor and Chartism: 'The cry of "O'Connor for ever" is singing through the town, and many who were wavering before are flocking to the Sturge standard.' It was an odd circumstance that Stephens was brought in by the Tories, together with Doherty of Manchester, to support Walter's candidature to the indignation of his old friend O'Connor. But the same number contains a violent denunciation of union with the middle classes by O'Brien, and reports from Sheffield a glorious victory of the Chartists and defeat of the Leaguers. For the Nottingham election, see R. G. Gammage, *History of the Chartist Movement*, p. 208; Thomas Cooper, *Life*, 2nd ed., chap. xv, pp. 159 sqq.: 'I was also present at the Nottingham election—where Chartists suddenly reversed their policy and voted against Walter and in favour of the noble philanthropist Joseph Sturge. Feargus O'Connor, while in York Castle, had advocated the policy of voting for the Tories in preference to the Whigs. But he came down to Nottingham, and by his speeches encouraged the Chartists to support Joseph Sturge. With the thought of rendering some help . . . other Chartists also came to Nottingham.'

The *Northern Star*, August 13, 1842: 'Every succeeding day furnishes additional proof of the villainy inherent in the despicable middle class; of their hostility to the interests of the mass; of their hatred of justice, and, consequently, of the absurdity of the doctrines propounded by the defunct "New Movers" and the expiring League, who profess to desire an amalgamation of the middle and lower classes.' Ibid., August 20: 'How will they compensate for the loss of life and the personal injuries, the shootings and cuttings and slashings, the imprisonments, and the transportings that are to follow? How will they compensate for those things which they and *they alone* have caused?' Thomas Cooper, *Life of* . . , 2nd ed., p. 190: ' "The Plug Plot" of 1842, as it is still called in Lancashire, began in a reduction of wages by the Anti-Corn-Law manufacturers who did not conceal their purpose of driving people to desperation in order to paralyse the Government.' Ibid., p. 209: The writer is giving an account of a meeting in Manchester: 'But now uprose William Hill, who had been a Swedenborgian minister, and so was often termed "Reverend", but who had for some years been O'Connor's servant, as editor of the *Northern Star*. He admired, he said, the clear intelligence which had led me to proclaim in so decided a manner that this strike meant fighting; but he wondered that so clear an intellect should dream of fighting. Fight! The people had nothing to fight with, and would be mown down by artillery if they attempted to fight. The strike had originated with the Anti-Corn-Law League, and we should simply be their tools if we helped to extend or prolong the strike.'

agitators, members of the Anti-Corn-Law League working for their own ends.

The executive of the League, on the other hand, when the strike broke out adopted an equivocal attitude of compassionate neutrality.[1] Mayors and town councillors who were free traders flatly refused to answer the appeal of the Tory gentry and organize resistance to the rioters. Their attitude was in many respects the same as that of many Tories in 1839 when the Whig Government had to repress rioting. It was not for the Whigs, said the Tories then, to put down an insurrection. For in 1832 they had not hesitated to carry the Reform Bill by incitements to revolt, yet by passing the Poor Law Amendment Bill and by consistently refusing to protect the workers against the servitude of the factory they had done everything in their power to inflame the passions of the masses. It was not for the Tory gentry, said the free traders now, to repress disorders for which they and they alone were responsible. For it was they who by their infamous Corn Law were ruining the manufacturers, starving the workers and plunging the country into the throes of revolution.[2]

When, however, the disturbances spread and threatened the safety, not only of the squires and their tenants, but of the shopkeepers and employers, the *Manchester Guardian*,[3] the accepted mouthpiece of Radical free trade, and even the official organ of the Anti-Corn-Law League,[4] began to dissociate itself from the

---

[1] Cobden, speech at Manchester, August 25, 1842: 'I think, notwithstanding the lamentable circumstances, the state of the public mind in this country, both with masters and men, will settle down into a more rational disposition to view this question apart from passion or prejudice than ever it did before; for I do think, gentlemen, that the present disturbances will leave less traces of prejudice or of resentment in the minds of the middle classes in this part of the country than any former tumults ever did before' (A. Prentice, *Hist. of the Anti-Corn-Law League*, vol. i, p. 387). Bright's address to the working men of Rochdale, August 17: 'A deep sympathy with you in the present circumstances induces me to address you. . . . Many of you know full well that neither an Act of Parliament nor the act of a multitude can keep up wages. . . . Against obtaining the Charter the laws of nature offer no impediment, as they do against a forcible advance of wages; but to obtain the Charter now is just as impossible as to raise wages by force. . . . Return to your employment. . . . Your first step to entire freedom must be commercial freedom—freedom of industry. . . . The aristocracy regard the Anti-Corn-Law League as their greatest enemy. That which is the greatest enemy of the remorseless aristocracy of Britain must almost of necessity be your firmest friend' (G. M. Trevelyan, *The Life of Bright*, pp. 81-2).

For accounts of the strike in August 1842, written from the standpoint of the League, see *The Nonconformist*, 'The Strike, its History, Causes, and Consequences', from a Manchester correspondent, November 9, 1842, February 1, 1843; Miss Martineau, *History of the Thirty Years' Peace*, book vi, chap. v; A. Prentice, *History of the Anti-Corn-Law League*, vol. i, pp. 370 sqq.

[3] *Manchester Guardian*, September 7, 1842.   [4] *Anti-Bread-Tax Circular*, August 25, 1842.

revolt and to denounce as its agents the Chartist agitators once more depicted as the rivals and foes of the missionaries of free trade.

Since the local authorities took no action the Government intervened. Wellington took over the command of the army from Lord Hill, and the extensive construction of railroads during the past three years made it possible to bring without delay into the disturbed areas forces sufficient to keep order. Except at Burslem, where the troops fired on the crowd and killed three persons, no blood was shed.[1] The Chartist ringleaders were imprisoned, but at the end of the winter or the beginning of spring were either acquitted or received mild sentences. And the disturbances died down. They gained no ground in Yorkshire, and the Midlands remained unaffected. In London nothing happened beyond some insignificant demonstrations and petty affrays with the police.

Parliament was in recess, having passed the fiscal measures introduced by Peel. The uncertainty, therefore, which had hampered business while their fate was unknown had been removed. Business was improving, and the agitation for free trade received a decisive blow when the price of wheat fell rapidly during the latter half of the year, from 64 shillings towards the end of July to 40 towards the end of December. It was no longer possible to argue that the new sliding scale was reducing the country to famine. The stroke had failed. The Government had overcome its difficulties, and the alliance between the free traders and Chartists, having so clearly proved barren, broke up. At Birmingham on December 27 Sturge invited a meeting of the Union for Complete Suffrage to go back on its decision of the previous spring and re-baptize its programme instead of the People's Charter, a Bill of Right. William Lovett protested against this abandonment of a standard for which for several years past so many workers had fought and suffered. He was supported by O'Connor, and when the proposal was rejected by a very large majority Sturge withdrew from the Union. Once more after a year's rapprochement the Chartists and free traders were at loggerheads.[2]

[1] For the Burslem incident, see the *Morning Herald*, July 23, and *The Times*, August 9, 1842.
[2] A special number of *The Nonconformist*, December 31, 1842, was entirely devoted to a report of the proceedings.

4

The Chartists, now more than ever O'Connor's fanatical
devotees, broke up so many meetings arranged by the free traders
that the latter were reduced to holding them in private.[1] But their
fanaticism may very well have been the result of their diminished
numbers, and the tactics adopted by Sturge, though Cobden
disapproved, had proved successful. As the Tories had profited
by the attitude of benevolent neutrality which they had adopted
towards the Chartist agitation between 1839 and 1841, so now the
manufacturers of the League, by the half-active sympathy they
displayed towards the Lancashire workers, made the class struggle
less bitter and effected a rapprochement between the middle and
the working classes which survived the quarrel between Chartism
and free trade.

In August the free traders had cleverly withdrawn from the
fray leaving their Chartist allies embroiled. In a country of artisans
and peasant proprietors Chartism would probably have succeeded,
the Anti-Corn-Law League failed. But in consequence of the distinctive social structure of Britain the contrary happened. It became a foregone conclusion a little later when O'Connor at last
worked out his project of social reform. He proposed to break
up the large estates and divide them among a number of small
freeholders, in short to get rid of the great landowners and bring
the workers back to the land as yeomen. It was the utopia of
reaction pure and simple. The free traders, on the other hand,
because, far from disliking the extreme industrialization of England they actively favoured it, stood for reality and the future.
Carlyle after the crisis of 1842 understood this. In his *Past and
Present* he portrays the civilization of Europe, not as tending to a
system of freedom, but as returning, after passing convulsions,
to a state of order. In his opinion, however, the old landed aristocracy was unworthy to preside over the birth of the new order.
It would perish and it deserved to perish because it had managed
to survive only by the artificial respiration of protection. To guide
the new society Carlyle looked to an oligarchy not agrarian but
industrial, to the men, in fact, who furnished Cobden with his
staff, and whose only fault was that they were deluded by the

[1] H. of C., February 2, 1843. Milner Gibson's speech (*Parliamentary Debates*, 3rd Ser.,
vol. lxvi, p. 154).

Liberal philosophy and, therefore, failed to perceive that their function in a community whose social structure was determined by the needs of production was to rule and serve at once.

Nevertheless, a gloomy outlook persisted among the ruling classes. 'There is an immense and continually increasing population,' the shrewd Greville wrote on November 2, 'deep distress and privation, no adequate demand for labour, no demand for anything, no confidence, but a universal alarm, disquietude and discontent. . . . Certainly I have never seen in the course of my life so serious a state of things as that which now stares us in the face. . . .' What a humiliation, he continues, for a nation which 'according to our own ideas' is 'not only the most free and powerful, but the most moral and the wisest people in the world'.[1]

And when at the close of the year Carlyle in his *Past and Present* attempted to draw the moral of the disturbances of 1842, as in his *Chartism* he had drawn the moral of the disturbances of 1839, he wrote, 'The condition of England on which many pamphlets are now in the course of publication, and many thoughts unpublished are going on in every reflective head is justly regarded as one of the most ominous, and withal one of the strangest, ever seen in this world. England is full of wealth, of multifarious produce, supply for human want in every kind; yet England is dying of inanition.'[2] In January the economic position deteriorated, as was acknowledged even by those whose hopes had revived in the autumn months. Though London was spared the worst sufferings of the crisis which it watched from outside, the bad news plunged the capital in gloom. The previous year, before the strikes, Londoners had been alarmed by two attempts against the Queen's life, and as the new year opened the alarm was

[1] *Greville Memoirs*, November 2, 1842.
[2] Carlyle, *Past and Present*, book 1, chap. 1, p. 1. We may compare the words of Samuel Bamford, an old Radical of 1819 turned philosopher, as he wrote them in the last pages of his book, *Passages in the Life of a Radical* (vol. ii, p. 235), on the very eve of the August strikes. His final page is dated July 27. 'Next come the manufacturers, working at the wrong end, and trying to make a pitiable impression on the heads and hearts of a class that never, since the days of Cromwell, was pervious to anything at variance with its own will save a battle-axe or a bullet. There they are, striving for cheap bread, as if it were present salvation, and forgetting what all history is constantly proclaiming, that nothing human is fixed; that crowns, sceptres, dominions, institutions, establishments, and monopolies are ever changing, ever departing from their old seats, springing up anew in other places and leaving deserts where they formerly flourished. Tyre, Sidon, Carthage, Greece, Rome! all the departed nations of the world warn us of this, and still we remain as if we were unconscious that our time comes, is coming, nay, is almost at the threshold.' The entire passage undoubtedly inspired chap. 4 ('Morison's Pill') of Carlyle's *Past and Present*.

renewed by a deed of blood which may be regarded as the tragic
epilogue to the troubles of 1842.

On January 21 Edward Drummond, Peel's private secretary,
was assassinated in the street, shot by a pistol fired at close range.
The murderer confessed that Drummond had been the victim of
a blunder. He had intended to shoot the Prime Minister. But who
was it who towards the end of the previous spring had, in language
thinly veiled, incited to Sir Robert's murder? When three weeks
later Parliament reassembled and the Corn Law was again discussed, Lord Francis Egerton, supporting his allegations with
copious evidence, accused the League of having provoked the
disorders of the previous year, and when he refused to give further
publicity by quoting them to speeches of which 'he had no doubt
the parties who made them were ashamed since' he made a
covert allusion to the strange language used in July on a League
platform. When Cobden replied, he did not refute Lord Egerton's
charges against the League, but attempted to shift the issue by
denouncing the equal incompetence of both parties, of the Prime
Minister above all, who, he declared, would be personally responsible for the misfortunes of the country if he refused to adopt the
measures necessary to save it. His speech had a chilly reception,
and he had hardly sat down when Peel got up to call attention to
the fact that Cobden had declared him 'individually responsible'
for the distress and suffering of the country. Cobden, before a
House alarmed by the turn which the debate had taken, excused
himself and explained that the responsibility he meant was purely
political, in virtue of 'Peel's office', and in sarcastic and haughty
terms the Prime Minister accepted his explanation.[1] The Tories
were delighted by what they mistakenly regarded as an irreconcil-
able quarrel between their leader and the apostle of free trade.

'He is afraid. We have him.' This is the burden of a letter
Cobden wrote at this time to his brother.[2] Though the strike of
last summer—a rising of the workers was to have terrified Peel

---

[1] H. of C., February 17, 1843 (*Parliamentary Debates*, 3rd Ser., vol. lxvi, pp. 823 and
839).
[2] R. Cobden to his brother, February 23, 1843: 'Peel has made a great fool of himself,
if not something more. . . . Lord . . . was joking with Ricardo in the House the other
night about him; pointing towards Peel, as he was leaning forward, he whispered,
"There, the fellow is afraid somebody is taking aim at him from the gallery." He is
looking twenty per cent worse since I came into the House, and if I had only Bright to
me, we would worry him out of office before the close of the session' (John Morley,
Life of Richard Cobden, 1902, p. 37).

into surrender—had not come off, he did not despair of succeeding sooner or later by less dramatic methods, not, as he once hoped, by agitation in the streets, but by harassing tactics in the House. Motion after motion in the Commons called for the repeal of the Corn Law. Naturally they were all defeated. But the free traders had the satisfaction of hearing Graham declare that 'free trade principles . . . are not much contested in this House. They are the principles of common sense',[1] and Gladstone stated that 'The difference between the Government and their antagonists was not really so great as the Opposition made out, but was one of degree only.'[2] Peel had, indeed, said as much in 1842, and in the autumn many country gentlemen addressing public meetings had seemed to be preparing their agricultural audiences for the introduction by the Government of some new measure which would be a concession to free trade. And this had undoubtedly been Peel's intention before the strikes.[3] He may even have entertained it later and have contemplated a further modification of the sliding scale. For at the close of the year Graham, who was convinced that the next two or three years would see the repeal of the Corn Law, for that very reason advised Peel against trying further half measures. 'The next change must be the last; it is not prudent to hurry it; next session is too soon and as you cannot make a decisive alteration it is far wiser to make none.'[4] The Budget which this year the Prime Minister left in Goulburn's charge[5] contained only one provision which could affect the price of wheat, namely the reduction of the duty on Canadian wheat to the nominal figure of 1

[1] H. of C., February 15, 1843 (*Parliamentary Debates*, 3rd Ser., vol. lxvi, p. 687).

[2] H. of C., February 13 (ibid., 3rd Ser., vol. lxvi, p. 490). *Annual Register*, 1843, p. 28. [Not in Hansard. From which I quote: 'The doctrines of free trade . . . are indisputable. . . . The whole question is . . : in what degree the actual circumstances of the country will bear their "application".'—*Trs. Note*.]

[3] Peel to Graham, July 26, 1842: 'I agree with you that we must advance in our present course of relaxation. Butter and cheese must share the fate of other articles of consumption. The sugar question we must most carefully and seriously consider' (C. S. Parker, *Sir Robert Peel*, vol. ii, p. 428).

[4] Graham to Peel, December 30, 1842 (C. S. Parker, *Sir Robert Peel*, vol. ii, p. 551). Peel, in fact, informed Parliament when the new session opened, that he had no intention at present of altering the Corn Law (*Parl. Deb.*, 3rd Ser., vol. lxvi, p. 178). When, in 1843, Lord John Russell summed up the work of the previous session in the department of finance, he remarked: 'I recollect the principles laid down by the Right Hon. Baronet last year. They applied to the articles of the tariff, but not to the Corn Laws. The Secretary of State for the Home Department said he did not consider the Corn Law a final measure.' He observed that the Minister had reduced his supporters to this difficulty, that they were obliged to vindicate the tariff on principles of free competition and the Corn Laws on principles of protection.

[5] H. of C., May 8, 1843: Goulburn's speech (*Parl. Deb.*, 3rd Ser., vol. lxviii, pp. 1391 sqq.).

shilling, in consideration of a duty of 3 shillings a quarter imposed on wheat imported into Canada from the United States. This, however, was colonial protection rather than British free trade. The clause, which was passed, was opposed by Cobden and the other uncompromising free traders.

Otherwise it was an unexciting Budget, and merely provisional. Goulburn's exposition began with a number of unpleasant disclosures. The customs had been expected to yield £21,500,000. The actual receipts were short of this figure by £800,000. The Excise had been expected to bring in fourteen millions. It had produced only thirteen. By a strange blunder the calculation had lost sight of the fact that the reduced duties would come into force immediately, whereas the new income tax would not be levied until the second half of the financial year following its imposition. The miscalculation had produced a new deficit. The Chancellor of the Exchequer had the consolation, however, of pointing out that if the reduced duties on coffee and timber had not produced an increase in the amount imported, sufficient to yield the larger revenue expected, other duties had produced a higher yield than before, and if the return from customs was so unsatisfactory its primary cause was a decrease in the importation of wines and spirits, the duties on which had not been lowered. It was also consoling to be able to state that the income tax was producing more than Peel had expected, and the deficit due to the fact that it had been levied only for half the year had been correspondingly diminished. And the general improvement of business, which took place while the Budget was being debated, guaranteed more satisfactory returns for the new financial year.

In these circumstances Peel and Goulburn did not consider it necessary to impose any new taxation. They proposed that the existing imposts should be left as they were for the following year to see whether the financial experiment made in 1842 would prove successful. Meanwhile, the deficit of £2,400,000 would be provisionally covered by issuing short-term loans, which would be called deficiency bills. This would mean an increase of the floating debt which, however, must not be regarded as the serious matter it had been in Baring's time. For the bills were due for repayment the following year when everything pointed to a surplus.[1]

[1] H. of C., May 8, 1843: Goulburn's speech (*Annual Register*, 1843, pp. 173 sqq.). St. Northcote, *Twenty Years of Financial Policy*, p. 376.

The session of 1843, therefore, ended like its predecessor on a note of patience. Better things had been hoped from Peel on the morrow of his victory at the polls in 1841. Voluble opposition, it is true, was confined to Cobden and his independent following. The official Opposition was as feeble and discredited as ever. And the excessive violence of Cobden's invectives against Peel had undoubtedly produced among many moderate men a reaction in his favour. Nevertheless, his popularity which could hardly have increased was on the wane. There was no one who seemed capable of taking his place, but the fact was regretted. This decline in popularity was the more marked because besides these financial and commercial problems, though they bulked very large in the public mind, other problems demanded the attention of the head of the Government, problems of foreign policy and colonial administration, religious problems and Irish problems. And all these, this summer of 1843, caused Peel serious anxiety.[1]

IV PROBLEMS OF FOREIGN POLICY

I

Did the foreign policy pursued by Lord Aberdeen, Foreign Secretary in the new Cabinet, play any considerable part in diminishing Peel's popularity? We might well think so if we were to take seriously the violent denunciations of it by Palmerston, once

[1] *Greville Memoirs*, January 16, 1843: 'As to the Ministry, if ever they had any popularity, they have now none left but their power as a government and their means of retaining office don't seem to be at all diminished. People are aware we must have a government, and tho' they feel no great affection for Sir Robert Peel and Co., they cannot look round and discover anybody else whom they would prefer to him.' June 6, 1843: 'Peel is become very unpopular. Ireland is in a flame. The whole country is full of distress, disquiet, and alarm. Religious feuds are rife. The Church and the Puseyites are at loggerheads here, and the Church and the Seceders in Scotland; and everybody says it is all very alarming, and God knows what will happen, and everybody goes on just the same and nobody cares except those who can't get bread to eat.' On August 1 Greville reports: 'Peel has fallen immensely in public opinion, and has so signally failed in his general administration of affairs as to have shown himself unequal to a great emergency and extraordinary difficulties and dangers.' Though he does not endorse this view, Greville considers that Peel 'acts rather like the cautious leader of a party, than like a great and powerful Minister determined to do what he thinks right' (August 6, 1843). 'Peel's policy appears to me to be in everything continually to advance, but to do so by such slow and insensible degrees that existing interests or, rather, existing powers may be as little frightened and as little hurt as possible' (September 10, 1843). Lord John Russell to Lord

more a member of the Opposition and in many respects its outstanding figure. When towards the end of the session, while the
battle was raging between Cobden and Peel, Lord John Russell,
entirely out of the public eye, was burying his chagrin in the
country, Palmerston on the front bench of the Opposition played
for six weeks the part of its leader. He did not, indeed, cherish
the hope of occupying a position no one offered him. His strong
and arrogant personality had made too many enemies in his own
party. But having ruled the Foreign Office almost without interruption for ten years he had come to regard it as his preserve where
he could act as he pleased without troubling about his colleagues'
views. When through their fault he was turned out of office, only
a few months after an unprecedented diplomatic triumph, he did
not consider himself as in the least involved in their unpopularity,
and regarded Lord Aberdeen as an intruder at the Foreign Office.
He instructed all the diplomatic representatives of England in
foreign capitals, as though they were his personal representatives,
not to resign but to remain at their posts. In this way his influence
would survive him until the day came when he would resume
control of foreign affairs. Only one of them, William Russell,
Ambassador at Berlin, was too fanatical a Whig to be retained in
the service of a Tory Cabinet.[1] By his speeches in Parliament
and the articles in the Press which he inspired or himself contributed to the *Morning Chronicle* he kept up a fire against the Government. Was he successful? The question admits no brief answer.
For we must distinguish between the different parts of the world
in which the Government had to make decisions, Asia, Europe,
and America.

Minto, August 5, 1843: 'Peel is tired and dispirited' (Sp. Walpole, *Life of Lord John
Russell*, vol. i, p. 390). John Foster to the Rev. Josiah Mill, 1843 (*Life and Correspondence
of John Foster*, vol. ii, p. 460): 'We are not to be suffered to go to sleep like our forefathers
in the dull quiet of their time. We should be able to live on "agitation", for we are to
have nothing else. The Corn-Law agitation—education agitation—Puseyism agitation—
Scotch Church agitation—and, most portentous of all, Irish agitation.' The *Quarterly
Review* (September 1843, an article entitled, 'Policy of Ministers', vol. lxxii, p. 553)
defends Peel. But the *Edinburgh Review* (October 1843, art. ix, 'The Ministry and the Late
Session', vol. lxxviii, pp. 517 sqq.) depicts a Ministry weakened after an unproductive
session. Cf. in the *Annual Register*, 1843, p. 27, Gladstone's admission: 'It was notorious,
that on the declaration of the changes intended to be effected, trade became stagnant,
employment was diminished, and capital rendered redundant. This was the temporary
effect of a plan which was defiant and specific.' See also Tooke, *History of Prices*, vol. i,
pp. 49–50.

[1] *Greville Memoirs*, December 16, 1841: 'Palmerston has ordered all his diplomatic
tribe to stick to their places, but William Russell should have felt in his case that it was
impossible.'

2

In Asia, in Afghanistan, and in China serious incidents—events, indeed, too serious to be called incidents—occurred. But they were the result of action taken before the Conservatives assumed office, and it was never possible to apportion between the two parties the responsibility for defeats or the credit for successes.

Afghanistan had always been the starting-point by which India was invaded through the Khyber Pass. Alexander, Timur, and Baber, the founder of the Mogul dynasty, had taken this route. The rumour had spread that if Napoleon completed the conquest of Europe he would attack Britain in India. And when with Russian aid Britain had overthrown Napoleon, a Russian invasion became the nightmare of the Indian Government. Since the death of a great sultan Afghanistan had fallen into a state of feudal anarchy, and was a prey to every influence from the East or West. To put an end to Russian intrigues the Indian Government had dispatched an expedition which crossed the Bolan pass and occupied Quetta, Kandahar, the stronghold of Ghazni, and finally Kabul. This happened in November 1840, and contributed to Palmerston's triumph.

Then exactly a year to the day after the surrender of Kabul the city rose. The British agent was assassinated, and his successor suffered the same fate. The garrison after a formal surrender, by whose terms they gave up their guns and ammunition, attempted to reach the eastern side of the Himalayas. The object of hostile attacks, they marched through snow over difficult mountains and among war-like tribes. Finally of several thousand men only one, Dr. Brydon, reached Jallalabad, wounded and half dead. It was a disaster unprecedented in the history of India. But regarded from the Parliamentary point of view it was a disaster for which Peel's Government had no responsibility.

The Governor-General of British India, Lord Auckland, decided that British honour must be avenged. Kabul was reoccupied. But while the campaign was in progress the government of India, as a result of the change of government at home, changed hands. Lord Ellenborough succeeded Lord Auckland. His policy, that of the new Cabinet, was retrenchment and peace. In Asia this meant a reaction against the policy of the Whig administration which had been too spectacular and too Palmerstonian. It was almost against the Viceroy's orders that the British army reached Kabul. It had scarcely arrived when it received the order to evacuate Afghanistan unconditionally, immediately, and completely. It withdrew, destroying, pillaging, and massacring as it went. When the evacuation was complete Lord Ellenborough issued a proclamation in which he expounded the principles of the Government's pacific and conservative policy. It would not interfere in Afghanistan nor spend another penny on it, but would leave it to the anarchy it deserved.

The Government of India did not, however, entirely renounce annexation. In 1838 one of the two armies preparing to occupy Afghanistan, starting from Karachi and advancing up the valley of the Indus, had concluded treaties with the local Mirs by which they accepted a British protectorate. Several years of intrigue had followed, during which the terms of these treaties had been respected neither by the British generals nor the native rulers. In 1843, after severe fighting, England annexed this region. Afghanistan remained independent between British India on the one frontier, Persia and Russia on others. But a buffer state no longer separated British India from Baluchistan and Afghanistan. Sind became British.

The annexation of Sind gave rise to protests at home. Even the Cabinet seemed none too pleased with the step the Governor-General had taken.[1] The horrible fate which befell the British army on its retreat from Kabul was the subject of protests equally strong. But no protests were raised against the evacuation of Afghanistan. Public opinion approved Lord Ellenborough's policy in so far as it was genuinely pacific and conservative. From beginning to end the policy followed by the Indian Government towards Afghanistan had been inconsistent and blundering. Both front benches, however, agreed to burke serious discussion of the matter. Responsibility was too equally divided. Moreover, it would have been impossible to discuss the question thoroughly without denouncing Russian intrigue in Central Asia. But this was just what the former and the present ministers were equally determined to avoid; the former, because, as we have seen,[2] Palmerston's policy had been to maintain a good understanding

---

[1] Gladstone wrote later (*Contemporary Review*, November 1876, p. 875): 'The conquest was disapproved, I believe unanimously, by the Cabinet of Sir Robert Peel, of which I can speak, as I had just entered it at the time.' Cf. *Greville Memoirs*, June 15, 1843.

[2] *History of the English People*, vol. iii, pp. 258-60.

with Russia, and he had, in fact, obtained from St. Petersburg a formal disavowal of the action taken by the Russian consuls in Persia and Afghanistan; the latter, because their pacific and conservative policy made them as determined as Palmerston had been, though for very different motives, to preserve at all costs friendly relations with the Powers of Northern Europe. The only overt criticism of British policy in India came from a group of Radicals, led by Roebuck and Hume, and an even smaller group of extreme Tories led by Disraeli.[1]

The situation in China was closely bound up with the situation in India. Trade with China was estimated to produce about two millions a year, a large part of which came from the trade in opium. The traffic in opium, though the point had not been very clearly determined, was illicit. And it was not favoured by the Chinese Government, which wanted to keep the sale of the drug its monopoly. The British Government became directly concerned in the matter when, in 1833, the East India Company lost its monopoly of trade with China, and to control it an Act of Parliament replaced the company's factor at Canton by a superintendent appointed by the British Government. The latter found himself in the ambiguous position of a British representative abroad who did not in any respect enjoy diplomatic status. In 1837 the Chinese authorities at Tonkin prohibited absolutely the import of opium. This led to a number of clashes, sometimes bloody, and finally, in 1840, to war. A British squadron occupied the island of Chusan and made a naval demonstration in the gulf of Chihli.

The forts of Canton were occupied and the protocol of a peace signed on January 7, 1841, by which the port and island of Hong Kong were to be ceded to England, import and export trade to be carried on there on the same terms as hitherto at Canton, and the Chinese Government undertook to pay within five years an indemnity of six million dollars. Military operations below Canton secured the immediate payment of the indemnity. But before the news of this further success reached England the Government, which regarded the amount of the indemnity as inadequate, objected to the time granted to the Chinese Government within which to pay it, and was displeased that the question of the importation of opium, required to balance the Budget of British

[1] H. of C., June 23, 1842, March 1, and July 23, 1843 (*Parliamentary Debates*, 3rd Ser., vol. lxiv, pp. 435 sqq.; vol. lxvii, p. 119; and vol. lxx, p. 1392).

India, had been shelved, refused to ratify the treaty, and recalled the superintendent responsible for concluding it. This happened in May 1841. Three months later the Tories took office just in time to reap the credit for retrieving the position. The British squadron sailing up the coast of China disembarked at Amoy, stormed the town and reoccupied the island of Chusan, took Ning-po, not far from the coast, Cha-pu on the opposite coast of the gulf of Hang-chow, and Wu-sung on the river below Shanghai and sailed up the Yangtze Kiang to the gates of Nankin. On August 26, 1842, a peace was concluded by which not only was the island of Hong Kong ceded to England and an indemnity of twenty-one million dollars imposed, but the five ports of Canton, Amoy, Fuchow, Ning-po, and Shanghai were opened to British trade and the right granted to England to appoint consuls.

Dreamers saw in this success an event comparable in importance to the discovery of America or the first beginnings of British rule in India, which had led by degrees to the conquest of the entire peninsula. They might surely hope to witness the conquest of China, now that she had lost the prestige conferred hitherto by her jealously maintained seclusion. But there is little evidence that these victories won on the coast of China aroused the enthusiasm of ardent patriots or, among those who objected on principle to armed conquest, the uneasiness and scruples they had felt and still felt at the news of the fighting in Afghanistan.

'The inglorious war in China,' wrote the *Annual Register*, 'in which success could be attended with little honour and failure would have been disgrace.'[1] The British dead were counted only by tens. The Chinese allowed themselves to be mown down when they did not fly too fast to be overtaken. Moreover, the result was not a conquest in the strict sense, simply the forcing open of markets badly needed in these hard times. The indemnity made up, in fact, part of the deficit of 1843. Philanthropists shocked by the opium traffic, Lord Ashley among the Conservatives, Brotherton among the Radicals, employed every possible argument to win British exporters to their point of view, reminding them that, since the object of the Chinese Government was to prevent too much currency leaving the country, the greater the amount of opium imported the fewer cotton goods would be admitted.

[1] *Annual Register*, 1842, p. 264.

But they were not heeded. The Radical free traders, though so ready to denounce policies of military honour, were delighted with a victory which, though no doubt British arms had contributed to it, was, take it all in all, a victory of commerce and, therefore, of civilization and peace.[1]

3

In Europe nothing was happening comparable in importance to the events in Afghanistan and China. But incidents occurred in Europe which were awkward from the British point of view. And Palmerston could exploit them more easily than the events in Asia, where he was responsible for all the mistakes made, and it was easy to represent any action taken by the Government which turned out badly as the result of their predecessors' blunders, any successes as the redress of their mistakes.

In Europe Palmerston had closed his term of office by his diplomatic triumph of 1840. Would the Government of Peel and Lord Aberdeen be able to maintain British prestige at the level to which he had raised it?

What, then, was the Europe of 1843? In the East there was Russia, a power half Asiatic, half European, whose ambitions on the Bosphorus and the Khyber Pass alarmed the English, but whose attitude as the result of Palmerston's policy was for the moment friendly. To the west of Russia was the Austrian Empire. It was in decay. But the ghost of her ancient supremacy still hovered over the German States. Liberals detested her reactionary policy. But British diplomacy without love or fear kept on good terms with her because she was regarded as an indispensable factor in maintaining the territorial *status quo* and the balance of power in Europe.

Can Italy be said to have existed? To English Liberals who visited her shores to warm and mellow in her southern sunshine their northern chilliness and austerity she was a hope dearly cherished. In all simplicity they constructed the imaginary creed of a Dante, depicted for no better reason perhaps than that he had been the foe of the Pope and France, as the great prophet of modern Liberalism.

[1] H. of C., April 7, 1843 (*Parliamentary Debates*, 3rd Ser., vol. lxviii, p. 362). Cf. Sp. Walpole, *History of England*, vol. vi, pp. 194 sqq.

Was there a Germany? Prussia already constituted the nucleus of a young and Protestant Germany capable of taking over the succession of the old Catholic Holy Roman Empire. She was a favourite of the Court, extremely Protestant and extremely German in sentiment, and popular with the army, for the memory of Waterloo was only twenty-five years old, in Evangelical circles (we have already remarked the influence wielded in London by the Prussian representative, Bunsen), and with the Liberal intelligentsia, which respected German science. Though Carlyle's diatribes annoyed a great many he was, nevertheless, a very real influence in the most diverse quarters. And his true fatherland was not England, nor even Scotland, but Protestant Prussia. Prussian policy, it is true, had already begun to cause a certain amount of anxiety in England. The Customs Union, the *Zollverein*, the first sketch of a Germany united under Prussian hegemony, was a direct blow launched by Prussia against the British exporter. And Friedrich List's important work, published in 1841, was a declaration of war in the name of the 'national' system of which he was the founder against the cosmopolitanism, insincere according to him, of English political economy. Palmerston disliked Prussia, not the less because the Court held her dear. But to allay English suspicions she had only to evoke the memory of Waterloo. And Austria's decline made her power an indispensable counterpoise to the power of France.[1]

---

[1] See an excellent article in the *Edinburgh Review* (1844, vol. lxxix, pp. 105 sqq.), entitled 'The German *Zollverein*'. After pointing out the value of British exports to Germany, the author continues: 'In every point of view, whether politically or commercially, we can have no better alliance than that of the German nation, spreading, as is does, its 42 millions of souls, without interruption, over the surface of Central Europe. Nor is it an unnatural sentiment for Englishmen to entertain towards Germany feelings of the same kind as the better class of Americans uniformly cherish for England, namely, those of reverence for the land of our forefathers, and of sympathy with that Teutonic race of which we are ourselves a continuing branch. Whenever the Continent shall be cursed with another war, the weight of the Germanic body will probably be sufficient to turn any doubtful balance, at its option, in favour of the East or West of Europe. We think it clear that English feeling and English policy ought to move alike in the direction of maintaining and strengthening our connection of friendship and alliance with the states of Germany.' He is aware, nevertheless, of the threat to British trade presented by the *Zollverein*. 'The *Zollvereinsblatt*, conducted by him [List] has acquired a large circulation, and his National System of Political Economy keeps up its reputation among those who either do not, or will not, know that the so-called system is utterly at variance with all sound political economy; and that the name of "National" is used as a cloak for the selfish claims of class interest.' But to seek to prevent the union of German States would be a shortsighted policy. The writer, on the contrary, expresses the hope that the entrance of the North German States into the *Zollverein* may 'liberalize the character of that association. The true object of British policy is not to counteract the extension of the *Zollverein* to the rest of Germany, but to weaken and destroy the mischievous influence

France, of which we have still to speak, had suffered at Trafalgar a defeat which, everybody in London was assured, could never be avenged. Nor did her reputation stand high. Some forty thousand voluntary exiles[1] attracted by the brilliance of Parisian life, sought in the French capital pleasure and luxury rather than culture, and the good name of France suffered from the ignoble character of their taste for her. Were the English ignorant, the French asked, of the existence of all their great scientists, poets, and novelists, that they persisted in regarding their country as a country which could not produce genius, a country of mere talent, a sceptical and critical cleverness, intelligent mediocrity.[2]

France was a troublesome neighbour, less hated in London than England in Paris, but a constant source of irritation. To ratify Trafalgar had required ten years of war and Waterloo. And quite recently to remind the French that another Trafalgar was always possible, France had been compelled to suffer a diplomatic Waterloo which had left behind it renewed bitterness in the hearts of Frenchmen. The Foreign Office, now under the control of Lord Aberdeen, attempted to take advantage of the change of government to seek reconciliation with a nation which had perhaps been too brutally humiliated. It was no easy task.

All over the world the English and the French habitually intrigued against each other. If England was confronted by a difficult situation in Northern India, she suspected the action of French as well as Russian agents. Syria, liberated by England from Egyptian rule, was a prey to anarchy. And the anarchy was made worse by the fact that here also England and France confronted each other. The military instructors of the Sultan's army were almost undisguisedly working to set up a species of British protectorate, and while the Jesuits were consolidating French influence over the Maronites the British were trying to convert the Druses to Protestantism. In Spain the two nations were engaged in a bitter struggle. When Espartero, the leader of the 'hotheads'

which is now by far too predominant—the influence of monopoly and class interest.' See, on the other hand, in the same *Review* (October 1845, vol. lxxxii, pp. 451 sqq.) an article protesting against the excessive admiration of German literature by the English; and another (January 1846, vol. lxxxiii, pp. 224 sqq.) expressing anxiety at the agitation conducted by the Prussian Liberals.

[1] For the English who settled in France after 1815, see R. Guyot, *La Première Entente Cordiale*, 1926, pp. 21 sqq.

[2] See the article by Charles de Remusat, 'Des Controverses Religieuses en Angleterre', *Revue des Deux-Mondes*, September 15, 1856, vol. v, p. 511, expounding Coleridge's philosophy.

(Exaltados), seized the person of the young Queen Isabella, the Queen Mother Christina fled to Paris, where she plotted against Espartero. When her supporters in turn gained the upper hand, it was in London that Espartero found asylum. Austria, which as the upholder of legitimacy cared nothing for the fate of the dynasty reigning in Madrid, watched with amusement England and France, whose joint action had placed it on the throne, quarrelling over their protégé. Metternich suspected that the King of the French wanted the Spanish crown for his son, the Queen of England for a cousin. Lord Aberdeen did everything in his power to smooth out conflicts which Palmerston's supporters could only too easily exacerbate. But the most thorny of the questions in dispute between England and France was none of these. It was, in fact, a question which concerned British relations with America as closely as those with the European Powers, namely the right of search.

On no other matter had the concord between British Liberalism and French, when they came into power in 1830, produced at first better results. Two treaties concluded in 1831 and 1833 had given the warships of either nation the right in specified areas and under specified conditions to search merchant vessels belonging to the other nation suspected of engaging in the slave trade.[1] To secure the adhesion of Russia, Austria, and Prussia a further treaty had been necessary which on two points altered the Anglo-French treaty of 1833. The areas within which the navies of the signatory Powers were granted the right of search were extended, and the clause which stipulated that the number of cruisers might not exceed by a half the cruisers of another signatory was dropped. The adhesion of Prussia whose navy was insignificant had made its application impossible. The treaty was ready for signature, when in 1840 the dispute arose between France and England on the question of Egypt. The right of search was one of the grievances which France exploited against England. In practice, the French complained, it worked in favour of the British navy, which was three times as large as their own and tended to strengthen what they called England's naval despotism. It must be added that philanthropic zeal was weaker in France than in Britain, and French naval officers were as remiss in chasing slavers as British were energetic. In Great Britain, a country proud to have been

[1] Treaties of November 30, 1831, and March 22, 1833.

the first to abolish by her solitary decision first the slave trade, then slavery, and where a philanthropic Evangelicalism had made its way into the Tory ranks, detestation of slavery was universal, and nobody supposed that the return of the Conservatives to power meant any alteration of the Liberal policy in this matter. Indeed, when an official at the Foreign Office named Bandinel published a volume giving a most optimistic account of the rapid decline of the slave trade, he was generally regarded as a mouthpiece of Lord Aberdeen, who wished to make the attitude of the Government clear.[1]

Guizot thought it advisable to refuse to sign the treaty so long as Palmerston remained in office. Everyone knew that Melbourne's Government was doomed. Had it been concluded after Palmerston's fall it would have been a triumph for Lord Aberdeen. Unhappily, French feeling against England was as strong and as vocal after his fall as before it. De Tocqueville made a speech against the treaty whose violence disconcerted his British friends. Though Guizot could give Lord Aberdeen no better reason than the hostility of French public opinion, he did not ask the French Chambers to ratify a treaty which in London he had assisted in drawing up. What was even worse, the Chamber of Deputies unanimously called upon him to place French commerce in future under the exclusive control of the national flag; in other words, to repudiate the treaties of 1831 and 1833. Once again France separated herself from the concert of the great Powers and this time in circumstances which did not enhance her moral prestige. It was an opportunity for Palmerston and his friends to exploit with every justification against the French Government what was at once a defeat of his policy and of the international crusade against slavery.

4

We have just represented France as isolated in the refusal of her Government to join England, Russia, Austria, and Prussia in signing the convention on the slave trade. Her isolation, however, was not in fact complete. For the Government of the United States stood with her in protesting against the right of search.

---

[1] James Bandinel, 'Some Account of the Trade in Slaves from Africa as connected with Europe and America . . . especially with reference to the efforts made by the British Government for its extinction', 1841. For this work, see *Edinburgh Review*, April 1844 (art. iii, vol. lxxix, p. 396).

Like the French, the Americans owned slaves and in far larger numbers. And they had their Anglophobes—as violent as the Parisian—who had not forgotten the War of Independence, the later war of 1814, and the sack of Washington. For these men an alliance with France against England was still a dearly cherished tradition. The American representative in Paris, General Cass, used all his influence to urge Guizot not to ratify the convention. English feeling towards America was not so simple. The United States was unpopular. When Radical speakers demanded that British institutions should be made democratic, their Conservative or Liberal opponents had only to mention the American democracy with its violence and corruption to reduce them to silence. Dickens's brilliant caricature of American life in *Martin Chuzzlewit* expressed perfectly the sentiments not only of the author, but the vast majority of his readers. But a more responsible group was making an effort to counteract the folly of allowing antipathies of this kind to foster enmity between the two great Anglo-Saxon peoples. Though American democracy jarred upon the conservative temper of the English, the latter were too bent on peace not to pursue a policy of conciliation towards the United States. Lord Ashburton, a member of the important financial house of Baring whose commercial relations with the States made him the ideal negotiator, visited Washington. Two questions had to be settled between the two nations. The boundary between American and British territories in the north-east, left undemarcated since the Treaty of Versailles, had to be drawn. Lord Ashburton gave the Americans all they asked, and since 1842 their territory has pushed upwards between New Brunswick and Canada as far as the most northerly point touched by the river St. John. The other was the slave trade. By a feat of diplomatic prestigitation England silently abandoned the right of search. It was agreed that to suppress the slave trade each of the two nations would maintain on the coast of Africa a squadron equipped with no less than eighty guns. The two squadrons would be mutually independent. But the two Governments undertook to give their respective commanders such orders as would enable them to act in concert after joint consultation. Palmerston and the *Morning Post* protested against these concessions.[1]

[1] C. F. Bell, *Lord Palmerston*, vol. i, pp. 332-5. H. L. Bulwer, *The Life of Viscount Palmerston*, vol. iii, pp. 59 sqq. T. Macknight, *Thirty Years of Foreign Policy*, 1855, pp.

They outraged patriotic feeling. And the abandonment of the right of search offended philanthropy and patriotism alike. Nevertheless, it was in vain that Palmerston attempted by noisy indignation to exploit these sentiments against the Government. He, rather than Lord Aberdeen, was the object of the general dissatisfaction.

The large number of opponents who in 1840 had spared no effort to thwart his rash policy but had been silenced by its success now returned to the attack. Prince Albert and the Queen were intensely relieved to be free from his heavy hand. The Duke of Bedford and Lord Spencer charged Lord John Russell to inform Palmerston, a mission which was very ill received by the latter, that his speeches in the Commons and articles in the *Morning Chronicle* were not approved by the leaders of the Whig aristocracy. Even at the Foreign Office his bullying and insolence were generally detested. The story went round that this man of untiring energy, who combined a life of pleasure and hard work, went to the Foreign Office one Sunday morning to work and was annoyed to find it empty. Lord Aberdeen's arrival was a welcome relief. Palmerston, it is true, could boast that his victory of 1840 had been won without war. For the naval demonstration under Sir Charles Napier could not be termed war. Nevertheless, in Asia his policy had led to war and an unpopular war at that. And speeches such as that which he had made at Tiverton[1] on the eve of the General Election were unpardonable. Delighted to insult the feelings of the French, he had drawn a contrast between the barbarous methods employed by France to conquer Algeria and the humane character of British annexation in Asia. In consequence, he told his audience, whereas an Englishman could go wherever he liked unarmed, a Frenchman could not venture far from the outposts without risk of assassination. By such language he had provided the French Press in advance with most welcome material for their hostile comment on the disasters and massacres in Afghanistan. And though he had fallen, it was, none the less, his fault that France went back on the policy of repressing the slave trade which she had pursued from 1830 until the eve of 1840. For she would not

298-302. See also *Greville Memoirs*, October 4, 5, and 12, 1842, and in the *Quarterly Review* the following articles: 'United States Boundary Questions', March 1841 (vol. lxvii, pp. 501 sqq.), and 'Treaty of Washington', March 1842 (vol. lxxi, pp. 560 sqq.).
[1] H. C. F. Bell, *Lord Palmerston*, vol. i, p. 316.

take joint action on any matter with a nation which, despite the change of government, was still Palmerston's.

In spite of everything England looked confidently to Lord Aberdeen to undo the mischief his predecessor had made. Reconciliation with France had been the traditional policy of the Whigs. Now, however, in opposition to Palmerston who had gone near to wrecking it—had he remained a few months longer at the Foreign Office, it was generally said, England and France would have been at war[1]—it had become, paradoxically, the policy of the Conservatives.

Guizot did a great deal to improve relations between the British and the French Conservatives. As the historian of England he knew better than any other Frenchman the right language to use in London, and during his embassy in London had made valuable English friendships. Moreover, as a philosophic historian he possessed the art of presenting the manœuvres of expediency as the dictates of a political ideal.

The Opposition in Paris exhumed the panegyric of the Holy Alliance he had written twenty years earlier, as a combination of the European monarchs 'to preserve order and peace'.[2] He replied by explaining that what was now called by the new name of the concert of Europe was the same thing as that formerly designated the Holy Alliance. 'What is termed the concert of Europe', he wrote, 'is nothing more than the determination of the great Powers to preserve peace.' If one liked to call it so it was in truth a kind of Holy Alliance, but a Holy Alliance whose object was peace rather than order. Conceived in this spirit the Franco-British understanding was an excellent thing, as had been proved when it made it possible to settle the questions of Belgium and Greece 'by amicable negotiation inspired by the sound sense of good Europeans'. It became dangerous only when it assumed the

[1] This was, for example, Francis Baring's opinion (*Greville Memoirs*, February 5, 1842). For criticisms of Palmerston, see, further, *Greville Memoirs*, September 29, 1841, January 11, and February 1, 1842. For Greville's dislike of Palmerston, see H. C. F. Bell, *Lord Palmerston*, vol. i, p. 305.

[2] *Le National*, of July 7, 1843, quotes Guizot's unfortunate eulogy of the Holy Alliance written in 1822: 'The monarchs of Europe, above all, the Czar Alexander, shocked by the excesses and crimes of our Revolution and fearful of the explosion of violent passions and the immorality which accompanied it . . . determined to secure Europe from similar upheavals in the future with their disastrous results. Accordingly *they formed an alliance to preserve order and peace.*' And the writer of the article concludes: 'Is the electorate prepared to leave it in M. Guizot's power to rebuild the Holy Alliance, renew this *solemn engagement* and sacrifice France to Europe?'

appearance of an alliance in the strict sense directed against the three Northern Powers.[1] The reorientation of French foreign policy thus clearly defined by Guizot received Peel's express approval.[2]

Napoleon's downfall had discredited once and for all the old belief that war can be self-supporting. The time had come for an agreement between the great Powers to limit armaments.

Though Cobden was absorbed at the moment by domestic questions, speaking one day in the House he warned Palmerston not to expect from the Manchester group any sympathy[3] with his

[1] Cf. also his *Memoires pour Servir à l'Histoire de Mon Temps* (vol. vi, pp. 8 and 9): 'I am well aware . . . that the progress of civilization and rational public opinion will not get rid of human passions, and that as a result of their operation, the spirit of conquest, propaganda backed by armed force, and inflexible adherence to a ready-made set of opinions will always play their part in the foreign policy of states. But I am equally certain that motives of this kind are no longer in harmony with the manners of the present day. The extent and vigour of manufacture and trade, the need for world-wide prosperity, frequent, easy, rapid, and regular communications between the different peoples, an invincible love of free association, examination, and discussion and unfettered publicity, all these characteristic features of modern society are already overcoming and will increasingly overcome dreams of military or diplomatic triumph. The language and childlike confidence of The Friends of Peace or Societies for promoting Peace may well raise a smile. But all the most potent aspirations and loftiest hopes of humanity have their dreamers and simpletons, their times of failure and disillusionment.' Guizot to St. Aulaire, December 10, 1840 (*Memoires*, vol. vi, pp. 38-9): 'Interests of a higher order enforce, and will long continue to enforce, European concert and unity, and there can be no concert or unity of Europe if France is left out of it. I am fresh from fighting for the maintenance of peace, and beyond that immediate object I have envisaged a restoration of the European concert.'

[2] H. of C., August 26, 1841, Peel's speech (*Annual Register*, 1841, p. 187). The *Quarterly Review* (March 1841, art. viii, 'Foreign Policy', vol. lxvii, pp. 254 sqq.), which censures Palmerston severely, expresses itself as follows on the subject of Franco-British relations: 'Nor can we say that we much regret this renunciation on the part of France of what they call the "English Alliance". . . . Let us have amity with France, sincere and open, and, if possible, solid—such as we have, or ought to have, with Russia or Prussia or Austria, but not in such secret and undefined obligations as would estrange us from the collective policy of the rest of Europe, and, after all, end on the very first untoward accident or occasion in a similar, or perhaps still worse, explosion of hostility than we have lately witnessed, and, as we hope, happily and honourably escaped.' The same review (March 1841, vol. lxvii, p. 397), in an article entitled, 'State of Society and Education in France' shows a profound distrust of the French: 'We are mistaken if in France there is not a much larger mass of energy and activity . . . almost entirely without regular or absorbing occupations and utterly stagnant and therefore liable to be ruffled and fiercely agitated by the slightest breath. What a nation might France have been if, to reckon only from the reign of Louis XIV, she had consumed the tenth part of the energy . . . which she has wasted in disturbing the peace of her neighbours . . . on the internal improvement of her provinces. She would cease to be Paris with a vast tributary domain, and become really France, with only a noble capital for the residence of her monarch and legislative.' The *Edinburgh Review* (April 1842, vol. lxxv, pp. 5-6) censures French pride: 'She is certainly eminent in war, in literature, and in the fine arts, but in education, in morality, in wealth, in the ordinary arts of life—in short, in all that contributes to the welfare of the mass of the people, the bulk of the population of France is far inferior to that of Holland, of Belgium, of Switzerland, of Great Britain, and of the greater part of Germany.'

[3] H. of C., August 10, 1842, Cobden's speech. He 'assured Lord Palmerston that there

meddlesome and war-mongering policy. And in saying this he had no intention of allying himself with a Cabinet whose Tory creed was anathema to him. It was, in fact, yet another instance of what we have already observed more than once, an unconcerted alliance between particular Conservative and particular Radical groups to oppose the bellicose Liberalism of Canning and Palmerston. On this point the antiquated ideal of the Holy Alliance was at one with the modern pacifist commercialism represented by Cobden. To sum up, the difficulties in the field of foreign policy were not such as to shake the solid ministerial majority or render either the Prime Minister or his Foreign Secretary unpopular.

Questions of another order caused the Cabinet serious, indeed grave, anxiety. And in the first place the religious question.

V RELIGIOUS QUESTIONS

I

Of the religious questions which would stir public opinion in 1842 and 1843, there was none in truth which had not been mooted already before the General Election. No religious issue, however, played an appreciable part in it. The Chartist agitation and the counter-agitation of the League had diverted political speakers to other topics. As we have already seen,[1] the growing indifference to the relations between Church and State had on the whole worked out to the profit of the former. Newman on his Romeward path, a leading Dissenter or so, and Chalmers, the great Scottish Presbyterian, had spoken or written in defence of her privileged position. Thus the election of 1841, which, it would be true to say, was totally unconcerned with ecclesiastical questions, might seem at first sight a victory for the Church.

But at this very juncture, as the Catholicizing movement gathered force in the Church of England, Newman was being gradually thrust from her communion. Among the Dissenters the

was a growing opinion in the country, that we had meddled too much in the affairs of foreign countries' (*Annual Register*, 1842, p. 230). According to the report in *The Times*, August 11, 1842, he added: 'It would be much better if our governors attended more closely to the conditions of our people at home. If that were not done, both parties, Whigs as well as Tories, would be shaken from their positions like dewdrops from a tree.'

[1] *History of the English People*, vol. iii, pp. 164 sqq., 182, 207-8.

old spirit, so bitter on the morrow of 1837, of uncompromising hostility to any State establishment of the Church revived, and in Scotland Chalmers led a great schism. 'Great and increasing', Greville wrote, 'is the interest felt in all the multifarious grievances or pretensions put forth by any and all of the denominations, and much are men's minds turned to religious subjects.'[1] A writer in the *Quarterly Review* referred to 'the spread, we had almost said the fashionable vogue, of religious literature'.[2] This intrusion of theology into the domain of politics, so disconcerting to statesmen, we must now describe as briefly as possible.

The crisis began, so far as the Anglican Church was concerned, with the publication on February 27, 1841, of the ninetieth of the *Tracts for the Times* entitled 'Remarks on certain Passages in the Thirty-nine Articles'.

The position hitherto taken up by the adherents of the Oxford Movement is quite clear. They were prepared to admit that the Thirty-nine Articles printed in the *Book of Common Prayer*, the doctrinal confession of the Anglican Church, were inspired by Protestant and Calvinist beliefs. But it was otherwise, they said, with the Liturgy and the Homilies whose formulas often imply the acceptance of a doctrine condemned by the articles as Romanist. This was, indeed, proved by the fact that the Evangelical party demanded a revision of the Prayer Book to bring it into complete harmony with the Articles. Newman, for he was the writer of Tract ninety, was daring enough to grapple with the Articles themselves, and displayed what we must term a frank and systematic bad faith in the attempt to show how an Anglican Protestant could by the intellectual subterfuges he suggested subscribe them. Following the unpleasant Tracts eighty and eighty-seven on Reserve in Communicating Religious Knowledge, with their disconcerting invitation to the clergy to practise mental reservation, Tract ninety could but strengthen the prejudices of those Englishmen who for some years had accused the Tractarians of disguised Romanism and Jesuitry. It was in truth a Jesuitry frank to the point of stupidity. Rules which it is practicable to observe in the secrecy of the Confessional were not devised for display in a work of public propaganda. The Tract,

---

[1] *Greville Memoirs*, January 16, 1843.
[2] *Quarterly Review*, May 1843, 'Rubric and Ritual of the Church of England' (vol. lxxii, p. 232).

indeed, had scarcely issued from the press when all the enemies of the men termed by Arnold the Oxford Malignants[1] were up in arms.[2]

Not only did the *Edinburgh Review* redouble its attacks, the *Quarterly* threw over a group it had originally defended. Thirteen bishops, among them avowed representatives of the High Church, such as the Bishop of London, the Bishop of Oxford, and even the fiery Bishop of Exeter issued charges condemning the position taken up by Tract ninety. At Oxford the enemies of the Tractarians attempted to secure an official condemnation of the Tract by the University. Had they succeeded, Newman's friends would not have found it easy to appeal to the tolerance which for the past century and a half the Church of England had displayed towards unorthodox theologies from the opposite quarter. For by the leading part they had taken in the demand for Hampden's condemnation,[3] they had done more than anyone to destroy this old Liberal tradition. They managed, however, to dissuade the Bishop from taking proceedings against the Tract, but only on condition the series was discontinued. Tractarianism was defunct. The appointment of Thomas Arnold as Regius Professor of History, and the brilliant success of his inaugural lecture in December, made it plain that at the very moment when the Conservative party returned to power the Tractarians had lost their citadel overnight.[4]

A curious episode of English Church history proved to the Tractarians—if so many episcopal charges against them were not sufficient proof—towards the end of this year 1841 that they no longer possessed a firm footing either in the University of Oxford or in the Church at large. It was the erection of the Protestant Bishopric of Jerusalem by the joint action of the British and Prussian Governments. The Bishop was to be in turn a German

---

[1] Stanley Arnold, vol. ii, p. 9. For this expression, however, see Sp. Walpole, *History of England*, vol. v, p. 275, note 2.

[2] Newman, however, was not the first to attempt a Catholic interpretation of the Thirty-nine Articles. In 1634 Franciscus a Sancta Clara (Christopher Davenport), chaplain to Queen Henrietta Maria, published his *Paraphrastica Expositio Articulorum Confessionis Anglicanae* in which he 'laboured' (*insudavi*) to reconcile the Articles with the doctrine of Trent.—*Trs. Note.*

[3] For the Hampden case, see below, pp. 355-6.

[4] Newman no doubt benefited by the fact that many bishops—the Bishops of London and Exeter, and even his own Bishop of Oxford—condemned him only with regret, because the imprudence of his writings forced their hand. Protestant circles considered that their charges made too many concessions to the new School of High Churchmen.

Lutheran and an Anglican.[1] The project originated with the Prussian minister, Bunsen, an outstanding and clever advocate of an understanding between these two Protestant bodies. From the outset the Court, which was the mainstay of this *entente*, was attracted by the plan. The leading Whigs also favoured it. It was a triumph for that alliance between Liberalism and Evangelicalism which was a prominent feature of the Whigs' ecclesiastical policy. And Palmerston saw in it a means of confronting the French protectorate of Catholic interests in the Near East and the Russian protectorate of the Orthodox with a protectorate of Protestant interests predominantly in British hands. And he also saw in it a British protectorate of the Eastern Jews. The belief was beginning to spread in British Protestant circles that the second advent of Jesus to judge the living and the dead must be preceded by a return of the Jews to Jerusalem, and the rebuilding of Solomon's temple that on the very spot where the Saviour had been crucified they might be confuted, converted and pardoned. The first Bishop of Jerusalem was, in fact, a Lutheran minister who was a converted German Jew. The Conservatives, who at this juncture came into power, did not go back on a decision already made by the Foreign Office. Peel was not a High Churchman.[2] There were Conservative as well as Liberal Evangelicals. Lord Ashley was an enthusiastic supporter of this fraternization between Lutheranism and Anglican Episcopalianism. Nor was it easy for the English Bishops, even the High Churchmen, to condemn the proposed Bishopric and Newman's Romanism in the same breath. Gladstone fully approved, even Pusey, at any rate at first. Newman felt himself more and more solitary in the Church of his birth, a Church which he dearly cherished and which he would fain regard as no worse than schismatic, but which seemed bent on deserving the label heretical affixed to it by the Roman Catholics.

On May 14, 1843, a sermon on the Eucharist preached by Pusey in Christ Church Cathedral was condemned within a fortnight by

---

[1] Sp. Walpole, op. cit., vol. v, pp. 277-8.
[2] Cf. Lord Ashley's judgment of Peel (*Diary*, July 24, 1841, in E. Hodder, *Life of the Seventh Earl of Shaftesbury*, vol. i, p. 342): 'He has abundance of human honesty and not much of Divine faith; he will never do a dishonourable thing, he will be ashamed of doing a religious one.' John Morley (*Life of W. E. Gladstone*, vol. i, p. 177) reports Gladstone's words to Monckton Milnes: 'Sir Robert Peel, who was a religious man, was wholly anti-church and unclerical and largely undogmatic. . . . By habit and education he was quite incapable of comprehending the movement of the Church, the strength it would reach and the exigencies it would entail.'

a commission of six doctors appointed for that purpose by the Vice-Chancellor. Several members of the group led by Newman and Pusey went over to Rome. Newman was at first shocked, then shaken by these conversions. 'The truth is,' he wrote to a friend, 'I am not a good enough son of the Church of England to feel I can in conscience hold preferment under her. I love the Church of Rome too well.'[1] On September 18 he resigned his benefice as Vicar of St. Mary's, preached his farewell sermon on September 25, and withdrew the following day to Littlemore, to live there with a few disciples a life of seclusion and meditation. But for the present he did not make his submission to Rome. He did not forget that when he launched the Oxford Movement his aim had been to fight the sacrilegious alliance between Irish Popery and English Radicalism. And that alliance which he never ceased to hate was as close as ever. Every day he found the prospect of conversion to Rome more attractive, and sooner or later, he felt sure, he would take the step. But would it not break up his life? He had dreamed of renewing the Anglican Church so as to make possible, when the time was ripe, collective reunion by a formal pact with her elder sister, the Church of Rome. To abandon by the act of a solitary individual the Church to whose priesthood he had been ordained would be a Protestant and individualistic, one might almost say a selfish, act. It would be to save his own soul, and at such a price he might not save it after all, by renouncing the attempt to save the soul of the Anglican Church.

2

It may seem paradoxical that it was the Conservative party, the High Churchmen's party, which by setting up the Jerusalem bishopric, scandalized the Oxford Tractarians and brought home to them the difficulty of their position in the Church of England. In fact, however, the incident proved how great was the ascendancy exercised by the Low Church over such moderate Conservatives as Peel and Graham. It is less surprising that under the influence of the same party Peel's Government immediately on taking office decided to tackle from another angle the problem of primary or 'popular' education. The Committee of the Privy Council on Education had hardly been set up by the Whigs,[2]

---

[1] Letter to J. B. Mosley, September 1, 1843 (*Letters and Correspondence of John Henry Newman*, 1891, vol. ii, p. 423).   [2] *History of the English People*, vol. iii, pp. 223-4.

when its attempts to bring the elementary schools under its authority had been confronted by the successful resistance of the Bishops, supported by the Wesleyans. Now that the Tories were in office, fortified by the sympathy of the Bishops and the Wesleyans, they would surely find a solution of this problem of primary education which the Dissenters could accept. They were doomed to disappointment.

The question had been officially studied since the end of 1841, and in 1843 everything was ready for legislation.[1] The disturbances among the working class in 1842 had undoubtedly contributed to impress the Government with the necessity for action. It was clear that the English governing classes who had done so much to increase the nation's material resources had not made sufficient provision for its moral and intellectual education. They were, therefore, running the risk of another French revolution, and British civilization might be exposed to the ravages of an ignorant and depraved populace. Parliamentary discussion of the question was opened by a speech from Lord Ashley, probably by prearrangement with the Cabinet. He called upon the Government to devise the best means to spread among the working classes 'the benefits and blessings of a moral and religious education'. Graham, in reply, expressed the hope that if the House would, as it seemed disposed to do, override differences of party and religious belief, neutral territory might be found on which to erect a system of national education which would take account both of the just wishes of the established Church and the Dissenters' legitimate scruples.[2] He then explained his plan, based

---

[1] For the history of the educational project of 1843, see J. L. and B. Hammond, *The Age of the Chartists*, pp. 192 sqq.

[2] H. of C., February 28, 1843. Lord Ashley's speech (*Parliamentary Debates*, 3rd Ser., vol. lxvii, p. 47), and Sir James Graham's speech (ibid., p. 77): 'I cannot but bear in mind that while all other governments of Europe, warned by the melancholy events which darkened the latter years of the last century . . . warned by those sad lessons, directed their earnest, their increasing attention to the moral training and religious education of their people, England alone, Protestant England, neglected this all-important duty of giving her people that training, that education which so intimately concerns not only their temporal but their eternal welfare.' Sir James Graham's speech, March 24 (ibid., p. 1440): 'If I had entertained any doubt upon the subject . . . the events of last autumn would have convinced us that not a moment should be lost in endeavouring to impart the blessings of a sound education to the rising generation in the manufacturing districts. . . . I am informed that the turbulent masses who, in the course of last autumn, threatened the safety of property . . . were remarkable for the youth of the parties composing them. . . . If some ten years ago we could have been so fortunate as to agree upon some . . . comprehensive scheme of education . . . my firm belief is that the outrages which took place last autumn . . . would never have taken place.'

on the Poor Law and the Factory Acts.[1]

District schools would be set up, connected with the work-houses, but empowered to take other children besides those of the paupers in receipt of relief. Their cost would be defrayed from the public funds, and they would be placed under the control of the Established Church. But the ministers of the different sects would have the right to give religious instruction to children whose parents asked for it. And the Factory Acts would be amended. Work of any kind would be forbidden to children below the age of eight, and between eight and thirteen restricted to six hours and a half, and all would be obliged to attend the courses of elementary education. These might be courses already organized by Anglican or Nonconformist societies. But the Government would be empowered to give financial aid to schools of a novel type, employers being compelled to keep back three-pence a day of the children's wages, to put it into a fund for the maintenance of these schools. 'The Holy Scriptures' would be 'taught daily in the version appointed by law to be used in churches. . . . The children of parents belonging to the Church of England would be instructed in the Catechism and Liturgy of the Church of England separately from the other children, and that daily.' 'The schools' would be 'managed by seven trustees; the clergyman, the two churchwardens, and four others nominated by the magistrates, two of them, if possible, being mill-owners, and inspected by the clerical trustees'.[2] Graham's speech was well received by the House. Lord John Russell merely expressed his regret that the application of the measure proposed was so restricted. It should have included agricultural as well as industrial districts. 'But it would', he said, 'not only be folly, it would be wickedness to oppose it.'[3] Sir Robert Inglis, speaking for the extreme Tories, complained that too many concessions were made to the Dissenters.[4] Strange to say, the Prime Minister

[1] Already, in 1841, before he came into power, Peel had suggested a measure on similar lines. See *History of the English People*, vol. iii, p. 222, note 3.

[2] See *Parliamentary Debates*, 3rd Ser., vol. lxvii, pp. 88-9. Also the analysis of the proposals and of the speeches they produced in J. L. and B. Hammond, *The Age of the Chartists*, pp. 193 sqq., and Frank Smith, *Life of Kay-Shuttleworth* (Secretary to the Education Committee set up in 1839). [The quotation in the text has been taken partly from *Parl. Deb.*, loc. cit., and partly from Hammond, loc. cit.—Trs. Note.]

[3] H. of C., February 28, 1843 (*Parl. Deb.*, 3rd Ser., vol. lxvii, p. 95).

[4] H. of C., March 24 (ibid., pp. 1144 sqq.).

while defending the measure let it be understood that, when all was said, he had little enthusiasm for this direct interference by the legislature in the sphere of education.[1]

Nevertheless, agreement seemed universal. But it soon became evident that a Nonconformist and a Catholic speaker who expressed their fears that the Bill would satisfy neither the Dissenters nor the Catholics had a truer view of the situation than the other members. When Sir James's proposals were made public, the storm broke. 'The Dissenting communities throughout the kingdom took up a general alarm on the subject and gave effect to their opposition with the zeal and activity commonly displayed by those bodies on similar occasions. Meetings were held at Liverpool, Manchester, Brighton, Bath, and other important towns, Roman Catholics as well as Protestant Nonconformists agreeing to denounce the Bill.'[2]

Petitions against the Bill received almost two million signatures. When the Bill, introduced on March 7, was read a second time on March 24, Graham asked that the discussion of the clauses providing for a system of national education should be postponed. But his attempt to appease the objectors by amending the Bill was fruitless. He pointed out that before a school of the new type could be erected in a particular locality the local ratepayers must carry out a number of formalities so complicated that for all practical purposes the Statute would be permissive rather than compulsory. He proposed an entire series of clauses guaranteeing the free exercise of their religion by children who were not members of the Church of England and a free choice of the form of religious instruction they would receive at school. And, finally, he proposed that of the trustees of the school one of the two churchwardens should be elected by a committee of the principal subscribers and the remaining four trustees by the ratepayers under conditions devised to secure the minority its just share of representation. All this meant concessions to which the Church would not have dreamed of consenting at an earlier date—a Conservative victory as Peel understood it.[3] And in the House many

---

[1] H. of C., February 28 (*Parliamentary Debates*, 3rd Ser., vol. lxvii, p. 107).

[2] *Annual Register*, 1843, p. 196. For the agitation against the Bill, the part played in it by Edward Baines, director of the *Leeds Mercury*, and the petitions which secured two million signatures, see J. L. and B. Hammond, *The Age of the Chartists*, pp. 197 and 199.

[3] *Parl. Deb.* 3rd Ser., vol. lxvii, pp. 1214 sqq. The amendments may be found in J. L. and B. Hammond, *The Age of the Chartists*, pp. 196-8.

members of the Opposition agreed with the Government's point of view, from Lord Howick, the most active of the younger members of the Whig aristocracy, to Cobden, who was not a Dissenter, was in fact rather proud of the fact, and had little liking for the fanatical hostility of so many of his Lancashire friends to a measure on the whole for the public good.[1] But the Dissenters would not accept a Bill which placed an Anglican at the head of the governing body of each school in the teeth of statutes which, with two or three exceptions at the summit of the political hierarchy, had thrown open all positions in the service of the Crown to Christians of every denomination. And their dissatisfaction was the greater because this Education Bill being grafted on to a Factory Act applied only to the manufacturing districts where the Dissenters boasted of being the progressive, wealthy, and most numerous element of the population. A feature of the opposition which caused the Government serious alarm was the attitude of the Wesleyans. In 1839 when the Committee of the Privy Council had been formed they had taken sides with the Church against the other Dissenters. Now they went over to the latter. Then, they had supported the Church against the impious alliance between the Dissenters and Catholics. Now, though still wishing to exclude Catholics from State aid of any kind, they could not accept the hegemony, even if friendly to themselves, of a Church contaminated by Puseyism.[2] Graham finally dropped

---

[1] H. of C., July 28, 1843. Lord Howick's speech (*Parliamentary Debates*, 3rd Ser., vol. lxx, p. 1430): 'His noble Friend had truly said that considering the state of public opinion, Her Majesty's Government had exercised a sound discretion in withdrawing the measures, and he could not help here saying that it was unfortunate such opinions prevailed on the subject which were not creditable to either of the great parties of the State. With that public opinion he did not sympathize, because he thought that the evil of having a large portion of the poor uneducated was so great as to overbalance other considerations, and he would make a great sacrifice of his own opinions to meet that evil. He was prepared to stretch to its uppermost the principle of religion, for the purpose of having a measure that would facilitate public education. He did not think that the opinion which prevailed was creditable to the Church, on the one side, or to Dissenters on the other. For that which had now taken place he was not disposed to blame Her Majesty's Government.' Cobden's speech (ibid., 3rd Ser., vol. lxvii, pp. 1469 sqq.): 'He would tell the Government that the Dissenters would resist the measure which had been brought forward. It would be the subject of a long controversy, and it was not worth it, after all. . . . And although he had received communications from various parts of the country hostile to the Bill, yet, if a division should take place, he would vote for the second reading and trust to amending the measure in Committee.' See also Miss Martineau, *History of the Thirty Years' Peace*, vol. iv, p. 450: 'The sectarian spirit which is the curse of English society has thus far condemned the children of the nation to a defective education, or to total ignorance.'

[2] For the attitude of the Wesleyans in 1839, see *History of the English People*, vol. iii, p. 224; J. L. and B. Hammond, *The Age of the Chartists*, p. 226; Sir James Graham to

the Bill, promising to reintroduce it in 1844 shorn of the clauses dealing with religious education. Peel deplored 'the sorry and lamentable triumph that Dissent had achieved'. And Lord Ashley while congratulating him on his courageous attempt was convinced by its failure that it must never be repeated.[1]

It was, in truth, a serious reverse for the cause of popular education in England. It was also a warning to the Church.

She may perhaps have been tempted to interpret the election of 1841 as the nation's deliberate return to the period before 1829. If so, she failed to see that it was a vote of confidence in Peel, and that if Peel had re-christened his party 'Conservative', it was to make it plain that it was not his intention to pursue in any respect a policy of reaction. If the failure of the Factory Bill of 1843 was a disappointment to all who wished to improve national education and were irritated to find that the conflicting bigotries of the Church and the sects made it impossible to achieve the reform they desired, it also shattered the delusion of High Church enthusiasts that the country was once more in their hands. The warning was underlined by further instances of refusal by the electorate and the country at large to accede to their wishes. The Church asked the Government to subsidize the building of new churches to meet the needs of areas where the population had enormously increased, and not to abandon these new urban or semi-urban populations to the activities of the sects. She was unsuccessful, and could obtain nothing more than an act authorizing the Ecclesiastical Commission set up in 1833 to raise, from the

Sir Robert Peel, April 13, 1843 (C. S. Parker, *Sir Robert Peel*, vol. ii, p. 560): 'I have received the enclosed communication from the Wesleyan body with great regret. It is more hostile than I anticipated, and marks distinctly a wide estrangement from the Church. In some of the principles announced, this declaration goes the whole length of the bitterest dissent, and the sole reservation opposed to perfect equality of sects is against the Roman Catholics alone. It is quite clear that the Pusey tendencies of the Established Church have operated powerfully on the Wesleyans, and are converting them rapidly into enemies.'

[1] Sir Robert Peel to Lord Ashley, June 16, 1843: 'My own opinion is, seeing what has passed, that there would be no advantage to the cause of religious education in trusting to the co-operation of the Dissenting Body in our measure, and that to abandon it is preferable to failure after religious strife. It is but a sorry and lamentable triumph that Dissent has achieved.' Lord Ashley to Sir Robert Peel, June 17, 1843: 'Let this last trial be taken as a sufficient proof that "United Education" is an impossibility. It ought never again to be attempted. The Dissenters and the Church have each laid down their limits, which they will not pass; and there is no power that can either force, persuade, or delude them. Your Government has nothing to regret, except the loss of a healing measure. You would have much to regret had you not propounded it. But you have endeavoured to remove a great evil, and in so doing have thrown the responsibility before God and man on the shoulders and conscience of others' (in Parker, op. cit., vol. ii, pp. 561-2).

Church's revenues, the funds required in its opinion for this purpose. The Church also asked for the erection of new Sees to meet this growth of population and at the same time increase the number of her clergy in the House of Lords. The Whigs had recognized the need for new bishoprics in Yorkshire and Lancashire. But as we have seen they proposed to compensate for the creation of two new Sees by unions which would suppress two others.[1] Though the union of the Welsh bishoprics of Bangor and Saint Asaph had not been effected, the High Churchmen asked for the establishment of a See at Manchester, and to make their request more acceptable, proposed, what from their point of view was a surrender, that the new bishopric should not confer on its occupant a seat in the Lords. This was not enough to win the approval of the Cabinet or the majority of Peers. They consoled themselves by procuring a succession of Acts of Parliament creating a large number of colonial Sees.[2]

What, then, would be the fate of popular education since British statesmen had been compelled by the electorate to sacrifice it reluctantly to an outburst of sectarian animosities? One resource alone was left, private enterprise.

Subscription lists were opened for the construction of schools and churches, and money poured in. As we have just seen, Peel had given only a qualified approval to the Bill for which his Government was responsible. It was not that he regarded the measure as too favourable to the Church. It was the principle of State intervention that was distasteful to him.[3] By this attitude the Conservative Prime Minister showed the extent to which he could be influenced by the growth of ideas flatly opposed to the principles of the party he led. Reaction against Graham's Bill was producing a revival of the opposition on principle to State action, the 'voluntarism' which had made such a stir in the two or three years following 1832.

We have already mentioned the foundation by Miall of *The Nonconformist* for the very purpose of preaching the reduction to a minimum of the activities of the State. And we have seen the

---

[1] *History of the English People*, vol. iii, pp. 204-5.
[2] See below, p. 340.
[3] Sir Robert set an example of private munificence by subscribing £5,000 to build schools, and giving a sum equally large for the construction of new churches (C. S. Parker, *Sir Robert Peel*, vol. ii, pp. 562 and 567). For his hostility to State action, and his attitude on the question of church building, see Parker, ibid., p. 563, and below, p. 343.

part it played in the economic sphere in the Cobdenites' free trade agitation. The agitation against the Factory Bill in 1843 gave Miall's propaganda new life. An important provincial organ, the *Leeds Mercury*, directed by Edward Baines, supported it. In reply to the blow which in their opinion the Church had attempted to deliver against the sects, these agitators did all they could to rouse the Dissenters from the torpor they had shown in the decade following the Reform Act, failing, therefore, to profit from what was or should have been their victory. And they attacked something worse than torpor in certain Dissenting circles. It was the active hostility of what they termed 'the aristocracy of Dissent', members of a wealthy and enlightened middle class, out of tune with the fanatical anti-clericalism in which they had been nurtured, and prepared to welcome the advances made to them by the leading statesmen of both the traditional parties, and accept without further scrutiny any compromise the Church might offer. Some about this time entertained the dream of a species of concordat by which the State, far from stripping the Church of her wealth, would admit Catholics and Dissenters to share in its favours. The aristocrats of Dissent were certainly not opposed to a system of which the *regium donum* might be regarded as a foretaste.[1]

The Factory Act had scarcely been dropped in June, when Miall suggested that the Dissenters should hold a convention to concentrate their efforts, too sporadic hitherto, on a programme of the complete emancipation of Christianity from a dishonourable bondage to the State. In September, seventy-six Dissenting ministers in the Midlands issued an appeal to the ministers of a London congregation to take the first steps to summon such a convention. They found themselves confronted with the opposition of the 'aristocracy of Dissent', which in spite of Miall's campaign was solidly entrenched in the metropolis. The provincial Dissenters then decided to take action themselves, and in June 1844 an Anti-State-Church Conference met in London, composed of seven hundred members elected in due form by all the Dissenting bodies in the United Kingdom to declare war against every form of alliance between the State and any religious communion. They based this campaign on the principle of the exclusive

---

[1] The *regium donum*, for which see below, p. 74, note 1, was a payment made by the State to the Irish Presbyterian clergy.—*Trs. Note.*

authority of Christ in His Church and the essentially spiritual character of His Kingdom.[1]

We shall have to follow the fortunes of this movement. For the present it will be enough to point out that those who launched it were encouraged by the conviction that their views were shared by the leaders of the Anti-Corn-Law League. They were fighting side by side with the latter for the repeal of the Corn Law. They felt assured that the Leaguers would fight by their side for Disestablishment.[2] They saw the success already obtained in the economic struggle and expected equal success for the campaign in the religious order which had been opened by the Anti-State-Church Association, founded by the Conference in 1844. They had, however, a further reason for optimism, the drama which was being enacted in Scotland, which would result in a secession costing the Church of Scotland a third of her ministers and more than a third of her flock.

3

To tell the story of this drama[3] we must go back a few years to the year 1834, when the General Assembly in the teeth of the Statute of 1711, which gave a lay patron the right to present the minister in each parish, conferred upon the majority of the heads of families duly registered in the parish the right to veto the patron's choice.[4]

The measure had hardly been passed by the Assembly when its opponents decided to contest its legality. When in the parish of Auchterarder the candidate presented by the patron had been rejected by the practically unanimous vote of three hundred heads of families, he appealed to the Synod of Perthshire and Stirling,

[1] For this movement, see the *Baptist Examiner*, January, April, and June 1844 (vol. I, pp. 10 sqq., 104 sqq., 174 sqq.). For the foundation of an Anti-State-Church Association, at a conference held in London, on April 30, 1844, see A. Miall, *Life of Edward Miall*, pp. 92 sqq. The resolution passed by the Conference declares: 'That this society be based on the following principle: that in matters of religion man is responsible to God alone; that all legislation by secular government in affairs of religion is an encroachment upon the rights of man and an invasion of the prerogative of God' (*Edinburgh Review*, April 1845, art. viii, 'The Churches of the Three Kingdoms', vol. lxxxi, pp. 532 sqq.).

[2] Rev. Thomas Spencer, *The People's Rights and How to get Them*, quoted by H. V. Faulkner, *Chartism and the Churches*, p. 113, note.

[3] For the Scottish schism, see Robert Buchanan, *The Ten Years' Conflict: being the History of the Disruption of the Church of Scotland*, 1849; Rev. William Hanna, *Memoirs of the Life and Writings of Thomas Chalmers*, 1849-52; A. T. Innes, *Law of Creeds in Scotland*, 1867; A. C. Dick, *Dissertation on Church Policy*, 1835.

[4] Cf. *History of the English People*, vol. iii, pp. 165-6.

to whose jurisdiction Auchterarder belonged, and when his appeal was refused, to the General Assembly of 1835, which remitted the matter to the Presbytery of Auchterarder on which more immediately than upon the Synod the parish depended.[1] The Presbytery rejected his appeal. He then decided to appeal not to the Assembly of the clergy, but to the supreme court of civil justice, the Court of Session. This time the decision was in his favour. The Assembly appealed to the House of Lords. No other course was open. But it was careful to circumscribe in advance the jurisdiction of a lay tribunal which it could recognize in a matter of this kind. It was competent to deal only with the civil rights and emoluments of ministers. All questions of ecclesiastical discipline pertained to the exclusive jurisdiction of Christ incarnate in His Church from which there could be no appeal to any other tribunal. In May 1839 the House of Lords, sitting as the Supreme Court of Justice and advised by Lords Brougham and Cottenham, decided that the Assembly of 1834 had no competence to alter the Act of 1711, which restored the rights of lay patrons. The Presbytery had the right to determine whether the patron's candidate possessed the necessary 'qualifications'. But these qualifications were the orthodoxy of his writings and the morality of his conduct. Rejection by a majority of the heads of families was not a disqualification within the meaning of the Act.[2]

It is important to grasp the character, by no means simple, of the legal struggle which after four years' combat led to the secession of 1843. It was in the first place a conflict in the Church of Scotland between the Evangelicals and the Moderates. The latter during the first quarter of the nineteenth century had been gaining ground uninterruptedly at the expense of what was then known as the Popular party. For Scotland had shared the general fate of Calvinism in decline.

In Edinburgh, as in Geneva, the creed of a body whose temper was reasoning and argumentative yielded by degrees to a more

[1] For the constitution of the Church of Scotland, see *History of the English People,* vol. i, pp. 462-4: 'The 900 Scottish parishes were divided into districts, each with its lay president, its elder. And each parish was governed by a council of elders. . . . Several parishes were united in a presbytery, to which each parish sent a minister and an elder. . . . Several presbyteries were grouped to form a provincial synod. At the head of the entire system was the General Assembly, which consisted of representatives of all the presbyteries together with representatives of the royal boroughs and the universities.'
[2] Rev. W. Hanna, *Memoirs of . . . Thomas Chalmers,* vol. iv, pp. 91 sqq. R. Buchanan, *The Ten Years' Conflict* (ed. 1852), vol. i, pp. 340 sqq.

or less radical rationalism, represented in Scotland by the ration-alism of a Dugald Stewart and the *Edinburgh Review*. It was the aim of the great Presbyterian minister Chalmers to regenerate and revive Scottish Calvinism by employing the revivalist methods which Wesley had employed with such success in England.

To counteract the separatist tendencies of his own new Evan-gelical party he had attempted to reconcile it with the Popular party by introducing the veto on the presentation of ministers which the Assembly had passed in 1834. In this way the simple faith of men in the humbler walks of life would counteract the scepticism of the aristocratic patrons. Years of prosperity had followed for the Scottish Evangelicals. The rapidity of their growth can be measured by the following fact. Whereas no more than sixty-three chapels of ease had been built between 1734 and 1834 to supply the deficiency of parish churches, the same number were erected by subscription in the single year 1835. In 1841 more than two hundred churches were built. And, as was not the case before 1834, the ministers of these non-parochial churches had their representatives, members, as the conditions of their appoint-ment ensured, of the Evangelical party, in all the clerical assemblies which governed the Church of Scotland.[1] It was to combat this invasion of evangelical pietism that the Moderates had engineered the incident at Auchterarder and finally had had recourse to their favourite weapon, appeal to the lay State and its civil tribunals. This gave rise to a new struggle, not this time between two views of Christian doctrine, but between two conceptions of the Church, or rather of the relation between the religious and the civil com-munity. For the question whether lay control of the Church should take the aristocratic form it had possessed between 1711 and 1834 or the democratic form, which in the latter year the General Assembly had substituted for the aristocratic, was a sub-ordinate issue.[2] Chalmers himself was a Conservative who had

---

[1] Rev. W. Hanna, *Memoirs of . . . Thomas Chalmers*, vol. iv, pp. 434 sqq. The Assembly of 1834 placed the ministers of chapels of ease on the same footing as parochial ministers. (Cf. Sp. Walpole, *History of England*, vol. v, p. 309.)

[2] 'The veto is a bagatelle and but dust in the balance, when compared with the proper independence of our Church in things ecclesiastical, and to which, in the case before us, there is super-added another object charged with essential principle, and where neglect or irresolution on our part would be followed by consequences the most ruinous—the proper subordination of our inferior to our superior courts' (Chalmers's speech before the General Assembly, December 11, 1839; W. Hanna, *Memoirs of . . . Thomas Chalmers*, vol. iv, p. 143).

championed the veto only as a matter of tactics and to prevent the democratic wing of the Evangelicals leaving the Church and by their secession weakening the Evangelicals in their struggle with the Moderates. But as time went on he became its zealous champion, until on this issue of the veto the man who had defended on doctrinal grounds the union of Church and State put himself at the head of the seceders, to be abandoned by the more conservative of his followers, who made common cause with the Moderates and refused to secede.[1]

The conflict became more acute every day. In two districts at least the Presbytery, relying on the decision of the Lords, took no notice of the parishioners' veto and ordained a minister whose ministrations his flock, supported by the General Assembly, refused to accept.[2] Such a state of anarchy could not continue. Since the courts refused to recognize the Assembly's jurisdiction, an Act of Parliament would be necessary if the Church of Scotland were not to be split by a secession. English public opinion, however, was at a loss. It was a Scottish question about which the English understood very little.

This was shown by the fact that Chalmers had the sympathy not only of the Dissenters, who wanted to see a new sect formed, and of the Wesleyans in particular, who were delighted to witness the Scottish Wesley driven by a degenerate Church to break with her against his will, but even of a number of High Churchmen, the Bishop of Exeter, for example, who approved of his struggle against the Erastianism they hated and his breach of the union between Church and State when the latter sought to transform alliance into subjection.[3] The politicians, on the other hand, Whigs as well as Tories, were all instinctively Erastian. Melbourne and Lord John Russell made a very half-hearted attempt to devise a legislative compromise which would satisfy both the Evangelicals and the Moderates. They quickly abandoned an undertaking which had no prospect of success. They were content with a

---

[1] When the split came, Chalmers declared: 'They were neither Voluntaries nor Anarchists; they quitted a vitiated Establishment, but would rejoice in returning to a poor one; they were advocates of a national recognition and support of religion.' And he told a deputation of the Presbyterian Church of Ireland: 'The Irish Presbyterian Church, with the help of the *Regium Donum*, presented an example of the best of all ecclesiastical systems: a clergy paid by the State and chosen by the people' (*Annual Register*, 1843, p. 251).

[2] At Lethendy and Marnoch (Rev. W. Hanna, *Memoirs of . . . Thomas Chalmers*, vol. iv, pp. 126 and 140).

[3] Sp. Walpole, *History of England*, vol. v, p. 238.

promise that the Government which held the patronage of a third of the Scottish parishes would never make use of it against the parishioners' will. In consequence, Chalmers, who had no affection for the Whigs, set his hopes on the Tories on their return to office in 1841, but only to be disappointed once more. And he came finally to prefer the Whigs, favourable at bottom to separation, to Peel and Graham, who could not conceive a union of Church and State which was not the bondage of the former.

Two measures of compromise were put forward by two prominent politicians. The Bill introduced by the Duke of Argyll sought to render the veto more democratic by extending it to all adult male communicants, but on the other hand provided that it could be overridden if it were proved to have been inspired by factious motives or unfounded prejudices. The Bill was not carried.[1] Lord Aberdeen, himself a Presbyterian, while refusing to admit a right of veto proposed to grant the parishioners the right to put forward objections which the ecclesiastical courts would be bound to take into consideration even if they did not concern matters of doctrine or flagrant immorality.[2] His Bill was finally passed. But it was not until 1843 after the secession. It therefore effected nothing beyond reassuring the consciences of those Evangelicals who had refused to leave the Church with Chalmers.[3]

On May 18, 1843, the General Assembly was in session. Four hundred ministers and a somewhat larger number of elders with-

---

[1] For the Duke of Argyll's Bill, introduced May 5, 1841, see W. Hanna, *Memoirs of . . . Thomas Chalmers*, vol. iv, p. 229.

[2] Lord Aberdeen's Bill was introduced on May 1, 1840, in spite of Chalmers's hostility to it (W. Hanna, *Memoirs of . . . Thomas Chalmers*, vol. iv, pp. 153 sqq.; *Parliamentary Debates*, 3rd Ser., vol. liii, p. 1209). It was passed on July 17, 1843 (*Parl. Deb.*, 3rd Ser., vol. lxx, p. 1206). But by that time Parliament was confronted by a resolution passed by the General Assembly of 1842, which declared that, 'Acts of the Parliament of Great Britain passed without the consent of the Church and nation in alteration of or derogation to the government, rights and privileges of the Church . . . are and shall be null and void' (Sp. Walpole, *History of England*, vol. v, p. 318). From that time Cabinet Ministers considered it their duty to uphold the authority of the State against the Church (see Sir James Graham's letter to the Moderator of the General Assembly, January 4, 1843, *Annual Register*, 1843, p. 243, and Peel's speech of March 8, 1843, *Parl. Deb.*, 3rd Ser., vol. lxvii, pp. 505-6). For the position taken up by the Government, see Torrens, *Life and Times of Sir James Graham*, vol. ii, pp. 230-1, and C. S. Parker, *Sir Robert Peel*, vol. iii, p. 93.

[3] See the severe judgment passed by the *Edinburgh Review* (October 1843, vol. lxxviii, pp. 534-5, and April 1845, vol. lxxxi, pp. 532-3). Also Harriett Martineau (*A History of the Thirty Years' Peace*, vol. iv, p. 264): 'There is now a general feeling that the affair is not over, that the Establishment in Scotland now remains a mere temporary arrangement, and that the Establishment in England and Ireland must sooner or later come into question in somewhat a similar way.'

drew in silence, and forming three abreast a column a quarter of a mile long, marched to a hall where three thousand supporters awaited their arrival. There Chalmers laid the foundation of a new organization, the Free Church of Scotland, and for the first time in the history of Protestant Scotland set up a rival General Assembly.[1] The Seceders were confronted by innumerable difficulties. They had expected to take with them half the clergy of the Established Church. In fact, less than a third seceded.[2] This was no inconsiderable success. For to follow Chalmers was to sacrifice an assured stipend and the social position occupied in his parish by a Presbyterian minister, a position like that of the Anglican parson beside the squire.[3] They took with them much more than a third of the laity. In the Highlands, it was calculated, the entire lower class followed them. It was no easy task to obtain sufficient ministers and churches to provide for the spiritual needs of this crowd. The wealthy classes, the gentry, and, with the exception of a few eccentric individuals, the entire nobility were for the Moderates. The chapels of ease which the Evangelicals had built in such large numbers since 1834 were taken over by the Moderates as being the property of the Establishment. The great landlords refused to sell the Free Church sites for churches. All these difficulties were overcome by a mighty outburst of popular enthusiasm. 'Never in the history of the Christian Church', wrote Chalmers's biographer, 'were so many sermons delivered, so many prayer meetings held, so many addresses

[1] W. Hanna, *Memoirs of . . . Thomas Chalmers*, vol. iv, pp. 335 sqq. For the history of the Free Church, see Rev. Thomas Brown, *Annals of the Disruption, with Extracts from the Narrative of Ministers who left the Scottish Establishment in 1843*, 1877.

[2] For the figures, see *Annual Register*, 1843, pp. 255-6. Of 1,430 ministers, 395 seceded. It is significant that of 947 parochial ministers, only 214 left the Church, whereas more than half the ministers serving chapels of ease seceded (144 out of 246). In a brochure entitled, *The Wheat and the Chaff gathered into Bundles: a Statistical Contribution towards the History of the Recent Disruption of the Scottish Ecclesiastical Establishment* (1843), James MacCosh shows that almost two-thirds of the Evangelical ministers left the Establishment. Moreover, he classifies the ministers in three groups: A, The Seceders; and among those who did not secede: B, the Moderates, C, the Evangelicals. The progress made by Evangelicalism is clearly shown, and the fact that the number of the seceders increased in proportion to their youth. Of the ministers, for example, ordained before 1800 and still living in 1843, there were only 12 seceders, and of those remaining in the Church, 59 Moderates as against 5 Evangelicals. Of the ministers ordained between 1830 and 1840, there were 208 seceders, and of those who did not secede, 91 Moderates and 90 Evangelicals.

[3] Chalmers (*Report on Sites*, vol. iii, p. 6436): 'I believe the upper classes very honestly thought ill of us, they looked at us as so many Radicals and Revolutionaries, and I have heard some of the higher classes, for whom I have the greatest respect, associate the Disruption with the idea of a coming revolution.' (Quoted by W. Hanna, *Memoirs of . . Thomas Chalmers*, vol. iv, p. 468.)

delivered by the same number of clergymen within the same period of time.'[1]

The financial organization of the new Church was firmly centralized by Chalmers on the Wesleyan model. In its ecclesiastical discipline, however, it was closer to Congregationalism than to the Connexionalism of the Wesleyans or even of Calvinist Presbyterianism. It is indeed arguable that the English Congregationalists and Baptists had more reason to be gratified by the birth of this new Church than the Wesleyans, however Wesleyan had been the original inspiration of the religious movement inaugurated by Chalmers. For the secession split the Scottish Evangelicals, and while on the one hand the position of those who remained in the Establishment was weakened in their struggle against the Latitudinarian rationalists of the Moderate party, those who seceded were influenced willy-nilly by the new spirit which had inspired Dissent for the past forty years. It was a spirit more political than theological—it was on an issue of political organization that the Free Church had seceded, and a spirit so strongly impregnated with Liberalism, commercial as well as political, that in the end this Liberalism was taken for the essence of Christian doctrine. From every point of view this unaccountable reaction of Scottish public opinion less than two years after the Conservative victory of 1841 was an unpleasant rebuff to the Government.

The entire episode embarrassed English journalists and members of Parliament. Though the English Nonconformists were lavish in noisy demonstrations of friendship for the new Nonconformists of Scotland, that Nonconformity was obviously of a different type, the offspring of a different Church. Obliged to follow, more or less inattentively, debates in which a Scottish problem, because it was Scottish, must be discussed in a language alien to her own religious institutions, England became aware that she presided over a kingdom less 'united' than disunited. Other events which occurred at the same time in other parts of the United Kingdom reminded the observer that the surface of a single constitution masked diversities of institutions and manners for which a confederation were better suited.

[1] W. Hanna, *Memoirs of . . . Thomas Chalmers*, vol. iv, p. 357.

VI THE IRISH AGITATION

I

Only a few words need be said of the revolt, strange, however, and characteristic, which for many months kept South Wales in unrest.[1] A conspiracy whose ramifications covered the entire country was formed with the queer name of Biblical flavour, 'Rebecca and her daughters'. Its members had sworn to destroy the too numerous and too expensive tolls which impeded road traffic. A man on horseback, masked and wearing a woman's clothes, and followed by other men similarly disguised and mounted, all armed with guns and axes, destroyed the toll-bar and demolished the toll-house. Then they rode away into the night to pursue elsewhere the same task of methodical destruction. No thefts were permitted or violence to persons. The entire countryside kept the secret of the culprits' names inviolate. In a short time the majority of the toll-bars had disappeared, and it had become almost impossible to levy the tolls. Rebecca and her daughters then turned their attention to the workhouses erected in accordance with the provisions of the new Poor Law. The authorities, who for a long time had shown indulgence to the rebels, took alarm. The troops were called out. A few arrests followed by mild sentences were sufficient to quell the disturbances. A Commission was appointed to inquire into the causes of the Welsh discontent.[2] Its report, issued in 1844, led to the passing of an Act the same year which completely reformed the administration of the Welsh roads.[3] This Welsh revolt is of interest because its theatre lay between the Chartist insurrection, of which the Welsh attack on the workhouses was an echo, and the Irish insurrection of which we must now speak, and which it strikingly resembled in being a movement of the peasantry, in its secret methods, and in the universal complicity of the country folk, though differing from it in its abstention from murder.

[1] *Annual Register*, 1843, pp. 257 sqq. Harriet Martineau, *A History of the Thirty Years' Peace*, book vi, chap. 5. S. and B. Webb, *English Local Government: The Story of the King's Highway*, 1913, pp. 217 sqq. (bibliography, p. 235). *Quarterly Review*, 1844, no. 117, art. v, 'Rebecca', vol. lxxiv, pp. 123 sqq. H. T. Evans, *Rebecca and Her Daughters*, 1910.

[2] Royal Commission of Enquiry into Turnpike Trusts, 1844.

[3] 7 & 8 Vict. Cap. 91: An Act to consolidate and amend the Laws relating to Turnpike Trusts in South Wales.

2

To understand the Irish revolt we must go back to the years of Whig rule.[1] Whatever the blunders with which the Whig ministry can be justly charged in other spheres, their government of Ireland had been undeniably marked by a combination of courage and skill.

The Lichfield House pact between the Prime Minister and O'Connell had been scrupulously observed on both sides. It was in constant consultation with O'Connell that the Whigs had ruled, and, what is more, administered Ireland. In consequence, particularly while Lord Normanby was Lord Lieutenant, political and religious passions became calmer and the material prosperity of the country increased. This co-operation between the Whigs and the Irish Catholics was, as we should have expected, the object of violent denunciations by the Tory Press and Tory speakers in Parliament. This, however, was a source of gratification to the Whigs rather than the reverse. For the Conservatives, they concluded, bound by what they had said in opposition, would be obliged when they returned to power to pursue in Ireland an impracticable policy which would soon prove fatal to them.[2] Their hopes were justified by the event. Peel, a man of moderate and conciliatory temper, chose for the post of Chief Secretary, the Minister responsible for Ireland, Lord Eliot, who shared his conciliatory dispositions. But he sent to Dublin as Lord Lieutenant, Lord de Grey, whose wife belonged to an Orange family. Under her influence, so it was generally said, de Grey made the Castle once more an exclusively Protestant stronghold, reserving all posts, great or small, for the Protestant gentry and their clients.[3] It was in vain that Peel, with Lord Eliot's support, tried to undo the mischief.[4] Once more the Catholic party was up in arms, and it had behind it six-sevenths of the population.

Nevertheless, the revolt of 1843 and the revolutionary attitude once more taken up by O'Connell cannot be sufficiently explained by the change of government in the summer of 1841. For O'Con-

[1] *History of the English People*, vol. iii, pp. 196-9.
[2] The most eminent of the Irish prelates said to a despairing Liberal, 'Be easy, Peel's past opposition will beat his future ministry' (*Reminiscences of Daniel O'Connell, Esq., M.P., during the Agitation of the Veto, Emancipation and Repeal*, by a Munster Farmer, 1847, p. 84).
[3] Ibid., pp. 84-5.
[4] C. S. Parker, *Sir Robert Peel*, vol. iii, pp. 34 sqq.

nell had prepared for, in fact begun, this change of tactics before 1841, partly no doubt because he foresaw that his enemies, the Tories, would return to power at no distant date, but also because his political position at home was such that he dared not make his alliance with the Whigs too close. For the past three-quarters of a century there had grown up in Ireland a tradition of secret societies—terrorists recruited from the peasantry and pursuing its interests, their aim being to expropriate the landlords and divide the great farms. When George III came to the throne they were called Whiteboys; at Victoria's accession, Ribbonmen. The agrarian outrages, so frequent in Ireland, which were so seldom punished and whose authors even were mostly undetected, were their work. O'Connell, a politician with a lawyer's mentality, distrusted these terrorists. Moreover, being warmly attached to the principle of private property, he disliked the forcible expropriation which was their objective and said as much in public. Nevertheless, he was not blind to the fact that they represented a distinctively Irish form of discontent which might become hostile to himself, if he became too friendly with the English Whigs. In these circumstances he devised a method of agitation intermediate between the Parliamentary action, which was the method he personally favoured, and the revolutionary action with which the national temper obliged him to make terms. His first experiment of this sort had been the foundation of the Catholic Association which within four years had won Catholic emancipation. It was, it would seem, in the same spirit that in 1837 he had advised the London Radicals to counter the Tory campaign against the Poor Law by launching the Chartist agitation.[1]

In 1838, to forestall the risk that an Irish revolutionary movement might capture without him, and indeed against him, the sympathies of the people he founded the Precursor Society, whose programme was to complete the union of the British and Irish legislatures by a thoroughgoing assimilation of the laws in force in the two countries.

The nature of this assimilation, as he conceived it, was explained in the text of a lengthy petition presented to Parliament. The franchise, to be extended later, should be made the same in the two countries, both for parliamentary and municipal elections, the number of Irish members increased to correspond with the

History of the English People, vol. iii, pp. 296-8.

growth of population, and the Established Church, which was in no respect national, disendowed and its revenues applied to national objects. As he foresaw, the Tories were violently hostile to his proposals, the Whig leaders unsympathetic. The extension of the Poor Law to Ireland and the reform of the Irish municipalities were not enough. The rejection in 1841 by a House of Commons, in which the Whig ministry presumably commanded a majority, of a Bill to extend the Irish county franchise was a decisive proof that they could go no further in granting the reforms demanded by Irish public opinion. The only conclusion which could be drawn was that the Union of Great Britain and Ireland was not and never would be genuine, and, therefore, if Ireland were to be governed by different laws from the British, they should be enacted not in London, but in Dublin by an Irish legislature. In other words, the Act of Union passed in 1801 must be repealed. This was the programme of a new association which O'Connell founded in 1840, and which was a reincarnation of the Society of Precursors as the latter had been of the Catholic Association. The new Association was called the National Loyal Repeal Association, whose object was to bring about the repeal of the Act of Union.[1]

3

A central committee met periodically in Dublin, discussed the Bills before Parliament and the Acts passed, and put forward its own demands. The Catholic Association had been elective from top to bottom and its electoral chart had copied the division of the country into counties and baronies. After this had been pronounced illegal, the Catholic Association and its successors were composed exclusively of officials, a large body consisting of a central committee, general inspectors, repeal wardens and collectors, chosen by co-optation on the recommendation of the priests. Their sole contact with the mass of their supporters was a public meeting, whose president had no official function other than keeping order while the meeting debated. As in 1825, the subscription was a shilling a year, a penny a month for associates,

---

[1] H. of C., February 23, 1844. Speech by O'Connell recalling his activities during the preceding years (*Parliamentary Debates*, 3rd Ser., vol. lxxiii, pp. 195 sqq.). For the Precursor Association, see *Annual Register*, 1839, pp. 40 and 55, and 1843, p. 138.

a pound a year for members.[1] The object of the Association was not to seize power by force. O'Connell repudiated the employment of what the Chartists called 'moral force'. It was to influence Parliament by methods of persuasion, by presenting petitions, by peaceable demonstrations which, nevertheless, had an intimidating aspect, and by mustering such enormous crowds that the Government could not but wonder what resistance it could oppose to such numbers, if their leaders' humour should suddenly dictate less peaceful tactics or if these masses were won over by a group of agitators and, defying their leaders, decided to rebel. And what after all was O'Connell's ultimate goal? Did he know himself? It was hinted that the agitation for repeal had not been to his liking and that he had finally launched it only to forestall others doing so.[2]

For the moment he was content to bask in the magnetic power exerted by his eloquence on the Irish masses, and enjoy the fear with which his enemies both in Ireland and England were inspired by the demonstrations his Association organized.

They were monster meetings in the open air, in themselves no novelty to the British public. But such meetings had never before been organized on so vast a scale. Nor had meetings, gathered to secure the signatures of a crowd to a particular petition, followed in such rapid succession and with such a huge growth in the numbers taking part. The agitation had begun even before the Whigs were turned out. Ten thousand attended a meeting held at Tuam on August 13, 1840, thirty thousand a meeting at Navan on September 1, two hundred thousand a meeting in October at Kilkenny.[3] And seditious speeches delivered by O'Connell at every meeting compelled Lord Fortescue, who had succeeded Lord Normanby as Lord Lieutenant, to make it known that he

---

[1] *Life and Times of D. O'Connell*, by James M'Cormick, 5th ed., 1846, pp. 128 sqq.

[2] 'We do not reckon Mr. O'Connell among the sincere Repealers. He knows too much to believe that repeal can be obtained except by force, and he has too much to lose to desire a sanguinary contest in which power would accompany not the qualities which he possesses, popular eloquence and legal knowledge, but those which he wants, military skill and indifference to danger' (*Edinburgh Review*, January 1844, vol. lxxix, p. 220). 'O'Connell showed unusual hesitation in opening his last repeal campaign. . . . O'Connell swept onward by the popular current, and, thoroughly frightened, unable to find footing as the waters rose around him. . . . He was more frightened by the monster meetings than the Government itself' (*Reminiscences of Daniel O'Connell*, by a Munster Farmer, 1847, pp. 84-5).

[3] H. of C., February 18, 1844. A speech by Sir James Graham proving that the agitation had begun before Peel's Cabinet took office (*Parliamentary Debates*, 3rd Ser., vol. lxxii, pp. 763-4).

must refuse his patronage to anyone who took part in the meetings for repeal.[1] The advent of a Tory administration inevitably
intensified the agitation and made O'Connell's eloquence more
revolutionary.

In 1843 panic took possession of Orange circles in Ireland, and
their English sympathizers began to tremble for the unity of the
kingdom. For the central committee was now in a position to
collect a monster meeting within forty-eight hours, at any place
it might choose. Five hundred thousand took part in a meeting
at Cork on May 21, seven hundred thousand in a meeting at
Clare on June 15, seven hundred and fifty thousand in a meeting
at Tara on August 15.[2] The Repeal Rent brought in £3,000 a
week. The middle classes and even a few of the aristocracy joined
the movement.[3]

The agitation, however, was not strictly speaking a rebellion.
That was not what O'Connell understood by agitation. He could
always claim that these meetings were perfectly lawful meetings,
convened to sign a petition. And he could also point out that the
result of the agitation had been to bring the agrarian outrages
almost completely to an end. And not these alone, but crime of
every description. Father Mathew, the apostle of temperance, had
converted the Irish masses, carried away by a wave of enthusiasm,
to total abstinence. His teetotallers as a body had joined the repealers. Never had Ireland been so sober as during these months
of semi-revolution.

The fact remains that the monster meeting at Cork had been
arranged for May 21, the anniversary of the battle of Vinegar Hill
at which the rebellion of 1798 had been crushed, and that on this
occasion handbills had been distributed in the barracks inciting
the troops to mutiny. And the movement was something more
than lawful petitioning. For 'agitation' O'Connell substituted or
rather superimposed upon it what he called 'organization'.
Attempts were made, though they were defeated by the quantity,
cheapness, and excellent quality of British manufactured articles,
to organize a consumers' strike, a general refusal to purchase goods
not made in Ireland. In Dublin a building was begun to house the

[1] *Annual Register*, 1843, p. 143.
[2] These are extreme figures—estimates vary widely.—*Trs. Note.*
[3] The repeal rent subscriptions received by the Repeal Association rose from £680
a week in May to £2,200 in June (Sp. Walpole, *History of England*, vol. v, p. 92). See
The Life and Times of Daniel O'Connell, p. 139.

Parliament which would shortly be elected by public meetings held under the auspices of the Association and would declare itself the sole lawful Irish legislature. In England the Radicals in 1819 and the Chartists in 1839 had cherished the same dream. The Repealers had obviously borrowed the project from them. But they went further than the Radicals or Chartists had ever thought of going. In opposition to the legally constituted courts, to which no genuine Irishman might appeal, they set up tribunals appointed by the executive committee of the Association, whose judgments though devoid of any sanction except that of public opinion were nevertheless obeyed. From the United States came funds, messages of support, and incitements to armed rebellion.[1]

On the morrow of his accession to power Peel informed Lord de Grey that he was opposed to prosecutions or the removal of justices of the peace for the expression of opinion. On the latter point he was compelled to some extent to yield. Several magistrates were removed for taking part in repeal meetings.[2] And he was obliged to take legal precautions against the possibility of an outbreak of serious disorder.

After lengthy debate an Irish Arms Bill was passed. In substance it did no more than re-enact the provisions of a Bill formerly passed on the initiative of a Whig Administration.[3]

Private persons were compelled to declare any firearms in their possession—the magistrates and police were given the necessary powers of search—and might retain them only if granted a licence to that effect in due form.[4] But no further action was taken. On May 9 Peel and Wellington stated in their respective Houses, with the all but unanimous assent of both, that the British Government would never even contemplate repealing the Union.[5] The Tories affected to believe that this declaration made the Association an unlawful body and that the Government, therefore, had both the

[1] H. of L., July 14, 1843. Speeches by Wellington and Brougham dealing with the foreign help given to the Association (*Parliamentary Debates*, 3rd Ser., vol. lxx, pp. 1113 sqq. and 1165 sqq.).

[2] Sir Robert Peel to Sir James Graham, December 19, 1841, and January 2, 1842 (C. S. Parker, *Sir Robert Peel*, vol. iii, pp. 37 and 51).

[3] In 1833. The Act revived Statutes passed by the Irish Parliament in 1793 and 1796.

[4] The Bill, which passed its second reading in the Commons on May 31, did not become law until the close of the session in August (*Parl. Deb.*, 3rd Ser., vol. lxix, pp. 1042 and 1378; vol. lxxi, pp. 470 and 912).

[5] H. of L. and H. of C., May 9, 1843 (ibid., 3rd Ser., vol. lxix, pp. 9 and 24). Sir Robert Peel to Lord de Grey, May 9 and 10, 1843 (C. S. Parker, *Sir Robert Peel*, vol. iii, pp. 47-8).

right and the duty to suppress it. Their view was not shared by the Prime Minister and his legal advisers. The declaration of two members, even though endorsed by Parliament, did not make it illegal to appeal by way of petition to a better-informed Parliament. But surely all these seditious speeches justified suppression? To which Peel replied that if the Repeal Association could be dissolved on this ground, the Anti-Corn-Law League, of which O'Connell was an active member and at whose meetings highly questionable speeches had been made by him and others, might with equal justice be suppressed.[1] But an Irish Procession Act was on the Statute Book, passed ten years earlier at the request of the Whig Government to put down certain Orange demonstrations which insulted Irish national sentiment. Surely its provisions could be employed now against the Catholic demonstrations? This was impossible, the Government replied. The Statute in question was couched in terms too precise to be applicable to the Association and its meetings.[2]

When Parliament was prorogued on August 24, the Government had taken no steps to stem the rising flood of meetings.

Certainly conditions at home were better than they had been when Parliament adjourned a year earlier. Then troops had to be dispatched in haste to Lancashire to suppress a widespread revolt of the workers. Now Lancashire was peaceful, the crisis had been overcome, business had undeniably improved, and the revenue from taxation was most satisfactory. Moreover, the Court was more gratified than ever by Peel's conservative and moderate policy. And nobody wanted to see the Home Office once more in the hands of Lord John, who was widely regarded as a statesman of mediocre ability, or the Foreign Office given back to Palmerston, discredited in too many quarters by pranks which according to his critics compromised British policy and endangered peace.

In spite of all this, Peel, after two years in office, had disappointed the almost unbounded hopes aroused by his accession to power. No doubt he was still regarded as an improvement on his Whig predecessors. This, however, was but a poor compliment in view

[1] Sir James Graham to Sir Robert Peel, May 7, 1843: 'The Duke is bent on immediate legislation. Stanley doubts the policy of it. He foresees also difficulty likely to arise from the proceedings of the Anti-Corn-Law League which are founded on the model of the Repeal Association; and if one be suppressed and the other be left untouched, there will be an appearance of unequal justice' (C. S. Parker, *Sir Robert Peel*, vol. iii, p. 47).
[2] H. of L., August 8, 1843. Lord Roden's motion and Wellington's reply (*Parliamentary Debates*, 3rd Ser., vol. lxxi, p. 372).

of the profound discredit into which the latter had fallen. The object of violent attacks not only in the organs of the Opposition, but also by the great independent paper *The Times*, whose policy was to flatter the passions and prejudices of the public, and viewed with distrust by an increasing section of the Tory Press, Peel began to wonder whether he would not be well advised to resign. Imagine, indeed, the feelings of a man opening his daily paper when he read that on a particular day the induction of a new minister in a Scottish parish had caused such serious rioting that the troops had to fire on the mob, or that in a Welsh borough rioters in control of the town were about to demolish the workhouse, when a squadron of cavalry arrived just in time to charge the crowd and save the building, and, finally, when news came from Ireland of these monster meetings, which might well prove the beginning of another rebellion like that of 1798. And if such a rebellion did break out, how delighted England's enemies would be in the United States, in France, and throughout the whole of Europe.

Two Years of Prosperity (1844-1845)

For this chapter M. Halévy has left only a very few pages fit for publication, but among his papers are notes and sketches so detailed that it has seemed possible to construct an outline of the themes he intended to develop. All passages not written by M. Halévy are indented.

I FOREIGN AFFAIRS AND IRELAND

I

THE autumn of 1843 witnessed two unexpected events when the Government surprised the public by the assurance and decisive action it displayed. The improvement of business brought easier times for Peel's Cabinet, though its difficulties were by no means at an end. The situation abroad and in Ireland continued to present awkward problems. But the Government seemed ready to face them. In September the Queen paid Louis Philippe an unexpected visit. In October the Government made up its mind to arrest O'Connell.

2

The meeting of the two sovereigns at the Château d'Eu promised to inaugurate a period of good relations between France and England, and Louis Philippe when he opened the French Chambers spoke with satisfaction of the friendly understanding which had been achieved. In any case, meetings between Guizot and Lord Aberdeen had removed the dangers to be apprehended from the rival policies pursued by the two Powers in Spain. France agreed that the young Queen Isabella should not marry a French prince, England that she should not marry a Coburg. The agreement, however, which was not set down in writing, was incomplete. Guizot attempted to secure British acceptance of a Bourbon husband, and put forward Count Trapani, the King of Naples' brother, in the hope of restoring between the three Bourbon dynasties an alliance which would be more valuable than ever to France now that she had occupied the southern shore of the Mediterranean. His diplomatic activities considerably embarrassed Lord Aberdeen, who countered them by putting forward a less dangerous suitor, the Count of Cadiz. But he was not prepared to put pressure on Spain, whose independence he was pledged to respect, or to break with Guizot, whose good intentions he was determined to credit. Peel, on the other hand, was far more suspicious of French policy. For the moment, however, the Spanish question did not produce an open breach between the two Governments. Later on, with another Government in office in England, it would become far more serious and destroy the good understanding with France. But this was reserved for the future.[1]

3

Two other matters, Morocco and the ridiculous incident of Pritchard, brought the two countries in 1844 to the verge of war. The news in February that Tahiti had been annexed by Dupetit-Thouars aroused no concern in London. Even Palmerston's organ, the *Morning Chronicle*, was reserved in its comment, and *The Times* soon reported with satisfaction a disavowal by Guizot which it had expected from the first.[2]

In June, however, the French launched an attack on Morocco, where Abd-el-Kader had taken refuge, which their fleet supported. It was commanded by Joinville, who had just given offence to the English by publishing his *Note sur les forces navales de la France*, in which he discussed the possibilities of a French invasion of England.[3] In August his fleet bombarded Tangier, and at the same moment the former consul at Tahiti, Pritchard, who had been expelled by the French, reached London. There was an explosion of anger throughout the country with which even Peel began to associate himself by complaining in the Commons of this 'gross insult'.[4] Lord Aberdeen, however, worked with Guizot to bring the crisis to an end. While the Whig Press was up in arms against France, *The Times* denied

[1] E. Jones-Parry, *The Spanish Marriages*, 1936, pp. 116 sqq.
[2] *Morning Chronicle*, February 28 and March 5. *The Times*, February 23 and March 4. *Examiner*, March 2 and 9, which ridicules the French.
[3] *The Times*, May 18 and June 4. 'The Prince of Joinville's Amateur Invasion of England', in *Punch*, 1844, p. 234.
[4] *Morning Post*, August 7, 9, and 19. *Morning Chronicle*, August 24 and 28.

that she had any intention of conquering Morocco and was simply doing what England had just done in China.[1] After the battle of Isly (August 14, 1844) the Moroccan crisis ended in September, when the Sultan decided to abandon Abd-el-Kader. At the same time the Tahiti dispute was settled by Guizot's expressing his disapproval of the treatment inflicted on Pritchard and his regret, and by his offer of an indemnity to the latter which was accepted. The settlement was on the whole favourable to France, who kept her protectorate over the Society Islands. Nevertheless, it aroused indignant French protests, though no one appears to have found fault with Guizot for evacuating Morocco. In England the agreement was no better received. When in October Louis Philippe returned the Queen's visit at Windsor, Lord Aberdeen's paper, the *Standard*, was alone in welcoming him as a European peace-maker. *The Times* maintained an attitude of reserve and the Opposition Press violently attacked the king of the French.[2]

The two Governments also settled their dispute about the right of search,[3] which had dragged on so long, by an agreement which the Duc de Broglie concluded in London on May 29, 1845. Concessions similar to those made to the United States in 1842 were extended to France. The Whig Press was forward in denouncing this surrender of the right of search. And *The Times* did not reply, but kept silence.[4]

The rivalry between the two countries continued all the world over. In the Lebanon, strife broke out in 1845 between the Druses and the Maronites. In Greece the Prime Minister, Mavrocordatos, was replaced by Guizot's friend, Collettis, and France, emerging from the background, where she had remained since the crisis of 1840, seemed to be doing her utmost to counteract British influence. On the west coast of Africa

[1] *The Times*, July 22, August 29, and September 2. The report of the bombardment of Tangier, which was published on August 24, had done much to excite popular indignation. For the relations between *The Times* and Lord Aberdeen, see *The History of 'The Times'*, vol. ii, pp. 95-8.

[2] *Standard*, October 8. The *Morning Chronicle*, October 10 and 14, spoke of the French as 'fools who have outraged every principle of humanity'. *The Examiner*, October 5, said that the country was honoured by the visit 'of all the French burglars that have lately roused John Bull from his easy chair. Now that John Bull is on his legs he will be glad to receive these princes and officers'. *The Morning Post*, October 9, protested against these attacks.

[3] Guizot, *Memoires*, vol. vi, pp. 235-6.

[4] *Morning Chronicle*, June 2 and 5, 1845. *Examiner*, June 21. *The Times*, May 13, 23, and 26.

a number of disputes were settled, not without difficulty. In 1843 Guizot agreed to keep out of Madagascar. But he allowed the governor of the Isle Bourbon to annex the neighbouring islands. In the Pacific, at the very moment of the Tahiti incident, the English witnessed a French attempt to establish a naval base at Basilan, near the Philippines. And they were confronted with yet another instance of French intrigue in the Argentine on the Cape Horn route.[1]

Whereas the British Empire was not the product of deliberate purpose, but, as it were, a spontaneous growth from the seed sown by her missionaries turned traders, France appeared to be seeking colonies for political reasons. Guizot's imagination—he was of an imaginative disposition—seemed to turn to the world beyond Europe, to satisfy by a policy of colonial expansion a minority of fervent patriots, concentrated in Paris, and craving for action and glory. He had to achieve the *tour de force* of carrying out this policy with the consent of the Power whose susceptibilities it must directly provoke, and at the risk of producing explosions of Anglophobia which would endanger the good understanding with England.

Guizot's policy caused the British Cabinet serious anxiety, which was voiced by Wellington, who persuaded Peel to overrule Lord Aberdeen and increase the national armaments.[2]

4

The Irish policy of Peel's Cabinet did not increase its reputation. It banished, it is true, the immediate danger to be feared from the agitation for Repeal. But far from providing a permanent solution of the Irish problems it gave rise to others equally formidable in England itself. At any rate, the Government did not shrink from courageous action.

When Parliament was prorogued in August 1843, no steps

[1] R. Guyot, *La Première Entente Cordiale*, pp. 256, 258, 281-3. Ch. Schefer, 'La Monarchie de Juillet et L'Expansion Coloniale' (*Revue des Deux-Mondes*, September 1912, 6th Ser., vol. xi, pp. 152 sqq.). *Edinburgh Review*, January 1844, art. ii, 'Proceedings of the French in the Pacific' (vol. lxxix, pp. 40 sqq.).
[2] C. S. Parker, *Sir Robert Peel*, vol. iii, pp. 195 sqq.

had been taken to restore tranquillity in Ireland.[1] The agitation for Repeal proceeded unchecked. A monster meeting was summoned to meet at Clontarf on Dublin Bay on October 8. The day before, the Government forbade it. Its intervention, justified by the fact that O'Connell's supporters had been told to come in military formation, proclaimed that the moment had come to suppress a revolutionary movement. O'Connell, in fact, to avoid a bloody encounter, revoked the order he had given. His surrender was a fatal blow to his influence, and from this moment the agitation began to wane.[2]

The following week the Government followed up its advantage and arrested O'Connell. His trial by a Dublin court was the occasion of discreditable manipulations which removed all the Catholics from the jury. O'Connell appealed to the House of Lords, which after protracted deliberations quashed the sentence.[3]

This result must not be regarded as a victory of justice. The Upper House left the decision to the Law Lords, of whom a majority were Whigs opposed to the Government's policy of repression. But although their judgment was dictated by party politics, it did not disturb Peel, who took advantage of it to adopt measures of conciliation and reform.[4]

In truth the Irish problem was incapable of immediate solution. All that could be done was to increase the county representation and assimilate the Irish franchise to the English.

In these circumstances the wiser policy was to deflect the attention of the Irish from their political claims by remedying their other grievances.

If the evil were to be attacked at its source, the agrarian problem, the system of landed property which was responsible for so much impoverishment and suffering, would have to be tackled. Of this Peel was well aware and to obtain the necessary information

[1] H. of C., July 11. Roebuck's speech. August 1, 1843. Ward's speech on the religious question in Ireland (*Parliamentary Debates*, 3rd Ser., vol. lxx, pp. 958 sqq., and lxxi, pp. 151 sqq.).

[2] *Annual Register*, 1844, pp. 60 sqq. H. of C., February 23, 1844. Peel's speech (*Parl. Deb.*, vol. lxxiii, pp. 206 sqq.). For the decline of the Repeal Movement, see *The Life and Times of Daniel O'Connell*, p. 139.

[3] Sp. Walpole, *History of England*, vol. v, pp. 108 sqq. *Reminiscences of Daniel O'Connell*, by a Munster Farmer, pp. 85 sqq.

[4] The Cabinet had been making preparations for them since the autumn of 1843 (C. S. Parker, *Sir Robert Peel*, vol. iii, pp. 63 sqq.).

appointed in 1843 a commission, over which Lord Devon presided, to inquire into the problem. But its report could not be ready before 1845, and until then could not produce any effect.[1] For the moment Peel did nothing.

5

It was the religious problem with which he grappled first. Attention had been drawn to it again by the refusal at O'Connell's trial to admit Catholic jurymen. In February 1844 it was the subject of debates which continued for nine sittings.[2]

In this connection we should observe that the attitude of the ministers was no longer that which had been prevalent in Tory circles twenty or thirty years earlier. They were no longer determined to defend uncompromisingly the privileges of the Anglican Church in Ireland against a Whig aristocracy always disposed to exploit against her the grievances of the Dissenters and Radical secularists. There was, in fact, no difference between the attitude of the Whig Cabinet then and the Tory Cabinet now. There was the same weariness of theological wrangles, and statesmen of both parties alike were disappointed by their revival in England and Scotland on the morrow of the election of 1841. We can, however, detect beneath this practical agreement a slightly different point of view. The Whigs were sceptics who regarded such disputes as out of date and hoped to see them obliterated by a universal indifference. The Tories on the other hand, troubled by the growth of this scepticism, thought it absurd that the different denominations should persist in fighting each other instead of realizing, as they should, how deep-seated their agreement was in face of the common foe, modern rationalism. Nevertheless, though perhaps from different motives, both parties pursued the same policy, a policy of active toleration prepared to patronize all forms of Christianity.

Unhappily it was by no means easy to see how religious peace could be made in Ireland.

[1] See below, pp. 158 sqq. In 1845 the Government introduced, through Lord Stanley, a Bill by which an evicted tenant could claim compensation for any improvements made during his tenure. But they gave way in face of the Lords' opposition (Sp. Walpole, *History of England*, vol. v, pp. 124-5).

[2] H. of C., February 13 to 23, 1844 (*Parliamentary Debates*, vol. lxxii, pp. 683 sqq.).

An Anglican Church furnished with wealthy endowments ministered to no more than an eighth of the population, whereas the Catholic Church subsisted in penury on the offerings of the poor.[1] It would have served no purpose to make the Catholic Church the established Church of Ireland unless at the same time it received the endowments of the Anglican. But a measure could not in prudence be adopted which must arouse a storm of indignation throughout Protestant England and Scotland. Nor could the problem be solved by disestablishing religion in Ireland as O'Connell desired, unless disestablishment were accompanied by disendowment of the Established Church. A third suggestion was the simultaneous establishment of two Churches, the Catholic and the Protestant. It was favoured by many politicians, particularly on the front bench of the Opposition, and possibly many Conservatives at the bottom of their hearts were not averse to it. But once more the question of endowments stood in the way. It would be impossible to divide them fairly without almost completely disendowing the Anglican Church.[2]

Yet another solution was possible, to leave the funds of the Anglican Church untouched but permit the Catholic Church to build up permanent endowments. In that case the latter would be brought into official relations with the State and to a certain extent subjected to its control.

This was, in fact, the policy which the Cabinet decided to pursue. An Act was passed legalizing bequests for the construction of Catholic churches and the support of their clergy. In accordance with its provisions three Catholic bishops were placed on the committee set up to administer such bequests and donations, which were thus secured against Protestant control. Peel, not without difficulty, secured the collaboration of the more moderate members of the Catholic hierarchy. His success in December 1844 was a victory over the extremists and O'Connell, who could no longer as hitherto count upon the support of the clergy.[3]

---

[1] G. de Beaumont, *L'Irlande Politique, Sociale et Religieuse*, ed. 7, vol. i, pp. 309 sqq.

[2] Lord Alvanby, *The State of Ireland Considered*, 1841. *Edinburgh Review*, January 1842, art. viii, 'Payment of the Catholic Clergy' (vol. lxxiv, pp. 474 sqq.). For the most moderate Catholic claims, see Lord Arran to Lord Heytesbury, August 1, 1844 (C. S. Parker, *Sir Robert Peel*, vol. iii, p. 119). See above all an anonymous publication believed to have been inspired by the Government, *Past and Present Policy towards Ireland*, 1845.

[3] 7 & 8 Vict. Cap. 97: An Act for the more effectual Application of Charitable Donations and Bequests in Ireland (C. S. Parker, *Sir Robert Peel*, vol. iii, pp. 126 sqq.).

6

Meanwhile Peel was preparing further measures of reform.[1] The contrast between Protestant wealth and Catholic poverty was nowhere more glaring than in the provision of educational facilities. The Protestants enjoyed the funds of the National Board and its three thousand schools. And the scholarships and chairs at Trinity College were reserved for them. On the other hand, Maynooth College, founded during the revolutionary wars to give candidates for the priesthood the education they could no longer receive on the Continent, presented visitors with a spectacle of indigence.[2] The Government brought in two Bills. The first founded three colleges to be provided with an endowment and an annual subsidy by the State, and together forming the University of Dublin. The University would not teach theology. In spite of the opposition of the more uncompromising Anglicans it was passed by a large majority.[3]

On the other hand, Peel proposed a grant of £30,000 for rebuilding Maynooth College and to triple the meagre subsidy hitherto paid annually. That England should pay for disseminating the superstitions of Popery was intolerable to Protestant consciences. Throughout the protracted debates which took place in April 1845 petitions against the Bill poured in, by the hundred at first, later by the thousand. Peel stood firm, and with great difficulty overcame an opposition which found adherents in every section of the House. He owed his victory not only to the discipline he imposed on his party, but also to the support of the Opposition leaders who saw, as he did, the political expediency of the step. In a celebrated and brilliant speech Macaulay made himself their mouthpiece.[4] The Bill was passed. But the feeling it had aroused had serious repercussions in Anglican circles, particularly among the High Churchmen. Gladstone was not prepared to oppose it; but, since he could‑

[1] In August 1844 he repealed no less than twenty-four penal Statutes against Catholics passed in the reign of Edward VI (7 & 8 Vict. Cap. 102: An Act to repeal certain Penal Enactments against H.M.'s Roman Catholic Subjects). See *Edinburgh Review*, October 1844, art. v, 'Results of Tory Rule', vol. lxxx, pp. 511 sqq.
[2] *Maynooth, The Crown and the Country*, 1845. By the same writer, *A Review of the Endowment Bill, showing its False Tendencies*, 1845. *Maynooth, Its Teaching and its Endowments*, 1845.
[3] *Annual Register*, 1845, pp. 141 sqq.
[4] For the debates, see *Ann. Reg.*, 1845, pp. 102 sqq. For the petitions, see Sp. Walpole, *History of England*, vol. v, p. 121, and S. Maccoby, *English Radicalism*, p. 259.

not reconcile it with the views he had hitherto expressed on ecclesiastical questions, he resigned from the Government.[1]

Pusey was shocked to see the Church of England, which claimed to possess the truth, consent to patronize error. The effect of the crisis on Newman was different. In October he left a Church which in his opinion admitted that she did not possess the truth and entered the Church of Rome.

II ECONOMIC POLICY

I

Thus, in the teeth of great difficulties, the Administration pursued its policy of a good understanding with France and conciliation in Ireland. But at the same time it was benefiting by the period of prosperity which had opened in England.

Good harvests in 1843 had cheapened the price of corn, and the same year business recovered, first, the Lancashire cotton industry, then the woollen industry, and finally the manufactures of the Midlands. The optimism which prevailed at the opening of 1844 was in striking contrast with the gloomy prognostications a year before.[2]

The improvement, however, was an obstacle to the adoption of certain reforms. On the other hand, it weakened the opposition to the Poor Law. In 1844 Sir James Graham reintroduced his Factory Bill shorn of the educational provisions, which had cost him such disappointment the previous year.[3]

In its new form the Bill forbade the employment in factories of children below the age of nine, instead of the eight years of the former Bill, restricted it to six hours and a half until the age of thirteen, to twelve till the age of eighteen. For those in the last category Lord Ashley asked for a ten-hour day. But it was argued that a mill could be run economically only if all its workers were subject to the same conditions of labour. It would, therefore, be necessary to reduce the working day of

---

[1] C. S. Parker, *Sir Robert Peel*, vol. iii, pp. 160 sqq. Nevertheless, Gladstone voted for the Bill. For his attitude, see J. Morley, *Life of W. E. Gladstone*, 1903, vol. i, p. 279.
[2] *Annual Register*, 1843, pp. 1 sqq., and 1844, pp. 1 sqq. Tooke, *History of Prices*, Preface to vol. iv.
[3] See above, pp. 63-7.

all the workers to ten hours. The House was prepared for a compromise between the twelve hours proposed by Graham and Lord Ashley's ten. But at this point the Government wound up the debate. The Act which was subsequently passed was a marked improvement on the statute of 1833. The working day for all female workers, even above eighteen, was restricted to twelve hours. A clause which forbade employers to interrupt these hours of work so as to spread them over the entire time the factory was open implemented the Government's avowed intention to extend by this indirect method the twelve-hour day to all workers. But it continued to be the working day for workers of both sexes between thirteen and eighteen.[1]

On the other hand, the rapid economic recovery made it necessary to protect the public against fraudulent company promoters. The Government carried an Act obliging joint-stock companies to publish a list of their shareholders and the distribution of their capital. But it did not apply to undertakings whose foundation had been sanctioned by Parliament, and it was precisely in respect of the latter that safeguards were most needed.[2] In no other department of industry had development been so rapid and so chaotic as in the case of the railways. There had been a boom accompanied by an epidemic of speculation. By 1843 some 2,000 miles of railroad had been built and their construction, which had slackened since 1836, was almost at a standstill in 1842. In 1844 Parliament sanctioned the construction of 800 miles of new railway. The figure rose in 1845 to 2,700. There was a mushroom growth of railway companies, though amalgamations of existing lines were effected on a wide scale on the initiative of G. Hudson.[3]

Gladstone at the Board of Trade attempted to keep this expansion in check. From the moment of his arrival at the Board he had tried without much success to extend the powers conferred on the Department of Railways which an Act of 1840

---

[1] The Act of 1833 forbade work before the age of nine, restricted it to nine hours between nine and thirteen, and to twelve until eighteen, for workers of both sexes. *Annual Register*, 1844, pp. 107 sqq. J. L. and B. Hammond, *The Age of the Chartists*, pp. 283-4, and *Lord Shaftesbury*, chap. viii. B. L. Hutchin and A. Harrison, *A History of Factory Legislation*.

[2] 7 & 8 Vict. Cap. 110, *Ann. Reg.*, 1844, p. 219. F. E. Hyde, *Mr. Gladstone at the Board of Trade*, pp. 198-200. Jelinger, C. Symons, *Railway Liabilities*, 1846.

[3] J. H. Clapham, *The Early Railway Age*, pp. 391-5. *The Times*, September 4, 1845. Tooke, *History of Prices*, vol. iv, pp. 63-4.

had set up.[1] In February 1844 he undertook an inquiry over which he presided in person, which at the end of six months published six reports. At the end of June he brought in a Bill to compel the companies to run particular trains with cheap fares, and empowering the Government to reduce fares or enforce the redemption of stock when a company after fifteen years had made a certain margin of profit.

But this interference by the State with private enterprise aroused an opposition which Peel made no attempt to overcome. Gladstone was obliged to be content with a more modest reform. Neither a reduction of fares nor redemption could be enforced before the end of twenty-one years, and then only if Parliament passed special legislation to that effect.[2] After Gladstone's resignation the Government once more concerned itself with the control of company amalgamations.[3] The functions of the Department of Railways were transferred in 1845 to a Committee of the Privy Council, and it was not until the following year, when Peel's Cabinet had resigned, that Commissioners of railways were appointed whose powers, however, were not clearly defined.[4] We shall see later how the speculation which the Government had failed to check involved the country in 1847 in a dangerous financial crisis. Ever since 1845 it had occasioned misgivings, and *The Times* pointed out with alarm that the railways were attracting a disproportionate amount of the nation's capital.[5]

But the prosperity which this growth seemed to reflect appeared, nevertheless, to justify the policy the Government had pursued, and was continuing to pursue, as it increased its control over the development of British finance.

2

In 1845 the agreement concluded in 1833 with the Bank of England came up for reconsideration.[6] Peel took advantage of

---

[1] 5 & 6 Vict. Cap. 55.
[2] 7 & 8 Vict. Cap. 85. F. E. Hyde, *Mr. Gladstone at the Board of Trade*, chap. vii. J. H. Clapham, *The Early Railway Age*, pp. 417 sqq.
[3] 8 & 9 Vict. Cap. 96.
[4] J. H. Clapham, op. cit., pp. 423-4.
[5] *The Times*, October 14, 1845.
[6] 3 & 4 William IV, Cap. 98. *History of the English People*, vol. iii, pp. 86-7.

the opportunity to effect a reform which had been widely discussed ever since the restoration of peace.

The dispute was still in process which had been fought years ago between the doctrine of Thomas Attwood who, in the interest of producers and of farmers in particular, opposed all restriction of credit and that of Ricardo, who held that the issue of currency should be limited and guaranteed. The dispute had been settled by the Act of 1819, for which Peel had asked as a young man, restoring payment in specie. The step Peel had taken at that time had never ceased to be the subject of hostile criticism, and the debate had been reopened by every economic crisis which befell the country.[1]

The decision, which had been taken to authorize besides the Bank of England other joint-stock banks, had been justified by the success of the latter, above all the London and Westminster Bank, and an Act carried by Peel in 1844 met with general approval. It required any joint-stock bank founded in future to possess capital of at least £100,000, of which a half must be paid up. But was it so wise to restrict the right of these joint-stock banks and private banks to issue notes, to give the Bank of England the monopoly of their issue in the London district, and, moreover, to authorize the Bank to open branches and put pressure on the provincial banks to abandon the issue of notes? On the other hand, the crisis of 1836 had regained favour for Ricardo's proposal that the privilege of issuing notes should be reserved to a State bank which should have no other function. And it had also given birth to the proposal that the Bank of England should be compelled to separate completely its issue of notes from its other operations.[2]

The Bank Charter Act of 1844 gave effect to the latter solution, which, indeed, the directors had begun to adopt voluntarily. In future the Banking Department would be entirely separate from the Issue Department, and the issue of the latter strictly limited. Notes might be issued to the value of £14,000,000 guaranteed by certain credits, and above all by the national debt owed to the Bank. But any increase of the issue must be covered by the metallic reserve, three-quarters of which must be gold. No new banks would be empowered to

[1] *History of the English People*, vol. ii, p. 53.
[2] Ibid., vol. ii, pp. 230-1, 292-4; vol. iii, pp. 277-82. Tooke, *History of Prices*, vol. v, p. 615.

issue notes. Those already in existence might not increase their issue and it was made easy for the Bank of England to call in their notes. Two further Acts extended the reform to Scotland and Ireland, adapting its principles to local conditions.[1]

These measures gave rise to very lively debates between financial experts which, it would seem, confused two distinct questions, the question of currency which the experts wished to restrict more or less according to the part which, in their opinion, it played in causing economic crises, and the question of credit and the part played in finance by this 'bankers' money', which consisted of bills of exchange. For it might be argued that the separation of the two departments of the Bank was not a sufficient safeguard, and the business world should also be protected against imprudent operations of the Banking Department.[2]

But discussions of this kind were pursued above the heads of the public, which left such matters to Peel, a statesman whose authority in the sphere of finance was enhanced by his high moral reputation. In consequence the passage of the Bill through Parliament was a triumphal progress which overawed all opposition.[3]

3

It was the success of his financial policy which at this juncture established the Prime Minister's authority so firmly. Whereas at the beginning of 1843 a short-term loan had been thought necessary to balance the Budget, the return of prosperity upsetting its calculations had produced by the end of the financial year a surplus more than sufficient to repay it. In 1844, therefore, the Government was in a position to effect a conversion on an unprecedented scale. The interest on the £250,000,000 of the national debt which had risen above par was reduced from $3\frac{1}{2}$ to $3\frac{1}{4}$ per cent for ten years, to be then further reduced to 3 per

[1] 7 & 8 Vict. Cap. 32. J. H. Clapham, *The Early Railway Age*, pp. 521 sqq.

[2] M. Halévy prefaced these observations with the words, 'So far as I can see at present'. On the other hand, the results the Bank could produce by varying rates of interest and discount were beginning to be better understood. See J. M. Keynes, *A Treatise on Money*, pp. 16–17; R. G. Hawtrey, *Trade and Credit*, chap. iv.

[3] *Annual Register*, 1844, pp. 190 sqq. *Quarterly Review*, June 1847, art. viii. 'The Financial Pressure' (vol. lxxxi, p. 252): 'The progress of Sir Robert Peel's Bill through the Houses of Parliament partook in some degree of the character of an ovation.'

cent. The operation effected an immediate economy of £625,000 which would ultimately be doubled.[1]

The Budget of 1844, presented by Goulburn on April 29, estimated the revenue at £51,790,000, the expenditure at £48,643,000, a surplus, that is to say, of more than three million.[2]

In spite of this the Cabinet would not consent to any substantial reduction of taxes. The income tax which brought in £5,000,000 would expire next year, and they must not anticipate the decision of Parliament. The only matter warmly debated was the sugar duty, and this was always a dangerous topic. For it called into action the defenders of the colonial planters. A motion by Lord John Russell asking that foreign sugar should be subject to no higher duty than colonial was easily defeated. Goulburn's sole concession was to reduce the duties to 34 and 24 shillings respectively. When the Commons passed an amendment making further reductions Peel forced the House to reverse its decision.[3]

The Government was criticized for its caution,[4], but it was due to its policy of waiting. At the beginning of 1845 Peel thought the time had come to act. On February 14 he made public the reforms he intended to effect. He was already in a position to look forward to a surplus of more than £5,000,000 at the end of the financial year. The uncertainty of Anglo-French relations compelled him, it was true, to increase the army estimates. But if the income tax were retained very considerable reductions would be possible in other directions. 813 articles were dutiable. He proposed to remove the duty on 430 of these, which together brought in a revenue of no more than £320,000. All taxes on exports, even the tax on coal imposed in 1842, would be abolished. Moreover, Peel, who expected a large increase in the use of glass, proposed to abolish the excise duty on it, and he was now prepared to reduce further the duties on sugar, while retaining the preference given to colonial sugar. In all, the reductions he proposed amounted to more than £3,000,000, and his programme of reform was obviously the continuation, if not the completion, of the work

[1] *Annual Register*, 1844, p. 153.
[2] Ibid., 1844, p. 156.
[3] Sp. Walpole, *History of England*, vol. v, pp. 33-4. F. E. Hyde, *Mr. Gladstone at the Board of Trade*, pp. 72-6.
[4] *The Times*, August 10, 1844.

of simplification and fiscal emancipation begun by his Budget of 1842.[1]

His proposals, however, did not go unopposed. The Radical, Roebuck, wanted the income tax to distinguish between different sources of income. And there was unmistakable evidence of dissatisfaction among the protectionists, who were alarmed to see their leader depriving farmers piecemeal of the protection they received from the tariff on imports. Peel had no difficulty in overcoming this opposition.[2] The country had confidence in him. Since he took office he had reduced taxation by £20,000,000. For the growth of trade had increased the revenue by £15,000,000, and the £5,000,000 brought in by the income tax kept the Budget balanced.[3]

The strength of his position was due in no small measure to his firm control over his own Cabinet. He followed his colleagues' activities and directed them in detail with a vigilance which won Gladstone's admiration.[4]

But Peel, determined as he was to prove a great statesman, had always to reckon with the serious difficulties, not yet settled, arising from the problem of Irish Catholicism and the insecure position abroad. His present success he won as an expert in finance.[5]

In this capacity he was brilliant. His enemies withdrew from the contest. Lord John Russell, leader of the Whigs, who were still unpopular, recognized the value of the work Peel was doing without regard to considerations of party to improve the condition of the people and saw the wisdom in the Whig interest of letting the Tory Prime Minister put Whig principles into practice.[6]

---

[1] *Annual Register*, 1845, pp. 22 sqq. Sp. Walpole, *History of England*, vol. v, pp. 43-8.
[2] S. Maccoby, *English Radicalism*, pp. 257-8.
[3] F. E. Hyde, *Mr. Gladstone at the Board of Trade*, pp. 21-2.
[4] W. I. Jennings, *Cabinet Government*, pp. 139-41.
[5] *Greville Memoirs*, August 21, 1845: 'There is no party distinguished by any particular badge of principle, with a distinct colour, and standing in open and defined antagonism to any other. . . . The world is absorbed by its material interest, railroads and speculation in its multiform aspect.' *Ann. Reg.*, 1845, pp. 213-14: 'The removal of the old landmarks of party warfare and the fusion or subdivision of the ancient Whig and Tory sections into fresh combinations, representing new shapes and modifications of opinion, afford unequivocal evidence of the transitional state which marks the political system of the country at the present day.'
[6] H. of C., August 9, 1844, and May 26, 1845. Lord John Russell's speech (*Ann. Reg.*, 1844, pp. 223-4, and 1845, p. 92). J. L. and B. Hammond, *Lord Shaftesbury*, p. 113.

Peel, in fact, had less support from his own party, in which grumbling was frequent, than from the country at large.

At the end of the session of 1845 a 'most complete repose'[1] prevailed in the world of politics. But it was the calm before a storm. For a problem still awaited solution of which politicians said very little, though it was in everybody's mind, the duties on imported corn and the campaign against them conducted by the Anti-Corn-Law League.

[1] *Annual Register*, 1846, p. 2.

CHAPTER III

The Revolution of 1846

I THE AGITATION FOR FREE TRADE

I

MANY times during the first chapter we have had occasion to speak of the part taken in Parliamentary debates by Villiers, Cobden, and other uncompromising free traders.[1] But the campaign up and down the country of the Anti-Corn-Law League was of far greater importance. And of this we have now to tell. It was this campaign that gave so much weight to the speeches made at St. Stephens by the representatives of this strange party which disclaimed being such, and was bound no more closely to the Whigs than to the Tories, a group outside and above the regular parties which existed to promote one object and one alone, which it claimed was the strictly logical consequence of the principles laid down by the science of political economy.

With the beginning of 1843, after the failure the previous autumn to engineer a revolution, the League extended and intensified its agitation. But though on a larger scale its character remained the same. It was an agitation of business men furnished to finance its activities with vast funds of which the League delighted to boast. A public subscription of £50,000, opened at the end of November 1842, brought in the entire sum within three months. Another subscription of £100,000 opened in November 1843 was fully subscribed by the summer of 1845.[2] And not only were these business men wealthy, they knew how to make good use of their wealth.

A German visitor has left an enthusiastic account of the magnificent organization of their headquarters at Manchester, the number of letters which poured in, the variety of their contents, and the speed with which they were read, classified, and a suitable answer returned to each correspondent. Their weekly organ *The*

---

[1] See Sp. Walpole, *History of England*, vol. v, p. 55.
[2] A. Prentice, *History of the Anti-Corn-Law League*, vol. ii, pp. 17-20, 131 sqq., 282, and 383. John Morley, *Life of Richard Cobden*, pp. 35 and 42.

League had a circulation of twenty thousand.[1] We should not, however, forget—I have already insisted on the point—the emotional appeal of the movement. Speakers on League platforms wept themselves and drew tears from their audience as they described the penury and sufferings of the British working class. In denouncing these evils they were on common ground with the Chartists, from whom they differed only in respect of the remedy to be applied. The remedy they advocated was not the Chartist prescription of a wider franchise, whose efficacy they pointed out must be very indirect, nor State intervention to regulate the conditions of labour which must be inefficacious because it did not touch the root of the evil. The true remedy, the panacea, in fact, was to abolish the duties on corn which benefited no one but the landlord, crippled the natural movement of trade, and starved the poor. The campaign took on a religious character: 'We bind ourselves to the League', said the Unitarian minister Fox, 'as to a Covenant', and he swore 'by Him who liveth for ever and ever' that it would not be long before the iniquitous Corn Law would be repealed which defied the will of God and made it impossible for the human race to enjoy in peace by the operation of free trade the diverse products of every climate and region of the globe.[2]

In this way political economy was transformed into theology, or rather perhaps theology into political economy. And the immediate demand for a definite fiscal reform passed over into the grandiose dream of mankind reconciled and disarmed by the universal levelling of frontiers. Moreover, the League—and this aspect of it has never been sufficiently emphasized—did not shrink from investing their campaign on occasion with the guise of a popular, we might almost say revolutionary, agitation. Such had been its character in 1842 and would be once more a year or two later. But the wealthy members of the middle class who pulled the strings of the League took alarm the moment popular discontent, aroused by their agitation, became more violent than they desired or took a different line from that which they had ex-

[1] A. Prentice, *History of the League*, vol. ii, pp. 117 and 281. *The League*, which succeeded the *Anti-Bread-Tax Circular*, issued its first number on September 30, 1843.

[2] Fox's speech at Drury Lane, March 30, 1843 (F. Bastiat, *Cobden et la Ligue*, p. 36). Villiers's speech: 'He thought that the Anti-Corn-Law League was well occupied in diffusing political truth. They were doing in their vocation what the religious societies were doing for religion' (Prentice, op. cit., vol. ii, p. 35).

pected. When this happened they contrived, as we have seen in 1842, a prudent retreat. They could sow the wind and disavow the whirlwind.

At the opening of 1842 they were confronted with the task of disabusing the public of the belief, fostered by their opponents, that their campaign was a device of the northern manufacturers to lower wages in proportion to the fall in the cost of food. On this point during the election of 1841 the Chartists had joined forces with the Tories against them. On the morrow of the election they had effected a reconciliation with the Chartists and, when their joint agitation failed, had saddled their allies with the responsibility for the riots and their suppression and had acquired with the more sober elements of the working class the influence lost by O'Connor's campaign. William Lovett and the London moderates broke with Chartism; many of the Chartist leaders arrested at the close of 1842 left prison, like Cooper, wiser men, and these two groups with their disciples were particularly open to the League propaganda. But this was not all. O'Connor, by the new form he gave to his agitation, contrived to alienate not only these moderates of yesterday or to-morrow, but the wild men led by O'Brien, who saw in Chartism the prelude to a social revolution. He abandoned the political programme of the six points of the Charter and launched a new one, exclusively economic and completely Utopian, a kind of 'snowball' to be set rolling by a subscription of £5,000 to be spent in the purchase of land. On the estates thus purchased, fifty smallholders chosen by lot would be settled and their number gradually and indefinitely increased.[1] The social reform which would be effected in this way without any aid from the State, the restoration of peasant proprietorship, could be secured, O'Connor maintained, only by retaining the Corn Law. On one occasion at a public meeting he had the hardihood to challenge, without much success, Cobden and Bright.[2] He still led a considerable body of fanatics. But he had forfeited the confidence of the great mass of his former supporters. If the programme of universal suffrage were to be dropped even for a time and Chartism must be content to press a purely economic reform, why not adopt the programme of the League,

---

[1] R. G. Gammage, *History of the Chartist Movement*, pp. 253, 268.
[2] A. Prentice, *History of the Anti-Corn-Law League*, vol. ii, pp. 228 sqq. Cf. R. G. Gammage, *History of the Chartist Movement* (pp. 270-1). He accuses O'Connor of collusion with Cobden.

less extravagant and better suited to the needs of the humble townspeople to whom the propaganda of Cobden and his group was at bottom addressed?

2

Another task which confronted the missionaries of the League was to make their campaign not only more intense, but more widespread. Its extent, it is true, had already by the end of 1842 impressed public opinion. But it was confined to the manufacturing areas of the north, the cotton and woollen districts. This was brought home to the League when, in August 1844, the iron-founders prevented the return of their candidate at Dudley.[1]

Nor would it be enough to convert the manufacturers of other districts. The financiers and bankers had turned a deaf ear to the propaganda for complete free trade, probably for social even more than for economic reasons. The bankers who despised the manufacturers were not likely to sympathize with an agitation they had launched. In the very heart of Lancashire at Manchester, a city of merchants rather than manufacturers, the free traders had been able to capture only one of the two seats. The League decided to extend its campaign throughout the entire country and to make a special attack on London, the metropolis of British, one is tempted to say of world, trade. Twenty-four mass meetings were held in Covent Garden Theatre, beginning in September 1843.[2] The success of the campaign was assured from the outset when the eminent banker, Samuel Jones Lloyd, joined the League, and at a by-election on October 23 it captured one of the two City seats.[3] Where the Chartists had failed, the free traders succeeded. Not only the manufacturing north but London was theirs.

With greater daring they extended the campaign to the country districts. Cobden had given the signal at Manchester in August 1842, when it had become evident that the extensive strike movement his supporters had encouraged and partly instigated was doomed to failure. It was obeyed. In this field the campaign was but partly successful. But we must not lose sight of it if we

[1] A. Prentice, op. cit., vol. ii, pp. 336 sqq.
[2] A. Prentice, op. cit., vol. ii, pp. 120 and 168. Already, in March and April 1843, a series of seven meetings had been held at Drury Lane Theatre (ibid., pp. 51 sqq., and J. Morley, *Life of Richard Cobden*, p. 38).
[3] A. Prentice, op. cit., vol. ii, pp. 127-8 and 130.

would keep every aspect of the League's activities in view.[1]

Cobden and his supporters denounced the wretched condition of the agricultural labourers. It was sound tactics. At the election of 1841 the Tories had successfully exploited against the manufacturers of the League the poverty of their workpeople. A Committee appointed in 1836 to inquire into agricultural distress had drawn the attention of the public to the hard lot of the labourers.[2] In 1843 Cobden obtained a further inquiry conducted by the Poor Law Commissioners. It finished its work quickly and issued its report[3] at the right moment to cause a sensation and embarrass the Tory members of Parliament who wanted the Factory Acts tightened up. It was now common knowledge that agricultural labourers were being paid seven shillings a week. None of his workers, Cobden stated, was paid less than twelve. It was widely known that since the Poor Law had been more strictly administered—indeed, in consequence of it—the labour of women and children was exploited more ruthlessly in the country districts of southern England than in the Lancashire mills. And the wretched housing of these unfortunates, packed as many as ten in a cramped hovel, had also been made public. The two brilliant orators, Cobden and Bright, made effective employment of the report, when in 1844 the new Factory Act was being debated. It was not surprising, they said, that agricultural labourers poured into the labour market of the great manufacturing towns to seek the happiness, comparative at least, which the advocates of the ten-hour day depicted as a hell. While Lord Ashley kept his eyes glued on Lancashire he was blind to what was going on under his nose in his native county of Dorset. Their argument was certainly not without effect on the debates, and as they must have expected influenced the agricultural labourers. The spirit of rebellion, dormant for the past ten years, revived. Ricks went up in flames.[4]

---

[1] A. Prentice, *History of the Anti-Corn-Law League*, vol. i, pp. 388-9. John Morley, *Life of Richard Cobden*, pp. 38-9.

[2] Report from the Select Committee appointed to enquire into the state of agriculture and into the causes and extent of the distress which still presses upon some important branches thereof, 1836. (In three parts, 76, 189, and 465, viii, 1.)

[3] Report of Special Assistant Poor-Law Commissioners on the Employment of Women and Children in Agriculture, 1843, xii.

[4] H. of C., May 3, 1844, Duncombe's speech (*Parliamentary Debates*, 3rd Ser., vol. lxxiv, pp. 609-11); June 25, Villiers's speech (ibid., vol. lxxv, p. 1353); and June 26, Milner Gibson's speech (ibid., p. 1493). J. L. and B. Hammond, *Lord Shaftesbury*, pp. 90 sqq. For the incendiarism, see *The Times*, December 8 and 18, 1843, and June 13 and 14, 1844.

Not seldom when the spokesmen of the League visited a rural district their arrival was greeted by a crowd of labourers armed with pitchforks and scythes, who asked if the great day had come at last.[1]

This new agrarian war was not altogether distasteful to Cobden and his friends. It intimidated their most powerful enemies, the landowners, the butt of their most impassioned eloquence, whose wealth, unearned by any form of work, incompetence, and idleness they denounced. They coupled with them in these invectives the Anglican clergymen, too often the relations and always the clients of the nobility and gentry whose income in so far as it was derived from the tithes rose with the price of wheat. The latter circumstance made an excellent theme for the denunciations of a League which was an alliance between the manufacturer and the dissenting minister against the squire and the parson.[2]

The League, however, was aware that in the existing state of public opinion they could never achieve their object until they had won to their cause a section at least of the Whig aristocracy. Already a few eccentric members of the great Whig families had subscribed to their loan and taken part in their public meetings. But it was a great day for them when the Marquis of Westminster subscribed. Henceforward they could count among their adherents not only the wealthiest manufacturer in the United Kingdom, Marshall, and the wealthiest banker, Samuel Jones Lloyd, but the wealthiest landowner.[3] If, however, the agrarian discontent took a more serious turn, it might well produce among the possessing classes a panic more favourable to the Tories than to the Manchester free traders. Indeed, had it not already ranged the farmers by the side of the landlords against the labourers, though the

---

[1] F. E. Hyde, *Gladstone at the Board of Trade*, p. 48, note.

[2] See Cobden's speech at Covent Garden Theatre, July 3, 1844: 'If there was a class which did benefit by the Corn Law it was the clergy. The Tithe Commutation Act fixed their income at a certain number of quarters of corn per annum. Was that a right position for the clergy to be placed in? That they who prayed for plenty should have an interest in the maintenance of scarcity? He put it to the clergy whether, with this one fact glaring forth to the world, they could, in consistency with their own character, be seen going about to Anti-League Meetings declaring for the maintenance of the Corn Law? They would not be fit to sit as jurors upon the Corn Law; they would be challenged as interested parties. All he asked of the clergy was to maintain a strictly neutral position' (A. Prentice, *History of the Anti-Corn Law League*, vol. ii, p. 219). Speech by J. W. Fox, February 15, 1844, in Bastiat, *Cobden et la Ligue*, p. 207.

[3] A. Prentice, *History of the Anti-Corn-Law League*, vol. ii, p. 145, where the Marquis of Westminster's letter of January 1, 1844, in which he expresses his intention of joining the League is given in full.

League had hoped when it extended its agitation to the country to combine the farmers and labourers against the landlords? It was all very well to explain to the farmers, in accordance with the doctrine of Ricardo, that any rise in the price of corn must increase not their profit but their rent, and to the labourers that the landowners were to blame for the wretched state of their cottages, and that the farmers, crushed by the high rents they had to pay, were not in a position to pay better wages.[1] It did not alter the fact that a war over wages was being fought, not between landlord and farmer, nor between landlord and labourer, but between farmer and labourer and that the farmers were not attracted by the prospect of a decrease in their rent, which would be immediately wiped out by an increase in their wages bill.

To judge by the reports published in the organ of the League you would think that the speakers in their rural campaign went from victory to victory. But in what proportion were their audiences composed of farmers and labourers? The latter certainly made up the bulk of them. And the more numerous they were the more likely was it that the farmers would be alarmed rather than persuaded by the orators' eloquence and be convinced, contrary to the intention of the latter, that their interest was bound up with the interest, not of their labourers, but of their landlords.[2]

We receive the impression that the leaders soon felt it advisable to turn against the movement they had provoked. We witness the diverting spectacle of their attempts to prove that the burning ricks were the work not of their disciples, but of those, who, wedded to the dogma of protection, were doing all they could to raise the price of corn by diminishing the supply.[3] And from the end of 1844 their propaganda took a new and more prudent form.

---

[1] See Cobden's speeches of March 12, 1844, and March 7, 1845, asking Parliament to institute an inquiry into the effect of the tariff on farmers and agricultural labourers (A. Prentice, *History of the Anti-Corn-Law League*, vol. ii, pp. 169 sqq., and 300 sqq.).

[2] In any case, when he was campaigning in the north and in Scotland, Cobden, carried away by the enthusiasm which is the professional agitator's breath of life, did not conceal his disgust with the farmers of Southern England. 'Our farmers cannot be brought to the Scotch standard by Lord Ducie, or a hundred Lord Ducies. The men are wanting' (J. Morley, *Life of Richard Cobden*, p. 41).

[3] Cobden's speech at Covent Garden Theatre, April 7, 1844 (A. Prentice, *History of the Anti-Corn-Law League*, vol. ii, pp. 224-5).

3

Three years had passed since the General Election. In three years' time another must be held. The League surely ought to prepare for it now and not leave in the hands of the two official parties that control of the voters' list which a public vote combined with a restricted franchise enabled them to exercise.

Before the election of 1841 Peel had perfected, almost created, this art of manipulating the lists. And in the opinion of many people his victory at the polls had been due as much to his practice of it as to his personal influence. Cobden determined to follow in his steps, indeed, to improve upon his methods. He began with Lancashire, the two county divisions as well as the boroughs, and after a few weeks could look forward with confidence to capturing a seat from the Protectionists in the southern division and winning all but three of the twenty-two borough seats. He then turned his attention to the rest of the country, boroughs and counties alike, and in the case of the latter had recourse to a novel device, legally unassailable, though the Tories spoke of it in tones of righteous indignation.

The Reform Act of 1832 gave a vote to all freeholders, that is to say to all who owned land whose annual rental value was not less than 40 shillings. The League set aside funds to purchase land and distribute it as freehold property to sympathisers of modest means.[1] It advised all who had the cause at heart to follow this example and provide their children with smallholdings. In this way it created as many new voters certain to vote for its candidates. And it claimed to be serving the cause of freedom at the same time by multiplying smallholders. It might seem that in doing this Cobden was copying O'Connor; for the latter at that very moment was endeavouring to increase the number of small landowners. But whereas O'Connor's land scheme was Utopian, Cobden's plan had in view nothing beyond the immediate benefit of his cause. Was this creation of new freeholders on a sufficiently large scale to alter the majority in many constituencies? The answer is not easy. For when the election of 1847 came the political situation had so completely changed that forecasts made in 1844 or 1845 had little relevance. One thing, at any rate, is

[1] This new branch of the League's activity began in the summer of 1844. A. Prentice, *History of the Anti-Corn-Law League*, vol. ii, pp. 220, 229, 249 sqq. John Morley, *Life of Richard Cobden*, p. 44. *Annual Register*, 1846, p. 67.

certain. The announcement of the creation by the free traders of an indefinite number of 40-shilling freeholders scared the Tories, who denounced the manœuvre most vehemently.[1]

This manipulation of the voters' lists to which the League now devoted so much of its activity was, however, an obscure and underground affair by contrast with the limelight which had invested their mass meetings of previous years. The Protectionists in consequence spread the report that the activity of the League was on the wane, indeed that it was doomed.[2]

The circumstances of the moment were, it is true, unpropitious. In 1842 a good harvest which accompanied, and to a certain extent assisted, the revival of trade had disappointed its hopes. The harvest of 1843 was again good, of 1844 excellent. Peel's ability was the subject of general praise. But the success of his financial policy had been due, the League maintained, to the accident of three good harvests in succession.

The first bad harvest and his overthrow was certain. For the most remarkable feature of the situation at the beginning of 1845 was the persistent vitality of the League in spite of circumstances so adverse to its propaganda. Never at a loss for an argument, it was not embarrassed by a fall in the price of corn which seemed to give the lie to all its denunciations of the Corn Law. For it now foretold that the repeal of the Corn Law would result in raising the price of wheat. For the growth of trade between the grain-producing countries and manufacturing Britain would enormously enrich the working class, and this increase of its purchasing power would make the farmers' fortune.[3] Moreover, as we have already seen, the influence exercised on members of Parlia-

---

[1] H. of C., January 27, 1846 (*Parliamentary Debates*, 3rd Ser., vol. lxxxiii, pp. 309-10).

[2] *Annual Register*, 1844, p. 225: Colonel Sibthorpe '. . . congratulated the country on the decline of the Anti-Corn-Law League.' Villiers's speech at Covent Garden Theatre, December 12, 1844: 'They are not standing still or, as our opponents say, dying, but they are trying something new' (A. Prentice, *History of the Anti-Corn-Law League*, vol. ii, p. 259). B. Disraeli, *Lord George Bentinck*, pp. 6 sqq.: 'Low prices, abundant harvests and a thriving commerce had rendered appeals, varied even by the persuasive ingenuity of Mr. Cobden, a wearisome iteration. The Manchester confederates seemed to be least in favour with Parliament and the country on the very eve of their triumph.'

[3] H. of C., February 26, 1846. Cardwell's speech: 'The repeal of these laws would promote the prosperity of commerce and manufactures; and that prosperity would increase, as it had increased, in past time, the rate of wages in the commercial and manufacturing districts. A man with 30s. a week would consume more bread, butter, beef, mutton, and other agricultural produce, than a man with 8s., or even 16s., and, when the consumption of agricultural produce was thus increased, the profits of the farmer would be increased likewise and the conditions of the agricultural labourer would be proportionately bettered.'

ment by the arguments in favour of free trade was as powerful as ever.[1] Only let the bad harvest so long desired come and the League would win a victory more decisive than that which it had expected in 1842 when it had increased its troops and improved its methods of propaganda.[2]

Who was the statesman destined to give effect to its wishes? Lord John Russell or Peel? It was indifferent to the League. It despised both alike. If, however, the quarrel of 1843 had not come between Peel and Cobden the latter would perhaps have preferred Peel. For in that case his victory would not be the victory of a party, above all not the victory of that odious clique of Whig aristocrats whose patronage the manufacturers of northern England were always hoping to throw off. Possibly he foresaw that Peel would, in fact, be the man. 'It is by no means inconceivable', wrote Bastiat in 1845, 'that this eminent statesman who can read the signs of the times better than anyone else and who sees the principles of the League advancing with giant strides to the conquest of England cherishes at the bottom of his heart a personal but noble ambition, to secure the support of the free traders before the day comes when they possess a majority, set his seal on the accomplishment of commercial emancipation and allow the name of no Minister save himself to be attached to the greatest revolution of modern times.'[3] Bastiat might put forward in tones almost of apology a conjecture for which he accepts the sole responsibility. It is not easy to believe that Cobden's disciple, the man who copied his methods and preached his doctrines in France, was not echoing a conversation with one or other of the leaders of the movement.

[1] See in A. Prentice (op. cit., vol. ii, pp. 376-7), the voting in the House of Commons on the motion in favour of free trade put forward annually by Villiers.

[2] H. of C., June 28, 1844, Bright's speech (*Parliamentary Debates*, 3rd Ser., vol. lxxv, p. 1544): 'The right honourable baronet owes his safety, as does the country, to the change in the seasons. What was the condition of the right honourable baronet some two years ago? . . . but good harvests will not always be granted.' Bright's speech at Manchester, October 24, 1844: 'The Providence which has given us two or three good harvests may give one or two, or three, more; but we must have in mind that the course of the seasons cannot be changed, will not be changed to suit the caprice, the folly, or the criminality of human legislation' (A. Prentice, *History of the Anti-Corn-Law League*, vol. ii, p. 256). Sir Robert Peel, to Croker, August 31, 1845: 'I should shudder at the recurrence of such a winter as those of 1841-2' (C. S. Parker, *Sir Robert Peel*, vol. ii, p. 194).

[3] Fred. Bastiat, *Cobden et la Ligue ou l'Association Anglaise pour la Liberté du Commerce*, 1845, Introduction, p. 63.

4

'What', Cobden asked at a public meeting in London on June 18, 'were the Government thinking of as a mode of repealing the Corn Laws?... They waited', he replied, 'for a period of famine. They waited for the day when Palace Yard should be crowded with famishing thousands.'[1]

We may picture, that is to say, the members of the League during the early months of 1845 as anxious students of the weather whose hopes rose when the barometer fell, fell when it rose. A wet May was followed by a fine June. 'The wonderful improvement in the weather', Prentice wrote in his diary at the beginning of June, 'has had a magical effect on vegetation and from present appearances we shall have an ample harvest. This will enable Sir Robert Peel to hold out a little longer against his own convictions of the necessity of a free trade in corn.'[2] In July the weather was changeable, the latter part of the month fine.

'Yesterday', Prentice wrote on July 19, 'the weather was not merely fine, but brilliant, and at the time of our going to press we have the prospect of its continuance and of the fair ripening of the crops now promising to be unusually abundant.'[3]

But shortly after a downpour began which lasted throughout August and, with a few intervals of finer weather, throughout September. The price of wheat which towards the end of March had barely exceeded 45 shillings, reached 60 on August 19. In September the weather was not so continuously wet as it had been in August. The corn merchants expected a moderately good harvest and the price fell to 54 shillings. By the beginning of October the emissaries of the League had resigned themselves to waiting a year longer until a second mediocre harvest in 1846 had succeeded the mediocre harvest of 1845 and their efforts, which they must redouble meanwhile, were at last crowned with victory.[4]

At this moment the news began to come in of a worse disaster, also to be attributed to the rain, a potato disease which rotted all the tubers not already dug up. For the English poor it was a further misfortune. For the Irish lower classes whose exclusive

[1] A. Prentice, *History of the Anti-Corn-Law League*, vol. ii, p. 384.
[2] A. Prentice, ibid., vol. ii, pp. 357-8.
[3] A. Prentice, ibid., p. 379.
[4] A. Prentice, ibid., vol. ii, p. 386.

diet was potatoes it was famine. The Irish question rose to the surface once more.

Four or five years before it had been a source of anxiety in its political aspect. Peel had successfully put an end to the agitation for repeal, had then attempted to divert public attention to the religious aspect of the Irish problem, and had found himself confronted, indeed was still confronted, by grave difficulties. Now he was suddenly faced with the economic problem which Cobden, Bright, and their supporters proposed to solve, like all other economic problems, by their panacea, complete free trade, and in the first place to prevent famine by the free importation of corn. By the end of October the price of corn had risen to 64 shillings. At this price by the operation of the sliding scale of 1842 the duty fell to 8 shillings, that is to say, to the figure formerly proposed by Lord John Russell. But it was not enough to satisfy Lord John. Still less did it satisfy the League which demanded 'complete, immediate and unconditional repeal' and was convinced that it was on the eve of obtaining it.

The League held a mass meeting on October 28 in the Free Trade Hall in Manchester at which an audience of eight thousand —hundreds were turned away—listened to the threatening speeches of Cobden and Bright.[1] On October 31 Peel, who understood better than anyone the gravity of the situation and was already all but converted to the creed of the League, called a meeting of the Cabinet.[2] Four meetings were held. Peel, while proposing a plan of public works on a large scale to give the Irish employment, insisted that the question of the Corn Law must be dealt with without further delay. It was a matter of urgency. The arguments put forward in defence of the sliding scale had proved unsound. At the last of these meetings, held on Thursday, November 6, he formally submitted the following proposals to his colleagues. The duties would be suspended by an Order in Council. Parliament would be summoned to approve

---

[1] A. Prentice, op. cit., vol. ii, pp. 399 sqq.

[2] For the Cabinet crisis at the close of 1845, see H. of C., January 22, 1846, speeches by Peel and Lord John Russell (*Parliamentary Debates*, 3rd Ser., vol. lxxxiii, pp. 67 and 95); H. of L., January 26, 1846, speeches by the Marquis of Lansdowne and Wellington (ibid., pp. 166 and 172). See further, Leon Faucher, 'De la Crise Ministerielle en Angleterre' (*Revue des Deux-Mondes*, January 1, 1846, vol. xiii, pp. 115 sqq.); *The Memoirs of Sir Robert Peel*, 1847; *The Later Correspondence of Lord John Russell*, 1930, vol. i; C. S. Parker, *Sir Robert Peel*, vol. iii, pp. 234 sqq.; Sp. Walpole, *Life of Lord John Russell*, vol. i, pp. 406 sqq.; *Greville Memoirs*; Harriet Martineau, *History of the Thirty Years' Peace*.

the Order, and be informed of the Government's intention to introduce a Bill to reform the Corn Law. All the ministers were unanimous that the propaganda of the League made it impossible to touch the tariff, without suspending its operation entirely, and that, if it were once suspended, it could not be restored. Suspension would amount to repeal.[1]

Only three ministers, Lord Aberdeen, Sidney Herbert, and Sir James Graham, supported Peel's proposals. The Cabinet separated without having reached any decision, which was in effect a decision to maintain the tariff as it was. The public, which knew nothing of the disagreement in the Cabinet, was informed by the official Press that in the opinion of the Government the situation was not sufficiently grave to justify free importation. An anxious fortnight followed. The propaganda of the League held the public ear. 'Our meetings', Cobden wrote to his wife, 'are everywhere gloriously attended. There is a perfect unanimity among all classes; not a syllable about Chartism or any other ism.'[2]

These words, it is true, were written on December 4, and the hopes of the League had just been raised high by a letter which Lord John Russell had addressed from Edinburgh on November 22 to his constituents of the City. He had, he told them, proposed in 1840 a fixed duty of 8 shillings. It should have been adopted at the time when, so he said, the compromise would have satisfied the League. But it was too late in the day for that. The nation would no longer accept it. Lord John advised the people to employ every lawful method of agitation to compel the Government to yield. 'The removal of restrictions on the admission of the main articles of food and clothing used by the mass of the people' would be 'useful to all great interests and indispensable to the progress of the nation'.[3] Thus, for the first time for many years, Lord John seemed to be the true leader of the nation and to have wrested from Peel, whose attitude at the Cabinet discussions at the beginning of the month was unknown, his monopoly of the public favour. We know that he is an honourable man, a country gentleman who was Russell's friend wrote to this

[1] H. of C., February 23, 1846, Sir George Clerk's speech (*Annual Register*, 1846, p. 62): 'We might have been justified in suspending the existing law, but, if the law were once suspended, away went for ever the great argument on which the sliding scale rested, and it was evident that along with it went the law itself.'

[2] J. Morley, *Life of Richard Cobden*, vol. i, p. 342.

[3] *Morning Chronicle*, November 25, 1845. The letter is printed in full in Spencer Walpole's *Life of Lord John Russell*, vol. i, p. 424.

effect to the Duke of Bedford; we did not know that he is such a clever man.[1]

Once more, this time in consequence of the action taken by the leader of the Whig Opposition, Peel called his colleagues together. Two meetings of the Cabinet were held on the 24th and the 26th without any decision being reached. A third held on December 2 was adjourned to the following day, December 3, when Peel seemed to have won over his colleagues. The next day, however, the opposition was renewed. The position, it is true, was not what it had been a month earlier. Now only two Ministers, Lord Stanley and the Duke of Buccleuch, were unyielding in their opposition. But too many of the others had given way so reluctantly that the Prime Minister felt that he could not rely on their support.[2] On the sixth he tendered his resignation to the Queen. It was in private. But a secret of this kind could not be kept long. When on the 10th Greville met all the Ministers at a meeting of the Privy Council, he was convinced that the Cabinet had resigned, when he saw them all as happy as schoolboys breaking up for the holidays. On the 11th the news became public. Cobden was enraptured, and addressing public meetings at Stockport and Covent Garden trampled on the body of his great adversary, prostrate at last.[3]

5

To all appearance it was a brilliant victory for Lord John. When, however, he dispatched his letter from Edinburgh on

[1] Sir John Shelley to the Duke of Bedford, November 30, 1845: 'If, instead of being the brightest ornament of the Senate, and the man to whom the country may point as that most rare of all beings, a truly honest politician, he had been a member of the prize-ring, he could not have known better how and where to apply his knock-down blow' (*The Later Correspondence of Lord John Russell*, vol. i, p. 85).

[2] Lord Ashley, Mr. Bickham Escott, and Captain Rous, hitherto staunch Protectionists, volunteered the avowal of their conviction individually that resistance was no longer tenable. Lord Morpeth gave in his adhesion to the Anti-Corn-Law League and re-entered Parliament, after four years' absence, as an unqualified free trader (MacCullagh Torrens, *Life and Times of Sir James Graham*, vol. ii, p. 420). Lord Morpeth's letter of November 24, announcing his support of the League, may be found in A. Prentice, *History of the Anti-Corn-Law League*, vol. ii, p. 406. For the discussions in the Cabinet, on December 4 and 5, see Sir Robert Peel to the Duke of Wellington, January 25, 1846 (C. S. Parker, *Sir Robert Peel*, vol. iii, p. 327).

[3] For Cobden's attacks on Peel, see his letters to G. Combe, of December 29, 1845, and February 1846, in J. Morley, *Life of Richard Cobden*, pp. 50-1. Harriet Martineau mediated between them. See her correspondence with Peel in C. S. Parker, *Sir Robert Peel*, vol. iii, pp. 331-2, and her *Autobiography*, vol. ii, pp. 259-62. For the reconciliation between Peel and Cobden, see C. S. Parker, op. cit., vol. iii, pp. 332-3.

November 22, he does not appear to have realized its significance. For the same day he received the news of old Lady Holland's death, went to England to attend her funeral and returned to Edinburgh on the 29th without, it would seem, the least suspicion that the political situation was sufficiently critical to keep him in London.[1] While still at Millbrook he learned from the newspapers that a meeting of the Cabinet had been held. But he had no suspicion that the Corn Law question, the campaign conducted by the League, or his own letter had anything to do with it. The public, however, even before December 6, was aware that a crisis was imminent. Lord Aberdeen, who warmly advocated the repeal of the Corn Law for the special reason that he hoped it would facilitate the very delicate negotiations then in progress with the United States, visited Delane, the editor of *The Times*, on December 3, when for a moment Peel appeared to have won his colleagues to his views, and informed him that the Corn Laws would be repealed and Parliament summoned for that purpose.[2] *The Times* published the information on the 4th, and it was denied by the *Standard* on the 5th. Though the denial was in fact true, it was not official, a significant circumstance which perplexed the politicians.

On the 6th Peel resigned. On the 8th Lord John, still in Edinburgh, received from the Queen a summons to Osborne. He arrived on the 10th. But the victor did not know what to do with his victory.[3]

The Whig leaders took fright.[4] They were being invited to take office with a minority of a hundred in the Commons. They could not carry the repeal of the Corn Law, for which Lord John intended to compensate the farmers by a very considerable reduction of taxes, unless they could obtain the support of a large section of the Tories. And they could obtain it only by favour of the former Prime Minister, in itself a humiliating position for them. But what was more serious, though in general terms Peel promised his assistance to the Whig Cabinet in course of formation, he refused to give a pledge in writing or even to promise Lord John his unconditional support, if, as he informed Peel it

---

[1] Sp. Walpole, *The Life of Lord John Russell*, vol. i, pp. 405–6, 409.
[2] *Greville Memoirs*, December 5 and 9, 1845.
[3] See Harriet Martineau's account in A. Prentice, *History of the Anti-Corn-Law League*, vol. ii, pp. 406 and 411.
[4] G. O. Trevelyan, *Life and Letters of Lord Macaulay*, vol. ii, pp. 161 sqq.

was his intention to do, he proposed the immediate and complete abolition of the duty on corn.[1] Even if Peel gave sufficient support to carry Lord John's measures through the Commons what would their fate be in the Lords? He could not count upon the fact that Prince Albert and the Queen had publicly expressed themselves in favour of repealing the Corn Law to overcome the opposition of the Tory majority in the Upper House.[2] If the Lords threw out the Bill, the Government could appeal to the country. Would it be on the programme of the League? And here we touch what was perhaps the true explanation of the vacillations of Whig policy. In consequence of its aristocratic composition the party was a party of landlords divided by everything, save an old tradition of political Liberalism, from the commercial Liberalism of Cobden and his supporters. Lord John's Edinburgh letter had won the approval of a country gentleman here and there, even of a few eccentric members of the Whig nobility. But as a body the latter had showered upon him, by word of mouth or in writing, their indignant protests against his foolish action. Palmerston was among his most violent critics.[3] If the Corn Law must be repealed, they had no desire to take the responsibility of doing so. They preferred to leave it to Peel.

Confusion prevailed among the Tories. Peel's resignation was a proof of it. But it prevailed equally among the Whigs as was manifest when day followed day and Lord John was still unable to form an administration. 'Ours is the only party', Cobden wrote on December 17, 'that is now solid, growing and consolidated in this country. . . . The League stands erect and aloft amidst the ruins of all factions.'[4] Moreover, Peel's standing in the country, shaken when his resignation was made public, improved as the impasse in which Lord John found himself continued, and it

[1] For Peel's attitude, see his letter to Lord Heytesbury, December 23, 1845 (C. S. Parker, *Sir Robert Peel*, vol. ii, pp. 288-9).

[2] For Prince Albert's influence at this moment, see *Greville Memoirs*, December 16, 1845: 'Formerly the Queen received the Ministers alone, with her alone they communicated, tho', of course, the Prince Albert knew everything; but now the Queen and Prince were together, received Lord L. and J. R. together, and both of them always said *We*; "We think or wish to do so-and-so; what had we better do?" The Prince is become so identified with the Queen, that they are one person, and as he likes business, it is obvious that while she has the title he is really discharging the functions of the Sovereign. He is King to all intents and purposes.'

[3] *Greville Memoirs*, December 12, 1845, and January 1, 1846. Sir James Graham to Sir Robert Peel, November 22, 1845, in C. S. Parker, *Life of Sir Robert Peel*, vol. iii, p. 524.

[4] Cobden, *Speeches on Questions of Public Policy*, vol. i, p. 349.

began to be whispered that his resignation on December 6 had been a device deliberately plotted to rob the writer of the Edinburgh letter of his laurels and in a short time re-occupy triumphantly the place the latter had shown himself incapable of filling.[1] And this was, in fact, what happened.

On December 18 Lord John decided to take the plunge and informed the Queen that he was prepared to form a Cabinet. He lost no time. Without further delay he began to choose his Ministers. Whig arrogance had nothing better to offer Cobden than the position, which he refused, of Vice-President of the Board of Trade. It was the post of a ministerial novice assigned to Gladstone in 1841.[2] But the following day, the 19th, his arrangements broke down. Palmerston wanted to be Foreign Secretary and would accept no other office. He felt the more confident of succeeding in his claim because Prince Albert, at first extremely hostile to the suggestion, had become reconciled to it after the Queen had received letters from Louis Philippe and Guizot saying that they had no objection to the choice. Lord Grey, however, not the Prime Minister of the Reform Bill, but his son Lord Howick who had succeeded his father three months before, flatly refused to enter the Cabinet if Palmerston were at the Foreign Office. Lord John on his part said that he could not dispense with Palmerston at the Foreign Office or Lord Grey as a Minister in the Lords. Why were these three statesmen so obstinate? In our opinion it was because all three shared the desire to escape a task highly distasteful to themselves and the rest of the party.[3]

[1] *Greville Memoirs*, December 19, 1845: 'There is such an inveterate distrust and suspicion of him that many people cannot be persuaded he is not hatching some secret and cunning plot to overthrow them in the end.' On the 21st, after Lord John's failure, he was himself converted to this opinion of 'many people'. 'I have', he wrote, 'a strong suspicion that he was reserved, and abstained from pledging himself, because he thought John Russell would very likely not be able to accomplish his task, that in case of failure the Government would fall back into his hands, and that he was resolved all the time to retake it if it was offered to him again.'

[2] See the correspondence between Lord John Russell and Cobden in John Morley, *Life of Richard Cobden*, p. 49. H. of C., January 27, 1846, Sir J. Tyrell's speech: 'The noble Lord . . . must include the hon. member for Stockport in any new Ministerial arrangements . . . but anyone could easily imagine how much that embarrassed the noble Lord, for he well knew that in acceding to such a proposition he should lose as much with the old constitutional Whigs, as he could possibly gain with the Liberal party' (*Parliamentary Debates*, 3rd Ser., vol. lxxxiii, p. 308).

[3] C. Greville, *Sir Robert Peel and the Corn-Law Crisis*, 1846, p. 162: 'He (Lord John Russell), in fact, never tried. He went to the Queen without any intention, as he afterwards expressly stated, and his Lordship's veracity is not open to question. Her Majesty much wished him to form a cabinet, but the Queen was, it seems, satisfied to abandon such desire on hearing that Earl Grey declined to take office.' The correspondence which

Peel was then recalled to Osborne on the 20th and within three days he had reconstituted his Cabinet. He did not propose to strengthen it by altering its composition. To show the country that he was once more master of his party after a passing revolt, he made his new Cabinet as much as possible a replica of the old. On the 19th Lord Wharncliffe had died of heart failure following an attack of gout. The Duke of Buccleuch, who at the beginning of the month had been among the obstinate rebels, consented to take his place as President of the Privy Council and was himself replaced as Lord Privy Seal by Lord Haddington. Lord Ellenborough took Lord Haddington's place at the Admiralty. Only one of the former Ministers refused to serve and his refusal was a more serious matter. He was Lord Stanley. Gladstone succeeded him at the Colonial Office. He had left the Administration the previous January for a theological reason.[1] Political economy brought him back in December. Lord Stanley, however, does not appear to have been an implacable foe of the Government to which he had belonged for four years. Gladstone asked his permission to take his place and he willingly gave it.[2]

The League was not displeased by this settlement of the crisis.

passed on this occasion between Lord John Russell and Lord Grey has been published in an anonymous article in the *English Historical Review*, vol. i, pp. 122-37. Lord Palmerston's return to the Foreign Office was, it would seem, the chief obstacle to their agreement. But they also disagreed about free trade, of which Lord Grey was a more wholehearted advocate than Lord John, and on the question of the Irish Church. Lord Grey was in favour of immediate religious equality in Ireland, whereas Lord John was opposed to making 'religions equal by laying a tax in Irish lands for the Catholic Church'. Their disagreement was aggravated by the fact that Edmund Ellice, to whom Lord Grey explained his views, did not pass them on accurately to Lord John Russell. But in any case, Lord Grey's letters leave the impression that he never really wanted Lord John to form a Cabinet. Cf. Sp. Walpole, *Life of Lord John Russell*, vol. i, pp. 410 sqq.; H. C. Bell, *Lord Palmerston*, vol. ii, pp. 355 sqq. On December 20, Macaulay wrote (G. O. Trevelyan, *Life and Letters of Lord Macaulay*, vol. i, p. 169): 'I do not blame Lord John, but Lord Grey and Lord Palmerston are both at fault. I think Lord Grey, highly as I esteem his integrity and ability, chiefly responsible for the unfortunate situation in which we are now placed; but I suspect that Palmerston will be made the scapegoat.' He would be blamed for refusing to accept any office except the Foreign Office. Cf. the violent attack on Lord Aberdeen's foreign policy in the *Morning Chronicle* of December 12, 1845.

[1] In January 1845 Gladstone had left the Board of Trade because he could not in conscience associate himself with Peel's policy in the matter of Maynooth. He had been succeeded by Lord Dalhousie, who, however, did not enter the Cabinet until December. Sir Edward Knatchbull had retired in 1843 (cf. Sp. Walpole, *History of England*, vol. v, p. 25, note 1, correcting a mistake of the *Annual Register*), and his successor as Postmaster-General, W. B. Baring, was not a member of the Cabinet (C. S. Parker, *Sir Robert Peel*, vol. iii, pp. 166-8 and 291).

[2] Sir Robert Peel to Sir James Graham, December 21, 1845: Lord Stanley to Sir Robert Peel, December 22, 1845 (C. S. Parker, *Sir Robert Peel*, vol. iii, pp. 286-7). J. Morley, *Life of Gladstone*, vol. i, p. 205. We have not mentioned a few unimportant changes among the Ministers not of Cabinet rank.

On December 23 in the Town Hall, Manchester, it held a mass meeting, attended by all the manufacturers and merchants of standing in the district. It made its balance sheet public. The receipts amounted not to £100,000 but £123,000, and in accordance with a resolution passed on the 16th a further subscription list of £250,000 was opened. Of this sum £60,000 were subscribed on the spot before the close of the meeting. Cobden, who had been blamed by several of his friends for his violent invective against Peel a fortnight earlier, spoke in more conciliatory terms. 'If Sir Robert Peel', he said, 'will go on in an intelligible and straightforward course . . . he will have the support of the League and the country as fully and as cordially as any other Prime Minister.'[1]

II THE REFORMS OF 1846

I

On December 23 the Cabinet was reconstituted, and within a month, on January 19, 1846, Parliament met to hear the Queen read in person the speech from the Throne. It was at once clear how far Peel's genius towered above the mediocrity of Whig statesmanship. We know that Lord John had intended to propose the immediate and complete abolition of the duty on corn. Certainly it would have been a daring if brusque measure. But it would have had the appearance of an expedient dictated by circumstances and carried through in haste under the pressure of events. On the other hand, with equal haste and as an isolated measure which could not be referred to any general policy he would have reduced a number of taxes which weighed particularly on landed property. Lord Lansdowne, who was unfavourable to the repeal of the Corn Law and for a moment, it would seem, entertained the dream of being himself Prime Minister in a Whig Administration, wanted these reductions raised to the figure of £1,000,000. Lord John wanted the Whig aristocracy to be content with a reduction of £700,000.[2] Had the latter

[1] J. Morley, *Life of Richard Cobden*, vol. i, p. 351. Harriet Martineau to Sir Robert Peel, February 22, 1846: 'I wrote a remonstrance, and his replies have done him great credit; he has never since fallen into the same mistake.' (C. S. Parker, *Sir Robert Peel*, vol. iii, p. 321. A. Prentice, *History of the Anti-Corn-Law League*, vol. ii, pp. 413 sqq.)
[2] *The Later Correspondence of Lord John Russell*, vol. i, pp. 94-8.

succeeded in forming a Cabinet, the acrimonious bargaining would no doubt have continued. Peel made a clean sweep of all this pettifogging. The repeal of the duty on imported corn was made part of a comprehensive measure of tariff reform, which carried further what had been already effected by the Budgets of 1842 and 1845.[1] We must now study the programme put forward by Peel which led immediately to the introduction of a Customs Bill and a Corn Bill.[2]

The Budgets of 1842 and 1845 had abolished almost completely the duties on the importation of the raw materials of manufacture. The duties on tallow and timber remained. But the duty on tallow had been more than halved, and a reduction on the duty on timber promised, if not at once, at any rate by degrees. Peel now tackled the problem which his two great former Budgets had not touched, the reduction, the abolition even, of the duties on the importation of manufactured articles. Since the Government proposed to permit the free import of corn, the Protectionists must be deprived of their favourite argument—why should we, the farmers and landowners, be made to suffer from foreign competition and not you manufacturers? And were the latter then so dubious of the superior quality of their products that they dared not dispense with the protection of a tariff?

Peel proposed to abolish a large number of duties on such articles, among many others, as boots and shoes, hats, leather goods, soaps and carriages. He treated as in a special category the reform of the tariff on manufacturered articles concerned with clothing, on cloth, woollen and cotton fabrics. Stuffs of a coarser quality would be free of duty. The duty on textiles of finer quality,

---

[1] Speech from the Throne, January 19, 1846 (*Parliamentary Debates*, 3rd Ser., vol. lxxxiii, p. 6): 'I recommend you to take into your early consideration, whether the principles on which you have acted may not with advantage be yet more extensively applied, and whether it may not be in your power, after a careful review of the existing duties upon many articles, the produce or manufacture of other countries, to make such further reductions and remissions as may tend to ensure the continuance of the great benefits to which I have adverted, and, by enlarging our commercial intercourse, to strengthen the bonds of amity with Foreign Powers.' Sir Robert Peel to Goulburn, December 27, 1845, to Lord Francis Egerton, January 6, 1846 (C. S. Parker, *Sir Robert Peel*, vol. iii, pp. 294, 323). Peel's speech, February 16, 1846 (*Annual Register*, 1846, pp. 54–5): 'Both Mr. Miles and Mr. S. O'Brien and, indeed, every speaker on their side, had treated the question as a Corn-Law question; but, in point of fact, it was not a Corn-Law but a great national and commercial question. That portion of his measure which related to the Corn Laws might be rejected, and the other portion accepted, or vice versa. He wished it, however, to be considered as a whole, and rejected or accepted as such.'

[2] Peel explained his proposals in his speeches of January 22, January 27, and February 16 (*Parl. Deb.*, 3rd Ser., vol. lxxxiii, pp. 67 sqq., 239 sqq., and 1024 sqq.).

cloth, woollen, cotton and silk fabrics would be reduced by half.
After this he was in a position to turn to the farmers and landowners and ask them to accept a reduction of half the duties on
butter, cheese, hops, preserved fish, a duty of no more than 5
shillings a bushel on seeds of all kinds, and the free importation of
all foodstuffs other than those abovementioned, except corn,
which would be the subject of special treatment, and livestock.
What, then, would be this special treatment of corn? The duty on
maize would be immediately and completely abolished. Wheat,
oats, barley, and rye would be subject from January 1, 1849, to a
fixed nominal duty of a shilling a quarter. Until that date a sliding
scale, greatly reduced throughout, would replace the scale of 1842.
When the price of corn was above 54 shillings, in other words,
the price at which it stood in January 1846, the duty would be
4 instead of 16 shillings.

Would nothing, then, be done to compensate agriculture for
the unconditional loss, almost immediate and all but complete, of
the tariff which had protected it hitherto, by lightening the
burden of taxation to which it was subject? The Whigs had
pledged themselves to do this when they made their attempt in
December to form a government. Peel proposed to do the same.
But his proposals were conceived in a much wider spirit than
those which the Whigs would have put forward had they been
in charge this January of the national finances. He proposed to
revise the system of local finance in such a way as to lighten the
landowners' burdens and at the same time effect an administrative
reform from which the entire nation would benefit. He determined to push forward with the task of administrative centralization which, ever since 1832, had been the programme of the
Liberals and Radicals, but which the Whigs had failed to carry
through. He proposed to amend the Highway Act of 1835 which
had restored the control of the roads to the parishes.[1] He proposed
to entrust it to the districts which constituted the Poor Law
Unions. He proposed at the same time to amend the Poor Law.

The law of settlement, as it stood at present, gave the pauper the
right to relief, not where he worked, but in the union where he
was born. This provision constituted a heavy burden on landed
property. In future the manufacturing districts would be responsible for all their paupers and would not be entitled to return to

[1] *History of the English People*, vol. iii, p. 219.

their native parishes in the country those who had come from outside. At the same time the cost of bringing criminals to justice would be transferred from the local authorities to the State. The latter would pay not, as at present, half, but the entire cost of the police, would share with the local authorities the cost of the medical provisions of the Poor Law and would support the work-house schools. And though it was a departure from the principles of the Liberal school of economics, farmers were promised credits, to be secured by short-term loans, to encourage them, under specified conditions, to improve their land.

On February 27 the Commons passed the second reading of the Corn Bill by 337 to 240 votes, and the third reading on May 15 by 327 to 229.[1] The Customs Bill passed its second reading in the Commons on March 26, its third on May 19.[2]

Interest was concentrated entirely on the question of corn. The debates on the Customs Bill therefore did not last long. Hops, silk, spirits, and timber were the only matters about which serious opposition was encountered. On May 29 when these preliminary successes had been achieved and it was regarded as certain that the Lords would pass the Customs Bill, the Government brought in the Budget. The financial situation was excellent. A revenue of £49,762,600 had been expected; £51,250,000 had been received.[3] The expenditure to date had been £49,400,157. When allowance had been made for expenditure still to be met there was a surplus of £2,380,600. The estimated revenue for the next financial year, though so many tariff reductions had been made, was £51,650,000. On the other hand, in spite of the credits advanced for public works in Ireland and an increase of the army and navy estimates, the estimated expenditure was no more than £50,874,000. That is to say, a surplus of £776,000 was expected.[4]

Thus, under Peel's guidance, the financial policy inaugurated by the Budget of 1842 pursued its triumphant and uninterrupted path.

Peel's victory was not only the success achieved by the new finance. It was the fact that public opinion put that success to his credit. Parliament, however, was not the country, and Sir Robert's

---

[1] *Parliamentary Debates*, 3rd Ser., vol. lxxxiv, p. 349, and vol. lxxxvi, p. 721.

[2] Ibid., 3rd Ser., vol. lxxxv, p. 136, and vol. lxxxvi, p. 874.

[3] In addition the Chinese indemnity had brought in £750,859.

[4] £700,000 of which was the fruit of the Chinese war (*Annual Register*, 1846, pp. 119 sqq.).

policy had thrown all party combinations into confusion. Peel and Cobden were not yet reconciled. It was not until after the session that they shook hands. But the Prime Minister and his subordinate, Sir James Graham, who had been so unpopular only a year ago, were already the object of Cobden's and Bright's praises.[1] Cobden and Bright—particularly the former—affected to despise party politics. But at Westminster they could not be ignored. The strength of Peel's position in the country was matched by the insecurity of his position in Parliament.

2

The ease with which at the end of December he had reconstituted his Cabinet had perhaps led Peel to cherish the illusion that he would remain the master of the majority at least of his party.[2] If so it was quickly shattered. All the old Tories were up in arms and were counting upon his fall before three months had passed. Even those who remained faithful to him witnessed many gaps in their ranks. Nine of them dared not brave the wrath of the great landowners to whose patronage they owed their seats. They resigned and were replaced by Protectionists, Lord Ashley, for example, in Dorset. Five Ministers, obliged by the fact of taking office to seek re-election, lost their seats. Lord Lincoln in Nottinghamshire and Gladstone at Newark, a borough of the

---

[1] On the morrow of Peel's speech, on February 16, Bright declared: 'I envied him the ennobling feelings which must have filled his breast after delivering that speech—a speech, I venture to say, more powerful and more to be admired than any which has been delivered within the memory of any man in this House' (H. of C., February 17; *Parliamentary Debates*, vol. lxxxiii, p. 1129). Cobden, obliged to be more reserved since he was not yet reconciled with Peel (cf. C. S. Parker, *Sir Robert Peel*, vol. iii, pp. 330-2), nevertheless expressed his satisfaction that his policy was approved by the country. 'Four-fifths of the Conservatives from the towns in the North of England were followers of Sir Robert Peel' (Cobden's speech in the Commons, February 27, in R. Cobden's *Speeches on Questions of Public Policy*, vol. i, p. 365). Cf. J. Morley, *Life of Richard Cobden*, 1902, p. 51.

The League, it is true, decided at a meeting in Manchester on January 29 to petition for the complete and immediate repeal of the Corn Law, and these petitions collected 1,414,303 signatures. Villiers, as in previous years, brought forward a motion to this effect which the Commons rejected on March 3 by 267 votes to 78. The League, however, knew very well that its campaign, far from making difficulties for the Prime Minister, must help him to overcome the opposition from his own party. Cf. A. Prentice, *History of the Anti-Corn-Law League*, vol. ii, pp. 422 sqq., and S. Maccoby, *English Radicalism, 1832-1852*, p. 263. Cf. Peel's view of the matter in C. S. Parker, vol. iii, p. 338, and Cobden's, in a letter to G. Combe, March 7: 'I rely upon his not compromising our principle beyond three years' (John Morley, *Life of Richard Cobden*, p. 53).

[2] According to Gladstone, Peel believed at this moment, 'that he would be able to carry his measure, and at the same time hold his party together' (John Morley, *Life of W. E. Gladstone*, 1903, vol. i, p. 283).

same county, found themselves powerless against the influence of the Duke of Newcastle, to whom they both had owed their original election. Another Minister, Captain Rous, was imprudent enough to stand for Westminster, where he and no doubt all his colleagues expected that he would benefit by the popularity which Peel must surely have gained in this urban constituency by his policy of commercial Liberalism. He was defeated, though not by a Protectionist, but by a Radical, Lacey Evans, for whom the Protectionists voted to ensure the defeat of the 'Peelite'.[1] For a distinct group of Peelites was already in existence and to fight it a Protectionist group had been systematically organized with its own Whips. In the Lords it was led by Lord Stanley, who had now definitely declared war on Peel, in the Commons by Lord George Bentinck, a puppet whose strings were pulled by Disraeli. And he pulled them with such devilment that Lord George amazed those who hitherto had encountered him only at race meetings by a flow of oratory which seemed inexhaustible. On February 11 Peel reckoned at 197 the Conservatives who would vote against him, those who would vote for him as no more than 123.[2] Even this estimate proved too hopeful. On February 27, on the second reading, 231 voted against the Corn Bill, only 112 for the Government.[3]

And how many even of these 112 were inspired by a genuine faith in free trade? There was, indeed, in Peel's entourage a small group of true believers. But many followed him against the grain because with that authority which emanates from the born leader he had convinced them that of all the British statesmen he alone was capable of governing the nation. Wellington, who was frankly opposed to the repeal of the Corn Law, bowed to his

[1] Annual Register, 1846, p. 41. C. S. Parker, Sir Robert Peel, vol. ii, pp. 333-7. Lord Lincoln, defeated in Nottinghamshire by a large majority in consequence of the intervention of his father, the Duke of Newcastle, found a Scottish seat in April through the influence of his father-in-law, the Duke of Hamilton (Ann. Reg., 1846, p. 69). For Gladstone, who gave up his intention to stand for Newark, see John Morley, Life of W. E. Gladstone, vol. i, p. 287. For the defeat of Rous, one of the Lords of the Admiralty, at Westminster, see C. S. Parker, Sir Robert Peel, vol. iii, p. 334.

[2] Sir Robert Peel, to the Queen, February 11, 1846 (C. S. Parker, Sir Robert Peel, vol. iii, p. 339).

[3] Peel to the Queen, January 28, 1846. He sent her an analysis of the voting the night before: 'It shows the relative strength of parties voting to have been—Government 112; Whigs and Radicals, 227; Protectionists, 231; Whig Protectionists, 11 (C. S. Parker, Sir Robert Peel, vol. iii, p. 342). See The Parliamentary Vote Book containing the Divisions of the House of Commons in the Session of 1846, compiled and arranged by Robert O'Byrne, June 1847.

will and the wishes of the Court in order, as he explained in words which became classic, 'to enable Her Majesty to meet her Parliament and carry on the business of the country'.[1] And the assistance which Peel could expect from the Whigs was very uncertain. Charles Villiers, a veteran champion of free trade, introduced a motion which was supported by Cobden and Bright in favour of the immediate abolition of the duty on corn without waiting three years.[2] Palmerston, on the other hand, who had been annoyed by the Edinburgh letter and was as hostile to the Corn Bill of 1846 as he had been to the Reform Bill of 1832, attempted, in collaboration with a number of Protectionists, to found a Whig-Tory coalition which, in opposition to the common programme of Russell and Peel, would uphold what until last November had been Lord John's programme, a fixed and moderate duty.[3] One feature alone of this labyrinth of intrigue was in Peel's favour, the divergences and inconsistency which resulted from its complications.

What precisely was the problem which confronted statesmen during these early months of 1846? It presented a double aspect, English and Irish, or rather consisted of two problems not only distinct but very dissimilar, an English and an Irish problem.

In England the price of wheat did not rise but fell during the winter. From 64 shillings at the end of October it fell to 63 shillings and 3d. in November, 61 shillings and 4d. in December, and 56 shillings and 8d. in January. And if it rose almost to 60 shillings in February, it fell below 55 in March. From January onwards the fall was no doubt due to the action of the farmers who, as they became more certain that the tariff would be abolished, unloaded their stocks as quickly as possible. This factor, however, did not begin to operate before January. Moreover, from January the price of potatoes also fell,[4] for a winter excep-

---

[1] For Wellington's attitude, see *The Correspondence and Diaries of Wilson Croker*, 1884, vol. iii, pp. 48-53, and Sir Herbert Maxwell, *Life of Wellington*, 1899, vol. ii, pp. 342 sqq.

[2] Villiers's motion was brought forward on March 2, 1846, was supported the same day by Bright and on March 3 by Cobden (*Parliamentary Debates*, 3rd Ser., vol. lxxxiv, pp. 422, 447, and 558).

[3] H. of C., March 27, 1846: Palmerston's speech (ibid., 3rd Ser., vol. lxxxv, pp. 252 sqq.). H. C. Bell, *Lord Palmerston*, vol. i, pp. 363-5. Cobden admitted later the alarm Palmerston's attitude had caused him (H. of C., November 26, 1852; *Parl. Deb.*, 3rd Ser., vol. cxxiii, p. 666).

[4] The price of potatoes, which had ranged from 50 to 80 shillings a ton in January 1845, had risen from 80 to 160 shillings by January 1846. (These are the figures given by Sir George Clerk, Vice-President of the Board of Trade. *Annual Register*, 1846, p. 62.)

tionally mild and wet made it possible to use fewer potatoes for human consumption or as food of pigs, cattle, and sheep. Grass, turnips, beetroot, and cabbages took the place of the scarcer potato. Moreover, wages remained high and there was little unemployment. The systematic pessimism of the League had foretold famine. Peel, the Protectionists said, had been caught in their trap and given way to panic. There was nothing in the situation to justify a measure so drastic as the complete abolition of protection.

3

In Ireland the situation was very different. Here the famine was only too real. Such a famine, however, was no novelty in Ireland. In 1831 there had been a famine in Galway and Mayo, on the western coast of Donegal in 1837. It could, indeed, be said that there was a famine every year from the time when the cottiers had exhausted their supply of last year's potatoes until the new potatoes could be dug up—a famine which usually lasted three or four months.[1] This permanent distress was due to two causes, the multiplication of small farms and the rapid increase in the cultivation of the potato which enabled the landlords progressively to reduce the value of what was left to the cottiers after the rent had been paid. The middlemen who formerly came between the landlords and the tenants, ruined since the close of the Napoleonic war by the impoverishment of agriculture, had disappeared.[2] The landlords were leaving the country in increasing numbers, less from fear of popular discontent than from the disgust inspired by the spectacle of Irish barbarism. The countryside was thus abandoned to an ignorant and famine-stricken peasantry.[3] The report of the Commission appointed in 1835 to inquire into Irish conditions revealed 1,131,000 Irish peasants living on no more than

[1] From the end of April to the end of August, according to G. de Beaumont, *L'Irelande Politique, Sociale et Religieuse*, 7th ed., 1863, vol. iii, p. 357. H. of C., March 30, 1846, O'Connell's speech: 'There was in Ireland what was called a "starving season" for about six weeks before the new harvest' (*Annual Register*, 1846, p. 131).

[2] For the 'middlemen', see the report of the *Devon Commission*, p. 15, and G. de Beaumont, op. cit., vol. i, pp. 237 sqq. Many landlords, heavily burdened with debt, were compelled to treat their tenants harshly, and the anger of the latter was directed against them instead of the true culprit—the moneylender. Cf. A. Pichot, *L'Irelande et le Pays de Galles*, 1850, vol. ii, p. 490.

[3] 'The Catholic population . . . free in theory to leave the land, but in practice bound to the soil as its only means of subsistence, is in truth worse off than the medieval serfs' (G. de Beaumont, op. cit., vol. i, p. 217). 'It will be seen in the Evidence that in many

2 shillings or 2 shillings and 6d. a week, 2,235,000 unemployed or in want of the necessities of life for an average of thirty weeks a year. If this were the normal state of the country, what would it be after the famine which had just devastated it? The last potato harvest—1,500,000 acres were devoted to growing potatoes—had produced only a quarter of the normal yield. The loss had exceeded £10 an acre, that is to say there was a total loss of £15,916,000 from the failure of the potato crop alone.[1]

What was the cause of this multiplication of small tenant farmers? The explanation often given in the early years of the century, that it was due to the landlords' desire to increase the number of electors who would vote as they were ordered, was no longer tenable. For the small tenant had revolted and had had the temerity to vote for O'Connell, and in consequence had lost his vote since 1829. It could be explained only by the rapid growth of the Irish population from about five million at the opening of the century to almost six in 1821, and to the round eight million two hundred thousand enumerated by the census of 1841. What remedy could be found for this superfluity of labour accompanied as it was by a decay of agriculture? What steps could be taken to prevent the productivity of the soil from diminishing as the number of those depending upon it for their livelihood increased? Should the small tenant farmers be turned into small freeholders? An entire group of economists, following John Stuart Mill, advocated this reform which many Repealers wished to effect brutally by expropriating the landlords. But even if we grant that the small farmers would have been relieved by such a measure from payment of a rent which rose as their labour increased the yield of their farms, the holdings of these Irish cottiers were in any case too small for scientific cultivation. Were, then, the majority of English economists justified in their view that the system of large farms should be introduced into Ireland and extended throughout the country, 'consolidating farms' as it was called?[2]

districts their only food is the potato, their only beverage water, that their cabins are seldom a protection against the weather, that a bed or blanket is a rare luxury, and that . . . their pig and manure heap constitute their only property' (*Devon Commission Report*, p. 35).
[1] *Annual Register*, 1847, p. 9.
[2] *Devon Commission Report*, pp. 17 sqq. The Commission did not recommend the unrestricted extension to the rest of Ireland of the tenant right already existing in Ulster, which compensated tenants for improvements made during their tenancy. See T. C.

Large farms of this kind already existed in Ireland which prospered in the midst of the general impoverishment and even by a shocking paradox were exporting wheat to England while the latter country was seeking the best way to save the Irish lower classes from dying of hunger.[1] But would this remedy cure the evil? The farms could be consolidated only by evicting a number of small tenants, evictions which a number of statutes passed during the last fifteen years had made easier.[2] What, then, would be the fate of the evicted tenants? Before eviction they were starving because their farms were too small and too poor. They would even more certainly starve after eviction. For they would no longer have anything at all to live on.

What plan, then, should be adopted to cure the sufferings of Ireland? A programme of public works? The vast bogs which covered the Irish plain could be drained and the area which could be brought under cultivation increased. Railways might be constructed. By all means, said the free traders, provided the work were left to private enterprise. Their principles or prejudices forbade State action. Unfortunately, private enterprise could not be counted upon to provide employment for the Irish poor. Every day Irish capital was being invested in Great Britain, not British capital in Ireland. To be sure, there was one region of Ireland where industry prospered. It was Ulster, or rather that part of Ulster where the preponderating element of the population was Scottish and Protestant. So far as the remainder of the country was concerned it was of little use for experts to point out the possibilities of creating Irish manufactures. An obstacle, racial and religious in character, stood all too plainly in the way.[3] Celtic and Catholic Ireland could not stomach the discipline of the factory and its monotonous toil. No doubt English and Scottish labour seemed at first sight dear. But it was in reality cheap, according

Foster's remarks on this subject, *Letters . . . Upon Ireland*, 1846, pp. 134 sqq.; Jonathan Pim, *Observations on the Evils Resulting to Ireland from the Insecurity of Title*, 1847; W. N. Hancock, *The Tenant Right of Ulster, considered Economically*, 1845.

[1] 'It is a remarkable fact that at the very moment when famine broke out in Ireland as a result of the potato disease, the export of cereals to England continued as before' (G. de Beaumont, *L'Irelande Politique, Sociale et Religieuse*, 7th ed., vol. i, p. 6, where the official figures are quoted). For these exportations, see John Gladstone, *The Repeal of the Corn Laws, with its Probable Consequences*, 2nd ed., 1839, p. 2; also *Annual Register*, 1847, p. 8.

[2] Letter from O'Connell to Charles Buller, 1844: 'There have, since the Union (I think), been seven statutes passed enhancing the landlords' power of distraint and eviction' (Sp. Walpole, *Life of Lord John Russell*, vol. i, p. 395).

[3] G. de Beaumont, *L'Irelande Politique, Sociale et Religieuse*, 7th ed., vol. i, pp. 329 sqq.

to Cobden the cheapest in the world, if the high quality of the work done were weighed against the wages paid. The Irish, on the other hand, the genuine Irish, would be content with low wages. But since the quality of its work would be lower still, Irish labour would prove on balance very dear.

What, then, could be done? Obviously the first and most urgent need was to relieve the starving by public and private charity on a large scale. It was not wanting. Such exhibitions of public generosity and compassion belong to the British moral tradition. The Government were hardly informed of the extent of the disaster when they purchased in America 100,000 quarters of maize at a cost of £100,000. This would, it was estimated, feed 500,000 people for three months. And another £100,000 was voted to cover Ireland with workshops where all the famine-stricken who came to work would be paid in kind. It was calculated that between November 1845 and February 1846 £852,000 was spent in relief.[1]

The repeal of the Corn Law was surely the programme dictated by this charitable temper. This, at any rate, was the burden of all the speeches delivered, all the tracts published by the League. But the policy suffered from a radical inconsistency which the Protectionists were not slow to point out. The remedy proposed for an immediate evil was total repeal in three years' time, when, though Irish agriculture might have recovered, the irrevocable step would be taken. To save the Irish peasant from starving here and now the most modern feature of Irish agriculture would be destroyed for ever, namely, the large arable farm modelled upon the British.

Perhaps the free traders dreamed of making Ireland an industrial country. If they did they were pursuing a phantom. Or possibly they were willing that the problem of Irish poverty should be solved by emigration, which for some years past had begun to assume the proportions of a mass movement. No; the League speakers never tired of denouncing emigration, flight from the evil, not its cure. The Irish members in the Commons voted as a body for complete free trade. They did so on O'Connell's orders, who apart from his personal belief, probably sincere, in free trade seems to have been moved by extremely plausible considerations

[1] H. of C., August 17, 1846: Lord John Russell's speech (*Parliamentary Debates*, vol. lxxxviii, p. 768).

of political strategy. He hoped to commit the British Radicals more thoroughly to the cause of Irish Home Rule by drawing closer his own ties with them. Cobden, however, was well aware how precarious was the support of these Irish politicians who voted for repeal only as a matter of party discipline. 'They are', he wrote, 'a very odd and unmanageable set, and I fear many of the most Liberal patriots amongst them would, if they could find an excuse, pick a quarrel with us and vote against free trade or stay away.'[1] He attributed this lack of conviction to the fact that they were landowners who were afraid for their rents. He persuaded himself that the small cultivators would be the gainers and agriculture the gainer by the relief from the burden of rent which free trade would effect. We have already observed the free traders attempting in vain to convince British farmers by this line of argument. They were not likely to succeed any better with the Irish tenant farmers. It is a singular circumstance that the great statesman, who at this moment had committed himself to repealing the duties on corn, was not himself convinced on this point. 'If there was any part of the United Kingdom', he said in the House, 'likely to suffer from the withdrawal of protection it was Ireland; for Ireland had not, as England had, the means of finding employment for her agricultural population in her manufacturing districts.'[2]

4

These were some of the arguments put forward by the Protectionists both in the House of Commons and in the Press against Peel's Corn Bill. They do not strike us as worthless to-day. But public opinion had been so thoroughly influenced by the skilful propaganda of the League that they came up against a wall of cast-iron conviction and seemed no better than dishonest sophistries. The Protectionist Opposition, however, was not content with these economic arguments.[3] It made a personal attack on

[1] R. Cobden to Mrs. Cobden, April 27, 1846 (John Morley, *Life of Richard Cobden*, vol. i, p. 380).

[2] H. of C., January 27, 1846 (*Annual Register*, 1846, p. 34). Cf. the peroration to his speech on June 10, 1845: 'It is because I believe the interest of Ireland would be prejudiced by a sudden importation of corn. . . . I shall give my decided vote against the proposition of the Hon. Gentleman' (*Parliamentary Debates*, vol. lxxxi, p. 378).

[3] And social as well. The Opposition was defending the aristocracy.

Peel as an inveterate traitor.[1] Peel's father, the first baronet, it was whispered, on the morrow of the peace, had obtained for him a place in Lord Liverpool's Cabinet by threatening that his son would otherwise go over to the Whigs.[2] His former treason was brought up against him, when in 1829 the Irish Catholics had been emancipated by the man who had pledged himself so often to defend to the last ditch the privileges of the Anglican Church.[3] 'Revelations', which Peel had a lengthy task to discredit, proved, his enemies said, that his change of front had been due to particularly scandalous motives. And now scarcely five years after winning an election on a programme of protection he had adopted the programme of the Anti-Corn-Law League. Peel replied by proving that his fiscal and tariff policy in 1846 did but carry further the policy begun on the morrow of the election of 1841 by the Budget of the following year. Possibly, Disraeli and his friends replied. But in that case you have been for the past two or three years engaged in betraying the cause of social conservatism and aristocratic government.[4] The memory of the election of 1841 must, in fact, have weighed heavily on Peel's conscience. For he had won that victory for himself and his followers in highly equivocal circumstances. When, on the morrow of the debacle of 1830, he had undertaken the task of modernizing the organization of the old Tory party and reconstituting it to be henceforward under his leadership the Conservative party, he had shared the erroneous belief of so many of his contemporaries that an extremely dangerous party of revolutionary democrats was in process of rapid formation, which by driving every day more members of the bourgeoisie into the Conservative ranks would enable him to play a double role, to be at once the accredited

---

[1] See the attacks by Disraeli and Lord George Bentinck (C. S. Parker, *Sir Robert Peel*, vol. iii, pp. 347 and 356, also the article entitled 'Peel Games', in *Punch*, 1845, vol. ii, p. 234). Contrast Cobden's judgment of Peel's conversion: 'Amongst all the converts and conformers, I class Sir Robert Peel as one of the most sincere and earnest. I have no doubt he is acting from strong conviction. . . . His mind has a natural leaning towards politico-economic truths. The man who could make it his hobby so early to work out the dry problems of the currency question, and arrive at such sound conclusions, could not fail to be equally able and willing to put in practice the other theories of Adam Smith' (R. Cobden to G. Combe, March 7, 1846, in J. Morley, *Life of Richard Cobden*, p. 53).
[2] *Greville Memoirs*, April 1846, vol. ii, p. 387.
[3] *History of the English People*, vol. ii, pp. 271-7.
[4] On April 24, 1846, a lively skirmish took place between Peel and Disraeli. The latter accused the Prime Minister of having given every sign of approving a statement by Cobden that the townsmen were in a position to impose their will on the 'Country party' (*Parliamentary Debates*, 3rd Ser., vol. lxxxv, p. 1014).

leader of the Conservatives and the hero of the middle classes. Events had upset his calculations and in 1841 he had found himself obliged to tolerate an almost open alliance between a large number of his followers and the Chartist agitators, whereas the Anti-Corn-Law League, whose views in spite of their unrestrained methods of propaganda were closer to his own than the Chartists', supported the Whig candidates. The statesman who ten years before had accomplished such an outstanding work of party organization had come by a most intelligible reaction to execrate the very notion of party politics.

'When I do fall,' Peel stated in the House, 'I shall have the satisfaction of reflecting that I do not fall because I have shown subservience to a party. I shall not fall because I preferred the interests of party to the general interests of the community.'[1] And Sidney Herbert, who of all the members of the House of Commons was, with Graham, the most in his confidence, used even stronger language. 'It has been said that party is part of our constitution. I think it is contrary to the whole spirit of our constitution.'[2]

So far as the Corn Bill was concerned, Peel was extricated from his awkward predicament at Westminster by the unswerving support he received from the leader of the Opposition, Lord John Russell. It was not in the least friendly. Lord John had never liked Peel and he liked him now less than ever. In his composition there was something petty. His small stature, both physical and moral, was a frequent butt of contemporary caricature. He was painfully aware of it and it made him all the readier to quarrel with those on the benches of the House who proved themselves greater men

[1] H. of C., March 27, 1846. Peel's speech (*Parliamentary Debates*, 3rd Ser., vol. lxxxv, pp. 247-8).

[2] H. of C., February 9, 1846. Sidney Herbert's speech. He continued as follows: 'I am not one of those who wish to see the constitution of this country rendered more democratic than it is; I cannot think that the public mind wishes it to be more democratic than it is. I think late events have rather shown that the mantles of despotic kings who disgraced the world have fallen upon democratic rather than upon temperate and mixed governments. I wish to see the aristocratic element preserved in our constitution; and it is upon that account I say: Do not peril it on a question in which your motives may be impugned, when once you are convinced, as I am, that these laws are not for the good of the community' (*Annual Register*, 1846, p. 43). *Parl. Deb.* (vol. lxxxiii, p. 630) gives a different version of the speech: 'I do not admit that this party, Conservative party or Tory party—call it by what name you will—is bound together by no greater object than a customs duty upon the importation of foreign corn. . . . We have had Corn Laws ever since the reign of Charles I, and since that time they have been constantly changed and constantly suspended. Was party, therefore, in each case weakened, broken up, dissolved? But it has been said that Corn Laws are part of our Constitution. Sir, if I am right in thinking that they impose a burden on one part of the community for the benefit of another, then I say they are contrary to the whole spirit of the Constitution.'

than himself.[1] Before 1841 he had been the official leader of the Commons. But the great commoner had not been himself but his colleague, Palmerston. In November he had taken the initiative in proposing the complete repeal of the Corn Law. But his opponent's manœuvres had been so successful that it was not he but Peel whom the League held up to the public as the great benefactor of England and humanity. Why not, then, undertake the easy task of overthrowing Peel? No course could be more fraught with danger, not only because of the unpopularity he would incur, but because his equivocal victory would place him in a most awkward position. He refused accordingly to support Villiers's motion, backed by Cobden, in favour of the immediate abolition for which he had himself asked in his Edinburgh letter. It, therefore, fell flat, obtaining no more than 78 votes.[2] He had even less difficulty in defeating the intrigue with the Tories, set afoot at Palmerston House.[3] In a few weeks the plot vanished into thin air.

Since the Whigs were certain that the Government must fall in a short time and in the ordinary course of things Lord John would take Peel's place, they thought it wiser to help it to settle the question of the Corn Law first. Then it would be time enough to withdraw their support and defeat it or let it be defeated.

The Bill, therefore, passed the Commons in spite of the fact that two-thirds of the House, so Cobden calculated, were hostile to the measure. It also passed the Lords, though the Peers were almost unanimously opposed to repeal. For they were aware how difficult their situation would be if they rejected it. In 1832 they had thrown out the Reform Bill. How disastrous and how useless their resistance had proved, and their position to-day was weaker than it had been then. They had not even the Court on their side.

---

[1] *Greville Memoirs*, January 30, 1846: 'In all this affair, so far, and since his speech the first night, which was very good, John Russell does not shine; he is a very clever, ingenious but *little* man, full of personal feelings and antipathies, and not, I suspect, without something of envy, which galls and provokes him and makes him lose his head and his temper together.'

[2] For Villiers's motion, see above, p. 112. For the relations between Cobden and Villiers, the latter not a little jealous of the former, and the former possibly disposed at first to reject the Government's Bill as not in strict conformity with the programme of the League, see *Greville Memoirs*, January 7, 1846. They finally agreed on a motion in favour of immediate repeal, not to overthrow the Government, but to strengthen its position by convincing the Protectionists that Peel's proposals were the least an angry nation would accept. See *Greville Memoirs*, January 30, 1846, and John Morley, *Life of Richard Cobden*, vol. i, p. 378. See also Cobden's letter to G. Combe, written on March 7, 1846, and quoted above, p. 133, n.1.

[3] *Greville Memoirs*, June 1, 1846.

Prince Albert and, therefore, the Queen were convinced free traders.[1]

If, then, they threw out the Bill a dissolution would be the result. Even if the impossible should be realized and the election result in a victory for protection against the expressed will of the electorate of London and the great manufacturing centres, it would be taken as proof that the franchise of 1832 still left too great a place to the influence of the aristocracy. That is to say, by forcing this appeal to the country they would be responsible for reviving the agitation not only of the League but of the Chartists, and might even bring about an alliance between the free traders and the democrats far more dangerous than that of 1842. The prospect, however, was that, on the contrary, the Protectionists would lose seats and the election prove the victory of neither of the old parties but of Cobden and his League. It was better to avoid battle than court defeat. On May 28 the Corn Bill passed its second reading in the Lords by 211 to 164 votes, a majority, that is to say, of 47.[2] On June 15 an amendment moved by the Duke of Buckingham that the new sliding scale, which the Bill provided should be in force until 1849, should be made permanent was rejected by 130 votes to 103, a majority of 27,[3] and the Bill was passed by show of hands without a division. In 1832 the nobility had sacrificed much of its political to save its economic privileges. Now it sacrificed the most valuable of the latter to save what the Reform Act had left of the former.

5

The enactment of the Customs Bill and the Corn Bill was the substantial achievement of the session of 1846. The session could, therefore, be regarded as a triumph for Peel's policy. It was so in truth, if this aspect of it is alone taken into consideration. But to obtain a complete view of it, other aspects must be considered.

---

[1] After Peel's speech on February 16, Prince Albert wrote to him: 'It cannot fail to produce a great effect even upon a party which is determined not to listen to the voice of reason.' The Queen added: 'The Queen must write a line to Sir Robert Peel to say how much she admired his speech' (C. S. Parker, *Sir Robert Peel*, vol. iii, pp. 339 and 340). The Queen wrote again on May 16: 'He possesses the confidence of the country, and he knows well how much he possesses ours' (ibid., p. 348). And when the Lords were debating the second reading of the Corn Bill, Wellington remarked: 'Without the House of Commons and the Crown, the House of Lords can do nothing' (*Parliamentary Debates*, 3rd Ser., vol. lxxxvi, p. 1404).

[2] Ibid., 3rd Ser., vol. lxxxvi, p. 1405.

[3] Ibid., 3rd Ser., vol. lxxxvii, p. 478.

Taken as a whole it was a medley of successes and failures, among the latter the final failure which brought about the fall of the ministry. We must briefly relate the history of both.

Peel, as we have already seen, to give some financial relief to the agricultural interest and thus compensate the landowners and farmers for the abolition of the tariff on corn, had proposed in January certain measures of administrative reform. In the first place a Highway Bill relieved the parishes of responsibility for the upkeep of the roads and assigned it to the new Poor Law unions. It thus revived the project, already twelve years old and cherished by the disciples of Bentham, of reforming the entire local administration and basing it on the Poor Law Amendment Act of 1834. But the Bill was attacked from many quarters by groups which regarded it as prejudicial to their interests and was dropped.[1]

A Poor Removal Bill, on the other hand, which gave effect to Peel's pledges in January was passed. The law of settlement, devised in the seventeenth century to repress vagabondage and bind the poor to the soil, forbade anyone to receive poor relief except in the parish of his birth. The rule had been maintained by the Poor Law of 1834, for two reasons presumably. It made it more difficult for the poor to receive relief, and in periods of unemployment it passed on to the landowners and farmers the cost of the relief sought by workers who had left the country to earn their livelihood in the manufacturing towns. And it was also from a double motive, humanity towards the poor and the desire to ease the financial burdens of agriculture, that it was abandoned in 1846. In future it would not be in their place of birth but in the place where they had resided for the past five years, and in certain specified cases this condition was dispensed with, that paupers would have the right to relief.[2]

The question of regulating the hours of work in factories

---

[1] Cf. *History of the English People*, vol. iii, pp. 219-20. An earlier act 'brought in by the Speaker' had permitted parishes to form themselves into groups for the purpose of administering the highways. The new Bill made it compulsory to do so. . . . The new districts would be identical with the 'registration districts' (the hateful name 'union' was avoided though the meaning was the same), and their number would be reduced from 1,400 or 1,500 to 550. The duty of forming them would be confided to the 'Enclosure Commissioners' recently appointed. (H. of C., April 2, 1846. Sir James Graham's speech, *Parliamentary Debates*, 3rd Ser., vol. lxxxv, pp. 489 sqq.) The Bill was dropped in July (H. of C., July 13, 1846, ibid., 3rd Ser., vol. lxxxvii, p. 1066).

[2] 9 & 10 Vict. Cap. 66: An Act to amend the Laws relating to the Removal of the Poor. H. of C., March 13, 1846: speeches by J. E. Denison and Sir James Graham (*Parl. Deb.*, 3rd Ser., vol. lxxxv, pp. 41 sqq.). S. and B. Webb, *History of the English Poor Law*, vol. i, pp. 421 sqq.

caused the Government more serious anxiety. As we have seen, when Lord Ashley declared himself in favour of Peel's policy, he had felt obliged in conscience to resign his seat as a country member for Dorset. On January 29, however, two days before his resignation, he brought in a Ten Hours' Bill, declaring himself prepared for a compromise, if the Government desired it. To win the good will of the House he contrasted the discretion with which his campaign was conducted with the methods of popular agitation employed by the free traders, to whom, nevertheless, he was in the act of surrender. After his disappearance from Parliament Fielden revived the Bill, which was debated on April 29.[1] The alignment of combatants was a strange one. The Peelite centre voted as a body, 73 out of 80 votes, against the Bill. But more than two-thirds of the Protectionist group, 117 to 51, in their hatred of the manufacturers supported on this issue the Tory social reform preached for several years past by Disraeli and his friends of the 'Young England' group. The Whig intelligentsia, Lord John Russell and Macaulay, who delivered an important speech, were delighted to display the breadth of their views in contrast with the narrow dogmatism of Peel and Graham, and declared themselves in favour of Lord Ashley's and Fielden's Bill. Almost half the Liberal members, 71 out of 81, followed their lead. In all, 195 voted for the Bill, 205 for the Government. Five more votes for the Bill and the ministry would have been defeated. In 1844 the same Bill had been defeated by a majority of 138. In 1846 it was supported by a queer combination of Whigs and Tories against the Peelites and their allies, the Manchester Radicals. The Corn Law crisis had broken up the old parties and the leaders of the Opposition groups were delighted to bring home to Peel the weakness of his position in Parliament.[2]

It was the Irish question which caused him the most serious difficulties. It had been the occasion and pretext for the repeal of the Corn Law and in this respect the cause of his victory. But it presented other aspects and finally proved the cause of his downfall.

---

[1] H. of C., April 29, 1846: Fielden's speech (*Parl. Deb.*, 3rd Ser., vol. lxxxv, pp. 1222 sqq.).
[2] H. of C., May 22, 1846 (*Parl. Deb.*, 3rd Ser., vol. lxxxvi, p. 1080). The *People's Journal*, June 6, 1846. J. L. and B. Hammond, *The Age of the Chartists*, p. 284.

6

It was inevitable and in accordance with the traditional behaviour of the Irish that their sufferings should result in a fresh outbreak of assault and murder. Not only were carts and ships taking corn to England looted, but agrarian outrages in the widest sense became more frequent. O'Connell's agitators had been able to win the cottiers to the cause of free trade only by turning their anger against the landlords, who alone, so they said, benefited by protection. They could not, perhaps they did not, wish to prevent their anger showing itself by acts of violence. In all the counties of central Ireland murderous assaults increased. The victims were chosen without discrimination between Whig and Tory, Catholic and Protestant. Once more economics took precedence of theology. But any cottier who occupied the farm of an evicted cottier was in danger of assassination, and if miraculously the assassin were arrested, woe to the members of a jury which dared to find him guilty.[1]

The speech from the Throne announced the Government's intention to introduce legislation to afford better protection to human life and secure the punishment of criminals. A Bill was brought into the House of Lords on February 16, withdrawn for amendment, reintroduced in its amended form on the 20th, passed its second reading on the 23rd and its third on March 13.[2] Too much time had been lost already in the opinion of those who regarded the Bill as an emergency measure. But progress would be slower still. On March 17 the Bill was brought down to the Commons. It was not until March 30 that the House agreed to take it into consideration. On May 1 it passed its first reading by a majority of 274 to 125. The second reading, fixed for May 25, did not in fact take place until June 8, and then the debate continued with intervals until June 25. That day, or rather June 26, for the debate lasted all night, the Bill was thrown out by a majority of 292 to 219 and the Government resigned the very day the Lords passed the third reading of the Bill repealing the Corn Law.[3]

[1] See the figures of these agrarian crimes given by Sir James Graham in Sp. Walpole, *History of England*, vol. v, p. 144.

[2] *Parliamentary Debates*, 3rd Ser., vol. lxxxiii, pp. 814, 1248 and 1348.

[3] Ibid., 3rd Ser., vol. lxxxiv, p. 1125, vol. lxxxv, pp. 1352 sqq., vol. lxxxvii, pp. 129 sqq., 265 sqq., and 1027. For the passing of the Corn Bill by the Lords, ibid., vol. lxxxvii, p. 961.

The, fluctuating fortunes of the Bill are significant, for they betray the confusion of the Parliamentary situation. The Cabinet was caught between two fires. At first this police measure seemed well received in all quarters. During the debates in the House of Lords the Tories made no opposition and the Whigs were content with an amendment, which they carried, making the Bill a temporary measure to expire at the end of three years. Then complications arose. In the Commons, as the debates dragged on, the Protectionists took heart, and consented to vote for the measure only on condition that it was passed quickly and its enactment should not be postponed until the Corn Bill had been debated.

Finally they voted as a body against the Bill. The Whigs could not very well object to the measure on principle. For they also had asked Parliament to pass special repressive legislation for Ireland. But they objected to particular clauses, especially the so-called curfew clause by which anyone out of doors at night was liable to a penalty which might be no less than deportation for fifteen years.[1] And they protested that, when they had had recourse to legislation of this kind, they had at the same time applied other remedies, measures of reform and prevention. The Government, it is true, had promised to introduce an Irish Landlord and Tenant Bill, an Irish Franchise Bill, and a Bill for the Amendment of the Municipal Corporations.[2] But they had in fact been content with enacting a batch of petty measures concerned with details of land tenure which were very far from realizing the hopes their pledges had raised.[3] On this question of the government of Ireland the great Whig families felt themselves on strong ground. However excellent Peel's intentions might be, in Ireland, as the leader of the Conservative party, he was a prisoner of the Orangemen and therefore incapable of governing the country in agreement with the Catholics, as the Whigs had done with such success from 1830 to 1841. Accordingly the Whigs adopted delaying tactics which left them free to vote against the Bill when the moment came to

---

[1] *Annual Register*, 1846, p. 143.
[2] H. of C., March 30, 1846. Sir W. Somerville's speech (*Ann. Reg.*, 1846, p. 127).
[3] An Act to amend the Law relating to the Valuation of rateable Property in Ireland (9 & 10 Vict. Cap. 110); An Act to amend the Law as to Ejectments and Distresses, and as to the Occupation of Lands (9 & 10 Vict. Cap. 111); An Act to facilitate and encourage the granting of certain Leases for Terms of Years in Ireland (9 & 10 Vict. Cap. 112); An Act to impose the Proceedings in Prohibition and on Writs of Mandamus in Ireland (9 & 10 Vict. Cap. 113).

overthrow the ministry, but made it possible to wait until the Corn Bill was safe.

It is not easy, by reading the papers from the ultra-Tory organs to the extreme Radical Press, to assess Peel's position in the country and in Parliament at this critical moment. With the exception of such an independent and central paper as *The Times* and those Northern papers directly influenced by the League, none of them approved his policy unreservedly.[1]

For the Tory Press from the respectable *Quarterly Review* to the venomous *Blackwood's* Peel was a guilty man. He had broken up the Conservative party which only a few years before he had led to victory. He was a demagogue who, having ruined the landowners by repealing the Corn Law, was preparing to ruin the owners of urban property and personal estate by progressively raising the income tax. He would then ruin the Church of England for the benefit of the Irish Catholics, would destroy the House of Lords and, finally, the Monarchy itself, though the Queen, misled by a foreign prince, was foolish enough to favour his policy.[2] The Liberals approved of Peel's financial policy. But it went against the grain to pay tribute to a statesman who, after all, had done no more than steal a plank of their platform. The Radicals could not forget that he was a Conservative, the Dissenters that he was a devoted member of the Anglican Church.[3] We are confronted, nevertheless, with the paradox that in a country so attached to its traditions and whose political tradition

---

[1] The *Standard*, June 27, protests against the attitude of *The Times*, and in its issue of June 30 expresses its satisfaction that Peel in his farewell speech declared his official career finally at an end. The *Morning Herald* of June 30 wrote: 'His offence is not merely an offence against party, but against morals.'

[2] *Quarterly Review*, December 1845: 'Ministerial Resignations', vol. lxxvii, pp. 298 sqq.; and September 1846: 'Close of Sir Robert Peel's Administration', vol. lxxviii, pp. 535 sqq. *Blackwood's Magazine*, August 1846, pp. 249 sqq.

[3] The *Daily News*, June 30: 'The sacrifice of life and power for a great end; that sacrifice made, moreover, in the plenitude of life and power and made with strong foresight and firm will: all these ennoble. They leave no room for pity, none for contempt. They silence hatred and redeem many faults.' The *Morning Chronicle*, June 29: 'There seems to be a very general disposition among all sections of the Liberal party to abstain from everything like searching and severe criticism of that extraordinary series of moral phenomena comprised within the last ten or twelve years of Sir Robert Peel's life.' The *Leeds Mercury*, June 27, regards Peel's character as an enigma: 'It is certainly not cast in the heroic mould,' and on July 4 points out that Peel has paid his political opponents the highest possible tribute by adopting their programme. *The Nonconformist* wrote: 'We recognize in his official ruin a just retribution for a lifetime of political crimes and follies . . . but the immediate cause of it . . . compels deep emotion.' *The Examiner*, June 27: 'To the many turns of Sir Robert Peel is now added the act of turning himself out.' The future will show 'whether politics with him is a game or a high patriotic duty'.

is one of party government, Peel acquired enormous popularity by breaking all the rules of the party game. A revolution more momentous than that of 1832, as momentous indeed as that of 1688, had been accomplished, and it was his work. When in the speech in which he explained to the Commons the circumstances of his resignation[1] he sketched the programme of Liberal reform which he said, not without a touch of haughtiness, he was prepared to support, if the Whigs were disposed to adopt it, the vast majority of the House rose to applaud him. Only the two hundred Protectionists and a few Whig politicians on the Opposition Front Bench kept silence. In the country his popularity was certainly far greater, and even the Conservative Press was compelled to take note, not without a certain patriotic pride, of the fact that the entire Continent felt astonishment and admiration at the spectacle presented by England under the rule, not of a party, but a man, of a revolution accomplished without bloodshed or rioting.[2] Miss Martineau, a philosopher of the new free trade Radicalism, expressed very happily the general view, when she had written to him a few months earlier, 'You are a great doer of the impossible.'[3] According to Disraeli, Peel lacked imagination.[4] True, if you mean the imagination of a man of letters, of Disraeli himself. His Budgets, nevertheless, were in their fashion works of imagination and spoke to the imagination of a nation of economists and business men. He is haughty and cold, Greville wrote;[5] he is followed, not loved. But the man in the street felt for him a respect so deep that in the end it was not unlike love.

[1] H. of C., June 29, 1846. Peel's speech (*Parliamentary Debates*, 3rd Ser., vol. lxxxvii, p. 1040).

[2] For foreign opinion, see C. S. Parker, *Sir Robert Peel*, vol. iii, pp. 372-4.

[3] Miss Martineau to Sir Robert Peel, February 22, 1846: 'You are a great doer of the impossible, in the government of yourself as well as in the government of the country. In the administration of public affairs, as surely as a great act or measure is declared impracticable, you forthwith achieve it' (C. S. Parker, *Sir Robert Peel*, vol. iii, p. 331).

[4] B. Disraeli, *Lord W. G. Bentinck* (ed. 1905), p. 198. In *Coningsby*, Disraeli wrote: 'A Parliamentary leader who possesses the faculty of inspiring enthusiasm doubles his majority; and he who has it not may shroud himself in artificial reserve . . . but he will nevertheless be as far from controlling the spirit as from captivating the hearts of his sullen followers' (W. F. Monypenny, *Life of Disraeli*, vol. ii, pp. 230-1).

[5] *Greville Memoirs*, August 1, 1843.

III FOREIGN POLICY

I

What, meanwhile, was befalling the other statesman who could boast of a popularity more solid and widespread than is given to a party politician? Palmerston, impatient as he was to take his revenge, was at the moment obviously defeated on his own ground, foreign politics.[1]

When we speak of the successes achieved by the foreign policy of Peel's Administration, we are not thinking of the two decisive victories won in Northern India on the Sutlej in December 1845, by Sir Henry Hardinge's army, victories which resulted in the British annexation of the Punjab in the following year. It is of greater interest to notice the effect produced by the news when it reached London in February 1846. It was not joy at the victory won, but horror at the losses it had cost. When Lord Lyndhurst drew up a resolution to be passed by the House of Lords returning thanks to God, Peel thought it unbecoming to thank Him for so much bloodshed and had the wording altered. That was the spirit of the times. England blushed at the thought that the conquest of an empire cost so many victims. Conquest and the glory of power were out of fashion.[2]

When we speak of the successes won by Lord Aberdeen's policy during this last session, we have in mind the relations, never easy, with France and the United States.

2

No important episode occurred to trouble relations with France. The Pritchard incident was already being forgotten. The improvement in Franco-British relations was aided by the success-

---

[1] In any case, the public took little interest just then in foreign politics. See Leon Faucher, 'De la Crise Ministerielle en Angleterre' (*Revue des Deux-Mondes*, January 1, 1846, vol. xiii, p. 118): 'As a result', he observes, 'of the insular position of the United Kingdom, her naval supremacy and the rapid growth of her colonial empire, foreign politics interest the public very little. They are left to the Government with a confidence born of security.'

[2] See the correspondence between Peel and Sir Henry Hardinge in C. S. Parker, *Sir Robert Peel*, vol. iii, pp. 296 sqq., and Peel's letter to Hardinge, written in April 1846, published in Charles Viscount Hardinge's *Rulers of India, Viscount Hardinge*, 1891, p. 143. H. of C., March 2, 1846. Speeches by Bright and Peel (*Parliamentary Debates*, 3rd Ser., vol. lxxxiv, pp. 385-6).

ful settlement in 1845 of the question of the slave trade. Both Governments were now engaged in giving effect to it. In South America, where hostilities between the Argentine Republic and the Republic of Montevideo had so often led to conflict between the English and French, the two navies took joint action to compel the combatants to make peace. At the very moment of Peel's fall, the death of Pope Gregory gave the French Ambassador at the Court of Rome, the Italian, Rossi, the opportunity to win a brilliant diplomatic success by securing the election of Pius IX, a Liberal and a patriot, hostile to the influence of Austria. It was now possible to entertain the dream of an Italy united, but not after the Jacobin fashion, a confederation of all its present rulers under the Presidency of the Pope.[1] For a moment there was a prospect that a liberal Conservatism might solve the Italian question without revolution or war. For once a diplomatic success won by the French Government caused no ill feeling in London. Peel was therefore justified when, in his speech on June 29 announcing his resignation, he boasted that by patiently pursuing the policy of cordial relations for five years in spite of so many checks, he had given it an aspect very different from that which it had presented to the world immediately after the fall of Charles X in France and the Tory Government in England. Then many saw, or at any rate wished to see, in this good understanding an alliance of the two Liberal Powers against the rest of Europe. Now under two Conservative Governments friendly relations with France did but complete friendly relations with the rest of Europe. What had been the fruit of that aggressive Liberalism of the thirties? Not even a Liberal crusade conducted jointly by England and France. It had brought the two countries to the verge of war and produced wars of conquest in remote regions of the world. Peel's administration, which had found England at war, was leaving her at peace with all nations.[2]

[1] *Morning Herald*, June 1846. *The Times*, July 9, 1846. Hildebrand, *Geschichte Frankreichs*, vol. ii, pp. 678-80. But, in fact, if we are to believe Thureau-Dangin, *Histoire de la Monarchie de Juillet*, vol. vi, pp. 230-1, the French Government had no part in this diplomatic intrigue which was due entirely to the initiative of Rossi acting without instructions.

[2] H. of C., June 29, 1846: Peel's speech (*Parliamentary Debates*, 3rd Ser., vol. lxxxvii, p. 1049). At the time of his previous resignation at the close of 1845, Peel wrote to Guizot, on December 18, to congratulate him on the character which the *entente cordiale* had assumed: 'We have succeeded in elevating the tone and spirit of the two nations, have taught them to regard something higher than paltry jealousies and hostile rivalries and to estimate the full value of that moral and social influence which cordial relations between England and France give to each for every good and beneficent purpose' (C. S. Parker,

3

We say with all nations and not only with France. For at the very moment of Peel's fall he was engaged by a dramatic coincidence in settling peaceably a dispute with the United States, which in other circumstances might have had disastrous results. An obscure Yankee politician named Polk who had risen to the White House had secured for his country the entire Pacific coast. At the northern extremity of this coastline he came into conflict with the rights of Britain. In 1818 the vast region of Oregon had been placed under a condominium of the two Powers and equal rights of hunting, fishing, travel, and navigation accorded to British subjects and American citizens. The United States had long wished to abolish this condominium. Many years ago Washington had proposed to the British Government that the 49th parallel of latitude, which was already the frontier between the United States and Canada to the east of the Rockies, should be made to the west of them the frontier between the States and British Columbia. The suggestion had been refused and in 1827 a new treaty continued the condominium. But American public opinion, or at least a noisy section of it, claimed that the boundary should run north along the crest of the Rockies and not turn westward until the 60th parallel was reached. In 1846 Congress denounced the treaty of 1827. Without losing a moment Lord Aberdeen declared himself willing to accept the boundary following the 49th parallel formerly proposed by the United States. Washington agreed. The American acceptance of this frontier was the more surprising, because it left England in possession of the entire island of Vancouver, even that portion of it situated to the south of the 49th parallel, and into the bargain the right of free navigation for her subjects on the lower reaches of the Columbia river within American territory.[1] The American Government had

Sir Robert Peel, vol. iii, p. 411). For the part played by Peel, in 1845, in reconciling Wellington's demand for measures of security against French armaments with Lord Aberdeen's fear that such a step might endanger friendly relations, see C. S. Parker, op. cit., vol. iii, pp. 396 sqq. For the attitude taken up by Peel and Lord Aberdeen in the difficult situation caused towards the end of the Conservative administration by the question of the Spanish marriages, see E. Jones Parry, _The Spanish Marriages_, chaps. viii and ix.

[1] _Edinburgh Review_, July 1845, art. viii, 'The Oregon Question', vol. lxxxii, pp. 238 sqq. _Annual Register_, 1845, pp. 279-80, and 1846, pp. 309 sqq. Lord Aberdeen informed the House of Lords of the agreement at the same sitting at which Wellington announced the resignation of the Cabinet. H. of L., June 29, 1846 (_Parliamentary Debates_, 3rd Ser., vol. lxxxvii, p. 1037).

two motives for being so accommodating. The annexation of Texas, Arizona, and California had just led to war with Mexico and the war not only claimed the Government's entire attention, but gave rise to a series of clashes with British interests which it would be imprudent to exacerbate by a further conflict. And in the second place the repeal of the Corn Law had won for Britain the good will of the American agricultural interest. The latter, moreover, was powerful in the Southern States, and, therefore, more concerned about Texas than Oregon. In America, in contrast to the position in Britain, the agriculturalists were free traders, the manufacturers of the North protectionists. This fact explains Lord Aberdeen's warm support of Peel in the Cabinet since the beginning of the previous November. Peel's ministry could, indeed, regard as the just reward of its policy of free trade the considerably lower tariff imposed by Washington in July.[1] The contention of the Manchester school that unconditional repeal of the tariff would obtain of itself reductions of foreign tariffs without the necessity of recourse to the complicated procedure of bilateral commercial treaties thus appeared to have been verified.

We must not forget, however, that if the new territorial arrangement was in some respects favourable to England it involved, nevertheless, a surrender of former rights sufficiently considerable to have aroused at another time vehement protest. After all, what America obtained now was what she had asked for in vain ten years earlier. We can picture Palmerston, therefore, denouncing what he could have represented as another version of Lord Ashburton's treaty. But times had changed. It was no longer a matter of attacking without circumspection a Cabinet certain to remain long in office. When the news reached London that the agreement had been signed the Government had been defeated. Palmerston was not prepared at the very moment of his return to the Foreign Office to alarm the pacific mood of the nation which had kept him out of it the previous December. He should rather be glad that the Oregon question had been settled just when it was, on the eve of his resumption of office. Speaking in the name of the Liberal Opposition he congratulated British diplo-

---

[1] For the new American tariff, see *Annual Register*, 1846, pp. 328–9. Three years later a Presidential message claimed that America had set England the example of free trade. 'Pursuing our example, the restrictive system of Great Britain, our principal foreign customer, has been relaxed' (*Ann. Reg.*, 1848, p. 439).

macy on having settled so quickly a lamentable dispute on terms equally honourable to both parties.[1]

Lord Aberdeen's foreign policy, still as pacific as it had been in the days of the Holy Alliance, was in harmony with the policy equally pacific, but inspired by a different spirit, of the Anti-Corn-Law League, and of Cobden in particular.

IV PEEL AND COBDEN

I

In his final speech, delivered in the Commons on June 29, 1846, the retiring Prime Minister paid a striking tribute to the head of the Anti-Corn-Law League. 'In proposing', he said, 'our measures of commercial policy, I had no wish to rob others of the credit justly due to them. . . . The name which ought to be associated with the success of those measures is not the name of the most noble Lord' (John Russell), 'the organ of the party of which he is the leader, nor is it mine. The name is the name of Richard Cobden.'[2]

Many in his audience were shocked by this panegyric of the great middle-class demagogue who for the last ten years had dragged the British aristocracy in the mud, depicting it as engaged in a deliberate design to enrich itself by impoverishing the lower classes.[3] They saw in Peel's words one of those outbursts of rhetoric which from time to time betrayed the impulsive temper hidden beneath the frigid surface. But perhaps there was more than this in Peel's peroration, and his language may not have meant exactly what at first hearing it could reasonably be understood to mean. He had just received a long letter from Cobden entreating him not to resign, but appeal to the country and on the ruins of the two old aristocratic factions found a new party, the

---

[1] H. of C., June 29, 1846. Palmerston's speech (*Parliamentary Debates*, 3rd Ser., vol. lxxxvii, p. 1057). H. C. Bell, *Lord Palmerston*, vol. i, pp. 369–70.

[2] John Morley, *Life of R. Cobden*, p. 57. *Parl. Deb.*, 3rd Ser., vol. lxxvii, p. 1054.

[3] Gladstone wrote in his diary, on June 30: 'Much comment is made upon Peel's declaration about Cobden last night. My objection to it is that it did not do full justice. For if his power of discussion has been great and his end good, his tone has been most harsh and his imputation of bad and vile motives to honourable men incessant. I do not think the thing was done in a manner altogether worthy of Peel's mind. But he, like some smaller men, is, I think, very sensible of the sweetness of the cheers of opponents.'

party of the middle classes of which he would be the predestined leader. For his creation of the party would have won him the enthusiastic devotion of the vast majority of the nation. Though Peel did not take this hazardous course, he could not but be flattered by Cobden's suggestion and the language in which it was made. 'You represent', Cobden told him, 'the *idea* of the age, and it has no other representative amongst statesmen.'[1] And since at the same moment he received from a man so different from Cobden as Carlyle a tribute couched in almost the same terms,[2] he must surely have been convinced that he was, in fact, in the eyes of the nation something other and something more than a party leader. Like Cobden? Perhaps, who could tell, greater than he. When, therefore, he said, 'Neither Lord John Russell nor myself, but Cobden', he may have been thinking and inviting his audience to think, 'not Lord John Russell, but Cobden and myself'.

With this reservation Peel was right. The entire credit for the radical abolition within a short time of the duties on corn belonged to Cobden and his League. If the Anti-Corn-Law League had never existed, England without the least doubt would have gradually adopted a very low tariff, that is to say, would have carried further the tariff reform inaugurated by Huskisson. Not more than a quarter of the population of Great Britain was engaged in agriculture. However great the improvement in methods of cultivation British farmers could hardly have retained permanently a monopoly of the country's food or provided every year the additional three hundred and sixty-five thousand quarters of wheat required to feed the three hundred and sixty-five thousand mouths added yearly to the population.[3] The surprising feature of the Repeal was the fact that a country always disposed in politics,

---

[1] R. Cobden to Sir Robert Peel, June 23, 1846 (John Morley, *Life of Richard Cobden*, vol. i, p. 392).

[2] Thomas Carlyle to Sir Robert Peel, June 19, 1846 (C. S. Parker, *Sir Robert Peel*, vol. iii, p. 377).

[3] H. of C., February 12, 1846. Lord Morpeth's speech: 'The fact was, and it could not be denied that with cheapness of bread there always came an increased demand for labour. He made a syllogism on this subject do the work of a speech. It was impossible to deny that there was not a sufficient quantity of food grown in this country for our population. There was a daily addition of 1,000 children to that population, or an addition of 365,000 in a year. But there was not an addition every year of 365,000 quarters of wheat to our native growth of corn. Ought we not then to procure a supply of corn from abroad, and at the cheapest possible rate, in order to be able to furnish the poorer classes of our community with a cheap and abundant supply of food?' (*Annual Register*, 1846, p. 48, and *Parliamentary Debates*, 3rd Ser., vol. lxxxiii, pp. 808 sqq.).

administration, and law to be satisfied with half measures had, for once, in the matter of the tariff carried out a principle with uncompromising logic. And this was due to the action of the League. And that in turn was the product of factors we have already had occasion to analyse. In the first place the Evangelical mission of the Methodist preachers had served as a model for Major Cartwright's Radical propaganda at the close of the eighteenth century, and later for the campaign conducted by Henry Hunt and his open-air speakers after the close of the Napoleonic war. Then the campaign for Catholic emancipation organized in Ireland by O'Connell had proved it possible, by concentrating the entire effort of what was already known as an 'agitation' on a single point to intimidate the British Parliament and compel it to surrender within a few months. After the passage of the Reform Bill, secured by an agitation which resembled O'Connell's in its methodical character, the Chartists had revived the Radical agitation of 1817 and 1819. Their first attempt made in 1839 had failed. But at the very time of their failure the Anti-Corn-Law League had already begun its activities. The campaign it conducted had many features in common with the earlier agitations, the emotional appeal of mass meetings, the concentration on a single object. It differed from them and improved upon them by the funds at its disposal and the skilful use made of them, by its newspapers and tracts. 'If a measure like that now proposed'— the reform urged by the League—'had been brought forward in 1842', the Radical Duncombe observed during the debates of 1846, 'there would have been no necessity for the guards and artillery, but contentment and peace could have been restored to the manufacturing districts.'[1] Peel, however, had answered him by anticipation when he had pointed out that in 1842 the reconciliation between employers and employed had not yet been effected.[2] The League had, it is true, made the attempt by concluding a species of alliance with the Chartists. But it was premature or, rather, misconceived. In their joint agitation the former was soon swamped by the latter. The position was very different now. If Cobden and his followers had stirred up a class war in the rural districts, they had restored social peace in the

[1] H. of C., February 19, 1846. Thomas Duncombe's speech (*Parliamentary Debates*, 3rd Ser., vol. lxxxiii, p. 1233. *Annual Register*, 1846, p. 61).
[2] H. of C., January 27, 1846 (*Ann. Reg.*, 1846, p. 25).

large towns. Chartism was hardly mentioned, and it was the entire population engaged in manufacture, without distinction of class, which within eight months won an overwhelming victory over the old landed gentry by enforcing the surrender of a Parliament in which the latter still disposed of a large majority of seats.

CHAPTER IV

From Peel's Fall to the European Crisis
of 1848

I THE WHIGS' DOMESTIC POLICY AND THE
GENERAL ELECTION OF 1847

I

LORD JOHN RUSSELL found no difficulty in reconstructing his Cabinet. The new Cabinet, with a few inevitable changes, was the Whig Cabinet of 1841. The Home Office was given to Sir George Grey, the Colonial Office to Lord Grey, and the Exchequer to Sir Charles Wood. In these circumstances the Greys raised no objection to Palmerston going back to the Foreign Office. He had just returned from a visit to Paris where he had been reconciled with Thiers, who had become the leader of the Liberal Opposition to Guizot, a Minister of extremely Conservative views and Lord Aberdeen's friend. Labouchere became Irish Secretary, leaving the Board of Trade to Lord Clarendon. Lord Morpeth, Irish Secretary in the last Whig administration, went to the Ministry of Woods and Forests. Lord Minto exchanged the Admiralty for the Privy Seal. As in 1841 Sir John Cam Hobhouse was at the Board of Control. Macaulay exchanged the War Office for a sinecure, the post of Paymaster-General of the Forces, which left him the leisure he needed to work at his great history. The composition of the Cabinet was exclusively aristocratic.[1] For Macaulay, a client of the Whig aristocracy, ended by persuading the country and possibly himself that he belonged to it. The true hero of the year, Cobden, had not even to refuse to join the new administration. In a very amicable letter Lord John told him that had he offered him any place it would have been a seat in the Cabinet. But he made his refusal in December and 'other circumstances' an excuse for offering him

[1] The *Edinburgh Review* could still write, in January 1848: 'Considered as a mere party combination and resting merely on the ancient Whig connection and the support of a few prominent and historical families, the present Government stands on too narrow a basis to be able to survive the first Parliamentary Storms' (vol. lxxxvii, p. 153. Cf. *People's Journal*, vol. i, p. 243).

nothing.[1] Three weeks before Peel's fall the Duke of Devonshire had given a large ball at Devonshire House to which, as though in anticipation of his friends' return to power, not a single Conservative family was invited. It was preceded by a banquet as formal and as dull as a banquet at the Guildhall or Buckingham Palace. Places were laid for forty guests, all of whom, except four, were Peers.[2] Once more, after an interval of five years during which the growth of Liberal ideas had disintegrated the Tory party, the great Whig houses were returning to power.

Placed at the head of this group of noble families, would Lord John show himself at last a statesman and impose his authority on Parliament and the country? At first sight he might well have seemed, this July of 1846, the great man of the hour. It was his letter from Edinburgh advocating the complete abolition of the duties on corn which had produced the political crisis. Peel had attempted too late in the day to make his party follow where Lord John had led the way. He had failed. It was no fault of Lord John's that disagreement among his followers had prevented him from forming the historic Cabinet which would have the glory of repealing the Corn Law. At any rate, when Peel finally formed an Administration with the mandate of repeal, the measure had been carried only by the consent, one might almost say under the aegis, of Lord John, whose followers made up three-quarters of the troops on whom Peel could rely. The Corn Law once repealed, the Whigs true to the Liberal tradition of which they were the guardians had refused to support Peel's Irish policy of reaction and coercion. In December Lord John had put Peel into office. In June he had turned him out. But though Whig journalists might depict the position in this light, they deceived nobody. The real arbiter of British politics, the hero of the day, was not the party politician who had just taken office, but the statesman who had fallen. He was not Lord John Russell. He was Sir Robert Peel.

[1] Lord John Russell to Richard Cobden, July 2, 1846 (John Morley, *Life of Richard Cobden*, p. 60). What were these other circumstances to which Lord John alluded? Cobden had been ruined financially, while he devoted his entire energies to the conduct of the League. His friends had opened a public subscription on his behalf. The noble members of the Cabinet could not bring themselves to tolerate in their ranks a man who had been the object of a public charity of this kind. If we can believe Bishop Wilberforce, Lord John had also thought of offering Colonel Hawes, a Nonconformist manufacturer, a place in his Cabinet. If such was his intention, he did not carry it out. (Letter from Wilberforce to Anson, June 29, 1846, published in *Letters of Queen Victoria*, 1837-61, ed. 1908, vol. ii, pp. 82-3.)

[2] Lord Broughton, *Recollections of a Long Life*, June 6, 1846 (vol. vi, p. 176).

In a country whose attachment to party politics we are perhaps prone to exaggerate, everyone was more or less consciously grateful to Peel for having chosen to be a national, not merely a party leader. The public felt, even before it knew, that he had not waited for the publication of the Edinburgh letter before attempting to win over his party to free trade and that Lord John had, in fact, published it only to anticipate Peel. It suspected that the reason why, shortly afterwards, the great Whig families had failed to form a Ministry was that at bottom they had little wish to do so, since the zeal they professed for free trade was not genuine.[1] It was glad that after so many tergiversations the reform had not been their work, and that Lord John, whose views on the Corn Law had changed so often to suit the circumstances of the moment, had paid Peel's genius the homage it deserved by replacing him in power. It was sorry that the tiresome Irish question which could never be solved had enabled Lord John to regain the upper hand, and waited, not without malice, to see how he would contrive to avoid in his government of the country the lamentable mistakes which had marked the years before 1841. For we must not suppose that the prestige of the great Whig families had benefited by their support of repeal. The Tory gentry accused them of betraying the interests of their class, and the Radical members of Parliament, the intelligentsia of Dissent, and the entire group of free traders declared that they had given way at the last moment only to preserve by this manœuvre the material advantages they derived from the possession of power.

In the eyes of all these convinced free traders Peel was the national benefactor, the man who thought and acted in the interest of the middle and lower classes. As for the Whig aristocracy, they hoped to compel it before long to make further surrenders.[2] Throughout 1847 *Punch* was publishing in successive

[1] *Economist*, January 9, 1847, vol. v, p. 33: 'The Whigs . . . consist essentially of two portions; the Liberals, who are for a continual and progressive advancement towards perfect free trade; and a large number of adherents of the mere landed interest who are in spirit if not in name Protectionists. Liberals are now much more allied in principle with the Peelites than with the Protectionist portion of the Whig party. These gentlemen looking only to the advancement of their principles, if they see a probability of them being better promoted by Sir Robert Peel and his friends than by Lord John Russell and his adherents will support the Right Hon. Baronet.'

[2] *Eclectic Review*, July 1847, art. i, 'The Late and the Present Administration', N.S., vol. xxii, pp. 1 sqq. See in particular p. 12: 'For our part, we have no hesitation in saying that we anticipate nothing else from the present ministry than the counterpart of the intelligent and sound measures which have marked the last two years of the administration of Sir Robert Peel, and a more disgraceful retreat from office than even their preceding

instalments Thackeray's violent attack upon the British aristocracy which would make 'snob' not only in England but the world over a household word.

Lord John was well aware how precarious his position was. In the circumstances he thought it prudent to adopt a modest, even a a humble, attitude. He disclaimed any intention of playing the Cabinet dictator after the fashion of Peel. He pointed out that agreement in principle between the members of a Cabinet did not of necessity involve complete agreement on all questions which might arise. Pitt, in 1784, Fox in 1806, and Lord Liverpool later had left their colleagues free to differ on questions which they regarded as non-essential. 'The right hon. gentleman, the Member for Tamworth (Sir Robert Peel), in forming his Government, certainly seems to have aimed at a much greater agreement of opinion, and at a much greater identity of conduct, on the part of the members of his Administration and of his party generally, but I own that, though the right hon. gentleman from his great talents, great powers in conducting a Ministry, from various circumstances succeeded for a time in his attempt, I do not think that it is an attempt likely to be very successful again.'[1] With these modest ambitions he might hope, if not to govern as Peel understood government, at least to dispatch current business freely in view of the state of disorder to which Parliament had been reduced since the last crisis. In his own party no doubt anarchy prevailed, and the advanced Liberals were in unavowed revolt against the persistent domination of the great Whig families. But in the ranks of the Opposition the anarchy was no less. On its front bench sat side by side Lord George Bentinck, Peel, and Peel's former colleagues with the exception of Sir James Graham, who sat apart four benches behind.[2] Peel had rejected the advances

shameful sinking down under the weight of their own blunders and misdeeds.' Also p. 17: 'In fact . . . we have Whig Ministers, but they have no policy; there is no Whig party. There is not even a ministerial party. . . . Divided among themselves, they have decomposed the grand Whig faction into two or three Whig cliques which their vanity, ambition and cupidity would soon again subdivide into smaller coteries, if some means were not found to consolidate them, and at the same time to disarm the hostility or even obtain the support of their adversaries.'

[1] H. of C., July 16, 1846. Lord John Russell's speech (*Parliamentary Debates*, 3rd Ser., vol. lxxxvii, pp. 1178-9).

[2] MacCullagh Torrens, *Life and Times of Sir James Graham*, vol. ii, pp. 476-7. Lord Palmerston to Lord Normanby, April 23, 1847: 'Graham . . . who sits under his old pillar, and never comes down to Peel's bench, even for personal communications, seems to keep himself aloof from everybody, and to hold himself free to act according to circumstances; but as yet he is not considered as the head of any party' (Lord Ashley, *Life of Viscount Palmerston*, vol. i, p. 22).

made to him by Lord John and refused to allow three of his colleagues to enter the new Ministry and thus make it a coalition.[1] Did he dream of winning the Tories over? He knew that the Protectionist leaders, if they hoped to bring back in time the main body of the hundred dissidents, had irrevocably repudiated him and three or four of his most intimate associates, Graham, Sidney Herbert, and one or two others.[2] In their hatred of this group which had brought the party to ruin they ostentatiously supported the Whig Cabinet, reassured by the consideration that its aristocratic composition doomed it to pursue a feeble and timid policy, confronted with the democratic sentiment of the nation which the repeal of the Corn Law had presumably fostered.[3] Peel from the opposite point of view was afraid the Protectionists might return to power if the Whig majority broke up. He, therefore, did everything in his power to buttress the weak position of a Government which possessed only a minority in the Commons and was unpopular with the Radical wing even of that minority and could, therefore, survive only with the support of his hundred followers. That is to say, though the situation was more complicated now, Lord John's Government like Melbourne's a few years earlier held office by its opponents' permission.

[1] Lord Dalhousie, Lord Lincoln, and Sidney Herbert (MacCullagh Torrens, *Life and Times of Sir James Graham*, vol. ii, pp. 475–6). Ellice, it would appear, revived the suggestion a few months later. But Lord John rejected it offhand, since he now felt securely entrenched in power (Lord Broughton, *Recollections of a Long Life*, April 12, 1847, vol. vi, p. 187). See, further, Duncombe's speech on July 16, 1846 (*Parliamentary Debates*, 3rd Ser., vol. lxxxvii, p. 1169).

[2] *Morning Herald*, July 4, 1846: 'The time for coalitions . . . has departed for ever. The country party will offer no opposition to the reconstruction of the Conservative party, provided only that Sir Robert Peel, Sir James Graham, Lord Aberdeen, Mr. Sidney Herbert and Lord Lincoln are excluded from the amnesty. These five ex-Ministers constituted, as is now ascertained, an interior Cabinet or *Camarilla*, which kept its projects as secret from the other members of the ostensible Cabinet as from the world outside.'

[3] *Morning Herald*, July 9th, 1846: 'The most encouraging circumstance connected with a recent change in Government is this, that, being confessedly weak in both Houses of Parliament and not strong among the people, the Whigs *must* strive to gain for themselves a good estimation by proposing measures the utility of which will be generally admitted. The same weakness, also, will probably deter them from taking bad and dangerous courses. Thus we do not think that they will be in any hurry either to pull down the Church of England or to establish Popery in that country (Ireland), because to attempt either of these things would be suicidal; and we incline to believe that, in their Cabinet councils, a majority at least would be opposed to self-destruction.' See also the *Morning Herald*, July 4, *apropos* of the advances which Lord John was reported to have made to certain members of the Country party: 'This is foolish. As a neutral party, honestly keeping the lists, until their own time shall come, as come it soon will, the Country party are really more useful to the new ministry than they can be (should they ever abandon their principles) in any other capacity.' Lord George Bentinck, speaking

Under such conditions it was extremely difficult to know what programme to adopt. Adopt none, was the advice given to Hobhouse by a city magnate:[1] do nothing during the approaching session, but mark time until the General Election which must be held next summer. Possibly this advice recommended itself to Lord John. But he was unable to follow it. Too many urgent questions pressed for settlement from day to day. The Government was, therefore, compelled to have a policy and, if that policy was unassuming and not always successful, at least it enabled the Cabinet, propped on one side by Lord George Bentinck and on the other by Peel, to survive until the General Election.

2

There was in the first place the problem of Ireland, the never-ending unhappy Irish question whose difficulties no statesman could escape. At the very outset, when the Tory Government after its unsuccessful attempt to carry an Irish coercion Bill had hardly disappeared from the scene, the new Ministry asked Parliament to renew the Irish Arms Act which was due to expire. The Liberal benches were up in arms. The fundamental principles of Liberalism would be jettisoned if, when Peel's Coercion Bill had been rejected in their name, the Government attempted to keep on the Statute Book an Act which was simply the Coercion Bill in a milder form. The new Irish secretary, Labouchere, attempted to satisfy the malcontents, explaining that the Government did not even propose that the Arms Act should be renewed for an entire year, but only until May 1, 1847, that is to say, only until they had had sufficient time to prepare a measure more in conformity with Liberal principles. He was unsuccessful. The second reading in an almost empty House of the Bill renewing the Arms Act secured a majority so slight that on August 17 Lord John informed Parliament that it had been dropped. For Liberalism it was a triumph. But for the Whig Ministry it was a pitiful, almost ignominious surrender, and it was as a ruler forcibly disarmed in face of possible rebellion that the Prime Minister had to take

in the House on February 3, 1848, still disclaimed any desire to see the Government turned out (*Annual Register*, 1848, p. 3).

[1] Henry Stephenson (Lord Broughton, *Recollections of a Long Life*, November 8, 1846, vol. vi, pp. 182-3).

emergency measures to deal with an economic situation which deteriorated every day.[1]

The potato disease, for all the pother made about it by the Anti-Corn-Law League, did not produce at first so serious a famine as had been feared. In the summer of 1846 there was ground for hope that the large sums expended to relieve distress in Ireland and the free or almost free importation of corn had together ensured the country against a repetition of such a disaster. But before autumn it became certain that the potato harvest was a complete failure and since, unlike the previous year, the Irish peasant no longer possessed a reserve of potatoes he was faced by a famine worse than that of the year before. And the lack of seed potatoes left little prospect of a harvest next year.[2]

Among the measures taken by the Government the first place must be given to two which applied the policy common to the League, Peel, and Lord John. The sufferings of the Irish, and to a certain extent, in spite of prosperous trade, of the British poor, were aggravated by a bad harvest in France, Germany, and many other parts of Western Europe. The price of wheat, 47 shillings at the beginning of August 1846, a month after the passing of the Bill which repealed the Corn Law, rose to 70 shillings and 3d. in January 1847. The Government proposed and carried a suspension of the duty of 6 shillings still levied on imported corn. The cost of carriage was also rising. To break the monopoly of the British merchant service the Navigation Acts were suspended until November 1.

Little more than a year earlier the Tories had rejected Peel's proposal to suspend the tariff on corn, foreseeing that the suspension must lead inevitably to total repeal. In the event it had been abolished at one blow. There was reason surely to fear that the suspension of the Navigation Acts would be followed, before the period had expired, by the abolition, not temporary but permanent, of the monopoly claimed for the British flag.[3]

But necessity knows no law. When he was inviting Parliament to repeal the Corn Law Peel did not hesitate to propose measures in flagrant violation of the philosophy of free trade. Now after its repeal Lord John was equally ready to do the same.

[1] *Parliamentary Debates*, 3rd Ser., vol. lxxxviii, pp. 575 and 753.
[2] Ibid., 3rd Ser., vol. lxxxix, p. 88 (Labouchere's speech).
[3] These two measures introduced at the beginning of the session were passed in a few days (ibid., 3rd Ser., vol. lxxxix, pp. 210 and 335).

These measures, like those of the previous year, were of two kinds. There were measures of relief, pure and simple, which differed from Peel's only in the smaller part assigned to officials in the distribution of relief in kind.[1] And there were measures to provide relief by public works, to be put into execution by the Lord Lieutenant and the Justices of the Peace.[2] But once more what were these works to be? At first, as under the late Government, they were confined to the construction of roads and bridges. There was nothing new in this. The most stalwart foe of State interference in the economic sphere admitted that construction of this kind was within the province of the State. Though large sums of money were undoubtedly squandered—almost eleven thousand functionaries, Lord John estimated, were employed in directing these undertakings—they proved most beneficial to Ireland, in this as in all other respects a backward country. Many people, however, invited the Government to go further. We have seen that, when England was being covered with a network of railways, the question arose whether the construction of these novel 'roads' and 'bridges' was not, like the construction of the old, a function of the State. It had been decided in favour of private enterprise, not only for Great Britain, but also for Ireland, though the latter had been the subject of a special inquiry.[3] But in the opinion of many people a country so poor must, unlike its wealthier and more civilized neighbour, be civilized from outside and from above. Later an eccentric member of the Whig aristocracy, Lord Morpeth, had submitted to the House of Commons a detailed plan for the construction of railways by the State,[4] and in 1845 this had been among the recommendations of the Devon Commission. In fact, neither private enterprise nor the State had done anything appreciable to construct railways in Ireland. Though Parliament had authorized the construction of 1,582,000 miles of railroad, only 123 had been built by the beginning of 1841. The question was raised again at the beginning

[1] For Peel's measures and the modifications introduced by the Russell Cabinet, see Sp. Walpole, *History of England*, vol. v, pp. 160-1.

[2] 9 & 10 Vict. Cap. 107: An Act to facilitate the Employment of the Labouring Poor for a limited Period in the distressed Districts of Ireland (*Parliamentary Debates*, 3rd Ser., vol. lxxxviii, pp. 775 and 999). See *The Condition and Prospects of Ireland*, by Jonathan Pim (an Irishman and a member of the Central Relief Association of the Society of Friends), 1862, pp. 76 sqq., also Sir C. Trevelyan, *The Irish Crisis*, 1848.

[3] *Report of the Commission of Enquiry into the Railroads of Ireland* (1836).

[4] For Lord Morpeth's Bill of 1839, see *Parliamentary Debates*, 3rd Ser., vol. xlv, pp. 1051, 1060, and 1100.

of 1847 and, it is of interest to observe, from the Tory benches. The Protectionist leader, Lord George Bentinck, laid before Parliament a carefully worked out plan according to which the State would advance £16,000,000 for the construction of Irish railways.[1]

The part to be played by the State in this scheme, which had been drawn up by two leading railway magnates, Hudson and Stephenson, was in fact less than it had been in the previous projects. It was confined to an advance to be made to the companies which would build the railways. For every sum of money invested by these companies in the construction of railways the State would advance double, to a total amount of £16,000,000 and at the rate of interest at which the company had borrowed from the private investor. The object of violent attacks from the Liberals and Peelites and from Lord John and Peel in person, the Bill was thrown out on the second reading by 332 to 118 votes.[2] Two months later, however, to the general surprise, Lord John revived Lord George Bentinck's proposal in a modified form. He brought in and carried a Bill authorizing the State to advance loans to the amount of £620,000 to companies building railways in Ireland.[3]

Nobody, however, even on the ministerial benches, believed that measures of this kind would suffice to cure the evil from which Ireland suffered, a deep-seated and chronic malady. The actual crisis, the famine, had at least the good effect of forcing roughly on the attention of the English nation, when her middle classes were being taxed to save the Irish from dying of starvation and her workers' wages threatened by the cheap labour of the Irish who, to escape the famine, were pouring into the country, the shocking disorder from which Ireland was suffering.

The great mass of the British public was convinced that it saw the remedy clearly. It was to substitute for a community whose classes impoverished each other by mutual exploitation a community in which they enriched each other by a fruitful co-operation. It was to get rid of a proletariat of small tenant farmers,

---

[1] H. of C., February 4, 1847. Lord George Bentinck's speech (*Parliamentary Debates*, 3rd Ser., vol. lxxxix, p. 773).
[2] February 16, 1847 (ibid., 3rd Ser., vol. xc, p. 123).
[3] April 26, 1847 (*Annual Register*, 1847, p. 68). Cf. also H. of C., June 28, speeches by Sir William Molesworth and Lord John Russell (*Parl. Deb.*, 3rd Ser., vol. xcii, pp. 975 and 981, also the *Economist*, July 3rd, 1847, vol. v, pp. 750-1).

doomed to live permanently on the verge of starvation and unable to cultivate profitably soil excessively divided, to abolish the system of the cornacre[1] and the cultivation of the potato as the staple crop and substitute for them a system of farms of a reasonable size—on the question of what exactly was a reasonable size economists differed—cultivated by labourers working for wages. Already before 1845 the first signs of such a development had been observed in Ireland, and there were those who cherished the secret hope that the crisis which had followed would hasten the change for the greater good of the country, that without interference by the Government the extremity of the disaster would automatically get rid of the small tenant farmers. 'The remedy', T. C. Foster wrote at the close of 1845 in letters to *The Times* which attracted wide attention, 'is a *social one*; a government can do little here.'[2]

It could, however, do something, and in the first place by repealing any legal provisions which interfered with the free transfer of landed property. A large part of Irish land was burdened with heavy mortgages. But in many cases the law made it practically impossible for a mortgagee who wished to call in his mortgage to do so by taking possession of the mortgaged land. Legislation should make it easier.[3] A large number of Irish tenant farmers held perpetual leases which made them in effect freeholders, but without the advantages attached to freehold property. A statute should be passed making such tenants legal freeholders. Lord John promised to introduce in the near future Bills to effect these reforms. But no one, however, could believe that these slight changes in the law of landed property would suffice to solve the problem. The evicted cottiers could not all find employment as labourers on the 'consolidated' farms. Nor could the same marvel recur in industrialized agriculture which had happened in industry, and the number of workers employed on the same job increase while the number required to accomplish a particular piece of work diminished. If the evicted cottiers were not to be compelled to emigrate and impoverish the country by their departure, they must be employed in bringing into cultivation those vast tracts of virgin soil whose extent in the west of Ireland amazed the English visitor. The soil of Ireland, far from being insufficient to

---

[1] For thi ssystem, see *Report of the Devon Commission*, p. 34.
[2] T. C. Foster, *Letters on the Condition of the People of Ireland*, p. 94.
[3] *Report of the Devon Commission*, p. 24.

support its six million inhabitants, could feed, some calculated, seventeen millions.[1] This, however, could not be brought about merely by hoping that a host of other landowners would follow voluntarily the example set by Lord George Hill in Donegal,[2] by being content to preach to the landowners, and remind them, as Lord Normanby had recently done in language whose vigour had annoyed those to whom it was addressed, that 'property has its duties as well as its rights'. The Government did a little more than this when by advancing money it encouraged groups of landowners to undertake jointly the drainage of their land, and Lord John extended the provisions of the Drainage Acts to cover any undertaking, even if it was not strictly drainage, which helped to bring virgin soil into cultivation.[3] But he went further still and, when the majority of the great Irish landlords proved too indolent to make use of the facilities offered by these measures, he claimed for the State the right to expropriate any landlord who refused to improve or sell his land. The land to which this new policy of expropriation would be applied must not exceed in value 2 shillings and 6d. an acre. The land thus obtained would be divided into farms of from 25 to 50 acres to be sold immediately or at a later date. Lord John estimated that in this way 4,600,000 acres of virgin soil could be brought under cultivation. He proposed to begin by devoting one million to the cost of expropriation.[4]

But even this measure, sensational though it was—and Trevelyan made the most of the new policy of expropriation when he explained it to the public[5]—did not arouse such widespread public interest as the reform of the Irish Poor Law which the Whig Government carried out in 1847.

[1] Sir Robert Kane, *The Industrial Resources of Ireland*, Dublin, 1844, p. 299.
[2] *Facts from Gweedore, complied from Notes by Lord George Hill*, Dublin, 1845. (Cf. the article in the *Edinburgh Review* reviewing the book, December 1847, art. vii.) For other good Irish landlords, see T. C. Foster, *Letters on . . . Ireland*, pp. 370, 397, 463.
[3] *Annual Register*, 1847, p. 21.
[4] *Parliamentary Debates*, 3rd Ser., vol. lxxxix, p. 440. Lord John made use of Robert Kane's work mentioned above.
[5] Sir Charles Trevelyan, a high official at the Treasury, was generally regarded as having inspired the Government's Irish policy (*Annual Register*, 1847, p. 14). An article by him which appeared in the *Edinburgh Review* (January 1848) was published as a pamphlet: *The Irish Crisis*, 1848.

3

When, towards the close of the session of 1846, the Whig Cabinet brought in their Public Works Bill it was provided that the local authorities should repay the Government loans by levying rates on the basis of the valuations prescribed by the Poor Law of 1838. And when at the beginning of the session of 1847 it brought in its Temporary Relief Bill,[1] the local committees entrusted with organizing relief works were to be financed from three sources—private charity, State grants, and rates. And if some critics protested against this indirect restoration of outdoor relief in Ireland, others on the contrary, more numerous and more noisy, complained that too much was being asked from the British taxpayer by way of credits and grants, too little from the Irish taxpayer and landlord. For many years past the taxpayers of Great Britain had felt it an intolerable grievance that landlords responsible, by the bad management of their estates, for the poverty of the Irish people should escape the burden of taxation borne by the English, Scottish, and Welsh. And Peel had already decided that Irish landowners, exempt from the payment of income tax, must pay it for the length of time they spent in Great Britain.[2] The crisis increased the public indignation. Complaints were raised that too much of the money spent by Britain to relieve the indigence of the Irish people went into the pockets of landowners who had contributed nothing themselves. The middle classes, emboldened by the triumph they had just won by the repeal of the Corn Law, were eager to win another victory over the landed gentry by transferring to their shoulders the burden of Irish poor relief. The Irish Poor Law of 1838 was by no means such a thoroughgoing measure as the British Poor Law, even as amended in 1834. On the one hand it compelled without exception a pauper in receipt of relief to go to the workhouse. But, on the other hand, though it empowered the local authorities to grant relief 'at their discretion', it did not recognize a right to relief. In consequence, therefore, of the combined operation of two causes, the loathing felt by the Irish poor for the workhouse and the farmers' strong aversion to paying rates, the Irish Poor

[1] H. of C., January 25, 1847. Lord John Russell's speech (*Parliamentary Debates*, 3rd Ser., vol. lxxxix, p. 435).

[2] Perraud (Cardinal A.), *Etudes sur l'Irelande Contemporaine*, 1862, vol. i, p. 235.

Law had remained as inefficient as it was cheap. The rates hardly
exceeded 6d. in the pound, the workhouses were usually three-
quarters empty. The Whig Government passed a Poor Law
Extension Bill which radically altered the administration of the
Irish Poor Law and sought to render unnecessary all the measures
of immediate relief which Parliament had passed, when brought
forward by Peel first, then by Lord John.[1]

The right to relief was recognized, the principle that it could be
given only in a workhouse maintained. That, after all, was the
British system. When, however, as would undoubtedly be the
case, the workhouses were full, outdoor relief might be given in
return for work to healthy paupers. This, indeed, was permitted
in England. The Opposition protested that the measure would
be the ruin of the landowners crushed by the excessive increase
in the rates, that, in the form proposed, the Poor Law was an act
of expropriation hypocritically disguised. And who would benefit
by it? Business men, the City, the men whose influence was preponderant in the present Parliament. But there was, in fact, no
reason to speak of hypocrisy. The most enthusiastic supporters of
the new Irish Poor Law on the Radical benches did not conceal
their object in voting for it. 'The Irish landlords', Molesworth
declared, 'must be got rid of—they must be treated as bankrupt
shopkeepers were treated—their estates must be sold, and the
proceeds divided among their creditors; and then their successors
might be expected to do their duty as proprietors of the soil.'[2]

A curious feature of the Bill was the insertion as an amendment
in the course of debate of a clause which by another route pursued
an objective no less revolutionary and tending in the last resort
to the same goal. Under the odd conditions obtaining in Ireland,

[1] For the Irish Poor Law, see the various works of G. Poulet Scrope, a member of
Parliament whose propaganda in support of the Act of 1838 played a large part in pre-
paring the Bill of 1847: *Remarks on the Irish Poor Law Relief Bill*, 1847; *Reply to the Speech
of the Archbishop of Dublin, delivered in the House of Lords on Friday, March 26, 1847,
and the Protest against the Poor Relief (Ireland) Bill, 1847, Draft Report Proposed to the Select
Committee of the H. of C. on the Kilrush Union, with Prefatory Remarks, 1850. The Irish
Poor Law: How Far it has Failed, and Why? A Question Addressed to the Common Sense of his
Countrymen*, 1849; also an excellent anonymous work attributed by common report to
the Poor Law Chief Commissioner for Ireland: *Irish Poor Law, Present and Future*, 1845.
Edinburgh Review, October 1846, art. i, 'Proposals for Extending the Irish Poor Law'
(vol. lxxxiv, pp. 267 sqq.).

[2] *Annual Register*, 1847, p. 44. And, in the same vein, Roebuck: 'did not hesitate to
avow the consequences which he expected from establishing the English Poor Law in
Ireland; it would, in nine cases out of ten, sweep away nominal landlords; and their
place must be taken by the mortgagees who must do as the English landlords do' (ibid.,
1847, p. 13).

Irish paupers were too often small tenant farmers. The clause in question provided that every such tenant who occupied more than a quarter of an acre could be relieved, only if he gave up all his land in excess of that amount. Since, however, he could not possibly subsist on the quarter of an acre left him, to be relieved, he must surrender his entire holding. The provision, that is to say, amounted to the eviction, by the indirect method of the Poor Law, of tenant farmers whose holding was too small, and their transformation into agricultural labourers on the 'consolidated' farms it was intended to form, their deliverance into the hands of a new middle class to rise on the ruin of the bankrupt landlords.

Such were the measures adopted by the Whig Administration, not only to meet the immediate disaster of the famine, but to improve permanently conditions in Ireland. In many respects, as we have seen, they did not lack courage and, as will appear later, in conjunction with other measures taken in the years immediately following, benefited the country considerably. Nevertheless, so far as its immediate effect was concerned, and from the strictly political point of view, Lord John's Irish policy could not in 1847 be pronounced successful. From 1835 to 1841 the Irish policy of the Whig Ministry of which he had been among the leaders had been violently attacked by the Tory members of Parliament and in the Tory Press. But it had won the good will of the Irish people led by O'Connell. Now the Whigs' Irish policy was not attacked by any English group, neither by the Radicals nor by either of the two sections into which the Conservative party was divided. But in Ireland they were becoming increasingly unpopular. It was in vain that O'Connell attempted to mediate between the revolutionaries and those who, in the days of his power, had been his friends in the Whig Cabinet. In 1842 he had imprudently launched the agitation for repeal and he could not suddenly suppress it now. He was a middle-class Radical who had no affection for the working class—his tirade in 1838 against the Dublin trade unions was not forgotten—whose Liberal orthodoxy was so pure that he opposed the extension to Ireland of any system of poor relief, and who did not find it easy to defend himself, when in 1846 a correspondent of *The Times*, visiting Kerry, discovered that, as a landlord he was no better than others and was a middleman into the bargain, renting land from the great landowners to sub-let it at a higher rental.[1] Moreover, he was first and foremost an obedient Catholic, and though he had professed himself an uncompromising believer in the freedom of religion from State control, he had shocked his Radical friends by declaring in favour of payment of the Irish Catholic clergy by the State. And now when agrarian outrages in Tipperary and elsewhere were rapidly increasing and Smith O'Brien with a few fellow plotters founded in Dublin in January 1847 an 'Irish Confederation' which demanded the repeal of the Act of Union and the restoration to their farms of the evicted tenant farmers and advocated the employment of 'physical force', he could not but feel, though still popular on the surface and cheered whenever he addressed an Irish audience, that he had been left behind. Old, in ill health, and obsessed by the fear of damnation, he decided to make a pilgrimage to Rome, and on May 15, 1847, died suddenly at Genoa before he could reach his journey's end, tormented by the belief that he was leaving his native land a prey to the hazards of insurrection.[2]

4

The noise made by the Irish question drowned all other clamours. Nevertheless, there were other questions which caused the Government more or less anxiety. There was first of all the annual Budget. On the surface the financial position, when the new session opened in January, was excellent, the Treasury richer than it had ever been since 1815. Goulburn had budgeted for a surplus of £76,000 which, when the indemnity of £700,000 due from China was added, meant a total surplus of £776,000. The receipts, however, from the Customs, increased by the import of foreign sugar, and Excise had risen so enormously that Sir Charles Wood expected by the end of the financial year in March a surplus of at least £2,846,000. It was a triumph for Peel's policy of free trade which the Whigs had made their own. Surely they could now with the aid of the Peelites go further along the same road and take advantage of so opulent an Exchequer to increase future revenue still more by further reductions of the tariff.

They did not do so, however. For, in spite of appearances, the financial situation was not quite so good as it seemed. In the first

---

[1] *The History of 'The Times'*, vol. ii, pp. 9-10.
[2] W. B. Maccabe, *The Last Days of O'Connell*, 1847.

place several signs warned experts that, excellent as it was in January, it was tending to deteriorate, that a new crisis was, in fact, brewing, like the others which periodically since the restoration of peace had disorganized the business of the nation. We shall have to return to it shortly. In the second place the position in Ireland must inevitably affect the Budget. The complete suspension for a time of duties on the importation of corn must make a hole in the estimated receipts. And the huge sums advanced by the Government to combat the famine in Ireland meant an increase of expenditure which could not have been anticipated in August 1846. The amount which must be spent before the next harvest was estimated at eight millions. How could it be found? By raising the taxes? By raising the income tax for certain classes of taxpayers? At a time when an income tax of any kind, always passed as an exceptional and temporary measure, was contested in principle, this was out of the question. By extending the tax to Ireland? Since the Poor Law in preparation would impose a heavy financial burden on Irish landed property, it could not be called upon to pay more. The Government obtained the sanction of Parliament for a loan at a nominal 3 per cent. That is to say, owing to circumstances rather than ministerial incompetence—Peel kept silence and Goulburn expressed his approval of Sir Charles Wood's first Budget—Whig finance after 1846 became once more as commonplace as it had been before 1841.[1]

5

In fact, paradoxical as it may seem, at the close of 1846 and the opening of 1847 there was no demand for a policy of free trade.

The victory won in 1846 by Cobden, Bright, and their League had been so brilliant and so dramatic that it left the impression that the question of free trade, like the question of the franchise in 1832, had been completely settled once for all. And at this juncture the 'social' question, the condition of the poorer classes, and the extensive measures of State intervention which seemed necessary to solve it suddenly assumed an importance which could not have been foreseen and which perhaps is not sufficiently recognized to-day.[2] The leaders of the Whig aristocracy, men cunning in the

[1] *Parliamentary Debates*, 3rd Ser., vol. xc, pp. 324 sqq. *Annual Register*, pp. 87 sqq.
[2] *The Times*, July 29, 1847: 'The stronger current opinion is that which demands the amelioration of the conditions of the poorer classes. This pervades all parties. . . .'

art of politics, were aware of it. Lord John, in an address to his constituents in 1846, declared that now that the great battle of the Corn Laws had been definitively won the Government must undertake the task of striking a balance between the interests of the different classes engaged in agriculture, manufacture, and commerce, and effecting 'great social improvements' not only in Ireland but in England in such matters as popular education, the prison system and urban sanitation.[1] Orthodox free traders were alarmed by this totally unexpected turn of public opinion. Distinguishing between 'government' and 'society' they complained that all these social reformers, however well intentioned or intelligent, confused the former with the latter and made the mistake of expecting from the intervention of the Government, which must in the nature of things be misconceived, what could be obtained only from the spontaneous progress of society.[2] 'We have embarked', Mill wrote to Auguste Comte, 'on a system of charitable government. . . . To-day all the cry is to provide the poor not only with money but, it is only fair to say, whatever is thought beneficial, shorter hours of work, for example, better sanitation, even education, primarily Christian and Protestant, but not excluding a modicum of secular information. That is to say, they are to be governed paternally, a course to which the Court, the nobility and the wealthy are quite agreeable. . . . They entirely forget or rather have never known that well-being cannot be secured by passive qualities alone and that, generally speaking, what is done for people benefits them only when it assists them in what they do for themselves.'[3] The Liberal Dissenters of the *Eclectic Review* and the Radicals of the *Westminster Review* agreed in reviving the old cries which after 1832 had been uttered by Conservatives denouncing the policy of the Whigs. This solicitude, they said, for the welfare of the lower classes was

[1] Sp. Walpole, *Life of Lord John Russell*, vol. i, p. 445.
[2] *The Nonconformist*, June 1846, article entitled 'Social Questions', perhaps from the pen of Herbert Spencer: 'The country will wake up one morning and find all vestiges of constitutional freedom gone. In the place of their civil rights they will have parks, museums and well-ventilated houses.' *The Nonconformist*, July 1846, article entitled 'What will the Whigs do?' *Edinburgh Review*, October 1849 (vol. xc, p. 496): 'Till the Continental convulsion of the past twelve months threw for the time all other matters into the shade, public attention seemed to be fixing itself upon the maladies of our population with an almost morbid intensity, and with an impatience of endurance and a craving for action as alarming to the philosopher as it was encouraging and consolatory to the mere philanthropist.'
[3] John Stuart Mill to A. Comte, May 17, 1847 (*Lettres inédites de John Stuart Mill à Auguste Comte. . . .* Edited by L. Lévy Bruhl, 1899, p. 549).

a mere pretext. The real aim of the great Whig families was to extend their patronage by creating a host of new officials.[1]

We have remarked upon the boldness of the Government's Irish policy. What in this matter of social reform were the objectives pursued in Great Britain itself by Lord John and his colleagues and how successful were they in attaining them?

6

We must notice first an important change in the Poor Law. Not only did an Act of Parliament alter the right of settlement in favour of the pauper by enacting among other provisions that five years' residence should confer the right to relief at the place of domicile.[2] What may be called the machinery of the Poor Law was radically altered. The rule of the three Somerset House dictators was brought to an end. There had been many protests against a Statute, unconstitutional, some said, which withdrew the entire administration of poor relief from the control of Parliament and, as one speaker put it, outlawed the paupers.[3] It had, in fact, proved impossible to observe rigidly the letter of the Act of 1834 and refuse all satisfaction to the complaints made from time to time by extreme Radicals or extreme Tories of the excessively harsh application of the Statute to particular cases.

The task of replying to such protests had devolved upon the Home Secretary, whose duties became constantly heavier as administrative machinery became more complicated and more centralized. They became, in fact, a crushing burden, and in this particular department were made heavier still by the anarchy which prevailed at the headquarters of the three Poor Law Commissioners. They were assisted by a secretary, Edwin Chadwick, who, far from being content to register passively the

---

[1] *Eclectic Review*, July 1847, art. i, 'The Late and the Present Administration', N.S., vol. xxii, pp. 1 sqq., esp. pp. 17 and 19. *Westminster Review*, October 1846, art. viii, 'Patronage of Commissions'. The increase in the number of civil servants is represented not as the first instalment of a nascent bureaucracy, but as a device of the aristocracy to increase the number of posts available for its clients.

[2] 9 & 10 Vict. Cap. 66: An Act to amend the Laws relating to the removal of Poor Persons from England and Scotland. 10 & 11 Vict. Cap. 110: An Act to amend the Laws relating to the removal of the Poor until the first day of October 1848. The second of these Acts made the Unions liable provisionally for the cost incurred by the parishes as a result of the former. See also H. of C., January 22, 1847, Lord John Russell's speech (*Parliamentary Debates*, 3rd Ser., vol. lxxxix, pp. 320 sqq.).

[3] H. of C., January 22, 1847. Borthwick's speech (ibid., 3rd Ser., vol. lxxxix, p. 345).

decisions taken by the Commissioners, regarded himself, not altogether without justification, as the author of the Act of 1834 and the only man capable of interpreting it correctly, and therefore as entitled to criticize constantly the Commissioners' decisions and, if his objections were not heeded, to denounce his superiors' stupidity to the Home Office or in the corridors of the House. The result was a general revolt against Chadwick. The enemies of the Poor Law complained of his systematic harshness. The Liberals distrusted his bureaucratic temper. That is to say, there was a Chadwick scandal which made a change in the system an urgent necessity. In future the Board of Commissioners for poor relief would, like the Board of Control for Indian affairs, consist of a President, a member of the House of Commons, assisted by two secretaries, one of whom might be a member of Parliament.[1] The Home Secretary was thus relieved of his burden, and irresponsible officials replaced by a genuine Minister responsible to Parliament. The Commissioners, it is true, retained the right to make administrative decisions which in other departments would require an Act of Parliament. This, however, under the new conditions was accepted without protest. The agitation against the Poor Law which ten or twelve years before had assumed almost revolutionary proportions, by a sort of 'mutation' had turned into the Chartist agitation and was still noisy on the eve of Peel's fall, ceased when the Whigs took office and passed the Act of 1847.

After all, the despotism of the three Somerset House 'Pashas' had not been so intolerable. It is instructive to compare the vehement denunciations of a system which, it was alleged, refused all relief outside the workhouse with the facts. The sick, the infirm, and persons over sixty received outdoor relief. And in districts where the number of paupers was particularly large it might with the formal sanction of the Commissioners be given even to the able-bodied.[2] The only feature of the old system which had

[1] 9 & 10 Vict. Cap. 109: An Act for the Administration of the Poor in England. The third reading of the Bill passed the Commons on June 24, 1847, by 105 votes to 35 (Parliamentary Debates, 3rd Ser., vol. xciii, p. 886). After it had been applied for thirteen years the principle of the separation of powers, too often regarded as the fundamental principle of the British Constitution, was abandoned in favour of a return to genuine constitutional practice, the combination of legislative and executive authority in the person of a responsible Minister.

[2] H. of C., March 12, 1847. Lord John Russell's speech: 'I was much concerned in the year 1834 with the Bill for the amendment of the Poor Law. But I do not remember that while we were reforming that law, the Government of the day ever contemplated that the starving able-bodied poor should not have a claim to relief. I believe that it is necessary

possibly vanished was the use of relief to make up an insufficient wage. But even this may have survived in a few parishes.[1] To sum up, as many as seven-eighths of those relieved under the new Poor Law were in receipt of outdoor relief and, when all is said, it differed from the old only by substituting, a difference certainly of capital importance, orderly administration for the former anarchy.[2] The reality was remote indeed from the Utopian dream cherished about 1830 by Liberal economists, when they asked not so much for the reform as for the abolition of the right to relief. To-day the principle was being extended to Ireland without a word of protest.[3] 'He should say', Lord John had pointed out some years earlier, 'that those countries in Europe in which there had been the greatest profusion, the greatest improvidence, the most extreme prodigality in administering compulsory relief to the poor were England, Holland and the canton of Berne. But if any person were to travel through England, Holland and the canton of Berne and were to compare the condition of the people in those countries with the condition of the people in other countries where Poor Laws were unknown, he would ask them to judge by the result whether general prosperity and general comfort did not exist in those countries where Poor Laws were established; and whether misery and destitution did not prevail in those countries where they were unknown? A Poor Law by giving the people the means of subsistence tended more certainly

for the peace and security of the country' (*Parliamentary Debates*, 3rd Ser., vol. xc, p. 1258). Cf. H. of C., June 24, 1847, Christopher's speech: 'In the most pauperized districts they would find that the Law with respect to the workhouse test was not carried out with great rigour, whilst in those counties that were better circumstanced, the law was stringently carried out' (ibid., 3rd Ser., vol. xciii, p. 892).

[1] 'In the Rye Union, for instance, it was the practice of the Commissioners to sanction, as a matter of course, small sums in aid of wages to lists of able-bodied men. In 1842, when the district including that Union was placed under my superintendence, I enquired into the subject, and I was told in the Commissioners' office that I was to overlook the existing compromises of the Law in that Union, for the population was too deeply pauperized for the Poor Law system to work beneficially there' (H. W. Parker, *Letters to . . . Sir James Graham . . . on the Subject of Recent Proceedings connected with the Andover Union*, 1845, p. 3, quoted by S. and B. Webb, *English Poor Law History*, part iii. *The Last Hundred Years*, vol. i, p. 146).

[2] H. of C., June 24, 1847. Wakley's speech, *Parl. Deb.*, 3rd Ser., vol. xciii, p. 842. Cf. *Irish Poor Law, Past, Present and Future*, 1849, p. 59: 'In England . . . outdoor relief is the general rule, and workhouse relief the exception, and this is the case in ordinary times as well as in times of severe distress.' For this work, see above, p. 163.

[3] H. of C., January 22, 1847. Lord John Russell's speech: 'He would guard the honourable gentlemen who wished to put an end at once to the present system against the results with which we might be visited, if we were without a proper establishment for the poor, should such a calamity as that which now prevailed in Ireland be felt in England' (*Parl. Deb.*, 3rd Ser., vol. lxxxix, pp. 320 sqq.).

than any direct law could possibly do to introduce prosperity at once among the inhabitants of any country.'[1]

7

In this same year, 1847, the opposition to the ten hours' day considerably weakened, as we have seen, during 1846, and was finally overcome,[2] though the victory won by its advocates cannot be regarded as a victory for the Government. In the absence of Lord Ashley, no longer a member of Parliament, Fielden brought in a Bill restricting the work of women of any age and of 'young persons' above thirteen and below eighteen to ten hours, five days in the week, and eight on Saturday, that is, to fifty-eight hours a week. The measure would come into force on May 1, 1848, after a preliminary transitional period of sixty-three hours a week, eleven hours on five days, eight on Saturday. In 1846 a Bill to the same effect had almost passed the Commons in spite of the opposition of a Cabinet strictly disciplined and subject to Peel's unremitting authority. This year the Cabinet was less united. Lord John declared the question one of those on which his colleagues would be free to vote as they thought best. Some Ministers voted in favour of the Bill, others against it. Others were in favour of a compromise by which the eleven-hour day would be made permanent. But even they were divided. Some, among them Lord John himself, stated that, if the Commons would not accept the eleven-hour compromise, they would vote for a ten hours' day. Others, like Sir George Grey, that in that case they would vote for retaining the twelve hours' day. It became evident that the compromise timidly put forward by Lord John would not be accepted when the Peelites—Peel and Graham spoke against Fielden's Bill—opposed it. No doubt they shared the opinion of those members who argued that, if the working day must be shortened, it would be wiser to accept at the outset the demand on which the working class had made up its mind so firmly. A half measure would fail to stop the agitation and might even lead to further demands, to the revival, for example, of the demand made in 1834 for an eight hours' day.

[1] H. of C., February 9, 1838 (*Parliamentary Debates*, 3rd Ser., vol. xl, pp. 966-7).
[2] See above, p. 138. The Factory Bill passed the Commons on May 3, 1847. Instead of the 203 adverse votes of the previous year, only 88 voted against the measure. The Opposition no longer included Cobden, Bright, or Lord Morpeth.

No novel argument emerged in the course of the debates, or rather perhaps only one, suggested by the circumstances of the moment. During the latter part of the winter the situation in Lancashire had been deteriorating and the factories were not working full time, not even ten hours a day. This surely was an excellent opportunity to limit working hours without causing manufacturers any immediate loss. For they would simply be prevented, when prosperity returned, from abusing it to prolong the working day excessively.[1]

The enactment of the Bill was the result of the war which for ten years had been fought on this issue between the Chartists and the free traders, a result, however, from which the Whig Cabinet derived no credit. For it had happened under its eyes while it looked on almost passively. We must, however, avoid the mistake, made by the great historian of the struggle to secure a legally restricted working day, Karl Marx, of confusing the Chartist agitation with the agitation for a ten hours' day and saying that the combined agitation reached its apogee in 1847.[2] Ever since 1843 Chartism had been on the decline and, so far as the Chartists were concerned, the enactment of the Ten Hours' Bill was but a victory of a rearguard over one wing of the enemy.

And it had been due to the untiring propaganda of the Evangelical philanthropists, supported by a considerable body of Protectionists inspired by hatred of the free traders, and to the disorganization of the Liberal front through the desertion of a large number of Whig politicians. The struggle, however, though a rearguard action, was none the less important for that. And this was well understood by contemporaries. The *Edinburgh Review*, obliged to lament the defection on this issue of its hero, Macaulay, called attention to it. 'It seems', wrote the reviewer, 'as if, in the inevitable succession of human delusions and errors, one false system of political economy must be enthroned as soon as another has been deposed, and that the system of commercial protection is to be immediately followed by the system of protection for labour. We fear . . . that we are destined to run a long career of legislative protection to labour, not confined to manufacturing

---

[1] H. of C., Feb. 10, 1847, Lord John Manners's speech (*Parliamentary Debates*, 3rd Ser., vol. lxxxix, p. 1105). For the speeches by Graham and Peel, see *Annual Register*, 1847, pp. 115 and 117.

[2] *Capital*, translated by Eden and Cedar Paul, Everyman's Library, vol. i, pp. 287, 289.

industry, until actual experience, as in the case of protection to trade, has demonstrated its mischievous operation.[1]

8

The education of the people, it was generally admitted, was another department in which the State was entitled to intervene.[2] This was, in fact, a tenet of Benthamite Radicalism.

The Liberals were hardly installed in office when the Education Committee of the Privy Council, no doubt on the initiative of the Ministry, took steps to improve the qualifications and the position of teachers. The necessary expenditure would be incurred to abolish the objectionable system of monitors, the use of pupils from the higher classes to assist in the teaching. For this purpose in particular schools, pronounced by the inspectors competent to undertake these new functions, a special category was created of 'apprentices' who, during the five years of their apprenticeship, would be paid salaries which would rise every year from £10 the first to £20 the last year. For instructing and training them their teachers would receive salaries in accordance with a scale fixed by the department. The most promising of these apprentices would receive exhibitions enabling them to carry their education further in a training college. When they were qualified to teach in a school inspected by the State, the latter would increase by half the salary they were receiving from a private source. Fifteen years' work in charge of a school would qualify for a retiring pension. That is to say, the State which hitherto had spent public money only on building schools, was creating for the first time a body of professional teachers controlled and, in part, paid by itself, methodically trained before beginning their work, salaried during its performance, and finally pensioned off.[3]

It was an extremely important departure. But Parliament does not seem to have been consulted. For it required no Act of Par-

---

[1] *Edinburgh Review*, January 1848, vol. lxxxvii, p. 162.

[2] See, however, an article in the *Eclectic Review*, September 1846, N.S., vol. xx, pp. 280 sqq., reviewing a work entitled, *On the Means of rendering more efficient the Education of the People: A Letter to the Lord Bishop of St. David's*, by *Walter Farquhar Hook, D.D., Vicar of Leeds*. The same *Review*, in January 1847 (N.S., vol. xxi, pp. 102 sqq.), expounded the views of Edward Baines on the Government's plan, and in November 1847 (N.S. vol. xxxi, pp. 589 sqq.) published an article, 'A Plan for the Establishment of a General System of Secular Education in the County of Lancashire'.

[3] Frank Smith, *Life of Kay-Shuttleworth*, pp. 531 sqq. J. L. and B. Hammond, *The Age of the Chartists*, p. 204.

liament. An administrative decision, a minute of the Committee was enough.[1] The matter would not come before Parliament until the Budget was introduced and it was called upon to vote the expenditure involved by the decision.[2] But the divines of every shade of doctrine were, as always, on the alert when it was a question of popular education and it suddenly became clear that a measure, calculated at first sight to strengthen the position of the Government, would prove a source of countless difficulties for it.

Which precisely were these schools defined by the minute of the Committee, in which the apprentices would first be trained, then authorized to teach? They were to be designated by the Government inspectors. But the latter, whose numbers and powers had been alike augmented, were a body of men decried in many quarters since 1839 as too obedient servants of the Established Church. To be approved by them a school need not be Anglican. The more tolerant ruling adopted approved not only schools founded by the Anglican National Society, but schools built by the Dissenters of the British and Foreign Schools Society and the Wesleyan Conference. This last case involved an innovation. Hitherto the Wesleyans had never asked for State aid.[3] Was it the Government's intention to reward them for having helped the Church in 1839 to resist the educational claims of the Catholics? Was there a secret compact between the Committee and the Wesleyans to exclude the Catholics? For according to the terms of the regulation no Catholic school could in any circumstances qualify for a grant. The supposed compact and the discrimination against Catholics occasioned a storm of protest from all the benches of the Commons except those occupied by the Tories. Peel himself took part in the debate.[4] Lord John found himself in an awkward predicament; for he shared the view of the critics and their Liberal opinions made his colleagues equally sympathetic to the Catholic claim. But on the eve of a General Election—for six years would soon have elapsed since the last

[1] See the Minutes of the Education Committee of the Privy Council, August and December 1846.
[2] The decision was debated in Parliament in April 1847. It was attacked by Bright and defended by Macaulay. Lord John was supported by Peel and Graham. The credits were finally voted by 372 to 47 votes (*Annual Register*, 1847, pp. 134 sqq.). For Peel's speech, see *Parliamentary Debates*, 3rd Ser., vol. xci, p. 1222.
[3] J. L. and B. Hammond, *The Age of the Chartists*, p. 206.
[4] April 19, *Parl. Deb.*, 3rd Ser., vol. xci, pp. 952 sqq.

election—it was hardly prudent to provoke an outburst of Protestant feeling. And a good Protestant could not stomach grants from the State to schools where children were taught not the pure Word of God, but the superstitions of Rome. In Liverpool, with an Irish Catholic population of thirty thousand, the Corporation had attempted to admit Catholic children to the schools, religious instruction being given to them in a separate building. But the municipal voters had risen in revolt, turned out the 'Popish' town council and replaced it by a 'Protestant'.[1] After some hesitation Lord John explained that in principle he was not opposed to the Catholic claim and was considering the possibility of making Catholic schools a special grant later on. What did he mean by later on? Before the election? Then why not make it at once? After the election? This would enable the Tories when the election came to exploit the Catholic question for their profit. Pressed for an answer he was on pins and needles. While he was thus confronted with the opposition of the Catholics and their allies, he had to face from the opposite quarter the attack of those Protestant Dissenters who since 1844 had combined to offer organized resistance to any intervention by the State in the sphere of education.[2]

Not 'Catholic' enough to please some, the system was too 'Catholic' to please other critics. To surrender the school to the Church was to surrender it sooner or later to the Ritualistic movement which in their eyes was a cancer devouring the entrails of the Establishment. They would, however, have opposed with equal determination, had a Liberal Cabinet dared to propose it, a system purely secular, holding impartially aloof from all forms of religious belief. For they prided themselves not only on being religious, but on possessing a monopoly of genuine religion. It was, they claimed, in their schools alone, free from State control, where secular and religious education were not separated, that true religion which of its nature is free could flourish. All other

---

[1] H. of C., April 19. Lord John Russell's speech (*Annual Register*, 1847, p. 147).

[2] For this controversy, see the *Economist*, April 24, 1847, article entitled, 'The Education Question—Mr. Macaulay', vol. v, p. 462. 'The editor of *Punch* makes common cause with the Bishop of London. The editor of the *Economist* finds himself compelled to enter the lists with Mr. Macaulay. The *Chronicle* attacks the Whigs and *The Times* is their defender. The author of the Test Act Repeal is at issue with the bulk of Nonconformists.' Edward Baines's criticisms of the regulation in the *Leeds Mercury* and Dr. Vaughan's led to the publication by Murray of a work, *The School in its Relations to the State, the Church and the Congregation*, defending the Government's point of view. The *Economist* replied to it on March 13 and April 10, 1847 (vol. v, pp. 294 and 410).

schools were in bondage to bureaucracy and 'clericalism', that is to say, to the exact opposite of religion, as England, alone of the European countries, could boast of understanding it. In Austria, Prussia, and France, the *Eclectic Review* declared, the Government was everything, the people nothing. The latter were swallowed up by the omnipresence of the former. And in consequence those habits of providence, self-respect, and personal independence which are indispensable to public virtue had been weakened, even extinguished.[1]

In Parliament, where it was represented only by Bright and a few eccentric individuals, this opposition caused the Government less difficulty than in the country. At the forthcoming election these fanatical individualists might perhaps set up candidates of their own in opposition to the official Government candidates, Whigs, Liberals, Radicals, secularists of Bentham's school, and those Congregationalists and Baptists who were prepared to accept government grants. It might mean so many seats lost to the Protectionists by the split Liberal vote.

9

The Government also tackled the problem of public health. It did so with the knowledge that the ground had been long prepared and that it was attempting to deal with a problem on the solution of which both parties had for the last decade been agreed. Even before the fall of the Whigs, the Radicals of the Poor Law Commission, Chadwick and Southwood Smith, had raised the question and secured, through the action of a member of Parliament named Slaney, the appointment of a Select Committee, which had recommended that in every town a Board of Health should be set up to control the water supply, cemeteries, open spaces, and workmen's dwellings. They had won over Lord Normanby to their cause, and he had persuaded the Lords to pass two Bills giving town councils the right to acquire by compulsory purchase land required for new or wider streets.[2] Peel

---

[1] *Eclectic Review*, March 1847, article entitled, 'National Education: the Government Plan' (N.S., vol. xxi, p. 360).

[2] On Chadwick's initiative the Poor Law Commission obtained, with the aid of Bishop Blomfield of London, a preliminary inquiry, whose report had been issued in 1842. In 1840 it secured through Slaney the appointment of the Select Committee which, in June 1840, reported in favour of several reforms. In 1841 Lord Normanby carried through the Lords a 'Borough Improvement Bill' and a 'Drainage and Building Bill'.

on the morrow of taking office had appointed—to study the question further—a Parliamentary Commission on which two eminent scientists sat and whose report was drawn up by Chadwick.[1]

Its report had hardly been published when Lord Normanby brought a Bill into the Lords to give effect to its recommendations. Peel replied to this move by getting a member of his Cabinet, Lord Lincoln, to introduce a Bill during the session of 1845 to the same effect. It was brought in too late to be debated before the close of the session. Then the Corn Law crisis supervened and diverted the attention of the political parties to other questions.[2] But in the country the campaign for the improvement of public health continued to be carried on by the traditional English methods, the creation of a society for the purpose, the publication of tracts, public meetings, and the floating of an important joint-stock company of which Thomas Baring and Samuel Jones were the two trustees, to provide any town which wanted it with the necessary apparatus of public hygiene. On the committee of patrons of the Health of Towns Association were Liberal philanthropists, Whig noblemen, Radicals, and ultra-Radicals. And 'Young England' was represented by Lord John Manners and Disraeli.[3]

The *Morning Herald*, a Protectionist organ, spoke of improving the housing conditions of the poor as one of the questions which afforded the Whigs, lacking as they did a majority in the House, an opportunity to win popularity by performing a useful task with general approval. Peel in his speech during the debate on the Address and again a little later, when he was speaking against the Ten Hours' Bill, declared himself in agreement with the Government's intention to introduce legislation to improve urban hygiene.[4]

See Sir Malcolm Morris, *The Story of English Public Health*, 1919. Sir John Simon, *English Sanitary Institutions*, 1900. B. W. Richards, *The Health of Nations*, 1887.

[1] *First Report of the Commissioners for Enquiring into the State of large Towns and popular Districts*, 1844 (572), vol. xvii, *Second Report* . . . 1845, part I (602), vol. xviii, p. 1; part II (610), vol. xviii, p. 299.

[2] Lord Lincoln's Bill passed its first reading on July 25, 1845, and was dropped in consequence of a speech by Sir James Graham, April 27, 1846 (*Parliamentary Debates*, 3rd Ser., vol. lxxxii, p. 1077, and vol. lxxxv, p. 1084).

[3] The Health of Towns Association, whose President was Lord Normanby, published in 1846 a *Report on Lord Lincoln's Bill*, and from January 1 until July 29, 1847, a periodical, *Weekly Sheet of Facts and Figures*. Its activities were summarized in the *Report of the Health of Towns Association, read at a Meeting held in the rooms of the Statistical Society*, February 24, 1847.

[4] *Parl. Deb.*, 3rd Ser., vol. lxxxix, p. 159. *Annual Register*, 1847, p. 118.

Even the adherents of the Manchester school, hostile as they were to any encroachment of public authority upon private enterprise, supported the movement. For they were delighted that the experts on public health had discovered that the manufacturing towns were not those with the highest rate of mortality. It was lower at Manchester, the typical manufacturing city, than at Liverpool, a huge urban agglomeration without factories; that is to say, the cause of disease was the wretched housing of the workers, not labour in factories. Nevertheless, in spite of this encouraging show of unanimity the Government met with a defeat.

Lord Morpeth introduced on its behalf a Bill which was Lord Lincoln's slightly altered.[1] As in the case of the Poor Law the measure started from the recognition that the Home Office was overburdened with work. Lord Lincoln's proposal to entrust the new functions to a Committee of the Privy Council was not adopted. In the matter of education and poor relief alike the system was too widely criticized to be acceptable. It was proposed, therefore, to set up a special Board whose composition would be the same as that of the Board of Control or the Railway Board set up the year before. It would consist of five members, three of them salaried officials, another unpaid who would be a member of the Government, and the fifth *ex officio* the First Commissioner of Woods and Forests. The Board, to be called the Board of Health and Public Works, would be empowered after an official inquiry undertaken at the inhabitants' request to devolve on a local authority 'the powers of sewerage, drainage, paving, cleansing and supplying water', all henceforward to be under the control of a single authority. This authority would not be a new organ of local government, elected for the purpose like the Boards of Guardians, but the corporation of the town as constituted by the Act of 1835. If it were shown that the urban area which should be dealt with as a single unit exceeded the boundaries of the corporation's jurisdiction, the Board could extend them. For towns which did not possess an elected corporation a new body might be set up, two-thirds of whose members would be elected by the ratepayers, the remaining third nominated by the Crown. The Board of Health would be equipped with extensive powers of inspection. In particular, inspectors of nuisances could take steps

[1] March 30, 1847 (*Parliamentary Debates*, 3rd Ser., vol. xci, pp. 617 sqq.).

to prevent the atmosphere of large towns being poisoned by fumes from factory chimneys. The local authority would be responsible for the lighting of towns. It would have no power to levy a rate or engage in municipal undertakings. Its authority would extend only to concluding agreements with private companies, borrowing the sums necessary to enable such companies to begin operations, and compelling the beneficiaries, not the landlords but the inhabitants, to pay the interest and redemption of the debt thus contracted.

The scheme was bold and comprehensive. And this proved fatal to it. The Bill was brought in on March 30, but by May it had not even been debated, and the Bill which Lord Morpeth then submitted to the House was a truncated measure. Thus mutilated it passed a second reading with a very large majority, though not until June 21.[1] But towards the close of a session members were not eager to pass a measure so complicated. The Tories denounced what they regarded not as a reform, but as a social revolution and demanded the substitution for this comprehensive measure, of a purely permissive Bill. That is to say, in their view the corporations should be invested with these new powers only in towns which wanted it.[2] The debates dragged on, and on July 8 Lord John informed the House that the Government had decided to drop the Bill for that session.[3] The decision caused widespread dissatisfaction with Lord John and his Cabinet. He was accused of bringing in Bills badly prepared with no great desire to get them passed, in the hope of impressing the public favourably on the eve of the General Election.

10

For a General Election could not be postponed now that a full six years had passed since the election which put Peel in office. It was not therefore a case of forcing a premature election in order to consult the electorate on a particular issue, as had happened in 1841. An election of this kind could have been held in 1846, when Peel's Cabinet, sufficiently strong to carry the repeal of the Corn

[1] *Parliamentary Debates*, 3rd Ser., vol. xciii, pp. 727 sqq.
[2] For the opposition to the reform, see *Health of Towns Association, Report of the Sub-Committee on the Answers returned to the Questions addressed to the principal towns of England and Wales and the Objections from Corporate Bodies to the Public Health Bill*, 1848.
[3] *Parl. Deb.*, 3rd Ser., vol. xcix, pp. 27 sqq.

Law, had proved too weak to obtain parliamentary sanction for its Irish policy. But the position of the parties in Parliament was too confused for the party leaders to desire to consult the people on a question to which they had no answer themselves. Accordingly they were satisfied to leave in the hands of Lord John and the great Whig families authority to dispatch the current business of government. The position in Parliament, however, was no clearer in the summer of 1847 than it had been a year before. The election, which nobody wanted, was held in an atmosphere of general indifference. The result on balance was a gain for the Liberal party, which in place of the 289 seats won in 1841 and the 282 they possessed at the dissolution, now had 337, only two less, that is to say, than in 1837.[1] But we have seen how precarious its position had been in 1837 with 339 votes. Was it any better now?

One result of the election was calculated to cause anxiety to the Whig aristocrats, the thoroughgoing change in the membership of the House which it produced. The reformers were delighted and did not conceal their hope that this 'infusion of new blood' would put an end to the apathy which had prevailed since the repeal of the Corn Laws.[2] The Conservatives were alarmed and feared a Parliament as disorderly as the first Parliament after the Reform Bill, packed as it had been with novices and enthusiasts. Both would prove mistaken, as indeed anyone who reflected on the cause of this change of membership could have foretold. It had been due not so much to the impatience of young men eager to make their mark in the arena of British political life as to the weariness of so many members who after the battles of the past years had decided not to stand again.[3] Their retirement left many vacant seats which were filled in many cases by men of business who wanted to defend and serve their private interests. They were more numerous, so far as we can judge, in this than in any previous Parliament. The manufacturers, it is true, were no better represented than before. Their creed of free trade and *laisser-faire* did not encourage political ambitions. They wanted to have as little to do with politics as possible. Let anyone else who pleased have a

[1] *Returns of the two last General Elections in 1841 and 1847. Westminster and Foreign Quarterly Review,* 1847, vol. xlviii, pp. 261 sqq.

[2] *Douglas Jerrold's Weekly Newspaper,* August 7, 1847: 'There is an infusion of new blood in the House.' *The Times,* August 18 and 21, 1847.

[3] *Annual Register,* 1847, pp. 95 sqq.: 'Numerous as were the changes which took place, they arose rather from the voluntary retirement of the old members, satiated with long enjoyment of parliamentary honours . . . than from political or religious opposition.'

seat in Parliament or a post in the government service provided they were left free to pile up wealth and in the process, they believed, foster the happiness of mankind. But railway promoters needed Parliament to sanction their companies and ensure that the State control of companies, which after all were public utilities, should not weigh too heavily. For a long time past they had beset the lobby of the House of Commons and they were determined to make their way in. The great George Hudson secured his own return for Sunderland, Robert Stephenson's return for Whitby, and forced upon the Tories a candidate of his own choosing as one of the two members for York, a puppet who would make way for his own son as soon as he came of age. In all, the railways were represented by no less than a hundred and two members of the new House.[1] The House of Commons had been industrialized.

How much longer could the great Whig families hold out against the irresistible trend of the times and defend their privileged position?

From one point of view the position of the Whigs was no better than in 1837. Their 337 members, like their 339 in 1837, were not a solid block, but a bundle of divergent groups with no great leader to compel them all to respect his strong will. In the first place there were the 63 Irish 'Liberals'. But apart from the fact that many of these Liberals, even of those justly regarded in Westminster as ardent defenders of Irish liberty—Richard Lalor Sheil, to mention one name—had barely kept their seats against the attacks of the Radical repealers, it was absurd to call Meagher and O'Connell's son Daniel Liberals, when they were, in fact, two revolutionaries who had just won their seats from two genuine Liberals, and even more absurd to reckon as a Liberal J. Reynolds, a violent repealer who had been returned at Dublin as the result of a scandalous bargain with the Orangemen to turn out the moderates who held the two city seats in favour of a repealer and a Tory.[2] A new Irish party was in process of formation, implacably hostile to England, which at elections lavished its abuse on both the English parties impartially, and far from feeling any gratitude to Lord John for the energetic measures he had taken with the unanimous approval of Parliament to relieve

---

[1] R. E. Lambert, *The Railway King*, pp. 217 sqq. See *Railway Times*, July 17, 1847, and *Railway Record*, August 7, 1847.
[2] *Annual Register*, 1847, p. 98. *The Times*, August 6, 1847.

the distress in Ireland, accused him of having engineered the famine to ruin the country. It was all very well for this party to flaunt O'Connell's name now that he was dead. It was they whose intransigence, after the return of the Tories in 1841, had embittered the leader's last days. If the close alliance before 1841 between the Irish patriots and the Whigs had made the latter unpopular with certain sections of the British public, it had undoubtedly strengthened their position in the House. It existed no longer.

The Chartist Opposition was but an echo of the past and only as such worth mention.[1] It could never have been very effective with the restricted franchise of 1832, and was even more impotent now when the party was decaying. It is true a few Chartist candidates presented themselves, but merely for form's sake. In some cases they wanted to discover the number of their supporters and went to the poll. But the number of votes they obtained at Glasgow and at Ipswich, where Edgar Vincent stood, was not even sufficient to prevent the return of a free trader. And they were often satisfied if the crowd accepted them as candidates on nomination day and left it at that. Harney took this course at Tiverton, where he delivered an attack on Palmerston to which the latter replied by a harangue which lasted five hours.[2] It is worth remarking that the moderates won two outstanding successes against two candidates of Chartist sympathies, the Tory Ferrand and the Radical Fielden. The former did not even attempt to repeat his exploit of 1841 and snatch a seat from the Whigs in their Knaresborough fief. The latter, who sought not only to retain his seat at Oldham but, in conjunction with Cobbett's son, to win both seats, was defeated by the combination of a leading free trader and a Peelite. In an urban district with a population of almost 100,000 but a very small electorate the free trader headed the poll with 719 votes; Fielden was at the bottom of it with 597. The same evening, in protest against the result, a riot occurred, so serious that the military had to be called out. But it did not alter the fact that Fielden had been defeated.[3] On the other hand, the Chartists, or rather the old electoral compact between Chartist and Tory, won at Nottingham a triumph the more remarkable

---

[1] R. G. Gammage, *History of the Chartist Movement*, pp. 283-5.
[2] *The Times*, August 3, 1847.
[3] J. L. and B. Hammond, *Lord Shaftesbury*, p. 121.

that it was unexpected. John Walter, the everlasting John Walter, was returned, but in alliance this time with O'Connor and by an overwhelming majority; a victory the more brilliant because it was won over a Cabinet Minister, Sir John Cam Hobhouse.[1] Thus, while Chartism lay on its death-bed, its leader returned to the House of Commons.

We must also notice an original feature of this election of 1847, the entry into the political arena of the Nonconformists organized as a distinct party.[2] We have watched the birth of this movement during the struggle provoked by the Educational Clauses of the Factory Bill of 1843.[3] We have spoken of the Southwark by-election at which Miall of the *Nonconformist* contested the seat with the orthodox Benthamite, Sir William Molesworth, who was an advocate of State action in the sphere of education, even if it involved the abandonment to some extent of consistent secularism, and we have seen how the agitation revived after the Minute of December 1846.[4] An Education Conference was held in April which decided that the Nonconformist vote should not be given to a candidate unless he had answered certain questions satisfactorily and that a number of independent candidates should be put forward. Throughout the month, as the result of an Anti-State-Church Conference, meetings of pastors and their flocks were held frequently in Yorkshire and Lancashire, also in some agricultural counties near London—Bedfordshire, Norfolk, and Essex. The results of the agitation were disappointing. It secured Perronet Thompson's return at Bradford and at Lambeth the Nonconformist candidate defeated Hawes, under-secretary at the War Office. And in Edinburgh these religious agitators won a sensational victory. Among the Whigs there were two intellectual luminaries of the House of Commons whose arrogance and unconcealed scorn for the petty fanaticism of the Protestant sects made them particularly odious to the latter. They were Lord John Russell and Macaulay. Against Lord John in the City his enemies were powerless. But they made war on Macaulay in his constituency, Edinburgh. His haughty demeanour had not en-

---

[1] *The Times*, July 30, 1847. M. Howell, *The Chartist Movement*, p. 283.
[2] For this new policy adopted by Dissent in the 1847 election, see an excellent article in the *Eclectic Review* for September 1847: 'The Electoral Policy of Dissenters: What are its Results?' (N.S., vol. xxii, pp. 354 sqq.).
[3] See above, pp. 63 sqq.
[4] See above, pp. 173 sqq.

deared him to his constituents. Certain regulations concerning the collection of excise duties had turned a large number against the Whig Government. Four hundred of the 440 voters who were members of the Free Church voted for Cowan against Macaulay, who failed to secure re-election.[1] His defeat made as much stir as O'Connor's victory. But like the latter it was an episode with no wider significance. For everywhere else the Nonconformist candidates were defeated: Sturge at Leeds by the combination of a Liberal and a Peelite, Miall at Halifax in stranger circumstances. In spite of an alliance with the Chartist—Ernest Jones—he was defeated by the combination of a Liberal and a Protectionist.[2] But though both were so weak there was this difference between Chartism and Nonconformist Neo-Liberalism—the former in 1847 was generally regarded as outmoded, whereas many people thought the latter might prove an important innovation, a political creed which gave philosophical expression to the victory won by free trade in 1846, free trade become a religion or rather perhaps a religion whose sum and substance was unqualified free trade.

For the moment, however, neither Chartism nor political Dissent was a serious source of weakness to the Ministry. What was serious was the fact that of little more than 300 members on the Government benches about 100 were Radicals. An exact figure cannot be given, for they were a trend of opinion rather than an organized group. Nor were their tenets susceptible of exact definition. The views of many Radicals were such that the Chartists on the one hand, the Nonconformists on the other, could claim their victories as their own, whether in the capital or in the industrial regions of the north. Some, Wakley for example, were democrats first, free traders afterwards. Others were free traders first, democrats afterwards. Such was Cobden, who, after a series of political journeys abroad, had returned to the political arena, and of whom everyone was asking by what new agitation he would continue a career which for the past ten years had been so marvellously successful. Others again, like Bright, were equally democrats and free traders. But all in different proportions were democrats and free traders. And all for diverse reasons, some because they had no religious belief, others on

[1] *The Times*, August 2. *Douglas Jerrold's Weekly Newspaper*, August 7, 1847.
[2] R. G. Gammage, *History of the Chartist Movement*, p. 284.

religious grounds, were political secularists. They all shared a common dislike of the Whig aristocracy which persisted in monopolizing the government of the party. And all professed that if they had to choose a leader outside their own group they would prefer Peel, the statesman, to a party politician like Lord John.

For in this stew-pot of warring groups Peel, there was no doubt of it, was the outstanding figure dominating all others. But if Lord John must endure the galling knowledge that for all that he was the Prime Minister nobody thought of him, compared with Peel, except as a front-bench politician, he also knew that Peel's position was such as must strengthen, not weaken, his Administration.

The party led by Lord John was numerically as strong, but in its composition as weak as the party which had supported Melbourne ten years earlier. But it was not, as then, confronted by a solid block of 310 Conservatives. The members who faced Lord John on the Opposition benches were divided into two hostile groups, 202 Protectionists and 116 Peelites. The figure of 202 Protectionists meant that the uncompromising Tories had lost 60 seats.

Disraeli had accomplished the *tour de force* of galvanizing into life not only Lord George Bentinck, but with him the old party of country gentlemen. And the election had been a further triumph for him when Tory patronage gave this young literary adventurer a county seat in Buckinghamshire. But he was partly responsible for leading his party into a blind alley from which it could escape only by retreat. For Peel the election had so far proved a success, that he now had behind him 116 members in place of the 112 who had seceded in 1846. But his group was in the awkward position occupied by every centre party. In some constituencies the Peelites had stood as Conservative candidates against the Liberals and Radicals. More frequently, however, this had been the case throughout Lancashire, where the election had wiped the Tories off the slate, the Liberals had combined with them to keep the Tories out. In the House many Peelites regarded themselves as being, apart from the single issue of free trade, Conservatives, and were waiting for the day when the Tory party would abandon protection and they could return to their former allegiance. On the other hand, the *Morning Chronicle*, which had recently become an organ of the group, advocated a union of Peelites and Liberals. Peel, whose personal authority kept the group together, would not pronounce for one side or the other and left his followers free within wide limits to vote as they thought fit on the questions which from day to day came before Parliament. As Premier he had been the despot of his Cabinet and party. But at present he was careful not to behave as the head of an obedient band of followers, manœuvring to sell its support to the Government on the most favourable terms. He preferred to occupy a position apart, above the conflicting groups, even his own, at the service of the nation rather than a party. Content to be the recognized adviser of his country he did not pursue an object at the moment beyond his grasp and aspire to become once more Prime Minister.[1]

The net result of all this was a situation, after as before the General Election, on the whole satisfactory to the Government. It would be misleading to say that in this new Parliament there were 339 Liberals to 319 Conservatives. It is truer to say that there were 453 free traders to 202 Protectionists. And since in this huge free trade majority the 200 Liberals were a centre party between 100 Radicals and 100 Peelites, the Whig aristocracy could feel itself comfortably installed in power. And their position was the more secure, because neither Lord George Bentinck nor Peel wished, any more than a year before, to overthrow the Ministry; Bentinck, because he feared that if he pulled down the Cabinet it might be for Peel's benefit, Peel because he feared that, if he did so, it might benefit Bentinck. Lord John therefore was certain to stay in office. Would he, however, be content to pursue a policy of inactivity and cautious moderation? Would he not rather be on the lookout for an opportunity to make himself by some positive programme the leader of Parliament and nation? If, however, on the morrow of the election he cherished an unavowed intention of this kind, circumstances did not leave him time to attempt to carry it out. Before the close of the year he found himself compelled to summon an extraordinary session of Parliament to help him solve the pressing problems presented by an economic crisis of extreme gravity, one of the gravest, in fact, which had befallen the country since 1815.

[1] See the view of Peel's attitude formed at this moment by two leading members of the Cabinet. Sir Charles Wood to Lord John Russell, August 14, 1847: 'I am convinced that he means to pursue the popular body-of-the-people line. They [Peel's people] and

II THE ECONOMIC CRISIS

I

The economic crisis whose history we have now to relate and which reached its peak in October had already begun to make itself felt before the election. Indeed, to discover its causes and understand all its aspects we must go back a considerable way, to the moment when Parliament was prorogued in the summer of 1845 before the Irish crisis and when a fever of speculation in industrial shares raged throughout the country. 'He never remembered in all his experience', the Governor of the Bank of England told Greville in October, 'anything like the present speculation; the operations of '25 which led to the great panic were nothing to it, and there could not fail to be a fearful reaction.'[1] Railway shares were in particular request with the public. It had long ceased to be a matter of purchasing shares newly issued or of considering their true long-time value. The affair had become a gamble. Shares passed from hand to hand, the purchaser buying only to sell again as soon as he considered it advisable to take his profit, and then he would proceed to stake the entire sum, investment and profit, on some other undertaking. When finally the number of cautious people who wanted to secure their profits exceeded the number of optimists who wanted to buy and become still richer, there must be a general crash. It occurred in October. 'The reaction', Greville tells us, 'came sooner than anybody expected it, but,' he adds, 'though it has blown many of the bubbles into the air, it has not been as yet so complete and so ruinous as many of the wise men of the East still expect and predict.'[2] He also remarks that business was already recovering, had, indeed, taken a new lease of life. Stocks were rising in value, new companies being launched. But if 'the wise men of the East', the City

we are the rivals for the lead of the great popular party. We have it in very difficult circumstances. He had it very much in favourable times, and has acquired a character which he does not deserve; but still there is a great leaning on the part of many of our friends towards him. This is what has always made me anxious to enlist some of his best men.' Lord John's reply, August 15, 1847: 'I am aware that the dishonesty of the country is prepared to rally round Peel at any time, but I think they are mistaken in their man. In the first place, he is not prepared to go headlong with Hume or Ellice into the adoption of radical changes; and in the next place, he would not make any sacrifices for the resumption of power' (*The Later Correspondence of Lord John Russell*, vol. i, pp. 179-81).

[1] *Greville Memoirs*, November 16, 1845.
[2] Ibid., November 16, 1845.

bankers, persisted in their pessimism they had very serious reasons for their anxiety.

The petty crisis of October 1845 was nothing more than the liquidation of some unfortunate speculators to the profit of others more shrewd. This transference of wealth from one individual to another in no way impoverished the nation. And if the recovery of business during the first half of 1846 disappointed expectations, it could be attributed to the violent parliamentary struggle provoked by the Government's policy of free trade, to the protracted debates, and the consequent uncertainty as to the economic policy which would finally be adopted. But the pessimism of 'the wise men of the East' was not removed by Peel's victory. In their opinion the fact that such a large amount of capital was taken up by the construction of railways to the detriment of other branches of industry threatened the balance of the national economy. An excessive amount of floating capital was being permanently tied up. For a railway and a factory differed in this respect. The capital tied up in a factory was transformed once more into free capital, into manufactured articles which could be exchanged for other articles or exported. Capital tied up in a railway, on the other hand, produced in return for the income it brought in only services, not goods. The danger, it is true, is not so great for a country when the lines it builds are on its own soil and not abroad, and in this respect the position at present differed from some of the earlier crises which had been due to foreign investment. It is also true that railways even while still under construction cause new mines to be opened to produce the necessary coal and iron, and the building of houses for the populations which will cluster round new stations. And these undertakings in turn will require the investment of capital. But owing to the infatuation of the public so much capital had been devoted to building these new railways that there might not be enough to spare even for these subsidiary undertakings. During the twelve years ending in 1844, £5,000,000 had been spent every year on the construction of railways. The promoters of new companies were now trying to persuade the public that they could spend twenty, thirty, even forty millions a year on railways. Statisticians, however, estimated the nation's annual savings at about £50,000,000. It was obviously absurd to allocate them in such a grotesquely unbalanced fashion. So long as more companies were floated than lines built, more capital accumulated in the banks than the companies drew out. But the number of lines could not be increased indefinitely. The moment was at hand when the network of British railways would be complete save for a few minor alterations and additions. And the moment was even closer when the flotation of new companies would slacken, while withdrawals of money invested in railway construction would become more frequent. One day or another, that is to say, and at a not distant future a crisis would supervene, not simply a crisis in the investment market in which some speculators would be ruined for the profit of others, but one of those crises of over-production which were apparently a normal occurrence in the new world of industry.[1]

As early as 1845 the *Economist*, the weekly organ of orthodox free trade, had warned its readers how grave the danger was.[2] Faithful, however, to its creed, it deprecated any safeguarding action by the State. But at the beginning of 1846 meetings were held at Liverpool and Glasgow to call upon the State to intervene. Parliament was asked to control more strictly the flotation of new companies, and government officials to exercise greater vigilance and see that the companies observed the conditions Parliament had imposed upon them. During the first half of 1846 Parliament was too occupied with the important problems of which we have spoken above to give the railway question the attention it demanded. It was only at the latter end of the session, when Peel's Government had already been succeeded by a Whig Cabinet, that to give effect to the recommendations of a Select Committee of the House of Commons an Act was passed abolishing the railway department of the Board of Trade and entrusting the control of the railways to a Board of Commissioners constituted on a novel principle.[3] In its original form the Bill, brought in by Lord John, not only transferred to the Board the powers hitherto possessed by the Railway Department of the Board of Trade, but in addition gave it authority to see that companies observed their statutory obligations and to undertake any inquiry Parliament might entrust to it. This was less than the companies'

---

[1] For the crisis of February 1846, see *Report from the Secret Committee . . . on Commercial Distress: Minutes of Evidence*. Evidence given by W. Cotton (q. 3953), and R. C. L. Bevan (qq. 2243-4).

[2] *Economist*, October 18, 1845, vol. iii, pp. 997-8.

[3] 9 & 10 Vict. Cap. 105: An Act for constituting Commissioners of Railways. H. of C., August 20 and 21, and H. of L., August 27, 1846 (*Parliamentary Debates*, 3rd Ser., vol. lxxxviii, pp. 891 sqq., 929 sqq., and 1057).

enemies asked for. But it was more than Parliament was willing to grant. The new Board merely took over the powers previously vested in the Board of Trade. These amounted to very little. There was, in fact, nothing more than the possibility, the hope, that later on the Board might receive wider powers and be able to do more. The most interesting feature of this Act of 1846 is the constitutional significance of the principle exemplified by the composition of the Board. It consisted of paid and unpaid members, members of Parliament, and officials without a seat in the House. Nor were all the members of Parliament unpaid. More exactly, there were five members of the Committee. The President, a member of Parliament and in receipt of a salary, would change with every change of government. There were two salaried members who might not sit in Parliament, two others unpaid who might be members of Parliament. This Board of 1846 with its deliberate confusion of executive and legislative functions was thus the prototype of the Poor Law Board of 1847 of which we have spoken already.

Parliament was prorogued at the end of August. Since the policy of free trade had been confirmed, not shaken, by the crisis which substituted Lord John Russell for Peel, a feeling of optimism prevailed throughout the country. The *Economist*, which in March had spoken anxiously about the pressure put upon the money market,[1] laid aside its fears and made no protest when in August the Bank lowered the rate of discount from $3\frac{1}{2}$ to 3 per cent.[2] It was a bounty given to the optimism which the state of its coffers seemed to justify.

Gold abounded in the cellars of the Bank of England, exceeding in the summer of 1846 £16,000,000.[3] The figure then reached was practically speaking a record. The question was asked, and it was not easy to reply, how long this optimism would last; how many months must pass before the over-capitalization of the railways would produce a crisis? In fact, this 'normal' crisis was precipitated, though at the same time disguised, in the course of the ensuing winter by the intervention of another crisis of an entirely different character.[4]

---

[1] *Economist*, March 14, 1846, vol. iv, pp. 325 sqq.
[2] Ibid., August 29, 1846, vol. iv, p. 437.   [3] Tooke, *History of Prices*, vol. iv, p. 302.
[4] The causes of the crisis of 1847 are explained in the *First Report from the Secret Committee . . . on Commercial Distress* (pp. 4 sqq.) and in an important article in the *Economist*, May 8, 1847: 'The Present Crisis, its Character and Remedy' (vol. v, pp. 517 sqq.).

2

It was a dearth—a crisis belonging to the old order—the last dearth, in fact, Europe has known up to the present day.[1] The unsatisfactory harvest of 1845 was followed by the disastrous autumn of 1846. The potato disease was worse than it had been the year before. The cereal harvest, moderately good in 1845, was a failure not only in the United Kingdom, but in France and throughout Western Europe. In 1845 Great Britain could still purchase corn even in Ireland, while the Irish poor were starving to death. Nothing of the kind was possible at the end of 1846. Britain could not even obtain wheat from France or Germany. In short, it was no longer Ireland alone, but the whole of Western Europe that had to be saved from famine. The United Kingdom, France, and Germany must import Russian and American wheat, the only sources available to supply the deficit. In consequence the price of wheat rose from 50 shillings and 2d. on August 22 to 65 shillings and 7d. on November 18. Reassuring accounts by the French Ministry of Commerce about the state of the harvest in France slightly lowered the price which fell to 59 shillings and 10d. on December 19. But it soon became known that these statements were unfounded and the price of wheat rose once more. It exceeded 70 shillings in January, 71 in February, and 78 in March, and in April appeared to be stationary at more than 77 shillings. In Germany and France, where another Jacquerie seemed to have begun, hunger caused an outbreak of rioting. The same happened in Scotland and the south of England. There was no bloodshed however. It was not even found necessary to call out the troops, except in Jersey, which after all is on the doorstep of France. But England suffered in common with Ireland and Continental Europe, and a drain on English gold began, to pay for the Russian and American wheat.

This would not have been altogether a bad thing if the sudden enrichment of Russia and the United States had meant a corresponding increase in the demand for the products of British manufacture. The drain of gold would have been checked by a simple balance of accounts, if the United States, for example, had bought more British cotton goods or paid a higher price for them. This, unfortunately, was not the case owing to yet another dearth, a

[1] Written before 1937.—*Trs. Note.*

partial failure of the American cotton crop. The prospect of a scarcity of cotton made the price rise from December 1846, and after a few weeks' pause, when the failure had become a certainty, prices began to rise still further. The amount imported was perhaps not less than in 1846, for in that year a third of the cotton used had been a reserve from the year before. But, since the price was half as high again, four or five million pounds more had to be paid to America. That is to say, the misfortune of a bad season hit very heavily, at a time when the situation was already so unfavourable, an industry which accounted for half the British exports. Some mills closed, others worked short time. Sir Charles Wood, when he presented his Budget on February 22, estimated that in January there were 2,638 unemployed in Manchester, and that, since then, there were no more than 2,900 working full time; 1,955 working short time.[1] On May 10 Lord George Bentinck gave figures, which no one disputed, which seemed to prove that the position in Lancashire had grown worse. Out of 1,061 mills 728 were either closed or working short time. Of 226,000 workers 100,000 were working short time, 23,000 were unemployed.[2]

The pressure which these forces in combination could exert upon the money market is obvious. The railway companies were asking for money, the importers of corn were asking for it, the importers of cotton were asking for it. The effect, however, was yet sensible in January, when the Bank of France, in difficulties, could borrow £1,000,000 from the Bank of England. But in March the Bank of England was also in difficulties. Both banks were delivered from their predicament by a sensational foreign intervention of which we must speak briefly to complete our picture of the European financial situation.

Russia, an exporter of cereals, saw the gold of Western Europe flowing into her coffers. Nicholas I and his advisers decided to turn her favourable position to a novel use. Instead of bringing this gold from the West to the East, they would spend it in the West on the purchase of State bonds. Russia would thus become a permanent creditor of the Western Powers. On March 11 she purchased 50,000,000 francs worth of 3 per cent bonds. This purchase definitely saved the Bank of France and gave the Bank of

[1] H. of C., February 22, 1847. Sir C. Wood's speech (*Parliamentary Debates*, 3rd Ser., vol. xc, p. 320).
[2] H. of C., May 10, 1847. Lord George Bentinck's speech (*Parl. Deb.*, 3rd Ser., vol. xcii, p. 621).

England temporary relief. For the Bank of France was now in a position to repay its January loan, and the sum thus placed at her disposal enabled England to purchase abroad the raw materials she needed. Moreover, six weeks later, on May 1, the Czar's Government, in pursuance of the same policy, bought £2,500,000 worth of Consols.[1] It must be added that since the discovery of the Ural goldfield in 1819 and the Siberian in 1829 gold mining in Russia had advanced rapidly every year. It is not sufficiently known how greatly, on the eve of the discovery of the Californian and Australian goldfields, this increase in the supply of Russian gold interested and worried the economists.[2] The assistance thus given by the Russian Government to the sale of British funds was, of course, a source of gratification to them. But the politicians were not so well pleased. They pictured the Russian Empire possessed of a species of monopoly, taking advantage of Western Europe's need of Russian corn to feed its population, to deplete it of its gold, and thus redouble its military strength by an economic power which, in conjunction with the former, might render it invincible.[3]

But the difficulties of the money market were by no means at an end. On January 21 the Bank had raised the rate of discount to 4 per cent, but had taken no steps since then to raise it further.[4] The Government, which could always give the Bank, if not orders, at least advice whose weight made it very like an order, did nothing. Possibly it was afraid that if it encouraged the Bank to raise the rate of discount it might jeopardize the success of its loan of £8,000,000.[5] Meanwhile there was a persistent drain upon the assets of the Bank. The amount of precious metal in its possession fell between January 23 and April 10 from £13,440,000 to £9,870,000, and between April 10 and April 17 from £9,870,000 to £9,330,000. During the same periods the reserve of the Banking Department—the only reserve from which in accordance with the Act of 1844 the Bank was permitted to draw— fell from £6,840,000 to £3,400,000, then to £3,080,000. For the Bank and the Government there was a further source of

[1] Tooke, *History of Prices*, vol. iv, pp. 73-4 and 393-4. *Economist*, May 8, 1847, vol. v, p. 525.
[2] Tooke, *History of Prices*, vol. iv, pp. 452-3.
[3] H. of C., December 2, 1847, C. N. Newdegate's speech, *Parliamentary Debates*, 3rd Ser., vol. xcv, p. 559. *Blackwood's Magazine*, December 1847, vol. lxii, p. 750.
[4] Tooke, *History of Prices*, vol. iv, pp. 302-3.
[5] See above, pp. 165-6.

anxiety. A time of year had been reached when the revenue from taxation diminished and expenditure increased. That is to say, since the Bank of England was the Government's bank of deposit, the nation's current account was becoming notably less favourable at the very time when the Bank's gold was being drained off through so many channels.[1]

On January 21 the Bank of England had timidly raised its rate of discount to 4 per cent. On April 8 very tardily it raised it to 5 per cent. This was not enough to meet the pressing danger. A weighty letter signed Mercator appeared in *The Times* on April 15. The writer, who was generally believed to be a person of importance, warned the public that this was the case. And the very same day, in fact, the Bank began a new discount policy.[2] The public were informed that the 5 per cent rate was a minimum which would apply only to bills for short-term discount, no longer than ten days or a fortnight. In the case of bills drawn for a longer period the Bank reserved the right to raise the rate in proportion to the length of time. In some cases, bills drawn for six months, by and in favour of firms whose financial position was unquestionably solid, rates of 12 and 13 per cent were reached. On the other hand, the Bank announced its intention to limit the amount of bills on which it would advance money and that when that limit had been reached it would refuse even the best guaranteed bills. It would even refuse to renew bills when they were due for payment—an unheard-of step. Then on May 1 the welcome purchase by the Russian Government occurred. And the Government supplemented the action of the Bank by two financial measures. On May 10 the Treasury raised to 5 per cent the rate of interest on its exchequer bills, and by a system of skilfully graduated bonuses encouraged subscribers to the Government loan to make their payments before the obligatory date. This device made the burden of debt heavier for the future. But it succeeded perfectly and the State obtained the cash it required.

---

[1] *Report from the Secret Committee . . . on Commercial Distress*; evidence given by Sir Joshua Bates, q. 2463. Lord Lansdowne's statement in the House (*Parliamentary Debates*, 3rd Ser., vol. xcii, p. 362).

[2] *The Times*, April 15, 1847. H. of C., December 3, 1847, Lord John Russell's speech: 'About the month of April last, a very remarkable letter appeared in *The Times* newspaper respecting the drain of gold that was then going on; and the Bank Directors immediately began to change their course by limiting their discount to a certain extent, and the circulation was diminished from the month of April to the beginning of June by about a million and a half' (*Parl. Deb.*, 3rd Ser., vol. xcv, p. 632).

At the same time the enemies of the railway promoters won a victory over Hudson and his associates. An influential member of Parliament, Ellice, nicknamed 'Bear' Ellice, entered the field against them. And he had with him, after all, the secret sympathy of the manufacturers, who looked askance at the ease with which, to their detriment, the railway promoters could always obtain the capital they needed for their railroads. And Conservatives were equally sympathetic. A Tory, Colonel Sibthorpe, the uncompromising enemy of modern industrialism in every aspect, and who saw in the expansion of the railways its most perfect expression, would have proposed, had it been possible, not stricter control, but the total abolition of railways. Ellice and Sibthorpe failed to carry a Railway Bill enlarging the powers of the Commissioners of Railways and giving them the right to inspect the companies' accounts. George Hudson's obstruction proved too strong for them. But at least they secured the passage by the Commons, acting in agreement with the Chancellor of the Exchequer, of eleven resolutions to restrain the companies' dubious activities. The two first sought to slacken the pace of construction. Companies who were asking Parliament for Bills must wait till the next session before the matter could go further. The three following forbade companies to pay interest out of capital before all the shares had been issued and the lines laid down. The last six condemned a number of scandalous practices too common among those who operated fusions of companies. Fusion was forbidden until at least half the capital had been paid up, and no fusions might be effected under which the capital of the fused companies was to be greater than the entire capital of the companies before fusion.[1]

The measures adopted, in conjunction with the Russian purchase, had extricated the Bank from its difficulties. At the beginning of May it was able to relax the extremely rigorous conditions it had imposed on borrowers towards the end of April. On May 10 the Chancellor of the Exchequer could inform the House that

---

[1] The first resolutions had been moved by Ellice and carried on February 23, 1847 (*Parliamentary Debates*, 3rd Ser., vol. xc, pp. 393 sqq.). They were repeated and completed in the course of debate on April 22 and May 14 and 17 (ibid., 3rd Ser., vol. xci, p. 1157; vol. xcii, pp. 821 and 947). The House finally passed them on June 10 (ibid. 3rd Ser., vol. xciii, pp. 310 sqq.). The *Economist* for June 12 gives their text. See, further, the *Economist*, September 18, 1847 (p. 1073), article entitled, 'The Railway Struggle for Capital', and October 2, 1847 (p. 1134), article entitled, 'Railway Calls and Railway Shareholders'.

gold and silver to the value of £400,000 had been placed in the cellars of the Bank and the number of bank-notes in circulation had been correspondingly increased. He was, however, careful to disclaim the view which had been attributed to him that the danger had been removed. The price of wheat continued to rise, and in the last week of May exceeded 100 shillings a quarter. At two sales it fetched respectively 115 and 124 shillings. And hunger rioting continued in Scotland and the south-west of England. Brougham, speaking about this time in the House of Lords, mentioned a county where 200 special constables had been sworn in and the yeomanry called out to deal with the rioters.[1] And there was another symptom of the persistent financial disorder. In April not a single firm or bank had failed. For that reason it was widely said that although there was pressure there was no panic. Now at the end of June a large firm which specialized in financing India failed;[2] then, on July 9, a bank at Preston. A series of minor bankruptcies followed in London and the provinces.[3] In the middle of July, when the interest on Consols fell due, the directors of the Bank and the public with them were alarmed to see the amount of their reserves once more diminishing.

The Bank did not delay to take the necessary steps to keep the bullion in its coffers. On August 2 the rate of discount was raised to 5 per cent for bills having at least a month to run, to $5\frac{1}{2}$ per cent for bills up to two months, and to 6 per cent for bills for longer periods. Bills having more than 95 days to run were refused altogether. On August 5 the minimum rate was raised to $5\frac{1}{2}$ per cent. This time, however, these measures were ineffective. The following day the crisis in the strict sense began and continued until October.

3

It began in August with the crash of speculators in the corn market. The price of wheat had fallen from 102 shillings at the end of May to an average of 75 shillings from the beginning of July to the beginning of August. After this date a rapid, con-

---

[1] H. of L., May 17. Lord Brougham's speech (*Parliamentary Debates*, 3rd Ser., vol. xcii p. 921).
[2] At this moment British India was itself passing through a commercial crisis, a crisis of over-production, due amongst other causes to the losses in the Mauritius market produced by the Sugar Bill.
[3] *Eclectic Review*, December 1847, art. viii, 'Commercial Failures in 1847' (N.S., vol. xxi, pp. 750 sqq.). *Economist*, March 4, 1848: 'List of Failures during the Commercial Crisis of 1847-8'.

tinuous, and regular fall reduced it from 75 shillings and 6d. to a minimum of 49 shillings and 6d. on September 18. That is to say, there was a fall of 50 per cent in four months. The corn factors who for months had been gambling on a rise had no time to retrace their steps and were ruined at a single blow.[1]

Comfort was sought from the reflection that the disaster was limited and the crisis had hit only a very small body of professional speculators. On September 10, however, the failure became public of the firm of Gower, Nephews and Co., which, since it discounted on a very large scale the corn factors' bills, had been involved in their ruin, and on the other hand, because its operations were not confined to them, involved in turn other firms in its failure. For the city merchants were not all in a sufficiently strong position to resist the blow. The railway companies' demand for money became more and more urgent. It was to stop this drain that the Bank had adopted its restrictions of discount at the end of July and the beginning of August. Firms of the highest standing and repute failed. A former Governor of the Bank of England, the present Governor, and three members of the Court of Directors were swept away by the current. While the Bank raised its rate of discount to 6, 7, and 8 per cent, and restricted the maximum period of its credits to 90, 60, and 30 days, Consols were falling by one, sometimes two, points a day, until by the end of the month they were at 84. Railway shares found no purchasers and collapsed.

In October the crisis reached the banks. On the 18th the Royal Bank of Liverpool, a house known everywhere, with a fully paid up capital of £800,000, stopped payment.[2] Other failures followed in Liverpool, Manchester, and the west of England. Consols fell to 77¾. And the Bank of England itself, the hub of the national system of credit, found itself progressively threatened, as in the previous April, but this time much more seriously.

At the beginning of September the Bank announced that it was prepared to make advances on suitable security repayable by October 14 at latest. It was perhaps an imprudent step. For it created in the public mind an unjustifiable optimism. In consequence the notes in circulation amounted to almost £18,000,000

---

[1] *Eclectic Review*, December 1847, art. viii, 'Commercial Failures in 1847' (N.S., vol. xxi, pp. 750 sqq.).
[2] *Report from the Secret Committee . . . on Commercial Distress: Minutes of Evidence.* Evidence given by A. Hodgson, director of the Bank of Liverpool, qq. 1 sqq.

by the middle of the month, to almost £19,000,000 by the beginning of October. The Bank decided that it had lent as much money as it could prudently part with. Accordingly on October 2 it issued an announcement refusing for the present any further advances and warning the public that on October 14 it would require repayment of all bills falling due on that date and in no circumstances would renew them. That was the date when dividends on Consols were due for payment, and it was only prudent to make sure that the April deficit should not recur and there should be sufficient funds available. The double decision was a shock to the world of commerce, and not only the Governor of the Bank, but the Prime Minister and the Chancellor of the Exchequer were bombarded with complaints. The critical day, October 14, passed without any untoward incident. With a few trifling exceptions the repayments were duly made and, surprisingly, without restricting the circulation of notes. But on Monday the 18th the Royal Bank of Liverpool suspended payment and many other failures followed after Thursday the 21st. The reserve of the Banking Department of the Bank of England, which on October 16 was as low as it had been at the end of April, was lower by a million on Saturday the 23rd, when it was £1,990,000 as against over £13,000,000 of deposits. Panic prevailed in financial circles. On October 21 instances were given of bills accepted by City bankers repayable in a week amounting in all to £10,000 and discounted at a rate which interest and commission together was no less than 13 per cent per annum.

On the morning of October 23 a leading financier asked the Bank for a loan of £200,000. He was asked to come back at noon and the loan was then granted, but at 10 per cent. When he protested and said that although personally he was ready to accept this exorbitant rate, the effect on the public would be disastrous, a compromise of 9 per cent was agreed upon.[1]

A crisis had been reached when the Bank of England, if it were to act as an ordinary bank and avoid failure, must bring down in ruin the entire edifice of British credit except itself. And this step must be taken, when besides the reserves of £1,900,000 still remaining in the Banking Department there was a further £10,000,000 in the coffers of the Issue Department which guar-

---

[1] *Report from the Secret Committee . . . on Commercial Distress: Minutes of Evidence.* Evidence of Sam. Gurney, 'billbroker', of London, q. 1599.

anteed the national currency and so could not be legally used for other purposes. Already in May, when the position of the Bank of England had been the subject of lively debates in Parliament, the critics of the Act of 1844 had protested against the absurdity and asked for the removal of this barrier between the Banking and the Issue Departments. And in July, when the financial situation had improved but was regarded by many people as precarious, a deputation of representative business men had urged the Prime Minister to prepare the public for a relaxation, if a crisis arose, of the too rigid provisions of Peel's Statute.[1] In October the pressure increased. The Government refused to give way. But when the crisis affected the banks and the Bank of England itself supported the appeals of the other banks the politicians could no longer hold out. The manager of the New-castle branch of the Bank of England, the brother of George Grote, the banker and historian, had saved the largest local bank by loans which enabled it to surmount three days of panic, but which exceeded his own financial resources. But without the express approval of the Government the Bank in London dared not risk such a step, which was, in fact, an indirect breach of the Act of 1844. On October 23 the Government gave its consent, and on Monday, October 25, the morning papers published a letter from Lord John Russell and Sir Charles Wood to the Governor and Deputy-Governor of the Bank authorizing them to extend the amount of their loans on approved security. The only safeguard against rash lending would be a charge of 8 per cent interest.

The effect of this step was 'instantaneous', 'magical'.[2] The Bank of England was not even obliged to draw upon the reserve of the Issue Department to furnish the credit required. The mere announcement that it was free to advance it was sufficient to reassure the public and make banks and private persons produce the notes in their possession. We must believe the word of the Chancellor of the Exchequer when, on November 30, he said that foreign orders were coming in, the demand for cotton, the number of mines working at full capacity, and the number of men employed were increasing, and that in view of the cheapness

[1] *Economist*, July 3, 1847, vol. v, pp. 749 sqq.
[2] *Report from the Secret Committee . . . on Commercial Distress: Minutes of Evidence.* Evidence of Thomas Birkbeck, qq. 5840, 5841.

of food there was every reason to expect that the winter would pass without the distress which had been feared.[1] He had spoken more cautiously in May, when the banks had surmounted their earlier difficulties. But he now shared the general opinion that the end had been reached, to use the language of a contemporary economist, of one of 'those periodical hurricanes which visit from time to time the great marts of industry'.[2] Or as another put it, 'That the cycle of events from the beginning to the end of the drainage of capital now, in December, completed its revolution.' Nevertheless, the 'hurricane' had been violent and the effects of such hurricanes are necessarily felt for a long time. Money remained dear, and the liquidation of superfluous railway companies had by no means ceased.

'Remarkable depression in the last months of this year,' Henry Reeve noted in his dairy; 'general illness; great mortality; innumerable failures; funds down to 76; want of money; no society at all.'[3]

And two months later Greville could still write: 'The impression is very bad; people are gloomy, frightened and angry.'[4] The question arises whether a disaster of this magnitude, occurring only a year after Peel's fall, should not be regarded as the condemnation of an economic policy which, when he fell, had been welcomed by the vast majority of the nation as being as beneficent as it was bold.

4

The free traders had promised that the abolition of duties on imported corn would put an end to speculation, and that when the British consumer could draw freely on the wheat of the entire world the price would be stable and moderate. Now, however, when the duties had been for all practical purposes abolished and those which were to remain in force for two years had been suspended to relieve the Irish famine, the price of corn rose and fell more violently than ever before. It rose 40 per cent in five

---

[1] For the history of these critical days, see H. of C., November 30, 1847. Sir C. Wood's speech (*Parliamentary Debates*, 3rd Ser., vol. xcv, pp. 374 sqq.); also *Secret Committee . . . on Commercial Distress: Minutes of Evidence*—evidence of Hodgson (q. 368), J. Morris (q. 273), and Bevan (q. 2271). Tooke, *History of Prices*, vol. v pp. 230-1.

[2] Fullarton, *Regulation of Prices*, quoted by Tooke, *History of Prices*, vol. iv, p. 290.

[3] Henry Reeve, *Life and Correspondence*, 1898, vol. i, p. 190.

[4] *Greville Memoirs*, February 20, 1848.

months to fall 50 per cent in less than three. At one moment it reached 100 shillings and hunger riots which had not been witnessed since the restoration of peace broke out once more. The free traders had explained that large imports of foodstuffs were no reason for alarm, for, by the operation of the mechanism of exchange they would be balanced by large exports of manufactured goods. The last two years, however, had witnessed an increase in the importation of foodstuffs, accompanied by a decline in the export of manufactured articles. Moreover, though Lord Overstone's theory of banking was not an article of the free trader's creed, the fact that Peel adopted it contemporaneously with his conversion to free trade had produced a confusion in the public mind between the two doctrines. What, in fact, was this theory of banking on which the Act of 1844 had been based? That the periodical crises to which British industry had been subject since the peace had been due to an excessive issue of currency, and, therefore, that if the Bank were divided into two watertight departments, one exclusively a bank of issue which would never swerve from certain rigid rules regulating the quantity of notes in circulation, the other exclusively a bank of deposit and a credit bank, a crisis of credit would in future be a mathematical impossibility. Now, three years after the Act of 1844 had been passed and two years after its principles had been extended to the Banks of Scotland and Ireland, the United Kingdom was in the throes of what might be regarded as the most serious economic crisis it had experienced since the peace. For it was possibly even more serious than the crisis of 1825.

The Tory Press renewed in violent terms their attacks upon the Statute of 1844. The more moderate organs, the *Quarterly Review*, for example,[1] distinguished between the Act of 1819 and the Act of 1844 and, while continuing to defend the former, directed their attacks exclusively against the latter. They expressed approval of a book published by Lord Ashburton immediately after the stringency in April which advocated the lowering of the barrier between the issue department and the banking department and the substitution of bimetalism for the monometalic system which, according to him, unduly restricted the currency.[2] But others

[1] *Quarterly Review*, June 1847 (vol. lxxxi, pp. 230 sqq.), art. viii, 'The Financial Pressure'.
[2] Lord Ashburton (Alexander Baring), *Financial and Commercial Crisis Considered*, 1847.

went further and Sir Archibald Alison, whose article attacking the Act of 1819 had been refused by *Blackwood's Magazine* in 1845, had the satisfaction of seeing that periodical, which had now broken with Peel, include in the same condemnation the two measures to which his name was attached and openly express its sympathy with the doctrines of the Birmingham school.[1]

Important London papers, the *Post*, the *Herald*, the *Standard*, *Douglas Jerrold's Weekly Newspaper*, the Birmingham Press, the *Midland Counties Herald*, and the *Liverpool Mercury* flew the banner of currency reform. As we should expect, these 'reformers' were not agreed on all points. The more cautious, for example the two members for Birmingham, Muntz and Spooner, were content to criticize the policy of deflation inaugurated in 1819, the devaluation of the pound, a policy which favoured those who lived idly on interest, to the detriment of the producer.[2] But the more radical views of Enderby and John Taylor also found advocates. And the Chartist, O'Brien, who in October 1846 had revived his *National Reformer*, had the pleasure in April 1847 of seeing his revolutionary programme justified, on one point at least, by the disorders produced by the monopoly of the Bank of England. His programme comprised, in addition to nationalization of land, abolition of the gold and silver coinage. He proposed that the State should empower all commercial houses to issue, subject to its control, bills secured by the deposit of valuable objects of every kind, among them gold and silver. These commercial bills, duly stamped, should be legal tender and exchangeable at any time for bank-notes or precious metals at their current valuation.

It seemed a distinct possibility that the financial crisis might produce an alliance, like that of 1841, between the Tories and the Chartists. But whereas that alliance had done so much to place Peel in office, its revival now would imply that recent events had killed his policy and lost him the confidence of those former supporters.

Nothing of the sort happened. The General Election began on

[1] *Blackwood's Magazine*, July 1847, 'Sir Robert Peel and the Currency' (vol. lxii, pp. 113 sqq.); December 1847, 'Our Currency, Our Trade and Our Tariff' (vol. lxii, pp. 744 sqq.).

[2] Muntz accordingly contradicted the other witnesses examined by the Committee of Enquiry and refused to agree that railway speculation had played an important part in leading up to the crisis. See *Report from the Secret Committee . . . on Commercial Distress: Minutes of Evidence*, pp. 1271 sqq.

July 29 and ended on August 18. The crisis, that is to say, the great crisis which lasted three months, began when the election was in full swing. But although some protests were raised against the existing monetary system by Tory and Chartist candidates and a few Whigs, Liberals, and eccentric Radicals, they played a very small part in the election and did not arouse the public from its apathy. To describe the place taken by the monetary question in the candidates' addresses *Blackwood's Magazine* used the enigmatic phrase, 'preponderant rather than vital', language which concealed its disappointment very badly or rather did not conceal it.[1]

Should we then reply with the Chartists that the opinion of a restricted electorate was not the genuine opinion of the nation? If that had been true, we should have expected a revival of the Chartist agitation, a revolt of the famished and a declaration of war by the malcontents upon the monopoly of the Bank. No Chartist revolt occurred. On May 29 lack of circulation compelled O'Brien to suspend publication of his *National Reformer*. He attributed his failure to the unsympathetic attitude towards himself adopted by the Chartist triumvirate: O'Connor, Vincent, and Lovett, who, moreover, were divided among themselves. The suspension, it is true, followed the April stringency, before the crisis which began in August and reached its sudden climax on October 25. But throughout that crisis the apathy of the working class was undisturbed.

On November 20, a month after the end of the crisis and a few days before the opening of the new Parliament, the Chartist executive committee, whose hopes had been raised by O'Connor's election, issued an appeal for a new National Petition. It went unheeded.[2] At the beginning of December Harvey's 'Fraternal Democrats' gave an official reception in London to the delegate of a Belgian group which styled itself the Democratic Association to promote Brotherhood among the Nations. The event marked an historic moment in the history of European Socialism. For the delegate in question was 'our esteemed friend and brother, Dr. Marx', and it was while making this contact with the London revolutionaries that Marx began to compose his Communist

---

[1] *Blackwood's Magazine*, December 1847, vol. lxii, pp. 744 sqq.

[2] *Northern Star*, November 20, 1847. The appeal continued with the following observations: 'Another important subject to which I have to call your attention is the state of the finances of the *National Charter Association* . . . our Exchequer is low, *almost empty*, and it requires to be immediately replenished.'

Manifesto. But the incident, which attracted no notice whatever in London, is without significance for the history of British labour. Chartism was moribund.[1]

5

How are we to explain this apathy? We shall understand it best if we turn our attention to Manchester, the industrial metropolis of the nation. We might even venture to call it the spiritual capital, inasmuch as political economy, understood, as it was understood at Manchester, had become more than a scientific doctrine; a moral, almost a religious, creed. For Manchester, far from being alarmed by the crisis, awaited it with a secret impatience, and far from being indignant when it actually broke out, welcomed its ravages with joy.[2]

When in August those who were speculating on the rise in the price of corn were hit, consternation prevailed in Liverpool, a leading port of importation, and the headquarters of merchants, billbrokers, and stockjobbers. But Manchester was delighted that those who for many months had battened on the impoverishment of the manufacturers of cotton and cotton goods, whose workers had been reduced to penury, were now feeling the pinch. The fall in the price of corn would compensate for the high price of raw cotton, which was likely to continue. Manchester men had never asked for the infliction of penalties on those who cornered foodstuffs. They were content to wait for the moment when, by the operation of natural laws, they would be ruined as quickly as they had grown wealthy. And in such hard times the Protectionists could not possibly demand the restoration of duties to safeguard the interests of the farmers to the immediate detriment of the workers. Manchester was triumphant.

It won a further victory, when in September so many important firms failed. Unperturbed, the Lancashire manufacturers and the publicists who expounded their views pointed out that the crisis of 1847, unlike that of 1825 and many others, was confined to commerce and did not affect the manufacturers and their workmen. They exaggerated as far as Lancashire was concerned, for there was unemployment there. Nevertheless there was much

[1] *Northern Star*, December 11, 1847.
[2] Tooke, *History of Prices*, vol. iv, p. 325. *Report from the Secret Committee . . . on Commercial Distress: Minutes of Evidence;* evidence of C. H. Turner, a Liverpool merchant, qq. 777 sqq. and 1027 sqq.

truth in their contention. Apart from the distress in Lancashire, due to the special causes already mentioned, industry as a whole, the entire woollen industry of the West Riding, for example, was unaffected by the crisis.[1] Industry was not suffering from a general crisis of over-production or excessive credit.

Alone, the railroad industry had overgrown the bounds of prudence, and in consequence so had a few other industries, coal mining, metal-working, and building. Otherwise British industry had suffered rather from insufficiency of capital, since the public infatuation had put such a vast amount into the construction of railways.[2] If many firms were now paying the penalty of their excessive trust in the prospectuses of the railway promoters, it was well deserved. And not only was it well deserved; it would benefit Lancashire, Yorkshire, and many other districts, since the capital hitherto withheld from them would be once more at their disposal. The Prime Minister and the Chancellor of the Exchequer had scarcely returned to London in October when they were overwhelmed with letters demanding that work on railways in course of construction should be stopped immediately, that for this purpose Parliament should be summoned without delay, or, for greater dispatch, the matter should be dealt with by an Order in Council.[3] The Cabinet turned a deaf ear. But when six or seven weeks later Parliament met in extraordinary session, the Chancellor of the Exchequer carried a Bill to retard still further the rate of railway construction, already checked by the Act passed the previous summer. The time granted to the companies by existing legislation for the purchase of land and the completion of preliminary work was extended, and an indemnity promised to the owners of land sold to compensate for any loss they might incur. And it was further enacted that companies which had not

---

[1] Report from the *Secret Committee . . . on Commercial Distress: Minutes of Evidence.* Evidence of J. Morris, Governor of the Bank of England, q. 2678.

[2] It is of interest to note that the demands of railway speculation, not satisfied by the great joint-stock banks, had given birth to companies called Commercial Exchange Companies, which, at a rate of interest little more than that charged by the banks in the normal course of business, made advances on securities, particularly railway shares. Disturbed by the growth of these new companies, the Bank of Scotland and the Royal Bank founded at their joint expense a British Trust Company to compete with them on their own ground.

See George Kinnear, *Banks and Exchange Companies. A Letter to Alexander Blair, Esq., Treasurer of the Bank of Scotland, in answer to the Prospectus issued by the proposed British Trust Company,* Glasgow, 1847.

[3] H. of C., November 26, 1847. Sir C. Wood's speech (*Parliamentary Debates,* 3rd Ser., vol. xcv, p. 235).

already begun to build might not commence construction without the sanction of the majority of their shareholders.[1]

In October the crisis had reached the banks, and the Bank of England saw its reserve in danger unless it suspended the discount of bills. The situation brought up more complicated problems on which the attitude of the Manchester free traders is less easy to define.

What reply was made by Peel and his supporters to the attacks made against the Act of 1844 as being responsible for the crisis? They put the responsibility on the directors of the Bank, whose policy, they said, had violated, if not the letter, at least the spirit of the Act. A feeble reply it would seem. For the Act of 1844 had left them as free to manage the affairs of the Bank as the directors of any other bank. If the Bank of England really differed in any essential respect from the other banks, why had it been given this liberty? If they had been mistaken in keeping the rate of interest very low too long, so that it had become necessary to raise it at a dangerous speed, the Statute ought surely to have subjected the rate of interest in the Banking Department to regulations as strict as those imposed on the circulation of notes by the Issue Department. Nevertheless, when two Parliamentary Committees were appointed at the close of autumn, one by the Commons and the other by the Lords, to inquire into the crisis and its causes,[2] not a single witness, it would appear, raised the question, which certainly has left no trace in either of the two reports. On the contrary the depositions were very largely concerned with the composition of the Court of Directors. Should it consist exclusively of London merchants[3] to the exclusion of traders in the strict sense, genuine bankers and manufacturers? Was it not desirable that it should be under the presidency of a permanent Governor

---

[1] 11 & 12 Vict. Cap. 3: An Act to give further Time for making certain Railways. See H. of C., November 26 and December 13, 1847. Ellice and Colonel Sibthorpe renewed their attack on the railway companies. We shall understand the nature of the social forces in conflict, if we read George Hudson's denunciation of the manufacturers of cotton goods in the House of Commons on November 26, and Lord George Bentinck's panegyric of the railways on December 13 (*Parliamentary Debates*, 3rd Ser., vol. xcv, pp. 228 sqq. and 991 sqq.).

[2] *Report from the Secret Committee of the House of Lords . . . on Commercial Distress* (July 24, 1848). *First Report from the Secret Committee* (of the House of Commons) *on Commercial Distress* (June 8, 1848). These Committees had been charged 'to inquire into the causes of the recent Commercial Distress, and how far it has been affected by the Laws for regulating the issue of the Bank Notes payable on Demand'.

[3] *Report from the Secret Committee . . . on Commercial Distress: with Minutes of Evidence.* Evidence given by R. C. L. Bevan, a London banker, qq. 2290 sqq.

or Deputy-Governor nominated by the State, instead of a Governor appointed only for a year and elected by the directors from among their own number?[1] No action, however, was taken to give effect to these suggestions, except for an unimportant change in the method of electing the Governor and Deputy-Governor, which, moreover, was made before either Committee had reported.[2]

To defend the Act of 1844 Peel and his supporters brought forward other and better arguments.[3] Far from agreeing that it was responsible for the crisis of 1847, they maintained that the latter would have been more serious if the system established by the Act of 1819 had not been reformed by the Act of 1844. It was absurd, the enemies of the Statute alleged, that the Bank should on two occasions have been compelled to refuse discount on the ground that its reserve no longer exceeded £3,000,000, when a further £6,000,000 were available, separated from the other reserve by a barrier legally insurmountable. The argument failed to take account of the fact that if the barrier had not been erected by the Statute of 1844 the £6,000,000 would have been quickly swallowed up and the Bank have found itself obliged not merely to refuse discount, but to suspend specie payments. It was, moreover, untrue that Peel had ever held the view that in no circumstances should the Issue Department come to the assistance of the Banking Department. He had always been of the opinion that Parliament might, if it were in session, meet a pressing need by repealing, for the occasion, the provisions of the Act of 1844. Nor, if the House were in recess, had he been opposed in principle to the Government acting on its own responsibility subject to the subsequent approval of Parliament.[4]

[1] *Report . . . on Commercial Distress*. Evidence of J. Morris, Governor of the Bank of England, qq. 2675 sqq., and Charles Turner, a Liverpool merchant, q. 676.

[2] *First Report from the Secret Committee . . . on Commercial Distress*, June 8, 1848, p. 5. 'Your Committee have learnt . . . with satisfaction that the attention of the Court of Directors has been given to the subject, and that a change has been made by them, as to the selection of the Governor and Deputy-Governor, calculated, in the opinion of your Committee, to improve the composition of the governing body of the Bank.'

[3] H. of C., May 10, 1847, Disraeli's speech and Peel's reply (*Parliamentary Debates*, 3rd Ser., vol. xcii, pp. 651-2, 665-6). Peel's speech of December 3, 1847 (*Annual Register*, 1847, pp. 217 sqq.).

[4] The contingency had, in fact, been foreseen by the framers of the Act of 1844, as William Cotton, Governor of the Bank of England at the time, deposed (*Report . . . on Commercial Distress* (q. 4057). Would it have been advisable to make an explicit provision for it in the Act? This view was taken by some of the witnesses who gave evidence before the Committee (ibid., qq. 166 and 672). But the majority considered that the Act had had a salutary effect, and the Committee did not recommend its alteration.

But to insert into the Statute, which set up the barrier between the two departments, a provision authorizing the Government or the Bank itself to meet an emergency by lowering it would have made the rule ineffective and created in the public mind the impression that the separation of the two reserves was no better than a fiction. The intention of those responsible for the Act of 1844 had been that the partition between the reserves should seem for all practical purposes insurmountable, and that the public and the Bank should regard it in that light. Moreover, the Act contained provisions restricting the issue of bills by private and joint-stock banks and the failure in October of three banks of issue had brought the day closer when the Bank of England would possess a monopoly of issue. The credit crisis had not been complicated by a currency crisis. Between the crisis of 1825 and the crisis of 1847 there was this difference among many others, that whereas in 1825 the members of the public tried to get rid of any bank-notes in their possession, in 1847 they treasured them and hid them away.[1] The difference was all in favour of the crisis of 1847 and the Act of 1844.

This being the defence made by Peel and his supporters, what attitude did Manchester take up? It was paradoxical, but intelligible. At the outset of his career as an agitator Cobden, it would seem, had been in favour of free banks, of free trade, that is to say, in banking as in all other departments. But he soon came to perceive that the policy of the Birmingham school was closely bound up with protection, and a policy of inflation and high prices. Accordingly, by his silence, if not by his formal assent, he had approved the extension of the Bank of England's monopoly by the Act of 1844 and the stricter regulation of the currency as producing deflation and low prices. And now, more uncompromising than Peel himself, the Manchester school was far from welcoming the letter of October 25. If the Act of 1844 had been strictly upheld the entire system of credit would have broken down, and prices crashed, and the consequent cheapness of all goods would have meant an unprecedented boom for the all-important Lancashire cotton industry.[2]

---

[1] *Report from the Secret Committee . . . on Commercial Distress: Minutes of Evidence.* Evidence of W. Cotton, former Governor of the Bank of England, q. 4065.

[2] *Committee of the House of Lords . . . on Commercial Distress:* Lord Overton's evidence, q. 1597. *Committee of the House of Commons on Commercial Distress:* Turner's evidence, qq. 1027, 1030. Tooke, *A History of Prices,* vol. iv, p. 325.

Manchester therefore supported Peel's policy in spite or rather because of the crisis. Indeed, its support was so ardent that its fanaticism went beyond Peel's opportunism. And how strange was the position which the great Whig families took up in this dispute about the Act of 1844. In one respect the crisis strengthened their influence. All those business men who during the four or five years of prosperity had amassed such huge fortunes and in larger numbers than ever before had invaded the benches of the House of Commons were demoralized and discredited.[1] And the public ready as it was to bow down to wealth would surely show more appreciation in future of the wealth of the landed aristocracy which, in striking contrast to the fluctuations to which these financial adventurers were subject, was stable and of a venerable antiquity.[2]

It was only with an effort, however, that this aristocracy, skilled as it was in the art of retaining power, could learn to speak or understand the language of political economy. This was as true of Lord John Russell, the most intellectual of the aristocrats, as of Macaulay, the most aristocratic of the intellectuals. The teachers of their Liberalism were Livy, Cicero, and Tacitus. To modernize their creed they must go to school with Peel, who was himself Cobden's pupil. The year 1847, therefore, proved a repetition of what had happened twenty years earlier. After the crises of 1817 and 1819 which had given birth to the Radical agitation, the far more serious crisis of 1825 had left the country in a state of dull calm. Triumph had crowned the policy of liberal Conservatism

---

[1] *Secret Committee . . . on Commercial Distress: Minutes of Evidence*, Charles Turner's evidence, qq. 1003-4. 'You have stated that, in your opinion, there were as many substantial men among Liverpool merchants as there were twenty-five years ago. Would you say that the credit of the London market in foreign countries was as high now as it was twenty-five years ago? No, . . . I think it was as good two or three years ago as ever; but . . . houses that were conceived to be enormously wealthy have now been shown to have been worth nothing; people have been so deceived in their estimate of persons whom they considered to be persons of great wealth, that the credit of their country has been seriously damaged.'

[2] *Eclectic Review*, December 1847, art. viii, 'Commercial Failures in 1847': 'Neither the abolition of the Bank Charter, nor the abolition of the Navigation Laws can be recommended on the ground that it will extend the operation of such houses as those of the Gowers, Rae Reid and Lesly Alexander. Speculation, rioting in its resources, and enhancing at one time the price of corn and cotton, stops the wheels of half the mills in Manchester, and becoming bankrupt at another throws the whole productive machinery of the country out of gear, threatening confusion, outrage and the sacrifice of liberty. That is too high a price to pay for the chance of enriching a few gambling merchants: and one of the most fatal effects of commercial bankruptcy is to diminish the political influence of our commercial classes. The discredit of trade tends to restore the ascendancy of landed aristocracy' (N.S., vol. xxi, p. 767).

and economic Liberalism inaugurated by Lord Liverpool, Huskisson and, even thus early, by Peel. In the same way after the crisis of 1837 and the following years and the Chartist agitation—in many respects a revival of the old Radical agitation—the far more serious crisis of 1847, comparable for its gravity with that of 1825, provoked no revolutionary disturbance and, far from shaking, consolidated the ascendancy of the economic policy initiated by Peel in 1842. But the piquant feature of the situation was that Peel was no longer in office, and a Whig Cabinet was reduced to living upon the credit of the man the Whigs had defeated a year earlier. But they did not count. The only man who counted was the fallen Prime Minister, Peel. The Whigs, Sir Charles Wood and the Duke of Bedford, had sought his approval before drawing up the letter of October 25,[1] and now that the crisis had been overcome the country resented more than ever being governed by Ministers no one respected. 'All eyes', Greville remarked, 'are turned upon Peel as if by a sort of fascination.'[2]

It was not only to ratify its banking policy that the Government summoned an extraordinary session of Parliament in November. It was also to pass an Irish Crime and Outrage Bill which the recrudescence of agrarian outrages in certain counties had made necessary. In many respects the Bill resembled the Coercion Bill which Peel had introduced the year before. But its fate was different. It was passed almost with unanimity. Only a handful of extremists, Irish members or Radicals, who never mustered more than twenty for any amendment, voted against it. The Tories, led by Lord George Bentinck and Disraeli, granted Lord John what they had refused Peel, the Liberals and Radicals likewise. Peel, not without irony, congratulated the Ministers on doing at last what they had not allowed him to do. He was the sole politician who remained true to himself and his stature towered above the shifting manœuvres of the various political groups.

When on the following February 3 Parliament reassembled

---

[1] *Greville Memoirs,* November 1, 1847.
[2] Ibid., October 23, 1847. *Blackwood's Magazine,* which, it is true, tended to exaggerate the part played by Peel in the economic crisis, and, accordingly, his responsibility, wrote (July 1847, vol. lxii, p. 114): 'We cannot explain, because we do not understand, the nature of that mysterious and undefinable power which Sir Robert Peel exercises over the proceedings of the present Cabinet.' And later (December 1847, vol. lxii, p. 744): 'Whether he was in office or not, that Parliament was the plaything of Peel. . . . True, he lost office . . . but he did not on that account surrender one iota of power.'

the crisis was a thing of the past. But it was common knowledge that the Government were going to ask for a considerable increase in the naval and army estimates in view of the persistent threat of war between France and England. That is to say, the new Whig Cabinet began as its predecessor had ended. For this deterioration in the relations between the two countries the Prime Minister bore no responsibility. Unfortunately, in every department he was eclipsed by a personality stronger than his own. On questions of political economy and in the Commons he was overshadowed by Peel, on questions of foreign policy and in his own Cabinet by the autocrat of the Foreign Office, Palmerston. We have now to describe Palmerston's attitude and relate his intrigues, and thus complete our account of the Whig Administration during the year and a half between Peel's fall in July 1846 and the revolution in Paris in February 1848.

III PALMERSTON AND GUIZOT (1846–1848)

I

The policy of a good understanding, an *entente cordiale*, which had been patiently pursued for three years by Lord Aberdeen and Guizot was a standing miracle. It was a state of unstable equilibrium which depended upon the fact that in England a Conservative Government with Liberal tendencies was in office, in France a Liberal Government with Conservative tendencies. Their respective paths seemed, therefore, to meet midway. The moment arrived when Peel went too far in the Liberal direction, split his party and handed the government over to the Liberals pure and simple. This upset the balance on which the understanding rested and contributed to hasten Guizot's advance to a purely Conservative policy, the more so because the new Foreign Minister was Palmerston, the avowed enemy of Lord Aberdeen's policy of a good understanding with France. His violent attacks upon it had been the reason why in December 1845 the Greys had refused to give him the Foreign Office. To reassure them he visited Paris at the end of the spring of 1846. He was received with courtesy by the Conservative statesmen, though not, as will appear, without distrust, was warmly welcomed by the leaders of the Opposition, a welcome which, as we shall see, was largely due to motives of political intrigue. The Greys, whose fears had been set at rest by the visit which they regarded as evidence of a desire to conciliate the French, were now ready to accept him as Foreign Secretary in the new Whig Cabinet. But only a few days had passed when their worst apprehensions were justified. The breach between the two Powers was sudden and dramatic.

Its immediate cause was the question which became more pressing as the young Queen Isabella reached marriageable age: what prince should she wed, a bridegroom favoured by London or a bridegroom favoured by Paris?[1] For some months the Queen Mother, Christina, who disliked Trapani, the French candidate for her daughter's hand, had favoured in default of the Duc d'Aumale or even the Duc de Montpensier, whom the French Government refused her, Leopold of Coburg, a candidate dear to the British court if not to the British nation. Lord Aberdeen had not found it easy to refuse Christina's choice formally expressed by her. Nevertheless, he did so. He fell, and Guizot, convinced that Palmerston would not maintain his predecessor's refusal, wrote on July 5 to Bresson instructing him to put forward as husband for the young Queen, not Trapani but the Duke of Cadiz, on condition, it must be clearly understood, that the Infanta's hand was given to Montpensier. 'Press the Duke of Cadiz's suit and place Montpensier beside him.'[2] At once or, as had been previously understood, when the Queen should become a mother? Immediately, there could be no doubt, if Bresson were to interpret Guizot's instruction, as it was interpreted in a letter written to him the same day by the Duke of Glucksberg, the son of Duke Decazes: 'Guizot will not give way about Coburg. He is not without anxiety as to the ill-feeling which the immediate conclusion of Montpensier's marriage may arouse in England. But since he considers himself no longer bound in that quarter he is determined to risk it.'[3] Bresson, therefore, on July 11, secretly proposed to the Queen Mother the simultaneous conclusion of the two marriages. She consented.

[1] For the crisis of the Spanish marriages, see Guizot, *Mémoires pour servir à l'Histoire de mon Temps*, vol. viii, pp. 100 sqq. A. d'Haussonville, *Histoire de la Politique extérieure du Gouvernement Français*, 1830–48, vol. ii, pp. 119 sqq. Sir Henry Lytton Bulwer (Lord Dalling), *The Life of Viscount Palmerston*, vol. iii, chaps. vii and viii, pp. 177 sqq. Paul Thureau-Dangin, *Histoire de la Monarchie de Juillet*, vol. vi, chap. v, pp. 203 sqq. (he makes use of unpublished sources). Herbert C. F. Bell, *Lord Palmerston*, 1936, vol. i, pp. 373 sqq.).
[2] F. Guizot, *Mémoires*, vol. viii, p. 286.
[3] Thureau-Dangin, *Histoire de la Monarchie de Juillet*, vol. vi, p. 207.

When Louis Philippe was informed after the event of the step taken by Bresson he warmly protested.[1] He had been made to break his pledged word. He insisted that Bresson's instructions should be corrected and the marriages should not take place at the same time. Guizot, however, could disregard the royal command without having to temporise long. For the very day, July 20, that Louis Philippe made his protest, Palmerston communicated to Jarnac, the chargé d'affaires in London, the instructions he had sent to Bulwer, the British Ambassador at Madrid. Having asserted the Queen's right to a free choice he went on to express the opinion that only three candidates were likely to be acceptable, Leopold of Saxe-Coburg to whom he gave the first place, and Francois de Paule's two sons, the Duke of Cadiz and the Duke of Seville. This amounted to a declaration of war on France. For it was a formal breach of the undertakings given by Lord Aberdeen. At bottom, however, Palmerston had little liking for this new Coburg. Neither the Brussels, nor the London, nor the Lisbon Coburg liked him and he liked them no better. Nor did he favour the Duke of Cadiz, whom the Queen disliked and who was suspected of being impotent and for that very reason perhaps was so acceptable to Bresson. He finished by proposing the Duke of Seville and for the Infanta, instead of Montpensier, Leopold of Saxe-Coburg. The declaration of war was even more undisguised and, as Palmerston desired, it assumed the aspect of a political rather than a dynastic struggle. For the Duke of Seville had put himself at the head of the Progressive party and Palmerston was no sooner installed at the Foreign Office than he restored what Lord Aberdeen had done his utmost to abolish. There would be once more at Madrid a pro-British party, the Progressives, enjoying the support of the British Embassy, and at loggerheads with the Moderate and Francophile party, supported by the French Embassy. If the match with the Duke of Seville could be brought about and Montpensier completely eliminated, it would be a double victory for the Anglophiles.

Bulwer obeyed his chief's instructions. But he did so with reluctance. For he foresaw the disastrous effect his interference might produce on Queen Christina's mind. 'Are your Ministers mad?' the Prime Minister, Isturiz, asked him. 'They wish for the independence of Spain—so do we, and we are in power; and

---

[1] Louis Philippe to Guizot, July 12, 20, 1846 (*Revue Retrospective*, p. 182).

instead of uniting with us they say in reality, *whatever they may say in words*, that their only conditions of an alliance are our surrender to our opponents. Supposing I were really willing to make this sacrifice, would the Court do so? Would my political friends do so? Would the officers now in command do so?'[1]

Rather than marry her daughter to the leader of the Progressives, Christina suddenly and warmly accepted the proposal of Guizot and Bresson: the Duke of Cadiz for the Queen, the Duke of Montpensier for the Infanta. The two marriages must take place at the same time, so that the Queen's marriage might be invested with the additional dignity accruing from her sister's marriage to the son of the King of the French. Louis Philippe was not easily reconciled to the simultaneous marriage. It was a breach of promise.[2] But since Queen Christina made it a condition of the match with the Duke of Cadiz, Guizot and Bresson declared his scruple of conscience impolitic and ridiculous. At the beginning of September the double marriage was announced and it took place on October 10.

It was a triumph for Guizot and a snub for Palmerston, and so soon after his victory in 1840. The ambitious design entertained by the French Minister was taking shape. France had been defeated in Egypt and Syria. But by making the Western Mediterranean her sphere of influence she would compensate herself for her losses in the Levant. At Naples the Court was closely bound by two marriages to the Court of the Tuileries. In Madrid the Francophiles had the upper hand. The entire coast of Algeria was French territory. The Western Mediterranean was in a fair way to become a French lake. 'In 1840,' Guizot wrote to a friend on November 4, 'on the trifling issue of Egypt, England was victorious in Europe. In 1846, on the important issue of Spain, she and she alone has been defeated.'[3]

But the victory had its dangers to which Guizot, unfortunately, was blind. Did he believe that Palmerston's defeat would be fatal to his position at home and that, like Thiers in 1840, he would be driven from office? If that was his belief, he could have had no notion of the truth, that in this matter of the Spanish marriages the entire country supported Palmerston. With the exception of

[1] Bulwer, *The Life of Viscount Palmerston*, vol. iii, p. 196.
[2] P. Thureau-Dangin, *Histoire de la Monarchie de Juillet*, vol. vi, p. 225.
[3] To Madame Auguste de Gasparin, *Lettres de M. Guizot à sa famille et à ses amis recueillies par Mme. de Witt née Guizot*, p. 245.

two Tory dailies and one Radical organ the entire Press, whatever its political complexion, came out strongly in his favour. Even the sympathies of the Court, annoyed by the rejection of a Coburg, were with him for the first time since the Queen's marriage to Prince Albert. Public indignation was increased by the breach of promise involved in the joint marriage and, since this double dealing seemed more in keeping with the king's character than his Minister's, Louis Philippe, not Guizot, was, most unjustly, made responsible for the intrigue. Two young girls, ran the cry, had been sacrificed to the anxiety of a middle-class monarch to make a brilliant match for his son. Sentiment had free play, and all England lamented these unhappy women, condemned for the first time in the history of European monarchies to make marriages that were not love matches. In reality it was a trifling matter which had put England and France at loggerheads. The Spain of 1846 was no longer the Spain of Charles V and Philip II. It was Spain without the Indies, a small country which had not learnt from its fall the prosaic virtues that make small nations great, a poor little country, the prey of civil war and party intrigue. But both Governments were victims of the same optical illusion and the conflict was as serious as if the stake had been more considerable.

Three months had sufficed to destroy the good understanding, jettisoned almost ostentatiously by the French Government and in circumstances which did it no credit. Palmerston swore revenge.

2

In the first place Palmerston attempted to restore the alignment of 1840, a return to 1814 and 1815, an alliance with the Northern Powers against France. He addressed himself to Metternich. A member of the British Embassy at Paris, Lord Howden, had discovered that the Duke of Montpensier's marriage with the Infanta contravened a provision of the Treaty of Utrecht. For that treaty laid down that the crowns of France and Spain might never be united in a single ruler. But if Queen Isabella were childless, Montpensier might become the Queen of Spain's husband. And it was not impossible that he himself or one of his descendants might one day succeed to the French throne. The contention was preposterous. For the Treaty of Utrecht had never debarred a Bourbon from the Spanish throne. Indeed, Philip V was himself a Bourbon. This did not prevent Lord Ponsonby, the British ambassador at Vienna, from making use of it to win Metternich over. The latter, however, was as favourably disposed to Guizot as he was hostile to Palmerston. For the former had just proposed and obtained his assent to an understanding between Austria and France to defend the principles of conservatism and order menaced by Palmerston. The barricades of 1830 were a remote memory, and when Ponsonby pressed Metternich he obtained no satisfaction. The Chancellor did not dispute the force of his argument, but said that it was no concern of his. He had no interest whatever in the dispute. For in his opinion the accession of Queen Isabella was itself a breach of the Treaty of Utrecht.

Palmerston turned to the Czar Nicholas and this time with more hope of success. For he was aware of the Emperor's invincible hostility to the July Monarchy, and he pursued on principle a policy of close and cordial relations with Russia.[1] It was, in fact, the policy he practised in Greece through 1847, where British and Russian agents fought side by side against the dictator, Colletti, a client of France. But on this matter of the Spanish marriage, Nicholas proved as adamant as Metternich and expressed his agreement with the Austrian point of view.

Finally, Palmerston turned to Prussia. At Berlin the Liberals, a very influential body, were urging the King of Prussia to break with Metternich and unite the whole of Germany under his ægis. In their view the *Zollverein* was but a preliminary sketch in the economic field of this political ideal. That the British Government was now Liberal might be expected to make it more favourable to these revolutionary ideas. It should be easier, therefore, for Lord John's Ministry than for Peel's to detach Prussia from Austria. But in history the individual counts for a great deal. Peel, though in the public view the pillar of the good understanding with France, was also, in full agreement with Prince Albert, Stockmar, and Bunsen, an admirer of Prussia, who wanted to see Germany a united nation and a treaty of alliance concluded between Prussia and England. Palmerston, on the other hand, though his return to the Foreign Office had sufficed to destroy the understanding with France, also entertained deep-rooted and persistent misgivings in regard to the

[1] Letter to Lord Bloomfield, January 23, 1847 (Bulwer, op. cit., vol. iii, p. 278).

Prussian monarchy and its territorial ambitions. In any case, whether for this reason or another, the negotiations were unsuccessful. Like Russia, Prussia adopted the Austrian attitude.

The only revenge Palmerston could take on Guizot at the moment was extremely complicated and indirect. At the beginning of 1846 an insurrection had occurred in the Polish provinces of Prussia and Austria. Since the Poles of the Republic of Cracow took part in the rising, the three Powers, Russia, Prussia, and Austria had occupied its territory. Paris and London had protested and obtained a pledge from the occupying Powers to evacuate Cracow as soon as order had been completely restored. The affair of the Spanish marriages, and the consequent quarrel between England and France, seemed a good opportunity to adopt a different course, and the Republic of Cracow was re-incorporated into Austria. Opinion in Paris was ardently pro-Polish, and Guizot was confronted with the problem of satisfying the French public without breaking with Metternich. English public opinion was not so favourable to Poland. Not only were the Conservatives as Protestants out of sympathy with Catholic Poland, but the Radicals, so ready to defend oppressed Catholics in other parts of the world, in Ireland, for example, did not favour a rising of the nobility against which the Austrian Government had been assisted in Galicia by an insurrection of the peasants.[1] Palmerston, moreover, was sceptical as to the effectiveness of any protest, even a joint protest by England and France. What, in fact, had the two Western Powers accomplished fifteen years earlier at the time of the great Polish rebellion? But he took care to put forward the dispute between England and France, when he refused to draw up a formal protest conjointly with the French Government. He saddled Guizot, as the author of the Spanish marriages and, therefore, the dissolution of the *entente cordiale*,

---

[1] See Harriet Martineau, *History of the Thirty Years' Peace*, chap. iii, *sub finem*. She recants the sympathy she had expressed with the Polish insurrection in 1830, and writes: 'It was not till long afterwards that the discovery was made that the Poles had been fighting—for nationality, it is true—but not for national freedom; that they had not the remotest idea of giving any liberty to the middle and lower classes of their people. . . . They themselves impute their latter disasters to dissensions among themselves. . . . But it also seems clear that their cause was doomed from the beginning, from the absence of any basis of popular sympathy. The great masses were indifferent, or, rather, more disposed in favour of Russian than of Polish rule.' Also *The Nonconformist*, December 30, 1846: 'We are not going to declaim on the subject of unhappy Poland. We think a good deal of sympathy has been wasted on it, and we advise its more sentimental advocates to read its history.'

with the entire responsibility for this crime against international law and national liberty.[1]

The twofold drama, the Spanish marriages and the annexation of Cracow, had been enacted during the recess of Parliament. When Parliament reassembled in January 1847 these incidents, which had caused such a stir in the Press, played no part in the debates. The leaders of the Conservative Opposition were not the men to blame the Government for having failed to uphold at Cracow the cause of Polish independence.[2] On the contrary, they justified the action of the Austrian Government.

They protested, it is true, against Palmerston's breach with a Conservative France. But the protest was a mere formality. Haunted, as they were, by the fear that a Ministerial crisis might restore Peel to office, they were not disposed to do anything which might shake the Cabinet of which Palmerston was a member. And the majority of the members, the Peelites, Whigs, and Radicals, who regularly supported the Government, had no quarrel with him. They agreed with him in condemning the dishonourable trick of which Louis Philippe and his Minister had been guilty in Madrid and the violation of the treaty by the Austrian Government at Cracow. Was he to be censured for not having gone further and broken more decisively with Guizot and Metternich? That would amount to a censure for not going to war.[3] And if there was anything which the country was determined to avoid at all costs it was war. Preoccupied by the grave situation in Ireland, the nation thought only of economic problems and showed an indifference, almost aversion, to problems of foreign policy.

'Foreign affairs', Brougham stated most truly during the debate on the Address, 'interested that House [the House of Lords] more

---

[1] T. Mackright, *Thirty Years of Foreign Policy*, 1855, p. 378: 'How could the perpetrator of the Spanish marriages remonstrate with any propriety against the iniquities of other statesmen? The injury done to Cracow was a grievous one; but the crime was not of a deeper dye than that committed in Spain.' See H. C. Bell, *Lord Palmerston*, vol. i, pp. 389–90.

[2] Bulwer, *Life of Viscount Palmerston*, vol. iii, p. 324.

[3] Lord Palmerston to Lord Normanby, February 23, 1847: 'We are very anxious to hear that the differences between you and Guizot have been in some way or other arranged. . . . You know how sensitive people are here about anything which, in their wisdom, or rather in their want of it, they may think likely to lead to war; and you are well aware that this feeling is perhaps strongest among our own friends and supporters, though it is also easily assumed by the other parties, who are in their hearts hostile to us, though for the moment they allow us to live on sufferance' (Bulwer, *Life of Viscount Palmerston*, vol. iii, p. 294).

than they did the other House; and they interested the other House much more than they did the country. He believed', he went on to say, 'that "foreign" royal marriages were as perfectly and entirely a matter of indifference to the good people of England, Ireland, and Scotland as they were to the inhabitants of the new planet discovered by M. Leverrier; except for those who read romances or who had nothing else to do, or whose affairs were in such a prosperous state that they had time to attend to matters of mere indifference.'[1]

A few months later, during the General Election, Palmerston, replying in his constituency to an attack by a Chartist speaker, delivered a long speech which lasted five hours, justifying the policy of the Government and, in particular, his own policy at the Foreign Office. But it fell flat in face of the universal indifference. It was neither applauded nor censured.

'Foreign affairs', The Times pointed out, 'had played no part in the combats and victories of the election. The struggle had been fought on British soil and beneath the British flag. Not a word had been heard of the Czar, of Louis Philippe, of the Spanish and Portuguese Queens, or even of the formidable Mr. Polk. Yet meanwhile two American generals were engaged in strangling Mexico and annexing territory as extensive as Europe. But John Bull cared little for the fate of continents.'[2]

3

Palmerston did not complain of this general indifference. When the session of 1847 opened it was far from his desire that questions of foreign policy should be discussed in Parliament or, if they were, made the subject of heated debate. Thanks to the apathy of

---

[1] H. of L., January 19, 1847, Brougham's speech (*Parliamentary Debates*, 3rd Ser., vol. lxxxix, p. 44). Cf. *Edinburgh Review*, April 1847, art. xi, 'The Spanish Marriages' (vol. lxxxv, pp. 490-1): 'Questions of foreign policy, unless when they bear directly upon the honour of the nation or the commercial interests of the empire, attract but little public attention in this country. Happily, the general course of our foreign policy is not subject to the same vicissitudes as belong to legislation on our domestic affairs. Continental alliances are no longer the rallying cries of party. The larger interests of England cannot now be sacrificed for the aggrandisement of the German dominions of her sovereign. She moves undisturbed in her own orbit, while she shares in the general motion of the system of civilized nations to which she belongs.' 'We think', the *Review* continues, 'that this indifference to questions of foreign policy, an indifference common to the public, to Parliament and to the Ministers, whether belonging to one party or the other, is pushed too far.'

[2] *The Times*, August 4, 1847.

the nation his policy escaped criticism. Remote from the scrutiny of the public, his colleagues, or the Court, he was free to make it increasingly what we may perhaps call a domestic foreign policy. Since he could no longer, as in 1840, play Metternich against Guizot, it was necessary and feasible to create difficulties for both by working up popular discontent against them. Would the bookish wisdom of these two statesmen be able to hold permanently in check the ferment and the impatient longing to renew the revolution of 1830 observable throughout Europe? Every element in the West that was youthful, liberal, and progressive sympathized without regard to national interests with the aspirations of young Germany and young Italy. It was a rich mine for a foreign secretary to exploit who was the heir of Canning's 'Æolian' policy. England, like the god of the winds, should unleash the tempest or lay it at her will.

In Paris, Palmerston replaced Lord Cowley by Lord Normanby, a great Whig nobleman who under Melbourne had aroused the wrath of the Tories by governing Ireland in agreement with O'Connell. He lost no time in adopting the typical attitude of the Palmerstonian diplomat and attempted to do in Paris what his fellows were doing in Madrid, Lisbon, and Athens, to make the Liberal Opposition an Anglophile party inspired and led by himself.

Among the Parisian politicians he found in the person of Thiers an ideal instrument of his purpose.[1] The victim in 1840 of Palmerston's policy, he had never ceased ever since to accuse Guizot of humiliating France before England and sacrificing her honour. And his motive in composing so laboriously his great history of the Revolution, Consulate, and Empire had been to denounce England's naval despotism. He surely was the very last man to advocate now friendly relations with a Government whose foreign policy was conducted by Palmerston. But he regarded the Spanish marriages as Guizot's revenge not only on the victor, but the vanquished of 1840, and was hungering to avenge himself in turn on Guizot even if he could do so only by allying

---

[1] For the estimate of Thiers formed by the English Liberals, see *Morning Chronicle*, July 10, 1846: 'He neither loves nor hates, but his little soul has a colossal aptitude for mischief. Revolution for revolution's sake, war for war's sake—such is his simple political creed; one, however, marvellously fitting him for the leadership of a many-sectioned opposition, each of which sections has its own object to gain; but, different as may be the object, to be gained only by revolution and war.'

himself with Palmerston. In 1840 Guizot had plotted against him in London. He would take his revenge by plotting against Guizot. And it was sauce to his revenge that it was in collusion with Palmerston, against whom as well as against himself Guizot had plotted with the Court of Windsor, that he undertook to make Louis Philippe, a royal 'coward', dismiss Guizot, if the British Government would help him to make the position of the latter impossible. He wrote to a Liberal Italian refugee in London, Panizzi, letters which the latter was to pass on to Palmerston and which were sent through the British Embassy to escape the search of Guizot's police.[1]

Immediately after the conclusion of the debate on the Address, whose unimportance had disappointed Guizot's opponents in Paris, Palmerston published a blue book containing diplomatic dispatches relative to the Spanish marriages. They made it plain that on August 31 Guizot had given a formal pledge that they should not take place at the same time. Palmerston, who had wanted the debate in the British Parliament to pass off quietly,[2] was determined to ensure that this would not be the case in the French Chamber. He was successful.

The Liberals and democrats joined the Catholics in accusing Guizot of betraying Poland and the Liberals accused him of destroying the good understanding with England for the sole purpose of procuring by dishonourable means an advantageous match for the King's son. In language carefully weighed Guizot protested against the publication by Palmerston in his blue book of dispatches, in which conversations he had held with Lord Normanby were published without having been first submitted to him in accordance with the accepted usage for any corrections he might think necessary. Whereupon, to the amazement of British politicians who regarded the protest as justified, his opponents launched out into denunciations of Guizot who, so they said, had insulted Lord Normanby by giving him the lie and

---

[1] For the full text of the letters written by Thiers to Panizzi, see Louis Fagan's *The Life of Anthony Panizzi*, 1880.

[2] On February 11 he wrote to Lord Normanby: 'I do not think we shall have any discussion upon these matters. . . . We are desirous of preventing discussion: the question cannot stand better than it does in public opinion as to the relative conduct of the two Governments; and as regards the conflicting interests of the two countries, nobody could, in our Parliament, add anything to the conviction that must be produced on the mind of every Englishman by the speeches in the French Chamber' (Bulwer, op. cit., vol. iii, p. 185).

owed the ambassador an apology.[1] The Opposition, however, though it made so much noise, had taken its stand on ground too obviously false after so many years of declamation against the selfishness of British policy, and Guizot, after a Parliamentary battle which lasted twelve days, obtained the largest majority he had ever secured from the Chamber of Deputies, 248 to 84. An incident followed which made considerable stir in Paris. A ball was given at the Embassy and an invitation sent to Guizot subsequently withdrawn with the explanation that it had been sent by mistake. Lord Normanby had to atone for this rudeness. For weeks the Opposition had been calling upon Guizot to apologize to the ambassador for his remarks about the blue book. He did nothing of the sort, and in the end it was the latter who had to apologize to Guizot for the incident of the ball.

In Portugal the Queen and her husband, Ferdinand of Saxe Coburg, the Prince Consort's first cousin, were confronted by an armed rebellion of the nation against the autocracy they had attempted to impose. The Portuguese Government invoked the treaty of the Quadruple Alliance and sought help in accordance with its terms from the three Governments of London, Paris, and Madrid. Palmerston, always eager to dissociate himself from the French, made Lord Methuen's old treaty the pretext for acting independently and offering the Queen of Portugal his good offices as an ally. He found himself obliged to consult Madrid and Paris. But he recovered the advantage by negotiating a peace between the Queen and the insurgents on the basis of mutual concessions. The rebels were granted an amnesty, and the leaders of the Liberal party received a pledge that they would eventually be admitted to share in the Government. But the Queen was barely secure on her throne when she broke her promises and restored the former despotism.

In Spain, Palmerston was prepared for any intrigue which might destroy French influence in Madrid. At one moment he even opened negotiations with the Carlists. He had solid ground for hope when the young Queen, loathing the imbecile husband

---

[1] *Greville Memoirs*, February 16, 1847: 'Normanby says all Paris considered that he was affronted by Guizot, and he was obliged to take it up. Here no one individual that I have seen construed what Guizot said in that sense. Such is the difference of the respective atmospheres of the two towns. There all fire, here all ice.' Cf. Palmerston to Lord Normanby, February 11, 23, 1847 (Bulwer, *The Life of Viscount Palmerston*, vol. iii, pp. 183, 293).

forced upon her, banished him to a suburb of Madrid and began a long series of love affairs by taking for her lover General Serrano, who put his influence at the service of the Progressives and the British Embassy. But Serrano fell from favour, the redoubtable Narvaez returned to power, and at Madrid, as elsewhere, the victory of the reactionaries was, paradoxical as it might seem at first sight, a victory for the policy of the July Monarchy.

Thus when the autumn of 1847 opened, Guizot's Mediterranean policy was everywhere successful, or at least had the appearance of success. And the seal was set on his triumph when in September the Duc d'Aumale was appointed Governor of Algeria—his father had wanted to make him viceroy[1]—amid the angry but impotent protests of the French Left and the London Press. He immediately began the campaign which ended in December with the surrender of Abd-el-Kader, whose raids had been equipped throughout by British money, and the completion of the French conquest.[2] But the moment was at hand when in other theatres Palmerston would take his revenge, or rather events would give it to him.

Switzerland was in the throes of civil war. The Radicals, who were winning all along the line, and who, since their conquest of the Canton of St. Gall at the beginning of 1847, had held the majority of the Cantons, were at war with the Conservatives on a constitutional issue. Should Switzerland become an organized federal State or remain the extremely loose federation of Cantons approved by the great Powers in 1815? And they also opposed the toleration of the Jesuits by the Cantons of the Conservative minority. Neither the English nor the French ruling class had much sympathy with the political aims of the Swiss Radicals. But neither liked the Jesuits. When, therefore, the absolutist Powers called for a diplomatic protest, even, if necessary, armed intervention, to compel the Radicals to respect the Swiss con-

[1] *Jerrold's Weekly Newspaper*, September 25, 1847: 'It is said that Lord Palmerston has protested against the continued occupation of Algeria by France, to which M. Guizot has replied by notifying the appointment of the Duc d'Aumale to the viceroyalty of their African possession.'

[2] See Lord Normanby's words to Brignoles, despatch of November 4, 1846, 'that his Government considered it its duty to support Abd-el-Kader as it had always done' (Hildebrand, *Geschichte Frankreichs*, vol. ii, p. 692). In London it was the subject of pleasantry, see *Jerrold's Weekly Newspaper*, September 25, 1847: 'By some mystery Abd-el-Kader has possessed himself of a park of cannons, and to crown the whole of these bellicose antecedents, two English vessels of war have been taking soundings at the mouth of the Po.'

stitution, they met with the same vacillations in London and in Paris. But the intentions of the respective Ministers for Foreign Affairs gave them a totally different significance. Palmerston wanted to prevent an understanding between Guizot and Metternich, Guizot to do nothing that would embroil him with Metternich. He might, indeed, have committed himself more decisively to the Austrian Chancellor if, on two occasions and on this particular issue of eventual military intervention, Louis Philippe's caution had not held him back. In any case, whatever the intentions of the two statesmen, they had recalled their Ministers at Berne—the Frenchman because he was suspected of being too hostile to Metternich; the Englishman because he was thought to be too favourable to him. The new French Minister, Bois-le-Comte, was an ardent Catholic and a violent opponent of the Radicals, the English was Jonathan Peel, a son of Sir Robert, passionately hostile to the cause of the Catholic Cantons. Guizot's tactics were to involve Palmerston in a joint intervention of the great Powers. Palmerston's were not to refuse outright, but to drag out the negotiations by proposing in opposition to the plan put forward by the Powers another conceived in a different spirit, and meanwhile to urge the Swiss Radicals through Jonathan Peel to act quickly and thus anticipate the intervention of the Powers. They acted quickly indeed. When on November 27 Sir Stratford Canning left London to present the same note to the Diet on the one part, to the Sonderbund of the revolting Cantons on the other, Lucerne had already surrendered three days before without resistance to the eighty thousand troops under the command of General Dufour.

Lucerne in 1847 avenged the fate of Cracow in 1846. It was a serious defeat for Metternich and, consequently, for Guizot, who had openly made common cause with him, and, therefore, an important victory for Palmerston and at the same time for Western Liberalism. For Radical Switzerland had become the refuge of all the revolutionaries persecuted in Germany and Italy. General Dufour's victory was their own. In this way events in Switzerland confronted the foreign policy of England and France respectively with novel problems. And their policies, if always opposed, were always inextricably linked.

4

The unrest in Italy, whose first symptom had been the election of Pius IX, grew more intense. The fortunate balance which had perhaps enabled the two Conservative Governments of London and Paris to entertain, for a time at least, the prospect of an Italian confederation which would take no account of Austria, to be formed by the Italian rulers under the presidency of the Holy See, was a thing of the past. That solution of the Italian question was no longer possible after Peel's fall, Palmerston's return to the Foreign Office, the Spanish marriages, the breach with France, and the rapprochement between France and Austria. Would the two nations then frankly oppose each other's policy in Italy, France taking sides with Austria against Italian independence, England for the Italian revolution against Metternich? The situation was far more complicated than that and the language addressed to Metternich by the representatives of the two Powers was practically identical. 'Take care,' Ponsonby warned him, 'an Austrian invasion of Italy would be met by French intervention and the effect of the latter, whatever the intentions of the French Government, would be a revival of revolutionary agitation.' 'Take care,' Flahaut told him, 'public opinion would not permit my Government to remain inactive in face of an Austrian expedition to Naples or Piedmont. The best safeguard of your position in Lombardy is to do nothing.' And when they addressed the various Italian Governments the language of the British and French representatives was still substantially the same. 'We are', they both said with equal sincerity, 'in favour of maintaining the *status quo* as regards your territorial arrangements. But if you desire to retain your power you would be well advised to concede to your subjects indispensable reforms.' But at this point the likeness between the two policies ceased. The reforms Guizot advised the Italian rulers to grant were the minimum which would enable him to state in Paris that he had not betrayed the Liberal cause, a minimum, however, which in his opinion was the maximum which ought to be granted. It should be an administrative not a political reform, nothing resembling the French 'Charter' of 1814. Palmerston, on the contrary, refused to attach any restriction to the legitimate demands of the Italian popular party, and it was a Constitution of the English type which he urged the Princes to have the courage to grant. What was the result of the attitudes adopted respectively by the two Powers? When Bresson on his appointment as Minister at the court of Naples stopped on his journey to visit the various Italian courts, he was received as a trusty adviser and admitted to the secret deliberations of the Cabinet, whereas the populace displayed a freezing hostility to ruler and diplomat alike. When, on the other hand, Palmerston obtained his colleagues' consent to dispatch Lord Minto, Lord Privy Seal, to Italy on an extraordinary mission to pass on from State to State the advice of the British Government, he cut the figure of a popular leader rather than a diplomatic agent. He had hardly arrived at an Italian city when, with his full approval, a public reception was arranged for him, and when from his hotel balcony he answered the plaudits of the crowd it was with the cry, 'Viva l'independenza Italiana.' After this he made his way to the palace to convey to the monarch the wishes of his own people rather than those of a foreign government. Both Foreign Ministers were playing a difficult hand and walking on a tight-rope. But though the temperaments of the prim Frenchman and the frivolous Englishman were in other respects so unlike, both had the same taste for this dangerous game, the same passion for the web of diplomatic intrigue.

Rome, where he arrived in January, was the avowed goal of Lord Minto's journey.[1] And it was the justification of this extraordinary mission of a British statesman to Italy. For England had no official representative at the Court of Rome. Moreover, Lord Minto had a difficult task to perform in his negotiations with the Holy See. He must persuade the Pope not to ban 'the godless colleges' which the British Government had founded in Ireland to facilitate contact between young Catholics and young Protestants. He must persuade him to put pressure on the Irish hierarchy to make them in turn restrain the priests under their authority and prevent them from conniving at agrarian crimes. In return the British Government undertook to carry a Bill establishing regular diplomatic relations between England and the Holy See. Moreover, it was most desirable, and the restoration of diplomatic relations would tend in that direction, that British influence in Rome should be strengthened to the detriment of French. This,

[1] For Lord Minto's mission, see Evelyn Ashley, *The Life of Henry John Temple, Viscount Palmerston*, 1846-65, vol. i, pp. 33 sqq.

however, was perhaps the most difficult of all Lord Minto's commissions. He found the influence of Guizot and his ambassador, Rossi, firmly entrenched.

In April 1847, in consequence of a popular rising, the Austrian Government had occupied Ferrara, a town of the Papal States, and in the teeth of the Cardinal Legate's protests. The Pope himself had protested publicly. The King of Sardinia, who had already carried out several reforms in his dominions, had placed his army at the Pope's disposition to resist an Austrian invasion. For this step he had been praised by Lord Minto, but blamed by the French Government which had warned him that, if he had to face an Austrian army and were defeated, he could not count on French help. And the Pope, who feared equally an Austrian invasion and the ostensible help of a Liberal Piedmont, was grateful to France for bringing about an amicable settlement of the dispute by the evacuation of Ferrara in December. And he was grateful to Rossi who, in accord with Guizot, while advising him to grant certain reforms—for example, to admit laymen to administrative posts and to his Ministry—encouraged him to refuse a system of constitutional government. French influence at the Court of Rome had never been more powerful and Lord Minto felt helpless to counteract it, when he received welcome news, not from Piedmont or Tuscany, through which he had passed and where he had observed so many favourable symptoms, but from Southern Italy where as yet he had not set foot.

On January 12, 1848, a rebellion broke out at Palermo. The entire population took part in it, the nobility, the middle class, and the populace. Paralysed by this unanimity the garrison did not move and let things take their course. The victorious revolutionaries demanded that the constitution of 1812 should be restored. The revolution spread to Naples and the entire country. At Naples, Turin, and Florence, formal constitutions were granted and even at Rome one was promised. It was a striking success for Palmerston's policy, and Lord Minto went on to Naples to act as mediator between the monarchy of the Two Sicilies and Sicilian separatism.

It was no easy task, and, if this revolutionary movement was from one point of view a triumph for Palmerston, it was in many respects a dangerous triumph. For France was not wholly Guizot's France, far from it. There was another France, Liberal, Jacobin, and revolutionary, which might profit by these insurrections in a fashion not at all to Palmerston's taste. But he was well aware that an Æolian policy involved these risks and he was gambler enough to incur them without raising an eyebrow. Guizot was his first consideration. De Montessuy, the French chargé d'affaires at Naples, invited the English representative, Lord Napier, to join with him in offering, as the King desired, their joint mediation to the Sicilian rebels. The latter refused. 'Go alone, if you think fit. But I must warn you that the boat which takes you to Sicily will also carry letters to our agents and influential Sicilians explaining why I have refused to accompany you. As for associating myself with you in this matter, believe me I am very sorry, but it is out of the question. Anywhere else, in any other region of the globe, in China itself, I could perhaps accede to your request. But in Sicily English and French interests are poles apart.'[1]

Why just here? Because British policy had found an unexpected opportunity to upset Guizot's new 'family compact'.

Thus the revolution at Palermo was Palmerston's revenge for the Spanish marriages, as the defeat of the Sonderbund had avenged the annexation of Cracow. But Guizot, thus twice defeated, did not relinquish the offensive. He kept a strict watch on Piedmont and had troops in readiness at Toulon, Port-Vendres, and in Algiers, where Abd-el-Kader's surrender had released large forces, to sail for Italy at the word of command.[2]

He continued to interest himself in the affairs of Switzerland and plotted with Metternich, who had not abandoned the cause of the Jesuits in the rebel Cantons and with Frederick William IV, who was furious with the Radicals of Neuchâtel for their disregard of his rights as suzerain. A meeting was arranged for March 15 at Paris to discuss with special representatives of Vienna and Berlin the situation in Switzerland, probably also in Germany and Italy. Guizot regarded the meeting, on the whole with good reason from the purely diplomatic standpoint,[3] as a victory for

---

[1] A. d'Haussonville, *Histoire de la Politique Extérieure du Gouvernement Français, 1830-48*, vol. ii, p. 271.

[2] Not to invade the United Kingdom, as J. F. C. Hearnshaw states (*Cambridge History of British Foreign Policy, 1783-1919*, vol. ii, p. 297) without referring to any other authorities than d'Haussonville, *Histoire de la Politique Extérieure . . .* , vol. ii, pp. 381 sqq., and Th. Martin, *Life of the Prince Consort*, vol. ii, p. 2, where nothing of the sort is to be found.

[3] His diplomatic victory would have proved a mare's nest from the military point of view. If the combination had materialized, it would have produced a coalition against England. Even if Louis Philippe's caution had allowed Guizot to return under another

his foreign policy. And British public opinion, in so far as it was vaguely aware of the new combination, gave the credit of it to Louis Philippe, though, in fact, the latter, more cautious by nature than Guizot, or become more timid with age, had often been taken by his Minister farther than he had wished to go and had sometimes even held him back. The King was unpopular in England. Every week for months *Punch* dragged him in the mud. But it was impossible to withhold a measure of admiration from this wily monarch who owed his throne to a revolution, and to whom the absolutist Powers were now turning for support when threatened in their turn by revolutionary Liberalism—Austria and Prussia at least, for Russia would not commit herself—and inviting him to preside over their policy of reaction.

This estimate of the situation, however, failed to grasp how insecure the position of Guizot and his sovereign really was. Could the British be ignorant that their government was based, in a country of thirty millions, on a 'legal country' of some two hundred thousand, was hated by the clergy in spite of all the advances it made to them, despised by the intelligentsia, respected but moderately by the army, though the military reputation of the King's sons stood high, and permanently threatened with a rising of the Parisian populace which had placed it in power and considered itself betrayed? Did they know nothing of that campaign of 'banquets' which had lasted for months to secure a reform of the franchise, a campaign secretly fostered by Thiers and perhaps also by the British Embassy? In fact, the true position was understood neither in Paris nor in London. It would, indeed, be an exaggeration to say that no one in England foresaw the overthrow of the Government. But this foresight was confined to isolated utterances in the Press. In the eyes of the vast mass of Englishmen, and probably in the opinion of the Foreign Office, the 'modern Ulysses' had successfully accomplished his *tour de force*, and by electoral corruption and administrative pressure, by strengthening the army and the fortifications of Paris, had entrenched himself securely in power. Men hoped that the Napoleon of peace would find his Moscow, but dared not believe it.[1] In

guise to Thiers's warlike dreams, though the nominal president of the coalition he would, in fact, have been assigned the most dangerous position by his allies, and have borne the entire brunt of British attacks.

[1] See, on this point, Wordsworth's conversation with Cooper in September 1846 (*Cooper's Journal*, p. 325).

Italy and Germany monarchs might surrender to the revolution. In Paris there would probably be nothing more than a riot, suppressed even more vigorously than that of 1834. It is not surprising, therefore, that when Parliament met in February 1848 the Government asked for credits to strengthen the army and navy. London had cherished too long the belief that the prestige achieved by her foreign policy would suffice with a minimum of military and naval expenditure to hold the Continental Powers in check. Now when the latter, with the exception of Russia, and for all Palmerston's advances to her she could not be counted upon, were united or preparing to unite, and moreover, under the presidency of France, it was high time to arm.

5

In the spring of 1847 Lord John had drawn his colleagues' attention to the unpreparedness of the country in the event of a war with France. He agreed with Palmerston that if a French army of thirty or forty thousand men succeeded in effecting a landing nothing could prevent them marching on London. Palmerston 'did not, indeed, imagine the capture of London would force England to peace. But how horrid it would be to have that capital of the commercial world sacked by an enraged soldiery.'[1]

In October, when the Cabinet met to discuss the emergency measures which must be taken to meet the economic crisis, Wellington, who had already been very pessimistic in the spring, pressed Lord John to insist once more on the urgent need to take precautions against the French peril. The regular army must be raised from fifty to seventy thousand and a hundred and fifty thousand militiamen should be available for service.[2] A rumour of these demands made by the Commander-in-Chief circulated in the Press. The alarmists still harped upon the pamphlet published by the Prince de Joinville some years previously, which was regarded by British public opinion as an attempt to prepare the French for a revival of Napoleon's project of invading England. And the matter had been brought before the public by a Press campaign which had continued for more than two months[3]

[1] Lord Broughton, *Recollections of a Long Life*, April 14 and 24, 1847, vol. vi, pp. 187 sqq.
[2] Ibid., October 19, 1847 (vol. vi, pp. 199 sqq.); also *Lord Palmerston's Memorandum*, December 1846 (Bulwer, *Life of Viscount Palmerston*, vol. iii, p. 325).
[3] *Morning Chronicle*, December 21, 1847; *The Times*, December 25, 1847; *Morning Chronicle*, January 3, 1848; *The Times*, January 5, 1848; *Morning Chronicle*, January 10, 1848.

when, on February 18, Lord John in his speech introducing the Budget drew his hearers' attention to the need to strengthen the national defences. He did not propose to increase the size of the regular army, but only to bring five thousand men back from India to England and undertake a reform of the militia which, if successful, would make it possible to avoid increasing the regular army in 1849. Additional expenditure must also be incurred to strengthen the navy. The total additional outlay for both services would be £358,000. In themselves his demands were moderate. But they were a serious burden coming at a time when months of economic distress had diminished the revenue. To meet them the Government proposed to raise the income tax from 3 to 5 per cent. These proposals were made by the Prime Minister in a rambling and ill-considered speech, whose worst blunder was a violent attack on the French military preparations in language which was not tempered by regard for the courtesies of diplomacy.

We should notice a feature peculiar to this 'scare'. It did not arise among the public and shake the Government's inertia. It was caused by the action of the Government, and from the outset, though the proposals made by the Cabinet were so moderate, was confronted by the hostility of the public.[1]

For in the public mind the brilliance of Palmerston's foreign policy had not compensated for the irritation caused by Lord John's feeble handling of domestic affairs. Indeed, in February 1848 the former appeared in many respects to be as discredited as the latter. Tory speakers replied to Lord John's demands for further armament by renewing the protests they had made the previous year against the results of his Foreign Secretary's mischief-making. The Tory Press accused the Prime Minister of attempting to escape from the difficulties produced by his Cabinet's domestic policy by engineering the diversion of a war.[2] And the Tories were aware that public opinion was on their side to a greater extent than it had been. Moreover, the Queen and the Prince Consort were now of their opinion. For they had begun to forget the affair of the Spanish marriages and

---

[1] Hobhouse had already recorded in his account of the Cabinet Meeting, held on October 19, 1847, Macaulay's fears on this score: 'Macaulay . . . said the proposal was quite right, although it would probably turn out the Government' (Lord Broughton, *Recollections of a Long Life*, vol. vi, pp. 199 and 200).

[2] *Standard*, September 5, 1847.

even to wonder whether, if in 1846 Lord Aberdeen had still been at the Foreign Office, the incident would have occurred. And the number of papers opposed to Palmerston's policy was increasing. In the opinion of *The Times* the apprehensions felt by the far-seeing, when, in July 1846, he returned to the Foreign Office, had been only too well justified.[1] In Switzerland the Radicals had received Stratford Canning's attempts at mediation unfavourably. And what were we heading for in Italy? The *Morning Chronicle* joined in the outcry. It had just left Radicalism for Peelism and, as everyone knew, Peel, passionately devoted to the cause of peace, had little sympathy with the revolutionary and bellicose programme of national liberty. In this perhaps he was once again representative of public opinion. The leading organ of advanced Liberalism, the *Daily News*, was compelled to admit that the Italian risings had by no means been greeted with the enthusiastic welcome accorded twenty years before to the Spanish and Greek revolutions.[2] And even within the Liberal ranks two eccentric publicists, Urquhart and Anstey, who had been returned to Parliament in August 1847, took up several sittings of the House with a lengthy denunciation of Palmerston's policy which, they said, had since 1830 been consistently anti-French and pro-Russian.

Palmerston received these attacks with his usual light-heartedness. He accused his critics of being in the pay of a foreign Government. The Tory morning and evening papers, the *Morning Herald* and the *Standard*, had, he said, been bought by the Government of Louis Philippe.[3] *The Times* was the mouthpiece of Vienna, the *Morning Chronicle* of Paris. The French King had financed the election of Urquhart and Anstey, and in the last ten years, he stated a little later, no less than £60,000 had been received by Urquhart, Anstey, and Westmacott, the editor of the *Portfolio*, for their unremitting campaign against him.[4] But he had to encounter more dangerous foes, and could not shut his eyes to the fact that they represented ideas and sentiments deep-rooted in the public mind. They came from the ranks of the economists, the victors in the great struggle of 1846. And foremost among them was Richard Cobden.

[1] *The Times*, January 27, 1848.   [2] *Daily News*, September 17, 1847.
[3] *Economist*, September 20, 1846.
[4] Lord Palmerston to his brother, Sir William Temple, July 24, 1852 (E. Ashley, *Life of Viscount Palmerston*, vol. i, pp. 364 sqq.).

A year and a half ago Cobden had emerged from his triumphant struggle for the repeal of the Corn Laws a ruined man. But a public subscription had made him once more wealthy, worth £80,000. He had decided to leave England for a time and, accompanied by his wife, to undertake a foreign tour to study conditions on the Continent. He did not return until the autumn of 1847. During his absence he had been returned for the West Riding of Yorkshire without spending a penny or taking the least action to secure his election.

We have just called his tour a tour of study. We should rather have called it a missionary journey. But his propaganda had no connection with that carried on by Palmerston's agents. To work for British free trade was, it is true, among the activities of the latter. For it was one of their objects to obtain from the Liberal Governments they supported in one or other of the Mediterranean peninsulas commercial treaties opening their markets to British goods. But their poor success in this respect contributed no doubt to the growing indifference, universally acknowledged, of the British public towards continental revolutions. A despot had often granted British trade more favourable terms than popular assemblies.[1]

Cobden took a more direct route. Instead of negotiating with statesmen he appealed to the economists of all countries to enlighten the public opinion of their respective peoples and, like his famous League in England, teach them the principles of political economy. When he visited Paris he was flattered by the welcome he received from Thiers, Odilon Barrot, and Guizot, the

[1] The admissions of the Liberal Press are illuminating. See *Daily News*, September 2, 1847: ' We have grown rather cold to constitution mongering, considering what it has produced to us in Greece and in the Peninsula; and the public, we fear, looks rather to the efforts of Pius IX with a dilettante feeling of pleasure, than with eager interest or sympathy in his cause.' And the reason? 'We trade less', we read in the issue of September 17, 'with the free Peninsula than we did with the enslaved. We have experienced as much commercial bigotry and political prejudices amongst the constitutional statesmen of these newly emancipated countries as we ever did from their courts, favourites and despotic Ministers.' It is not, therefore, surprising that to-day we show less enthusiasm for the Italian agitation than we did twenty-five years ago for the risings in Spain and Greece. 'On looking forward to a free Italy, we cannot but look forward to the usual combination of madness and ingratitude and discontent.' For the growing indifference of the public to purely political questions, see, further, the interesting admissions made about the same time by the great Liberal quarterly, the *Edinburgh Review*, January 1848 (vol. lxxxvii, p. 1091): 'The fanaticism about political forms and the tendency to expect that good laws will be produced mechanically by a good constitution of the legislature, is greatly diminished. People have begun to see that, though some governments are nearly always bad, none are always good. There is neither a royal nor a democratic road to perpetual good government.'

last named, no doubt, the most sincere of the three in his expressions of intellectual and moral sympathy. But he and his entire following were delighted when at a congress of economists held in Brussels free trade carried the day, and, moreover, largely owing to the intervention of the French members, Michel Chevalier and Blanqui. And it was encouraging to see Bastiat begin his career as a writer and show promise of becoming perhaps the French Cobden, and societies for advocating free trade founded in many provincial towns. In the opinion of the *Economist* France had adopted or almost adopted free trade.[1] This surely was the right way to bring about, outside the political sphere, a good understanding between the two countries which, moreover, would not preclude a similar understanding with any other. There would be no more wars for liberty, but liberty achieved and secured by peace. No longer would the revolutionaries in every nation receive encouragement with the distrust aroused in consequence throughout the Conservative classes. There could, therefore, be no need to arm, and as a result of the heavy burden of taxation to return, under pretext of a war for freedom, to poverty and servitude. When, towards the close of December, the campaign of which we have just spoken for a policy of rearmament opened, Cobden publicly protested. And whereas he had seldom taken part in debate during the November session he spoke in the debate on the Address.[2] He thus opened the ten years' war he would wage with varying success against Palmerston's policy. Against Palmerston's policy, but not on this occasion against Palmerston personally. For the latter thought it wise to repair his chief's blunder by a pacific speech. He disclaimed the desire to do anything calculated to endanger good relations between England and France. It was, indeed, in the interest of such good relations that the Government was taking steps to improve the national defences. For a genuine friendship can exist only between equals. He did not believe that war was imminent. The long peace did not mean that the time was now ripe for another war, but, on the contrary, that Europe was losing the fighting habit and

---

[1] September 12, 1847. A year earlier, the *Economist* had expressed the same hope in respect of Italy. 'In such a country free trade ought to find a congenial home, and sure we are that the good and great Pius IX, the most enlightened Pontiff that ever reigned, will interpose no obstacle, for already he has given his sanction to the credit of railways, in the way of which helps and promoters of civilization his predecessor threw every obstacle' (*Economist*, October 10, 1846).

[2] See below, pp. 281-2.

would lose it more and more as communications became quicker and trade freer. In short, it was just such a speech as Cobden himself might have delivered. But all this prudence did not appease the ill-humour of the public. In spite of the Chancellor of the Exchequer's denials the increased expenditure on the armed forces was obviously responsible for the Government's decision to impose new taxes and in particular to raise the income tax, a step taken by the very men who five years earlier had so bitterly opposed the imposition of such a tax. The Cabinet was compelled to consent to the appointment by the Commons of a committee to inquire into the expenditure on the army, navy, and artillery. And on February 23, 1848, it was also forced to agree that this inquiry which it had intended to be secret should be conducted in public.

The same day, however, an event took place in Paris which stultified all the forecasts and plans of the professional diplomats. And three weeks later, on the date fixed for the meeting in Paris of representatives of the French, Austrian, and Prussian Governments to deliberate in common on the best way to save by their joint action the cause of order in Europe, a republic had been proclaimed in Paris, revolution broke out in Vienna and Berlin, and Louis Philippe, Guizot, and Metternich, driven into exile, were all three in receipt of British hospitality.

CHAPTER V

The European Revolution and the End of Chartism

I APRIL 10, 1848

I

ON February 25, 1848, the news reached London that Louis Philippe had surrendered to the insurgents, dismissed Guizot and replaced him by Comte Molé, and on the following day that, in spite of this surrender and others which followed it, the insurrection had degenerated into a revolution, the King had abdicated, and a Republic had been proclaimed.[1] On February 29, when a regular postal service with Paris was restored, the details became known of the amazing upheaval which after two days' fighting had made France a Republic founded on universal suffrage and semi-Socialist. Chartism had triumphed, but in France, not in England. On March 2 the deposed French King, loaded with the scorn of the entire nation, which had indeed always approved though without enthusiasm his policy of a good understanding with England, but could not pardon his new policy inaugurated, it would seem, by the Spanish marriages, of rupture with England and friendship for the absolutist Powers, arrived at Newhaven with his Queen on an English steamer on which the British Government had secured him a passage under an incognito. He received from everyone the attentions and courtesy which the powerful take pleasure in showing their former rivals when they are weak and defeated.

The revolution in Paris completely changed the aspect of the European revolution. Until the end of February all Englishmen had viewed it as a German and Italian affair. If disturbances broke out in Paris they would, it was believed, be repressed more easily than in 1834, and it was even feared that Paris would assist Vienna, Berlin, and Rome to put down their rebels. Now Paris seemed the

---

[1] *Annual Register*, 1848, Chron., p. 28. *The Times, Morning Chronicle,* and *Daily News,* February 25 and 26, 1848. The news of Louis Philippe's fall began to be circulated on the 25th. But Palmerston did not receive it until shortly before midnight. See H. of C., February 25 (*Parliamentary Debates,* 3rd Ser., vol. xcvi, p. 1334). Also Palmerston to Lord Normanby, February 26, in Ashley, *Life of Viscount Palmerston,* vol. ii, p. 76.

heart of the general revolution, and even in consequence of a strange optical illusion which has persisted until the present day, as the source of a movement which in fact originated in Berne and Palermo. On March 5 fifty-one Republicans from the South German States combined at Heidelberg to set up a German Parliament elected by universal suffrage. The same day a rebellion broke out in Hungary and forced the Austrian Government to yield to the rebels' demands. In Vienna on March 15, after an insurrection which lasted two days, Metternich fell from power. Three days later the revolution reached Prussia—'Prussia, too,' Carlyle lamented, 'solid Germany itself'[1]—and triumphed on March 21.

What, then, of England? In 1830 the July revolution had caused a ferment almost as serious as that in France itself. The infection surely could not fail to reach the country now, at a moment moreover when England had just emerged from a commercial crisis graver than any of those from which she had suffered since 1830. It did, in fact, reach England, but in a form so extremely superficial that the Continental rulers could not fail to perceive the humiliating contrast between the weakness of their own Governments and the solid strength of her social and political fabric.[2]

We have seen how the new National Petition for the People's Charter launched in December 1847 had proved a damp squib.[3] On January 1, 1848, the *Northern Star* admitted that the Chartists' party fund did not amount to £60, just sufficient to defray the expenses of a single candidate. The appeal made every week by O'Connor's paper to the members of the party, addressed to *The Old Guard of Chartism* and headed by the slogan, 'The People's Charter. No Surrender', betrayed old age, discouragement, and defeat. Nevertheless, the tone of the paper became more lively after the outbreak of revolution in Palermo. Signatures to the National Petition began to come in in a steady stream. Meetings multiplied and were encouraged by those freelance Conservatives, the currency men of Birmingham, who gave the Chartists the use of the town hall, also by the London Radicals,

---

[1] Carlyle, *Latter Day Pamphlets*, 1850 (Pamphlet 1, *The Present Time*, p. 36).
[2] See E. Halévy, *English Public Opinion and the French Revolutions of the Nineteenth Century*, published in A. Colville and H. Temperley, *Studies in Anglo-French History*, 1935.
[3] See above, p. 203.

Duncombe and Wakley. 'To your tents, Chartists,' wrote O'Connor. 'We are becoming stronger and more united every day.' Towards the end of February the excitement increased still further. The Chartist organ was jubilant. The news from Italy, Naples, and Sicily, it declared, was extremely important. And the concessions granted by the Pope were even more significant. But the outstanding event of the week had been the victorious insurrection in Paris. How glorious it was for the Parisians. Once again they had taught tyrants a lesson and set an example to the oppressed in every nation.[1]

The immediate effect, moreover, of the revolution in Paris, which spread at once throughout Central Europe, was to paralyse business everywhere and to revive the economic crisis in England, which for the last two months had seemed to be dying down. At this season of the year the difficulties of navigation in winter brought trade with Northern Europe practically to a standstill. And the adverse circumstances of the previous year continued to interfere with exports to the West Indies and the United States. There remained the French market, which absorbed as many British imports as the West Indies, and the European market in general, which absorbed three times the amount of goods exported to the remainder of the globe. Now these were closed. The result was a fresh crop of failures, failures this time of manufacturing firms, and in consequence a rise in unemployment. It should be an easy task for the Chartists to exploit the discontent thus caused.[2]

On March 5 a riot which might seem serious broke out at Glasgow. The mob, armed with pikes, made a surprise attack on the city, looted fifty shops, chiefly gunsmiths' and jewellers', and did damage to the tune of £60,000. Inadequate measures of repression left the ringleaders at large and enabled them to concert a more methodical insurrection for the following day. The mob was to march *en masse* upon the manufacturing quarters and compel the factories to close, take possession of the gasometers and plunge the city in darkness the ensuing night, then seize the gaols and free the prisoners. They would thus become masters of Glasgow. The military, however, checked the 10,000 rioters at the outset by firing upon the crowd and making casualties. But the work had to be completed by the dispatch of a regiment of

---

[1] *Northern Star*, February 26, 1848.
[2] *Annual Register*, 1848, p. 31.

cavalry.[1] Rioting also occurred in all the great manufacturing centres, in Manchester where the mob gathered in front of the workhouse and clamoured for the discharge of its inmates, at Oldham, Preston, Newcastle, Sunderland, in the Potteries at Hanley, where O'Connor received a triumphal reception, at Nottingham, and Birmingham. Finally the movement reached London, which had not been the case in 1839 and 1842.

On March 6, when a Radical meeting to demand the abolition of the income tax has been banned by the police, it was captured by G. W. M. Reynolds and transformed into a Chartist meeting. There were skirmishes round Trafalgar Square in the direction of the Strand and in the direction of Buckingham Palace on which the demonstrators had announced their intention to march after the meeting. On March 13 a mass meeting of 20,000 was held on Kennington Common, controlled by 4,000 armed policemen, and another on the 15th at Blackheath where the rain assisted the police by damping the spirits of the assemblage. Several meetings were also held in private, among them a meeting to receive the delegates whom the Chartists had sent to Paris to fraternize with the victorious revolutionaries. But no particular object was consistently pursued nor was a general revolt attempted. Conservative even in revolution, the Chartists followed the procedure canonical since 1817 and to which they had conformed already in 1839 and 1842. They decided to elect at a public meeting representatives of the people, to constitute a National Convention which would sit in London and in its turn elect delegates to take to Parliament a petition for universal suffrage and the other points of the Charter. When, as could not fail to happen, the petition was rejected by an overwhelming majority, what would they do next? If they were in earnest with their revolution, they should have made up their minds quite clearly beforehand. But at this point hesitation and vacillation prevailed at the would-be headquarters of the revolution.[2]

The thirty-nine delegates who composed the National Convention had scarcely met on April 4 in John Street off the Tottenham Court Road when the battle broke out between those who advised caution and those who wanted to take risks. The revolu-

---

[1] For the disturbances in Glasgow, see Sir Archibald Allison, *Some Account of my Life and Writings*, 1883, vol. i, pp. 571 sqq.
[2] R. G. Gammage, *History of the Chartist Movement*, pp. 293 sqq. M. Hovell, *Chartist Movement*, p. 288.

tionaries proposed that as soon as the petition had been rejected the Convention should proclaim itself the sole legitimate authority as against a House of Commons elected by a restricted suffrage, in other words, should give the signal for a civil war.[1] The plan actually adopted played for time. When the petition was rejected the Convention would content itself with drawing up a National Memorial, to be presented to the Queen, calling upon her to dismiss her Ministers and choose others who would make the six points of the Charter a question of confidence. Then meetings held simultaneously, a procedure borrowed from 1819, would elect in every constituency delegates to constitute in London a National Assembly and present the National Memorial to the Queen. The sole concession to the revolutionaries was an amendment providing that the Convention should remain in session until the National Assembly had met.[2] One of the most violent opponents of the revolutionaries was O'Brien. He denied that the Convention could claim to represent the majority of the nation. He had himself been elected by no more than 2,000 of the 2,000,000 inhabitants of London. And of these 2,000 how many had confidence in himself or O'Connor. He did not believe that the population of London was with them or that they were ready to adopt further measures. He was not prepared to defy the law so long as he regarded it as just. It was only on the day that he believed it to be unjust and was also convinced that the people were stronger than the law that he would be ready to cry 'to hell with the law'. He even refused to take part in the final meetings. For the motion carried was too revolutionary for his approval. It was criminal to launch an unarmed populace against a Government which had taken all the necessary steps to deprive it of arms. Not that O'Brien had become a moderate like Lovett, Hetherington, and Cooper. More than ever he was what we should call to-day an orthodox social democrat. But he hated O'Connor and deplored what his stupidity had made of the movement.[3]

In O'Brien's opinion, as in that of many others, O'Connor was a charlatan. He could not be relied upon when battle was joined. A boaster before the decisive moment, he was a coward when the

[1] G. Reynolds's motion (R. G. Gammage, *History of the Chartist Movement*, p. 308).
[2] Ernest Jones's amendment (R. G. Gammage, op. cit., p. 309). *Northern Star*, April 8, 1848.
[3] E. Dolléans, *Le Chartisme*, vol. ii, pp. 428 and 432. R. G. Gammage, *History of the Chartist Movement*, p. 312.

storm broke. O'Brien did not even consider him an honourable man. He believed that he had sold himself to the Anti-Corn-Law League three years earlier, and he took seriously the charges made against him in 1847 of misappropriating the funds of his National Charter Association.

Moreover, O'Connor was not a Socialist. It was all very well for him to declare now that he would not care a fig for the Charter, unless it would bring about a social revolution, and that the entire issue at stake was the question of labour. Either he understood by the social question something very different from what O'Brien meant by it and regarded the establishment on the land of a multitude of peasant proprietors a sufficient social reform, or he was deliberately using ambiguous language, because he realized that after the events in Paris and the formation there of a Government which contained some at least who called for the 'organization of labour' by the State and declared that 'the exploitation of men by their fellows' must cease, he must court the favour of the masses by speaking the language of Socialism. The latter was O'Brien's opinion. But he regarded O'Connor as an unrepentant individualist at the bottom of his heart and, therefore, unfit to lead a movement of which henceforward such men as himself, Julian Harney, and Ernest Jones were the rightful leaders.

Finally, O'Connor was an Irishman and an Irish patriot, and as such he compromised Chartism, as O'Connell had compromised Radicalism, when he forced himself upon it as its official demagogue. Anyone looking through the numbers of the *Northern Star* which appeared between November 1847 and February 1848 will be at a loss to decide to which programme it attached more importance, universal suffrage for the United Kingdom or the repeal of the Act of Union with Ireland.

As a matter of principle, O'Brien disapproved of combining the two programmes. In his view the cause of universal suffrage should be bound up not with Irish Nationalism but with Socialism. And as a matter of political strategy O'Connor's double programme was not calculated to win favour in England and Scotland, for the Irish were unpopular with the masses of Great Britain.

2

The Government was well informed, if only from their *agents provocateurs*, of these internal dissensions and vacillations. But the public was more ignorant and, therefore, could not fail to be impressed by the announcement of the mass meeting to be held in London on April 10 when the National Petition would be presented to Parliament, bearing, it was claimed, almost six million signatures. The Chartists were expecting a procession of 500,000 to accompany it from Kennington Common on the south bank of the Thames to Westminster. Nothing of the sort had been witnessed in 1839 or 1842. Men were reminded of 1832 and, what was more alarming, of the events which had just taken place in Paris, Vienna, and Berlin. The royal family left London and took refuge in the Isle of Wight.[1] Many middle-class families followed the royal example. But this panic, if there really was a panic, was a proof that the situation was not so dangerous as it had been in the great continental cities. There had been no panic among the bourgeoisie of Paris on the morning of February 23. And after all, there was not strictly speaking a panic in London. The leading newspapers had refused to take the sanguinary affray in Glasgow too seriously, and on that occasion had contrasted the good humour of the British lower classes with the violence of the continental proletariat.[2] Business men were equally unconcerned. When the February revolution brought British trade to a temporary standstill, the *Economist*, while noticing this renewal of the crisis, said that its end was not far off and recovery would be rapid.[3] What is more surprising is the fact that, although the Committee appointed by the House of Commons to inquire into the causes of the crisis sat from January till June, not a single allusion to the European revolution can be found in its proceedings. Nor was this all. A member of the House of Baring, Sir Joshua Bates, when questioned by the Committee on March 3

[1] R. G. Gammage, *History of the Chartist Movement*, p. 248.
[2] *The Times*, March 9: 'A London mob, though neither heroic, nor poetical, nor patriotic, nor enlightened, nor clean, is a comparatively good-natured and harmless body.' See also *The Times* April 8 and 10. Even so, the *Daily News*, April 15, blamed *The Times* for being too timid. The *Morning Chronicle* wrote, on April 8: 'In the present disposition of the London householders, we are by no means sure that the police are not more likely to be called on to protect the Chartists from them, than them from the Chartists.'
[3] *Economist*, March 4, 1848, vol. vi, pp. 254-5.

about the management of the Bank of France during the last few years, replied that the problems with which it had to cope were far simpler than those which confronted the Bank of England. How, he asked, could the fluctuations to which a 'great commercial country' like England was exposed be compared with the conditions of a country like France where 'everything is quiet'.[1]

A brawl, a skirmish, perhaps even the beginnings of a riot might be expected. The Government and the nation adopted the necessary measures to teach the English revolutionaries, and indirectly the continental, a salutary lesson.

The Government, well aware of their internal dissensions, took steps to profit by them. A Crown and Government Security Bill was brought in, ostensibly to meet the threat of an Irish rebellion, but drawn up in terms applicable to the entire United Kingdom. In this way the Chartist agitators were made to appear, as it were, British Irishmen.[2] At the same time an Aliens Removal Bill was introduced authorizing the summary expulsion of foreign revolutionaries. It encouraged the British people in sentiments of hostility to foreigners at a moment when they were in little need of the encouragement.[3] For there had been strange happenings in France on the morrow of the February revolution. While in Paris revolutionaries from all countries were fraternizing with their Paris confreres, scenes of a very different character had been enacted in the provinces and even in the suburbs of the capital. For many years past engineers, foremen and skilled workmen, had been flocking into France from England to teach the French the processes of manufacture. The Revolution produced a crisis of unemployment during which the working class in Paris, at Havre, and elsewhere, turned against these competitors and intruders from abroad, Piedmontese, Belgians, and Englishmen. They were driven into flight, leaving behind them savings-bank deposits and arrears of wages unpaid, and landed in England infuriated with France and spreading their anger far and wide. The world of

[1] *Report from the Secret Committee . . . on Commercial Distress: Minutes of Evidence.* Evidence of Sir Joshua Bates, q. 2429 and q. 2493.

[2] The Crown and Government Security Bill, introduced on April 7, passed its third reading on April 18. It extended to Ireland a statute of 1795, and modified certain of its provisions to make the measure easier to apply, but at the same time created new offences (*Parliamentary Debates*, 3rd Ser., vol. xcvi, pp. 22 sqq., 33, 223 sqq., and 480).

[3] The Aliens Removal Bill, introduced on April 11, passed its third reading on May 11 (ibid., 3rd Ser., vol. xcviii, pp. 135 sqq., 264 sqq., and 870).

fashion by way of reprisal boycotted French silks.[1] When some French actors, ruined by the revolutionary disorders in Paris, came to London in the hope of earning a livelihood by theatrical performances, the English employees of the theatre demonstrated so noisily against them that the performances could not be given.[2] The public imagination, it would seem, confused the Irish with the French. 'A Frenchman', a journalist wrote, 'is a civilized Celt, an Irishman is a Gallic barbarian. What is Communism in France is brigandage in Ireland.'[3] It was quite clear that the nation would have nothing to do with a movement led by Irishmen to launch in England a revolution after the French pattern.

Wellington, on the other hand, took the necessary precautions to safeguard public order in the metropolis. He drafted into London a large force of troops from the provinces. But he did not allow the soldiers to be in evidence. He concealed them in a number of buildings, transformed into forts, the Tower, the Bank, Millbank prison and some others, and requisitioned steamers to be in readiness to transport them quickly by river if the need arose, to any point where reinforcements might be required. In the streets were seen only the members of the regular police force, mounted or on foot, and a large body of special constables, volunteers enrolled as the result of an appeal made to citizens in a proclamation of April 6. It had met with an enthusiastic response from the public. Applications for enrolment had come from every class of society. Half the members of the House of Lords, it was said, were special constables. Peel himself was enrolled, a sure sign, jested a Radical paper, that he was planning to carry the People's Charter through Parliament before many years had passed.[4] Prince Louis Napoleon, who had taken refuge in London after his escape from imprisonment at Ham, and who a month later would play through his agents a very different part in Paris,

---

[1] *The Times*, March 8, 1848. Pierre Quentin Bauchart, *Lamartine et la Politique étrangère de la Révolution de Février*, 1913, pp. 104 sqq. See also H. of C., March 27, 1848: Sir C. H. Wood's speech (*Parliamentary Debates*, 3rd Ser., vol. xcvii, p. 1027).

[2] *Annual Register*, 1848, Chron., p. 79.

[3] *Economist*, April 28, 1848, vol. vi, p. 477: 'Thank God we are Saxons! Flanked by the savage Celt on one side and the flighty Gaul on the other—the one a slave to the passions, the other a victim to the theories of the hour—we feel deeply grateful from our inmost hearts, that we belong to a race, which, if it cannot boast the flowing fancy of one of its neighbours, nor the brilliant *esprit* of the other, has an ample compensation in the solid, slow, reflective, phlegmatic temperament which has saved us from so many errors, spared us so many experiments, and purchased for us so many real, though incomplete and unsystematic blessings.'

[4] *Jerrold's Weekly Newspaper*, April 15, 1848.

offered his services. Merchants and tradesmen enrolled *en masse*. It was noticed that among the working classes, those who belonged to the aristocracy of labour—the members of trade unions —while refusing to take part in the revolutionary demonstration, also refused to participate in the counter-demonstration of the middle class and fight their comrades. On the other hand, many volunteers came in from the rabble of the docks.[1] How unlike the situation in London was to the situation in Paris, Vienna, and Berlin. On the Continent the Government, without any support except the army, was impotent in face of a popular rising and the discontent of the middle classes. In England the Government kept its troops hidden and encouraged the people to defend itself against revolution.

3

On the morning of April 10[2] the demonstrators, perfectly organized, set out from several starting points to the north of the river and marched in procession over the bridges to Kennington. A body that attracted particular attention started from Bloomsbury, marched down Holborn, and crossed Blackfriars bridge. It escorted two carriages. One of them, drawn by six horses, contained all the members of the National Convention, headed by O'Connor and Ernest Jones. The other, drawn by four horses, carried the enormous scroll on which the National Petition was written. These processions, however, were not greeted by any sign of sympathy or by an applauding crowd. The streets emptied, tradesmen put up their shutters. The Chartists felt frozen by the atmosphere of hostility. How many were they when they all assembled on Kennington Common? 150,000 the Chartists claimed, far less than the half-million advertised. Even so, their figure was contested. The number of demonstrators was generally estimated at twenty-five to thirty thousand. Some even maintained that it did not exceed eight. For the sake of argument we will accept the Chartist extravagant estimate. There were 170,000 special constables. It could not be said that the majority were rising against the tyranny of a small minority. A minority was demonstrating against the overwhelming majority of the nation.

[1] *Parliamentary Debates*, 3rd Ser., vol. xcvii, pp. 458–60.
[2] For the events of April 10, see the account in R. G. Gammage, *History of the Chartis Movement*, pp. 312 sqq. E. Dolléans, *Le Chartisme*, vol. ii, pp. 462 sqq.

The meeting had scarcely opened when a police inspector made his way through the crowd and summoned O'Connor to speak with the Commissioners of Police. He obeyed. A disturbance broke out among the bystanders. Either they suspected the police of attempting to arrest O'Connor or O'Connor of a secret understanding with the police. But order was restored, and O'Connor had no great difficulty in explaining to his audience that a Chartist procession to Westminster had been forbidden and that to avoid useless bloodshed he advised the Chartists to obey. He himself with a few friends would go to the House. 'So help me, God,' he exclaimed. 'I will die upon the floor of the House or get your rights for you.' The meeting expressed its approval, and three cabs conveyed the petition to Westminster. The police had not allowed the demonstrators to cross the Thames. They dispersed without even a brawl, without a single window broken. The same evening a jubilant middle class walked the streets of London singing *God Save the Queen*. 'God save our shops is what they ought to be singing,' the Chartists muttered as, swamped in the crowd, they witnessed this collapse of their hopes.

Chartism, moribund since 1842, had produced by a final convulsion the semblance of a recovery. On April 10 it foundered not in blood, but in ridicule. At Westminster a committee, appointed to verify the signatures to the petition, reported that the number of genuine signatures did not reach two millions and that many of them were imaginary, Wellington for example, the Queen herself, or grotesque or obscene nicknames. Would the result have been different if the same trouble had been taken to check the signatures to the petitions of 1842 and 1839, or the innumerable petitions of 1831 and 1832? Possibly, but, that is the significant fact, they had not been checked.[1] Now the vanquished were trampled underfoot. The defeat of Chartism undoubtedly produced an appreciable effect on the Continent. Six days later in Paris, for the first time since February, the workers who assembled on the Champs de Mars and went to the Hôtel de Ville to demand 'the organization of labour by association' were dispersed by the National Guard of the middle-class districts, while the crowd of onlookers shouted 'Down with the Communists'. April 10 had

---

[1] Ch. Kingsley, *Alton Locke*, 3rd ed., 1852, p. 300: ' "Why, my dear MacKaye," said I, "you know the Reform Bill Petitions were just as bad." "And the Anti-Corn-Law ones too, for that matter," said Crossthwaite.'

restored confidence to the Parisian middle class, given the signal for a reaction against the general revolution. Even in London the revival of business, uncertain before, was unmistakable from that day forward. Shares rose in value, even foreign shares which had fallen when April 10 lay ahead. The rise in the value of British stocks can be measured by the following instance. In a single day, railway shares rose by at least £5, in some cases even £10, a share.[1]

At the end of April the 'Convention' was succeeded by the 'National Assembly', whose sessions began on May 1. It contained neither O'Brien, who had broken with the movement on the eve of April 10, nor O'Connor, who declared this assembly of more than fifty persons illegal[2] and maintained that the Chartists must in future keep strictly within the law. It was, he claimed, the 'Physical Force' men who had made the movement unpopular and thus brought about the fiasco of April 10. Nevertheless, when the Assembly, in whose proceedings sixty at most of the hundred members elected took part,[3] had brought its sessions to an inglorious close on May 12 a last convulsion occurred. The occasion of this final outbreak was the condemnation in Ireland of the revolutionary Mitchell to fourteen years' deportation. In this instance, therefore, the movement was of Irish rather than French origin, and since the 'Physical Force' men were for the moment supreme at the headquarters of Chartism it assumed in Lancashire and Yorkshire the character of an insurrection. Pikes were manufactured, an armed force organized, military training given. The Government replied by banning the meetings, breaking them up by force, if the Chartists persisted in holding them, and bringing the ringleaders to trial. The penalties inflicted were not very heavy, at most, in a few exceptional cases, two years' imprisonment.[4] But in London in August the police made public, the more confidently because it had been organized by *agents provocateurs*, the details of an extraordinary conspiracy. A procession was to have started at midnight. If the police had attempted to interfere, an armed rising would have followed at several points in the capital and the chief public buildings would have been set

---

[1] *Annual Register*, 1848, pp. 60–1.
[2] *Northern Star*, April 22, 1848.
[3] R. G. Gammage, *History of the Chartist Movement*, p. 329.
[4] *Northern Star*, May 6 and 13, 1848. R. G. Gammage, *History of the Chartist Movement*, p. 332. For the agitation in Ireland, see below, pp. 292–3.

on fire.[1] All the troops garrisoned in London were ostentatiously called out, the rebels' dumps of arms confiscated, all the revolutionary clubs closed, and some thirty obscure individuals imprisoned and tried. Four were sentenced to deportation for life.[2]

4

Every time Chartism had collapsed after some years or months of revolutionary effervescence a group of Chartists, advocates of 'moral force', had withdrawn from the movement to explore the possibilities of an alliance with the democrats of the lower middle class, the Nonconformists of the manufacturing centres, to put forward a programme of parliamentary reform less extreme than universal suffrage. The attempt had been made after 1842, with a programme of household instead of manhood suffrage, triennial instead of annual parliaments, a reduction of the existing inequality of constituencies instead of absolute equality. The secret ballot was the only point common to both programmes, the old and the new.[3]

But, as we have seen, the moderate Radicals had merged with the members of the Anti-Corn-Law League and decided to wait for the time when, if possible without a prior reform of the suffrage, they had secured the repeal of the Corn Laws, before recommencing, in concert they expected with their free trade allies, the campaign for household suffrage. They were quickly disillusioned. The free traders saw no point in a reform of the franchise. It was untrue that the franchise established in 1832 subjected Parliament to the influence, still omnipotent, of an oligarchy of landowners. For it had proved possible with the existing franchise to inflict on that oligarchy a defeat so serious as the repeal of the Corn Laws. In February 1848 the introduction in France of manhood suffrage contemporaneously with the final Chartist rising revived this moderate and legal campaign under the leadership of Joseph Hume. He secured the support—wholly platonic—of a few eccentric Whigs. He had to face the attacks

[1] *Annual Register*, Chron., pp. 103 and 104.
[2] R. G. Gammage, *History of the Chartist Movement*, pp. 39-40. In December there were five similar condemnations at Liverpool (ibid., p. 342).
[3] See above, pp. 29-30, 38.

—equally platonic—of Chartist speakers.[1] In face of an indifferent public his campaign fell flat.[2]

In 1832, Hume and his supporters argued—in contrast with the purely nominal revolution which had substituted Louis Philippe, King of the French, for Charles X, King of France—we English had effected a genuine revolution, and if we had not achieved democracy, had gone much farther in that direction than any other European nation. Now surely, when France was taking the initiative, we could not be content to remain as we were regardless of the fact that, as statistics proved, not only had the number of voters not increased in proportion to the increase of the population, but had, it would seem, actually diminished on the whole, certainly in many counties.[3] But what object, answered the advocates of the *status quo*, will be served by this reform of the franchise? The introduction of Socialism on the French pattern? Nothing was farther from the intentions of Hume, an orthodox opponent of Socialism. And he did not fail to point out that the experiments in Socialism made in Paris and elsewhere in France had been the work of a Provisional Government not approved by universal suffrage, and that as soon as a genuinely democratic assembly had been elected the reaction against Socialism had begun.[4]

If, however, this reaction found favour with the advocates of household suffrage, why were they not satisfied with the franchise which had enabled the nation to shake off the yoke of the great landowners without falling into the servitude of a socializing State? In 1848 Hume obtained only 84 votes;[5] in 1849, 82,[6] and

[1] On May 6 the Chartist National Assembly advised Chartists to take part in meetings in support of household suffrage. 'Not for purposes of obstruction or moving factious amendments, but for showing calmly and rationally the superiority of the Charter' (R. G. Gammage, *History of the Chartist Movement*, p. 326). O'Connor, however, began in 1848 to support Hume's campaign. If in the following year he appeared to have left the movement, when he decided to bring forward in the Commons a motion in favour of the Charter, he rejoined Hume immediately after its defeat (R. G. Gammage, op. cit., pp. 327 and 347-8).

[2] It gave occasion to Disraeli's ironical comment: 'Those who are interested in finding employment for the rising generation will be glad to learn that a new profession has been discovered, and that is the profession of agitation. . . . The remarkable circumstance is that the present movement has not in the slightest degree originated in any class of the people, even if the people had been misled. It is a possibility that there might be a popular movement, and yet erroneous; but this is erroneous and yet not popular' (H. of C., June 21, 1848. *Annual Register*, 1848, p. 150). [3] Ibid,, 1848, p. 152.

[4] H. of C., June 21, 1848: Hume's speech (*Parliamentary Debates*, 3rd Ser., vol. xcix, pp. 879 sqq.).

[5] H. of C., July 6, 1848 (ibid., 3rd Ser., vol. c, pp. 226 sqq.).

[6] H. of C., June 5, 1849 (ibid., 3rd Ser., vol. cv, p. 1233).

in 1850, 96.[1] It was very slow progress. The time was not far off when the question would be regarded as urgent. But as the revolutionary phase of the European crisis receded into the past, members were less afraid to vote for the reform, more willing, that is to say, to vote in principle for a measure to which the country attached no importance. In one of his speeches Hume admitted bitterly that the campaign which he led had no possibility of success so long as its advocates were opposed by both the historic parties.[2] It was perfectly true.

II ENGLAND AND THE SOCIALISM OF 1848

I

Though Peel disclaimed any desire to intervene in the domestic affairs of France and professed his determination to let the French make whatever social experiments they wished without any interference from outside, he knew that the vast majority of his fellow countrymen agreed with him in thinking these experiments extremely dangerous. If England must choose between the Socialist will-o'-the-wisp and the teachings of political economy, her choice was certain. For several years a Parliament elected on the franchise of 1832 had fulfilled the expectations of the nation. There was, therefore, no need for a further reform.[3] The Protectionists could not speak quite the same language. They disliked the economic Liberalism whose victory in England they were invited to applaud. But the continental disorder furnished cheap material for their sneers. 'I find in France', Disraeli observed, 'a republic without republicans, and in Germany an empire without an emperor; and this is progress. This is the brilliant achievement of universal suffrage—the high politic consummation of the sovereignty of the people.'[4]

As for the Whig aristocracy it was becoming more conservative, while remaining as haughty as ever.[5] It had witnessed with

---

[1] H. of C., February 22, 1850 (*Annual Register*, 1850, pp. 20 sqq.). For the campaign for household suffrage after 1850, see below, p. 283.

[2] H. of C., June 5, 1849. Hume's speech (*Parliamentary Debates.*, 3rd Ser., vol. cv, p. 1156).

[3] H. of C., April 10, 1848. Peel's speech (ibid., 3rd Ser., vol. xcviii, pp. 453 sqq.).

[4] H. of C., February 1, 1849. Disraeli's speech (ibid., 3rd Ser., vol. cii, p. 103).

[5] 'The Whigs, having effected a triumph over O'Connor and his boasting physical-force followers . . . resolved to crush, if possible, the right of petitioning altogether.

anxiety the February revolution, when for a moment it had feared that its repercussions might possibly shake the British Constitution. It continued to watch with anxiety its effects on the Continent and the danger, never dispelled, of further civil or foreign wars. 'A change came over the world', Lord Lansdowne declared, 'which entirely reversed the order of things throughout Europe. After that which took place at Paris—I mean the revolution with all its consequences—the danger which arose was not as before the interference of governments with the independence of States', but 'that a democracy without a throne would overturn all the crowns of Europe.'[1]

Lord John Russell, the theorist of the party, expressed the most conservative view of the British Constitution he had ever entertained. Three great nations, he said, had come through the crisis unscathed, despotic Russia, the democratic United States, and England with her mixed Constitution, which therefore suited England, as despotism suited Russia and democracy the United States. That is to say, he depicted it as good not in itself, but for England alone. It could, however, be regarded as excellent in itself, but not for the reason, alleged by many Whig publicists, because it established a balance of powers between monarchy, aristocracy, and democracy. For if that theory were pushed to its logical conclusion, since the House of Commons represented democracy, it should be elected by a democratic franchise. He regarded the British Constitution not as a balance between rival powers, a regulated condition of civil war, so to speak, but as a coalition of powers effected by the collaboration of monarchy, aristocracy, and democracy. In his opinion, therefore, the composition of the House of Commons should not be wholly democratic.[2]

By this conservative tendency the Whigs infuriated many Radicals who had always found their arrogance hard to stomach.[3]

They thought to silence effectually the public voice by raking up an old law of the Stuarts, which declares that political petitions shall not have more than twenty signatures. And this, be it remembered, was effected by *Whig Reformers*' (William Lovett, *Life and Struggles*, 1876, p. 341).
[1] H. of L., March 22, 1849. Lord Lansdowne's speech (*Parliamentary Debates*, 3rd Ser., vol. ciii, p. 1105).
[2] H. of C., June 5, 1849. Lord John Russell's speech (ibid., 3rd Ser., vol. cv, p. 1224).
[3] Harriet Martineau was annoyed by the attitude they adopted after April 10, 1848: 'I have seen a good deal of life and many varieties of manners; and it now appears to me that the broadest vulgarity I have encountered is in the families of official Whigs who conceive themselves the cream of society and the lights and rulers of the world of our

But one cannot be blind to the significance of the involuntary tribute paid to them by Bright at the very moment when in 1849 he was demanding a democratic reform of the franchise. 'There is not a man in this House who objects less than I do to any of the noble Lords who hold positions in the Government. It is quite possible you could not find in this House an equal number of men against whom so little objection could be raised.'[1] Their position was undoubtedly more secure after February than it had been before.

Guizot, flotsam from the Continental reaction and an excellent observer of conditions in England, which he judged from the Conservative standpoint, summed up the situation correctly when he wrote to a French correspondent on July 1, 1848. 'The Cabinet will not die because everybody wants it to live. Everyone is delighted that at this juncture there is a Whig Ministry and a Conservative Opposition. They argue that if the Whigs were in Opposition they would be Radicals, even Chartists, and there would be a new Reform Bill, if not worse. The country is Conservative but timid, anxious as to the issue of a great struggle should it take place, looking back to the days of the mighty conflicts between the parties, between Pitt and Fox, as heroic times, long past, which it has no particular desire to see return, and hoping that a halt may be made at a cheaper rate on the slippery slope on which it feels itself placed. Maybe they are right.'[2]

Nevertheless, the great victim of the February revolution was mistaken in regarding April 10 as the complete victory of Conservatism as he understood it and the unqualified repudiation of Socialism by British public opinion. In fact, there is discernible in the public mind a movement in the opposite direction whose character we must now describe and whose influence we must measure. We have already insisted, when telling the story of the years preceding 1848, on the widespread philanthropic enthusiasm and the uneasy conscience felt by the middle class at the spectacle of the poverty in which the workers were condemned to live.

Empire. The time is not far off, though I shall not live to see it, when that coterie will be found to have brought about a social revolution, more disastrous to themselves than anything that could have been rationally anticipated from poor Feargus O'Connor and his Chartist host of April 10, 1848' (*Autobiography*, 1877, vol. ii, pp. 297 sqq.).

[1] *Parliamentary Debates*, 3rd Ser., vol. cv, p. 210.
[2] Guizot to Vitet, July 1, 1848 (*Lettres de M. Guizot à sa famille et à ses amis*, 1884, p. 256).

This philanthropy was not likely to have been silenced by fear of revolution. On the contrary, the ruling classes, to judge by their most representative elements, seem to have argued as follows. Nothing could be more absurd or more dangerous than to entrust the government of the country to a populace incapable of governing themselves. But the structure of society surely is responsible for the existence of this proletariat. The most prudent course therefore to adopt, if future revolutionary outbreaks are to be prevented, is indirect, to endeavour to raise the moral level of these degraded masses. That is to say, Socialism contained a core of truth which it was for British wisdom to extract. *Punch* joked when Prince Albert presided over the inaugural meeting of a 'Society to improve the Condition of the Labouring Classes', which was addressed by Lord Ashley.[1] A little later, by newspaper articles, speeches, and books, Mayhew launched an impassioned campaign against the evils of sweating, rampant among the East End tailors. Sweating was a novelty scarcely ten years old. West End tailors gave out orders wholesale to sub-contractors, often Jews, who made their profit by exploiting the workers, usually Irish, who executed their orders at home. In France this sweating was called 'marchandage', and the new Republic claimed that its decree had abolished 'marchandage' at a single blow. England, Mayhew pleaded, should pursue the same goal, but by methods less spectacular perhaps, but more efficacious.[2]

It would be easy to multiply instances.

Socialism, so the *Economist* summed up the position, was making progress in England as abroad. It was patronized by a number of clergymen and men of letters. There was a party in the Church which looked to it for support, saw in it the ally, possibly the final realization of Christianity. It was, we were told, the last word of science, that it reconciled the past with the future, political economy with progress. And it was accordingly gaining ground in the country. Moreover, it was a novelty and as such gave free scope to the imagination to picture the numerous blessings it would bring forth. It was smiled upon by philanthropists and ladies, and promised, such was the bitter comment

[1] *Punch*, 1848, vol. i, p. 228.
[2] Henry Mayhew, *London Labour and London Poor*, 1851. (See the article on Mayhew in the *Edinburgh Review*, May 1852.) *People's Journal*, vol. v, Appendix, pp. 6, 11, 28; vol. vi, pp. 32 sqq. *Economist*, November 16, 1850. See *The Times* Leader, December 28, 1849, on the philanthropic experiments being made in England.

of this organ of orthodox Liberalism, distinction and influence to those ambitious men whose creed was a successful career. Any opinion which favoured their designs was a further and a welcome article of their faith.[1]

2

We shall understand better this sentimental attitude to social problems, this infatuation for a particular type of 'Socialism', if we first study a few individuals who may be regarded as representative in this respect. We shall select some of them from the party of liberty, others from the party hostile to liberty. And the better to place them we shall relate the men of our choice to two writers whose acquaintance we have already made, who, in fact, prided themselves on not belonging to any party, for they regarded themselves as occupying a position above party membership, as instructors of the national conscience, friends of fifteen years' standing, but friends no longer, yet continuing to follow paths less divergent than parallel, John Stuart Mill and Carlyle.

The *Principles of Political Economy* which Mill published immediately after the revolution of 1848 had been written and printed before it broke out. It was a magnificent textbook of political economy whose success, as we know, has been enormous and lasting. Nothing like it had appeared in England since *The Wealth of Nations*.[2] Its superiority over the works of Ricardo and James Mill was due to the method employed. Unlike the Benthamites of the first generation, Mill did not regard political economy as the whole of sociology. On the contrary, he regarded it as but one department of a social science, wider and more complex. Viewing its laws in the light of this new conception he reached views broader and more supple than the rigid dogmatism of James Mill. Indeed, if we can believe what he tells us in the *Autobiography* he wrote later, already before 1848 he felt himself strongly attracted to Socialism. 'We were now', he wrote, speaking of Mrs. Taylor and himself, 'much less democrats than I had been, because so long as education continues to be so wretchedly imperfect, we dreaded the ignorance and especially the selfishness and brutality of the mass: but our ideal of ultimate improvement

---

[1] *Economist*, May 4, 1850.
[2] See article in the *Edinburgh Review*, October 1848, on Mill's *Political Economy*, vol. lxxxviii, pp. 337 sqq.

went far beyond democracy and would class us decidedly under the general designation of Socialists.'[1] The revolution in France did but embolden him to express publicly views for which before it occurred he had not thought the public ripe. But did he not deceive himself? Is this not one of the numerous instances in which our memory betrays us or, when we are relating the history of a conversion, we are disposed either to dramatize it unduly or deny that it was so sudden as, in fact, it was? For in the first edition of his *Political Economy*, Socialist doctrines, though treated with respect, are radically refuted. With the single exception of child labour, and, even so, only after considerable hesitation, Mill was the determined opponent of any legislation to protect the workers. If society in its actual state, based on private property, was the scene of so much suffering, this was due according to him not so much to private property as to the shackles which still fettered enterprise. The solution of the social problem must in his opinion be found not in abolishing private property, but in freeing it completely.

February 1848 changed his entire outlook. His enthusiasm was aroused and he wanted to believe that the British public was interested in the social experiments being made across the Channel. Though, as he confessed, sceptical about many of them, he was, nevertheless, glad that they were being tried. And in the second edition of his treatise published in 1849 and the third published in 1852, under the influence of events in France, he made most far-reaching alterations throughout, but above all in his chapters on 'Property' and 'The Futurity of the Labouring Classes'. To a criticism of Saint-Simon he added a most sympathetic appreciation of Fourierism.[2] He refused to pronounce on the question whether freedom and justice would be reconciled on a basis of private property or of Communism. The Socialists he pronounced 'one of the most valuable elements of human improvement now existing',[3] and declared that, if he must choose between society as it was with its iniquitous inequalities in the distribution of wealth and Communism, 'all the difficulties, great or small, of Communism would be but as dust in the balance'.[4]

It is interesting to observe in the most enlightened Dissenting

[1] J. Stuart Mill, *Autobiography*, 1873, p. 231.
[2] 2nd ed., pp. 260 sqq., and 3rd ed., pp. 258 sqq.
[3] 2nd ed., p. 255.
[4] 3rd ed., pp. 253-4.

circles, in particular in the extremely intellectual Unitarian body, the expression of similar sentiments. Miss Evans, the future George Eliot, who had long been unhappy because she was, she believed, compelled to live in one of those purely negative epochs of which the Saint-Simonians spoke, began to feel proud of her age. 'I would consent', she wrote, 'to have a year clipt off my life for the sake of witnessing such a scene as that of the men of the barricades bowing to the image of Christ who first taught fraternity to men.'[1] In 1848, Miss Gaskell's *Mary Barton* was published, a novel which was an apology for the crime which despair drove the workers to commit during a strike. And Miss Martineau, generally regarded as nothing but a popularizer of orthodox utilitarianism in its most commonplace and middle-class form, ends her *History of England during the Thirty Years' Peace* on a very different note. 'While all this is done—so much progress achieved that appears to be incontrovertible—what remains to be done? Something greater than all that has been achieved. The tremendous Labour question remains absolutely untouched. . . . The question of the Rights of Labour is pressing upon us.' Its 'solution may probably be the central fact of the next period of British history; and then, better than now, it may be seen that in preparation for it lies the chief interest of the preceding Thirty Years' Peace'.[2] These, it may be said, were isolated voices; in any case they came from narrowly restricted circles, and perhaps were spoken into the void. The continued success of Mill's *Political Economy* after the sensational additions introduced in 1849 and 1852 testifies to the contrary.

Carlyle on his part continued his prophesyings. He had in truth nothing to say in view of the convulsions of 1848 on the Continent which he had not said already on occasion of the disturbances in England in 1839 and 1842. But his tone became, if possible, even harsher in his *Latter Day Pamphlets*, published in 1850. Democracy, he said, has arrived and will invade the entire world. But does the overthrow by the West of its monarchies and

---

[1] Miss Evans to V. Sidbree, February 1848 (*George Eliot's Life*, 1886, vol. i, p. 145). See also a letter to Charles Bray, June 5, 1848: 'Poor Louis Blanc! The newspapers make me melancholy. . . . I worship the man who has written as the climax of his appeal against society: "L'inégalité des talents *doit aboutir* non à l'inégalité des retributions mais à l'inégalité des devoirs" . . . I feel that society is training men and women for hell' (ibid., vol. i, p. 153).

[2] Harriet Martineau, *The History of England during the Thirty Years' Peace*, 1850, book vi, ch. 17, pp. 715-16.

aristocracies mean that it will be able to dispense permanently with monarchy and aristocracy? Not at all. The nature of society, indeed nature universally, is monarchic and aristocratic. Europe is merely ridding herself of sham monarchies and sham aristocracies, of governments whose illegitimacy has been proved by the mere fact of their collapse. We are witnessing 'the universal bankruptcy of imposture'. Freedom, on the other hand, the absence of all government, is not itself a legitimate form of government. 'West Indian blacks are emancipated and, it appears, refuse to work. Irish whites have long been entirely emancipated; and nobody asks them to work.'[1]

What, then, of England, whose peace has not been troubled by the revolution of 1848, the country which shocks Carlyle so deeply, where everyone is willing to practise rituals, monarchic, religious, and parliamentary, which represent no profound conviction, provided cotton gets duly spun, the pastures produce enough beef, spices come from the West Indies, shares continue to be marketable, and the banks make payment in specie? Even England will be carried away by the universal movement, though, we may hope, not 'in the form of street barricades and insurrectionary pikes'.[2]

The same problem must be solved in the same fashion. An aristocracy incapable of ruling must be replaced by a new governing class fit to rule. It already existed in England. It consisted of the 'captains of industry' who had proved their capacity by the management of their factories. But they must free themselves from the philosophy of *laisser faire* and acquiescence and understand that their capability, while conferring rights, imposes duties. The workers who toil at present for a starvation wage or are unemployed must become soldiers of industry serving under their command. They must be given Ireland to cultivate, the commons of England and the waste lands of Scotland to plough, three kingdoms and forty colonies to exploit. Accompanied by the new expression, 'captain of industry', which would become a cliché, Saint-Simon's prescription of a regimented industry seemed to him, as earlier after 1830, the solution of the labour problem. And we must give the recipe, the organization of labour, which fifteen years before had attracted Carlyle and in the open-

---

[1] Carlyle, *Latter Day Pamphlets*, 1850. Pamphlet i, p. 30.
[2] Carlyle, op. cit., p. 11.

ing months of 1848 was bruited so noisily in the streets of Paris, its original Saint-Simonian meaning which was undoubtedly Socialism, but also, Carlyle would say for that very reason, a hierarchical order.

Carlyle was an isolated voice. He plumed himself on being so. But his spectacular isolation was perhaps a means of keeping himself in the limelight. Even when his countrymen were taking a road other than that on which he would set their feet, he exercised over them a queer kind of influence, in a sense against the grain and not easy to define. It was not limited to the Tories, who sympathized with his constant eulogies of strong governments, though they dared not subscribe to his opinions and were scandalized by his unorthodox religious and political views. It was the most advanced democrats who delighted to quote his denunciations of the hypocrisy of the Whigs and the crimes of Mammon.[1] And through the channel of a curious group founded on the morrow of the February revolution and as its repercussion, what we may term Carlylian Socialism became in a considerably modified form influential.

3

Charles Kingsley, an Anglican clergyman and the son of a clergyman, came of a good family. When obliged later than usual to choose a profession, he had hesitated between the Army and the Church and finally chose the Church, because he could not afford a commission. He was a typical Tory clergyman, but a man who took his clerical duties very seriously and who had early come under the influence of Carlyle's ideas as conveyed by the writings of an eccentric theologian, Frederick Dennison Maurice. The religion he professed combined reverence for the heroism and nobility of Protestant Christianity with an equally profound contempt for all the dogmas in which the Churches sought to confine Christian sentiment, whether they emanated from Geneva or Rome. He had, moreover, been persuaded to read, and had read with admiration, the writings in which about the beginning of 1840 Carlyle expounded his social views. He

---

[1] For Carlyle's influence on the working class, see Charles Kingsley, *Alton Locke, Tailor and Poet: an Autobiography*: 'It shook a little of my faith in the infallibility of my own class to hear such severe animadversion on them, from a person who professed herself as much a disciple of Carlyle as any working man' (ed. 1852, p. 167).

was, therefore, ripe for conversion to what he would term Christian Socialism. But to effect that conversion it required 1848.

On Monday, April 10, Kingsley decided to accompany back to London Parker, a publisher who had spent the week-end with him in his country parish of Eversley, that he might see for himself what would happen at Westminster. Parker, as he bade good-bye to his host's family, said, with a smile, that on arrival he might find his shop plundered or he might himself be thrown into the fountain in Trafalgar Square. When they reached London, and still more when they made their way to Kennington, they found that the expected insurrection had vanished into thin air.[1] But when four or five friends met the same evening in Parker's shop they refused to be satisfied with the victory, and agreed in the conclusion that England was heading for further crises unless she learned the lesson of that day's events.

One of the group present, Ludlow, had been educated in a Parisian *lycée* and strongly influenced by French Socialism.[2] He explained to the others, and Kingsley's Carlylism had prepared him to grasp at once what he meant, the need to distinguish in Chartism between its empty democratic formulas which had so signally failed and the Socialist aspirations concealed beneath them, which were the life and soul of the movement. They were excited by the reports in the papers of a meeting held in Manchester on April 20 which demanded bread for those who are starving and the regulation of wages as it had been practised in the Middle Ages, of another meeting in the same city on the same evening which called for Boards of Trade to be set up everywhere for the amicable settlement of labour disputes, and of a lecturer who had been applauded by his audience when he stated that the time had gone by when it was sufficient to dismiss Communism with scorn. For Communism, he said, was an attempt to discover a better substitute for competition.[3]

The group addressed an appeal to the Chartists asking them whether they sincerely believed that, if they obtained the six points of the Charter, it would make them free in the only sense

---

[1] Ch. Kingsley, *His Letters and Memoirs of His Life*, 1877, vol. i, p. 154.

[2] On the front page of a collection of *Tracts on Socialism* made by F. J. Furnivall, now in the British Museum, the latter wrote: 'J. M. Ludlow was the mainspring of our Christian Socialist Movement. Maurice and the rest of us knew nothing about Socialism. Ludlow, educated in Paris, knew all. He got us round Maurice, and really led us.'

[3] Résumé of a lecture given by A. Y. Scott, 'On the Development of the Principle of Socialism in France' (*Politics for the People*. Supplement for May 1848, p. 90).

in which a Christian could understand freedom. And at the same time they asked Christians how they could hope to enlighten the ignorant masses, if they left them to wallow in their destitution.[1] They cherished the hope of saving Socialism from the ruin of Chartism, and considered it the strict duty of a genuine Christian to replace the selfish system of competition by a system of co-operation. In their eyes April 10 acquired a mystic significance imparted by the myth which had become for them the centre round which the entire Christian religion revolved. April 10 was the day when Socialism had perished in its materialistic form of Chartism to be reborn in the spiritual form of Christian Socialism.[2] They organized propaganda by tracts,[3] periodicals,[4] and books. In 1850 and 1851 Kingsley published two novels which were widely read and discussed. They told the story, the first of a young workman, the second of a young gamekeeper who after many storms found in Christian Socialism intellectual satisfaction and spiritual peace.[5]

Not even a brief sketch of this group, however, could be considered satisfactory which did not mention the influence exercised over it and over Kingsley in particular by the opinions of a young art critic, John Ruskin, who was himself a disciple of Carlyle. It was only at a later period and under the influence of the Christian Socialists that Ruskin would become a champion of English Socialism. But he was already helping Kingsley to complete his theology and politics by an appropriate æsthetic.[6]

The propaganda of Kingsley and his friends won for 'Socialism' an entrance into circles which would otherwise have been closed to it. By the omnipotence of a book Mill was able to shake the anti-Socialist prejudices of his Liberal and free trade readers. By

[1] Kingsley, *His Letters and Memories of His Life*, 4th ed., 1877, vol. i, pp. 156 sqq.
[2] Kingsley, *Alton Locke*, ed. 1852, p. 368: 'Believe me, that tenth of April, which you fancied the death-day of liberty, has awakened a spirit in high as well as in low life, which children yet unborn will bless.'
[3] *Tracts by Christian Socialists*, 1850.
[4] *Politics for the People*, published by John W. Parker, May 6 till July 29, 1848, with two supplements dating from July. The *Christian Socialist*, a journal conducted by several of the promoters of the London Working Men's Association, was published in a large format from November 2 till June 28, 1851, and in a small format from July 5 till December 27, 1851.
[5] *Alton Locke*, 1850. *Yeast*, 1851 (the novel had appeared in *Fraser's Magazine* in 1848). For these novels and for Christian Socialism in general, L. Cazamian, *Le Roman Social en Angleterre* (1830-1850), 1904: Dickens, Disraeli, Mrs. Gaskell, Kingsley, pp. 436 sqq.
[6] See the review n the *Economist*, May 26, 1849, of Ruskin's *The Seven Lamps of Architecture*.

the esteem in which his writings were held as literature Carlyle wielded a certain influence in Tory circles and could complete the work of Young England, a group which was on the decline and whose showiness he had always disliked. Of the religious groups, which alone were sufficiently organized for effective social action, the Christian Socialists undoubtedly occupied a stronger position in the Establishment than such Unitarians as Miss Evans, Mrs. Gaskell, or Miss Martineau held in Nonconformity. The latter were scarcely Christian and suspect *a priori* to the pietists of the Evangelical sects. The former in spite of Maurice's heterodox views attracted the sympathies of the Low Church by their ardent Protestantism, of the High Church by a corporatism which seemed more in harmony with their emphasis on the Church than with their opponents' individualism.[1] We can hardly exaggerate the importance of the part played by the Christian Socialists after the first anti-French panic had passed in dispelling the terror of Socialism felt by the middle classes and reconciling them to it or at least to a particular version of it.

We must now inquire how deep this current of Socialist feeling flowed and there is no better method of measuring this than to discover what influence it may have exercised on contemporary legislation.

III   SOCIAL REFORMS AND
THE DEMISE OF CHARTISM

I

Christian Socialism certainly does not appear to have influenced factory legislation at this period. We have seen that after strenuous and prolonged efforts the Ten Hours' Act had been passed in 1847. It came into force on May 1, 1848.[2] But the attempt to execute its provisions proved that factory owners were able to make it a dead letter. When an inspector of labour

[1] In the *Christian Socialist* of May 22, 1851, a correspondent calls attention to a series of articles favourable to the Christian Socialists which had appeared in the *Guardian*, the organ of the High Church party, and comments: 'There are several reasons, I think, why they should understand our movement. They, at all events, acknowledge the importance of corporate life, and assert a ground of fellowship which does not rest upon the state of the individual man, but upon a divine fact.' See H. U. Faulkner, *Chartism and the Churches*, 1916.

[2] See above, pp. 171-3.

tried to put it into force, legal decisions reduced him to impotence.[1] The courts refused to enforce the provision of the Act of 1844 prohibiting interruptions of labour and thus enabled millowners without breaking the Ten Hours' Act to keep all their workers in the factory till closing time. The Government gave up the attempt to enforce the Statute. And even Lord Ashley resigned himself to the admission that his work had been 'nullified'.[2]

On the other hand, 1848 saw the reform of public hygiene, whose fate had been in doubt for the last five years.[3] On February 11 Lord Morpeth, the Commissioner for Waters and Forests, reintroduced the Bill he had been compelled to drop the previous year.[4] It was a timid measure. For it did not apply to London. And the local committees for whose formation it provided, in the boroughs the municipal authorities, elsewhere boards elected for the purpose, were entrusted with only a few compulsory functions, others, sewerage, for example, and street paving, remaining optional. The Bill, however, like its predecessor of 1847, established a central authority, analogous to the Poor Law Commission, the Board of Health. This brought it once more into collision with the borough corporations and all who were opposed to centralization 'after the French pattern'. In spite of the efforts of *The Times* and a section of the local Press which recognized its merits,[5] the Bill emerged seriously mutilated from the debates in Parliament in May and June.[6]

The Public Health Act as finally passed on August 15[7] set up a Board of Health, consisting of no more than three members, of whom only one was a salaried civil servant. He, it is true, was Edwin Chadwick, the Secretary of the Poor Law Commission, who might be expected to make the new Board

---

[1] For the fruitless attempts made by Inspector Horner in Lancashire, see the *Economist* December 16 and 30, 1848, January 6, 1849.

[2] Lord Ashley's *Diary*, February 1, 1850: 'The Attorney-General said to me this afternoon, "They will give judgment not according to law, but on policy."' February 15, 1850, 'The Ten Hours' Act nullified. The work to be done all over again' (J. L. and B. Hammond, *Lord Shaftesbury*, 1923, pp. 135-6).

[3] See above, pp. 176-9.

[4] *Parliamentary Debates*, 3rd Ser., vol. xcvi, p. 385.

[5] J. L. and B. Hammond, *The Age of the Chartists*, pp. 304-5 and 310.

[6] H. of C., May 5, 8, 11, 18, and 25; June 15, 1848 (*Parl. Deb.*, 3rd Ser., vol. xcviii, pp. 713, 764, 872, 1172, and 1414; vol. xcix, p. 689).

[7] H. of L., Aug. 15, 1848 (ibid., 3rd Ser., vol. ci, p. 141).

active—and unpopular. But it had no powers of compulsion. The utmost it could do was to enforce the creation of a local Health Council, in districts where the rate of mortality exceeded 23 per cent. For adoption of the reform remained optional, and these councils could function only with the consent of the local authorities. That is to say, it was left to the decision in the ensuing years of some 200 corporations, among them the corporations of the important manufacturing towns. Indirectly the measure had a good effect. For fear of government interference induced towns not coming within the scope of the Act to undertake reforms on their own initiative.[1] The work achieved in 1848 cannot, however, be connected with the movement of ideas which the Continental revolutions had provoked. On the contrary, it fell short of the hopes expressed, as we have seen, in 1847. The progress of Socialism was not calculated to reconcile the English to centralization.

2

Another important social measure passed by Parliament during the period treated in this chapter was the Act of 1852 'to legalize the Formation of Industrial and Provident Societies'.[2] Unlike earlier legislation this was due directly to the Christian Socialists. In 1851, towards the close of the session, they were pressing the Whig Cabinet to introduce a Bill into the Commons. They were defeated by the direct refusal of Labouchere, the President of the Board of Trade.[3] The following spring, however, the Conservatives, in the circumstances which we shall describe later, were in office for some months. Disraeli, Chancellor of the Exchequer and Leader in the Commons, persuaded his colleagues to prove by passing the measure quickly that, unlike Whigism, a regenerated Toryism was in truth the people's friend, genuinely eager to tackle the social problem.[4] The Bill gave the co-operative societies legal status, and the fact that its enactment was a victory won by Kingsley and his friends throws light on the character of Christian Socialism.

[1] J. L. and B. Hammond, *The Age of the Chartists*, pp. 308-9.
[2] 15 & 16 Vict. Cap. 31: An Act to legalize the formation of Industrial and Provident Societies.
[3] *Christian Socialist*, July 12, 1851, p. 23.
[4] H. of C., March 8, 1852: Slaney and Walpole's speeches (*Parliamentary Debates*, 3rd Ser., vol. cxix, pp. 1256 sqq.). Ch. Kingsley, *Life and Memories*, vol. i, pp. 313 sqq.

When the Chartist rising collapsed in 1842 many of the disillusioned revolutionaries fell back on co-operation. And the technical invention of the Rochdale Pioneers coming thus at a particularly opportune moment had fostered the growth of co-operative societies. Goods were sold at a price little lower than the current market price to shareholders of the Society. At the end of the year the profits were divided among the members, not in proportion to the amount of capital represented by their shares, but in proportion to their purchases. And a portion was retained for the final establishment of the complete co-operation preached by Owen. But it was not long before the co-operators lost sight of this ulterior aim and the distribution of profits in proportion to purchases had become the essential feature of the institution. In Lancashire and also in other districts the success of the Rochdale co-operative had produced imitators who had been equally successful. It had been the first to institute a wholesale department, conducted on the same principle as the local co-operatives which purchased from it, and at the end of the year sharing its profit between the latter in proportion to their purchases. It had also been the first to institute productive departments, a bakery and a weaving factory. And though the first attempt had proved for the moment a failure, a second had been a complete success and been copied by many other groups.

The founders of these co-operatives were secularists, avowed enemies of religion and religious morality, as being not only useless but actually harmful to mankind. The ideological goal of Owenite co-operation was to regenerate man by changing the environment in which he grew up and creating an environment in which it would be to his interest to be good, and he would promote the welfare of all by promoting his own. The irreligion of Owen and his disciples shocked the public. Nevertheless, they benefited by their hostility to the Chartists, as the Quakers at the beginning of the eighteenth century had benefited by their opposition to the three Nonconformist denominations. Then the Tories had overlooked the extreme unorthodoxy of Quaker beliefs, because their uncompromising pacifism made them repudiate rebellion, as they repudiated war. Now the Conservatives were equally grateful to the co-operators for keeping aloof from politics of any description, even democratic, and refusing on principle to participate in the Chartist agitations of the last few years. And it was not surprising that before long some Conservative philanthropists reached the conclusion that the principle of co-operation should be retained, the materialism and atheism on which Owen had based it dropped, and his order of ideas in a sense reversed. Owen had treated the moral problem as a social problem. On the contrary, the social problem is a moral problem and should be treated as such and co-operation in particular can flourish only on the foundation of charity. This was the view expressed by James Pierrepont Greaves in his *Sacred Socialists.* Instead of looking for scientific arrangements so skilfully contrived that the abundance of wealth produced would exceed men's needs, he wanted men everywhere to learn to live contented without needing or desiring riches.[1] This point of view gave birth to the Communist Church, and the Leeds Redemption Society, in Ireland to the Community of White Friends, in Scotland to the Alva Associative Society.[2] Young England itself took the field, and on May 27, 1846, the Bishop of Norwich, supported by Lord John Manners, inaugurated at Exeter Hall a Church of England Self-supporting Village Society.[3] That evening of April 10, 1848, Maurice, Ludlow, Kingsley, and their friends had simply decided to continue a movement already begun and purely English in origin. Nor should we forget that before the stir produced by Parisian Socialism the term Socialism meant Owen's co-operation and nothing else. When Kingsley's group called themselves Christian Socialists they did so to make it clear that they were not Chartists, but Christian Owenites.

This does not mean, however, that Paris had no influence on the movement. On the contrary, it exercised through Ludlow an influence which can be precisely determined. The English co-operatives, already so prosperous, were all copies of the Rochdale model. They were all co-operative stores, that is to say, what we should now call consumers' co-operatives. The Christian Socialists made two criticisms of them. In the first place they were open only to their shareholders. That is to say, their members must be in a position to save at least a pound. And they sold only for cash payments. In consequence the lowest strata of the working class,

---

[1] *Christian Socialist,* March 22, 1851, vol. i, pp. 164–5. Lecture by E. Vansittart Neale on 'Socialist Systems'.

[2] *People's Journal* (vol. iii, p. 253). Article by Godwin Barnby, 'Defence of Communism. On Religion, Family, Country Property and Government: in answer to Joseph Mazzini'.

[3] *People's Journal,* June 6, 1846, 'Annals of Industry', p. 46.

those whose moral degradation lay so heavy on the Christian Socialists' conscience, could not benefit by them.[1] In the second place almost all the co-operative stores sold to the general public. So long as they sold only to their members the dividend which returned to the co-operators what would otherwise have been the shopkeeper's profit was a socialist feature. But sale to the public could not be defended on Owen's principles. For the co-operators thus became a collective business enterprise, making profit at the expense of the public. In Paris, on the other hand, where the co-operative movement had been influenced by Socialists such as Buchez and Louis Blanc, a type of workers' association had been adopted, the working association, which was a producers' co-operative and, in the opinion of the Christian Socialists, was not open to the objections they brought against the English consumers' co-operatives. It was, it is true, liable to criticism on other grounds. The members of a producers' co-operative were apt, when business was prosperous, to refuse to accept new members who would be a burden upon them if a slump came. They preferred to hire for the time wage labour and, therefore, tended to repeat in their own movement that contempt for the wage-earner which it was their professed aim to get rid of. To this objection, however, the Christian Socialists replied that a rule could be introduced, to which the entire movement would be bound, forbidding producers' co-operatives to engage temporary labour on terms less favourable than they accepted for themselves. Accordingly to the English and Rochdalian consumers' co-operative, the Christian Socialists, opposed the Parisian and Buchezian producers' co-operative.

By their zeal, intelligence, talents, and social position Kingsley's group rendered invaluable service to the co-operative movement without distinction of religious allegiance. What in particular was the purpose of that Act of 1852 mentioned above? To secure the co-operative societies in the possession of their capital, hitherto precarious. In Common Law, if their membership were less than twenty-five, they were private partnerships dissolved by the death or withdrawal of any one of their members, and in which each member had the same power as another over the entire property of the association and each was individually responsible for all the

---

[1] *Christian Socialist*, June 28, 1851, 'Co-operative Stores and their Management', vol. i, pp. 273 sqq.

debts contracted by it. There were, indeed, legal devices by which the co-operatives could protect themselves against unjust claims by their members. But they had no protection against unjust claims by persons who were not members. If their membership exceeded twenty-five, they could take advantage of the Joint Stock Companies Act of 1844.[1] But to do this a co-operative must be registered as a public company. Complicated formalities must be complied with at a cost of from fifty to a hundred pounds. And a co-operative just founded was in no position to afford such a sum. The usual procedure, therefore, was to be registered as a Friendly Society, so as to take advantage of a provision of the Friendly Societies' Act of 1846,[2] known as the Frugal Investment Clause, which permitted these societies to invest their members' savings 'for better enabling them to purchase food, clothes or other necessaries or the tools or implements of their trade or calling', provided the 'shares shall not be transferable'. It required the vigilance of the Christian Socialists to prevent this Clause being dropped in a Statute of 1850 consolidating previous legislation concerning Friendly Societies.[3] But the Clause did not apply to the working associations whose object was not purchase but sale. The only way by which they could bring themselves within the Act was to effect at every sale a fictitious sale to one of their members who would then be reputed to sell outside. But not only was this a complicated procedure, it made the society dependent on the good faith of the individual in question. And the lawyers of the group pointed out that even the co-operative stores forfeited the protection of the Friendly Societies Act when, as they nearly all did, they sold to the public. They brought home to the entire co-operative movement their urgent need of a measure directly legalizing their position. In 1852 they obtained it.[4]

[1] 7 & 8 Vict. Cap. 110: An Act for the Registration, Incorporation and Regulation of Joint Stock Companies.
[2] 9 & 10 Vict. Cap. 27.
[3] 13 & 14 Vict. Cap. 115: An Act to Consolidate and Amend the Laws relating to Friendly Societies. H. of C., June 19, 1850, and H. of L., August 12, 1850 (*Parliamentary Debates*, 3rd Ser., vol. xcii, pp. 95 sqq., and vol. cxiii, pp. 1017-18). For previous legislation, see 4 & 5 Will. IV Cap. 40, and 3 & 4 Vict. Cap. 73.
[4] The Act to Legalize the Formation of Industrial and Provident Societies with model rules for the Formation of Productive Associations, prepared by a committee appointed at the Co-operative Conference, held in London, and approved by the Registrar of Friendly Societies, accompanied by an explanatory statement and suggestions. Drawn up by Members of the Society for Promoting Working Men's Associations, London. Printed by the Working Printers' Association.

3

The Act of 1852 may be regarded as a political and legal seal set upon the influence of the Christian Socialists. It was a powerful influence. They had created a new type of Socialism calculated to attract, by reassuring them, those who had been alarmed by some extreme doctrines preached by Owen. In the first place, of course, there was no hostility to Christianity. But there was also no Communism. 'Go through all our associations,' wrote a member of the group; 'you will find men throwing in common a certain number of hours of their time, selling their labour under common management, devoting a certain proportion of its produce to common purposes—nothing more. The members do not live together. They not only do not throw their private property into a common stock, but they divide their weekly allowances in varying proportions. They divide their profits amongst themselves.'[1] Though in sympathy with the group led by Lord Ashley they were suspicious of anything approaching State Socialism. They were, indeed, prepared for occasional measures of State regulation, to protect, for example, the men who unloaded timber at the London docks, who were mercilessly exploited by the publicans employed as agents to hire them.[2] But at no time in their zealous campaign against the scandalous sweating by London tailors does the notion of a State regulation of the trade appear to have crossed their minds. What they wanted was a league of consumers who would refuse to buy clothes made by employers of sweated labour. And in 1849 the Christian Socialists founded an association of journeyman tailors to inaugurate a new era when they would no longer work under the yoke of employers. They advocated the foundation of a Society to assist associations of labourers to be formed.

They proceeded to elaborate a more ambitious scheme and Christian Socialism culminated in Utopia. At Bury they founded among the railwaymen a General Labour Redemption Society which they dreamed of extending to the entire Kingdom. By paying a penny a head every week the working class would accumulate enough money to buy up the entire capital of the nation and transform a capitalist society into a vast co-operative

[1] J. M. Ludlow, *Christian Socialism and its Opponents*, 1851, p. 9.
[2] *Christian Socialist*, February 22 and March 22, 1851 (vol. i, pp. 134 and 166).

based on the right to subsistence and the obligation to work.[1] The Society, however, was open to members of all classes; and one of the rules expressly condemned any member who failed to understand that his membership of the Society made him independent of his employer. The Christian Socialists had little liking for the militant Trade Unions.[2] They wanted to establish their Socialism by reconciling the classes, not by class war. Obedient to the spirit of the times and disagreeing on this point fundamentally with Carlyle and approaching Mill, whose chapter on the 'futurity of the labouring classes' was their breviary, they sought by co-operation to reconcile not only Christianity and Socialism, but Socialism and freedom. We cannot over-estimate the influence of the co-operative ideal in the England of 1850. It was the same, it is true, in contemporary Paris. But the Parisian movement was cut short by the *coup d'état* of December. The English developed peaceably.

The hold which co-operation had taken on the imagination of the working class may be judged by the fact that several of the large Unions formed about this time—the Amalgamated Engineers, for example, and the Amalgamated Iron Trades— decided to set aside by a formal provision of their constitution a portion of their funds for the purpose of organizing producers' co-operatives among their unemployed members, and that the innovation became sufficiently popular to alarm the Chartist leaders who were concerned to keep the Unions true to uncompromising democracy and class warfare.[3] They had a further cause for anxiety when in the very bosom of Chartism the co-operators, in Lancashire chiefly, formed themselves into a regular party with recognized leaders.[4]

In speaking of these leaders we are not thinking of Thomas Cooper, the author of the *Purgatory of Suicides*, a convert from

---

[1] *Christian Socialist*, December 14, 1850 (vol. i, pp. 52 sqq.). *Tracts by Christian Socialists*, iv; *Labour and the People*, part II (pp. 12-13). For the Christian Socialists' co-operative Utopia the concluding chapters of *Alton Locke* should be read, in particular pp. 426, 433, and 437 (ed. 1882).

[2] Their attitude towards the Unions was, in fact, one of considerable embarrassment. See Ch. Kingsley to Tom Hughes, January 28, 1852 (*Life of Kingsley*, vol. i, pp. 311 sqq.). Address 'To the Members of the Typographical Profession' (in the *Christian Socialist*, June 28, 1851, vol. i, p. 276). See, on the other hand, S. and B. Webb, *History of Trade Unionism*, p. 215.

[3] R. G. Gammage, *History of the Chartist Movement*, pp. 382-3.

[4] F. Engels to Karl Marx, January 8, 1851 (*Der Briefwechsel zwischen F. Engels und Karl Marx*, vol. i, pp. 124 sqq.).

Chartism, who became an orthodox Christian Socialist,[1] but of the youthful Holyoake, destined to become the leading figure and finally the patriarch of British co-operation—at the opening of the twentieth century I was able to make his personal acquaintance—who, in 1851, captured the Chartist executive and obtained its sanction for a programme of free trade, fiscal economies, and a reform of the franchise which would not necessarily go as far as universal suffrage.[2]

The Social democrats, however, made an effort to stem the rising tide of Liberalism. O'Brien, the most powerful mind among them, had finally broken with Chartism. In Reynolds's *Political Instructor*[3] he published a series of articles entitled 'The Rise, Progress and Phases of Human Slavery; how it came into the world, and how it shall be made to go out'. In these he drew up in 1851 the programme of a new league which he founded, the National Reform League. The State should purchase land and lease it to the unemployed. A currency guaranteed by the precious metals, which was the cause of all our economic disorders, must be replaced by a currency guaranteed by the real wealth of the nation or the credit of the State. Markets or public stores should be opened in every town to organize the barter of goods by impartial officials, their value to be measured by corn or labour.[4] Meanwhile, Ernest Jones and Julian Harney wearied the Chartist world with their quarrels. Harney disappeared from the executive, and Jones resigned in his turn.[5]

In 1851 O'Connor returned to Chartism. Harney and Jones were reconciled with each other and with O'Connor, and in concert summoned a Convention to meet on the anniversary of April 10, which was honoured by a leader in *The Times*.[6] It

---

[1] Th. Cooper quarrelled with O'Connor and founded, in January 1849, a new weekly, *The Plain Speaker*, which survived until July. In January 1850 *Cooper's Journal* began to appear. See R. G. Gammage, *History of the Chartist Movement*, p. 346, and for Cooper's first relations with Kingsley, *Life and Memoirs*, vol. i, pp. 183-4.

[2] R. G. Gammage, *History of the Chartist Movement*, pp. 384 and 388.

[3] For Reynold's's *Political Instructor*, whose first number appeared on November 10, 1848, and O'Brien's activities after his rupture with Chartism, see R. G. Gammage, *History of the Chartist Movement*, pp. 346 and 351; M. Hovell, *The Chartist Movement*, pp. 297-9.

[4] The articles were collected in one volume in 1885. For O'Brien's social programme, see pp. 174 sqq.

[5] R. G. Gammage, *History of the Chartist Movement*, pp. 352-3, 385, and 388. Karl Marx to F. Engels, March 3, 1852 (*Der Briefwechsel zwischen F. Engels und Karl Marx*, vol. i, p. 304).

[6] *The Times*, April 22, 1851: 'The six points of the Charter are pure democracy; the programme before us attempts to reconcile us with Socialism.' See in *The Times* of April

declared that a political revolution would be ineffective unless it were accompanied by a social revolution, called for the nationalization of the land, and made considerable use of the co-operative principle to solve the question of labour. 'They are stealing from us,' said the Christian Socialists.[1] Thus O'Connor for the first time accepted Socialism. But it was on his political death-bed. A year later the aged demagogue lost his reason.

Nothing more was heard in England now of simultaneous meetings, conventions, national petitions, and general strikes. Chartism as it receded into the past became an heroic legend. The veteran Chartist no longer inspired loathing or terror as an imitator or accomplice of the revolutionaries of Paris and the Irish assassins. He was recognized as a genuine product of British civilization, a man brave, patient, and tenacious, who could suffer for an ideal, whose nobility was admitted when there was no prospect of its speedy realization, a man who had been dismissed by his employer for his beliefs or gone to prison for them. He was respected, the object of a naïve flattery. He was conscious of being in his place a person of importance. His intelligence was blunt, his knowledge limited. But he played a distinctive part in the national life, preaching an extension of the franchise, running co-operative societies, working for the cause of popular education, and contributing to periodicals written for the instruction of the masses. Nor did he despair of seeing England one day reach the Chartist goal, though by other paths than those Chartism had foreseen. For he witnessed the silent achievement with the connivance of the political economists of a species of undogmatic Socialism which had not issued from the brain of a social philosopher, a framer of systems, but was the spontaneous birth of practical necessities. There were the laws protecting labour in factories, the improvement of public health in the large towns, the progress of popular education. And co-operation was advancing triumphantly. These movements would surely produce one day, in a form at present unpredictable, Socialism of one kind or another, possibly even Communism. But the time was not yet. So many privileges and monopolies had still to be destroyed that for a long time to come there would be ample scope for the

23 a reproduction *in extenso* of the programme adopted by the Convention and a complete list of the thirty signatories.

[1] *Christian Socialist*, April 26, 1851 (vol. i, p. 205). See also the same periodical, June 7, 1851 (vol. i, p. 250).

Liberals, free traders, and upholders of *laisser faire* to pursue their negative but salutary task.[1]

[1] A remarkable exposition of this point of view will be found in a little book by James Hole, *Lectures on Social Science and the Organization of Labour*, 1851. The Conservative Press went further on the road of optimism. What was the reason, asked *The Times*, that England had been so little affected by the general upheaval? Because she was already reaping, where the other nations were sowing. She already possessed a free Press, a representative Government, hardly any monopolies, no army to speak of. 'In point of fact, under very great hindrances and drawbacks, the dream of the Communist and Socialist receives (in England) its nearest fulfilment!' (We have been unable to trace this quotation.—*Editor*.)

CHAPTER VI

Financial and Domestic Politics 1848–1852

I THE REPEAL OF THE NAVIGATION LAWS

I

WHATEVER the influence exercised by Socialist ideals in the England of 1848, English legislation pursued the tenor of its way, as though no revolution had taken place on the Continent. The free traders, however, were convinced that they held the key to the solution of the social problem. For in their opinion the welfare of the working classes could be secured, not only without interference by the State, but on the contrary by reducing to the utmost its functions and, in consequence, its expenditure. Their agitation accordingly assumed new forms.

When the Irish famine had made it necessary to suspend the duties on imported corn, the campaign conducted by the Anti-Corn-Law League which for many years had assumed such formidable proportions, made it obviously out of the question ever to reimpose them. Therefore, the sole course open to a British Prime Minister was to propose their repeal without further delay. Much the same thing happened in the case of the Navigation Laws. When their application was suspended in favour of foreign vessels importing corn there had not, it is true, been any organized campaign for their abolition. But the suspension immediately gave birth to it.

It alarmed British shipowners, who protested to the Government against any alteration of the law should it be contemplated. In October 1846 Lord Clarendon, President of the Board of Trade, gave them the assurances they sought. In the following March, however, the Government consented to an inquiry, and though the Committee to which it was entrusted had reached no conclusion, when the dissolution of Parliament terminated its existence, it did not pass unnoticed that the majority of witnesses heard by it had been in favour of repealing the Navigation Laws.[1] The shipowners' fears were justified.

[1] For these events, see Lord Hardwicke's speech, H. of L., February 25, 1848 (*Parliamentary Debates*, 3rd Ser., vol. xcvi, pp. 1314 sqq.).

At the opening of the new Parliament, the speech from the Throne recommended the legislature to study the changes it might be advisable to make in the law as it stood.[1]

What had won the Cabinet over to this reform? A few weeks earlier the United States had taken diplomatic action. Their ambassador, Bancroft, had proposed to Palmerston a system of complete mutual reciprocity by which British and American vessels would enjoy equal freedom of trade in the ports of both countries. Palmerston, while pointing out that the final decision must rest with the Parliament shortly to assemble, had expressed himself so favourably that the American Press which made the negotiations public treated his reply as a definite promise.[2]

But to give satisfaction to the United States was not the Government's sole motive. It was being pressed by the Colonies which, like the States, asked for the repeal of the Navigation Laws. Canadian corn had benefited since 1843 by a preferential tariff which reduced the duty on its importation by the fixed amount of one shilling a quarter. The repeal of the Corn Law effected by Peel deprived them of this preference. And at the same time the alterations he had made in the tariff had been prejudicial to the import of Canadian timber. In consequence, since August, Canada had made repeated representations in London.[3] The revision of the duties on sugar undertaken by Lord John Russell had caused discontent in the West Indies. Lord George Bentinck made himself the planters' mouthpiece and took advantage of the unpopularity of a measure which would profit the slave-owning States to demand its repeal. Lord John could escape a hostile vote only by agreeing to postpone until 1854 the application of the new tariff on sugar which should have come into force in 1851.[4] In these circumstances it was not easy to disregard the wishes of Canada when she asked that to compensate her for the sacrifices forced upon her by free trade she should be relieved in future from the excessively high freightage which their monopoly enabled British

---

[1] Speech from the throne, November 23, 1847.
[2] Lord Hardwicke's speech mentioned above. J. H. Clapham, *Economic History of Modern Britain*, vol. i, p. 505.
[3] Ibid., vol. i, p. 504.
[4] Lord John made this concession on June 16, 1848. Even so, on June 29 he could secure, even with Peel's help, a majority of no more than 15 (Sp. Walpole, *Life of Lord John Russell*, vol. ii, pp. 4-5. Maccoby, *English Radicalism*, pp. 300-1).

shipowners to exact. And satisfaction must also be given to the West Indian colonists who obtained their corn and timber from the United States by enabling them to employ the American ships which brought them to carry their sugar to Great Britain.

Finally, on the Continent the enforcement of the Navigation Laws provoked protests and threats of reprisal. For the past twenty years relaxations of their strict tenor had been permitted. Though goods not brought in vessels belonging to the country of their origin were not permitted to enter the country,[1] certain ports were treated as the natural outlets of countries without direct access to the sea. Mecklenburg-Strelitz, for example, was allowed to ship its produce to Britain in vessels sailing from Danzig or Antwerp. But these privileges excited the jealousy of the Dutch and above all of Prussia, which rightly saw in this policy an attempt to combat the extension of the *Zollverein* in Germany. When the repeal of the Corn Law was decided, Bunsen, the influential Prussian Minister in London, began to press for the simultaneous repeal of the Navigation Laws. In the course of the next few years his demands became more insistent and were accompanied by a hint that the *Zollverein* might find itself compelled to take steps to defend itself against treatment intolerable to German honour.[2]

2

Though for all these reasons it was favourable to the Reform the Cabinet was in no hurry to undertake it. It was not until May 15, 1848, that Labouchere introduced a measure to that effect.[3] He did not fail to point out that the system it was proposed to abolish was not that of Elizabeth and Cromwell. At present the Navigation Laws were, as Peel expressed it, 'mutilated and shattered'.[4] Nor was it even the legislation of

---

[1] After 1825, however, a list was drawn up of European goods which might be imported in ships not of the country of their origin, but this concession did not apply to non-European products. In effect, this discriminated against America.
[2] J. H. Clapham, *Economic History of Modern Britain*, vol. i, p. 503.
[3] H. of C., May 15, 1848. Labouchere's speech (*Parliamentary Debates*, 3rd Ser., vol. xcviii, pp. 992 sqq.).
[4] Sir Robert Peel (H. of C., May 29, 1848): 'the mutilated and shattered state of the Navigation Laws as they now exist' (*Annual Register*, 1848, p. 79). Cf. Lord Lansdowne (H. of L., May 7, 1849): 'Instead of being to commerce a suit of impenetrable armour, it was a mere clothing of shreds and patches' (Ibid., 1849, p. 39).

1660 and 1662, but the Wallace Acts of 1822[1] and Huskisson's Navigation Acts of 1825[2] with the amendments which on the outbreak of the Irish famine had been adopted without discussion.[3] American produce entering England to be consumed there must be brought by vessels of the country of origin. European produce received more liberal treatment. It was not necessary that the European port where they had been embarked should belong to the country of their origin.[4] It was enough if the vessel belonged to the port in question.[5] Colonial trade had been left by Huskisson on the same footing as British coastal trade and remained a British monopoly. The Colonies, however, had been authorized to trade directly with other countries subject, like England herself, to the provisions of the Navigation Laws.[6] The United States had secured the admission of their vessels to British colonial ports, where, however, their produce was not accorded equal treatment with colonial.[7]

Very few, in fact, in 1848, understood in detail a system so complicated. But the notion persisted that, as Adam Smith had believed, its maintenance was necessary in the interest of national security. The proposals of the Government, therefore, met with vigorous opposition, which the Protectionists did not fail to exploit. They claimed to be the defenders of Huskisson's work and argued that the British mercantile marine, since it was obliged to pay its crews higher wages, could not possibly compete with foreign competition on an equal footing. Their arguments were refuted by G. L. Ricardo, Cobden, and James Wilson. On June 9 Peel set out all the reasons which made the reform imperative. The same day, the Cabinet obtained a majority for the measure of 294 to 177. Nevertheless, it obtained little support from a public still terrified by the memory of the previous year's crisis, and even among the working class, still hostile to the programme of the free traders,

[1] 3 Geo. IV Cap. 41, 42, 43, 44, and 45. See *History of the English People*, vol. ii, p. 124.
[2] 6 Geo. IV Cap. 109. See *History of the English People*, vol. ii, pp. 201-2.
[3] 8 & 9 Vict. Cap. 88.
[4] See footnote [1] p. 275.
[5] *History of the English People*, vol. ii, pp. 124-5. See Clapham, op. cit., vol. i, p. 331. A Portuguese vessel, therefore, might carry Spanish wine, but an American vessel might not carry Cuban sugar.
[6] *History of the English People*, vol. ii, p. 200.
[7] Ibid., vol. ii, pp. 124, 199-200.

it met with much criticism. Lord John thought it advisable to shelve the Bill.[1]

He reintroduced it the following year, but in different circumstances. The Colonial protests had become more pressing and the Governor-General of Canada had transmitted to London a warning which could not safely be disregarded. The Protectionists took advantage of these protests to demand openly a return to protection which, they said, could alone allay the discontent of the Colonies. But in a speech which produced a considerable effect Sir James Graham declared that the reform they were debating was indispensable if Canada were to remain in the Empire. The Bill became the battleground between progress and reaction. The Government, compelled to act, was victorious in the Commons. In the Lords it barely escaped defeat. Its majority on the second reading was only ten. Nevertheless, the Bill was carried, thanks to Wellington, who refused to support the Protectionist attack led by Stanley, and even more to the vote of the Bishops, the majority of whom supported the Bill.[2]

On June 26, 1849, the Navigation Laws were repealed.[3]

This thoroughgoing reform left nothing of them except the provision which gave British vessels a monopoly of the coasting trade, and that which required the crews of British merchantmen to be at least two-thirds British.[4] But the shipowners were relieved of the obligation to employ a number of apprentices proportionate to the tonnage of their vessels. While, however, the form of State interference represented by the Navigation Laws was thus abolished, the State undertook the task of securing through the Board of Trade and local committees set up in the ports better conditions of labour for the sailors and better provision for the passengers' safety and comfort.[5]

[1] *Annual Register*, 1848, pp. 69 sqq. H. of C., May 29 and June 9, 1848 (*Parliamentary Debates*, 3rd Ser., vol. xcix, pp. 24 sqq. and 646 sqq.).

[2] *Ann. Reg.*, 1849, pp. 34 sqq. For the Canadian attitude, see Lord Grey's speech (*Parl. Deb.*, 3rd Ser., vol. cv, p. 71). For Graham's speech, see *Parl. Deb.*, 3rd Ser., vol. iv, p. 675. For the voting in the Lords, see *Parl. Deb.*, 3rd Ser., vol. cv, p. 117. See, further, an excellent account in Sp. Walpole, *History of England*, vol. v, pp. 217-19.

[3] 12 & 13 Vict. Cap. 29: An Act to amend the Laws in force for the encouragement of British Shipping and Navigation.

[4] J. E. Clapham, *Economic History of Modern Britain*, vol. i, p. 505.

[5] A Statute passed in 1850 (13 & 14 Vict. Cap. 93) set up local marine boards, and a further Statute passed in 1854, the Merchant Shipping Act (17 & 18 Vict. Cap. 18), consolidated a number of previous enactments. See J. E. Clapham, op. cit., vol. ii, pp. 409, 410.

The tonnage of the British mercantile marine which in 1846 amounted to 3,199,000 tons rose to 3,759,000 in 1852. Exports rose from £57,786,000 in 1846 to £78,076,000 in 1852. The fears expressed during the debates of 1848 and 1849 were very soon discredited and the shipbuilders had no difficulty in meeting foreign competition.[1]

As a matter of fact, this success was not due primarily to Lord John, who in the debates of 1849, as in those of the previous year, had let the Peelites take the leading part.[2] On the contrary, the reform continued Peel's work, and coming, as it did, after the many alterations of the tariff he had made and at the moment when the Act of 1846 took effect on February 1, 1849, and the duty on corn was reduced to a purely nominal figure, seemed the final victory of free trade.[3]

II FISCAL POLICY

I

The repeal of the Navigation Laws was undoubtedly a signal triumph for the free traders. Emboldened by their victory they might surely have been expected to attempt to make use of it to win further conquests. Cobden called attention to the fact that, in spite of all the advances made along the road to free trade, of all European countries the United Kingdom was still the one in receipt of the greatest revenue from duties levied on foreign food-stuffs and goods, no less in fact than twenty millions a year. Of every twenty shillings spent by the poor man on the purchase of tea, ten represented duty on it, of every twenty spent on sugar, six.[4]

These duties were not protective, and the Manchester school attacked them only inasmuch as they hampered trade with the

---

[1] The natural advantages possessed by America for building wooden ships was lost when about this time vessels of iron came into general use. See Cunningham, *Growth of English Industry and Commerce, Modern Times*, vol. ii, pp. 832-3.

[2] 'Lord John Russell briefly wound up the debate, the necessity for a lengthened speech being obviated, as he said, by Sir Robert Peel's excellent speech' (*Annual Register*, 1848, p. 20). 'Lord John Russell thought it almost needless to add anything after the masterly and unanswered speech by Sir James Graham' (ibid., 1848, p. 37).

[3] Ibid., 1849, pp. 49 sqq.

[4] H. of C., March 13, 1848. Cobden's speech (*Parliamentary Debates*, 3rd Ser., vol. xcvii, pp. 505 sqq.).

countries producing tea and sugar. But the tariff still contained a large number of duties protecting manufactured or partly manufactured articles. Surely the time had come to complete the work of clearance Peel had begun and introduce another Budget like those of 1842, 1845, and 1846. The Whigs had not done so in 1847, 1848, or 1849. Nor did they dare make the attempt in the years which immediately followed the repeal of the Navigation Laws. The experiment would not be made until the Whig Ministry had fallen and been succeeded, after a Tory interregnum, by a Cabinet not purely Whig but formed by a coalition of the Whigs and Peelites, when a Peelite would be Chancellor of the Exchequer. Meanwhile, it was customary to applaud the repeal of the Corn Laws, then of the Navigation Laws as the final victory of free trade which left nothing further to be done. This halt after such sweeping reforms cannot be sufficiently explained as due to the fact that the Government was in the hands of politicians incapable of going further than the opinion of the moment and seeing what must be done to satisfy the public opinion of the morrow. For these Ministers, just because they were politicians, would have bowed to public opinion, if it had demanded immediate reductions in the tariff. But it took, in fact, another direction and let itself be guided, and in the first place by the great leaders of the Manchester school, along another path.

To understand this we must study the fiscal problem as it presented itself at the opening of 1848.

Whig finance was in difficulties. The financial year 1847–1848, not yet expired, had been disastrous. If the revenue from income tax, land and assessed taxes, and the Post Office had slightly increased, the revenue from all other sources had fallen. The revenue actually received had been only £51,362,000 instead of the estimated £52,065,000. Expenditure on the contrary had risen. The navy had cost an additional £245,000, the service of the debt incurred to relieve the distress in Ireland amounted to £422,000, and the Kaffir war had cost more than a million. In all, the expenditure, instead of the estimated £51,576,000, had reached the sum of £53,660,000. But the Kaffir war was not at an end and the unfriendly relations with France which had led her to increase her naval expenditure made it necessary for England to strengthen her army, navy, and artillery. For the following year a total expenditure of £54,596,000 was expected, a revenue of only £51,250,000.[1]

In these circumstances Lord John proposed to continue for another five years the income tax due to expire in April and to raise it from 7d. to 1s. in the pound, that is to say, from 3 to 5 per cent during the next two years. It would have been only fair to extend the tax to Ireland. But Lord John pointed out that to do so would hamper the economic recovery of the United Kingdom. The increase in the income tax would produce £3,500,000, bring the revenue up to £54,750,000, and thus balance the Budget. When money was no longer required for the Kaffir war, there would once more be a surplus which would make it possible to reduce the burden of taxation borne by industry.[2]

These proposals were greeted in the Commons with shouts of indignation. With what face could Lord John who, in 1842, had opposed Peel's restoration of the income tax, come forward now under his former adversary's indulgent eye and ask for its increase? The Protectionists expressed their surprise that in his estimates he did not dare to count upon a rapid revival of trade and a consequent increase in the revenue from the customs. But above all there was a cry for retrenchment. A motion by Hume that a committee should be appointed to effect economies indeed lost. But the Government was obliged to agree to the appointment of two committees, to inquire into expenditure.[3]

The increase in taxation was chiefly due to the expenditure on the armed forces. As we have seen, it was fear of a French attack which had led the Cabinet to undertake it. The February revolution most opportunely came to its assistance and put an end to the danger. Ten days after Lord John's speech the Chancellor of the Exchequer, Sir Charles Wood, was able to inform the House that the measures proposed were no longer necessary. It would be sufficient to continue the income tax at the present rate of 7d. and that only for three years.

The Opposition would have been obliged to content them-

[1] *Parliamentary Debates*, 3rd Ser., vol. xcvi, pp. 905-6.
[2] H. of C., February 18, 1848. Lord John Russell's speech. Lord John presented the Budget in person (*Parl. Deb.*, 3rd Ser., vol. xcvi, pp. 921 sqq., and *Annual Register*, 1848, pp. 34 sqq.).
[3] H. of C., February 18, 1848. Hume's and Granbys' speeches (*Parl. Deb.*, 3rd Ser., vol. xcvi, pp. 926 and 935. *Ann. Reg.*, 1848, p. 41).

selves with expressing their surprise at such a rapid *volte face* if Lord John's proposals had not suggested a demand for a more equitable apportionment of taxation.

On February 18 Bright had announced his intention to move in the matter, and on the 28th he returned to the subject.[1]

Landed property must bear a heavier and fairer share of the burden. On the other hand, and this also Bright demanded, the middle classes, at present overburdened by taxation, must be relieved by a just discrimination between different sources of income. A motion brought forward by Horsman with this object on March 3 proposed to raise to 8d. in the pound the tax 'on incomes arising from realized property', but to reduce it by a quarter on incomes derived from 'trade, commerce, and manufactures', by a half on incomes derived from 'professional and other precarious sources'.[2] And on no less than three occasions during this month of March the Government was faced with the demand that, if the income tax was to be retained, landed property should pay a larger share of it.[3]

2

Cobden could not refuse to endorse the proposals of Bright and Joseph Hume. But he does not seem to have shown any enthusiasm for them. He probably thought it impolitic to launch this new attack on the landowners so soon after the victory won in 1846, in fact before it had been completed. It was not until 1849 that the Act of 1846 would take full effect, and corn be for all practical purposes unprotected. This further assault might well drive many members of the governing aristocracy into the Protectionist ranks. Even if there were no danger of a Protectionist reaction, and Cobden, it would seem, did not share Peel's apprehensions on this score, many landowners would be antagonized who were resigned to the abolition of the Corn Law, but would certainly not accept this further sacrifice meekly. Proposals of this kind, therefore, courted certain defeat in Parliament. Moreover, in Cobden's opinion the proposed reform of the income tax, though

[1] H. of C., February 18 and 28, 1848 (*Parliamentary Debates*, 3rd Ser., vol. xcvi, pp. 975 sqq. and 1440 sqq.).
[2] *Annual Register*, 1848, p. 47.
[3] Motions brought forward by Hume on March 6, by Lacy Evans on March 20, and a second time by Hume on March 27 (*Parl. Deb.*, 3rd Ser., vol. xcvii, pp. 712 and 1021). Sp. Walpole, *Life of Lord John Russell*, vol. ii, p. 27.

it made the tax more equitable, made it at the same time more inquisitorial. A Liberal rather than a democrat and opposed on principle to any policy of using taxation for social reform, Cobden concluded that he would be well advised to turn his efforts in another direction and demand not a reform, but a reduction of taxation.[1]

The belief that the State could and should provide more cheaply for the public services and the needs of national defence was very widespread at this period, and in the principal towns associations were formed to secure retrenchment. The Association founded by the Liverpool merchants attracted Cobden's notice. He joined it and decided to launch a new agitation for 'Fiscal reform'.[2]

He found himself, in fact, confronted by serious difficulties due to the more democratic members of his following who wanted the Association to pursue two objects at the same time, fiscal reform and reform of the franchise. He protested. As he explained to Bright, it would be bad tactics to pursue two aims simultaneously. The mistake might be excusable if there were reason to believe that to combine the cause of fiscal reform with the cause of a reformed franchise would strengthen the former. But in his opinion Bright failed to realize the strength of the movement in favour of fiscal reform which had, he said, 'far more hold upon the public mind than we (the League) had, even after three years' agitation'.[3]

At bottom, Cobden, passionately devoted to the cause of fiscal reform, had no enthusiasm for a reform of the franchise. He admitted that the electorate could be widened without detriment to the indispensable campaign to secure administrative economies. But where were they to stop? And what security was there that the reform would not be carried too far and give the vote to an improvident class which would be easily persuaded to demand financial assistance from the State for all sorts of objects?[4]

---

[1] H. of C., February 18, Cobden's speech, and March 27, Sir Charles Wood's speech (*Parliamentary Debates*, 3rd Ser., vol. xcvi, pp. 964-5, and vol. xcvii, pp. 1034 sqq.).

[2] *Annual Register*, 1849, p. 153, Maccoby, *English Radicalism*, p. 314. On March 10, 1848, Disraeli protested against the activities of a League for Fiscal Reform (*Parl. Deb.*, 3rd Ser., vol. xcvii, p. 436).

[3] Cobden to Bright, December 23, 1848 (J. Morley, *Life of Richard Cobden*, 1905, vol. ii, p. 502. See also his letter to Bright of November 16, 1848 (ibid., vol. ii, pp. 498-9).

[4] For Cobden's views on this subject, see Maccoby, *English Radicalism*, pp. 317-18.

The financial aim which free traders should pursue was not only to foster the growth of trade by lowering fiscal barriers, but also, by depriving the State of revenue, to compel it to reduce its expenditure on the civil services and above all on the army and navy. But the success of Peel's fiscal policy in the former respect threatened to make the latter objective unattainable. For the volume of trade was growing so rapidly that, although some duties had been removed, others reduced, the revenue from customs was increasing. Accordingly the State, not being obliged to retrench, was spending more. Expenditure had risen from £50,819,000 in 1842 to £52,183,000 in 1847, £54,164,000 in 1848. The cost of the army and navy had reached the sum of £17,645,000 in 1848, whereas it had been only £15,440,000 in 1842, and did not exceed £11,657,000 in 1835. A few years before, Joseph Hume had wearied the House with his complaints of the monstrous increase of expenditure due to the Napoleonic war, and had put forward as the goal of British finance a return to the expenditure of 1792. The fiscal reformers of 1849 were less Utopian, though, as the event would prove, Utopian still when they adopted as their slogan a return to the expenditure of 1835.

To combat the encroachments of bureaucracy they revived the arguments the Tories had employed against the Whigs on the morrow of 1835. If, however, he shrank from committing the fate of his fiscal reform to the issue of an agitation for a wider franchise, Cobden saw in fiscal reform a means of effecting that reduction of expenditure on armaments which he had most at heart. His new campaign was inspired by his pacifism. Fiscal reform, he thought, would rally public opinion to the cause of peace, less attractive to the public than the former. For, as he saw it, the cause of free trade would not win its definitive victory, until it had brought about universal peace.[1]

The campaign opened in 1849 with a meeting at Manchester at which Cobden spoke in support of fiscal reform, Bright on behalf of a reformed franchise. Then in February Cobden

---

[1] Cobden was faithful to the line of action he had adopted in 1842. He refused then to link the cause of free trade with reform of the franchise, and wrote to Wilson, February 27, 1842: 'We must keep the League as a body wholly distinct from the suffrage movement.' On the other hand, he wrote to H. Ashworth, on April 12, 1842: 'It has struck me hat it would be well to engraft our free trade agitation upon the Peace movement. They are one and the same cause' (J. Morley, *Life of Cobden*, 1902, pp. 31-2).

brought forward a motion in the Commons demanding that naval and military expenditure should be reduced with the least possible delay by ten millions, which would bring it back to the figure of 1835.[1]

3

At the same time the Protectionists, whom the fluctuations in the price of corn had not reconciled to the new fiscal policy, turned their efforts in another direction. After the crisis of speculation which in June 1847 had raised the quarter of wheat to 92 shillings and 10d., the price fell to 53 shillings and 11d. on January 1, 1848, and to 46 shillings and 10d. on June 17, a figure to which, after a slight rise, it had returned by the end of December. The fall continued in 1849 after the Act of 1846 came into full operation in February and was maintained throughout the year, the price falling to 38 shillings and 9d. on December 15. In 1850, for two weeks in August, the figure of 36 shillings was reached. The price had never fallen lower since 1836. The farmers could, therefore, justly maintain that the free traders had been mistaken, if indeed they had not deliberately lied, when they had brought forward a host of arguments, often inconsistent with each other, to prove that the repeal of the Corn Law would not lower the price of corn. Their complaints, already voluble, when in 1848 and the early part of 1849 there was a general fall in prices, became louder still when they all began once more to rise, except the prices of their produce. For what then did they ask? A return to protection as it existed before 1846? They soon ceased to agitate for this.[2] Did they ask then for a reduction of the duties on manufactured articles and raw materials indispensable for manufacture, that the decrease in their profits might at any rate be compensated by a decrease in the cost of the manufactured articles of all kinds which they were obliged to purchase? Instinctively hostile to the abandonment of protection in any department, they had no such

---

[1] Cobden's motion was defeated by 197 to 78 votes. Once before, on March 30, 1848, he had called for a reduction of armaments, and his motion had obtained only 38 votes (J. Morley, *Life of Richard Cobden*, p. 67).

[2] Lord George Bentinck and, after his death in September 1848, the Protectionist, Herries, still thought a return to protection possible. Disraeli, however, who succeeded Bentinck as leader of the Protectionists, recognized that their programme must be refashioned, and when, at the opening of the Session of 1849, Lord Stanley attempted to resume the old struggle, he disavowed him. See Sp. Walpole, *History of England*, vol. v, p. 206.

thought. And this was possibly one of the reasons why Cobden, Hume, and their supporters thought it advisable for the present to turn their attention elsewhere. What the farmers asked for was the reduction of particular taxes, the malt tax and window tax, which directly affected them. When during the years which followed the restoration of peace a policy of deflation had been pursued, the attempt had been made to safeguard agriculture against the evil effects it must inevitably produce by protective measures. Now, when that protection had been abandoned, the farmer must be compensated in some other way. This was Disraeli's aim when, by Lord George Bentinck's death, he became in 1848 the leader of the Protectionists. The land, he maintained, was overburdened with taxation. For it had to bear the entire burden of the rates, county rate, highway rate, church rate and poor rate, and the land tax into the bargain. At least half these imposts should be transferred to the Budget and made chargeable upon the entire nation.

At the opening of 1849 Disraeli made a first attempt to persuade Parliament to come to the help of the distressed farmers.[1] A few weeks later during the debates on the Navigation Laws he took the opportunity to denounce once more the intolerable burden imposed by the poor rate on agriculture.[2]

The campaign thus launched by the Protectionists was diametrically opposed to that which Cobden was conducting at the same time for fiscal reform. At the close of the year Cobden was at pains to prove that the measures demanded by Disraeli would benefit the landlords far more than the farmers. But the discontent fostered in rural districts by the persistent fall in the price of corn embarrassed the free traders and favoured Disraeli's campaign.[3]

During the early months of 1850 the Protectionists seemed on the verge of success. A motion brought forward by Disraeli on February 19 skilfully presented his demands in a moderate

[1] March 15, 1849 (*Parliamentary Debates*, 3rd Ser., vol. ciii, p. 424). Sidney Herbert pointed out that the distressed state of agriculture was not due to free trade, and Sir Charles Wood that, in spite of free trade, the price of farm produce was higher in 1848 than in 1844 (*Annual Register*, 1849, pp. 51-2).

[2] H. of C., April 23, 1849. Disraeli's speech (*Parl. Deb.*, 3rd Ser., vol. civ, p. 701).

[3] See Cobden's speech at Leeds, December 19, 1849, and at Aylesbury in Disraeli's territory at the opening of 1850. See also S. Maccoby, *English Radicalism, 1832-1852*, pp. 305-6.

form. He contented himself with asking for the transference from local to national taxation of rates to the amount of two millions. He had the satisfaction of seeing Gladstone bring over to his side a section of the Peelites in the hope of a cheap guarantee against the danger of a return to protection and hearing Peel himself pay tribute to his skill and moderation. Though his motion was lost it obtained 252 votes.[1] A motion, on the other hand, which Cobden defended the following month asking for a large reduction in the expenditure on armaments secured only 89.[2]

The Protectionists, however, at this juncture, began to support the agitation for fiscal reform, and to relieve the farmers called for retrenchment. The member for Oxford, Henley, one of their leading champions, brought forward a motion asking for a general reduction of civil servants' salaries, and Lord John's Cabinet had to agree to the appointment of a committee of experts to study the question.[3]

4

The debates on the Budget of 1850 which were taking place at the same time showed the farmers how far they might expect to benefit from a larger surplus. As the crisis of 1847, prolonged, as it had been, by the outbreaks of revolution on the Continent, receded into the past, the financial position improved. In 1848 the Ministry had presented a sorry spectacle of weakness and hesitation. To the two Budgets of which we have spoken, presented successively in February, it had been obliged to add two more. In June the alterations in the sugar duty secured by Lord George Bentinck compelled Sir Charles Wood to revise his estimates once again. In August, however, he had to confess

---

[1] *Annual Register*, 1850, pp. 19-20. *Parliamentary Debates*, 3rd Ser., vol. cviii, p. 272. The Protectionists, however, had been defeated by a far larger majority on an amendment to the address attributing the distressed state of agriculture to free trade (ibid., 3rd Ser., vol. cviii, p. 253). See Sp. Walpole, *History of England*, vol. v, p. 226.

[2] March 8, 1849 (*Ann. Reg.*, 1850, p. 127).

[3] April 12. *Ann. Reg.*, 1850, p. 123: 'The representatives of the agricultural interest, still suffering under some depression, declared their resolution to carry out the principles of retrenchment into every department of the State, by way of relieving their constituents from the burdens of which the reduced prices of their produce had made them now doubly sensible.' The Committee reported on July 25: *Report from the Select Committee on Official Salaries* (1850, xv). For the results, see *Copy of Treasury Minute, dated the 20th of May, 1851, recording the steps which have been taken for giving Effect to the Recommendations of the Select Committee of 1850 on Official Salaries* (1851, xxxi).

that they had proved mistaken and that a loan was inevitable. 'We had', Disraeli exclaimed, 'some time ago the Government of all the talents: this is the Government of all the *Budgets*.'[1]

When in 1849 he came to draw up the balance sheet of the financial year which had expired on March 31, Sir Charles was in fact obliged to admit a deficit of £269,378. But the relief granted to the starving Irish peasants had to be taken into account, also a naval expenditure in excess of the credits voted, an excess which might, he claimed, be fairly regarded as due to exceptional circumstances. Had it not been for these two items, not only would the Budget have been balanced, there would have been a surplus of £444,329.

Sir Charles estimated the revenue for the financial year 1849–1850 at £52,252,000, the expenditure at £52,157,696. That would mean a small surplus of £94,304. Moreover, account must be taken of the fact that £642,639 would be required to meet the exceptional expenditure previously incurred. Otherwise there would have been a surplus of £736,943. During the year the revival of trade exceeded expectations, and sufficient economies were effected to produce, in conjunction with that revival and leaving out of account the expenditure required to make up past deficits, a surplus for the financial year 1849–1850 of £1,895,000.

The estimated expenditure for the year 1850–1851 could be reduced from the original estimate of £51,515,000 to £50,763,000. The estimated revenue, if the taxes remained as they were, was £52,285,000. There would, therefore, be a surplus of £1,522,000. Of this surplus Sir Charles proposed to devote half to relieving the burden borne by agriculture.

He proposed to abolish the tax on bricks and thus assist the construction of cottages and farm buildings, and to reduce considerably the stamp duties on the sale, mortgage, or lease of land. A large part of the remaining surplus would be devoted to debt redemption and the rest placed at the disposal of the Treasury, which would advance loans to the farmers of the United Kingdom to the amount of three millions for draining and improving the soil.[2]

[1] For the four Budgets of 1848, see the excellent account in Sp. Walpole, *History of England*, vol. v, pp. 198 sqq. and 204. H. of C., April 30, 1848, Disraeli's speech (*Parliamentary Debates*, 3rd Ser., vol. ci, p. 685).
[2] *Annual Register*, 1850, p. 118. *Parl. Deb.*, 3rd Ser., vol. cix, p. 990.

Evidently it was a Budget which took account of the farmers' well-justified complaints. And it also met the wishes of the economists, such as John Stuart Mill, who wanted landed property made more fluid and a class fostered of small land-owners and small tenant farmers. But it did not satisfy those who in every party were opposed to the existing taxation and who were encouraged by the revival of trade. On almost every point Sir Charles successfully beat off their attacks. In the matter, however, of the reform of the stamp duties he was obliged to yield to the great landowners, when they urged that, although the new scale of duties made the transfer of small properties easier, it would increase the taxation they had to bear. The Government was unable to carry its proposals as they stood, and it was only with great difficulty that a compromise secured a majority.[1]

5

At this point we may pause in our study of the Budgets. In the years immediately following the question once more came up whether the income tax should be continued and, if so, for how many years. On the other hand, new aspects assumed by the strife of parties would impart, as we shall shortly see, a novel character to the contest over the Budget. But already in 1850 the character of the Whig fiscal policy is clear. It proved successful, and the country was finally rescued from the disastrous tradition of chronic deficit which had marked the period before 1841. It was economical and gave the landowners and farmers sufficient relief to make them forgive the complete abandonment of protection which the Whig aristocracy had forced upon them. But if respectable, it was commonplace. It was made possible by the country's favourable financial situation for which everyone gave the credit, not to the Whigs, but to Peel. Peel remained the cynosure of all eyes. During his five years in office he had given the economic policy of the country the shape which for a long while before everyone had more or less consciously desired but which neither of the two historic parties had been able to give it. It was always possible, it is true, to cherish the hope of abolishing other taxes than the income tax, those, perhaps, whose abolition was de-

[1] *Parliamentary Debates*, 3rd Ser., vol. cx, p. 340. Sp. Walpole, *History of England*, vol. v, pp. 227-9.

manded by the bulk of the malcontents. The financial burdens might be reduced which weighed on the production and consumption of the poor. But who among the Whigs would have the courage to undertake it?

England was witnessing at this moment the opening of an era of prosperity. From the close of 1849 the first results began to be felt of an event which coincided exactly with the revolution of 1848, and was destined to affect the economic history of the civilized world as powerfully as the latter affected the political history of Europe, namely, the discovery of the Californian goldfield. It immediately caused an influx of gold throughout the United States, and, in consequence, an increased demand for the articles which British manufacture could supply. And this in turn produced a rise in prices and an expansion of trade.[1]

In 1850 the financial surplus and the growth of exports were calculated to remove any misgiving which might still linger in the public mind about the effects of the victory of free trade.[2]

The political stability of the country might, indeed, be explained by this spectacle of economic prosperity. The mass of the British people might have persuaded itself that this prosperity was, in fact, due to the excellence of its political system. It is not easy to believe this in view of the fact that the passing of the Bank of England Act and the Corn Law Repeal Act had been followed by a crisis of such extreme gravity that it had appeared to disprove all the forecasts of Peel and the supporters of his policy. Nevertheless, the confidence of the nation that this policy was the right one had not been shaken. Though Peel had been turned out of office he remained the unavowed leader of the entire country. It may even be said that the stability then experienced was actually deeper and more paradoxical than later on. For as a repercussion of the February revolution there had been a revival of the Chartist agitation on a small scale, it is true, but real enough to alarm many people. It had been dissipated and brought to an end by the general prosperity. This, however, did but set a seal to the unshakable optimism which had prevailed before the February revolution during the period from 1844 to 1846.

[1] For the price movements, see Tooke, *History of Prices*, vol. v, p. 258.
[2] *Annual Register*, 1850, p. 2.

To understand the character of this equilibrium we must go back to the years immediately following the restoration of peace in 1815. Two hostile systems then confronted each other. One of these, the Radical programme, advocated by men so unlike as Hunt, Cobbett, and Jeremy Bentham, put in the first place a 'Radical' reform of the franchise, the adoption of universal suffrage, and looked forward to the eventual abolition of the House of Lords and the monarchy itself. What results did the Radicals expect from the realization of their programme? Repudiation of the national debt? The devaluation of the pound? A ruthless reduction of public expenditure and taxation, the abolition in the first place of the odious duty on the importation of corn imposed by a Parliament of landlords? The answer is by no means clear.

Another programme confronted the Radical. It was the programme advocated by the school of Adam Smith, a programme exclusively economic which would leave the country's political institutions untouched. There must be a sound currency, the State must fulfil scrupulously its obligations as a debtor, taxation must be reduced, and all fiscal barriers to the freedom of manufacture and commerce removed, in the first place the duties on imports.

Nor should we forget that it was the moderate section of the Tories which about 1820 adopted, or more truly, initiated this programme when the Whig aristocracy had no interest in it. At an even earlier date, in fact, Pitt, when in 1786 he became leader of the Tories, had adopted this policy and he had been followed by Huskisson and the young Peel. It had been put into practice, not unsuccessfully, between 1820 and 1826 with the active support of Lord Liverpool and, during the last years of his administration, of Castlereagh. The seal was set on its success when the crisis of 1825, graver than those of 1816 and 1819, unlike the latter, failed to produce an explosion of Radicalism.

Precisely the same thing happened now. Peel, Prime Minister and leader of the Tory party, which under his leadership became the 'Conservative' party, had taken for his programme this policy of 1820. We have seen the amplitude he gave it and its success, evident when the crisis of 1847 was no more able to shake his authority than the crisis of 1825 had damaged Huskisson's. It is obvious which was the true national policy of England, not the programme of the malcontents of 1817, 1819, 1837, and 1839, but the programme of the reformers of 1820 and the succeeding years, not Radicalism or Chartism, but the Liberalism of the political economists.

III IRELAND

I

During this calm of political and social passions when the country as a whole supported the policy of free trade gradually extended, the only questions which engaged the attention of Parliament and the people were such as might more or less be regarded as belonging to foreign politics.

In the first place there was the Irish question which cannot be regarded as, in the strict sense, a domestic issue. For a section and a growing section of the Irish people refused to regard Ireland as a part of the United Kingdom. And those who were demanding separation from Great Britain, to be accomplished, if necessary, by violence, and whose hands had been untied by the recent death of the great protagonist of lawful agitation were encouraged at the beginning of 1848 by the events in Paris. The French had always entertained strong Irish sympathies, the Catholics because they hated English Protestantism—they had not forgotten the attempts made by Louis XIV to snatch Ireland from the yoke of the unbeliever—the democrats because they remembered the two landings made half a century before by the Jacobins to rescue the land of Ireland from the yoke of the alien aristocracy which had stolen it. To-day, when a combination of Catholics and democrats had overthrown the unpopular Orleans dynasty, these sympathies in Paris could not fail to explode and heat Irish hopes to boiling point. Government circles in London were seriously afraid that the European conflict might take the form of war against England. But 1848 was not 1792; and desire for peace, with England in particular, was stronger in Paris than the desire of particular groups to intervene. This was recognized by the Provisional Government. The British Embassy, alarmed by noisy manifestations in the revolutionary clubs in favour of Ireland, asked and received from Lamartine assurances that his Government had no hostile intentions. When, on March 17, four days after the rising in Vienna, a deputation presented him with an address and, as an act of homage, gave him an Irish flag, Lamartine thought it prudent to recall the memory of O'Connell and advise the employment of those methods of peaceable agitation which had won civil liberty for the Irish, had almost won constitutional liberty and independence, and might do so in future. But even this was not enough to satisfy the British ambassador. Speaking with the spirit and language of an agent of Palmerston he rebuked Lamartine, informing him that 'the spokesman of a government is not justified in expressing any opinion which reflects in any way on the domestic affairs of another nation'. After this, when, on April 13, he received an Irish deputation headed by Smith O'Brien, Lamartine delivered himself in terms as plain as the most sensitive English patriotism could require. 'We are', he said, 'at peace and we desire to remain on friendly terms not with any isolated section of the British, but with the entire country. We believe that this peace is beneficial and honourable, not only to Great Britain and the French Republic, but to the human race.' His speech was warmly welcomed in Parliament and by the London Press.[1]

April 10 had witnessed the irretrievable defeat of the English Chartists. And we have seen that the fact that the movement was led by an Irishman, that the Chartist leaders were in permanent alliance with an Irish revolutionary, and that to the six points of the Charter there had been added a seventh, the repeal of the Union, had contributed not a little to the growing unpopularity of Chartism. We have also seen that on the very day of the great fiasco the Commons were debating at the request of the Government a Bill extending to Ireland the provisions of a repressive Statute passed during the reaction against Jacobinism. And in Ireland itself the threatened rebellion hung fire. Probably the abandonment of the Irish cause by the French revolutionary Government, though the Irish revolutionaries did their utmost to conceal it, produced a demoralizing effect. It became known, moreover, that the great majority of the Irish Catholic priests refused to have anything to do with a movement which had

[1] E. Ashley, *Life of Viscount Palmerston*, vol. i, pp. 87-9. Palmerston wrote to Lord Normanby, on April 18: 'Lamartine is really a wonderful fellow, and is endowed with great qualities. It is much to be desired that he should swim through the breakers and carry his country safe into port' (ibid., p. 94).

assumed a Jacobin and Socialist character.[1] And it caused amusement in London when the news arrived that at Limerick on April 30 the partisans of moral force, O'Connell's party, had recourse to the brutal method of physical force to break up a meeting of conspirators over which Smith O'Brien presided in person. Days passed, then weeks. June marked the turning point at Paris, and with Paris Europe as a whole definitively escaped the clutches of the revolution. In Ireland no one stirred. The moment had come when governments everywhere took courage and, because they were no longer afraid, crushed a party which had ceased to be dangerous but could not be forgiven the terror it had once inspired.

Already, in May, the Lord Lieutenant had made an unsuccessful attempt to secure the condemnation of a number of agitators on a charge of arousing hatred and contempt of the Queen and inciting to revolt. He had failed to obtain a verdict against O'Brien and Thomas Francis Meagher. But he had been more fortunate in the case of John Mitchell, charged with a breach of the Statute[2] passed in April and sentenced on May 27 to fourteen years' transportation.[3] We have already noticed the repercussion of this condemnation in England, a final paroxysm of Chartism followed by arrests and sentences. Events took the same course in Ireland, and there was a modicum of truth in the reports which reached the authorities of preparations for rebellion being made by the leaders of the 'Irish Confederation'. What was untrue was the dangerous character attributed to the movement. An army of determined revolutionaries cannot be recruited from helots reduced to beggary, and the accounts we read of crowds in which only one man in twenty was armed and their arms the queerest medley in the world, a few muskets, pikes, scythes attached to the end of poles, should have inspired pity rather than alarm. Nevertheless, Lord John on July 21 brought in a Bill in the Commons empowering the Irish Government to suspend Habeas Corpus for nine months. To make it plain that he was resolved to act with the utmost vigour, he declared, straight away and even before Parliament had time to pass the Bill, that in virtue of an Act discovered in the storehouse of old Irish Statutes passed before

[1] H. of L. and H. of C., July 21 and 22, 1848. Lord Lansdowne's and Lord John Russell's speeches (*Annual Register*, 1848, pp. 98 sqq.).
[2] Crown and Government Security Act, see above, p. 243.
[3] *Ann. Reg.*, 1848, pp. 364 and 384.

the Union the Lord Lieutenant had authority to arrest any person suspected of taking part in seditious activities. On July 26 the Bill passed both Houses and became law the same day.[1]

Next morning *The Times* alarmed its readers by the news that the entire South of Ireland was in revolt, that a demoralized army had retreated before the rebels, and that there was no news from Waterford and Cork.[2] There was a panic on the Stock Exchange. But within three days the public alarm was allayed. Fifty policemen had sufficed to suppress a feeble show, a mere gesture of rebellion. Smith O'Brien and his subordinates, abandoned by their followers, had taken to flight. Within a fortnight they had been arrested without resistance by themselves or the people. Further prosecutions for breaches of the Statute passed in April, undertaken in August at the very moment when O'Brien and his subordinates were arrested, disappointed the hopes of the Government. All the accused save one were acquitted. What would be the fate of the new batch of accused, not merely guilty of preaching rebellion, but actual rebels? Tried by a special commission which sat in September and October, they were found guilty in turn, but recommended to mercy. In every case the death sentence was commuted to transportation for life.[3]

The extraordinary legislation to which Ireland was subjected in 1847 and 1848 would be continued by successive prolongations, often under new names, throughout the following years.[4] But would not a Liberal Government, so untrue to all the principles for which it stood and which, had Parliamentary institutions functioned normally, should have left the responsibility of this

---

[1] *Parliamentary Debates*, 3rd Ser., vol. c, pp. 696 and 779. Sp. Walpole, *Life of Lord John Russell*, vol. ii, p. 72.

[2] *The Times*, July 27, 1848. See Sp. Walpole, *Life of Lord John Russell*, vol. ii, p. 73.

[3] *Annual Register*, 1848, Chron., pp. 389 sqq.

[4] These coercive measures were the following: *A*, Coercion Bill (11 & 12 Vict. Cap. 2), passed in December 1847, at the request of the Lord-Lieutenant, Lord Clarendon, who was thus empowered to take special police measures in districts where he judged them necessary (*Parl. Deb.*, 3rd Ser., vol. xcv, pp. 270 and 310, also Sp. Walpole, *Life of Lord John Russell*, vol. i, pp. 462 sqq., for the correspondence on the subject between Lord John and Clarendon). For the prolongation of the Coercion Bill in the following years, see Cardinal A. Perraud, *Etudes sur L'Irelande Contemporaine*, 1862, vol. i, pp. 189-90. *B*, A Crown and Government Security Bill (11 & 12 Vict. Cap. 12), passed in April 1848, to make it possible to sentence the Irish rebels to transportation (*Parl. Deb.*, 3rd Ser., vol. xcviii, pp. 20, 420, and 537); and an Aliens Removal Bill (11 & 12 Vict. Cap. 20), passed in May 1848 (*Parl. Deb.*, 3rd Ser., vol. xcviii, pp. 135 and 560). For these two Statutes, see above. *C*, Suspension of the Habeas Corpus Act, passed in July 1848, prolonged in 1849 (*Parl. Deb.*, 3rd Ser., vol. cii, p. 306).

policy of repression to the Tories, at least seek to compensate for it by a policy of reform?

2

When in 1847 Lord John resigned himself to take repressive measures he had seemed to recognize the need of legislation to protect the tenants.[1] At the opening of the session of 1848, before the February revolution broke out, and there was not as yet even a semblance of seditious activities in Ireland, the Government had brought in a Bill granting tenants with the landlord's consent or without it, if the claim were approved by arbitrators, compensation for improvements made during their leases. But almost immediately Parliament was permitted to shelve the Bill.[2]

In 1848 a Bill was passed which Lord John had introduced the previous year to facilitate the transfer of mortgaged estates. But the measure ill-conceived would remain a dead letter.[3] And nothing more in the way of reform in Ireland was effected by the Prime Minister in 1848.

Lord John, whose impulsive tergiversations are often as difficult to follow as to understand, seems to have thought that in existing circumstances all he had to do in Ireland was to suppress disorder by extraordinary measures of coercion. What now was left of the alliance concluded with O'Connell in the years before 1841? O'Connell was dead. What had become of the imposing programme of reform outlined by the Prime Minister at the beginning of 1847? The revolution of 1848 had made him, it would seem, a hardened Conservative, instinctively hostile to anything Irish and treating the Irish agitations as part of the upheaval

[1] Lord John Russell to Lord Clarendon, November 10, 1847: 'That which presses at present is the habit of driving out cottier tenants from their homes without compensation or prospect of employment. . . . It is clear to me that you do not meet this evil by the best law possible giving tenants compensation for improvements. . . . Therefore it seems to me a remedy for this evil must strike deeper and wider. It must embrace all who have occupied the land for a certain number of years (say five), and must give them something like the tenant right of Ulster.' And on November 15, 1847: 'I am not ready to bring in any restrictive law without at the same time restraining the power of the landlord' (Sp. Walpole, *Life of Lord John Russell*, vol. i, pp. 463-5). Lord John spoke to the same effect in Parliament (ibid., p. 473.)

[2] The Bill, introduced immediately after the Christmas recess of 1847 by Somerville, Labouchere's successor as Irish Secretary, was remitted for examination to a special committee (*Parliamentary Debates*, 3rd Ser., vol. xcviii, p. 69, and vol. xcvi, p. 673).

[3] See below, p. 303. 12 & 13 Vict. Cap. 77 (Encumbered Estates Act). For the debates, see *Parl. Deb.*, 3rd Ser., vol. xcvi, pp. 1249 sqq.

produced in a democratic Europe by the co-operation of revolutionary demagogues and priests.[1]

It therefore fell to Peel, though he did not occupy a responsible position, except inasmuch as he was the leader of public opinion, to sketch in 1849 the comprehensive programme of constructive reform which Lord John seemed to have entirely forgotten. But did not the persistence of Irish poverty condemn the policy of agricultural free trade which in 1846 he had put forward as the cure for the evils which afflicted Ireland? However that may be, his influence was unimpaired. He was the adviser to whom his countrymen loved to have recourse, while Lord John, exciting neither enthusiasm nor interest and kept in office only by the mutual hostility of the two sections which divided the Tory party, managed the current business of State.[2]

3

It was Peel who on March 30, 1849, was the outstanding figure of a debate in the Commons on the Irish question. He explained how necessary it was to study all its aspects, with a passionate conviction which suggests to a reader of his speech that this congenital reformer, after so often giving up the Irish problem in despair, cherished the dream of finishing his career by finding the solution which had escaped all his predecessors. It was, he insisted, impossible to maintain permanently a force of fifty thousand men—thirty thousand soldiers and twenty thousand constables—to keep order on the other side of St. George's Channel, or to be

[1] In a latter written to Peel on January 16, 1849 (C. S. Parker, *Sir Robert Peel*, vol. iii, p. 501), Sir James Graham relates a conversation with Lord John, in which the latter said to him: ' "With respect to Ireland (in strict confidence, I may tell you), the renewal of the Suspension of the Habeas Corpus Act is intended without any comprehensive measure prepared for the improvement of the future social condition of that unhappy country." I told Lord John that somebody had observed, "It was occupied, not governed," that this could not be maintained as the permanent policy of England; and that I feared the proposal of continued coercion without any concomitant would be most violently resisted. Lord John thought otherwise. He believed that Great Britain, for the present, would be satisfied if tranquillity were procured in Ireland, even by force.' Lord John had, however, proposed to provide payment for the Irish Catholic clergy, and later had wished to take steps to assist emigration. But he had been confronted by the opposition of his colleagues, in particular of the Grey group, and by January 1849 had lost heart. (Cf. Sp. Walpole, *Life of Lord John Russell*, vol. ii, pp. 81 and 98.)

[2] At the opening of the session of 1849 Lord John proposed to alter the Irish Poor Law by limiting the possible amount of the poor rate in any union, and by introducing a national rate in aid to assist unions too impoverished to support their paupers. But the Lords mutilated the Bill, and Lord John persuaded the Commons to give way. See Sp. Walpole, *Life of Lord John Russell*, vol. ii, pp. 83-4, and his *History of England*, vol. v, pp. 209 sqq. It was during the debate on this Bill that Peel spoke.

resigned to the chronic poverty, persistent crime, and recurrent famines.[1]

In 1848, while so much fuss was being made about the unimportant incidents of an abortive rising, the peasants, after two years of famine, were making a last desperate effort to save themselves from starvation by replanting the potato. In a single night the potato disease had once more destroyed the entire crop. What could be done? Peel submitted to the Commons a plan which his audience received with applause. He had the gift of interpreting by instinct the wishes of enlightened public opinion. We will summarize this great constructive plan, not following the detail of his speech, but endeavouring to make its substance clear.

He first dealt with the operation of the Poor Law in Ireland.[2] By imposing on the State for the first time an obligation to relieve all paupers, and moreover, even if they were healthy, to grant outdoor relief,[3] it was rapidly bringing Ireland to ruin. A quarter of the unions—all those in Munster and Connaught, and of those in Ulster, all in Donegal—that is to say, all the unions of western and Catholic Ulster, were insolvent. What return was being received for this ill-considered expenditure which it had been hoped to make Ireland pay, but which must be met once again by England? The procedure followed had been the exact opposite of that which should have been adopted. On this point Peel was in agreement with all who approved the principles of the English Poor Law of 1834, betrayed by the Irish Poor Law of 1847.[4] In 1848 Lord John Russell had attributed the evils which afflicted Ireland chiefly to the early marriages and improvident habits of the people. The Act of 1847 did everything possible to promote this fatal improvidence. In the language of Mill's *Political Economy*, published in 1848, the growth of population was fostered, when it was production that should have been promoted.[5]

For this lavish system of poor relief there could be only one possible justification. In each union since the insolvent farms could not pay the rate its entire amount had to be paid by the solvent farms which in consequence could not prosper.[6] Was it possibly

[1] *Parliamentary Debates*, 3rd Ser., vol. civ, p. 90. [2] Ibid., 3rd Ser., vol. civ, pp. 91 sqq.
[3] In practice, not altogether in theory. See above, p. 163.—*Trs. Note.*
[4] *Parl. Deb.*, 3rd Ser., vol. civ, p. 107.
[5] John Stuart Mill, *Political Economy*, p. 200.
[6] *Parl. Deb.*, 3rd Ser., vol. civ, p. 98.

the Government's intention to ruin the large estates and thus compel expropriation and transfer the soil of the country to the tenants? In 1847, when the Poor Law was debated, strange language had been heard from members of Parliament, even from members of the Government. Since then, in February 1848, the national workshops had been set up in Paris, the Socialists had come into power, and the June massacres had followed. No one any longer spoke the language of O'Connor and Louis Blanc. Peel himself had never done so. The Act of 1847, that is to say, must be repealed as soon as possible and the principles of the English Poor Law applied, a more parsimonious measure, but in the long run serving better the permanent interests of the poor. The workhouse test must be restored. But as soon as possible did not mean immediately. The test could not be reimposed without providing work, and Peel proposed that the change should be effected in the following way.

Committees should be set up invested with full powers, though they were so unpopular in England that in 1847 it had been found necessary to abolish the Poor Law Commission and the unpopularity of the committees set up by the Public Health Act of 1848 was already threatening to wreck the reform. These committees, working in close collaboration with the Board of Works, would relieve the burden upon the Poor Law by employing immediately as large a number of paupers as possible in bringing virgin soil into cultivation.[1] The task, performed under the direction of the committees, themselves advised by the Board of Works, would provide the Irish with employment for many years. And when the land had been brought into cultivation, it would provide further employment for all those Irishmen who, instead of colonizing America and Australia, would colonize their native country, and would remain agricultural labourers instead of coming to England to compete with British workmen in the Lancashire mills and reduce their wages.

Did Peel and his supporters contemplate the settlement on these reclaimed lands of further hoards of peasants living in squalid poverty and glued to their little parcel of ground like human vermin? Far from it. His dream and theirs were very different.[2]

---

[1] *Parliamentary Debates*, 3rd Ser., vol. civ, pp. 101 sqq. For the land to be brought under cultivation, see A. Pichot, *L'Irlande et le Pays de Galles*, 1850, pp. 429 and 479.

[2] *Parl. Deb.*, 3rd Ser., vol. civ, pp. 104 sqq. G. de Beaumont, *L'Irlande sociale, politique et*

How would this work of preparing the ground for cultivation be carried out? The ground would first be broken up. Then stones and sand would be laid between the clods of turf to expose the soil to the air and prevent the rain water lodging on the surface. The next step would be to grow a crop of potatoes which would be followed the next year, after further preparation of the soil, by a crop of oats.[1] It would then be possible to establish regular cultivation, to grow wheat or lay down pasture. But these new farms, thus won from the waste, would not be tiny like the cottiers'. They would be as large as British farms. This would do away with what the British economist regarded as the original sin of Irish agriculture, that it did not make the distinction, made everywhere else, between the landlord, the capitalist, and the wage-earning labourer. The tenant who in the normal order of things should be a capitalist was a proletarian in Ireland, whose remuneration, though answering pretty exactly to Ricardo's definition of a wage, was not a wage. For the entire surplus was taken from him not by a capitalist, but by a landlord. Except in the form of money-lending, capitalism did not exist in Ireland. And in the country districts the money-lenders' extortion was added to the landlords'. To create large farms in Ireland and introduce capitalism in its English form was the great object of Englishmen, who for the benefit of Ireland desired to solve her agrarian problem and banish pauperism.

For this was the paradox to which the English Liberals called attention when the Chartists attempted to acclimatize the theories of the French Social Democrats. It was precisely in Ireland, a country without capitalism, that all the evils, due elsewhere to the new capitalism, were most rife.

'In every nation there are poor people, more or less numerous. But an entire nation of paupers is something never witnessed before.' This is not a quotation from Marx denouncing what according to him was a novelty peculiar to the industrialized modern society, the creation of a proletariat. It is a quotation from a French observer describing the conditions prevalent in Ireland, the one portion of the United Kingdom where none of the phenomena which accompanied in Lancashire the birth

religieuse, 7th ed., 1863, vol. i, p. 246: 'It would be impossible to imagine anything worse than the condition of these poor labourers swarming on the soil and attached to it like human vermin.'

[1] A. Pichot, L'Irlande et le Pays de Galles, 1850, p. 417.

of modern large-scale industry had made their appearance.[1]

And what was the remedy for these evils? To introduce manufacture into Ireland. 'In Ireland', said the same traveller, 'there is a productive potential of several million arms idle or ill-employed. It is a power which industry would put into action, where it is inert, and would fertilize, where it is barren.' Nor is this all. 'From every point of view,' he continues, 'the development of industry in Ireland is desirable. Not only is the physical existence of the working class at stake, but the future also of those middle classes, called, as we have seen, to play so important a part. Industry alone can feed the former and enrich the latter.'[2] This was the conclusion of a competent observer at a time when Chartism was widespread in England and Scotland. His prescription to rescue the lower class from its penury and call into existence an almost non-existent middle class was to import into Ireland industrial capitalism of the English type.

Another French student of Ireland, equally competent, De Lasteyrie, wrote fifteen years later that a decrease in the number of smallholdings and the creation of moderate-sized farms where the farmer is a capitalist employer was proving the true solution of the agrarian problem in the country districts, while the surplus population was being disposed of by emigration to the towns, the colonies or the United States. 'Many small tenants are becoming labourers. They work on farms constituted by the union of smallholdings and are in receipt of a wage paid by the day. If in consequence the total yield of the soil is less, the cultivator derives a higher return from his labour, and the number of those unfortunates whose existence depends entirely on the potato crop has enormously diminished. The wealthy farmers, therefore, and these labourers sure of employment'—in other words these capitalists and wage-earners—'are the first step to the abolition of pauperism in Ireland.' But this was exactly the process described by Sismondi and after him by so many French Socialists as the cause in their opinion of modern pauperization. Of this, De Lasteyrie was well aware and he realized the controversial implications of the passage we have just quoted. 'The facts', he concludes, 'evidently do not support Socialist theories.'[3]

[1] G. de Beaumont, *L'Irlande sociale, politique et religieuse*, 7th ed., 1863, vol. i, p. 223.
[2] Ibid., 7th ed., 1863, vol. ii, p. 83.
[3] J. de Lasteyrie, 'L'Irlande depuis la dernière Famine' (*Revue des Deux-Mondes*, August 1, 1853, vol. iii, p. 513).

What, then, was the right course to pursue? Not to expropriate the great landowners for the benefit of the small tenants as Mill, Bright, and many Radicals advocated. Such a proposal, regularly supported by the example of the French peasantry, made no appeal whatever to the British public. The English, extremely proud of their agriculture, regarded no system of cultivation as truly progressive which was not based on the large farm of the British type. Peel was, therefore, in accord with the unanimous opinion of the ruling classes when he was content to ask that the recommendation of the Devon Commission, and the programme sketched by Lord John in 1847 which Parliament had begun to implement in 1848, though by a measure which was misconceived and must be completely remodelled if it were not to remain a dead letter, should be effectively carried out and the transfer of mortgaged lands made easier, even in certain cases compulsory. The compulsion, though out of harmony with the Liberal principles of the English, would in this instance be warranted. For in a case of urgent necessity the Government should have the courage to employ dictatorial methods and, moreover, from the Liberal point of view the end justified the means. For in this way something would be done towards breaking up the large estates, not to benefit the small owner, but to create farms of a reasonable size, farms of about 100 acres. On one point, however, Peel and his supporters agreed with the Radicals. A feudal system of landed property which seemed calculated to render any transference of land impossible must be abolished. Land must be a marketable commodity. There must be free trade in land.[1]

[1] Peel seems to have thought that the measures he proposed would attract English and Scottish capital to Ireland, and settle in that country colonists of a novel sort to run Irish agriculture as good capitalists, with native wage-earners working for them. Sir James Graham showed more sagacity when he expressed the hope that Irish capital might find profitable investment in the country where it had been earned, the persistent Irish emigration to England be checked, and an Irish middle class thus come into existence in Ireland itself. Peel seems also to have contemplated the formation of arable farms in Ireland. It would justify his repeal of the Corn Law in 1846. Under free trade, however, Irish wheat could not compete successfully with foreign. But he was not blind to the fact that cattle-raising could prove a source of prosperity to the Irish farmer. For in this case the geographical neighbourhood of the two countries would discourage foreign competition. In the event the area of pasture was extended as a result of the Encumbered Estates Bill, and of the consequent evictions which no longer shocked the public conscience to the same degree as in the past. For emigration had relieved the pressure on the means of subsistence and on the soil itself. (Cf. Perraud, op. cit., vol. i, pp. 285-6.)

4

The programme sketched by Peel in 1849 was very imperfectly carried out. When we inquire what was done in the years immediately following 1848 to satisfy Irish grievances, we find a Statute, purely political in character, which, by reducing the property qualification in the country districts of Ireland, increased the county electorate.[1] We also find two measures dealing with the Poor Law, one of 1849 whose sole object was to relieve the ratepayers and which must, therefore, render the law still harder to work, if the difficulties which had begun to make their appearance in 1846 should continue,[2] and another of 1850 subsidizing distressed unions, a measure which returned to the old mistakes and did nothing but supply the Irish deficit at the British taxpayer's expense.[3]

We find, in fact, only one measure of genuine reform which implemented an item of Peel's programme, namely, the Encumbered Estates Bill of 1849. The measure revived an Act passed in 1848 which was vitiated by the mistake of assigning the transfer of the land in question to the Court of Chancery whose expensiveness and delays were a public scandal.[4] It was not until 1849 that, at the urgent request of the creditors of the Irish aristocracy, Parliament authorized the sale of property encumbered with debt. Entrusted at first to a temporary commission of three members, the Commission for the sale of Encumbered Estates in Ireland, these sales were finally placed under the jurisdiction of a Court which had already been in existence for twelve years,

---

[1] 13 & 14 Vict. Cap. 69. Lord John Russell, in 1850, carried this Bill which he had been compelled to drop in 1848 and 1849. But the House of Lords had considerably reduced its effectiveness by raising the qualification from the £8 proposed by the Government to £12 (*Parliamentary Debates*, 3rd Ser., vol. cviii, p. 699, also Perraud, *Etudes sur l'Irlande contemporaine*, vol. i, p. 89). Lord John's proposal to abolish the office of Lord-Lieutenant and admit the Irish Secretary to Cabinet rank was unsuccessful (*Parl. Deb.*, 3rd Ser., vol. cxi, p. 1464, and cxii, p. 899).

[2] 12 & 13 Vict. Cap. 114. The most important clauses of the Bill had been removed by the Lords. See above, p. 296, note 2.

[3] In 1849 the Government had obtained from Parliament the grant of a subsidy of £50,000 (12 & 13 Vict. Cap. 5), and another later of £500,000 (12 & 13 Vict. Cap. 25), for the distressed unions. In 1850, Parliament granted a further subsidy of £300,000 for the same purpose.

[4] The Act of 1848 was modified in the following year (12 & 13 Vict. Cap. 77) on Peel's initiative, who pointed out that the Chancellor himself dissuaded his friends from having recourse to the Court of Chancery. H. of C., Peel's speech, March 30, 1849 (*Parl. Deb.*, 3rd Ser., vol. civ, p. 112).

the Transferred Estates Court, whose records inform us what they had effected each year.[1]

The Court on the mere petition of a creditor or the owner himself ordered the sale by auction in the most informal fashion of mortgaged land and the delivery to the purchaser of a title giving him a freehold of it. Those who before had claims on the land had them now only on the purchase price. It was for the Court to examine the validity of their claims and pay out what was due to them.[2]

5

Ireland was once more at peace. For the first time for many years the Irish question ceased to obsess Parliament. In August 1849 the Queen and the Prince Consort visited Ireland and were warmly welcomed.[3] The same year, it is true, a bloody affray occurred which cost several lives, led to the removal of Lord Roden's name from the list of magistrates, and obliged the Lord-Lieutenant to visit London and give an explanation.[4] And in 1852 there were several murders which caused passing anxiety. But it vanished when it was realized that these acts of lawlessness were confined to an extremely small area and the rest of the coun-

---

[1] For the operation of this Act, see the details in Perraud, op. cit., vol. i, pp. 370 sqq.

Mill (*Political Economy*, p. 204), remarking the decrease of small tenants, does justice to the important part played by the Encumbered Estates Act. 'It is probable that the repeal of the Corn Laws necessitating a change in the exports of Ireland from the products of tillage to those of pasturage would of itself have sufficed to bring about this revolution in the future. A grazing farm can only be managed by the landlord. But a change involving so great a displacement of the population had been immensely facilitated, and made more rapid by the vast emigration, as well as by the greatest boon ever conferred on Ireland by any government, the Encumbered Estates Act, the best provisions of which have since, through the Landed Estates Court, been permanently incorporated into the social system of the country.'

[2] A considerable number of these purchases of land were, in fact, forced upon the purchaser, a creditor who had no other means of securing payment. Many lots were bought by former middlemen who held mortgages on the estates they had administered.

[3] After this visit, the speech from the Throne, delivered on January 31, 1850, remarked on the peaceful state of the country: 'H.M., in her late visit to Ireland, derived the highest gratification from the loyalty and attachment manifested by all classes of her subjects. Although the effects of former years of scarcity are painfully felt in that part of the United Kingdom, they are mitigated by the present abundance of food and the tranquillity which prevails.' See also Lord John Russell's speech, H. of C., February 15, 1850 (*Parliamentary Debates*, vol. cviii, p. 823). On February 18, Lord Clarendon, the Lord-Lieutenant of Ireland, spoke to the same effect. 'Ireland was then more free, on the whole, from religious as well as political agitation and agrarian outrage, than at any period within recollection' (*Annual Register*, 1850, p. 114).

[4] The skirmish which took place at Dolly's Brae, in the county of Armagh, was provoked by Orangemen who had gone to Lord Roden's estate to celebrate the anniversary of the battle of the Boyne (Sp. Walpole, *History of England*, vol. v, p. 219).

try was undisturbed. A French traveller who paid two visits to Ireland, the first at the beginning of 1852, the second in 1853, remarks how speedy the improvement had been. 'If', he wrote, 'we compare the state of Irish cottages in 1853 with what it was at the beginning of 1852, we notice signs of care, and there is no better proof that hope has revived than care of one's person and poor home. The population also appears better nourished and the number of wretches seeking admission to the workhouses has been halved.'[1] Nor was this improvement temporary.

Another French observer stated as a well-known fact that 'since 1848 as a result of the severe and more or less illegal measures which have sent into exile in different parts of the globe the most influential leaders of the National party, peace has been restored in Ireland. It must not, indeed, be regarded as due to any taste for British rule or trust in the Government. Nevertheless, tranquillity prevails, the law is obeyed, the administration of the country is carried on, and the courts function, unimpeded, and with no opposition other than untrammelled discussion by speech and in the Press as its exists in England.'[2]

Was the writer just quoted correct in ascribing, as he seems to do, the restoration of order to the arbitrary measures of repression taken in 1848? Or should it be regarded as the effect of free trade? No direct connection of cause and effect can be established between the repeal of the Corn Law in 1846 and the pacification of Ireland. For its only result was to destroy the cultivation of corn in Ireland. But the emigration which removed from the country not only a considerable part of the population but the most discontented made possible a large reduction in the cost of poor relief and the union of small farms, which in turn enabled farmers to raise cattle profitably. When all is said, the recovery of Ireland was due not to government action, subsidies, or the inauguration of public works, but to the free sale of Irish cattle in the English market and the voluntary emigration of Irishmen to America and Australia.[3] Therefore this economic recovery and the appease-

[1] J. de Lasteyrie, 'L'Irlande depuis la dernière Famine', in the *Revue des Deux-Mondes*, August 1, 1853, vol. iii, p. 514.

[2] Perraud, op. cit., vol. i, p. 129.

[3] In 1847, 1848, and 1849 the number of emigrants exceeded 250,000. The population of Ireland, 8,196,000 in 1841, was only 6,574,000 in 1851, less than the 6,801,000 recorded by the census of 1821. The fall in population was far greater in Munster, and even more in Connaught, than in the other parts of the country, and did not affect the towns, whose population, on the contrary, continued to rise. The emigration, however, occurred at

ment of discontent were in this sense a victory of the Liberalism which had produced the Act of 1846 and thus an indirect result of that revolutionary measure.

A study of colonial questions should have followed this section on Ireland. M. Halévy would have proceeded to recount Palmerston's foreign policy down to the famous debates of June 1850 on the Pacifico incident.[1] On that occasion Peel spoke for the last time. The next day he was thrown from his horse and died in agony on July 2. M. Halévy had collected a large number of notes showing the impression produced by his death in England and abroad.

IV DOMESTIC POLICY FROM 1850 TO 1852

I

Palmerston's victory in Parliament[2] and Peel's death might have seemed at first sight a double victory for the Whig Cabinet. Peel the real, because the moral, leader of the Commons had made room by his death for the official leader. One of the principal members of the Cabinet appeared to possess the unquestioning confidence of the nation. These things surely were enough to establish the Whig aristocracy firmly in power. In fact the situation was not so simple. Palmerston's triumph and Peel's death made Lord John's political position very difficult. Without speaking here of the legislation passed in 1851 and 1852 we propose to relate the history during the next two years and a half, not so much of the English people as of their political parties, a story of real, if limited, interest.

a moment when in any case an arrest in the growth of the population might have been expected. The increase, 14.2 per cent in the decade of 1821-31, had already fallen to 5.5 per cent in the following decade.

[1] [*Trs. Note.*—David 'Don' Pacifico, a Portuguese Jew, was born at Gibraltar, and was, therefore, a British subject. A merchant at Athens, he claimed damages from the Greek Government when in 1847 his house was burned down in an anti-Semitic riot. In 1850 Palmerston, to enforce his claim, ordered naval action against Greece. Russia and France protested, and the matter was debated in Parliament. The House of Lords condemned Palmerston's action (June 17). A week later, however, the House of Commons reversed the Lords' condemnation by a majority of 46. In the course of his speech, which lasted five hours, Palmerston declared that a British subject—*civis Romanus sum*—should be able to count upon British protection of his rights in any part of the world. Eventually Don Pacifico received a considerable sum in compensation. (This note has been taken from the *Encyclopædia Britannica*, art. 'Palmerston', 13th ed., vol. xx, p. 648.)]

[2] On June 25, 1850, Palmerston made his famous speech in the debate about the episode of Don Pacifico. (See *Trs. Note*[1] above.)

On June 25, 1850, Palmerston had inflicted a heavy defeat upon the Court. It was now more difficult than ever, in fact it was literally impossible, for Lord John to keep his promise to the Queen, which, indeed, was also his personal desire, and inform Palmerston that he must exchange the Foreign Office for another post in the Cabinet.[1] But the greater his difficulty in this respect, the more uneasy his position became as head of the Government. It was not that he disagreed in principle with Palmerston's policy. It was the traditional Whig policy which he had often laid down himself. But in the first place it was far from agreeable to so vain a politician to see it practised with such brilliant success by another man and himself reduced by his unruly colleague to the second place in his own party. And if he approved of Palmerston's policy, he certainly did not approve of his methods. The two statesmen differed as an artist and a pedant. Moreover, the revolutionary abroad became an obstinate conservative at home. Whenever Lord John attempted to take the initiative and bring forward a measure of parliamentary reform to give some satisfaction to Radical opinion, he was confronted in the Cabinet by Palmerston's uncompromising opposition. If on the other hand he should ever succeed in removing his colleague from the Foreign Office, he might expect Palmerston to rouse Radical sentiment against him and in conjunction with the Radicals carry on an opposition to the Ministry, as embarrassing as it would be disloyal.[2]

The Court, however, though defeated by the Commons, did not abandon the contest. On August 12 the Queen drew up a Memorandum to be given to Lord John which stated in precise terms the rights of a Queen of England in relation to her Ministers

---

[1] An attempt made at this time failed. See Greville (*Memoirs*, July 28, 1850), whose informant was Reeve: 'In spite of the triumph Lord Palmerston had obtained in the House of Commons, the evils of his arbitrary mode of conducting foreign affairs continued to excite the anxiety of his colleagues and something more than the distrust of the Court, and an attempt was made with the concurrence of Lord John Russell, the Duke of Bedford, Lord Lansdowne, and Lord Clarendon to induce him to take some other office in the Government, which, of course, he declined to do.' The Queen persisted in demanding Palmerston's removal. Letter to Lord John Russell, July 28, 1850, *Letters of Queen Victoria*, vol. ii, p. 305.

[2] Memorandum by Prince Albert, August 5, 1850: 'In conversation with me Lord Clarendon spoke in his old strain of Lord Palmerston, but very strongly too of the damage of turning him out and of making him the leader of the Radicals, who were anxiously waiting for that, were much dissatisfied with Lord John Russell and free from control by the death of Sir Robert Peel' (ibid., vol. ii, p. 310). For the attitude of the Radicals to Palmerston, see H. C. F. Bell, *Lord Palmerston*, vol. ii, pp. 29-30.

and her Foreign Minister in particular. There was nothing in the Memorandum approaching an attempt to encroach upon the recognized constitutional rights of the responsible Minister. The Queen simply asked in the first place to be informed in advance of any action contemplated in the field of diplomacy, and in the second place that a measure which had received her approval should not afterwards be arbitrarily changed by the Minister in question. Palmerston promised Lord John that he would 'punctually obey' these 'directions' and asked for a personal interview with Prince Albert. It took place on the 15th. 'He was very much agitated,' wrote the Prince Consort, 'shook, and had tears in his eyes, so as quite to move me, who never under any circumstances had known him otherwise than with a bland smile on his face.' Palmerston gave Prince Albert the promises for which he asked, and the following day Lord John informed the Prince that 'he thought what had passed had done a great deal of good'.[1]

It is plain, however, to anyone who reads Prince Albert's Memorandum to-day that the moment the Prince tried to go beyond generalities and obtain on a concrete issue more definite pledges, Palmerston, however 'low and agitated' he might be, managed to evade giving them. A German, indeed a Prussian, patriot such as Prince Albert was deeply concerned over the issue of Schleswig-Holstein. Once again he protested against the protocol by which England, France, Austria, and Russia had guaranteed the integrity of Danish territory.[2] If Prussia took action, would not Russia intervene? If she intervened, would it not mean a general war? What action would England take in that case? What action would Palmerston take if the Queen were at Balmoral and Lord John in Scotland? Palmerston, who refused to believe war possible, talked for an hour and managed to reach the moment when the conversation broke off without having pledged himself to anything.[3]

In the event Palmerston won yet another bloodless victory. The King of Prussia gave way and at Olmutz yielded to the demands of Austria. Possibly a secret delight in annoying the

[1] Sir Th. Martin, *Life of H.R.H. The Prince Consort*, vol. ii, pp. 307 sqq. *Letters of Queen Victoria*, vol. ii, p. 315.
[2] H. C. F. Bell, *Lord Palmerston*, vol. ii, p. 11. Lord Palmerston to Lord John Russell, une 23, 1850 (*Later Correspondence of Lord John Russell*, vol. ii, p. 26).
[3] See Lord John Russell's letter to Palmerston of November 18, 1850, and Lord Palmerston's to Lord John Russell, November 26, 1850, proving their disagreement (ibid., vol. ii, pp. 33-5).

Court entered into Palmerston's hostility to Prussia. No diplomat was more liable to be influenced by motives of this kind. But his policy was determined by far more reputable motives. Strictly speaking, he was not anti-Prussian. But he considered that any attempt to upset the territorial arrangements of 1815 was a threat to the peace of Europe. For it would justify military intervention by France and her Jacobin and Napoleonic aggression would be renewed. If France were to be kept peaceful, peace must be universal. In any case his temporary opposition to Prussia was not inspired by any prejudice in favour of Austria. The Austrian Government was planning to bring all its non-German possessions into the German confederation. After some hesitation the Russian Government consented. It was England that in concert with France opposed its veto. Provided the consent of the Diet was obtained, the proposed step did not constitute from the juridical standpoint a breach of the treaty of 1815. Nevertheless, it altered the European balance of power as established at that time. And this was sufficient to bring Palmerston into the field against it.[1]

On this point he was for once in agreement with Prince Albert. But his insolent conduct towards Austria soon embroiled him with the Court. It was nothing more than an incident. But Palmerston's entire career was made up of such stormy incidents. At the beginning of September an Austrian general, General Haynau, visited England. He was detested by the whole of Liberal Europe for the harshness, the savagery they said, with which he had repressed the revolutions in Italy and Hungary. When he paid a visit to a large London brewery, his presence became known and he was obliged to take flight from a riot of the employees. Even in the street he was hustled, stoned, and struck. Since he refused to prosecute no one was brought to trial. But Palmerston was obliged to send a letter of apology. He submitted the draft to the Queen as he had undertaken to do on August 14. But when she asked him to omit a particular phrase, she found that the letter had already been dispatched. This time the Court scored. Palmerston had to send another without the objectionable words.[2]

So the warfare went on between Palmerston, now more popular than ever, and the unyielding Prince Albert. Lord John was

---

[1] For Palmerston's German policy, see H. C. F. Bell, *Lord Palmerston*, vol. ii, pp. 1 sqq.
[2] Sir Th. Martin, *Life of the Prince Consort*, vol. ii, pp. 266-7. H. C. F. Bell, *Lord Palmerston*, vol. ii, p. 40.

caught between the two combatants. And he had other difficulties
to face. In the first place there was Peel's disappearance from the
political scene. Contrary to what might have been expected it
weakened the Prime Minister's position. Ever since he took office
in July 1846 Lord John had been, so to speak, buttressed by the
Peelites and the Protectionist Opposition. The hatred entertained
by the Tories for the man whom they regarded as an incorrigible
traitor, a turncoat on principle, made them indulgent to the
Whig Ministry. And, on the other hand, Peel's fear, which remained with him to the last, that the Protectionists might return
to power made him a staunch defender of the Cabinet. Though
this patronage was not a little humiliating, at any rate it secured
the life of the Government. Now, however, Peel's party had been
weakened by his death. In 1847 the Peelites had exceeded a hundred in number. To-day they were not more than sixty. The
remainder had returned to their old party. What would be their
line of action under Sir James Graham's more timid leadership?
Their choice was important from two points of view. The
Government needed them because, though they were so weak
numerically, they were the buttress of their majority. On the
other hand, they had a first-rate staff composed of Peel's most
competent assistants. And the Tories, who suffered from the lack
of trained leaders, had great need of them. This, however, made
it difficult for the Whigs to admit them into a coalition, as many
people expected. It would mean almost too much talent for one
Cabinet. A decision one way or the other seemed urgent when the
Session of 1851 opened.[1]

2

Never, in all the four years and a half it had been in office, had
the Whig Ministry, dependent now on its own strength, been so
conscious of its weakness, as at the opening of 1851.

[1] For the Peelites after Peel's death, see Palmerston's letter to his brother, September
1, 1850 (E. Ashley, *Life of Viscount Palmerston*, vol. i, p. 229). The Whigs who, in January
1849, had tried to persuade Sir James Graham to join the Cabinet (see C. S. Parker, *Sir
Robert Peel*, vol. iii, pp. 500-2) were afraid now that he might insist on the retrenchments
demanded by Cobden and the Radicals (*Greville Memoirs*, March 24, 1850). If we can
trust the explanation given by Lord John to the Queen, Sir James did not think his
following sufficiently strong. 'He did wish to support the Government, but he thought
he would be of more use if he did not join the Government and was able to give them an
independent support. He had not attempted to lead Sir Robert Peel's followers. Many
who followed Sir Robert Peel would not follow him' (Memorandum by the Queen,
February 17, 1851, in *Letters of Queen Victoria*, 1907, vol. ii, p. 344).

On February 11 the debate on the Address had scarcely been concluded, when Disraeli invited the House of Commons to vote on a resolution he had drawn up calling for immediate measures to assist landowners and tenant farmers, not a return to the Corn Laws—he bowed before the *fait accompli*—but the abolition of a large number of taxes to which land was subject and which, justified so long as the cultivators of the soil had been protected against foreign competition, had now become a crushing burden, when they had to face this competition unprotected. He was defeated, but by a narrow margin. His motion obtained 267 votes as against 281 for the Government. The Government majority, that is to say, was only 14.[1]

A few days later the Chancellor of the Exchequer brought in his Budget.[2] The financial position was excellent. The expenditure had been £629,000 less than the estimated amount, the revenue £371,000 more. The total surplus was thus no less than £2,521,000. For the financial year commencing on April 5 the Chancellor estimated an expenditure of £50,247,171 and a revenue of £52,140,000, that is to say, a surplus of £1,892,829. What would he do with it? The Chancellor would not give up the income tax nor even, as he was asked to do, reduce it by reducing the amount levied on certain categories of income. He proposed to employ a million of the surplus to pay off debt, to reduce the tax on fruit and the duties on imported chicory, foreign or colonial, on timber and seed, and to abolish the window tax, a reform which had been demanded for many years in the interest of public health, while restoring the house tax abolished in 1834,[3] and to transfer to the State part of the cost of maintaining pauper lunatics. It was not enough to satisfy all the appetites aroused by this large surplus. The Radicals asked for further economies and the abolition of the income tax; the champions of agriculture protested that the relief granted to the landowners and farmers was trifling. It became clear at once that Sir Charles Wood's Budget would not be passed without very considerable alterations.

---

[1] *Parliamentary Debates*, 3rd Ser., vol. cxiv, p. 604. Disraeli thus renewed the campaign he had conducted the previous year (see above, pp. 284-6). He was supported by a section of the Peelites and even by Muntz, the Radical member for Birmingham. Cobden, however, and the other Radicals voted for the Government (S. Maccoby, *English Radicalism*, p. 307).　　[2] *Parl. Deb.*, 3rd Ser., vol. cxiv, pp. 703 sqq.

[3] For the history of the window tax and house tax, see Sp. Walpole, *History of England*, vol. v, pp. 426-7.

The position was even worse the following week when the question of reforming the franchise came up. Lord John was in favour of reform. He had already proposed to deal with the matter, but had been prevented by the majority of his colleagues, from Lord Lansdowne to Palmerston.[1] He had, however, obtained a promise that, if the Whigs were still in office next year, he might bring forward then the measure he had in mind. This accounts for the vagueness of his reply on February 11 to a question in the House. He agreed that 'certain amendments' and 'certain extensions of the Reform Act' were desirable and added, 'I shall act on that opinion when I think the proper time has come'.[2]

On the 20th a member of Parliament, Locke King, brought forward a motion with the object of placing the county franchise on the same footing as the borough. Lord John made reservations with regard to the proposal. Its effect, he said, would be to increase in country districts the number of voters subject to the influence of the great landowners, while weakening the proportional strength of the really sound element of the country electorate, namely the freeholders. He expressed himself, however, in favour of reforming the franchise in another way and even pledged himself, were he still in office, to introduce at the opening of the next session a Bill extending the suffrage.[3]

If he thought this pledge would disarm the Radicals and dissuade them from supporting Locke King's motion, he was disappointed. On the 11th his language had been vague. To-day he had spoken plainly. The change must obviously be due to his fear of the Radicals. This salutary fear must be maintained. A Radical speaker declared that the best way to make Lord John keep his promise next year was to defeat him to-day. The motion was passed by 100 votes to 52, twenty-five of which were Conservative.[4]

As Lord John bitterly remarked, Palmerston had not taken the trouble to come and vote.[5]

[1] Sp. Walpole, *Life of Lord John Russell*, vol. ii, p. 123. Memorandum, by Prince Albert, February 22, 1851: 'We agreed with Lord John, praised his speech on the suffrage, which is admirable, and regretted that his colleagues had prevented him from bringing in a measure this year' (*Letters of Queen Victoria*, vol. ii, p. 347).

[2] *Parliamentary Debates*, 3rd Ser., vol. cxiv, pp. 373-4.

[3] Ibid., 3rd Ser., vol. cxiv, pp. 857 sqq.

[4] Ibid., 3rd Ser., vol. cxiv, p. 869. *Greville Memoirs*, February 24, 1851: Lord Stanley observed that, 'In the minority had voted only 27 members of the Government side, the rest had been of his party.' See also Memorandum, by Prince Albert, February 22, 1851 (*Letters of Queen Victoria*, vol. ii, p. 346).

[5] *Greville Memoirs*, February 28, 1851. He relates Lord John's remark: 'If Palmerston

The Prime Minister now decided that he no longer possessed sufficient authority to govern the country, and, since his colleagues were of the same opinion, tendered his resignation to the Queen, who accepted it. The oddest Cabinet crisis England has ever known began and lasted from February 21 to March 3, when the Whig leaders in both Houses informed the nation that the existing Cabinet would return to office, were it only 'to carry on Her Majesty's Government'. For no other political combination had proved practicable.

3

It was, as we have just said, an odd crisis and one whose nature reveals the increasing stability at this date of the nation's political institutions. Before 1830, parties had at times been as divided as they were now. But the sections had not been so disturbed by the fact nor so unanimous in desiring that the divided parties might be reconstituted on a firmer foundation and, in consequence, be better balanced. It was not the extremists who confronted statesmen of every political group with an awkward problem or, if they did, it was only inasmuch as there was a danger that if they were no longer wedged between two parties solidly organized to their right and left, they might, the Radicals in particular, profit by the disorganization of the moderate elements of the nation. The stumbling block was the centre group constituted by the Peelites, a group which could not make up its mind whether it would play its part as a group at once Conservative and Liberal more effectively by supporting the Conservatives or the Liberals. Some of them, the Duke of Newcastle for instance, seem to have believed that the party could continue to exist separately as a centre party, and might in the end become sufficiently numerous to govern the country in opposition to the Protectionists on the right, the Radicals on the left. But few held that opinion. Sir James Graham, who refused to regard himself as the leader of the group, had already for all practical purposes joined the Whigs,[1] Goulburn, on the other hand, the Conservatives. The others

had chosen to be present on Locke King's motion, and had spoken, it probably would not have happened at all.'
[1] Graham, however, of all the Peelites the most inclined to an alliance with the Whigs, thought that this should follow not precede the experiment of a Tory administration.

were undecided. The Court wanted to put an end to their hesitation and hoped they would enter a coalition with the Whigs.[1]

It was essential that they should make a choice one way or the other and thus enable two-party government to function normally, as it had functioned, it would seem, since 1832. We must not, therefore, think of Lord John Russell and Lord Lansdowne on the one side, Lord Stanley on the other, battling for office. Assisted by Prince Albert and in perfect harmony they were considering what could be done with the Peelites to ensure the normal working of parliamentary government.

Lord Stanley, for whom the Queen sent first, advised her to invite Lord Aberdeen and Sir James Graham to form a Coalition Government with Lord John. Negotiations were actually begun. But they were broken off even before the difficult stage had been reached of apportioning Cabinet offices. It was not because the Peelites thought the Liberalism of the Whigs too advanced that they refused to enter into a coalition with them. On the contrary, the views of Lord Aberdeen and Graham on the franchise were more advanced than those of Lord Lansdowne and Palmerston. Nor did they part company on the question of Palmerston's foreign policy.[2] What made agreement impossible was the sudden emergence of a novel issue, Papal Aggression and the Ecclesiastical Titles Bill.[3]

The decision of the Holy See to restore a regular hierarchy in England had aroused keen indignation. Lord John made himself the mouthpiece of public feeling in an open letter to the Bishop of Durham[4] and had brought in a Bill imposing upon anyone who assumed the ecclesiastical titles thus created a fine of £100. On February 14 the Commons passed the first reading.[5] But several

---

[1] Sir Th. Martin (*Life of the Prince Consort*, vol. i, p. 353) mentions a 'Scheme for a Coalition Government of Whigs and Peelites sketched by the Prince for his own amusement'.

[2] Lord Aberdeen and Sir James Graham were as opposed as Lord John to keeping Palmerston at the Foreign Office. See H. C. F. Bell, *Lord Palmerston*, vol. ii, pp. 41-2.

[3] The memoranda drawn up during these negotiations by Lord John on the one hand, and by Lord Aberdeen and Sir James on the other, have been published by Sp. Walpole (*Life of Lord John Russell*, vol. ii, pp. 124-8). They conclude with Lord John's statement: 'Lord Aberdeen and Sir James Graham object decidedly to *any* legislative measure on the subject of the Ecclesiastical Titles Bill. This put an end to the negotiations. There has been no question between Lord Aberdeen, Sir James Graham and himself with regard to persons.' For the Ecclesiastical Titles Bill, see below, pp. 366-71.

[4] For the text of the letter, see Sp. Walpole, *Life of Lord John Russell*, vol. ii, pp. 120-1.

[5] *Parliamentary Debates*, 3rd Ser., vol. cxiv, p. 999.

of his colleagues disapproved of the step he had taken.[1] The Radicals declared against the Bill and the Peelites had not concealed their dislike of it.

On this point at least the Peelites were unanimous, and suddenly became aware of a united front against the Tories and Whigs brought together for the nonce by their common hatred of Rome. The Tories remained the anti-Catholic party they had become since 1815; the Whigs became once more the anti-Catholic party they had been in the eighteenth century. Only the Peelites remained 'Catholic' as Peel himself had been since 1829. Agreement was impossible.

Without Lord John, Lord Aberdeen could not take the responsibility of forming a Cabinet. He lost no time in refusing, and the Queen invited Stanley to attempt a coalition of Tories and Peelites. The disappearance of Peel and shortly after of Bentinck, who had worked, up to a point successfully, to rebuild the Tory party on the foundation of a strictly Protectionist programme might seem to have made it easier. To be sure, there was Disraeli. But though his brilliant gifts gave him an ascendency in the Commons, he was still regarded with considerable distrust by the Tory gentlemen. The young Jewish adventurer was, in fact, the leader of the Tories in the Commons—though without the official title—because in the void created by the defection of Peel's entire staff he was indispensable. But he did not yet wield the authority he would soon acquire. Lord Stanley was no fanatic on the subject of protection or any other. Nevertheless, so soon after the rupture with Peel and well acquainted as he was with Conservative opinion, he dared not promise the Peelites the formal repudiation of protection which they made the indispensable condition of entering his Cabinet. A Tory-Peelite coalition thus proved as impracticable as a Peelite-Whig.

Lord Stanley was then urged to form a purely Tory Administration. He did not refuse point blank. Disraeli, afraid of nothing and attracted by the prospect of making his début, were it but for a few weeks, as official leader in the Commons, was all in favour of making the experiment. But Stanley's other subordinates were more timid. They were conscious of their own deficiencies as a party executive, and their inability to manage a Parliament in which, as a minority, they would be compelled to count upon the

[1] Letters from Lord Palmerston to Lord John Russell, January 16 and 18, 1851.

divisions of the majority. Lord Stanley, therefore, abandoned the attempt, and Lord John returned to office with the same Ministers and the same discredit to confront a nation which, rejoicing in the general prosperity and more uninterested than ever in questions of ministerial politics, watched these disputes with boredom and an indifference even more complete.[1]

4

Public interest turned away more than ever from the wrangles in Parliament when the great Universal Exhibition was opened in Hyde Park. The nation saw in it the triumph of British industry and British wealth. But it was also a personal triumph for Prince Albert.[2] For the Exhibition was his work. It was he whom its promoters had approached a year earlier when the success of a National Exhibition of arts and manufactures had suggested the project of an international exhibition.[3] Its realization was due to him. His able diplomacy had successfully overcome the attacks of his enemies who, at the moment when Palmerston was arousing national feeling over the affair of Don Pacifico, attempted to ruin the enterprise by preventing the Exhibition buildings being erected in Hyde Park.[4]

The success of the Exhibition was universally regarded as a victory for the ideal of international peace—the official speeches with perfect sincerity harped on this point—a victory also for the ideal of a reconciliation of all parties, to be the work of a country which had been the refuge of political exiles and to-day offered her hospitality to monarchs. Though some dared not accept the invitation, at least those who did were not victims of an assassin.

And Tennyson, who had just succeeded Wordsworth as Poet Laureate, hymned England's majesty.[5]

[1] Lord Malmesbury, *Memoirs of an Ex-Minister*, pp. 203 sqq.

[2] The Queen wrote to Lord John on June 18, 1851: 'The Queen, at the risk of not appearing sufficiently modest (and yet, why should a wife ever be modest about her husband's merits?), must say that she thinks Lord John Russell will admit now that the Prince is possessed of very extraordinary powers of mind and head' (Sir Th. Martin, *Life of the Prince Consort*, vol. ii, p. 378).

[3] For the origin of the Exhibition, see *The Life of Wentworth Dilke*, vol. i, p. 7.

[4] Prince Albert to Stockmar, June 28, 1850: 'The Exhibition is now attacked furiously by *The Times*, and the House of Commons is going to drive us out of the Park. There is immense excitement on the subject' (Sir Th. Martin, *Life of the Prince Consort*, vol. ii, p. 285).

[5] Fear not, isle of blowing woodland, isle of silvery parapets !
Tho' the Roman eagle shadow thee, tho' the gathering enemy narrow thee,

In the shadow then of these festivities and demonstrations Lord John's Cabinet continued its life without too many difficulties until the recess. After interminable debates he passed his Ecclesiastical Titles Bill,[1] but not until a determined minority of Whigs and Peelites had considerably watered down its provisions. It was made illegal for Catholic priests to take in England the title of Bishop. But the fine imposed for disobedience was never inflicted. In short, the Bill, from being a serious measure of repression, became a mere gesture of protest. Sir Charles Wood carried his Budget, but only with important amendments and a sufficient reduction of his house tax to satisfy the Opposition.[2] On the other hand, when the income tax expired and the Government proposed to continue it for a further three years, Hume, who advocated a thoroughgoing reform of the tax, to force the Government to effect it quickly, moved that it should be continued only for one year. Since all the enemies of the tax and the entire Opposition supported him, the Government was defeated by 244 to 230 votes.[3] But the Cabinet gave way. It therefore remained in office, and that was all it asked. It would receive its death blow from Palmerston's hand.

At first, indeed, Palmerston's foreign policy did not disturb his relations with his colleagues. On the contrary the Cabinet had been strengthened by the fact that his diplomacy made a convert, the most unlikely of converts, namely Gladstone. He was a Conservative, one of the rebels, it is true, since he had supported Peel, but a Conservative all the same. In religion he was a Puseyite and convinced that, if the growth of irreligion were to be checked and peace promoted, England must make common cause with the Continental monarchies. But after a visit to Italy in the winter of

Thou shalt wax and he shall dwindle, thou shalt be the mighty one yet!
Thine the liberty, thine the glory, thine the deeds to be celebrated.
Thine the myriad-rolling ocean, light and shadow illimitable,
Thine the lands of lasting summer, many blossoming Paradises:
Thine the North and thine the South and thine the battle-thunder of God. (*Boadicea.*)
[1] The passage of the second reading was secured only after a debate lasting seven days (*Parliamentary Debates*, 3rd Ser., vol. cxv, p. 618). The third reading was not passed until July 4 (ibid., cxviii, p. 240). And the Lords did not pass the Bill until the end of July.
[2] *Parl. Deb.*, 3rd Ser., vol. cxv, p. 1058. *Annual Register*, 1851, pp. 29 sqq.
[3] On May 2, 1851 (*Parl. Deb.*, 3rd Ser., vol. cxvi, p. 496), *Ann. Reg.*, 1851, p. 85. Hume's motion was passed with the help of the Protectionists. Cobden opposed it (S. Maccoby, *English Radicalism*, p. 308).

1850–1,[1] and conversations with the British Minister at Naples and with Italians hostile to the despotic government, alike of the Pope and secular rulers, he made up his mind to expose the ruthless repression of the democrats by the Neapolitan Government which formed part of the powerful movement of reaction that prevailed throughout Europe. He attended the trial of Poerio and was shocked by the procedure and the sentence, twenty-five years in irons for no other offence than having been a Liberal politician. Twenty thousand persons were deprived of their civil rights, among them a former Prime Minister and the majority of the suppressed Parliament. And the prisoners in irons were tied together in couples. Gladstone returned to London boiling with indignation and called on Lord Aberdeen. They agreed that any representations made by Palmerston, morally isolated as he was from contemporary Europe, would do more harm than good, but that something might be accomplished if Lord Aberdeen, though in opposition, were to follow the line of action pursued formerly by Guizot and make friendly representations to the courts of Naples and Vienna in the interests of legitimate government. But time passed and he did nothing. Gladstone lost patience. Without consulting Lord Aberdeen he published, one after the other, two letters to him in which he denounced the Neapolitan scandals.[2] The effect was enormous. Palmerston had an edition printed at the Government's expense and copies were sent officially to every court in Europe.[3] That one of Peel's leading henchmen should have thus adopted so wholeheartedly the principle, if not the methods, of his foreign policy, was a great victory for him.[4] As a result of Gladstone's action Conservative circles gradually took the infection of his anger, even the Court.[5] The entire country, in protest against the Neapolitan atrocities, became Palmerstonian.

[1] For Gladstone's journey and the political campaign he launched on his return, see John Morley, *Life of W. E. Gladstone*, book iii, ch. 6.

[2] *Letters to the Earl of Aberdeen, on the State Prosecutions of the Neapolitan Government*, 1851.

[3] *Annual Register*, 1851, pp. 138–9.

[4] Lord Palmerston, to his brother, April 3, 1851: 'Gladstone and Molesworth are full of the abominable tyranny exercised by the Neapolitan and Roman Governments. . . . Both of them say that they were wrong last year in their attacks on my foreign policy, but they did not know the truth. This is satisfactory as far as I am concerned, though very unsatisfactory as regards the state of Italy' (E. Ashley, *Life of Viscount Palmerston*, vol. ii, pp. 256–7).

[5] Prince Albert to Stockmar, August 1, 1851, and the Queen to Stockmar, April 17, 1851 (Sir Th. Martin, *The Life of the Prince Consort*, vol. ii, pp. 389–90).

But this state of affairs could not last. A section of the Press continued to wage unremitting warfare against Palmerston,[1] and the latter would soon rekindle by his caprices the feuds which perhaps gave his life its savour.

At the end of October, Kossuth, the hero of Hungarian independence, arrived in London. Against his colleagues' wishes, Palmerston was determined to give him an official reception at the Foreign Office. To prevent him from doing so required the Prime Minister's formal prohibition, supported by a decision of the Cabinet and the pressing instances of the Court. But a few days later, receiving a deputation of Radicals, who had come to pay tribute to him as a champion of liberty, he allowed them without protest to denounce in his presence the odious tyranny of Russia and Austria. His removal from the Foreign Office was once more considered. But once more it was found impossible to dismiss so popular a Minister.[2]

In this matter of Kossuth the Court was openly hostile to Palmerston, and the majority of his colleagues unsympathetic. But he had behind him the enthusiastic support of the public. On another issue he would provoke the combined hostility of the Court and his fellow Ministers, and disconcert the mass of his supporters by the most extraordinary of all his diplomatic interventions.

Reaction on the Continent was making rapid progress. It had but to reach its goal in France. The struggle in that country was being waged between the Reds, a minority in the Chamber and country, but inspiring in the majority a terror out of proportion to their real strength, the Royalists, a majority in the Legislative Assembly, but weakened by the division between the supporters of the elder branch of the Bourbons and the supporters of the younger, the latter being the more numerous and cherishing an illusory prospect of returning to power, and finally, Louis Napoleon and the mysterious party of the Elysée which aimed at the restoration of a democratic empire and dreamed of a new

---

[1] *The Times*, with its editor, Delane, and its chief foreign editor, Reeve, fought Palmerston. So did the *Morning Chronicle*, which since 1848 had been under Peelite influence. Palmerston, inadequately supported by the *Globe*, had found a more effective defender in the *Morning Post*, whose circulation had greatly increased since 1850. See H. C. F. Bell, *Lord Palmerston*, vol. ii, pp. 32-4; *The History of 'The Times'*, vol. ii, pp. 106-8.

[2] See in Sp. Walpole, *Life of Lord John Russell*, vol. ii, pp. 132-8, the principal correspondence on the Kossuth episode.

eighteenth Brumaire. The Orleanists who thought themselves all-powerful, not only at the Palais Bourbon, but in the army, were planning a military *coup d'état*. On December 2 they were anticipated by Louis Napoleon.

What attitude would Palmerston adopt? His hatred of the House of Orleans proved stronger than his love of liberty. A Government which, to judge by everything he had said and done for many years past, should have excited his most violent antipathy received his wholehearted sympathy. It made no difference that his arch-enemy Louis Philippe had been dead a year. His sons Joinville, Aumale, and Nemours were in London, received as personal friends by the Court. For they were related through the King of the Belgians to the Queen and Prince Albert. And they had belonged to that Holy Alliance of Western Europe which, in the days of Lord Aberdeen and Guizot, had attempted to restore cordial relations with the Northern Powers. The death of Louis Philippe's daughter, Queen Louise of the Belgians, had been an occasion for family mourning at Windsor, as well as at Twickenham. An Orleanist restoration would have confronted Palmerston with Prince Albert's opposition in Paris as well as in London. Nor was it so surprising, as it might seem, that Palmerston, once so obsessed by the desire to hold the military ambitions of France in check, should have preferred to see in The Tuileries the heir of Napoleon's name rather than a boy of twelve, heir of the most bourgeois of monarchs. For Louis Napoleon did not strike those who knew him as a Caesar, and seemed to have adopted for his programme not the legend of Napoleonic war, but Napoleon's political legacy, the Memorial from Saint Helena. On the other hand, Louis Philippe's sons were the least bourgeois of princes. Their democratic education in a Parisian *lycée* in companionship with the sons of the most enlightened section of the population of Paris had combined with their natural gifts to make them far superior to the average member of the European royal families. And their tastes were thoroughly military.

Joinville had been the outstanding figure of the French navy throughout the latter part of his father's reign, and Palmerston had not forgotten the anti-British manifesto by which he had done more than anyone else to make the King unpopular with the British. Aumale was the conqueror of Isly and military governor of Algeria when the February revolution broke out. He might well be suspected of cherishing the design to make the tricolour monarchy once more popular by victories won in Italy or on the Rhine, and steal Palmerston's programme of Liberal propaganda to exploit it for the benefit of French expansion. Far better then this queer bumpkin, the Prince President.[1]

When the news of the *coup d'état* was received the Cabinet met in haste to discuss the situation. The Ministers decided, in entire agreement with the Court, to adopt towards the new *de facto* Government the attitude England had adopted towards the Republican Government after the fall of the July monarchy, an attitude neither of approval nor systematic hostility. But when Lord Normanby communicated this decision to the Prince President's Foreign Minister, the latter replied that he already knew Palmerston's attitude to the *coup d'état*, of which he had been informed by Walewski, the French ambassador in London, and that it was one of benevolence and sincere approval. Once more Palmerston had acted without consulting his colleagues or informing the Court. His action aroused the anger of Prince Albert and the Queen, and offended at once Lord John's susceptibilities and his Whig principles. 'I am most reluctantly compelled', the latter wrote to Palmerston, 'to come to the conclusion that the conduct of foreign affairs can no longer be left in your hands with advantage to the country.'[2] In exchange for the Foreign Office he offered Palmerston the Lord-Lieutenancy of Ireland, even an English peerage, if he wished for one. Palmerston refused the

---

[1] Lord Palmerston to Lord Normanby, November 20, 1851: 'It seems to me that Louis Napoleon is master of the field of battle and will carry the day. I have always thought that such a result would be the best thing for both France and for England. There is no other person at present competent to be at the head of affairs in France, and if Louis Napoleon should end by founding a dynasty, I do not see that we need regret it, as far as English interests are concerned. The Family of Bourbons have already been most hostile to England. . . . What should we gain by substituting Henry V or the Orleans family for the race of Buonaparte?' (E. Ashley, *Life of Viscount Palmerston*, vol. i, p. 270). See, further, Lord Palmerston's letters to Lord Normanby, January 24, 1851 (ibid., vol. i, pp. 285-6), and Lord John Russell, October 24, 1851: 'The chances are in favour of the President, but if the Reds were to triumph or Joinville to succeed we should have to sleep with one eye open' (*The Later Correspondence of Lord John Russell*, vol. i, pp. 269-70). The Queen's sympathies, on the other hand, were with the Orleans family. On December 20 she wrote to Lord John: 'It was quite clear to the Queen that we were entering upon most dangerous times in which Military Despotism and Red Republicanism will for some time be the only powers on the Continent' (Sir Th. Martin, *Life of the Prince Consort*, vol. ii, p. 419).

[2] Lord John Russell to Lord Palmerston, December 17, 1851 (Sp. Walpole, *Life of Lord John Russell*, vol. ii, p. 139). For this crisis, see E. Ashley, *Life of Viscount Palmerston*, vol. i, pp. 286 sqq.; H. C. F. Bell, *Lord Palmerston*, vol. i, pp. 46 sqq.; Sp. Walpole, *Life of Lord John Russell*, vol. ii, pp. 138-42.

Government of Ireland and vanished. It was suggested that the vacant office should be offered to Lord Clarendon. But since the latter was not *persona grata* either with Lord John or Prince Albert, Lord Granville was appointed, and thus owed to a political accident entrance upon his career as Foreign Secretary. He was recommended to Lord John by his popularity with the Manchester free traders and by the fact that he was in favour of reforming the franchise.[1]

It was a victory for Lord John; but a victory, and he was not blind to the fact, more apparent than real. For he was well aware that, if he was disposed to look upon himself as a statesman of the first rank, the accredited heir of a great parliamentary tradition, public opinion was far from agreeing with him. Even after the unfortunate episode of his interviews with Walewski a considerable section of the Liberal Press remained loyal to Palmerston.[2] He saw Prince Albert, even more relieved than himself by the disappearance of this overwhelming personality, taking every day a more active, though it was necessarily unavowed, part in politics.[3] Now that Peel was dead and Palmerston put out of action for a long while to come, it was galling to hear political wiseacres lament, as though he did not exist, the mediocrity of Ministers and the dearth of great men. It seemed as though the country, blessed by an ever-increasing prosperity, felt the need to be ruled by what was called a great man. It was not the hostility but the indifference of the public with which Lord John had to contend. To buttress a shaky Administration he once more suggested to his colleagues the possibility of a coalition with the Peelites, if not with the entire group with some of them at least, perhaps even with Graham alone. Their response was not encouraging. It was, therefore, except for the loss of Palmerston's powerful personality, with the same Cabinet as before that Lord John met Parliament when the Session of 1852 opened.[4]

---

[1] For the part played by the Queen in the choice of Lord Granville, see H. C. F. Bell, *Lord Palmerston*, vol. ii, pp. 51-2.

[2] For the effect produced abroad by Palmerston's fall, see E. Ashley, *Life of Viscount Palmerston*, vol. i, p. 308; H. C. F. Bell, *Lord Palmerston*, vol. ii, pp. 52 sqq.

[3] The Queen to King Leopold, February 3, 1852: 'Albert grows daily fonder and fonder of politics and business, and is wonderfully fit for both' (Sir Th. Martin, *Life of the Prince Consort*, vol. ii, p. 432).

[4] John Morley, *Life of W. E. Gladstone*, vol. i, p. 416.

6

Parliament reassembled on February 3 and its opening session was marked by an oratorical victory for the Prime Minister. Called upon to explain the circumstances of his breach with his Foreign Secretary, he had only to read the Queen's Memorandum of August 15, 1850, mention Palmerston's acceptance of the rulings laid down in it, and relate how he had broken his promise, to justify himself completely. Palmerston's reply was generally regarded as feeble and was applauded only by a small group.[1] It was the general impression that evening in the lobbies and in the clubs that his career was finished.[2] But the Prime Minister's position remained difficult.

To prove his ability to get something done now that he was free from Palmerston's opposition in the Cabinet to his projects of reform, Lord John extorted his colleagues' permission to keep the promise he had made the year before and bring in a Bill to extend the franchise. On February 9 he explained its main provisions in the Commons. In the English boroughs the household qualification would be reduced from 10 shillings to 5, in the counties the qualification would not exceed 20 shillings, and in the case of copyholders and long leaseholders would be reduced from 10 to 5 shillings. Boroughs considered too small would not be disfranchised, but enlarged by taking in part of the adjoining county. There would no longer be any property qualification for membership of Parliament. The oath would be so modified as to make it possible for Jews to be members. Members of Parliament who exchanged one ministerial office for another would no longer have to seek re-election. Similar provisions would be applied to Scotland and Ireland. The House listened to this preparatory speech, not even accompanied by a formal measure, without dislike or pleasure. It was obvious at once that the project would be killed by the universal indifference.[3]

---

[1] *Parliamentary Debates*, 3rd Ser., vol. cxix, pp. 84 sqq. E. Ashley, *Life of Viscount Palmerston*, vol. i, pp. 318 sqq. H. C. F. Bell, *Lord Palmerston*, vol. ii, pp. 54-6. For Lord John's victory, see Sp. Walpole, *Life of Lord John Russell*, vol. ii, p. 143.

[2] See Lord Dalling's account, quoted by E. Ashley, op. cit., p. 331: 'I think it was the night after the debate, that meeting Mr. Disraeli on the staircase of Ashburnham House, which was then the Russian Embassy, he said, in his peculiar manner: "There *was* a Palmerston." "Palmerston is smashed," was indeed the expression generally used at the clubs.' The Marchioness of Dufferin wrote: 'Palmerston is completely floored, and people think he is not likely to rise again' (H. C. F. Bell, *Lord Palmerston*, vol. ii, p. 57).

[3] The Radicals criticized Lord John's proposals, mainly on the ground that the ballot formed no part of them (Maccoby, *English Radicalism*, pp. 320-3). The Protectionists had

The moment had come for Palmerston to take his revenge.[1]

The Parliamentary Reform Bill had been inspired by the desire to prove—in the void, as it were, and without any public demand —that the Whig Government stood for reform. Another measure introduced by the Cabinet was inspired by very different motives. It had yielded, as any other Cabinet would have done, to the irresistible pressure of public opinion. The same panic once more prevailed as had prevailed on the eve of the February revolution, fear of a war with France which, if launched suddenly, would find the country unprepared.[2] For two or three years the internal troubles which had made French history so stormy had made England secure. Now, when the President had received dictatorial powers, was about to declare himself Emperor, and was called Napoleon, anything might be expected. There was even danger that a French army would invade England, but after invading Belgium first. The panic, therefore, was even greater in Brussels, where King Leopold was seeking assurances of English help, than in London. Lord John was not content with asking for a stronger army, he proposed to reorganize the local militia, a reserve force for home defence.

On this subject Palmerston, ever since 1840, had consistently differed from his Whig colleagues. For he wanted not a local but a national militia.[3]

Palmerston now moved that the word local should be dropped from the title of the Bill, and he carried his motion by a majority of 136 to 125 votes, a majority of eleven.

already committed themselves in advance to a hostile attitude by Lord Derby's and Disraeli's speeches on February 3, during the debate on the Address (*Parliamentary Debates*, 3rd Ser., vol. cxix, pp. 15 and 135), and the Queen regretted their opposition— The Queen to the King of the Belgians, March 17, 1852 (*The Letters of Queen Victoria*, vol. ii, p. 463). But on February 9 they did not think it worth while to carry their attack further. For the general indifference, see *Annual Register*, 1852, pp. 17 and 21.

[1] Palmerston wrote to his brother on February 24, after the fall of the Cabinet: 'I have had my tit-for-tat with John Russell, and I turned him out on Friday last.' See E. Ashley, *Life of Viscount Palmerston*, vol. i, p. 334.

[2] This was the second of the 'panics' which Cobden described in 1862 in his book, *The Three Panics* (*Political Writings*, vol. ii, p. 235).

[3] For the militia, see Sp. Walpole, *History of England*, vol. v, pp. 428-9. There had been two distinct militias in England. (1) The militia created in the reign of Charles II, and transformed in 1757 into a national militia, recruited by lot from a list of able-bodied men drawn up in each parish and placed under the direct control of the central Government. (2) The militia created during the Napoleonic wars. Although its recruitment was the same as that of the former, it was called the local militia, because its purpose was to keep order or resist an invader in its own locality. Neither had been called out since 1815. It was the second which Lord John proposed to revive, whereas Palmerston wanted to revive the former.

Lord John had declared the issue a question of confidence in the Government.[1] Accordingly, after holding office for five years and eight months—during which the prestige and power of the country had greatly increased, but the Cabinet had had no share of either, the Whig Ministry was turned out.

7

There was a general agreement now to try the experiment of a Tory Government which had proved impossible a year before. Though the Tories were in a minority in the Commons, the divisions which weakened the other parties should make it possible for them to govern. The Whigs were paralysed by the incubus of Palmerston's personality and the discontent apparent even among Lord John's followers. The Peelites were equally disunited, some of them supporting Aberdeen and Graham who leant towards the Whigs, others Gladstone and Sidney Herbert, whose sympathies lay more with their old Tory friends. But the latter group could not contemplate rejoining them so long as they clung to protection.[2] The Tories, therefore, must carry on the Government alone, and their adversaries were content to leave it in their hands until the rapidly approaching General Election.

Stanley, now Lord Derby, for he had just succeeded his father, to whom it fell to preside over the new Cabinet, did not, it would seem, make the experiment without considerable misgivings. But his principal subordinate, Disraeli, was enthusiastic.[3] Lord Derby had attempted to bring Palmerston into his Administration, and had even secured the Queen's permission to offer him the post of Chancellor of the Exchequer by convincing her that his acceptance would make his future

[1] February 20, 1852 (*Parliamentary Debates*, 3rd Ser., vol. cxix, pp. 550 sqq. and 849 sqq.); H. C. F. Bell, *Lord Palmerston*, vol. ii, p. 58. Cobden made an unsuccessful protest against reviving the militia in any form (John Morley, *Life of Richard Cobden*, p. 75).

[2] The Peelites, who had kept their seats on the Opposition benches, now found themselves sitting with the Whigs. Sir James Graham even took his place on the front Opposition bench beside Lord John. For the divisions among the Peelites, see *Greville Memoirs*, January 11, 1852; John Morley, *Life of W. E. Gladstone*, 1903, vol. i, p. 417.

[3] Malmesbury, *Memoirs of an Ex-Minister*, February 21, 1852, ed. 1885, p. 227. Lord Derby, however, according to Palmerston, was not in favour at the Court. Palmerston wrote to his brother on June 20, 1852: 'Derby has an offhand and sarcastic way about him, which is not the manner of the courtier' (E. Ashley, *Life of Viscount Palmerston*, vol. i, p. 349). Disraeli, on the other hand, began to court the Queen's favour. He made the success of the Exhibition the occasion for a panegyric of Prince Albert (Monypenny, *Life of Disraeli*, vol. iii, p. 303).

return to the Foreign Office more unlikely. Palmerston, however, refused on the ground that he differed from the Tories on the issue of free trade. He preferred to retain an independence whose advantages he appreciated. He would promise the new Government nothing more than a benevolent neutrality.[1] Lord Derby had to be content with a Cabinet of novices. For his party suffered very seriously from the lack of experienced statesmen. Of the new Ministers only two had held Cabinet office before, and it was necessary to make no less than seventeen of them members of the Privy Council. The new Cabinet was nicknamed the 'Who? Who? Cabinet', for when the aged Wellington was told the names of its members, they had to be repeated to him, so unfamiliar were they. The Foreign Office was given to the young Earl of Malmesbury, and Palmerston was most willing to be his mentor.[2] Disraeli, on the other hand, who in spite of the fact that he had no experience whatever of finance, did not hesitate to accept the Treasury together with the leadership of the Commons, was confident of making his way by his unaided abilities.

Everyone, of course, was asking whether the return of the Protectionists to power would reopen the issue of free trade. On this point Lord Derby spoke with considerable embarrassment, giving it to be understood that a decision would be postponed until after the approaching election. This was not enough to reassure the Manchester group, who at Cobden's suggestion declared their intention to revive the League.[3] But the House had no desire to press the Government, and was satisfied when Disraeli, without the least embarrassment, spoke of the benefits the country had derived from free trade.[4]

When Hume brought up once more the question of parliamentary reform, Disraeli adroitly argued that it was not only the manufacturing population that was inadequately represented and that many rural constituencies had more voters than the urban. Only the Radicals voted for Hume's motion.[5]

[1] E. Ashley, *Life of Viscount Palmerston*, pp. 334 sqq. H. C. F. Bell, *Lord Palmerston*, vol. ii, pp. 60-1. [2] Ibid., vol. ii, p. 61.
[3] *Parliamentary Debates*, 3rd Ser., vol. cxix, pp. 898 sqq. J. Morley, *Life of Richard Cobden*, p. 75.
[4] Disraeli's speech, April 30, presenting a provisional Budget (*Annual Register*, 1852, pp. 111 sqq.). See Sp. Walpole, *History of England*, vol. v, p. 462. Walpole was himself Home Secretary in the Derby Cabinet.
[5] It was defeated on March 25 by 244 to 89 (Maccoby, *English Radicalism*, p. 324).

The Ministry won a further victory in April when it proposed to revive the militia, not Lord John's local militia, but the national militia advocated by Palmerston. Lord John was sufficiently ill-advised to oppose the Bill and seek his revenge on the very ground on which he had been defeated. His imprudence cost him a second defeat, and procured the Cabinet the satisfaction of a large majority.[1]

But it was not long before their opponents reminded the Government how weak its position was. Two boroughs, Sudbury and St. Albans, had been disfranchised for corruption, and the Government proposed to give the vacant seats to the West Riding and South Lancashire. Without discussing the proposal on its merits, Gladstone, as mouthpiece of the Opposition, declared that in taking this step the Government had exceeded the authority granted to it by Parliament pending the election, and by a majority of 86 it was prevented from effecting a reform as Liberal as it was wise.[2]

The Tory Cabinet, therefore, to which in April Parliament had granted nothing more than a provisional Budget to meet current expenses,[3] dragged out an inglorious life till the close of the session.

The dissolution at the end of July was followed by the General Election. It should have been fought on the issue of free trade. But many Government candidates, convinced that the question had been definitely settled against them, refrained from placing protection on their electoral programme. Disraeli himself declared in July that no one could possibly credit the Government with the intention to go back on the decision taken in 1846. But it was possible to do something for its victims and compensate the farmers and landlords by measures favouring their interests. Religious differences played an important part in the campaign. The no-Popery issue on which Lord John had taken up so decided an attitude furnished one battle-cry, and in particular the religious policy in Ireland inaugurated by Peel's Maynooth grant. Since the parties were so disorganized, the struggle was a confused mêlée and its result not easy to interpret.

---

[1] 315 votes to 165 (*Parliamentary Debates*, 3rd Ser., vol. cxx, p. 1085).
[2] J. Morley, *Life of W. E. Gladstone*, vol. i, p. 424.
[3] The income tax had been continued for a year (*Annual Register*, 1852, p. 115).

The Government secured roughly 300 seats. The Whigs kept a little less than 200. Almost 100 went to the Radicals. It is not surprising that the Peelites who had numbered 112 in 1846 lost two-thirds of their strength. We might rather be surprised that they were still able to muster forty members, a group still to be reckoned with for the calibre of its leaders. But they had lost their former position as arbiters between the Tories and the Whigs. In the new Parliament the balance between the Protectionists and free traders was held by the Irish brigade.[1]

8

The success of the Government at the polls, which had surprised its opponents, enabled it to continue in office, and the more easily since the dissatisfaction with Lord John still prevalent among the Whigs would have made his return to power difficult. The Manchester group, therefore, decided to take the offensive and prevent the Government undoing their work, were it only by the indirect method of compensating the farmers.[2]

When the new Parliament assembled on November 11 the speech from the Throne did not allay their apprehensions. The Queen observed that the measures establishing free trade had inevitably injured an important section of the community and recommended Parliament to study the best method of enabling that section to prosper under the system of unrestricted competition which it had in its wisdom established.[3]

On November 23, Villiers, who had put forward so many motions in favour of free trade, introduced another. It declared the measures passed in 1846 wise, just, and 'beneficial', and demanded that they should not only be maintained but carried further.[4] Disraeli denounced these 'odious' epithets and proposed as an amendment a more neutral statement, which did no more than recognize the benefits the lower classes had derived from free trade and the principle of free competition on which the country's commercial policy must in future be founded.[5]

---

[1] Sp. Walpole, *Life of Lord John Russell*, vol. ii, pp. 150-1.
[2] Maccoby, *English Radicalism*, p. 310. J. Morley, *Life of Cobden*, p. 76.
[3] *Parliamentary Debates*, 3rd Ser., vol. cxxiii, p. 20.
[4] Ibid., 3rd Ser., vol. cxxiii, p. 351.
[5] Ibid., 3rd Ser., vol. cxxiii, p. 411.

At this point, to rescue the Ministry from this dangerous situation, Palmerston intervened. In concert with the Peelites and no doubt at their instigation,[1] he proposed a third version, declaring that free trade must be 'firmly maintained and prudently extended', but without inflicting injury on any important interest.[2] On November 26 the House rejected Villiers's motion by 336 votes to 256 and passed Palmerston's by 468 to 53.[3]

From one point of view this result was a striking victory for free trade which, after the country had been consulted, was condemned by no more than some fifty Protectionist diehards. And it seemed as if it might strengthen the position of the Government by enabling it to win those who had come to its assistance. Lord Derby wanted to have Palmerston, Lord John's implacable enemy, in his Cabinet, also certain Peelites, Gladstone in particular, who after the settlement of the free trade issue had no longer any reason for remaining aloof from their former party. But the negotiations for a coalition conducted between the leaders of the different parties were complicated and made still more complicated by Palmerston's formidable personality. Nothing, therefore, had been settled, and the composition of the Cabinet was unchanged when Disraeli, eager to display his capacities, introduced his Budget.[4]

As it listened on December 3 to his speech, which took over five hours to deliver, the House admired the speaker's brilliant oratory and the cleverness of his proposals. Disraeli accepted the result of the election as the definitive condemnation of protection and claimed to do nothing more than help the country to adapt itself to free trade which must henceforth prevail. He even pronounced obsolete his own former proposals to reform the system of local taxation and thus compensate Peel's agricultural victims.[5] His language was ambiguous. But his aim was undoubtedly under colour of removing the tram-

[1] J. Morley, *Life of W. E. Gladstone*, vol. i, p. 433. H. C. F. Bell, *Lord Palmerston*, vol. ii, p. บ๖.
[2] *Parliamentary Debates*, 3rd Ser., vol. cxxiii, pp. 451 sqq.
[3] Ibid., 3rd Ser., vol. cxxiii, pp. 696 and 711.
[4] J. Morley, *Life of W. E. Gladstone*, vol. i, pp. 434-5. H. C. F. Bell, *Lord Palmerston*, pp. 69-70. Malmesbury, *Memoirs of an Ex-Minister*, November 24, 25, and 28, pp. 281-2. *Greville Memoirs*, December 4 and 6.
[5] Cobden wrote to George Wilson on December 4: 'The Budget has finally closed the controversy with Protection. Dizzy has in the most impudent way thrown over the "local burdens" as he did before a fixed duty. The League may be dissolved when you like' (J. Morley, *Life of Richard Cobden*, p. 76).

mels which still fettered the classes of producer for whose benefit a system of free trade had been introduced in 1846, 1848, and 1849, to compensate by financial relief those who had been deprived of protection. Shipowners would be relieved of certain duties. The growers of colonial sugar would receive special facilities for refining their produce which would better enable them to meet foreign competition. For the benefit of agriculture the duties on malt and hops would be reduced by half. The duty on tea would be gradually reduced. But these reforms would be effected in the train of bolder changes. Compelled to ask for a further continuation of the income tax, Disraeli would take advantage of it to differentiate between various sources of income. Farmers, traders, and those in receipt of salaries would pay only 5d. in the pound, the amount which earned income would pay in future, whereas unearned would continue to pay 7d. in the pound. To balance the Budget, however, he was obliged to lower the limit of exemption from income tax to £100 a year and liability to the house tax from a rental value of £20 to a rental value of £10. He was also obliged to double the house tax. On the other hand, the taxable income of farmers would in future be a third of their rent, instead of half.[1]

The Budget was calculated at once to attract and disconcert all the reformers whose ideas it appropriated.[2] Had not Cobden himself during his campaign for fiscal reform demanded the abolition of the malt tax?[3] Did not the Radicals ask for a reform of the income tax by differentiating between sources of income? But this did not alter the fact that the daring proposals of the young Minister would benefit rural England at the expense of the great urban centres, and create an unfair disparity of treatment between the townsman of modest means, with an income of £100 to £150, who would have to pay income tax and a double house tax and the countryman paying a rent of almost £300 who would be exempt from taxation.[4]

[1] *Parliamentary Debates*, 3rd Ser., vol. cxxiii, pp. 836 sqq. See also Disraeli, *Speeches*, pp. 347 sqq.; Monypenny, *Life of Disraeli*, vol. i, p. 1242.

[2] See above, pp. 280-1. On the eve of his fall, Disraeli, to win over the Manchester group, was prepared to risk a step which caused wide scandal. After a long conversation with him, Bright concluded: 'This remarkable man is ambitious, most able, and without prejudices. . . . He seems unable to comprehend the morality of our political course' (*Diary of John Bright*, December 15, 1852, pp. 128-30). See also J. Morley, *Life of Richard Cobden*, p. 76.

[3] *Annual Register*, 1849, p. 153.

[4] Tooke, *History of Prices*, vol. v, pp. 440 sqq. Maccoby, *English Radicalism*, p. 312.

At first, Disraeli's proposals were well received. Since the Whigs were undecided and Cobden's attacks made little impression,[1] he might have carried his Budget had it not been for Gladstone's indignant protest.

Gladstone was too well acquainted with the technical aspect of finance not to be shocked by the improvisations of his inexperienced adversary. He was indignant at his evasions, the 'foxchase', in which he was engaging Parliament.[2] But his anger was aroused above all by the revolutionary nature of the Budget, shown by the proposed reform of the income tax and the house tax, against which he felt it his duty to protest.[3] His revolt was the revolt of a Conservative Peelite against 'the least conservative Budget he had ever known'.[4]

He did not speak until the close of the debate, on December 16, when an unforgettable duel was fought between the two combatants. Replying to a masterpiece of oratory in which Disraeli employed every resource of sarcasm and invective,[5] Gladstone proceeded to slaughter his rival and concluded in accents of convincing sincerity by appealing against 'enchanters and magicians' who sought to govern the country by 'parading' their financial 'operations' to the moral principles of 'men of sense and honour'.[6]

In the division which followed at four o'clock in the morn-

---

[1] J. Morley, *Life of Richard Cobden*, p. 76.

[2] Gladstone, to his wife, December 18: 'The intense efforts which we made to obtain and the Government to escape a definite issue were like a fox-chase, and prepared us all for excitement. . . . My great object was to show the Conservative party how their leader was hoodwinking and bewildering them' (J. Morley, *Life of W. E. Gladstone*, vol. i, p. 438).

[3] Note by Gladstone: 'It was a measure essentially bad to repeal half the malt tax. But the flagrantly vicious element in Disraeli's Budget was his proposal to reduce the income tax on Schedule D to fivepence in the pound.' Letter to his wife, December 14: 'Whether they win or not . . . they cannot carry this house tax nor their Budget. But the mischief of the proposals they have launched will not die with them' (J. Morley, op. cit., pp. 436-7). It is a curious fact, worth remark, that to compensate for the abolition of so many duties on imports Gladstone would have introduced in the Budget of 1842, not an income tax, but a house tax. This, perhaps, was known to no one outside the small group of Peel's friends. But could Gladstone have forgotten it himself when he denounced Disraeli's Budget so violently? (See Francis Hyde, *Gladstone at the Board of Trade*, pp. 12 sqq.).

[4] Gladstone to his wife, December 8: 'I am convinced that Disraeli's is the least conservative Budget I have ever known' (J. Morley, op. cit., vol. i, p. 437).

[5] *Parliamentary Debates*, 3rd Ser., vol. cxxiii, pp. 1629 sqq.

[6] H. of C., December 16, 1852: Gladstone's speech (*Parl. Deb.*, 3rd Ser., vol. cxxiii, pp. 1690-1). See in J. Morley, *Life of Gladstone* (vol. i, pp. 439-40), the impression made by Disraeli's speech on *The Times*, and on Gladstone himself: 'His superlative acting and brilliant oratory from time to time absorbed me and made me quite *forget* that I had to follow him.'

ing the Peelites voted for the occasion with the Radicals and Whigs. Palmerston was prevented by illness from being present. The Government was defeated by a majority of nineteen.[1]

Thus ended the first of many fights between the two statesmen who twenty years later would be the official leaders of the two great British parties. But not until twenty years had passed. For the moment the country could be governed only by a coalition.

9

Disraeli had never been under any illusion as to the weakness of the party he led in the Commons. But he exaggerated the weakness of the Opposition. He saw it split into hostile groups, the Peelites who loathed the arrogance of the Whig aristocracy and their lip-service to Liberalism, Palmerston a solitary and in so far less formidable figure, but a man who hated Lord John and whom in turn Lord John hated, the Radicals who went further than the Peelites but preferred them to the Whig aristocrats, who, however, could not be denied credit for their skill in keeping office so long in face of so much hostility, and finally the Irish who could not pardon Lord John the Protestant policy he had pursued during his last days in power. 'I know', said Disraeli in the classic peroration with which he concluded his speech of December 16, 'what I have to face. I have to face a coalition. The combination may be successful. A coalition has before this been successful. But coalitions, although successful, have always found this, that their triumph has been brief. This, too, I know, that England does not love coalitions. I appeal from the coalition to that public opinion which governs this country.'[2]

He was mistaken. The man who had understood the power wielded in England above parties by public opinion and who had been appointed by public opinion a national leader, superior to the parties and mediating between them, was the man whom Disraeli had attacked so bitterly, just because he had broken the rules of party government. He was dead. But it was now apparent how great the influence of his name and the authority of his tradition still remained. The policy pursued by Disraeli in 1852

[1] *Parliamentary Debates*, 3rd Ser., vol. cxxiii, p. 1693. After his defeat Lord Derby could not conceal his resentment against the Peelites. Disraeli's gracious manners, on the other hand, won forgiveness for his attacks (J. Morley, op. cit., pp. 441-2).
[2] *Parl. Deb.*, 3rd Ser., vol. cxxiii, p. 1665.

gave Peel a posthumous victory over the Tory gentlemen, who were obliged to own themselves defeated, and the Whig aristocracy which must lower its ensign.

In September, when uncertainty as to the verdict of the General Election seemed to justify any political intrigue, the Duke and Duchess of Bedford had sounded Palmerston and asked him if he would be prepared in any circumstances to overlook the past and serve under Lord John. Palmerston had retorted upon Lord John the charges he and his friends had so often brought against himself and replied that his experience during the last few years had shown him that Lord John wanted the tact and cool judgment required in a Prime Minister. He was extremely sceptical as to the possibility of forming a Whig Cabinet, for the Peelites, whose support was indispensable, would not allow themselves to be swallowed up by the Whigs. However, he would be willing to serve in the same Cabinet as Lord John under another Prime Minister sitting in the Lords, Lord Lansdowne, for example.[1]

But would Lord Lansdowne, who was old and in bad health, consent to undertake a task so onerous? It would seem, in fact, that during the next two months Palmerston turned to the Peelites, and in November, when Villiers brought forward his motion, he made himself their mouthpiece. At this moment Lord Derby began his conversations with the Peelites in which Palmerston probably took no part. But it was precisely the question of Palmerston which led to the negotiations being broken off almost immediately. For the Peelites would consent to enter a coalition with the Tories only in company with Palmerston and under his leadership in the Commons. This, however, was unacceptable to the Court and, it would appear, to Disraeli.[2] On December 16, when Palmerston was kept away by illness, the Peelites overthrew the Cabinet they had saved in November. What would the Queen do?

With the full approval of Lord Derby, whose advice she had asked,[3] she sent for Lord Lansdowne and Lord Aberdeen. The veteran of the Whig aristocracy, a sick man, pleaded his inability to accept the task offered and pressed Lord Aberdeen to attempt

---

[1] Sp. Walpole, *Life of Lord John Russell*, vol. ii, pp. 157 sqq. E. Ashley, *Life of Viscount Palmerston*, vol. i, pp. 374-6.

[2] See above, p. 328. H. C. F. Bell, *Lord Palmerston*, vol. ii, pp. 64-74. Gladstone, on the other hand, would not enter a government in which Disraeli was leader in the Commons.

[3] Malmesbury, *Memoirs of an Ex-Minister*, December 18, 1852, p. 286.

to form a government.[1] The latter consented. It was the Peelites' first victory over the Whigs. Lord John, invited by Lord Aberdeen, made difficulties encouraged by a number of disgruntled members of his party. He declined at first and gave way only at the instance of Macaulay, whose advice was asked.[2]

He was to be given the Foreign Office and with it the leadership of the Commons. Lord Aberdeen, he understood, agreed that he might, when he thought fit, resign the Foreign Office which might be taken over by Lord Clarendon, and retain, together with the leadership of the Commons, a general control over the policy of the Cabinet, and that he would be recognized as entitled to succeed Lord Aberdeen when the weariness of age should compel his resignation. The fact, however, remains that the man who was Whiggery incarnate agreed to serve here and now under the man who in the Upper House embodied Peel's political tradition.[3]

Palmerston had still to be won. At first he refused point blank. If he had consented to serve in the same Cabinet as Lord John it was to be under Lord Lansdowne, not Lord Aberdeen. Apparently the fall of Lord Derby's Ministry which had happened in his absence had taken him by surprise, and he was persuaded that, if he had been present, he would have prevented what he regarded as a disaster, and still dreamed of a coalition of the Conservatives and Peelites, in which he would have led the Commons in opposition to the Whigs and Radicals. Possibly he came to see that in

---

[1] The Queen saw the necessity of a coalition government. On December 19 she wrote to Lord John: 'The Queen thinks the moment to have arrived when a popular, efficient and durable government could be formed by the sincere and united efforts of all parties professing Conservative and Liberal opinions' (Sp. Walpole, *Life of Lord John Russell*, vol. ii, p. 161). She had written, however, to the King of the Belgians, March 17, 1852 (*Letters of Queen Victoria*, vol. ii, p. 464): 'One thing is pretty certain, that out of the present state of confusion and discordance, a sound state of parties will be obtained, and two parties, as of old, will again exist without which it is impossible to have a strong government.' The Queen was, moreover, predisposed to entrust the Government to Lord Aberdeen. On September 17, after Wellington's death, she wrote to the King of the Belgians: 'We shall soon stand sadly alone; Aberdeen is almost the only personal friend of that kind we have left. Melbourne, Peel—and now the Duke—all gone' (ibid., vol. ii, p. 478).

[2] For Macaulay's intervention, see Sp. Walpole, *Life of Lord John Russell*, vol. ii, pp. 161-2. When he described, in his *History*, the origin in the seventeenth century of the parties embodying respectively the conservative and the progressive political outlook, Macaulay remarked, in a well-known passage, that the best statesmen were those who were closest to the boundary line between the parties: 'In the sentiment of both . . . there is something to approve. But of both, the best specimens will be found not far from the common frontier' (*History of England*, ed. 1849, vol. i, pp. 98-9).

[3] Sp. Walpole, *Life of Lord John Russell*, vol. ii, pp. 162 sqq.

the existing state of parties such a combination was out of the question. For at the end of two days he gave way. He accepted the Home Office under Lord Aberdeen, in a sense, indeed, under Lord John himself, since the latter would be leader of the Commons. No doubt he was planning future intrigues to be conducted within the Cabinet. But for the moment he yielded.[1]

In the Cabinet, as finally constituted, the Peelites, who mustered thirty to forty votes in the House, had six seats. Lord Aberdeen, Peel's Foreign Secretary, went to the Treasury, Gladstone, his Colonial Secretary, to the Exchequer,[2] Newcastle, who had governed Ireland in 1846, became Colonial Secretary, Sidney Herbert returned to his old place at the War Office, Sir James Graham exchanged the Home Office for the Admiralty.[3] The Whigs and Radicals who reckoned that together they had 270 seats in the House,[4] divided almost equally between them, received no more than seven in the Cabinet. Of these, six went to the Whigs. Lord Granville became President of the Privy Council, the Duke of Argyll, Lord Privy Seal, Palmerston, Home Secretary, Lord John, Foreign Secretary, Sir Charles Wood, Secretary for India, and Lord Lansdowne, Minister without Portfolio. The Radicals obtained only one seat. Cobden and Bright made way for Molesworth. Their turn had not yet come.[5] Some time before, immediately after the General Election, Lord Aberdeen had advised Lord John to abandon the unpopular designation—Whig. He would be better advised to call his party Conservative-Liberal. Lord John had refused. For the term Whig was part of his inheritance.[6] When Lord Aberdeen became head of the December coalition the victory was his. For this correspondence with Lord John in September was no doubt in his mind

[1] For Palmerston's attitude, see E. Ashley, *Life of Viscount Palmerston*, vol. ii, pp. 1 sqq.; H. C. F. Bell, *Lord Palmerston*, vol. ii, pp. 70-2; J. Morley, *Life of W. E. Gladstone*, vol. i, p. 445.

[2] It was at Prince Albert's suggestion that the Exchequer was entrusted to Gladstone (Memorandum, by Prince Albert, December 22, *Letters of Queen Victoria*, vol. ii, pp. 510 sqq.). But Lord Aberdeen had another motive for giving Gladstone a key position. His 'Catholic' views might disarm Irish hostility.

[3] The sixth Peelite was Lord Cranworth, Robert Rolfe, who became Lord Chancellor. He had sat in Melbourne's Cabinet, and had since kept aloof from political life. Lord John's objection excluded from the Cabinet the Peelite Cardwell, formerly President of the Board of Trade (*Greville Memoirs*, December 28, 1852).

[4] This was Lord John's estimate. (See J. Morley, *Life of W. E. Gladstone*, vol. i, p. 446.)

[5] Sir William Molesworth became First Commissioner of Works. For the exclusion of Bright and Cobden, see *Diary of John Bright*, pp. 130-1, and J. Morley, *Life of Richard Cobden*, p. 76.

[6] Sp. Walpole, *Life of Lord John Russell*, vol. ii, p. 156.

when he made his statement in the House of Lords. 'The Earl of Derby, he was informed, had spoken of a conservative form of government, and wondered how he (Lord Aberdeen) and his associates would be able to carry on the service of the Crown; but the truth was, no government was possible at present except it were Conservative, nor was any government possible except it were Liberal. Those terms had ceased to have any definite meaning except as party cries and the country was sick of them. The measures, therefore, of the government would be Conservative as well as Liberal, for both were essentially necessary.'[1]

In France the cycle of events which opened with the revolution of 1848 ended with the establishment of a democratic Empire, a military dictatorship. In England the cycle which opened with the revolution of 1846, like previous English revolutions a Conservative revolution, ended with the formation of a Cabinet under the patronage of the statesman who had abolished entirely the duties on corn.

Fragment of an Earlier Version of this concluding Passage

Perhaps the best way to understand the development of public opinion between 1841 and 1851 is to observe the changes in the formation of political parties and see in them the reflection of changes in the formation of public opinion.

In 1841 Peel won the election on a programme not reactionary, but distinctly Conservative, as the head of a large party, which, he expected, would finally embrace the entire nation with the exception of unrepresentative Radical extremists. What this new configuration of parties expressed in the temporal order, the Established Church expressed in the spiritual.

In 1852 his shadow lay over the political landscape. The Cabinet which took office in December 1852 was the Cabinet he would have formed had he been still living. And like the former this Government was a national Government, which this time managed to include from the outset the entire nation except the Tory extremists. And Protestantism no longer meant Anglicanism. On the contrary, Anglicanism, after having got rid of the converts to the Catholic Church, meant Protestantism which in turn meant Liberalism.

[1] H of L., December 27, 1852. Lord Aberdeen's speech (*Annual Register*, 1852, p. 156).

CHAPTER VII

England in 1852

INTRODUCTION

THE picture of England in the middle of the century should have consisted of three chapters. Of these, M. Halévy had written only the third, devoted to religious beliefs.

For the first chapter, entitled 'The National Wealth', he had collected a large number of notes arranged under two headings.

(*a*) *Progress in Quantity*.—Notes proving that the increase of wealth since 1815 had outstripped the growth of population.

(*b*) *Progress in Quality*.—Notes dealing with various manifestations of this wealth, in particular the Universal Exhibition of 1851.

The collection of notes for the second chapter, to be entitled 'The Social Classes', began with the following passage:

'We have seen that the total amount of national wealth had increased. But how was this wealth distributed? If we are to believe those contemporaries whose judgment seems at first sight most authoritative, namely, the politicians, it was distributed most unequally. The Marxist doctrine that there is a natural law governing human society, in virtue of which an increasingly small minority accumulates wealth and an increasingly large majority is reduced to destitution was not derived solely from the writings of the French Socialists. Engels and, after him, Marx found it a current belief in England. Was it borne out by the facts?

M. Halévy had collected and arranged a number of documents supporting or refuting this Marxian dogma, also copious notes dealing with the aristocracy, proletariat, and middle classes.

The conclusion he reached would appear to be stated in the following passage:

England, far from being the country in which wealth was most unequally distributed, was the country where the middle class was strongest.

There is this much truth in the Marxian view. There was enormous wealth and extreme poverty. But the wide gap between them was filled by the wide extent of the middle classes.

Religious Beliefs

I THE CHURCH OF ENGLAND

I

IN its economic aspect British society was well balanced, and, far from being divided and increasingly divided into two classes—the one composed of extremely wealthy persons, the other of paupers—was pre-eminently a society in which the extreme wealth of some and the extreme poverty of others were balanced by the existence of a middle class, itself subdivided into a very large number of sections, a class extremely numerous, extremely powerful, and fully conscious of its power. This being the case, we have no longer any need to seek, as we sought in our first volume,[1] outside the economic sphere the explanation of the stability and balance of such a society. The religious and moral agencies we then described—a number of institutions which gave the middle class distinctive beliefs, a distinctive religious organization and a self-respect which respected without envying the aristocracy—had already done their work. The failure of the Chartist movement of 1842, and the victory won in 1846 by free trade and the middle class, were alike proofs of the influence these beliefs and institutions had exercised in the past. To maintain the balance of English society they need but continue their action.

But we must now inquire, if we are to give an accurate and complete account of the moral condition of the country in the middle of the nineteenth century, how far the effects produced by its religious institutions in 1850 were the same as in 1815, how far the Established Church, whose constitution was so free and so loose and which was exposed to so many diverse influences, was subject in 1850 to exactly the same influences as in 1815, and if the Nonconformist sects, a buffer state between the conservatism of the Establishment and the irreligion, indeed the gross ignorance of religion, of the lower classes remained exactly what they had been thirty-five years earlier, and if not, in what way and to what extent they had changed.

[1] *History of the English People*, vol. i, in particular Part iii.—*Trs. Note.*

2

If we would study the social composition of a nation we must begin by studying its religion. And a study of the religion of England must obviously begin with the Church of England. We have spoken of the reaction in its favour which followed, towards the close of the same decade, the outbursts of anti-clerical violence which had marked the years round 1832, and have seen how this growing popularity of the Church had contributed to the Conservative victory at the polls in the summer of 1841.[1]

We have also described the religious policy of Peel's Cabinet and its failure,[2] a failure which could be obscured only by the ambiguous triumph he won in 1846, when, acting outside and above the conflict of the official parties, he made himself responsible for establishing a system of free trade. What, then, after so many troublous years, when she had been threatened in turn by secularism from without and schism from within, was the spiritual and moral condition of the Church in the middle of the century?

At first sight she seemed her old self, a Church closely linked with the ruling aristocracy, a wealthy Church and a Church of the wealthy. Twenty years earlier this had justified the violent Radical attacks. To-day, however, these denunciations were scarcely audible. The reforms which had been effected were certainly not sufficient. One day or another further steps would have to be taken along the same road. But for the moment the zeal of the reformers had died down. The Church was reaping the fruit of the reforms which under the Whig Government she had accepted without much demur.

The difference between the organization of the Church at the opening of the century and her organization fifty years later consisted in the fact that, as a result of the reforms effected by the Whigs in 1830 and the following years, the State now intervened between the clergy and their flocks and administered their property, treated henceforward as belonging not to the parson, in virtue of his clerical status, but collectively to the Church, or, if you prefer, to the State itself in its spiritual aspect. The State redistributed this collective revenue among the clergy in proportion

[1] *History of the English People*, vol. iii, pp. 181-2, 207 sqq.
[2] See above, pp. 59 sqq., 92 sqq.

to the importance of their functions. The incumbent of a living no longer levied tithe on the farmers of his benefice.[1] The tithe was now collected by the State which then paid the clergyman its value, which varied according to the price of wheat, by which it was calculated. In spite of protection the latter had fallen. And it might be expected to fall lower still under the new system of free trade. Rents were falling more slowly, or not at all, so that, although the payment of Church rates remained a grievance for the taxpayer, which the Dissenters assiduously nursed, the tithe had, in fact, lost a considerable part of its former value. Everyone, whether Protectionist or Liberal, agreed that the real sufferer from the repeal of the Corn Laws was the clergyman.

3

Meanwhile the Ecclesiastical Commission had come into existence.[2] Created in 1836 it had already been reorganized several times. In 1836 it consisted of the two archbishops, three bishops and three laymen, together with five high officials, members *ex-officio*. Its functions were limited. They were to revise the incomes of the episcopal Sees, and advise on the creation of new Sees.

In 1840 its composition was considerably enlarged. The admission of some judges and six other laymen did not balance the membership of the entire Episcopate and three deans. That is to say, whereas in the Commission as originally constituted laymen were a majority, the majority now consisted of clergymen. The functions of the Commission were enlarged at the same time. Besides dealing with the creation of new Sees, it was to make further provision for parishes where the supply of clergy was most inadequate.[3] To pay the new clergy in such parishes a fund

---

[1] 6 & 7 Will. IV Cap. 71 (see *History of the English People*, vol. iii, pp. 209-10).

[2] 6 & 7 Will. IV Cap. 77. See *History of the English People*, vol. iii, pp. 208-12. For the history of the Commission, see an article by Sir George Middleton, which appeared in *The Times* of August 13, 1936, the centenary of its birth. See also *First General Report from the Ecclesiastical Commissioners for England*, 1846, *Second Report*, 1847, *Third Report*, 1851; H. of L., February 11, 1850: Lord Lansdowne's speech (*Parliamentary Debates*, 3rd Ser., vol. cviii, pp. 626 sqq.).

[3] The Act of 1840 (3 & 4 Vict. Cap. 13) phrases it: 'For the cure of souls in parishes where such assistance is most required.' The *First Report from the Ecclesiastical Commissioners* defines their functions, 'To establish out of the surplus of Cathedral Revenue a fund to be applied to the purpose of making better provision for the cure of souls.'

was provided by abolishing a number of minor Cathedral dignitaries deemed superfluous.[1]

Further legislation progressively increased the funds at the Commission's disposal, and by renewing the leases of its property on more favourable terms it obtained a higher income from it. In 1850, however, the discovery of its secretary's fraudulent practices occasioned the passing of a new Statute. It set up a Commission of three laymen, the Church Estates Commissioners, to which the Commission's funds and the execution of its decisions were entrusted.[2]

In this way Parliament, without making the Church a grant from the national revenue, took steps to improve gradually the distribution of her income. In this respect the Act of 1840 marked a new departure. It fixed the stipend of deans at £1,000, of canons between £500 and £600. The Act of 1850 fixed the stipend of future bishops at a definite sum. In 1852 the Commission was able to abolish a large number of benefices whose total income amounted to £130,000.[3]

4

What should be done with the funds thus made available? In the first place the original intention should be carried out and new Sees created. It was surely unreasonable that in spite of the growth of the population their number should remain the same. In the years following the Reform Bill of 1832 a proposal which emanated from the High Church Party was not well received by the nation. The bishops were unpopular. Why, then, add to their number? At any rate, it should be possible to redistribute the

[1] For this fund, see Peel's speech, May 5, 1843 (*Parliamentary Debates*, 3rd Ser., vol. lviii, pp. 1278 sqq.). Peel carried an act empowering the Commission to borrow from Queen Anne's Bounty (6 & 7 Vict. Cap. 37: An Act to make better provision for the Spiritual Care of Populous Parishes).
[2] 13 & 14 Vict. Cap. 94. See *Third Report from the Ecclesiastical Commissioners*, 1851; H. of L., February 11, 1850, and H. of C., April 29 and July 8, 1850 (*Parl. Deb.*, 3rd Ser., vol. cviii, p. 625, vol. cx, p. 938, and vol. cxii, p. 1079).
[3] See the Marquis of Blandford's important speech (H. of C., April 29, 1852): 'In 1840 the Act was passed which removed all obstacles to Parliament interfering in the distribution and arrangements of the revenue of the Church.' The Act of 1840 'provided that the clergy should receive their income in money payments, and there was introduced a third party by whom the revenues were collected and paid over to the clergy' (*Parl. Deb.*, 3rd Ser., vol. cxx, pp. 1322-3). See also *Fourth Report from the Ecclesiastical Commissioners*, 1852.

bishoprics without adding to them. The population of southern England was declining. The former wastes of the north were being settled by a huge population. It was unreasonable surely that the former should have as many bishops as in the past, and, if any southern Sees were suppressed, new Sees should be set up where the need was making itself felt. This, after all, was the principle on which constituencies had been redistributed by the Reform Bill. In 1836 the Government proposed to unite the dioceses of Bristol and Gloucester, and of Saint Asaph and Bangor, and in return to create two new Sees, one at Ripon for industrial Yorkshire, the other at Manchester for Lancashire. It had to be content with a bishopric at Ripon and the union of Bristol with Gloucester. Throughout the years following, the question of a Manchester bishopric continued to be hotly debated.[1]

Did hostility towards the capital of free trade weigh more with the Conservatives than the desire to increase at the same time the influence of the Church and the Tory party? Or was it on the contrary the opposition of the Radical free traders which stood in the way of the reform? In any case it was not until 1847 that Lord John Russell obtained the creation of the bishopric. It was provided that the new bishop should not sit in the House of Lords, but must wait before taking his seat for the next vacancy on the bench. This provision reassured those who feared that the increase in the number of bishops might increase the political influence of the Episcopate.[2]

Lord John had also asked for authority to create three more Sees. But the hostility with which the proposal was received by his own party and generally by Parliament compelled him to give up the attempt. The question, therefore, of increasing the Episcopate remained open. The suggestion was mooted that suffragan bishops should be created with modest stipends and without a seat in the Lords. They would be appointed in each diocese by the diocesan to exercise under his authority a number of episcopal functions. On one occasion Gladstone took his hearers aback and showed those who regarded him as a Conservative, the reformer, and the reformer, gifted with imagination,

---

[1] The Welsh, who opposed a union of Saint Asaph and Bangor, introduced a number of Bills between 1843 and 1846 to prevent it. Peel's Cabinet secured their rejection. For the numerous debates on the subject, see Sp. Walpole, *History of England*, vol. v, p. 260, note 2.

[2] The Bishop of St. Asaph's death provided the opportunity for this reform. In future the Bishop most recently appointed would not sit in the Lords.

he had it in him to become, by suggesting the appointment of a Bishop to be paid no more than £1,500 and without a seat in the Lords in any district where churchmen might ask for one and would undertake to raise half the stipend.[1]

It was only outside England that the Church could contemplate with pride a very rapid increase in the number of her bishops. Eleven colonial Sees had been created between 1825 and 1847, and during the same period the number of clergy rose from 290 to 652. The position of these Churches was anomalous. For the bishoprics had been set up by Acts which bestowed on their Churches an authority which made it unnecessary to have any recourse to the Archbishop of Canterbury. But the lawyers pronounced these statutes unconstitutional. It was not until 1852 that Parliament on Gladstone's initiative made the colonial Churches completely independent of the Mother Church. But at the same time it furnished them with a distinctive constitution which gave the laity seats in the assemblies of the clergy, and on the other hand laid it down clearly that any decisions taken by these Churches could bind only their own members, so that every colonial Church was autonomous and on an equal footing with the rest.[2]

In the colonies, in short, the Anglican Church was divided into a number of independent Churches which expressly and in advance renounced all the privileges of an establishment, and while in the colonies episcopal government displayed such vitality, at home the Episcopate remained what it had always been, a small body whose number had not appreciably increased, of extremely wealthy princes of the Church.[3]

---

[1] H. of C., July 8 and 15, 1850. Gladstone's speeches (*Parliamentary Debates*, 3rd Ser., vol. cxii, pp. 1124 and 1402).

[2] See Gladstone's speeches during the debates on the Australian Colonies Government Bill (H. of C., May 6 and July 15, 1850; *Parl. Deb.*, 3rd Ser., vol. cx, p. 1199, and vol. cxii, p. 1404), also during the debates on the Colonial Bishops Bill (H. of C., August 28, 1852; *Parl. Deb.*, 3rd Ser., vol. cxx, p. 1264).

[3] They lived in state and visited the Whig and Tory noblemen on an equal footing. Legislation had indeed limited their control over their wealth. But the management of diocesan property remained in their hands, and they were obliged to hand over to the Ecclesiastical Commission only the income in excess of the stipend permitted by law. And it was in their power when a lease was renewed to grant the tenant very favourable terms in return for the payment of a 'fine', which they could keep for themselves. The Bishop of Durham and the Bishop of Salisbury gave scandal by the practice.

Moreover, in the eyes of many the bishops' statutory stipends, on an average £5,000, seemed excessive. But were they? A judge received £6,000, and a fashionable London doctor could earn £4,000. Would it be fair to place the bishops, members of the same class, and whose palaces were very expensive to keep up, below them in the social scale?

5

The most powerful obstacle to the creation of new Sees was the widespread opinion that the funds at the disposal of the Ecclesiastical Commissioners should not be used to support new bishops. For they were needed to increase the stipends and numbers of the parochial clergy. That, in fact, had been the Government's policy in 1840 and again in 1843. In 1852 the Marquis of Blandford in an important speech in the Commons,[1] while acknowledging how much had been done, pointed out that the programme laid down in 1835 by Peel's Commission of Enquiry was still a long way from fulfilment. Much, nevertheless, had been accomplished, in close collaboration, practical and financial, with various diocesan societies and the important Pastoral Aid Society.

During the eight years which followed 1835, as Peel pointed out in 1843, 525 new churches had been consecrated, during the first eight years of the century no more than 20.[2]

During the eighteen years between 1835 and 1853 the number of livings in England and Wales had increased by 1552, having risen from 10,718 to 12,270, an average increase of almost 100 a year. And every year the rate of increase was greater. The number of curates on the other hand was diminishing. It fell from 5,320 in 1835 to 4,885 in 1853, and, whereas in 1835 four-fifths of the curates were supplying for non-resident vicars, in 1853 no more than two-fifths were doing so. Moreover, it was not difficult to maintain the constantly increasing supply of clergy. Around 1850 the average yearly excess of ordinations over deaths was about 300.[3]

The defenders of the Church were, moreover, justified in protesting against statements that Anglican incumbents were over-paid. Stipends of £1,000 were denounced as excessive. But as we have seen, these were not fixed, but dependent upon the rise and fall of the tithe, which was in fact falling. The incumbent had to pay the poor rate and the highway rate and, when necessary, an assistant curate. He was also obliged to subscribe to a host of local charities, constantly increasing in number with the growth

[1] H. of C., April 29, 1852. Marquis of Blandford's speech (*Parliamentary Debates*, 3rd Ser., vol. cxx, pp. 1317 sqq.).
[2] H. of C., May 5, 1843. Sir Robert Peel's speech (ibid., 3rd Ser., vol. lxviii, p. 1291).
[3] *Edinburgh Review*, January 1854, art. entitled 'Ecclesiastical Economy', vol. xcix, p. 96.

of modern philanthropy, and pay a portion of the stipend attached to his benefice to the administrators of Queen Anne's Bounty. When all these deductions had been made, of that stipend of £1,000, which shocked the critics, little more than half was left him to meet the cost of living. Moreover, stipends of this amount were received only by a privileged minority of the clergy, not more, in fact, than 174. Only 1,000 stipends exceeded the sum of £500, only 8,000, £300.[1] And inquiries conducted by the Ecclesiastical Commissioners had discovered and made public the existence of a veritable proletariat among the Anglican clergy, hidden among the hills of Wales and Cumberland, uncultured, of worse than indifferent morals, and recruited from the children of the scarcely civilized farmers of these poor districts.[2] On the same financial level were those unfortunate curates who, if they failed to obtain a living, were the helots of the clergy, wretchedly poor, crushed with work, and burdened with the support of a family. Their poverty may be judged from the number of instances in Lancashire and Yorkshire in which the Ecclesiastical Commissioners took credit for having raised their stipend to £150. When in 1850 the Archbishop of Canterbury was urging a reform of the Commission he called the attention of the House of Lords to this state of things. 'It can be nothing', he said, 'but injurious to the Church, when the feelings of the inferior clergy are alienated from those who are above them in rank and fortune, though often in nothing else.'[3]

We cannot deny the existence of this danger, since the Primate himself called attention to it. On the other hand, there is no evidence in the England of 1850 of revolt among the lower clergy. The poor clergy seem to have been more concerned to conceal their poverty than to complain of the riches enjoyed by their more favoured brethren. The latter, however, did nothing to conceal their wealth. On the contrary, they displayed it to the world.

[1] H. of C., July 8, 1850. Sir B. Hall's speech (*Parliamentary Debates*, 3rd Ser., pp. 1087 sqq.).
[2] *Edinburgh Review*, April 1853, art. v, 'The Church of England in the Mountain' (vol. xcvii, pp. 342 sqq.).
[3] H. of L., February 11, 1850 (*Parl. Deb.*, 3rd Ser., vol. cviii, p. 630). 'It can be nothing but injurious to the Church when the feelings of the inferior clergy are alienated from those who are above them in rank and fortune, though often in nothing else, and who probably at the very moment when they lie under the imputation of selfishness, are employing their time, their thoughts, their influence, and often not sparing their purse in promoting the comfort and increasing the means of usefulness of their humble brethren.'

Though as we have just seen, the largest stipends were, after all, not so enormous when the expenses attached to the incumbency of a parish are taken into account, the majority of the parochial clergy lived on a lavish scale. This was due to the fact that though they were not a wealthy clergy, they were a body of wealthy men. For livings were sought by young men who enjoyed a private income equal to, or even greater than, the stipend attached to them. They valued them for the sake of the position which in the society of rural England such a living had always conferred on its incumbent, and now more than ever.

At the summit of the clerical ladder were those who belonged to the class of country gentlemen and regarded themselves as forming within the ranks of the clergy something in the nature of an exclusive club open to nobody not qualified by his birth and his education, social not intellectual or theological, at Oxford or Cambridge. Immediately below them were the sons of wealthy members of the middle class who liked to find a place for some of their children in the ministry of the National Church. If they had been to Oxford or Cambridge, they formed a link with the higher class. The majority, however, two-thirds about 1850, had been to neither of the Universities and, in consequence, occupied positions inferior to that of the country gentlemen. Lower still, the sons of farmers and small shopkeepers were to be found in vicarages or curacies to which a small or even a tiny stipend was attached. Though their income was so small, consisting chiefly, or perhaps wholly, of their stipend, the public lumped them together with their superiors and regarded them as belonging to a species of aristocracy.[1] Such was the Church of England, a faithful reflection of England herself. She was an aristocracy, but an aristocracy in which no rank was a closed caste, an aristocracy in which the inferior regarded the superior not with envy but respect. It was not impossible to climb into a superior class and those who respected those above them were respected in turn by those below them and by those outside the Church, whether ministers or laymen. That is to say the Anglican hierarchy was a hierarchy whose social structure was modelled on the economic structure of the nation in which, in spite of so many misleading statements, there was no sharp cleavage between extremes of riches and poverty, but an imperceptible gradation of wealth and social status.

[1] *Edinburgh Review*, January 1854, art. entitled 'Ecclesiastical Economy', vol. xcix, p. 105.

6

A Church so secular, so deeply involved in what devout souls called the world, was not, it would seem, a Church to harbour fanatics. And this will, in fact, be the conclusion we shall reach when we turn from studying the organization of the Church of England to study the beliefs which found a home in her. Nevertheless, about the middle of the nineteenth century the Church seemed the prey of a most acute conflict between two hostile fanaticisms, the one Protestant, the other Catholic.

We became acquainted long ago with the origin and nature of the Protestant fanaticism. It was reborn of the Methodist revival which, outside the Establishment, created the Wesleyan Church and other Methodist sects, and gave new life to the entire body of Dissent and within the Church of England produced the Evangelical movement and party. By 1850 the Evangelical party had outgrown the stages of infancy and adolescence and reached maturity. The time was no more, when, younger by thirty years, it saw in the conquest of a single See matter for congratulation. The long possession of office by the Whigs, who, hostile on principle to the Tory High Church, divided their favours between the Liberals, and the orthodox Evangelicals, had given them five bishops, among them the Archbishops of Canterbury and York.[1] They were far, it is true, from having a majority on the bench. But they were resigned to the appointment of so many latitudinarian prelates, since that was the price of excluding High Churchmen. Neither were they a majority of the lower clergy. But they did their utmost to secure for Evangelicals livings in the gift of the Crown, the nobility, and the gentry. And they created clerical trusts to amass from legacies and subscriptions the necessary funds to purchase advowsons for the party. More than a third of the benefices, it was calculated, were in their hands. But their influence in the Church did not stop at the frontier of their party. They could boast that they set the tone of almost the entire Church. Gladstone was a High Churchman. But the language of Evangelical piety was often on his lips. Nor, save from the strictly doctrinal standpoint, were they mistaken in claiming for their own Thomas Arnold, though he made a point of professing himself a Liberal.

[1] *Edinburgh Review*, October 1853, art. entitled 'Church Parties', vol. xcviii, pp. 273 sqq.

When all is said, their doctrine was very simple, nothing but the doctrine of justification by faith which Luther and Calvin following St. Augustine had built on the foundation of St. Paul's epistles. They had no other dogmas. It was not, to be sure, a bulky theology, but it was the entire theology of the Evangelicals. They had, it is true, in reply to the editions of the Fathers, published by Newman and his friends, founded the Parker Society in 1840 to reprint the works of the sixteenth-century Reformers, and had collected 7,000 subscribers, published fifty-five volumes. But we can hardly believe that the result had answered to the effort made and that this abundant supply of literature had made students of the Evangelical clergymen. They were men not of theory but of practice, content to base their activities on an uncompromising affirmation of their faith in the fundamental principle of Protestant religion. This Protestant belief brought them close to the Dissenters, and in 1846 they founded in conjunction with the latter the Evangelical Alliance, which, though not without friction from both sides, united all English Protestants, Churchmen and Nonconformists, in a common hatred of Roman Catholicism and of every Catholic influence in the Church of England. Their Protestantism narrowed the gap between clergyman and layman, and it was still further diminished by the rudimentary nature of their theology. For a trained clergy was not required to expound and comment upon a doctrine so simple. The unreflecting faith of the most uneducated believer was sufficient. It was characteristic from this point of view that the Evangelical party had two leaders, two 'popes'. One of them was a clergyman, the pious Archbishop of Canterbury, famous before his elevation to the primacy for his government of the Chester diocese; the other a layman, a nobleman, Lord Ashley, whose philanthropic activities we have encountered on more than one occasion. It was not the sole object of the powerful Church Pastoral Aid Society, which they founded in 1836, the heart of their entire organization, with 3,000 subscribers and an income of £40,000, to provide additional curates in thickly populated districts, where the supply of clergy was so inadequate, but also to train lay scripture readers to assist rectors and curates.[1] The idea had been borrowed from the

---

[1] For the attempt of the bishops to regulate the use of Scripture readers and Bishop Phillpotts's protest, see *Scripture Readers: Letter to the Venerable the Archdeacons of the Diocese of Exeter*, by the Right Rev. Henry (Phillpotts), Bishop of Exeter.

Wesleyan lay preachers. Nor was this their only scandalous practice. In defiance of the provisions of the New Toleration Act of 1812 they presumed to celebrate the Anglican offices in places not officially recognized as places of public worship, and even in unconsecrated buildings. It was not until 1855 that Lord Ashley got the practice legalized.

Such was the party which had every reason to be proud of its achievement during the previous twenty-five years. It could boast of having brought about the reform of the Church which had saved her from the dangers produced by the combined operation of Tory inertia and Radical enmity. Their laicism and Protestant Erastianism had enabled them to devise an intervention by the State which, without confiscating the possessions of the Church, redistributed them in accordance with the needs of the time. They had waged war against pluralism and the scandal of non-residence which it produced, and by 1850 might well hope that the evil was rapidly disappearing.[1] By their prudent action they had reinvigorated diocesan and parochial life. They had divided parishes of unwieldy size into districts regularly visited from house to house by curates and lay helpers. In the parishes they had multiplied Sunday Schools, infant schools, and lending libraries, and founded friendly societies and clubs to provide the poor with clothing. With the subscriptions, collected by their large Church Building Society, they had built new churches throughout the country. During his nineteen years as Bishop of Chester, Bishop Sumner had consecrated 232. They had revived the missionary spirit in the Church and persuaded some bishops to risk what seemed a daring innovation and ordain priests not to officiate in their diocese but to preach the Word of God in every part of the globe. And when their Church Missionary Society celebrated its jubilee in 1848, it could boast of its 166 European missionaries, and 1,300 native preachers, fourteen of them in priest's Orders, that it had converted 10,000 negroes in Sierra Leone, the entire

---

[1] The Pluralities Bill passed in 1838 (1 & 2 Vict. Cap. 106) made it illegal to hold two benefices more than ten miles apart, if their combined value exceeded £1,000, or the population of either exceeded 3,000. (See *History of the English People*, vol. iii, p. 200.) In 1850, on Gladstone's initiative, another and a stricter measure was passed (13 & 14 Vict. Cap. 98) reducing the distance to three miles and the value to £100; H. of C., July 26, 1850 (*Parliamentary Debates*, 3rd Ser., vol. cxiii, p. 291). On the latter occasion the Bishop of Salisbury, speaking on July 4, had made it clear to what extent the previous measure had already reduced non-residence. The number of non-resident incumbents had fallen from 4,307 in 1838 to 3,094 in 1849, the number of resident incumbents risen from 5,859 in 1838 to 7,779 in 1848 (ibid., 3rd Ser., vol. cxii, pp. 891-2).

Maori population of New Zealand, and 20,000 Indians.[1] Nearer home they cherished hopes of converting the Catholics of the Irish countryside where, they claimed, they had already made several thousand converts.[2]

Not content with these purely religious activities, they had made themselves remarkable for their philanthropic zeal, and had played a leading part in the campaign against slavery and in the agitation which obtained from successive governments legislation protecting the workers. Prison reform, moreover, was largely their work and, if the introduction of a system of solitary confinement by which prisoners were kept in complete solitude and unbroken silence, with no other reading than the Bible or any converse with their fellows save for a short daily visit from the chaplain, would shortly be the subject of severe criticism, as calculated rather to brutalize than reform a criminal, it was, nevertheless, an indubitable improvement on the previous system of a hideous promiscuity and a stage on the road to future progress.

7

But we must look at the other side of the shield. The Evangelicals had their shortcomings which were serious and became worse as time went on. For the movement had lost the freshness of youth, and as it grew older the party had become bigoted and morose. In matters of doctrine it was the most inflexibly conservative party, the most determined in its opposition to any kind of free study of Biblical history, the most attached to the belief in the verbal inspiration of Scripture. It was also the most inflexible in the brutal simplicity of its theology, in its untiring insistence on predestination and the unprofitableness of good works. If there were a subject on which Evangelicals gave free rein to theological speculation, it was the conversion of the Jews and their return to Jerusalem, which must take place before the second coming of Jesus to pronounce the irrevocable sentences of the Last Judgment and, since there was room for differences of opinion as to the date, more or less close, of that event, an entire

---

[1] *Church Missionary Society Jubilee Paper. Address of the Committee*, p. 6.

[2] Lord Shaftesbury to Lord John Russell, October 16, 1851: 'I rejoice that I have not deceived you respecting Ireland. I told you of the progress of Gospel truth there. Depend upon it, you have seen but the beginning. A mighty change is at hand' (*The Later Correspondence of Lord John Russell*, vol. i, p. 313). For Protestant proselytism in Ireland, see G. de Beaumont, *L'Irlande sociale, politique et religieuse*, 7th ed., 1863, vol. i, pp. xiv sqq.

press and an entire body of literature came into existence to interpret on this point the Old Testament prophecies.[1] In consequence, the stricter members of the party lost interest in any measures to improve the lot of the poor and oppressed in this world, disposed rather to believe that to attempt to make men better by making them happier was a mistake, since they could be made truly happy only by being made better in the religious understanding of the term, when they would be happy because they had learned resignation to the suffering which is man's lot on earth. The more human aspect of Evangelical religion found expression in the weekly *Christian Witness*, its more inhuman in the *Record*, an acrimonious paper appearing twice a week, which, under the editorship of the redoubtable Alexander Haldane, had constituted itself the political as well as the theological organ of the group, maker of bishops, archdeacons, deans, and clergymen, and censor of clerical morals. Woe to the clergyman seen at a theatre—Shakespeare alone was tolerated on patriotic grounds provided his plays were read, not seen on the stage—or on a racecourse. Regattas were permissible. Woe to him if he took part in or even watched a cricket match or were caught hunting or even smoking, if he played cards, or attended a ball. Only 'at homes' were lawful. He was held up to public disgrace. And, with the exception of the oratorio, all forms of music were suspect.

A favourite target with men of letters and caricaturists was the unctuous and lugubrious clergyman, clad from head to foot in black, who would have thought himself doomed to hell fire had he even once read his sermon, but with whom eloquence, which professed to be the spontaneous utterance of the heart, had degenerated into a dreary and mechanical parade of words, and who had learned from the Methodists the secret of those devout effusions with which Wesley had, so to speak, feminized the austere and sombre Puritanism of the seventeenth century. One feature of the party was the small gathering in the evening round a tea table in the house of some tradesman in a large or small town, concluded, after two or three hours of edifying conversation, by a more formal discourse delivered by the clergyman. The women of the lower middle and middle class delighted in these little love-

---

[1] See the publications mentioned by G. R. Balleine. *A History of the Evangelical Party in the Church of England*, 1908, p. 207.

feasts. Often they were in love with the clergyman himself. And if he were a bachelor and one of the group a widow, well off into the bargain, spiteful gossips remarked it might end in a marriage and the parish or district henceforward have a two-headed Cerberus for its pastor.

In the political field the alliance continued between the Evangelicals and the Whigs. But so far as the more conservative members of the party were concerned, it was a *marriage de convenance*, not a love match. Since the Tories were allied with the High Church party, it was only from the Whigs that the Evangelicals could expect promotion in the Church. In many respects, however, they felt themselves genuine Tories. At the back of their minds they considered that it was they who should be the High Church party, if only the latter would understand that a patriotic Englishman must not toy with Rome.

8

But the High Church was Romanizing and it was this Romanizing, this Italianizing, of the Church of England which the Evangelicals were determined to prevent. For the innovators of the past fifteen years were High Churchmen. Or to speak more accurately, they were members of the High Church party. For there was another High Church, 'High and dry', which liked these foreign novelties no better than the Evangelicals. No one, for example, could suspect of Italianizing such a man as the Bishop of Carlisle, Hugh Percy, the son of Lord Beverley, nephew of the Duke of Northumberland and son-in-law of Manners Sutton, an extremely wealthy nobleman, who laid out £40,000 on restoring his Episcopal palace, and a lover of horses, who, when the House of Lords reassembled, travelled up to town driving the four horses of his mailcoach himself. In this display he was one of the last survivors of a type of bishop rapidly becoming extinct; and the death at the beginning of 1848 of Howley, the Archbishop of Canterbury, who, though of less exalted origin than Percy, kept even greater state, had marked an epoch in the history of the Anglican episcopate. He drove to Westminster from Lambeth in a coach flanked by outriders. Once a week during the season he kept open house. Thirty flunkeys in livery, fifteen without livery, served the dishes and wine. Anyone was welcome who wore court dress.

His death made a revolution. His successor, Charles Sumner, led at Lambeth the simple life of a country clergyman. He rose early, lit his own fire, and dealt with his vast correspondence before breakfast. And he walked to the House of Lords carrying an umbrella under his arm. That is to say, the substitution of a Low for a High Churchman was a victory for the most modern type of Protestantism. But at the same time a novel form of English religion was making its way, not indeed on to the Episcopal bench, but into the parishes, that, namely, which Newman and his friends had begun to preach at Oxford almost twenty years earlier.

9

This High Church, revived by returning to the theology of the fathers and the customs of the Middle Ages, was old enough already to have insensibly changed its character. In their desire to obey more strictly than hitherto the rubrics of the *Book of Common Prayer*, not to be content with Sunday worship, but to recite morning and evening prayer, daily or at least on Wednesdays and Fridays, and the Litany, the Tractarians had been at the outset at one with the Evangelicals. And in their extreme, even horrifying, asceticism, the original Tractarians had rivalled the Evangelicals in austerity.[1] During the first five or six years of the movement they were, so to speak, the Jansenists of Anglicanism confronting the Jesuits. But gradually in both respects the divergence between the two reforming parties widened. The Puseyites attached more and more importance to a ritual increasingly elaborate, and they turned away more markedly every year from asceticism or, at any rate, from the appearance of it. The Tractarians became the Ritualists.

This new direction taken by the Oxford Movement, at the moment when it left Oxford, was the result of influences which had not touched Newman and his associates of 1833. Theology had brought them back to Catholicism. In the case of their successors it was art. Romanticism was charmed by the medieval cathedrals. And it was scarcely possible to feel their charm without

---

[1] See the rule of life Pusey imposed on himself: '. . . to keep the eyes down when walking except for the sight of nature . . . to make the fire to me from time to time the sign of hell. Always to lie down in bed confessing that I am unworthy to lie down except in hell, but praying to lie down in the Everlasting Arms. Not to smile, if I can help it, except with children . . .' (H. P. Liddon, *Life of E. B. Pusey*, vol. iii, pp. 104-5).

understanding and loving their symbolism. And those who the better to love their Christian faith set themselves to study and learned to love its outward forms, alike architectural and devotional, were led to espouse a form of Christianity less ruthless than that for which an impassable gulf divides spirit and matter, for which, on the contrary, matter can express spirit and in so doing be reconciled with it.

Under these conditions the liturgical war broke out. The Evangelicals who valued the Prayer Book highly had pleaded for a revision which would get rid of any surviving vestige of Roman Catholicism, shocking to a Protestant conscience. From the opposite point of view the adherents of the new High Church party demanded its strict observance, until the day when they took a further step and reintroduced into the Anglican ritual ceremonies which went back to the pre-Reformation period, or went further still and invented new rites more Catholic in their opinion than the Catholic rites themselves.

They wanted, for example, Baptism administered no longer in a hole-and-corner fashion, but in the presence of the congregation, and the ceremony made the central point of a Sunday service. They wanted the communion table to be once more an altar on which the sacrifice of the Divine Saviour is really renewed, made, therefore, of stone and adorned with flowers and candles. The celebrant must no longer face northward, but eastward with his back to the congregation. The bread and wine must not be placed on the altar before the service by a mere clerk, but by the clergyman in the course of the rite, and should meanwhile be placed on a credence table near the altar. They wanted to restore several features of Sunday worship which had fallen into disuse, the bidding prayer before the sermon, and after the sermon the recitation of an offertory text while the collection was being taken. By these additional ceremonies they sought to make it more burdensome and difficult, even impossible, for the clergyman to take off the white surplice he wore at the altar and preach in a black gown. For he must not be a priest only while he was actually officiating and become once more in the pulpit an ordinary man, as fallible as the congregation he was addressing and in whose company he was studying Christian doctrine. He must enjoy throughout the mystic prerogative with which he had been invested by his ordination.

The Ecclesiastical authorities took alarm. In a lengthy charge Bishop Blomfield of London attempted to regulate the liturgical position afresh and decide which of the innovations were permissible, which must be forbidden.[1] Candles might be placed on the altar, but they must not be lighted. A clergyman might preach in his surplice in the morning, but must wear a black gown in the evening. The public laughed at these ridiculous compromises and the Ritualists disobeyed regulations which even in Blomfield's own diocese had no binding force. The Court of Arches,[2] called upon to pronounce upon the legality of stone altars, condemned them. The Ritualists disregarded the condemnation. Riots broke out in several places, organized by the Evangelicals to protest against these Italianizing novelties. A surplice worn in the pulpit provoked an uproar which might spread from the church to the street. These disorders assumed a very serious character after the conversion of Newman and his friends had in the eyes of the public torn down the curtain behind which the Ritualists' dishonesty concealed their ulterior aim. Ritualism was discredited, but it was not killed. The dry Pusey held firm, though forced to keep silence, because no Bishop dared allow him to preach. Phillpotts of Exeter, however, at the bottom of his heart sympathized with Pusey. And the clergy of the new school continued to shock the public and take pleasure in doing so. Like the Evangelicals, they were a party. Like the former they had their organs, the *Chronicle* and the *Guardian*, and their associations; the Church Union and the Curates' Pastoral Aid Society. And they had their distinctive dress, the cassock, a spectacle strange to a public accustomed to seeing clergymen in a different garb.

They displayed no philanthropic enthusiasm or zeal for the education of the poor, whom they visited only to hear the confessions of the sick and give them extreme unction. They disapproved of Sabbatarianism, encouraged Sunday games, and seemed to make a point of attending balls, as though to prove they were no Puritans. Their attitude smacked a little of Young England. They were less serious, more childish than Keble, Newman, and Pusey had been about 1835, and despite their attempts

---

[1] *A Charge delivered to the Clergy of the Diocese of London at the visitation in October 1842, by Charles James (Blomfield), Bishop of London.*

[2] The Archbishop's Court was so called because it met in the Church of St. Mary le Bow.

to make themselves popular by the more human character they deliberately gave to their religion, all these puerilities of vestment and ceremonial earned them nothing save a reputation for Jesuitry and dishonesty.[1] But although they were so unpopular they had made undeniable progress in particular parishes. The reaction produced by the conversion of the clergy of Saint Saviour's, Leeds,[2] and Newman's spectacular conversion,[3] might halt this progress—it could not undo it. The Bishops were obviously powerless, and they all, even Phillpotts, were dismayed by these conversions to Rome. They decided to seek legislation to strengthen their hands.

10

In 1847 the Bishop of London, Blomfield, at Phillpotts's instigation, introduced a Bill with this object. It proposed on the one hand to reorganize the Bishops' diocesan courts, on the other to revive the Court of Delegates to judge appeals from these courts to the Crown. But this attempt to strengthen the Bishops' authority in their struggle against the Ritualists' innovations came up against the obstacles which for a long while past had prevented any reform of the ecclesiastical courts. Blomfield's proposals were debated in 1847, 1848, and 1849, and got no further.[4]

Meanwhile, a new crisis had arisen in the Church in consequence of Dr. Hampden's appointment in 1847 by Lord John Russell to the See of Hereford. By his heterodox views this Oxford professor of Divinity had already incurred the hostility of the High Church which in 1836 had secured his condemnation by the University. The conflict, which had died down, was reopened

---

[1] For Ritualism, see the *Quarterly Review*, May 1843, art. iii, 'Rubrics and Rituals of the Church of England' (vol. lxxii, pp. 232 sqq.), and June 1851, art. viii, 'Rubrics versus Usage' (vol. lxxxix, pp. 203 sqq.).

[2] The Church had been built by Pusey's friends in a particularly poor quarter of Leeds. But nine members of the staff were converted to Catholicism (P. Thureau-Dangin, *La Renaissance Catholique en Angleterre*, vol. ii, pp. 120 sqq. and 234–5).

[3] Newman was received into the Catholic Church on October 9, 1845.

[4] See, in particular, the debates in the H. of L. on May 20, 1847 (*Parliamentary Debates*, 3rd Ser., vol. xcii, pp. 1095 sqq.), and the Bishop of London's speech on June 3, 1850 (vol. cxi, pp. 598 sqq.). The Church Courts were archidiaconal, diocesan, and provincial. Until 1832 appeals to the Crown had been heard by a Court of Delegates. Since 1832 they had been heard by the Judicial Committee of the Privy Council. For the question of the reform of the Ecclesiastical Courts, see Sp. Walpole, *History of England*, vol. v, pp. 262–4. The Tories, who wanted to preserve the diocesan courts, were opposed by the Whigs, who wanted to abolish the lower courts and keep only the Court of Arches. For this reason the Bill of 1847 left the plaintiff the option of taking his case to the diocesan court, or directly to the Court of Arches.

355

by his elevation to the episcopal bench. Thirteen bishops sent the Prime Minister a protest against his choice of a theologian who had been the subject of official censure by the University. Lord John, however, would not allow the prerogative of the Crown to be called in question and compelled the Hereford chapter, in spite of an attempt at resistance made by the Dean, to elect his candidate. Hampden's enemies then attempted to get the Court of Arches to refuse to confirm the election. But the Archbishop of Canterbury, the Evangelical Sumner, decided that he must obey the decision of the Government.[1]

Hampden's Bishopric was certainly not a victory of the Low over the High Church. In 1836, Low and High Churchmen had joined forces against Hampden. It was, however, the work of the Whig Government which preferred the Low to the High Church. And an Evangelical Archbishop began his tenure of the primacy by subscribing to the Erastian principle of the spiritual supremacy of the Crown.

At the moment, however, when the Archbishop's decision settled the question of Hampden, the revolutions in France and elsewhere on the Continent distracted public attention almost completely from the dispute. About the same time, however, another theological battle was waged, this time between the Evangelicals and the High Churchmen.

The question at issue was the doctrine of Baptismal Regeneration. Like the Real Presence, it was a battle-ground between the High Church and the Evangelical Low Church. Does the baptismal rite possess a magic power which transforms the soul of the baptized infant, justifies and saves it without its conscious collaboration? Protestant spiritualism in its most logical, its Calvinist form, rejected the belief. Hence strange disputes. That baptism is not indispensable is proved by the case of the Good Thief. Perhaps, however, he had been sprinkled by the blood and water drawn by the soldier's lance from the Lord's side and therefore baptized more perfectly than any other mortal. The Baptists rejected infant baptism, holding that no one should be baptized until he knew himself to be fit to be so, as had been the case with the first Christians and Jesus Himself. To this, it was replied, that when Jesus said, 'Suffer little children to come unto Me', He instituted infant baptism. But were those words anything more

[1] Sp. Walpole, *Life of Lord John Russell*, vol. i, pp. 475-80.

than an expression of God's tender love for all human beings, even children? It was easy for those who were Protestants pure and simple to be content with this view of baptism. But for Anglicans it was more difficult. For not only did the language of the baptismal service imply the doctrine of Baptismal Regeneration, Article twenty-seven was couched in language too cautious to be called strictly Calvinist. The Tractarians, therefore, felt themselves on firmer ground here than on the question of the Real Presence, and in 1835 Pusey had devoted a bulky theological monograph to the dogma of Baptismal Regeneration, which had filled three successive tracts and created a flutter in ecclesiastical dovecots.[1]

When an Evangelical bishop attempted to enforce his views on the Real Presence upon the clergy of his diocese and refused ordination to those whose opinions on the question seemed to him unorthodox, it was only natural that the High Church bishops should reply by turning their attention to the unorthodoxy of those among their clergy who were suspected of holding unsound opinions in regard to Baptismal Regeneration.[2] When in 1846 and 1847 they asked for legislation to strengthen their hands, the *Record* suspected that their object was to make it easier for them to persecute what they regarded as the fundamental heresy of the Evangelical party.[3] The theological device which enabled the Evangelicals to refuse to baptism the value ascribed to it by the Catholic Church, without altogether emptying it of value, was to oppose to the doctrine of unconditional, a doctrine of conditional regeneration. Baptism, they taught, made its recipients fit for salvation, saved them on condition they merited later on by their faith the prevenient grace they had received.

The pugnacious Bishop of Exeter suspected of heresy a clergyman named Gorham, on whom the Chancellor had just conferred

---

[1] *Scriptural Views on Holy Baptism*. Tracts 67, 68, and 69, published in 1835.
[2] When the University of Oxford condemned Ward for his interpretation of the Thirty-nine Articles in his *The Ideal of a Christian Church*, Pusey wrote to Hook, December 18, 1844: 'For a Low Church who cannot receive the Baptismal Service except by some violent perversion, to help to hunt down Ward is most outrageous.' It is curious, however, to find Pusey, in 1846, when it was a question of strengthening the Bishops' authority advise the toleration he needed himself. Letter to Hook, November 14, 1846: 'We cannot afford to part with the Evangelicals as a body, nor all who at present deny Baptismal Regeneration. Our sins have brought us into this state of confusion, and we must pray God to pardon them and bring us out of it' (H. P. Liddon, *Life of E. B. Pusey*, vol. ii, p. 421; and vol. iii, p. 118).
[3] *Record*, April 4 and May 22, 1847.

a living in his diocese which was in the gift of the Crown. Three clergymen of the diocese had signed on Gorham's behalf the customary testimonial of orthodox belief and moral behaviour. Phillpotts refused his signature. In spite of this, the Chancellor presented Gorham on November 2, 1847. The Bishop then subjected him to a theological examination which occupied eight sittings and took up in all fifty-two hours. He was called upon to reply to 149 questions. On March 11 he received a letter from Phillpotts refusing to institute him. He appealed to the Court of Arches, which, after a judicial inquiry, confirmed the Bishop's decision. He then appealed to the Judicial Committee of the Privy Council.

The matter came up for trial on November 11, 1849. There were three clerical judges, the two Archbishops of Canterbury and York, both Evangelicals, and the Bishop of London, a moderate High Churchman, and seven laymen—three ministers (the President of the Privy Council, Lord Lansdowne; the Master of the Rolls, a sort of Vice-Chancellor; and the Chancellor of the Duchy of Lancaster, Lord Campbell) and four judges.

> Their judgment quashed that of the Court of Arches, and not only condemned the Bishop's claim to judge the theological views of a candidate presented to him, but definitely laid it down that Gorham's opinions did not disqualify him from holding the living to which he had been presented.[1]

The decision of the Judicial Committee came as a thunderbolt to the High Churchmen. A controversy followed on the competence of a committee, the majority of whose members were laymen and not necessarily even Anglicans, to make the final pronouncement on ecclesiastical questions.

> The Bishop of London took the opportunity to bring forward once more the Bill on which in previous years Parliament had refused the necessary time to pronounce.[2] This time he proposed to substitute for the Judicial Committee of the Privy

---

[1] See Lord John Russell's letters to the Bishop of London and the Archbishop of Canterbury, February 25 and March 15, 1850; Sp. Walpole's *Life of Lord John Russell*, vol. ii, pp. 117-18. For criticisms of the Bishop of Exeter's action, see Thomas Binney, *Conscientious Clerical Nonconformity: with Introductory remarks on the imputed conduct of the Bishop of Exeter in the cases of the Rev. T. Shore and the Rev. G. C. Gorham*, 1848.

[2] See above, p. 355.

Council a special court to be composed entirely of the clergy. The Government opposed a reform which in their view derogated directly from the prerogatives of the Crown.[1] But the Bishop of London deplored equally the fact that Convocation no longer met,[2] and, in default of a new tribunal, it was proposed to make Convocation the supreme court.

II

Convocation (it would be more correct to speak of Convocations, for there are two, one for the province of Canterbury, the other for the province of York) is the assembly of the clergy, meeting annually, and originally possessing the power to tax the clergy. Like the lay Parliament, it consists of two Chambers, an Upper House composed of the Bishops under the presidency of the Archbishops, and a Lower House consisting of the Deans of cathedral chapters, an elected representative of each chapter, the Archdeacons, and a number of elected representatives of the parochial clergy. In addition to its right of taxation it possessed the right to legislate on ecclesiastical questions. And although this right was narrowly restricted by the Royal Prerogative, in the sixteenth and in the early seventeenth century Convocation had been very active in this respect. It had laid down regulations for Divine Worship, drawn up rubrics, and issued Canons. Since they emanated from a period of reaction, many of these Canons left the devout Anglican two centuries later the alternative of breaking the law of the State or the law of the Church. Immediately after the restoration Convocation had been deprived of the right to tax itself. Otherwise its prerogatives had remained intact. But in the early eighteenth century, for political reasons,[3] Walpole

---

[1] H. of L., June 3, 1850, The Bishop of London's speech (*Parliamentary Debates*, 3rd Ser., vol. cxi, pp. 598 sqq.). Lord Lansdowne replied to it: 'The particular measure was objectionable in the strongest degree, as striking a blow at the Queen's prerogative. It introduced a tribunal the decisions of which were for the first time in this country to be, in the language of the Bill, "Binding and conductive", on H.M.'s opinions, and it, therefore, took from H.M. that which from the earliest to the present time had been deemed the essential prerogative of the Crown, the government of the Church' (*Annual Register*, 1850, p. 143). Lord John Russell pointed out to the Bishop of London: 'If the Supreme Court of Appeal in heresy were formed solely of the clergy, their opinions would probably be founded on the prevailing theological opinions of the Judicial Bishops, which might be one day Calvinistic and the next Romish' (Sp. Walpole, *Life of Lord John Russell*, vol. ii, p. 117). The Bill was thrown out by 84 votes to 51.

[2] *Parl. Deb.*, vol. cxi, p. 606.

[3] The members of the Lower House, Tories opposed to the Hanoverian dynasty, were in a state of permanent revolt against the Bishops who, as nominees of the Government, were attached to the Whig party.

had prorogued it and had never summoned it again. His successors had followed his example. Convocation, indeed, whenever a new session of Parliament opened, met at the same time. But the meeting was a mere formality. It drew up an address to the Crown and was prorogued. Why should not the Queen employ her prerogative to make it once more a reality?

This has been suggested fifteen years earlier by the Evangelicals, who wanted the Prayer Book reformed by the excision of everything in it out of harmony with Calvinism and, therefore, with the Thirty-Nine Articles. For they were in a false position when they maintained that a High Churchman could not subscribe the Articles without perjury, since they were themselves guilty of the same dishonesty in the opposite direction when they used a liturgy whose formulas so often contradicted their dearest convictions.[1] To-day, however, it was the High Churchmen, shocked by the Gorham judgment, who were asking for the revival of Convocation. The Evangelicals on the contrary were unsympathetic to the proposal and agreed with those shrewd politicians who considered that at a time of such bitter controversy it would be imprudent to reverse Walpole's decision. A Church without a representative assembly might indeed be an anomaly in a country whose entire constitution was based on the representative principle. But it might well be among those anomalies which were the boast of British institutions. It would not make for public tranquillity to have a Parliament of theologians sitting beside the Parliament of politicians and debating passionately, in full view of the Press, questions of doctrine and discipline and, moreover, as being so important that the wellbeing of the Church depended upon their solution. Instead of making a settlement easier it would fan the flames of party strife, and far from contributing to the peace of the Church, might even lead to schism. The combatants were better separated and lost in remote dioceses from the public view.

If, however, Convocation must be revived and perform some useful function, many Evangelicals advocated changes in its composition, and on this point many moderate High Churchmen shared their opinion. The unnecessary distinction of two Convocations should be abolished. There should be a single Convocation

---

[1] John Kempthorne, *The Church's Self-Regulating Privilege*, 1835. See G. R. Balleine, *History of the Evangelical Party*, p. 269.

for England and Wales to which the Church of Ireland and the new Colonial Churches scattered over the globe might also send representatives. The electoral body of the Lower House should be enlarged and a vote given not only to the incumbents of the new parishes set up by the Church Building Acts, but also to stipendiary curates. Cathedral chapters should no longer be represented in the Lower House, and the archdeacons should elect representatives of the clergy, together with an equal number of laymen. And there was much to be said for admitting to the Upper House lay peers in equal number with the bishops. These suggestions raised the serious question of admitting laymen to the assembly of the clergy. Though the novelty attracted such a leading High Churchman as Gladstone, who at this very time introduced it into the constitution of the colonial Churches, the majority of the High Church party, as was only to be expected, took alarm. They were eager to shake off the bondage of the Church of England to the secular State. Some even entertained the hope of a separation between Church and State, which would give them the same preponderance in the Church of England which the Ritualists possessed in the Episcopal Church of Scotland, which was a free Church. But nothing would be gained by getting rid of the Erastianism from which the Church suffered if it were to be replaced by a species of Presbyterianism. The question remained undecided.[1]

12

What we have said up to the present, however, has drawn a deliberately over-simplified picture of the party struggle in the Church. A third party was growing up destined to be victorious. It was a revival of the old Liberal or Latitudinarian party under the name of the Broad Church.[2]

It was the Liberals, tolerant on principle, who in 1836 had saved Hampden from the persecution to which a combination of the Low and High Church had sought to subject him. In 1841 they

[1] Ecclesiastes (a pseudonym for H. H. Wood), *Church Emancipation and Church Reform*, 1847; *Reasons for Reviving the Action of the Convocation: printed for the Chester and Manchester Church Union*, 1850; *The Law, Constitution and Reform of Convocation*, 1852; *A Charge to the Clergy of the Archdeaconry of Lewes*, 1854. See Thureau-Dangin, *La Renaissance Catholique en Angleterre*, vol. ii, p. 245.

[2] For the origin of the name Broad Church, see Thureau-Dangin, vol. ii, p. 392; John Tulloch, *Movements of Religious Thought in Britain*, 1885, p. 260; *Memorials of W. C. Lake, Dean of Durham*, 1901, p. 35.

had saved Newman from the excommunication demanded by the Low Churchmen, and, finally, in 1850 had made common cause with the Low Church against the High Church fanatics. And in that combination they had taken the lead. The Gorham judgment had been inspired by them. They had refused to decide the doctrinal issue between Phillpotts and Gorham. Their judgment amounted to a declaration that such controversies were obsolete, matters in which the common sense of the nation had no interest. Manning's conversion was a protest against the victory not so much of Evangelicalism as of Liberalism.[1]

We must be quite clear as to the significance of this Liberalism. It expressed the deep-seated conviction of the enlightened section of the Church, often driven into the background by the outbreak of some fanaticism or another, but which re-emerged within a few years, possibly as a reaction against the noisy theological brawls between the High Churchmen and the Low.[2] The Whig statesmen, like their philosopher and historian, Macaulay, were religious sceptics bound to the Establishment by its beautiful liturgy and historic traditions, and because they saw in it the expression of a mean between the conflicting extremes of Roman Catholicism and the Calvinist sects. A century and a half earlier, Swift, though no Whig, had brilliantly defended this point of view. Accordingly, Lord Melbourne between 1835 and 1841 and Lord John Russell between 1846 and 1852 had given preference to Liberals over Evangelicals in their appointments. Such Liberal appointments were Maltby to the See of Durham, Thirlwall to St. David's, and Hampden to Hereford, Milman made Dean of St. Paul's, and Tait Dean of Carlisle. In 1853, therefore, the *Edinburgh Review* reckoned only thirteen High Church bishops, ten Broad Churchmen, and five Evangelicals.[3] But paradoxical as it may appear at first sight a tacit understanding existed between the Evangelical and the Liberal Protestants against the High Church. 'The Low Church party', wrote Macaulay, 'contained, as it still contains, two very different elements, a Puritan element and a Latitudinarian element. On almost every question, however,

---

[1] *Edinburgh Review*, July 1850, art. entitled 'General Advantages of Comprehension', by the future Dean Stanley (vol. xcii, pp. 272-3).

[2] Ibid., October 1853, art. entitled 'Church Parties', vol. xcviii, pp. 341-2. *Cooper's Journal*, March 30, 1850.

[3] *Ed. Rev.*, October 1853, art. entitled 'Church Parties', vol. xcviii, p. 338. Sp. Walpole, *Life of Lord John Russell*, vol. ii, pp. 116-17.

relating either to ecclesiastical polity or the ceremonial of public worship, the Puritan Low Churchman and the Latitudinarian Low Churchman were perfectly agreed.'[1] The Archbishop of York was a Latitudinarian, the Archbishop of Canterbury a Puritan. But the Evangelicals claimed them both. And when Lord John resigned office in February 1852, Lord Ashley wrote him a farewell letter, thanking him for the 'excellent and invaluable appointments which he had made in Church matters. No Prime Minister', he said, 'has ever surpassed you in this respect; nay, I do not believe has equalled you.'[2]

But we must look beyond the boundaries of the Whig party if we would measure the full extent of the progress made in the Church of England by modern Liberalism. If there were Liberal Evangelicals there were also moderate High Churchmen. To whom on the Episcopal Bench could the Tractarians, the Ritualists, look for support? To Phillpotts and Bagot, though the latter had come into conflict with the Tractarians when he was Bishop of Oxford, and it was to escape from the difficulties they caused him that he had taken refuge in the See of Bath. Even Blomfield, Bishop of London, could not be counted upon, nor any other of the ten High Church bishops. Dogmatic Tractarianism could not flourish in so undogmatic a Church.[3]

No Church on the contrary was more favourable soil for the growth of a Latitudinarian party. The *Edinburgh Review* reckoned the number of Broad Churchmen among the Anglican clergy at three thousand five hundred; of whom a thousand were fully conscious of their allegiance, 'theoretical' Latitudinarians.[4] Nor can it be doubted that in the ranks of those classified by the review as Low or High Church there were many whose convictions were so lukewarm that they scarcely differed from Broad Churchmen. For the Broad Church was not a definite party like

---

[1] *History of England*, 1855, vol. iii, pp. 72–3.

[2] Lord Shaftesbury to Lord John Russell, February 24, 1852 (*The Later Correspondence of Lord John Russell*, vol. i, p. 216).

[3] In such a body the clergyman who cherished ambitions was careful not to be involved in doctrinal disputes. 'He is usually distinguished in early life by academical success, which forms the appropriate basis of his subsequent career; when he has entered on the business of mature years he seldom ventures upon the dangerous experiment of authorship; or if he chooses that mode of launching himself upon the notice of the world, he commits himself to nothing by his publications, but edits a "Father" with uncontroversial notes, or publishes a volume of sermons, polished in style and neutral in sentiment' (*Edinburgh Review*, January 1854, art. entitled 'Ecclesiastical Economy', vol. xcix, p. 108).

[4] *Ed. Rev.*, October 1853, art. entitled 'Church Parties' (vol. xcviii, p. 338).

the other two, with its associations, its organized propaganda, and its press. It was simply an attitude of mind, a tendency, we might even say in the widest sense of the term, a group, within which several subordinate groups may be more or less roughly distinguished.

One of these, which we may call the broad and dry, was a survival of the old Latitudinarian party, still steeped in rationalism of the eighteenth-century type.

In Thomas Arnold, on the other hand, and his disciple, the future Dean Stanley, the combined influence is visible of German rationalism and Evangelical pietism.

Robert Vaughan, seeking to describe Arnold's position in the Church, pointed out that although his beliefs were closely akin to those of the Evangelicals, a 'spiritual liberty which he felt to be so joyous' divided him from their dogmatic orthodoxy. And although, on the other hand, he agreed with the Tractarians in the importance he attached to the part played in theology by history, imagination, and poetry, he kept himself free from their excesses and held fast to 'the substance of Evangelical truth'.[1]

A third group was centred round Cambridge. For though no tracts issued from that University, it had its own school of theology. It was influenced by Platonism and German metaphysics. It was voiced by men who had sat at Coleridge's feet at his Highgate soirées, Julius Hare, the translator of Schleiermacher, and Frederick Denison Maurice,[2] and, though in his life of John Stirling (1851) Carlyle scoffed at the Highgate philosophizings, he was, perhaps, less remote from them than he thought.[3]

[1] Robert Vaughan, *Essays*, vol. i, p. 117.
[2] James Martineau, *Essays Philosophical and Theological*, vol. i, pp. 334 sqq. *Quarterly Review*, June 1855, art. entitled 'Archdeacon Hare' (vol. xcvii, pp. 1 sqq.).
[3] James Martineau, op. cit., p. 389.

II THE CATHOLICS

I

We have sought to depict, without crossing the boundaries of the Established Church, the general orientation of English religious thought about the middle of the nineteenth century. But if we cross them we shall understand it even better. And in the first place we shall learn more of the two movements whose fortunes within the Church we have related, the Evangelical movement and the Oxford movement. For these movements were, in fact, simply two forms, distinctively English, of the two great forces which struggled for supremacy over Western Christianity, the Protestant and the Catholic religions. Within a Church which was essentially a Church of compromise, neither appeared or could possibly appear in its pure form. And in England there was a Roman Catholicism more Catholic than Pusey's Anglo-Catholicism, and on the other hand the Protestantism of the Dissenting sects, more Protestant than the Protestanism of the Evangelical Anglicans. What was the condition about 1852 of these two religious groups outside the Establishment?

Let us go back to the date when the conversion of Newman[1] and his most intimate friends first interfered with the progress of the Oxford movement. Its effect, we may remember, had been double. On the one hand it had weakened the Oxford movement and provoked a reaction, Protestant, Liberal, often sceptical. On the other hand, it had chilled the enthusiasm of those High Churchmen who had been tempted to give their party a Roman colouring and brought them back—and as a defence against the suspicions Newman's defection had not unreasonably aroused they made a great point of it—to the old strictly Anglican type of High Churchmanship. They had not, however, been content to remain on the defensive. Under the leadership of the untiring Bishop of Exeter they had gone over to the offensive and taken the field against Gorham to affirm the right of the Episcopate to exercise a firmer control than hitherto over the theological opinions of the clergy. Unhappily they had failed. Judges, the majority of whom were laymen, had condemned episcopal pretensions and pronounced a judgment, which could be understood

[1] Newman was received into the Church of Rome in 1845.

as Protestant or, what was worse, as infected with Latitudinarianism. The judgment, therefore, made many High Churchmen move in the direction opposite to that which they had taken when Newman's 'treason' had wounded, so to speak, their ecclesiastical patriotism. They asked themselves whether after all he had not been right, if the Church of England really deserved to be called a Church, as they understood the word, and if sooner or later they might not find themselves compelled to follow him.

2

Another episode in the ecclesiastical history of England which followed the Gorham judgment by a few months confirmed waverers in this point of view. It was the 'Papal Aggression' and the storm it roused. When three years earlier Lord Minto left for Italy,[1] Rome had been the goal of his journey. He went there, Lord Palmerston informed him, 'not as a Minister accredited to the Pope, but merely as an authentic organ of the British Government'.[2] Palmerston, however, in agreement on this point with his colleagues, and encouraged by the full approval of the leaders of the Opposition, cherished the hope that before Lord Minto left Rome regular diplomatic relations might be established between the Court of Rome and the Court of St. James. A Bill was, in fact, introduced at the opening of the session of 1848 and passed by both Houses, which would have settled the question, if an amendment introduced with the approval of the Government had not provided that the diplomatic representative of Rome in London must be a layman.[3]

This was unacceptable to the Pope, and the Act remained a dead letter. And at the same time the execution of another design conceived about this time by the Pope was suspended. The aristocracy which governed England wished to treat the Catholic Church as a normal Christian Church to be placed on a footing of complete legal equality with the Anglican, possibly even

---

[1] See above, p. 225.

[2] Lord Palmerston to Lord Minto: 'You will be at Rome not as a Minister accredited to the Pope, but as an authentic organ of the British Government enabled to explain its views' (E. Ashley, *Life of Viscount Palmerston*, vol. i, pp. 34-5). For Lord Minto's mission, see H. C. F. Bell, *Lord Palmerston*, vol. i, pp. 416 sqq.

[3] The Bill was introduced by Lord Lansdowne on February 7, 1848 (*Parliamentary Debates*, 3rd Ser., vol. xcvi, p. 169). The amendment was accepted by the Lords on February 18 (ibid., p. 876).

enjoying the benefits of a concordat and in receipt of financial assistance from the State. But it quite rightly thought it ridiculous that the Roman Church in England should still be organized in a fashion which the repeal of the penal laws had made an anachronism, that England should be treated by Rome as a heathen country in which the Church is governed not by a regular hierarchy, but by simple vicars apostolic, missionaries among the enemy. At the opening of the century the old English Catholic families, inspired by a 'Cisalpine' outlook, had advocated a restoration of the hierarchy which had become extinct in the sixteenth century. The bishops, assembled eventually in a national synod, would, they hoped, resist the Pope on points of discipline or even dogma. Now it was the Curia that revived the project which was warmly encouraged by Wiseman, who was very influential at the court of Rome. The moment seemed favourable. In Ireland a Catholic hierarchy had always confronted the Anglican. And up to the present the Government had shut its eyes to the fact. From time to time, indeed, an Irish priest had been allowed to sign an official document with his title as bishop, and an individual bishop had been given precedence on a ceremonial occasion.[1] When in 1839 Wiseman had asked the Colonial Office if there was any objection to the creation of a Catholic hierarchy in Canada he had been told: 'Call yourselves by any name you please, bishops, muftis, mandarins. What is it to us?' And more recently, when he asked the same Minister the same question in regard to Australia, he received the answer: 'Do as you please, but don't ask us.'[2] Three years later, when the revolutionary crisis of 1848 had passed, Pius XI decided to revive the project of 1847.

On August 16, 1850, summoned by the Pope, Wiseman left London for Rome. Before his departure he had an interview with the Prime Minister, at which he seems to have given Lord John more or less clearly to understand what the Pope's intention was in recalling him to Rome and the Prime Minister raised no objection. In September he took part in a Consistory at which fourteen new Cardinals were created, ten of them non-Italians and among them Wiseman himself. In this way the Papacy strikingly emphasized its international or rather supernatural character. On

---

[1] See the incident occasioned in 1838 by the Catholic Bishop of Tuam, and Lord Melbourne's decision not to carry the matter further (*Annual Register*, 1838, p. 106).
[2] Wilfrid Ward, *The Life and Times of Cardinal Wiseman*, 1897, vol. i, p. 474.

September 29 the Pope published a brief by which he re-established the hierarchy in England. The eight vicars apostolic would be replaced by a metropolitan Archbishop and twelve suffragan bishops. The new bishops were not given titles already borne by the Anglican Bishops. This not only avoided any breach of the Statute of 1829, but brought the arrangement of the dioceses into greater harmony with the actual distribution of the population than was the case with the Anglican Sees. At the head of the hierarchy, in place of an Archbishop of Canterbury flanked by an Archbishop of York, was an Archbishop of Westminster, whose See was thus placed at the national centre and included the place where Parliament sat. The south of England was given fewer bishops than the centre and north, and Birmingham and Nottingham received bishops, when no Anglican bishop had as yet been appointed. The step was taken without any formal agreement with the British Government. The latter, after all, would hardly have wished to be asked for its official sanction. And it was invested with further solemnity by the pastoral letter, theatrical in style and circumstance, which Wiseman, the new Cardinal and first Archbishop of Westminster, issued eight days later from Rome itself. 'Your beloved country has received a place among the fair churches which, normally constituted, form the splendid aggregate of Catholic Communion; Catholic England has been restored to its orbit in the ecclesiastical firmament from which its light had long vanished, and begins now anew its course of regularly adjusted action round the centre of unity, the source of light and of vigour.'[1]

Thereupon, as on many previous occasions, but now more strikingly than ever, the power of anti-Catholic feeling in England was displayed. It was as though, after three centuries of liberty, the Pope and the Cardinal were seeking to reduce the country once more to subjection, spiritual, and even temporal. In the dead calm which prevailed in the world of politics the 'Papal Aggression' monopolized public attention. Almost without exception the Press, headed by *The Times*, fulminated against Rome. Numerous country meetings were held. Many Catholic churches were objects of rioting, sometimes even Anglican

---

[1] Wilfrid Ward, *The Life and Times of Cardinal Wiseman*, 1897, vol. i, pp. 525 sqq. and 542. P. Thureau-Dangin, *La Renaissance Catholique en Angleterre*, 1903, vol. ii, pp. 202 sqq.

churches where the parson was a Ritualist. Lord John was carried away by one of those emotional outbursts which chequered so oddly his political career. The same Liberalism which had often brought upon him, as on so many other members of the Whig aristocracy, the charge of Catholic sympathies, now made him declare war on Roman ultramontanism. He wrote an open letter, published in the Press on November 4, addressed to the Whig Bishop of Durham, in which he declared that 'no foreign prince or potentate will be at liberty to fasten his fetters upon a nation which has so long and so nobly vindicated its right to freedom of opinion, civil, political, and religious'. He took the opportunity to denounce those clergymen of the Church of England who, by their blameworthy innovations, 'honour paid to saints, the claim of infallibility for the Church, the superstitious use of the Sign of the Cross, the muttering of the Liturgy so as to disguise the language in which it is written, the recommendation of auricular confession, the administration of penance and absolution', had 'been most forward in leading their flocks step by step to the very verge of the precipice'.[1]

Next day, November 5, was the anniversary of the Gunpowder Plot, and it was not Guy Fawkes, but Pius IX and Wiseman whom the London urchins burned in effigy.

3

What action must now be taken? For the letter to the Bishop of Durham was not sufficient to satisfy public feeling. 'The worst point', Stockmar had written three years earlier to Prince Albert, 'in the attitude of Protestantism towards Romanism is that it cannot venture to be tolerant. Romanism which denounces and excludes every other creed and never surrenders the smallest tittle of its infallibility, forces Protestantism for toleration's sake into acts which are occasionally intolerant in fact, but more commonly have only the semblance of being so.'[2] What 'intolerant' measure could be devised to safeguard English toleration?

The lawyers got to work and produced a Bill of three Clauses forbidding Catholic priests under penalty of a fine to take terri-

[1] Lord John Russell to the Bishop of Durham, November 4, 1850: 'I agree with you in considering the late aggression of the Pope upon our Protestantism as insolent and insidious' (Walpole, *Life of Lord John Russell*, vol. ii, pp. 120-1).
[2] Stockmar to Prince Albert, August 5 (Sir Th. Martin, *The Life of the Prince Consort*, 1876, vol. ii, p. 455).

torial titles, declaring all gifts made to them and all acts performed by them under such titles null and void, and confiscating to the Crown any property bequeathed to them under these titles. Heated and lengthy debates followed. Introduced by Lord John on February 7, the Ecclesiastical Titles Bill did not pass its third reading in the Commons until July 4.[1] At every stage it secured huge majorities. But the minority put up an obstinate fight. Nor was it confined to the English and Irish Catholics whose opposition too directly interested could be ignored. It included the Radicals, and in particular those among them—Bright was their mouthpiece—who, being Dissenters and opposed in principle to a State Church, could not champion the privileges of the Church of England against a dissident Church, even though it was the Church of Rome.[2]

It also included a handful of Peelites, Sir James Graham, and Gladstone, and, in the Upper House, Lord Aberdeen, who were faithful to the ideal of a concordat which their leader had entertained during his memorable ministry.[3] And if the attitude of the majority was predetermined, and Lord John himself could not draw back from the line of policy on which he had embarked, it became clear, as the debates dragged on, that he and Parliament in his steps were heading for an impasse. Before Parliament met, Wiseman had published a letter explaining the papal brief, which *The Times* had reproduced in full[4] and of which fifty thousand copies had been printed, a letter as conciliatory in tone as his pastoral of October had been provocative. He had convinced a large number of readers that the toleration which was the boast of modern Protestants obliged them to tolerate even Roman intolerance. The Catholic members of the Commons by abstention from voting gave themselves the pleasure of seeing the Government defeated by the Protestant bigots. In consequence the preamble of

[1] *Parliamentary Debates*, 3rd Ser., vol. cxiv, p. 211, and vol. cxviii, p. 240.

[2] H. of C., February 7 and May 12, 1851: Bright's speech (ibid., 3rd Ser., vol. cxiv p. 242, and vol. cxvi, p. 917). Compare the attitude expressed by Edward Miall when, at an Islington meeting, he proposed an amendment expressing the astonishment and indignation of the meeting at the Papal Aggression, but adding: 'But at the same time it is no less strongly opposed to the assumption and exercise of similar claims and authority by any other hierarchy from whatever quarter it may profess to derive authority' (A. Miall, *Life of Edward Miall*, p. 164).

[3] H. of C., March 20, 1851: Sir James Graham's speech (*Parl. Deb.*, 3rd Ser., vol. cxv, p. 280); March 25: Gladstone's speech (ibid., vol. cxv, p. 579). H. of L., July 21: Lord Aberdeen's speech (ibid., vol. cxviii, p. 1072).

[4] *The Times*, November 20, 1850.

the Bill, as it was passed, was more anti-Catholic in its language than originally it had been. Nevertheless, the provisions of the measure had been considerably weakened. Only one of its clauses had survived; that which imposed a fine of £100 for a breach of the new law. But everybody knew that it was a mere statement of principle, and that no Catholic prelate would, in fact, be fined, that the Irish bishops would continue to use their territorial titles, and that the new English bishops would in future do what their Irish brethren had always done with impunity.

4

That is to say, the English Catholic clergy, indeed, English Catholics as a body, had won a victory. And their victory was confirmed by an increase in the number of converts from Anglo-Catholicism. The influx began with the blow which the Gorham judgment inflicted on the latter. It was reinforced by the violent reaction of public opinion to the 'Papal Aggression'. Included in the unpopularity of the Roman Catholics, handed over in a sense by the Prime Minister to public vengeance, many lacked the courage to cling to a Church which loaded them with abuse. While Parliament was debating the Ecclesiastical Titles Bill, the Bishop of Chichester instructed his archdeacon to call a meeting to denounce the aggression of Rome. Manning obeyed, but, when the assembly met, he informed them officially that in doing so he had acted for the last time as archdeacon. Shortly after he was received into the Catholic Church. This sensational conversion bore little resemblance to Newman's equally sensational conversion six years before. The latter had left the Church of his birth in search of intellectual satisfactions she could not provide. Manning was no philosopher. He was a politician for whom a dogma was a ticket rather than a truth. A politician or rather, perhaps, a soldier; born a priest, as other men are born soldiers, this worldly ascetic of austere ambition had dreamed of rising in the Anglican hierarchy until he became, who could tell, the new Laud of a regenerated Church. Such hopes were at an end. To judge by the outburst of anti-Catholic feeling he might well be doomed to remain Archdeacon of Chichester to the close of his life. His ambition took another direction. The die was cast. He would cross the Rubicon. He would join the Church of Rome and aim at becoming a Roman prelate while remaining a great Englishman. It would be an extremely difficult task, but no undertaking could be difficult enough to daunt his indomitable and devouring ambition.[1]

He submitted to Rome, was warmly welcomed by Wiseman, and ordained priest with the least possible delay. Others followed him, and the flow of conversions, which had slackened since Newman's, returned to or rather increased and permanently increased its normal volume. Confronted with these conversions, Liberal Protestantism felt at once indignant and impotent. When in 1853 Parliament passed an Act giving the State control over donations for charitable purposes, the clause subjecting Catholic donations to this control was dropped,[2] and two years later a special Act was passed according the latter distinctive and preferential treatment.[3]

Thus the Catholics who in 1850 had claimed in the name of the Common Law the right to possess their archbishop and bishops, had now obtained special legislation exempting them from it.

Does this mean that the victory won in 1851 by the English Catholics was more important than it could have seemed at the time? Would it prove the prelude to future victories even more decisive? Would the Earl of Arundel, who in 1847 had created a sensation in Parliament by predicting that one day the entire nation would return to the Catholic fold, prove after all a true prophet?[4]

Such a view would have underestimated the strength of anti-Catholic feeling which had just shown itself so violently. And although the enemies of Rome had to admit that the Catholic minority must be tolerated, the position of Catholics in England remained, nevertheless, difficult and abnormal.

[1] P. Thureau-Dangin, *La Renaissance Catholique en Angleterre*, vol. ii, pp. 129 sqq. and 218 sqq.
[2] 16 & 17 Vict. Cap. 127: An Act for the better Administration of Charitable Trusts.
[3] 18 & 19 Vict. Cap. 124: An Act to amend the Charitable Trusts Act. Catholics had already secured the partial removal of the disabilities to which they had been subjected by the Acts of 1844 (7 & 8 Vict. Cap. 102), and 1846 (9 & 10 Vict. Cap. 59). See during the debate on the latter enactment the speeches of Lord Campbell, H. of L., April 30, 1846 (*Parliamentary Debates*, 3rd Ser., vol. lxxv, p. 1287), and Lord John Russell (H. of C., August 6, 1846, ibid., vol. lxxxviii, p. 360).
[4] Ibid., 3rd Ser., vol. xci, pp. 763-5. Broughton, *Recollections of a Long Life*, vol. vi, p. 187.

5

It was difficult because they were deeply divided. The new-comers felt lost in an unknown world and, moreover, a world which in some respects seemed less Catholic than themselves. Artificially cut off from the Continent by centuries of persecution, the English Catholics had finally, in spite of the suspicion with which they were regarded, become more English than Catholic.. The extremely difficult conditions under which Catholic wor-ship had to be carried on had prevented English Catholics, lay-men or priests, from sharing fully Continental devotion. There were no retreats, little extra-liturgical cultus of the reserved Sacrament, no public veneration of images, no devotion to the Sacred Heart. The religious Orders had but lately returned from exile abroad, and when, in spite of the law forbidding it, religious congregations began to be established in England, among them Jesuits, Redemptorists, Passionists, and Marists, they and the Jesuits in particular were often exposed to the undisguised hostility of the leading English Catholics. We are not speaking of the Irish proletariat. In Liverpool, where only four chapels and fourteen priests served the needs of 39,000 adult Catholics, the Jesuits, supported by O'Connell, attempted to open a church. The secular clergy were up in arms and organized violent demon-strations against them. Rome, though deciding in favour of the Jesuits, to give time for hostile passions to subside, forbade the church to be opened till six years had passed. Many of these old Catholics merged unobtrusively with the Protestants among whom they lived. And this conversion of the lukewarm to Angli-canism increased, it would seem, after 1829, at the very time when the counter-movement of conversions of zealous Anglo-Catholics to Rome was beginning. This Cisalpinism and Liber-alism of the old English Catholic gentry and middle class, akin to French Jansenism and Gallicanism, has usually been treated with contumely by Catholic historians of English Catholicism. The representatives, they tell us, of the old English Catholicism were human fossils, and Catholicism in their hands in mortal danger when the infusion of new blood by the arrival of the converts from Anglicanism reinvigorated the anaemic body.

The 'Papal Aggression' and the debates which followed it made

373

the conflict between the Cisalpines and Ultramontanes only more acute. Some of the former, in the Press and even in Parliament, denounced the restoration of the hierarchy as warmly as if they were Protestants.[1] When the change had been made, they continued to protest against what they regarded as the superstitious practices of Continental Catholicism and the Jesuit invasion. They had once been in favour of a territorial episcopate, hoping that Bishops more firmly planted on English soil would be in a stronger position than the vicars apostolic to resist the autocracy of the Roman Curia. The attitude of the first Archbishop of Westminster, Cardinal Wiseman, had changed their opinion, and they were now asking that England should be divided into parishes, in which the parish priest would enjoy the same rights, as against his bishop, as he enjoyed in Catholic countries. Wiseman waged ruthless war upon them, and in the political sphere did all he could to detach the English Catholics from the Liberal party, to which they had belonged hitherto, and bring them back to the Tories. In his war against the Cisalpines he provided himself with a staff of converts whose zeal adopted the most advanced Ultramontane views. By birth more foreign than English, in his connections extremely Continental and Roman,[2] he was aware that these neophytes, because they were thoroughly English, would be more persuasive missionaries of Ultramontanism in England than himself. But even in their ranks disagreements arose. The Catholic Newman could not get rid of the intellectual restlessness which had detached him from the national Church. For it was his nature. The Church of Rome, however, does not look with favour on restless intellects. The new form of apologetic he had worked out in process of conversion was not strictly orthodox and, when he was placed at the head of a Catholic university in Dublin, which, it was hoped, would raise the intellectual level of the Irish priesthood, he was confronted by the hostility of a conservative clergy. In vain he asked Wiseman, who had adopted Manning as the predestined heir of his office and influence, to obtain for him from Rome the bishopric which would have given him the authority he needed to defeat his adversaries.

[1] The Duke of Norfolk associated himself with Lord John's protest and joined the Church of England, though he was reconverted to the Catholic Church on his death-bed. —Trs. Note.

[2] John Stoughton, *Religion in England from* 1850 *to* 1866, vol. ii, p. 257. Wilfrid Ward, *Life of Cardinal Wiseman*.

Deserted by everyone, he resigned. The long struggle between Newman and Manning had begun.[1]

We must not, however, exaggerate the gravity of these disagreements. Above all, we must not look upon them as necessarily a symptom or cause of decadence. Quarrels are often a mark of life and growth. To grasp the weakness of English Catholicism at grips with the attacks of its foes we must look at it from a different point of view.

We must go back in imagination to the year 1850 when the 'Papal Aggression' caused such a stir in England. Throughout Latin Europe, in Austria, and in Belgium, Catholicism had defeated Liberalism, atheism, and Socialism. Before the close of 1851 Louis Napoleon, with the blessing of the entire Episcopate, would overthrow the Constitution in France. Papal Aggression was but the prolongation beyond the Channel of this Catholic reaction against the hostile forces which, ever since 1789 and with renewed strength since 1830, threatened it everywhere.[2] It was not, therefore, surprising that British public opinion took alarm. On the Continent the defeat of the revolution of 1848 had been the victory of Catholicism. But England had escaped that revolution; and, when the Catholic reaction reached England, it encountered an obstacle which had no existence on the Continent, the victory of the revolution of 1846, the victory of Liberalism.[3] The Catholics could boast that in spite of everything they were gaining ground.[4] But had they gained as much as Pusey's

---

[1] P. Thureau-Dangin, *La Renaissance Catholique en Angleterre*, vol. ii, pp. 275-9.

[2] The favourite argument of Anglicans, even High Churchmen, against the Romanizers was the degraded condition of the Church of Rome, which seemed to leave the Latin nations no other choice than between debased superstition and complete irreligion. The Protestant nations had avoided this impasse and prospered. Now, however, Catholicism was reviving, gaining strength and emerging victorious from the crisis of 1848. It was, therefore, once more a danger in itself, not only as opening the way to irreligion.

[3] See Gladstone's speech during the debates on the Ecclesiastical Titles Bill, March 25, 1851: 'Oh, recollect the functions you have to perform in face of the world. Recollect that Europe and the whole of the civilized world look to England at this moment not less, no, but even more than ever they looked to her before, as the mistress and guide of nations. . . . They know that you are not a monarchy to-day, a republic to-morrow, and a military despotism the day after. . . . Show, I beseech you, have the courage to show the Pope of Rome and his Cardinals and his Church that England too, as well as Rome, has her *semper eadem*' (J. Morley, *Life of W. E. Gladstone*, vol. i, pp. 412-13).

[4] The religious census of 1851 (see below, pp. 391 sqq.) showed that at that time there were 186,111 sittings in the Catholic churches and chapels of England and Wales, and that 252,873 persons had attended them. These figures seemed to prove that during the previous thirty years the increase in the number of Catholic churches (87 per cent) had been more rapid than the increase in the number of Protestant (66 per cent). The number of Catholic chapels had doubled between 1829 and 1853, and during the same period the

Ritualists, who had remained faithful to the Church of their fathers? Eminent men of letters, it is true, Thackeray and Dickens, attended in 1852 the series of lectures in which Newman sought to lay bare the "Difficulties of Anglicans'. The literary world of London had always prided itself on its freedom from anti-Catholic bigotry. Nevertheless, there can be no doubt that for many years after 1850 Protestant Liberalism became increasingly anti-Catholic. Wiseman, who had hitherto been welcomed in London society, saw many doors closed against him. Many middle-class families would not employ Catholic servants. Catholics delighted to depict the Church of England as dull, prosaic, without principles, and infected with Erastianism. But the suffering a Newman and a Manning felt in wrenching themselves from her proved how many and how strong were the roots which had bound her up with every fibre of their being. Weakened though she was by so many warring parties, and threatened by the growth of popular scepticism, she was still the most perfect expression of England's spiritual unity in face of the Continent and against it. Conversions to Catholicism might be multiplied. Each, in the convert's mind, was a protest against the spirit of the age, which was unalterably anti-Catholic. By birth or choice Catholics were aliens at home. The history of the growth of English Roman Catholicism is no part of English history.

III DISSENT

I

What we have just said of Catholic Dissent is obviously untrue of Protestant. It cannot possibly be regarded as a foreign body embedded in English society. Though outside the national Church the Protestant sects were, nevertheless, a distinctive national feature differentiating the English from all other European nations, Protestant as well as Catholic. Nor could the country forget, even when the sects were regarded with suspicion or disdain, that, in

number of priests had risen from 477 to 823 (Stoughton, *Religion in England*, vol. ii, p. 264). On the other hand, *The Times* of January 10, 1854, commenting on the results of the census, reached the conclusion that when allowance had been made for the large number of Irish and foreigners attending Catholic churches: 'We may very safely put 150,000 as the sum total of the sittings required for bona fide English Papists; nor should we, indeed, have much hesitation in reducing even this amount by fully one-third.'

her hour of need, the three ancient dissenting bodies had assisted the Anglican Church to shake off the yoke of James II and the Jesuits. Nor could it fail to recognize what the new Nonconformity of Wesley and Whitefield had done to transform and regenerate the moral life of the entire nation and the Church in particular. We might, therefore, have supposed that, when about the middle of the nineteenth century England reaffirmed so decisively her religious independence in face of the Catholic reaction which was sweeping through Europe, the sects, Pre-Methodist and Methodist alike, would have stood forth proudly as living symbols of this independence and prospered as never before. In fact, paradoxical as it may seem, for the Nonconformists these years were troubled years of dissension and decline.

Among the Wesleyans a schism took place in 1849 which made a great stir in the Press, almost as great indeed as the Scottish schism of 1843, which in view of the fact that the Wesleyans were so few in comparison with the numbers of Scottish Calvinists proves how high their prestige stood.

The Rev. Jabez Bunting, a great man in his way, had established a dictatorship from which the Society had in many respects benefited. Its organization had made uninterrupted progress,[1] the management of its finances steadily improved. But this despotism of an individual was out of tune with the times. Once already, in 1834,[2] a rebel, the Rev. Warren, had not only weakened the Society by a schism, but compelled Bunting to make concessions to the malcontents lest it should spread still further. As in the case of all previous secessions, the grievance was concerned with a question not of doctrine, but organization. The malcontents wanted to extend the rights of the laity, of the rank and file, in the assemblies which governed the Wesleyan body and thus protect them against the domination of the collective pastorate which had inherited Wesley's authority on his death, and in which Bunting in the name of the legal hundred exercised power almost equal to that of the founder himself. In consequence, the Conference of 1835 decreed for the first time that the Society's funds, since they were entirely or mainly provided by the general body of members, must without any exception be administered under the control of Conference by mixed committees, to be

---

[1] For this organization, see *History of the English People*, vol. i, pp. 412 sqq.
[2] Ibid., vol. iii, pp. 154 sqq.

composed of ministers and laymen in equal numbers. Moreover, the Conference agreed to relax the rigour of the old rules governing the expulsion of members and forbade arbitrary expulsions. It instructed superintendents in difficult or doubtful cases not to demand an expulsion without first consulting the most judicious and experienced members. It gave members sentenced to expulsion the right of appeal to the annual district meeting, to Conference or to a district meeting specially summoned, where the president would be advised by two preachers chosen by the appellant and two others chosen by the superintendent. Conference had further decided that after each quarterly district meeting, to sound the opinion of the circuit and become acquainted with any serious grievances that might be current, the superintendent must call into consultation the most important laymen in the circuit. Nevertheless, it was to a clerical tribunal, whatever its composition, that the right of appeal lay from a sentence of expulsion. And the obligation placed on the superintendents to consult at regular intervals the leading laymen of the connection was regulated so minutely by the terms of the enactment of 1835 that it was rendered to a large extent ineffective. Jabez Bunting remained the Methodist Pope. When he persuaded Conference to found a theological college, he had himself appointed president and distributed the teaching posts among his partisans. The voice of complaint, therefore, was not silenced.[1]

In 1846 the discontent came to a head. The breach between Peel and the bulk of the Tory party made Bunting's intransigent Conservatism intolerable. Their social position and turn of mind made the wealthy and most prominent Methodists the predestined adherents of the new economic creed of free trade of which Peel was now, together with Cobden, the hero. An independent press came into existence among the Methodists which opposed Bunting's political views.[2] For the first time in Wesleyan history the deaths exceeded the converts in number.[3] In 1846 the gain in membership for the whole of the United Kingdom was only 310, in 1847 there was a loss of 5,000. Bunting and his supporters

---

[1] George Smith, *History of Wesleyan Methodism*, 1861, vol. iii, pp. 344 sqq.
[2] *Eclectic Review*, August 1846, art. entitled 'Methodism as it is' (N.S. vol. xx, pp. 129 sqq.).
[3] At this date the number of Wesleyan Methodists was about 350,000, of members of the New Connexion founded in 1797 about 15,000, of Primitive Methodists who had seceded in 1812 about 100,000 (J. L. and B. Hammond, *The Age of the Chartists*, p. 239).

laid the blame for this on the malcontents, who, they said, were bringing the Society into discredit by shaking the authority of its rulers. The latter retorted the blame on Bunting and his partisans who, according to them, had isolated the Society from the mass of the nation. Bunting took the bold step of expelling three ministers for collaborating with the Opposition press. His action provoked an outburst of indignation, not only among Protestants of other sects who invited the expelled ministers to their pulpits, but in the Liberal organs. *The Times* declared the decision of Conference a threat to the liberty of the Press and gave its blessing to the attempts made by the victims of an irresponsible tyranny to reform the constitution of a Church whose political conservatism it pronounced detestable.[1] With this powerful support the rebellion spread. The original policy of the rebels was not to break with the Church of which they were members, but to reform it, while clinging to its membership, and compel its rulers to surrender by the traditional method of withholding supplies. *No surrender, No secession* was their slogan. But the tension became too acute. A secession took place, the most serious which had yet occurred in Methodist history; and a new group was founded, the United Methodist Free Churches. As we have seen, it owed its foundation not to a doctrinal but a political issue. The gravity of the schism may be measured by the fact that within a year the Society lost 56,068 members and, whereas it had hitherto boasted of its financial prosperity, it was left at the end of three years with a deficit of £50,000. To cope with the disaster, Conference in 1852 acted, as it had acted before, when faced with Warren's secession in 1835. A large number of duly qualified laymen were given the right to take part in the quarterly meeting. To provide against the danger of too hasty expulsions, special circuit meetings were set up composed exclusively of laymen to report to the superintendent. Having given the malcontents this satisfaction, Conference counter-balanced its concessions by tightening up the machinery of expulsion. Anyone who refused to pay his subscription would be expelled automatically and without right of appeal. Nor might any proposal made by a circuit receive a hearing if it was obviously of a revolutionary nature, or in revolt

---

[1] The ministers in question were Everett, Dunn, and Griffith. The last of these, Radical in politics, was constantly charged with being a Chartist (Faulkner, *Chartism and the Churches*, pp. 92-3). E. R. Taylor, *Methodism and Politics*, p. 186.

against the system of doctrine and discipline bequeathed by Mr. Wesley to Conference as a sacred deposit, and which it regarded as having been entrusted to it by God's providence and grace. In this way by modernizing and to a certain extent laicizing the Methodist body, Bunting, like the statesman he was, contrived to save his authority. But two or three years must elapse before the numbers of the sect began to increase once more, and as a result of the secession it had lost over 100,000 members at a time when the progress of political Liberalism gravely imperilled the High Church of Nonconformity.[1]

2

If this was the condition of Methodism what of the other sects? Though their troubles were less obvious and made less noise and outside restricted circles little was heard of them, they were serious. For English Dissent as a whole the years immediately before and after 1850 was a period of decline.

The better to understand its nature and causes we will first study two sects on the opposite boundary of Dissent to Methodism, the Unitarians, a mutation of the old English Presbyterian body dating from the eighteenth century and, therefore, contemporary with the Evangelical revival, and the Quakers, a seventeenth-century sect akin to the Unitarians in so far as they do not profess a definitely formulated Trinitarian creed, and are in agreement with their refusal to believe in the mystical or magical efficacy of the Sacraments to which, indeed, the Quakers deny even a symbolic value. But in other respects the two sects differ widely. The Unitarians, Priestley's disciples, are Deists of the eighteenth-century type, who prove the existence of God by abstract arguments. The Quakers' religion, on the other hand, is of a mystical type. They believe that the human soul can make direct contact with the Godhead by an interior illumination, an immediate intuition, for which even the intervention of Christ is not required.

The Unitarians were few in number. There were, it is true, in the United Kingdom some 300 Unitarian congregations and

---

[1] George Smith, *History of Wesleyan Methodism.* See also T. P. Bunting, *The Life of Jabez Bunting.*

250 ministers. But the resources at their disposal, now secured
to them by the decision of Parliament which left them in
possession of funds formerly bequeathed to the Presbyterians,
which had gradually come into their hands, enabled them to
support even moribund congregations.[1] In the cities, in Birmingham, for example, and London, their small groups were
closely allied with the Radicals. Nevertheless, they prided
themselves on their Liberal opinions, which often, in fact,
brought them close to the Conservatives.[2]

The sect, however, had no uniformity of organization or
doctrine. A meeting of their congregations, held in London in
1838 for the purpose of tightening the bonds between them,
had passed resolutions affirming 'the complete and thorough
independence of our separate religious societies as to all matters
of internal arrangement and discipline', and 'while professing
its attachment to Unitarian Christianity as at once scriptural
and rational . . .' at the same time recognized 'the essential
worth of that principle of free inquiry to which we are in-
debted for . . . that spirit of deep and vital religion which may
exist under various forms of theological sentiment'.[3]

The Unitarians exercised an influence out of proportion to
their small numbers. But was restricted by an unorthodoxy
which caused wide scandal, shocking easygoing Anglicans
equally with fanatical Calvinists.[4]

Was their doctrine any longer religious at all? One might
have doubted it, but for the efforts made by some of them to
breathe life into it, and Frederick Newman might well be
surprised by a remarkable sermon in which James Martineau
spoke of Christ in language as devotional as though he believed
in His divinity.[5] For Martineau had felt the influence of German

[1] 7 & 8 Vict. Cap. 45. The House of Lords, in 1844, had decided that the Unitarians
were not entitled to benefit by a foundation made by Lady Hewley in the eighteenth
century because they denied the doctrine of the Trinity. The following year, however,
Parliament enacted that, in the absence of an explicit provision by the founder, those who
had benefited by the foundation for twenty-five years should retain possession.

[2] History of the English People, vol. ii, p. 264; vol. iii, pp. 157-8.

[3] James Drummond and C. B. Upton, Life and Letters of James Martineau, vol. i, p. 94.

[4] Unitarianism confuted: A series of lectures delivered in Christ Church, Liverpool, in 1839,
by thirteen clergymen of the Church of England. Unitarianism defended: A series of lectures
by three Protestant Dissenting Ministers of Liverpool, 1839.

[5] James Martineau, Endeavours after the Christian Life, 1843: 'His unity of soul, the
unalterable spirit pervading all his altering moods of thought, in short, his identity with
himself is altogether divine.' F. Newman, Phases of Faith, p. 99. [Frederick Newman, the
Cardinal's brother, became a Unitarian.—Trs. Note.]

idealist philosophy and had returned from Germany in 1849 filled with admiration for Schleiermacher's theology.[1] We shall have to notice the influence exercised by another German, D. F. Strauss, on George Eliot, Bray, and their entourage.[2]

Like the Unitarians, the Quakers were influential, but very few in number. Ten years after the death of their founder, George Fox, there were 40,000 of them in Great Britain and Ireland. To escape the persecutions to which they were subject at home, large numbers emigrated to America, where the sect had prospered. At the beginning of the nineteenth century they were only 20,000 and their numbers were declining, while the population of the country was advancing by leaps and bounds.[3] To what was this stagnation due? It alarmed the Quakers, who sought to find the explanation. They found it in the deliberately exclusive nature of the sect, which had become more and more a closed caste. Until recently no one who had not received the Divine illumination could become a member. The children of Quakers were accepted only when they had professed themselves enlightened by the inner light and the elders of the Society had attested the truth of their profession. But for some years past every child of a Quaker was presumed to be a Quaker from birth and enrolled as such in the registers of the sect. He was then educated at a Quaker school. If he were poor he was given help and hospitality by the wealthy Quakers. He was married and buried in the fashion prescribed by the Society. A distinctive costume must be worn by men and women. The Quaker must not use those words of pagan origin employed in western Europe to designate the months and the days of the week. Nor must he use the conventional formulas of politeness, not even 'you' when addressing a single person. God alone might be addressed in terms of ceremony. Thus a religious body which on principle condemned every kind of superstition and formality had become involved in an extremely superstitious formalism, which an age of progressive Liberalism found intolerable.

Therefore, though the sect survived, many members were repelled and left it, though they took with them much of that

---

[1] *Life and Letters of James Martineau*, vol. i, p. 189.
[2] See below, p. 400.
[3] Sir Robert Inglis, in 1847, reckoned the number of Quaker families at 4,000 (*Annual Register*, 1847, p. 31).

spirit of peace and philanthropy for which it was distinguished. Nineteenth-century England owed much to these former Quakers. Many also were expelled, though they had no desire to go: anyone, for example, who took a wife outside the sect save for the extremely rare case in which the bride was not only willing but after a meticulous examination judged worthy to become a Friend.[1]

The formalism, however, was itself on the decline. Individual Quakers revolted in increasing numbers against the puerile singularity of the old usages. And they were revolting more and more against more important rules, the prohibition, for example, to take part in politics. For politics, according to the Quakers of the old school, were necessarily a more or less attenuated form of the revolution or war which their religion condemned without qualification. But in spite of this ban, when the legal barriers to their entrance into Parliament had been removed in 1832,[2] Quakers could not resist the temptation to enter it. And Bright triumphed over strong opposition and succeeded in remaining a Quaker, while becoming one of the leaders of British Radicalism.

Moreover, their philanthropic zeal was constantly bringing the leading Quakers, the wealthiest in particular, into close contact with the members of the ruling class, and the Evangelical philanthropists, as participants in their charitable activities. Such men often became ashamed of what was shockingly unorthodox in the Quaker doctrines as they had been canonized by Barclay in the seventeenth century. In 1825 the devout banker, Gurney, had published Essays on Christianity which attracted considerable attention, in which he subscribed to the dogmas of the Trinity, original sin, and imputed righteousness.[3] Thus interpreted the Quakers' belief no longer differed essentially from that of the Calvinist sects or Anglican Evangelicals. That is to say, the Quaker pride had lost its foundation. The young people, bored on Sunday mornings by the silence of the Quaker meeting, went in the afternoon to hear a Methodist or Baptist preacher. And the

---

[1] According to The Reasoner, 1851 (vol. xi, p. 87), this was the reason why there were about eleven women in the Society for every seven men.

[2] In 1832 Joseph Pease had been allowed to take his seat without having sworn the oath.

[3] Joseph John Gurney, Essays on the Evidences, Doctrines and Practical Operations of Christianity, 1825. It reached its sixth edition in 1840. A Letter on the Authority, Purpose and Effects of Christianity, 1824, by the same author, ran into twenty-five editions, and four editions of a French translation. See J. Gurney, Memoirs, 1854.

saying was current that no wealthy family, and too many Quaker families were rich, indeed extremely rich, remained faithful to the Society of Friends for more than three generations. It became merged with its Anglican environment.

3

If these were the troubles and difficulties with which about 1850 the important Wesleyan Church on the one hand, and on the other the small Unitarian and Quaker groups had to contend, how did things stand with the two large and old sects, the Baptists and Congregationalists?

Both were declining in numbers or at best at a standstill. The Baptists were in a position to measure exactly the extent of the decline. For many years ago they had overcome the prejudice against centralization of any kind, against anything which would detract from the independence of the local groups.[1] They had provided themselves with a solid organization, in a position to collect, at the annual conference of the Baptist Union, all the statistical information required by the governing body of the sect to determine its policy. The number of members of the Baptist associations, which between 1834 and 1845 had risen from 40,763 to 89,269, that is to say, had more than doubled in eleven years, fell to 85,148 in 1846, 84,362 in 1847, and 82,871 in 1848. In 1849 a slight increase was registered. But the Baptists refused to regard it as a matter for congratulation. For it was due to a revival in the South-West, from which the sect had profited, and which masked a continued decline everywhere else. The increase, however, was maintained in the following years, and the number of Baptists rose from 82,871 in 1848 to 106,448 in 1852. The Baptists, however, were not satisfied with a growth too slow in proportion to the growth of population. And there was good reason to think that the disintegration of Wesleyan Methodism about this date had caused a considerable number of Wesleyans to join other Nonconformist bodies. In 1854 the number had fallen back to 85,245, that is, practically the figure for 1846.[2] That is to say, when flow and ebb were balanced, a decade of progress

---

[1] *History of the English People*, vol. i, pp. 422-3.

[2] These figures have been taken from the *Baptist Examiner*. See, in particular, in the issue for October 1845 (vol. ii, pp. 421-3), its gloomy observations on the membership of the various Dissenting sects.

had been followed by a decade during which the sect was at a standstill.

For the Congregationalists such exact figures are lacking. For the sect was too loosely organized to obtain them.[1]

Possibly because its sole distinctive doctrine was the independence of each congregation, it was more hostile than the Baptists, distinguished also by the doctrine of adult baptism, to any centralized government. Like the latter, the Congregationalists had, it is true, been affected by the general tendency of the period and had followed, though to a comparatively slight extent, the example which the new Methodist Churches had given British Nonconformity. As we already know,[2] the Congregationalists had founded in 1831 a Union, with the same object as similar Nonconformist organizations, to improve their pastors' theological education and financial position, and, since they were no longer content with providing for the spiritual needs of existing congregations, to launch a missionary campaign throughout the country to win more souls. The next twenty-five years were devoted to the work of developing patiently the collective undertakings of the Union. Patience was needed. For it was no easy task. It had to contend with the Congregationalists' uncompromising and traditional independence. About the middle fifties the Union almost succumbed to the attacks made upon it.[3] Meanwhile, complaints were universal of the slow progress made by the sect, which was accepted as an indubitable fact, though its extent could not be measured.

How are we to explain this check to the growth of the Nonconformist sects about the middle of the century? Perhaps what we have just said of the causes, political and doctrinal, which produced the decline in the case of the Wesleyans, Unitarians, and Quakers, will help us to answer the question.

4

The progress of the Anglo-Catholic party in the Church of England and its challenging attitude might have been expected

---

[1] *The Congregational Year Book* for 1848 shows that in Great Britain and Ireland at that date there were 2,173 churches and 1,979 ministers. A. Peel, *These Hundred Years: A History of the Congregational Union of England and Wales*, 1831-1931, p. 169.

[2] *History of the English People*, vol. iii, pp. 136-7. A. Peel, *These Hundred Years*, chap. v: 'The Launching', p. 134.

[3] Ibid., chap. xi: 'Almost Wrecked', 1848-58.

to produce defections from the Church and conversions to Non-conformity. This did not happen. Why not?

Let us consider first the laity. Instances, it is true, are known in which in towns or, more often, in villages, Anglicans left a church where a Romanizing clergyman had introduced novel usages, and sat at the feet of a Nonconformist preacher, preferably a Methodist. For his doctrine and form of worship approximated most closely to the Anglican. Except indeed for his rejection of the Anglican hierarchy, his creed was the same as the Low Churchman's. But in the vast majority of cases these malcontents did not go over to Nonconformity. On Sunday morning and Sunday evening they attended the Methodist chapel. But they continued to be married and buried and had their children baptized by the clergyman of the national Church, the Church of the general public, the Church to which they felt themselves attached by roots which had struck deep. There may, indeed, have been conversions to Nonconformity due to reaction against the Tractarianism of the thirties, the Ritualism of the forties. For between 1840 and 1845 the number of Nonconformists was on the increase. It declined on the other hand or remained stationary from the moment that Newman's conversion made the Ritualists' position in the Church of England difficult, and the Evangelical opposition to Catholicism gathered strength within her communion. But it was a poor reason for leaving the Church that an individual clergyman, disowned by his brethren, disgusted his parishioners by the eccentricities of an Italianate Anglicanism. He was to blame, not the Church, which remained Protestant and was invested with an atmosphere of traditional poetry totally lacking to the stark and mean Dissenting chapels, even the Wesleyan.

We will now turn to the clergy. There were cases of clergymen who left the Church to become pastors of some Nonconformist sect. Among them was the Rev. B. W. Noel, who became one of the leading Baptists. Another was the Rev. James Shore, whose battle with the Bishop of Exeter made such a stir in 1849. The Duke of Somerset wanted to put him in charge of a chapel in the diocese he had built at his own expense. The Bishop refused to license him. Whereupon the Duke registered the chapel as a non-Anglican place of worship, where Mr. Shore would officiate with the status of a Dissenting minister. The Bishop prosecuted Mr. Shore before the Church Courts and secured a sentence of one year's imprisonment for his breach of the obligations imposed by his ordination, by thus officiating as a Nonconformist pastor. The case aroused considerable excitement and gave rise to a protracted agitation against a Prelate who enjoyed this kind of unpopularity.[1]

But these were isolated incidents. The number who went over to the enemy's camp could probably be counted on the fingers of one hand. There were, no doubt, far more pastors who joined the Established Church. And even of those few who left her some returned to the fold. Once more, what was the reason?

The explanation must be sought in the wide gulf which separated the respective social positions of the Anglican clergyman and the Nonconformist pastor. The former, as we have already pointed out, was not without its drawbacks. But they were due chiefly to the fact that too often the parson was not rich enough to keep up without countless difficulties and privations the position his benefice gave him the right to occupy. For he was a member of the ruling class. In the country the squire and he were the natural lords of the village. Between the former and the villagers, even the poorest, he was the accredited mediator. On the other hand, the pastor of a Nonconformist congregation, the walls of whose humble chapel confronted the Anglican Church on the parcel of ground, which the tolerance of the great landowner had permitted him to purchase, had no contact with the latter or with any of his circle. Nor had he contact with the working people, farm labourers or others, except those who by their deliberate choice belonged to his flock. Too frequently he had no other resources save the generosity of his congregation on whom he was financially and morally dependent. He was confined to the narrow circle of small farmers and small shopkeepers who were members of his sect. Everyone else despised or disliked him, or at best regarded him with complete indifference. If, into the bargain, he were a new convert, who had left the Established Church, he was made to feel that the members of the sect he had joined, even his fellow pastors, were unsympathetic and suspicious. For he was an intruder, whose upbringing had been very different from theirs. His family tradition and the pieties of his

[1] Thomas Binney, *Conscientious Clerical Nonconformity: with Introductory Remarks on the Imputed Conduct of the Bishop of Exeter, in the Cases of the Rev. J. Shore and the Rev. G. C. Gorham*, 1848.

childhood had not been Methodist, Baptist, or Congregationalist.[1] If he had not been queer he would not have joined them. There was no knowing where his vagaries might not take him. Other clergymen who had broken with the Church had founded new and extreme sects without a clergy to serve them, sects like the Plymouth Brethren, or the strange sect founded by the former Presbyterian minister, Edward Irving.[2]

5

This distrust of religious eccentricity expressed the character of Dissent in the middle of the nineteenth century. It had something of the chill of the older Dissent, before the storm of the Wesleyan revival had shaken it from its slumber. It was becoming bureaucratic and intellectual. Bunting, as we have said, gave Wesleyan Methodism a theological college. It was a proof that he did not consider the summary training which was all preachers had received hitherto, a sufficient preparation for the pastoral office. It was no longer enough to teach Jesus Christ crucified or rather the art of stirring the masses by bringing Him vividly before the imagination. In a Church increasingly organized, the pastorate was becoming more and more a regular profession which required an organized theological education. Open-air preaching was now a thing of the past. And those little groups for mutual edification which Wesley had called classes and had made the living cells of the vast body he had founded, were losing their importance, were, indeed, doomed finally to disappear altogether. The rebels of 1849 were therefore justified in their rejoinder to Bunting's claim that he was defending the order established by Wesley, that in several respects he was destroying it, and that Methodism, as it was, was no longer Methodism as it had been. But what was true of Wesleyanism was even truer of the other sects which had been affected only indirectly by the Wesleyans' emotional piety.

The influence of this emotional religion had brought about at the close of the eighteenth century the decay of the Academies

---

[1] Robert Vaughan, *Essays*, vol. i, p. 130. John Forster to Sir C. E. Smith, March 9, 1840 (*The Life and Correspondence of John Forster*, 1846, vol. ii, pp. 382-3).

[2] The Plymouth Brethren had been founded by the Rev. J. N. Darby. See Teulon, *History and Doctrines of the Plymouth Brethren*, 1883. Edward Irving, expelled from the Church of Scotland, had founded in 1832 a 'Holy Catholic Apostolic Church', whose headquarters is the Church in Gordon Square.

which had once been the boast of English Nonconformity.[1] But they were now being revived under new names, inferior no doubt to the old Academies, but far superior to the little schools of emotional preaching which had satisfied Nonconformity at the beginning of the century.[2]

Over these institutions and over the press—weekly or quarterly—with which Dissent equipped itself about the same time presided what the malcontents in the lower ranks of Nonconformity called ironically 'the aristocracy of Dissent'. Robert Vaughan and Edward Baines wrote books of high quality, valued even outside Dissenting circles, and which would have been even more successful had their authors been Anglican clergymen. Occasional articles published in the *Eclectic Review* during its best years reached the standard of the *Edinburgh* or *Quarterly*. These intellectual aristocrats of Nonconformity, thoroughly conscious of their own superiority, flattered by the hearing they obtained outside the frontiers of their sect and eager to extend it still further, made a point of dissociating themselves from the fanatical democracy of Dissent. They were well aware that, although Liberalism had penetrated every Congregationalist institution, the Church of England did not recognize the fact and persisted, not altogether without reason, in regarding herself, in spite of her noisy Anglo-Catholics, as more Liberal than the sects which prided themselves on their Liberalism. Accordingly they refused to identify themselves with the propaganda of the extreme sectarian fanatics and support these self-appointed champions of a free Anglican Church.[3] What good purpose would it serve to separate Church and State, if the former were prepared to tolerate all forms of Christianity and even the Jews? Nor should all proposals put forward for a system of State-sponsored popular education meet with an uncompromising rejection, simply because the Church sought to exercise a measure of control over it.

Their moderation was opposed by those who for some years past had become known as the Political Dissenters, who sought by unintermittent political propaganda to regenerate and thus

[1] *History of the English People*, vol. i, p. 418.

[2] For these educational establishments, see A. Peel, *These Hundred Years*, p. 286, also a monograph which was the prize essay in a competition organized by the Congregationalists, entitled *Jethro: A System of Lay Agency in connexion with Congregational Churches for the Diffusion of the Gospel among our Home Population*, 1839.

[3] For the views of Baines and Vaughan on the relations between Church and State, see my *History of the English People*, vol. iii, pp. 209-210.

strengthen British Radicalism. In 1841 Edward Miall founded his famous weekly *The Nonconformist*[1] to defend against this luke-warmness 'The Dissidence of Dissent and the Protestantism of the Protestant Religion'. And shortly afterwards he drove Vaughan from the editorial chair of the *Eclectic Review* and replaced him by Dr. Price.[2] But the success Miall achieved and the noise made by his polemics were as dangerous to Protestant Evangelicalism as Vaughan's intellectual Liberalism. Readers of this excellent periodical will look in vain for an article of mystical aspiration or religious meditation. Under colour of making war against clericalism, embodied in the worship of the Establishment, it spoke of nothing but free trade, the franchise, and the individual's political rights, and thus, instead of making Radicalism Christian it ended by secularizing Christianity.[3] A reaction was overdue, as much against Miall's Radicalism as Vaughan's moderation.

A Congregationalist pastor, John Campbell, nicknamed the Son of Thunder,[4] began his career by conducting a series of campaigns to obtain for the Congregationalists the possession of certain Methodist chapels in London. He had already founded Nonconformist periodicals, notorious for their virulent polemics, the *Christian Witness* and the *Christian's Penny Magazine*. In 1847 he started a weekly, the *British Banner*. It appeared every Saturday to combat what Campbell regarded as the pernicious influence of the Sunday papers. It had 16 pages and 64 columns and cost 4d. This was the usual format, size, and price of a Sunday newspaper. Like these, it discussed all topical questions, and it professed the political opinions of Nonconformity. But its avowed object was to fight against the prevalent infidelity and revive Evangelical orthodoxy. Campbell's ambition was to reach a circulation of

---

[1] The first number appeared on April 14, 1841. Miall denounced the 'sensitive reluc-tance' to offend 'shown by a secti n of Dissent' a little compact ambition to behave as 'respectable, well-trained gentlemanly members of society', and concluded, 'Theirs is the *ne plus ultra* of passivity of spirit' (A. Miall, *Life of Edward Miall*, pp. 68-9).

[2] H. U. Faulkner, *Chartism and the Churches*, pp. 98-9: 'The aim of Dr. Price was to win the mass of the people by advocating their cause in relation to political rights.' Vaughan and his supporters founded in their turn the *British Quarterly Review*.

[3] See Edward Miall, *The Politics of Christianity, reprinted from 'The Nonconformist'*, 1847-8 (1863).

[4] A. Peel, *These Hundred Years*, p. 129: 'He was truly a son of thunder, and storms naturally gathered round him.' For Campbell's political attitude, see H. U. Faulkner, *Chartism and the Churches*, p. 100: 'While believing there was no great discontent in the country, he was willing to advocate a reformation of the House of Lords and triennial Parliaments. Universal suffrage, however, was entirely out of question; the utmost that could 'rationally be expected or prudently desired', said he, 'is household suffrage'.

100,000. Though he did not achieve it, the circulation reached 60,000, a figure unprecedented in the history of Nonconformist journalism. His success won him considerable influence in Dissenting circles, and he finally wielded behind the scenes an authority parallel with that exercised by the official organs of Congregationalism.

No pastor, in fact, whom he thought undesirable could be elected. As the years passed the extent of his sway increased, until it provoked a crisis. For the moment, however, his activities were an influential protest against the relaxation of the Evangelical spirit in the sects, the dangerous growth of rationalism, and what may be termed political secularization.[1]

6

In 1854 the Nonconformists drew comfort from the publication of the results of the religious census held in 1851 on the occasion of the general census.[2] No attempt was made to discover the denominational allegiance of individuals. When ten years later such a census was mooted, the Nonconformists were up in arms. For they knew how unfavourable the result must prove for them. All the indifferent, all those who practised no form of worship would, with rare exceptions, declare themselves out of apathy members of the Establishment. But Palmerston had proposed a complete census of the places of worship belonging to the various denominations and of those who attended any of these churches or chapels on a particular Sunday selected at random. His proposal had been carried out and, though for the first time, very efficiently. The results were extremely favourable to the Nonconformists.

The Census returns showed 34,467 places of worship, seating 10,212,563. But of this total only 14,077 places of worship, seating 5,317,915, belonged to the Established Church. That is to say, of the total sittings not more than 52 per cent, a little over half, were Anglican. And the same proportion obtained as regards the number of persons who had attended a place of worship on March 30, 1851, 3,773,474 of the total 7,261,032. In particular regions the results were even more unfavourable to the Establishment. In

[1] For Campbell's career, see the sermon preached by Robert Ferguson at his funeral in 1867.
[2] *Census of Great Britain*, 1851. *Religious Worship—England and Wales*, 1853. See further the study of the Census in the *Congregational Year Book for* 1854, pp. 33 sqq.

Lancashire there were only 529 Anglican places of worship, seating 383,466, as against 1,098 places of worship belonging to other denominations, seating 407,408; in Yorkshire, 1,143 places of worship, seating 423,966, as against 2,273, seating 582,190;[1] in Wales, 979 places of worship as against 2,498, sittings for 236,630 as against sittings for 541,572. The figures for church attendance in Wales gave similar results: at the morning service 83,089 Anglicans as against 247,394, at the afternoon service 40,525 as against 134,835, at the evening service 31,452 as against 324,859.[2]

Nor were the Anglicans left the consolation that as time went on their position was improving. For the official figures seemed to prove that the opposite was the case. During the past century 2,698 Anglican churches and chapels had been built with 1,028,032 sittings as against 16,689 non-Anglican places of worship with 4,013,408 sittings.[3] Evidently the Established Church could hardly be called the Church of the nation. Soon she would have no title whatever to be regarded as such. Statistics justified the advocates of disestablishment.

Her position seemed even more unfavourable when her worshippers were compared not with those other Protestant denominations, nor even with all the denominations taken together, but with the population as a whole. Her 5,317,915 sittings did not represent quite 30 per cent of the population. And the 3,773,474 persons who on March 30 had worshipped at her services were little more than 20 per cent. This proportion, however, was by no means an unqualified triumph for the Dissenters. For its significance was double-edged. If to this number of Anglican worshippers we add the number of those attending non-Anglican worship, the result is still far from satisfactory. According to Mann, the official statistician, when infants, the sick, the infirm, and those prevented by some professional reason from attendance were left out of account, the possible number of regular Sunday worshippers amounted to 58 per cent of the population. But there were three services every Sunday and the 58 per cent could not have been equally divided between them. A good 70 per cent of

---

[1] A previous investigation carried out by Edward Baines in the manufacturing districts had shown that there were sittings in the Churches for about half the population (Edward Baines, *The Social Educational and Religious State of the Manufacturing Districts, with Statistical returns of the Means of Education and Religious Instruction in the Manufacturing Districts of Yorkshire, Lancashire and Cheshire*, 1843).

[2] *Census . . . Religious Worship*, pp. 233-4.

[3] Ibid., pp. 131 and 140.

the possible worshippers must certainly have attended one of the three. Let us, however, accept for the sake of argument the proportion of 58 per cent. It should have involved the attendance at Divine worship of 10,398,013 persons. In fact, on that Sunday, March 30, 1851, there were no more than 4,647,482 attendances in the morning, 3,184,135 in the afternoon, 3,064,449 in the evening. Over half of those who should have attended had stayed away. And for this state of things the Dissenters must share the responsibility with the Anglicans.[1]

The number of available sittings, it is true, was almost sufficient for 58 per cent of the population. It was, in fact, little more than one per cent less. When, however, we distinguish between town and country it is clear that the position was very different. In the country there was a positive superfluity of sittings. Nor was this due only to the large number of parish churches. Though the Nonconformists were more or less resigned to concentrating their efforts on the towns and leaving the countryside to the alliance of squire and parson, they observed to their satisfaction that, even in the country, their zeal had proved far more effective against the traditional Anglican monopoly than they had expected. And in the small towns dependent on the surrounding country the provision for public worship was adequate. But in the great urban agglomerations it was glaringly inadequate. In Sheffield there were sittings for only 33.9 per cent of the inhabitants, in Manchester for 31.6 per cent, in Liverpool for 31.4 per cent, in Birmingham for 28.7 per cent, in London for 29.7 per cent.[2]

The contrast was striking between the large number of city churches and the extremely inadequate provision of places of worship in working-class districts. But even in the centre of the capital there were sittings for no more than a third of the population.[3]

Everyone was ready to agree that the Church had failed to make provision for the vast influx of people into the large towns.

---

[1] Census . . . Religious Worship, pp. 120 sqq. and 151.

[2] Ibid., p. 129. In London there were 504,914 attendances; 276,685 Anglicans, 186,321 Dissenting, 36,334 Catholic, and 5,374 of other denominations. See The Times, January 7, 1854.

[3] This was the conclusion reached by the inquiry, whose results were published by the Congregationalists under the title, Jethro: A System of Lay Agency in connexion with Congregational Churches for the Diffusion of the Gospel among our Home Population, 1839. See above, p. 389, note 2. See also Congregational Magazine, June 1838, N.S., vol., ii, pp. 325 sqq., and January 1839, vol. iii, pp. 30 sqq.

But the Nonconformists cherished the belief, whose supposed truth was admitted and lamented in Anglican circles, that the gap had been filled by the Dissenting sects. Plainly this was very far from the case.

7

The Nonconformist sects were not Churches of the proletariat. The only Nonconformists who set out to evangelize the working classes were the Methodists. It was in the open air that Wesley and his first followers had reached the weavers and miners, and Wesley had instituted by the side of his regularly ordained ministers, 'lay preachers', unpaid assistants of the latter in their work of preaching, whose unofficial character would reassure their audiences and bridge the gap between the pastors and their flocks. There were roughly 20,000 of these preachers belonging to the Wesleyan and other Methodist bodies about the middle of the century. But did they not leave the masses to join either in person or in the persons of their children the lower middle class, and did not their converts in turn gravitate to the lower middle class? And what of the other sects?

A member of the Society of Friends tells us that when he became engaged to a girl who did not belong to it he resigned his own membership. At first, on his persuasion, his fiancée had determined to apply for admission into the Society. But he had finally come to the conclusion that his most honourable course was to resign. One of his reasons for marrying outside the Society was prudential. For the daughters of Friends were brought up to expect a wealth, ease, and luxury not in keeping with the life of an artisan.

No doubt the Quakers were distinguished by their notorious wealth from the other sects who were inclined to scoff at it. But the latter were by no means poor Churches themselves. The arrangement of their chapels, the division between the rented sittings and the free seats, above all the fact that only those who rented a sitting had the right to vote on the affairs of the congregation, combined to make the poor when they sat down humbly in the worst seats in the chapel, feel that they were to all intents and purposes strangers.[1] The Baptists, it is true, and the

[1] Here in Great Britain we carry our class distinctions into the House of God. We have no negro pews, for we have no prejudice against colour—but we have distinct

Congregationalists[1] had attempted to copy the Methodist mission to the lower classes, but it was but a simulacrum and their Home Missions gave poor results.[2] 'So long as their zeal fires them,' a French observer wrote, 'the Protestant sects can still make converts, but by violating not charming souls. . . . Where this uncultured enthusiasm is extinct society is cut literally into two. Take your stand in Briggate Street, Leeds, in Mosley Street, Manchester, in Lord or Dale Street in Liverpool. What kind of families are they you observe walking to a church in silence and with a devout mien? There can be no mistake about it. They belong almost exclusively to the middle class. The workers stand on their doorsteps or collect in groups until the time when service is over and the public houses open. Religion presents itself to them in such sombre colours and with so harsh an aspect and refuses so consistently to speak to the senses, imagination or heart, that it is not surprising that it remains the patrimony and privilege of the well-to-do and treats the poor man as a pariah.'[3]

If, therefore, the influence of Nonconformity had contributed to paralyse the efforts of revolutionary Chartism, it had not been by making the life of the proletariat Christian. Had it done so, Protestantism might have assumed a revolutionary form, as in other days it had done in England and in Germany. But by becoming the religion of the middle classes it had separated the latter, not only the upper middle, but the lower and the lowest middle class, from the common people and had deprived the latter of the leaders they required to wage the war against the rich which they wanted to wage. Deprived of leaders, the populace fell back into a state of incoherence, demoralization, and at last apathy. From one point of view, indeed, there was greater hostility between the lower middle class and the proletariat than between

places for the penniless, for we have a morbid horror of poverty (E. Miall, *British Churches in relation to the British People*, 1849, p. 201). See also J. L. and B. Hammond, *The Age of the Chartists*, pp. 243 sqq.

[1] 'We (the Congregationalists) are generally reputed to be a respectable body; in learning and intelligence second only to the Establishment; in the average quality of our preaching, somewhat above it; chiefly composed of the middle classes; in Christian activity and benevolence proportionally second to none; generally liberal though not extreme in our sentiments; altogether a very decent, great, respectable people' (G. W. Conder, *Congregationalism and Modern Church Movements*, 1856).

[2] 'The dissenting clergy, with a few noble exceptions among the Independents, are not the strong men of the day—none knew that better than the workmen' (Ch. Kingsley, *Alton Locke*, p. 30).

[3] L. Faucher, *Etudes sur l'Angleterre*, 1845, vol. i, pp. 351-2. On the passage in Faucher, see J. L. and B. Hammond, *The Age of the Chartists*, p. 241, note 3.

the proletariat and the upper class. For to the latter the working class was a mysterious world of whose sufferings its members knew little. But they were disposed to look with indulgence on the gross pleasures of the masses, so long as they kept them contented. The member of the lower middle class, on the other hand, knew the workers only too well. He or his father had risen from their ranks. He had risen by hard work. He was twice 'saved', if, in addition, he belonged to a religious sect, saved by his faith in himself and saved by his faith in God, saved in the temporal and saved in the spiritual order. Let the others follow his example and save themselves as he had done. If not, so much the worse for them. They deserved their hell.[1]

It is not, therefore, surprising that, during the past decade, the Nonconformists had shown so little enthusiasm for the cause of the workers. They had agitated for the abolition of slavery in the colonies. But the annual discussions of the Baptist or Congregationalist Union showed no interest whatever in legislation to improve the conditions of labour. For this was a case not of emancipation but legal protection, and their ingrained individualism was as stubbornly opposed to any interference by the State with labour as to its intervention in the field of education.[2]

We have noticed already the policy of *The Nonconformist*. The same outlook appears in the prospectus in which the *British Banner* expounded its policy. It would be the programme supported by the great body of English Nonconformists, Liberal in the widest acceptation of the term, but reasonable, free from anything doctrinaire, extravagant or visionary. They would never be weary of insisting that national regeneration could be achieved only by the regeneration of individuals. In the economic sphere they would defend the rights of labour, but they would not be afraid to maintain that capital also has rights as well as duties. The programme of the Young England Group was in many respects artificial, theatrical, and superficial. Nevertheless, they showed more understanding of the workers' claims when they invited the ruling class to be reconciled with the poor and form a common front with

---

[1] For the relations between the Chartists and religion, see H. U. Faulkner, *Chartism and the Churches*, pp. 12, 17, and 18.

[2] A. Peel (*These Hundred Years*, pp. 105 sqq.) remarks on the indifference to such questions shown by the Congregationalists. In 1839 Nonconformity was equally uninterested in the temperance campaign with which only the Quakers and Anglicans concerned themselves, and which was also opposed by the *British Banner*. See E. Thomas Beggs, *Teetotallers and Teetotalism: A Letter to the Rev. Dr. Campbell*, 1854.

them against the selfishness of the lower middle class. And although the names they bestowed on the schools and churches they built for the benefit of the destitute, 'ragged' schools and 'ragged' churches, was patronizing, illiberal, and humiliating, the social policy pursued by such Anglicans as Lord Ashley was inspired by a more realistic understanding of the immediate needs of the proletariat than the programme of the Dissenting Evangelicals.

The Nonconformists, the Congregationalists in particular, had not waited for the publication of the religious census of 1851 to take alarm at the divorce between their sects and the working class. In October 1848 the annual meeting of the Congregational Union had given the problem its anxious consideration and heard three papers on the subject.[1] Miall opened the correspondence columns of *The Nonconformist* to letters from workmen whom he asked to explain the reasons why the Protestantism of the Dissenting sects had so little hold on the masses. And he delivered a series of lectures at the City of London Literary Institute which were collected and published towards the end of 1849 under the title *The British Churches in Relation to the British People*. To combat the indifference of the lower classes to religion, he advised that full use should be made of lay preachers, pew rents abolished,[2] and the Gospel preached, not only in regular places of worship, but in public assembly rooms of all kinds, and, on the other hand, that places of worship should be used for non-religious but charitable purposes and meetings arranged to attract the workers which would not be distinctively religious in character.[3] This secularization of Christianity roused the ire of Campbell's orthodox Evangelicalism. He charged Miall with founding 'a school of anarchy' and making the Anti-State-Church Association the instrument of his political ambitions, and resigned from it.

How far the recovery of British Dissent a few years later was

[1] *Thoughts on the need for increased efforts to promote the Religious Welfare of the Working Classes in England by the Independent Churches and their Pastors*: read by the Rev. A. Wells (*Congregational Year Book*, 1848, pp. 80 sqq.). *By what means we can, as a body of Christians, best promote the Religious Good of the Working Classes*: read by Edw. Swaine, Esq. (ibid., pp. 91 sqq.). *How far have the Labouring Classes, especially of mechanical occupations, become interested in our religious movements and identified with Nonconformists: and how can their sympathy be increased or perpetuated for the prosperity of our Church*: read by Rev. Dr. Mass (ibid., p. 100).

[2] See above, p. 394.

[3] A. Miall, *Life of Edward Miall*, pp. 151 sqq. Preface to Edward Miall's book, *The British Churches in Relation to the British People*, pp. III sqq.

due to the methods advocated by Miall, or to the Evangelical revival demanded by Campbell, we must consider hereafter. For the present we must be content with calling attention to the anxiety prevalent in the leading circles of Nonconformity about 1850, or rather on the morrow of 1848. For although the crisis was settled so peacefully in England—in fact, when we view the situation in the right perspective, it is clear that, strictly speaking, there was no crisis—we have seen how terrified the middle classes were that April and subsequently.

The alarm was intensified in religious circles by the fact that a very active and methodically organized anti-religious propaganda was at work among the working class, which bade fair to become eventually a serious rival to the preaching of the sects and the Church alike.

IV THE GROWTH OF SECULARISM

I

This new campaign against religion originated in 'Socialist' or, in other words, co-operative circles.[1]

The most significant event in this secularist movement was the foundation by Holyoake in 1846 of a weekly, the *Reasoner*.[2]

It was in the order of things that the initiative should be taken by a disciple of Owen's. For Owen had based his 'new moral world' on a mechanical arrangement of the passions which was a deliberate rejection of Christian morality. Nevertheless, the founders of the *Reasoner* did not place their periodical under his patronage. At the time of its foundation they were displeased with the man who should have been their hero. For he had abandoned a Communist experiment called Harmony, which many of Holyoake's friends, his collaborators in founding the *Reasoner*, had

---

[1] For this movement, see in particular the writings of George Jacob Holyoake: *Christianity and Secularism*, 1854, and *The Logic of Death*, 1849 (written during a cholera epidemic). On Holyoake, see Charles de Remusat, 'Des Controverses Religieuses en Angleterre' (*Revue des Deux-Mondes*, September 15, 1856, vol. v, p. 503). See further, Ioseph Barker, *Confessions of a Convert from Christianity*, 1858; Rev. J. Gregory, *Modern Atheism or The Pretensions of Secularism Examined*, 1852; Rev. J. H. Hinton, *Secular Tracts*, 1853; Rev. F. Meyrick, *The Outcast and the Poor of London*, 1858, pp. 91 sqq.

[2] The motto prefixed to the first number was a quotation from Sir James Mackintosh: 'It is time that men should tolerate nothing ancient that reason does not respect, and shrink from no novelty to which reason may conduct.'

helped to finance.[1] And there was some reason to believe that his motive in doing so had been his persistent dislike of the revolutionary and democratic ideas which he feared his followers might adopt. He was at present travelling in America, calling for a united effort by all classes to solve the social problem and even appealing to the Christians with whom he professed himself in fundamental agreement.

It was a medallion portrait of Bentham which made its appearance on the title page of the *Reasoner*, at the moment, unpropitious for such a step when under the influence of the events of 1848 it adopted the sub-title: *A Weekly Journal, Utilitarian, Republican and Communist*.[2] From one point of view Bentham was an appropriate patron. The violent pamphlets against Christianity which he had published anonymously thirty years earlier had not been forgotten. But the choice did not mean that Holyoake and his friends entertained relations with the remnant of his disciples. About 1820 his friends had been appalled by the virulence of his anti-Christian sentiments, and those who in their youth had shared his violence, ripened now by age, though as anti-Christian as ever, were careful not to make a frontal attack on religion or Christianity. 'To present positivism in open conflict with religion of any kind,' Mill wrote to Auguste Comte, 'is perhaps the one way of presenting it, which, in my opinion, it would be most inopportune to employ in England to-day. Under existing circumstances, I believe, those who write for the English public should say nothing directly about religion, while making as many indirect attacks on religious beliefs as they have an opportunity to make.'[3]

Moreover, though Holyoake and his supporters revived the secularist tradition of Benthamism, they avoided the virulent

---

[1] The Communist community at Queenwood (Hampshire), where Owen had repeated the experiment made in America by the Community called *The New Harmony*.

[2] On the twenty-seventh number published in May 1847 the title had been already altered. It read: *The Reasoner and Utilitarian Record*. But it was not until the seventy-ninth number, in 1848, that it bore the sub-title given in the text with Bentham's portrait, and the motto: 'They who believe that they have the Truth ask no favour save that of being heard. . . . Refused Co-operation, they invoke Opposition, for Opposition is their Opportunity.'

[3] *Lettres inédites de John Stuart Mill à Auguste Comte*, published by L. Lévy-Bruhl, 1899: letter written July 8, 1845 (p. 447). See also a letter of April 3, 1844 (p. 307): 'The time has not come when it is possible without prejudice to our cause to make open attacks in England upon theology, even Christian. All we can do is to pass it by quietly, leaving it out of all philosophical or sociological discussions and refusing to discuss any question distinctively theological.'

language which had marked Bentham's attacks on religion. Their line of attack was far more restrained. Instead of attacking religion directly, they were content to argue that whether true or false, it should be left on one side as useless. They advocated not only a separation of Church and State, in which the Dissenting pietists would have agreed with them, but the separation of religion from education and morality, in short, the secularization of society. Accordingly, they called themselves 'secularists', a term which Holyoake invented and which caught on.[1]

Holyoake was a missionary pure and simple.

He never claimed to be anything more and there does not appear to have been any thinker behind the group. The fact remains, however, that, at this juncture, Continental free thought invaded England, like some exotic plant, which would never fully acclimatize itself in the land of Wesley.

Auguste Comte, whose *Cours de Philosophie Positive* had just been translated into English, was known in England and possibly taken more seriously than in France.[2]

The influence of George Sand's novels and French anti-clericalism is undoubtedly visible in the youthful Fróude's revolutionary novel *The Nemesis of Faith*.[3] And Michelet's fulminations against the Jesuits found an echo in England, where they confirmed the fears of a Lord John Russell or an Edward Miall.[4]

German influences, however, appear to have been stronger: Feuerbach and, above all, D. F. Strauss. The latter's *Life of Jesus* excited the admiration of Charles Hennell, who had himself published a few years before an *Enquiry into the Origins of Christianity* by his brother-in-law, Charles Bray. And the translation of Strauss's book which Miss Brabant began on her marriage to Hennell was completed by Miss Evans (George Eliot).[5] Published at a low price and widely circulated, it

[1] After running for fourteen years the *Reasoner* became a monthly, the *Counsellor*, which in 1862 was absorbed in its turn by the *National Reformer*. Holyoake became its chief editor. See *Westminster Review*, January 1862, art. iii, 'The Religious Heresies of the Working Classes' (vol. xxii, p. 86).

[2] The *Cours de Philosophie Positive* was translated in 1847, by G. H. Lewes—*Lettres de John Stuart Mill à Auguste Comte* (1899); August 23, 1844, April 26 and June 21, 1845, pp. 346, 415, and 427.　　　　　　　　　　　　　　　[3] *The Nemesis of Faith*, 1848.

[4] Michelet, *Priests, Women and Families*, 1846. The work ran to eighteen editions.

[5] Miss Evans's translations appeared in 1846 (*Life of George Eliot*, vol. i, pp. 100 and 152-3).

became the subject of a widespread controversy, in which the young workman who was the hero of Kingsley's *Alton Locke* took part.[1]

At this point M. Halévy intended to study the conflict between Christianity and Science at the Universities of Oxford and Cambridge at the time when the appointment of Commissions raised the question of University reform.

2

'It is a dishonourable characteristic of the present age', the Unitarian leader, James Martineau, wrote at the beginning of 1846, 'that on its most marked intellectual tendencies is impressed a character of *Fear*. While its great practical agitations exhibit a progress towards some positive and attainable good, all its conspicuous movements of thought seem to be mere retreats from some apprehended evil.'[2] This evil, this alarming foe against whose assaults the defence was entrenching itself, was science. The conflict between the Christian tradition on the one hand and the progress of science on the other is undoubtedly the outstanding feature of the intellectual and spiritual history of the West in modern times. Religion no longer asserts her truth as something to be taken for granted. She pleads her cause before a hostile tribunal. She has become, to use the current phrase, apologetic.

The object of the Bridgewater Treatises which, in accordance with the terms of Lord Bridgewater's will, were to be selected for publication by four clergymen and four doctors of medicine to be appointed for the purpose by the Archbishop of Canterbury and the President of the Royal Society was to demonstrate 'the Power, Wisdom and Goodness of God as manifested in the creation'. Among other arguments they must employ must be 'the variety and formation of God's creatures, in the animal, vegetable and mineral kingdoms, the effect of Digestion, the construction of the hand of Man'.[3] In other words, they must reconcile Christian doctrine with the conclusions of modern physiology. Chalmers, Buckland, Whewell, and Babbage had

[1] *Eclectic Review*, March 1846, art. x, 'The Straussian Controversy'. Ch. Kingsley, *Alton Locke*, ed. 1852, p. 276.
[2] James Martineau, *Miscellanies*, p. 162. An article which appeared in the *Prospective Review*, February, 1846.
[3] *Edinburgh Review* (vol. lviii, pp. 422 sqq.), art. entitled 'The Bridgewater Bequest'. Lord Bridgewater died in 1829.

contributed more or less directly to the series.[1] Martineau, however, in the article from which we have just quoted, would seem
to have misconceived the true nature of the effect on western
thought of this sentiment of intellectual fear. As he saw it, through
the fault of the clergy, and in consequence of this novel desire to
find a safe rather than a true belief, this intellectual cowardice saw
itself confronted, as a natural reaction against it, by a state of
indifference to all religious belief. This might be true of Catholic
Europe. But it certainly was not true of Protestant. Martineau
had been unduly impressed by the noise made in the Anglican
Church by a group of Tractarians. 'The history of the past errors
of our parent Church', Babbage wrote in his Bridgewater treatise,
'supplies us with a lesson of caution which ought not to be lost
by its reformed successors. The fact that the venerable Galileo was
compelled publicly to deny on bended knee a truth of which he
had the most convincing demonstration remains as a beacon to
all aftertime.'[2]

We do not propose to describe the state of the sciences in England about 1850. We shall not speak of Faraday or Joule. For their
researches were in a field of science unconnected with theology,
and our concern at present is with the relations, the hostile relations, between religion and science. We shall not even discuss the
general question of miracles, though it is a question with which
religion and science are most intimately concerned. For it is a
permanent issue. And it was not the issue on which controversy
turned in England about the middle of last century.[3]

3

It was when science became history, was or claimed to be a
cosmogony, that the English were painfully surprised to discover
how wide was the gulf between the scientists' picture of the origin
of the universe and that depicted in the Bible. According to the
latter the story of the world began with its creation in six days,

---

[1] Th. Chalmers, On the Adaptation of External Nature to the Moral and Intellectual Constitution of Man. William Buckland, On Geology and Mineralogy. Whewell, On Astronomy
and General Physics. Charles Babbage had added to the series of Treatises a supplementary
volume, The Ninth Bridgewater Treatise: A Fragment, 1837.

[2] Charles Babbage, The Ninth Bridgewater Treatise: A Fragment, 1837, p. 80.

[3] Babbage, however, the inventor of a calculating machine, made it the foundation
of an ingenious argument, which attracted a certain amount of attention, to prove the
impossibility of a determinist explanation of the universe as the product of blind forces
(The Ninth Bridgewater Treatise, p. 133).

continued with the death on the Cross of the Son of God, and would conclude with the final revelation of God to damn and save and the absorption of earth by heaven. According to the former our world began as a primordial nebula and would conclude with the reign of mankind on earth, under the sway throughout of a rigid determinism unbroken from beginning to end by a single miracle. In this respect two books in particular, some twenty years earlier, had burst as bombs upon the intellectual world.

The first of these was Lyell's *Geology*, the first edition of which had been published in 1830 and which had gone into a large number of editions by 1852. Its title, quoted here in full, summarized the entire thesis of the book: 'Principles of Geology. Being an attempt to explain the former Changes of the Earth's Surface by reference to Causes now in Operation.'[1] Lyell, that is to say, postulated no extraordinary intervention, no miracle.

The geological record, however, could not be discussed without raising the question of the origin of species.[2]

Did they owe their origin to a miracle, the arbitrary product of the Creator's fiat? Such a view was repugnant to reason. Should their successive appearance be explained by the transformation of previously existing species? As yet, science was unable to answer. Lyell, though he tried to account for the extinction of species by the action of natural causes, dared not explain in the same way how others had originated and might in future originate. But he was so obviously looking for a rational explanation of the origin of species, on similar lines to the explanation he gave and proved to the satisfaction of the public mind of the changes which had taken place in the earth's surface, that theologians could not fail to suspect him of what they regarded as the most serious of heresies. If the Biblical account of the special creation of species was no longer to be accepted literally, it would be no longer

[1] Vol. i (1830), vol. ii (1832), vol. iii (1833). Lyell also published, in 1838, *Elements of Geology*, of which a second edition appeared in 1842, a third in 1851.

[2] For discussions of this question, see J. Pye Smith, *On the Relation between the Holy Scriptures and some parts of Geological Science*, 1839. On the other hand, reverence for the Biblical tradition led James Cowles Pritchard to transformism, *The Natural History of Man: Comprising Enquiries into the Modifying Influence of Physical and Moral Agencies on the Different Tribes of the Human Family*, 1843, which sought to prove that the races of mankind are varieties of a single species. See also the works of the Rev. W. Whewell, *History of the Inductive Sciences*, 1837, and *The Philosophy of the Inductive Sciences founded upon their History*, 1840, vol. ii, p. 137: 'It is not only an interruption, but an abyss, which interposes itself between us and any intelligible beginning of things.'

possible to believe in the special creation of the first man and the first woman. Man was no longer nature's miracle. In spite of his cautious disclaimers, Lyell found himself in the end charged, not unfairly, with holding this evolutionary view.[1]

His young disciple, Darwin, already an eminent scientist, famous not only for the help his geological researches had given to Lyell, but for his original application of his master's ideas to other problems, had composed in the seclusion of his study—in 1850 he had been working on the subject for over ten years—a complete explanation of the evolution of species on Lyell's lines. But the work was kept secret, its existence known to nobody, and would remain a secret for several years to come. It was another book which broke to the world the shocking truth. It was the *Vestiges of the Natural History of Creation*, published anonymously by its cautious author in 1844. For his name was never disclosed in his lifetime.[2] The book has fallen into a well-merited oblivion. For its scientific documentation, in the earlier editions above all, was grossly inadequate. But it was well written and well planned, and its enormous success, totally unexpected by the author, shows how ripe the times were for the novel idea.[3]

It became a storm-centre, the subject of refutations proportionate in number and virulence to its success. Rather surprisingly, to lay the scene of its speculations in the centre of the universe, it began by expounding the theory of Laplace. In a subsequent edition the author explained that it was the study of this theory which had led him, as he reflected on the uniformity of natural laws, to his views on the transformation of species.[4] At this weak point his opponents attacked. In 1845 Sir John Herschel took the

---

[1] Lyell was careful to write, p. 3 (1847 edition): 'An attempt will be made in the sequel of this work to demonstrate that geology differs as widely from cosmogony as speculations concerning the mode of the first creation of man differ from history.' See also his *Lectures on Geology* given in New York in 1842, p. 42. He wrote, however, to Whewell, on March 7, 1837: 'If I had stated as plainly as he [Herschel] has done, the possibility of the introduction or origination of fresh species by a natural, in contradistinction to a miraculous process, I should have raised a host of prejudices against me which are, unfortunately, opposed at every step to any philosopher who attempts to address the public on these mysterious subjects.' See further, his letter to Sedgwick, January 20, 1838: 'I have admitted that we have only data for *Extinctions*, and I have left it rather to be inferred, instead of enunciating it ever as my opinion, that the place of lost species is filled up (as it was of old) from time to time by new species' (*Life of Lyell*, vol. ii, pp. 5 and 36).

[2] The author's name (he was the publisher Robert Chambers) was revealed only in 1884 in the preface to the twelfth edition.

[3] *Vestiges of the Natural History of Creation*, 1844. The book reached its tenth edition in 1853.

[4] Preface to the tenth edition.

field against him at a meeting of the British Association, and shortly afterwards Sedgwick published a venomous criticism in the *Edinburgh Review*.[1]

Immediately after the meeting at which Herschel spoke, a simple-minded Baptist exclaimed: 'Cuvier refuted Buffon. Herschel has silenced Laplace.'[2] Had Herschel silenced Laplace? If Cuvier could boast of refuting Buffon and even Lamarck, he had certainly not silenced Geoffroy Saint-Hilaire, and now when the *Vestiges* was published in London its success was enormous. The author was content with maintaining that organisms had a tendency to change in order to adapt themselves to their environment. He did not explain this adaptation by the action of the environment, but was content to affirm transmutation as a fact without attempting to explain it. Darwin, however, would pay tribute to the *Vestiges* and the good influence it exerted;[3] and some writers had already reached the conclusion that, after all, it might perhaps be absurd to regard transformism as an irreligious hypothesis.[4]

4

The controversies of which we have just spoken were concerned only with *accidents* of the Christian religion, with some queer doctrines contained in the book which Christians regard as sacred and particularly in the pre-Christian part of it. They did not touch the *substance* of the Christian religion. Of far greater significance was the conflict between Christianity and certain entirely modern 'moral' and 'human' sciences, which professed to study from an empirical and positive standpoint what every form of religion declares to exceed the scope of science. At this point the

---

[1] *Edinburgh Review*, July 1845, art. i, 'Natural History of Creation' (vol. lxxxii, pp. 1 sqq.). On July 18, 1845, Mill wrote to Comte about 'a long article full of professorial and priestly rancour, which I know on reliable authority to have been written by a man named Sedgwick, professor of geology at Cambridge. . . . The author of *Vestiges* appeals to your verification of Laplace's hypothesis. It was this, I believe, which decided Herschel to make his attack and Sedgwick also has his knife into you' (*Lettres de John Stuart Mill à Auguste Comte*, pp. 466–7). For the subsequent course of the controversy, see Th. Monck Mason, *Creation by the Immediate Agency of God, as Opposed to Creation by Natural Law*, 1845, and, above all, the rejoinder made by the author of *Vestiges—Explanations: A Sequel to Vestiges of the Natural History of Creation*, 1845.

[2] *Baptist Examiner*, July 1845, p. 258.

[3] Charles Darwin, *Origin of Species*, 6th ed., 1872, pp. xvi and xvii.

[4] They saw in the evolution of nature the accomplishment of a Divine plan. See John Harris, *Man Primeval: or The Constitution and Primitive Condition of the Human Being*, pp. 203 sqq.; the Rev. Alex. Crombie, *Natural Theology*, 1829, p. 178.

conflict should have been most bitter. Actually, in England it was not so serious as the controversy about the origins of the world and mankind. The problem of the consequences for ethics of these new sciences might well have become tragic, had any writer decided to make a frontal attack. But the leading representative of this point of view, John Stuart Mill, had chosen to write not a treatise dealing with philosophy as a whole but a Logic, not a study of ethics but a Political Economy. And it was only indirectly that he dealt with the critical issue of the ends of morally good conduct. It was his determination to take this line that he was explaining to Comte when he told him that in England one must keep silence on the question of religion and be content with attacking it indirectly.[1] 'The favourable reception which my Logic has had here', he wrote to Comte on another occasion, 'is one proof among many others that there is a public in England capable of appreciating discussions conducted even on a very high level in the field of positive science, if only a few indispensable but easy reservations are made.' And again, 'Anti-religious language is feared and denounced here far more than the thing itself.'[2]

De Tocqueville's study of the ethos of American democracy enjoyed an enormous success in England. For the English recognized many features common to the Anglo-Saxon countries overseas and the mother-country, so far, at any rate, as some of their most modern characteristics were concerned. In the course of his study, De Tocqueville observed, 'In the United States you hardly ever hear virtue called good. . . . They say it is useful and prove their point every day. . . . The doctrine of enlightened self-interest, that is to say, has been universally accepted. . . . You hear it as often on the lips of the poor as on the lips of the wealthy.' Far from being scandalized, this Christian moralist resigned himself to this state of things. 'It is', he writes, 'a point of view which, if not elevated, is clear and safe. Possibly it prevents some individuals from rising much above the ordinary level of humanity. But a large number of others, in danger of falling below it, are confronted and held back by it. Those few individuals it debases. But humanity in general it raises.' Nor did he shrink from saying

[1] *Lettres de John Stuart Mill à Auguste Comte*, 1899, letter of July 8, 1845, pp. 447-8. See above, p. 399.
[2] Ibid., letters of June 21 and July 8, 1845, pp. 427 and 448. The same point of view is expressed on pp. 13, 152, and 403.

.that in his opinion, 'Of all ethical doctrines that of enlightened
self-interest suits best the needs of our contemporaries and is the
strongest defence left them against themselves.' He advised
moralists to give it their careful consideration. 'It may, perhaps,
be imperfect, but in the actual state of civilization it is indispensable.'[1]

This morality which De Tocqueville accepted, on one level at
any rate of his thought, was Bentham's utilitarian morality, the
morality of the greatest happiness of the greatest number. At a
time, that is to say, when Bentham's name was being forgotten
in England and America alike, his language was in everybody's
mouth.

It would be an intriguing task to seek the explanation of this
combination of Christian religion and the ethics of enlightened
selfishness, of a religion which teaches that God Himself was
incarnate as a man to redeem the entire world by the unreserved
sacrifice of His life and a morality which can conceive sacrifice
only as the surrender of a lesser for a greater gain. Was it a reasoned
conclusion, a deliberate capitulation, as was the case with such a
Christian sociologist as De Tocqueville? Such an explanation
allows too much to reason. Or was it the effect of an historical
accident, a consequence of the fact that the dominant social classes
in Protestant Europe, not indeed always, but very often, and
particularly in the Anglo-Saxon countries, have been the commercial classes? But we have still to explain why this has been
the case, what pre-established harmony exists between Protestant
morality and the utilitarian ethics of a mercantile society. The
harmony, we have discovered, is a harmony between a particular
type of Christian asceticism and the stern law of labour which,
the more gladly its harsh yoke is accepted, enriches willing
obedience and increases the earthly prosperity of those who have
the strength of mind to refrain resolutely from indulgence in the
softer pleasures. For the moment, however, it was in commerce
rather than industry, in the field of trade rather than in the field of
production, that British Christians sought a religious justification
for their love of money-making.

In a world of commerce, Adam Smith taught, everything
happens as though Providence intervenes to harmonize the
interests of the individual and the public interest and ensure that

---

[1] *A De Tocqueville de la Democratie en Amérique*, 13th ed., 1850, vol. ii, pp. 136 sqq.

the machinery of exchange shall produce the same effects as a universal benevolence. We have only, therefore, to consider the goal pursued to discover in the ideology of free trade, the simple philosophy of the commercial traveller, a philosophy of love, the love of all for each and each for all. The campaign conducted by the Anti-Corn-Law League had in fact consistently preached this identification. After all, you cannot move men's hearts if you speak no language but that of self-interest.

Carlyle's object in writing his *Cromwell* had been to combat his compatriots' secularization of the Christian ideal, and since, though completely unorthodox in matters of doctrine he was a consistent admirer of Puritan heroism, he had sought to confront what he regarded as the hypocrisy of contemporary Protestantism with the portrait of a man who exemplified what Puritanism had once been, in all the nobility of its first youth. But who was prepared to follow his lead?

Far more representative of England at this period were the views of *The Nonconformist*, Christian and Liberal at the same time. For its Liberalism was hatred of the artificiality and unnatural character of State interference which was, therefore, incompatible with religion. 'The first thought', wrote Miall, 'that presents itself to view, calculated to aid us in our present inquiry, is that religion, or Christianity, in the soul of man is *Life*. . . . Institutions, rules, habits, associations, are of use only as they induce spiritual vitality to unfold. The self-acting evolution of the quickened soul . . . the ripening into strength and perfection of powers yet undeveloped—this is the single end of all.'[1]

Here is the entire programme of *Social Statics* which Herbert Spencer published in 1850, in which he expounded for the first time the principles of a new philosophy which expresses this confusion between political economy and a morality not content to be merely Utilitarian.[2]

[1] Edward Miall, *The British Churches in Relation to the British People*, p. 12 and pp. 35-6.
[2] Spencer quotes, in support of his new philosophy, the following passage from Coleridge: 'The distinct foresight of consequences belongs exclusively to the Infinite Wisdom which is one with the Almighty Will, on which all consequences depend; but . . . for man, to obey the simple unconditional commandment of eschewing every act that implies a self-contradiction or, in other words, to produce and maintain the greatest possible harmony in the component impulses and faculties of his nature, involves the effect of prudence' (Herbert Spencer, *Social Statics*, ed. 1851, p. 43, note).

5

When on July 31, 1847, Palmerston was attempting to define for his constituents' benefit the essence of good government, he said, 'It is by comparing opinions—by a collision of opinions—by rubbing one man's opinions against those of another and seeing which are the hardest and will bear the friction best—that men, in or out of office, can most justly arrive at the knowledge of what is most advantageous to the interests of the whole community.'[1]

He did not tell his audience what precisely the aims of a good government should be. He was content to say that they are truth and justice. He simply pointed out the best method of discovering them, namely, free inquiry.

Six months later the writer of an article in the *Edinburgh Review* asked himself what is meant by 'a liberal system of government'. And he admitted that he did not find it easy to reply. For 'the phrase, we confess, is not very precise'. He then had recourse 'to Kant's notion of an enlightened state of society, characterized by a readiness to submit all opinions to the test of reason'.[2]

This was exactly Palmerston's definition, though he, of course, did not refer to Kant. Once again a Liberal Government was defined not so much by its aim, as by the method employed to pursue it. The writer in the *Edinburgh Review* added, however, 'By a liberal system of government we mean such a system of government as is indicated by the opinions of the old Whig party of England, improved and enlarged by modern speculation, particularly in questions of public economy and jurisprudence.'

Liberalism, that is to say, meant something more than a method of government. It had, in addition, a positive content, namely, certain reforms which had been effected under the influence of Bentham and Ricardo, amelioration of the penal code, a guarantee for the citizen against the greed or injustice of the professional judges and free trade, the right of every man to buy in any market and from any vendor. Thus understood, Liberalism had been victorious in 1846. It had not been a sudden victory, a theatrical revolution, an act of violence, but the goal of a progres-

[1] *The Times*, August 2, 1847, Palmerston's language reminds us of Cromwell's address to the army at Putney in 1647. See Ernest Barker, *Oliver Cromwell*, 1937, pp. 55-6.
[2] *Edinburgh Review*, January 1848, art. iv, 'The Ministry and the New Parliament' (vol. lxxxvii, p. 152).

sive movement, begun in 1688, from liberty and by means of it to further liberty. Let us now hear Lord John Russell's protest against Disraeli's assertion, extremely paradoxical at the date it was published, that it is the distinctive character of the English nation always to go back on its steps. 'Ever since we had been in the enjoyment of a regular government, nothing was more beautiful to the reader of history than to see the progress which this country had constitutionally made and the determination with which it had adhered to the conquests of truth and reason. The Habeas Corpus Act, the Bill of Rights, the Abolition of the Censorship of the Press, the Toleration Act, the Act for the Abolition of the Slave Trade, the Emancipation Act: who had ever wished to repeal them or to restore the oppression, disabilities and disqualifications which they abolished? The triumphs of liberty, of reason and of truth had, in this country, always been permanent and had remained without any risk of subsequent defeat.'[1]

It is thus that the child grows up to manhood, capable of more and more liberty as he becomes older, and with no possibility of a return to infancy. In 1850 the English in their optimism seemed blind to the possibility, the inevitability perhaps, of a later progress to senility.

'The Englishman', Faucher wrote, 'is disposed to believe that all the nations of mankind, with the single exception of the British, who in his opinion have reached maturity, are children.'[2]

Still children, perhaps to remain children always, for a long time to come in any case, to judge by the lamentable spectacle presented by Europe since 1848. It was falling back under the yoke of an aristocratic and military despotism, because it was puerile and, therefore, incapable of self-government. It was because it was an adult nation that Britain, unlike the infantile nations of the Continent, needed only a minimum of armed force to secure it against domestic rebellion or foreign attack. 'The life of savages', the editors of the census of 1851 observe, 'is spent in war; but the civilized populations, who are born courageous, have only to dedicate a portion of their time and of their people to the pursuit of arms, in order to ensure ten times as much security as the savage enjoys.'[3]

[1] H. of C., July 26, 1846. *Annual Register*, 1846, p. 184.
[2] Léon Faucher, *Etudes sur l'Angleterre*, 1845, vol. i, p. 8.
[3] *Census of* . . . 1851. *Report*, p. 63.

6

British Liberalism, that is to say, was regarded by the English themselves as intimately bound up with the solidity of their institutions. Was the Liberalism a result of the solidity, or the solidity of the Liberalism?

The English were inclined to accept the latter explanation. Gladstone, the high Tory of ten years previously, expressed his admiration for 'the great and noble secret of constitutional freedom which has given to us the largest liberties, with the steadiest throne and the most vigorous executive in Christendom'. And he attributed to the sense of individual responsibility, the attachment to the principle of freedom spread uniformly through all classes of society, the fact that England escaped the disorder of class warfare which afflicted the Continent.[1]

England, it is true, though if not unarmed, at least very slightly armed and most reluctant to grant its Government any increase in military expenditure it might ask for, did not for all that restrict the extent of her possessions overseas. But her motive was neither love of conquest nor greed of gain. Her overflowing population swarmed, and those Englishmen who founded Anglo-Saxon colonies beyond the seas were inspired by the loftiest of motives, 'the desire of spreading throughout the habitable globe all the characteristics of Englishmen—their energy, their civilization, their religion and their freedom'.[2]

We do not propose to inquire how far this view of their political and social institutions current among the English in 1850 corresponded with the facts or how far it cloaked illusions, even half conscious self-deception, how true it really was that the colonial policy pursued by the English conqueror of India was uninfluenced by motives of greed or conquest, or whether political institutions were free which refused the vast majority of the people the right to vote their own taxation, or how far the factory

[1] W. E. Gladstone, *Letter to . . . William Skinner, Bishop of Aberdeen* (published in *Gleanings*, vol. vi, pp. 16-17): 'I am deeply convinced that among us all systems, whether religious or political, which rest on a principle of absolutism, must of necessity be, not indeed tyrannical, but feeble and ineffective systems; and that methodically to enlist the members of a community, with due regard to their several capacities, in the performance of its public duties, is the way to make that community powerful and healthful, to give a firm seat to its rulers, and to engender a warm and intelligent devotion in those beneath their sway.'

[2] H. of C., 1850: Adderley's speech (*Annual Register*, 1850, p. 32).

workers, who in the England of Peel and Cobden must be protected from their employers' exploitation by legislative measures
still very far from adequate, could, except in a purely technical
sense, be considered free. We are content to point out that it was
the accepted view, and that, to justify it, facts which contradicted
it flatly, such as the labour legislation or even the Poor Law which
had not, as the orthodox economists desired, been abolished but
merely made uniform, were glossed over or it was argued that
liberty must necessarily be restricted, for by definition it was a
progressive achievement to be won by degrees and the more
secure the more gradually it was attained. Where had unqualified
democracy taken France? Twice over to the despotism of a
Napoleon. The ruling classes, therefore, were glad, when they
passed from the temporal to the spiritual order, to find in the
national Church the most perfect embodiment of this liberty,
always limited because always growing.[1]

Here, too, there are reservations to be made. They were made in
England itself. Uncompromising Dissenters would not have endorsed this favourable appreciation of the Anglican Church.
Nevertheless, they resigned themselves to live beside her, as she
in turn tolerated their existence at her feet. And perhaps the best
way to understand the structure of English society about the
middle of the nineteenth century is to study its religious aspect.

Ten years before, the disintegration of the majority returned to
Parliament by the first general elections held under the franchise
of the Reform Act, had brought back the Conservatives to power.
To this result religious factors had contributed. The Church might
well have seemed to stand for the majority which in the newly
elected Parliament supported Peel's ministry. The hope of the
party was the young Gladstone, who had just come before the
public as the obstinate defender of an indissoluble union between
Church and State. But it was not long before it became evident
even to Peel himself that the Conservative victory of 1841 had
been due to a misconception, to the combined effect of a movement of reaction against a democratic Radicalism, not, after all,
formidable, and a movement in the direction of a high Toryism
which the nation did not want. English history, therefore, was on

[1] 'That religion which most courts inquiry, most desires self-judgment, and rests
upon the basis of intellectual strength' (H. of C., 1847: Sir Robert Peel's speech. *Annual
Register*, 1847, p. 151).

the road to the double crisis of 1845. Within the Church the tension increased as the new High Church party progressed. Its most outstanding leader and many of his friends left her for the Church of Rome. In consequence the position of the High Church party within the Church of England was weakened, and for the benefit not of the Evangelicals, but of the Liberals. On the other hand, there was a growth of doubt and scepticism. Latitudinarianism was reborn as the Broad Church. At the same time there was a decline of evangelical fervour in the sects and the important Wesleyan body split. Meanwhile, among the supporters of the Government a rupture took place between the majority of the Conservative party and the majority of the Cabinet, the latter led by the man who had been so largely responsible for rebaptizing his party Conservative to bring it up-to-date, but who now found himself too progressive to impose his moderation on a party of ingrained Tories. The Government fell and when reconstituted was compelled to rely on the support of the Liberal Opposition to carry through the revolution of 1846 by completely repealing the Corn Laws. Then the Cabinet was turned out and the Liberals took office, but kept it only with the support of the Peelites, without whom they would not have possessed a majority. The political disintegration paralleled the religious of which we have just spoken. And the former was, perhaps, but the reverse of the latter.

In 1848, however, revolution broke out on the Continent, and brought its trail of destruction. Everywhere revolutionaries were massacred, there was disorder and reaction. England, alone exempt from both, realized, after witnessing four years of anarchy abroad, that the superficial disintegration of 1847 had concealed from her how solid her institutions really were. They were free, yet firm. Why not say they were firm because they were free? And a stable government could surely be found, not as in 1841 a Conservative Cabinet opposing Radical disorder, but a Cabinet formed by a coalition of all those who despite minor differences of all kinds believed in liberty, which would be led not by Peel in person, for he had been dead for two years, but by the statesman of his group who seemed most capable of carrying on his tradition. But what should be the policy of this new Cabinet? Should it be content to maintain the conquests already made by British Liberalism or should it make new? If so, what should they be?

That was the secret of the future. One thing alone was certain. The formation of parties in Parliament, of public opinion in the country, was polarized by the ideal of freedom. Against the clerical reaction England reasserted her creed, at once Protestant and Liberal, but even more Liberal than Protestant, for though she was averse to separating the two, she was no longer so ready as in the past to define Liberalism in terms of Protestantism, but disposed rather to proclaim herself Protestant, because in her eyes Protestantism was the form of Christianity most favourable to the progress of intellectual and political freedom.

Fragment of an Earlier Version

Two outstanding events marked in the religious sphere the period of English history which followed immediately the repeal of the Corn Laws and the European revolution of 1848. One was the schism in the Wesleyan body and the reform of Wesleyanism. It was a double movement of Wesleyanism towards the Left. The Dissidents, separatists against their will, and expelled by the orthodox did not witness after their secession an uncompromising maintenance of tradition by the latter. On the contrary, the orthodox, having driven them out, surrendered, at least in part, to their demands, and made their organization more democratic.

The other was the restoration by Rome of the Catholic hierarchy in England and a fresh wave of conversions to Catholicism, Manning's in particular. It was but a backwash of the widespread movement of Catholic reaction which swept Europe. That movement, however, cannot be said to have affected the English nation as a whole. If the outburst of indignation aroused by the restoration of the hierarchy did not lead to measures of persecution against the Catholics, it was because Liberal sentiment was more powerful than even anti-Catholic feeling. And the latter, indeed, was in its way a manifestation of Liberal sentiment. For the conversions to Rome at this period were not a ferment leavening the nation but a self-elimination, a secession, an emigration at home. And the Anglican Church, her ballast lightened by this partial riddance of the High Church element, turned her face, like Nonconformity, to the Left. Her interpretation of her traditional creed became more liberal. The Broad Church, a blend of Latitudinarianism and Puritanism, patronized by 'King' Albert, came to the fore. England was conscious of being Protestant and, because she was Protestant, Liberal.

PART II

1852 TO 1895

By R. B. McCALLUM

From 1852 to 1895

WHEN the great Sir Robert Peel died in 1850 he left something of a vacuum in English politics. The period of nearly twenty years which followed his death is looked upon sometimes as an interregnum or break in the normal flow of party development. This is partly explained by the disappearance of so important a personality, and partly by the dislocation—there are those who would say the ravages—which Peel had wrought to the party system by his great conversion or apostasy when he not only espoused but actually carried through the repeal of the Corn Laws. How high he is to be rated will always be a matter of dispute, but he represented that orderly and reforming conservatism which was characteristic of the times and he executed the measures of government with a degree of firmness and perfection which made him the model of future statesmen. Even Gladstone, a greater figure, a more powerful influence, never failed to attest his discipleship of Peel. Yet if Peel was in himself the golden mean and the master craftsman, he was never the happy warrior; party broke in his hand as an instrument too brittle for his use. His followers, who expected him to lead to battle, found that they had at their head not a commander but an explorer. That element of political activity which is the expression of merely combative emotion was not encouraged by his leadership. His former henchmen in the Tory party nursed an undying resentment, and two generations later, a great and wise Conservative, Balfour, could say that he could never hear Peel praised with patience.

The year 1852 opened with the Tory party in office once again. Its leader, Lord Derby, a former Whig, had now become established in a position of unchallenged influence, but he could not give the party the *élan* which would take it to power. Lofty, insouciant, and not notably industrious, he could march at the head of his forces but neither form them up nor inspire them to charge. His lieutenant, Benjamin Disraeli, however, had won his way to the leadership of his party in the Commons by combative qualities, but more in speech than in deed. He was, perhaps, too calm, too coolly imaginative, too carefully calculating in political

417

issues to snatch victory from defeat. To victory he did indeed lead his party, but not until 1874; the process is too slow to be called snatching. Indeed, it was not easy for Conservatism in these days to make headway. It was not merely that Peel had gone, and with him the sagacious Graham, the skilful and industrious Cardwell and Herbert, and the brooding and energetic if enigmatical Gladstone. They had more than losses to deplore. They had heavy obstacles to overcome. The spirit of the age was against them. Protectionist at heart, they had sullenly to accept free trade, and Disraeli's budget of 1852, thrown out by Gladstone's harsh attacks, had attempted little more than to apply some palliatives to the farming and landed interest. Palliatives, it should be added, to bruises rather than to wounds, for the expected evils of free trade were still afar off and delayed till the last three decades of the century.

The spirit of the age was against them in other matters. The Tories were *par excellence* the defenders of the Church interest. Yet slowly the Dissenters were establishing their claim to equality. Relief from most civil disabilities they had won in 1829 with the repeal of the Test and Corporation Acts, but they were pressing for equal rights in marriage and burial, for admission to the old universities, and with them went the plea for the remission of Jewish disabilities. Behind all this lay the great question of the disestablishment of the Anglican Church—in Ireland, in Wales, in England itself. The first two measures lay in the future; the disestablishment of the Church in England itself has never come, and the average Churchman of the eighteen-fifties would have been as surprised and relieved to have been told that his Church would still be safe a century hence as the Dissenter would have been astonished and indignant to learn of its survival. But there was no general battle to be joined. So far as England went, the establishment was not assaulted; the Dissenters might snipe and press, but there was no general engagement. The Whig leaders, Erastian and indifferent, would not burn their hands in such a struggle. Moreover, there were large numbers of the British people who were turning their minds from Church questions to secular realms—to science, to new processes of production. This absorbed much of the energy of the liveliest spirits of the time. England and Scotland and Wales were deeply religious communities, but not everywhere and in all circles. Behind the

Broad Churchman lay the free-thinker, behind the Methodist preacher the atheist cobbler. There were many who would not stir a finger either to disestablish a Church or establish it, but were concerned to know more about geology, biology, chemistry, the new wonders of electricity, to improve drains, to eradicate disease. Now, with some exceptions, these men tended to call themselves 'Liberal'; the Tory Party could not claim their strong allegiance and, in so far as their earnest mental activity was neglected, resented, or despised by more conservative people, they placed themselves on the side (a word already becoming popular and soon to become magical) of Progress. Much radical thought was going on in England, but very little in the way of a radical movement. Chartism was almost dead as an organized force although it was to linger as an influence. It had been woefully weak in middle-class membership and without that was doomed to fail. There was therefore no very obvious enemy for the Conservatives to fight, no scare or terror to send people to their side. The more fashionable nostrums were more in their opponents' keeping. If England wanted to be reformed it was, in the long run, the task of the Liberals. And as for preserving England, the English people were doing it so well themselves—good trade, steady agriculture, a free constitution, an apparently inviolable security, a loyal people—all this left the politicians a little short of raw material. The question which party should rule England never was, it never can be, unimportant. But it has often mattered much more than in the period between 1850 and 1868.

Now, although it is dangerous to suppose that the Parliamentary life of England was similar to that of the present century, it is safe to say that by the mid-nineteenth century it had been established that no Government could hold office without the habitual support of the House of Commons. The Court and the House of Lords had greater influence than in later times, but the choice of a Government rested with the Commons. The easiest way, probably the best way, to find a consistent and stable administration was to have one party dominant by a secure majority. In the period from the death of Peel to the accession of Gladstone in 1868 there was only a small margin between the Conservatives, always in a minority, and the Whigs, Peelites, Radicals, and Irish, whose total formed the majority of the House, but could not always maintain a constant and coherent majority in support of any one administration. For politics to settle down, for one party to have a long and secure tenure of power, it seemed that the nation would require to be consulted and give a verdict.

Yet to speak in these terms is to think too much in the notions of our own day when it is common to consider, in a loose phrase, a general election as a 'plebiscite' by which the 'people' chose a government. In the period between 1832 and 1867 the 'people' is an ambiguous term. In its narrowest sense it meant the electorate —what the French called the *pays légal*—those citizens whose property or superior incomes entitled them to the franchise. This figure was rising from about 600,000 in 1832 to nearly a million in 1865. Behind them was the totality of the people of England, many of them ignorant, drunken, feckless, distressed. Yet no government could ignore the general mood of the populace. England was growing into the orderly community we now know; it was being policed; it was submitting reluctantly to more government and regulation. Yet even those who had no votes and no formal power could grumble and threaten, assemble and riot. If a candidate need not listen to their pleas, he might none the less be compelled to hear their curses; if he did not require to seek their votes, he might be unable to evade their brickbats. When he spoke from the hustings he spoke to all and sundry; he stood, to take a famous phrase of Burke exactly and literally, 'upon a conspicuous stage'. After the failure of the Chartists in 1848 to bring about a head-on clash between the people at large and the legal people, the electorate and their Parliamentary representatives, the country lay for the most part at rest. Cerberus slumbered; but in 1867, when some not very serious rioting took place in London, it was quickly thrown a sop in the form of an extended franchise to the householders of the towns.

But not only was the greater part of the people excluded from direct participation in national government, even the legal electors were very far from having full initiative and choice in elections. Custom, tradition, and local interest determined the result of elections in many constituencies. Unopposed returns were common. In 1857 as many as 308 members were unopposed in 206 constituencies. In 1865 there were 289 members unopposed in 185 constituencies. Even where a contest was forced, in many county divisions or smaller boroughs the dominant family would secure the seat. Thus the borough of Bridgenorth, which had returned a Whitmore since 1712, continued to return a Whitmore until 1865. A Clive continued to sit for Ludlow. At Woodstock, a son of the Duke of Marlborough was rarely without a seat. In Sutherland, the nominee of the Duke, and very often a member of the Leveson-Gower family, represented the county, nor was it ever contested. In Cumberland and Westmorland, the great Lowther interest prevailed, and even in 1918 two Lowthers, the Speaker and his cousin, sat for this region. Some places never varied in their party allegiance. The Borough of Eye never returned a Liberal; the Burgh of Paisley never returned a Conservative. Now, all this meant that there was not much leeway for the parties to manoeuvre in. It was idle to expect that one party would sweep the country. The landslide of modern times was not yet possible. The balance of personal and local considerations which determined the choice of a candidate was delicate. It is true that party leaders gave much time to this; the whips were busy and the Reform and Carlton Clubs occupied themselves in promoting candidatures. But the number of constituencies in which a change of allegiance was possible was not large enough to permit of a sweep, in default of some strong and dominant issue such as the aftermath of the Reform Bill in 1832, which had reduced the Conservatives to about 150 members, or the weary distate with the Whigs which had brought Peel into power in 1841 with a moderate and compact majority. We are not in the period of spring tides.

While, therefore, public opinion was relatively calm and politics relatively uncombative, Ministries changed frequently. In December 1852, the first Derby-Disraeli Ministry (it is not without significance that historians always refer to these Ministries with a hyphen) fell, and the logic of the situation demanded a coalition. Lord Aberdeen, a Peelite Tory, became Prime Minister and formed a distinguished administration of Whigs and Peelites. Russell was at the Foreign Office, Palmerston was Home Secretary, Gladstone at the Exchequer, Graham at the Admiralty. This Ministry might have lasted long had it not stumbled into the Crimean War. It fell when the public, distressed at the slow progress of the war, incensed at the maladministration of the Army and its supplies, and from the first distrustful of Aberdeen's pacific nature, demanded more vigorous measures. The result of this crisis was that Lord Palmerston was called to power. Although the occasion was less perilous, this event is of the same pattern as British politics in other wars. In the Seven Years' War the Elder Pitt had to take the helm at the imperious demand of the public. Later, Lloyd George was to succeed Asquith, and in our own time Churchill was to succeed Chamberlain. It might have been expected that Palmerston would continue safely in office and that his ministry would last.

It was not to be. In 1857 he was defeated on his rough and stern action against the Chinese at Canton over the seizure of an alleged British vessel, the *Arrow*. He secured a dissolution, and there was in the constituencies a perceptible movement in his favour. But a few months later, in February 1858, he was defeated in the House and for the moment lost his popularity in the country. The Emperor Louis Napoleon had been attacked in Paris, and while he himself escaped there had been many casualties. The French Press clamoured for redress from Britain, where the conspiracy had been hatched and the bomb manufactured, and Palmerston, never afraid to take his own course, brought in a Conspiracy to Murder Bill, which appeared to be truckling to the foreigner. Once more the Queen turned to the Tory minority in the House and the Derby-Disraeli combination was set up again. It served until June 1859, when it was again compelled to resign. Then Palmerston returned to power, for the last time but for a long, secure tenure of six years. For now the political position was becoming clearer. The country—that is to say, the active, moveable, and free part of the electorate—would produce no major change in the balance of the House of Commons. It fell, therefore, to the members of the House and to the principal political leaders to sort themselves out and act on the great maxim that the Queen's Government must be carried on. What actually was happening?

On one side of the House, short of a majority by anything from forty to eighty votes, were the Tories or Conservatives proper led by Disraeli, and owing allegiance to the old Earl of Derby. If they could at any time have attracted any one group to them they might have won securely to power.

Their leader, Disraeli, tried hard. He knew that he himself, a baptized Jew, a littérateur, a suspected political adventurer, held the respect of his party by a slender thread. He had at different times angled for the support of Palmerston, who in most things, except his tendency to support 'liberal' movements abroad, was a conservative statesman.

But Palmerston would not move. Gladstone, the most brilliant of the Peelites, was approached, and Disraeli made the greatest sacrifice that an ambitious politician can make in offering to take the second place. But Gladstone, for all his dislike of Palmerston, disliked Disraeli even more, both for his personal qualities and for his record; by Gladstone and the Peelites, Disraeli and his friends were never forgiven for their assault on the Master; they were the men whose daggers had slain Caesar. It is even on record that Disraeli made suggestions to the men of the Manchester School, to Bright and Cobden, hinting that the Tories, now purged of protectionism, were more suitable allies than the stiff, bellicose, disdainful, insouciant Whig noblemen like Russell and Palmerston. When, therefore, no substantial group of the House would secede to the Tory side, it was essential that all non-Tory groups should swallow their mutual dislikes and cohere together. And this is what happened. The surviving Peelites— Gladstone, Cardwell, and Herbert—threw in their lot with the Whigs, or, as they were now more commonly called, the Liberals. If it meant sacrificing old loyalties, if it put them in an uncomfortable position as High Churchmen, doomed now to associate with Erastians and Dissenters, it put them also on the side of progress, of the most representative and characteristic ideas of the expanding age. They were free to spread their wings.

But to complete the combination one other element was necessary; the Radicals, the 'Manchester men', had to be not merely neutralized but conciliated and drawn in. Who were these men? To the world, then and now, the answer is given in two names—Cobden and Bright. They were very different men. Bright, a Lancashire man and a Quaker, was the great orator; Cobden, a Sussex man and merely an emigrant to Lancashire, was the great demonstrator of the movement. Where Bright exhorted, he proved. He had been the brain of the Anti-Corn-Law League, and Peel himself had paid tribute to his convincing power. Both were cotton manufacturers; both were animated by an intellectual belief in *laisser-faire* economics and an almost mystical faith in the merits of free trade as a moral and political good; both had a strong class sense. They believed in the intellectual and moral superiority of the middle class which they represented, the real, middle middle class, successful enough to be affluent but not aping the aristocracy, receiving baronetcies, and sending their sons to Eton and Harrow like the founders of the houses of Gladstone and Peel. To the working classes, the artisans or labouring poor, they were benevolent monitors. They believed in the identity of interest between master and man and called on the working men to unite behind radical leadership against the patricians with their pride, exclusiveness, and militarism. Yet they could not in themselves dominate the House; they could not form a national party, and in 1859 they came to heel and followed Palmerston's lead. Cobden refused the Board of Trade, but his colleague and friend, Milner Gibson, a Manchester School man, accepted this office. Mr. Guedalla has stated that the Liberal party was born on June 6, 1859, at a meeting at Willis's Rooms in London when the three elements—Peelites, Whigs, and Radicals—agreed to support Palmerston's new administration, with Gladstone at the Exchequer and Russell at the Foreign Office. If a date must be sought, no better date could be found.

It was, of course, an uneasy alliance. Neither Gladstone nor the Radicals liked Palmerston. They thought him careless, rash, bellicose, too zealous for military expenditure, and yet too reluctant for the reforms that might make such expenditure more effective. Palmerston stood in a position of curious isolation. The élite of English politicians all distrusted him. In his major Parliamentary struggles over Don Pacifico in 1850 and later over the Canton forts in 1857 he stood out against nearly all the great men of his day—Peel, Aberdeen, Derby, Disraeli, Gladstone, Cobden, Bright. And he was successful. The public turned to him. Since 1830 he had been a Whig. He could not be accused of reaction. If he was no reformer at home, he did at least show himself as an enemy of 'despotism' abroad. In these days the way of Liberalism could also be the way of 'patriotism'. The extreme moral scrupulosity of later nineteenth-century Liberalism had yet to arise. Men were not ashamed to be Liberals and yet to have a strong hand, to take strong measures. He could minister to the nation's pride and preserve its security. If some 'reforms' were wanted also, his subordinates, within limits, could be permitted to cater for that fashionable craving.

During the decade of the eighteen-fifties British politics were disturbed by two external events, the Crimean War and the Indian Mutiny. The war between Great Britain, France, and Turkey on the one hand and the Russian Empire on the other has been considered as an example of a war that came about by a mixture of blundering by some statesmen and scheming by others. A dispute between Latins and Greeks as to the custody of the Holy Places in Jerusalem raised the question of the right of the Tsar of Russia to protect his Greek Orthodox brethren in the Turkish Empire. The ground of dispute was changed from Palestine to Constantinople, and France and Great Britain supported the Turks in resisting Russian demands. Two strong ambassadors, Lord Stratford de Redcliffe for Great Britain and Prince Menshikoff for Russia, opposed each other in the Turkish capital. Lord Aberdeen was reluctant to resort to extreme measures, but the more bellicose members of the Cabinet feared the danger of yielding to Russian pressure and advised strong support for Turkey. The French Emperor desired to maintain French influence and to show the power of his arms. When, in 1854, Russia invaded the Danubian Principalities and after a declaration of war destroyed the Turkish fleet at Sinope, public opinion in this country could no longer be held back. France and Britain declared war and sent fleets and armies to the Black Sea. After landing first on the Bulgarian coast, the armies were sent to the Crimean Peninsula as it was considered an outlying and vulnerable spot were Russia could be not indeed conquered but taught a lesson. There followed the siege of the fortress of Sebastopol, prolonged for nearly two years and successful in the end. The war is famous for the sufferings of the troops in the winter, their valour in the Battles of Balaclava and Inkerman, and for the lamentable breakdown in supplies—errors indeed which when exposed were remedied with remarkable speed; and the end of the campaign saw a newly laid railway supplying our army from the base and improved hospital treatment celebrated by the name of Florence Nightingale. At the end, the Allied Powers, joined by the forces of Sardinia (Piedmont), were able to impose severe terms on Russia, which forced upon her the dismantling of Sebastopol and restricted her naval power in the Black Sea. The Ottoman Empire remained intact. The objects of the war had been attained, but the public were left with an uneasy feeling that it had been more glorious than successful and more costly than was necessary.

One effect we have seen was to bring the Aberdeen coalition to an end and to raise Palmerston to the highest place in British politics. It had, however, other more subtle and lasting effects. The public in general, after nearly forty years of peace, showed much martial enthusiasm, and the critics and opponents of the war were unpopular at the time and later punished by loss of their seats in the election of 1857. Still, in the end they won. Cobden and Bright were true to their principles of foreign policy, which laid down the absolute minimum of intervention in European affairs and a deep moral reprobation of war. Bright rose at this time to his greatest heights as an orator. We remember his most famous periods such as his 'Angel of death' speech, but he also showed a remarkable power of sustained argument in the diplomatic details. Some few years later he suffered from a mental affliction, after which he had never the same abilities. When the first enthusiasm was passed, when the dead were mourned, the sufferings revealed, and the cost counted, when in 1870 Russia was able calmly to secure the revocation of the Treaty which disarmed her in the Black Sea, the view became general that the war was stupid and unnecessary and effected nothing. It is not certain that this view is necessarily right. Opinion as to the magnitude or the reality of the Russian menace in the Levant will always vary according to time and circumstance. But the Crimean War remained as a classic example, a perfect demonstration-piece, of how governments may plunge into war, how strong ambassadors may mislead weak prime ministers, how the public may be worked up into a facile fury, and how the achievements of the war may crumble to nothing. The Bright-Cobden criticism of the war was remembered and to a large extent accepted. Isolation from European entanglements seemed more than ever desirable. To several generations of Englishmen there loomed before their minds this awful warning. The Cobdenite leaven worked far and long in the Liberal Party. It may be that in the present century we have encountered more danger and disaster from our reluctance to accept alliances or to prepare in time against our dangers. If this is so, then it may be that the Crimean War by its example has killed more Englishmen in the twentieth century than it did at the time in the nineteenth. In 1914, when Great Britain declared war on Germany, one Minister of great eminence resigned. He was Lord Morley, the biographer and avowed disciple of Cobden.

No sooner was the Crimean War over than the public was startled by the outbreak of the Indian Mutiny, which began in March 1857. For a time it seemed as if the ascendancy of the British in India might be terminated, but armed forces were sent in time, and as the mutiny was not universal throughout British India, it was subdued. The Governor-General, Lord Canning, showed calmness and courage. Many feats of generalship and soldierly valour earned the grateful applause of popular opinion. When order was restored the Government resolved to bring to an end the East India Company, and in November 1858 its lands were annexed to the Crown, while a Secretary of State was made responsible for Indian affairs. When votes of thanks had been passed to the generals and troops and statues in due time erected, a backwash of criticism and heart-searching set in. Stories of ferocious punishments carried out first in panic and continued in sustained anger became known. The sensitive English conscience was troubled. British India flourished and expanded. In 1876 Queen Victoria was proclaimed Empress. The British Raj was still to rise to new heights of power and splendour, to exercise in many fields a wise and beneficent authority, but an uneasy doubt as to British justice and humanity lingered.

The Crimean War and the Indian Mutiny may well have done much to dispose the British people to peace by allowing a generation to know of war and to be sure of the valour of their race. Although no other major effort of British arms was required till the end of the century, when the Sudan was reconquered and the South African Republics overrun, British armies were not entirely without action on the long frontiers of Empire. We may compare with this the experience of the Germans, who between 1871 and 1914 saw no other use for their tremendous forces than their part in the Boxer expedition in China. Englishmen were blooded in the two great struggles of the fifties. They were also troubled. From this time, perhaps, we may trace the growth of that movement called anti-imperialism, which became in the end an accepted creed of almost half the nation. In part it was the heart-searching of a deeply Christian people, and this was aided by the ethical doubts of those who took their inspiration from secular philosophy. In part it was the reasonable restraint of prudent men, who saw the dangers of too great an Empire both to defend

427

materially or justify morally. Less worthy motives also entered in. In some breasts it may have been little more than hatred of social superiors, since both the glory and emolument of Empire seemed to accrue to the patrician and the wealthy. In others it may have been the rancour of the more timid and unadventurous towards those of whatever class who went forth to travel, to explore, to trade, or to fight in distant parts. But whatever its source, it became a major factor in British politics, and the most scornful imperialist could never deny its power nor even fail to admit some small grain of reason in it. After the apotheosis of Empire at the Great Jubilee, the poet of Empire, Rudyard Kipling, wrote his *Recessional*. Even if it be considered as the most grotesque and shallow essay in humility that literary records disclose, the fact remains that it was written; it is to be found in hymn-books even now. The sentiment of anti-imperialism which was developing in our period was to reach its heights in the period after 1918, until shortly before 1939 our friends feared and our enemies hoped that Britain was a power that would never fight again. In one view anti-imperialism has brought most of the disasters of the twentieth century upon us. In another view it has been a principle of sanity and restraint, a saving grace which has averted the evil eye of an envious world and left us with friends who found their interest in our survival rather than their pleasure in our destruction.

In 1860 the names of Imperialist and anti-Imperialist, jingo and little-Englander lay still in the future. Yet under Palmerston's presidency moral and political forces were drawing together which were to recast entirely the old mould of mid-Victorian Whiggery. Gladstone was moving up in the political firmament, recognized by far-seeing observers as the lord of the ascendant. And in conjunction with him was John Bright, the Quaker, the Pacifist, the idol of the Radical artisan. Long before the century ended their portraits were to hang side by side as the household gods of countless Liberal homes.

The junction was not swiftly or easily achieved. Bright's mind and personality and creed were simple, Gladstone's complex. He was a man of wide learning, of brooding and reflective mind, of long experience in office, familiar with the dilemmas and difficulties of government. His Liberalism would appear in bursts and flashes, and would often be qualified by retractions and conditions. Since 1851, when in a famous public letter to Lord Aberdeen he had denounced the despotic government of Naples, he had been on the side of Italian Liberalism and unity. He admired Cavour, and when in 1859 Sardinia, in alliance with France, attacked Austria and won Lombardy and later, with the adherence of the northern Italian states, founded the Kingdom of Italy, Gladstone rejoiced. With Palmerston and Russell he supported the new kingdom, and when Garibaldi in 1860 overran Sicily and Naples, Gladstone, with his colleagues, used British influence to prevent interference with this further extension of Italian unity. The Conservative statesmen looked with some dismay on these radical changes, and at Court there was much sympathy with Austria. But Cavour, and still more Garibaldi, were heroes to Liberal Englishmen, and the Italian question was a tide bearing Gladstone towards the Radical ranks.

The American civil war, however, had the contrary effect. Englishmen were much divided over this question. While positive zeal for slavery was unknown in this country, the plea of the Southern States that they had a juridical right to secede was weighty and convinced many. Gladstone, in a speech at Newcastle on October 7, 1862, gave much encouragement to the South by admitting that Jefferson Davis had made a nation. Palmerston's Government did its best to remain neutral in the struggle, but had to concede belligerent rights to the South. When in November 1861 Confederate envoys were forcibly removed from a British ship, the Trent, by a United States warship, war seemed near, and a too strongly worded despatch by Palmerston was watered down at the suggestion of Prince Albert, shortly before his fatal illness. An ironclad cruiser, the Alabama, was allowed to leave the Mersey partly by dilatoriness on the part of the Home Office and partly by sheer mischance—the sudden illness of the legal officer whose advice was asked. Opinion in the Northern States was embittered and in London was answered by much hostility to the Northern cause; the Times and Punch gave much offence to Americans by their satirical remarks. English opinion found it difficult to follow the movement of American opinion, which began the war as a defence of the Union and were ending it in avowed determination to abolish slavery. And as the war went on, the brilliance of Lee's generalship and the gallantry of the weaker South attracted a natural sympathy. Englishmen were to show the same sympathy to France in 1870 after, but not before, her first defeats. So far as a generalization can be made, upper-class opinion and opinion in Southern England favoured, without necessarily approving, the Southern cause. Radical, middle-, and working-class opinion was strong for the North. It was difficult for British statesmen to avoid giving deep offence to one side or the other. It has been observed that one British statesman only succeeded—Benjamin Disraeli kept his head and held his tongue. The rewards of a negative wisdom were due to him. But Bright and, while he lived Cobden, played a more positive part. They firmly took the Northern side, and under their influence the Radical masses followed. Even in Lancashire, stricken by the cotton famine which was caused by the Federal blockade of the Southern ports, allegiance to the cause of human liberty did not falter. The distressed unemployed workmen, whose sufferings are still a live memory in the cotton towns, commemorated in songs, such as 'Brother's fainting at the door', held firm. Bright's political principles had taken him to the side that was afterwards to be acknowledged as right, and also to the side that won. Had there not been in England this body of popular opinion, animated and dignified by so great a leader, England might have incurred in America an enmity so deeply rooted that friendship could never have been securely restored.

It was to Gladstone, as Prime Minister, that was left the final work of conciliation. For six years the United States demanded, often harshly and with menaces, compensation for the ravages of the *Alabama* and her consorts. The extreme claims for indirect and secondary damage were not in the end taken into account by the arbitration tribunal which was appointed. The sum of £3,250,000 was paid in the end. It was more than British opinion thought was just; it was more actually than the American Government could easily find claimants for, since it lingered for many years in the United States Treasury not completely exhausted. But it settled a difficult account; it provided an inspiring example of the possi-bilities of arbitration. Perhaps there was a danger in this. The Liberal belief that all international disputes could and should be made justiciable was much encouraged by the successful issue of the *Alabama* dispute. Yet it was a case in which the precedents of international law were not indeed easy but possible of applica-tion, and it was one in which the claims could be measured in figures and settled by payment. Very different was the problem that faced European diplomatists when Prussia and Austria, supported by all German States, insisted by force on the withdrawal of all Danish claims of sovereignty over the provinces of Schleswig and Holstein. In this matter, juridical and historical rights were in conflict with the pride and spirit of a great European nation, conscious of its imperfect recognition and its still incomplete unity. The two senior Ministers, Palmerston and Russell, favoured British intervention in support of Denmark and treaty rights. Other members, such as Gladstone, opposed armed action. Opinion in London was much divided, the Queen favouring the German point of view, and the Prince of Wales, with his young Danish bride, Alexandra, that of Denmark. Fundamentally the weakness of the small British Army, unprepared for rapid mobilization and transport to the Continent, reduced our statesmanship to helplessness. Two years later another war, the war between Austria and Prussia, broke out, and Bismarck established himself as the leading statesman of Europe. Here was a force that would yield to no persuasion or arbitration if it hindered settled policies and long-matured plans. Both wars were short and peace quickly established. Englishmen had scarcely time to digest the issue before a settlement was reached, dictated in each case by the victor.

In home affairs the Liberal Cabinet of Palmerston was under much strain and stress, which it successfully survived. Palmerston's principal opponent was his destined successor, Gladstone. They clashed over urgent demands for military and naval expenditure. French armaments and policy appeared to be threatening. In particular, the rapid development of steamships and ironclads made it appear that the power of the British Navy to hold the Channel against invasion might be overcome by superior French naval units. The result was a scare that took three forms. First, increased expenditure on the Navy; secondly, the building of stronger fortifications on the south coast; and thirdly, a sudden stimulus of the Volunteer movement in order to add to the number of trained defenders of our shores. The danger did not materialize. French power was to suffer a blow from Prussia in 1870, which drove thoughts of French invasion from our minds. The political effect of this was to bring Gladstone, who at the Exchequer set himself against increases in expenditure, more and more in touch with Bright and the Radical wing. On another issue they were also allies. In 1860, Gladstone proposed the repeal of duties on paper, which was to have the effect of making newspapers and, indeed, all printed matter cheaper and more easily available to all classes. The House of Lords feared the radical effects of such a measure and rejected the bill repealing the paper duties. Palmerston was indifferent to this rebuff, but under Gladstone's pressure he was compelled to force the issue in the next session. This time all the financial proposals for the year were embodied in one measure, the finance bill or unified 'budget' with which we are now familiar. Lord Derby did not feel it prudent to urge the Tory majority in the Lords to reject it, for it would have led to a severe clash with the Commons over the Commons primacy in finance, a clash in which the Commons would have a good case in constitutional theory and strong Radical support. It was another great victory for Gladstone and his element in the party, that element which was beginning to take as its slogan, 'Peace, Retrenchment, and Reform'.

For Gladstone was now increasingly the object of public admiration for his marvellous skill at the Exchequer. His first great budget in 1853 had established him securely as a great financier; now he went from triumph to triumph. Free trade and economy in public spending were accepted generally as self-evident benefits. In free trade the chief event of the period was a treaty with France negotiated by Cobden and put into operation in 1861 by Gladstone. This treaty encouraged trade between the two countries by a mutual lowering of duties so that France would receive British coal and manufactures and Britain, French wines, brandy, and other products. All the tremendous logic of free trade was behind it. The two nations were to take from each other their most suitable and characteristic products. It was never a popular measure in France, where the organized manufacturers protested and the wine-growers seem to have made their case heard less effectively. In Britain, in spite of some local protests where special interests were threatened, it was hailed as a masterpiece of statesmanship, and Gladstone's speech introducing the measure was regarded as one of his greatest. In cold print now, it does not seem so remarkable. But it was notable for two reasons. Gladstone made the tariff changes at the earliest possible moment, without hesitation, higgling, or delay. In this way he made out of a mere commercial agreement an act of moral virtue. And also the treaty appeared to contemporaries to be another splendid and, it was hoped, irreversible movement in the progress of world freedom of trade, with all the merits, real and supposed, attaching to free trade, peace through the interdependence and association of nations, prosperity through the wider and more rapid flow of goods. These expectations were by no means realized, for France and Germany and America were to increase their tariffs ideas. The Liberals of Gladstone's day scarcely realized how difficult it might be to maintain free trade against political pressure from those who feared economic or social disturbance. The rulers of Germany, military and agrarian in their outlook, had an eye to national economic security and to the maintenance of the healthy and loyal elements in the country against the more corrupt, liberal, even socialist ethos of the towns. French peasants, like English landlords, were to care for the price of their crops, and American manufacturers, masters and men, had an interest in maintaining their wages and profits.

Still, while the century lasted, the aura was never to depart from the Cobden treaty in the minds of Englishmen. They looked also with gratitude to Gladstone for his skill in reducing taxation while maintaining the necessary revenue. It was then all but universally accepted that wealth expended by the Government was less usefully employed than wealth saved, invested, and employed by individuals. Every pound spared from taxation would, it was assumed, be invested, in general, with profit. The private company or individual entrepreneur knew better than any department of the State how to enhance national and private wealth. In retrospect, this view has encountered criticism, and it is easy for us now to think of many ways in which government might have used the nation's wealth for public works, health, or education. Yet if any large sum had been subtracted from the sums available for investment, then many sources of wealth would have run dry. Factories, machines, railways, and docks at home or in far distant countries would have lacked that flow of capital which thrifty, enterprising England could alone supply, and to attempt any dogmatic judgment on whether this country or the world would have been wealthier or happier under some different economic régime, is to trench upon the province of divine omniscience. The men of that day had few doubts, and they looked to Gladstone as the supreme artificer. The magnitudes of his budgets seem small, his savings, his surpluses, sometimes were only measured in hundreds of thousands, but compared with the budgets of other Chancellors of the age, they show that margin of superiority which is the proof of greatness. They reveal the major qualities of statesmanship, a firm grasp of principle, a combination of imaginative mind with meticulous care for detail, and incessant, indefatigable labour.

To many Englishmen, looking back on the decade of the eighteen-sixties, the most vivid memory might be, not any act of statesmanship at home or war abroad, but something more vivid and personal. Some would recollect the day in December 1861 when they heard that Albert, the Prince Consort, was dead and their Queen left in early middle life a widow. Others would remember October 1865, when the news went round that old Lord Palmerston had died. That indeed seemed the end of an epoch; Palmerston, who had played for Harrow against Eton in 1794, who had held a subordinate post at the War Office before the Battle of Waterloo, who had been playing a skilful game to secure the neutrality of Belgium while his colleagues were pressing on with the great Reform Bill, who for twenty-eight years, either as Foreign Secretary or as Prime Minister, had vindicated what Englishmen held to be their just rights and dignity and troubled those whom Englishmen were pleased to think of as tyrants, Palmerston had gone. While he lived, Reform on a large scale was held back. His outlook has been described as sceptical, cynical, philistine, but never as stupid and never weary. It was with energy, sense, and spirit that he governed Great Britain, not by doctrine or by passion. Others would remember most keenly the terrible day in May 1866 when the bankers, Overend and Gurney, closed their doors, when the Government suspended the Bank Charter Act, and panic shook the City. Many individuals and families faced sudden ruin.

It has been common to speak of the mid-Victorian epoch. If we consider the reign carefully we will find that there never was any mid-Victorian epoch. The Queen's reign of sixty-four years divides itself best into two halves, the earlier and the later. The line may be taken in 1861 at the Prince Consort's death, although that is really too soon; the death of Palmerston in 1865 is another mark, as is also the passing of the second Reform Bill in 1867, or the accession of Gladstone to power in 1868. In foreign affairs, the end of the American civil war in 1865 or the victory of Prussia over France in 1870 are dates that divide. But somewhere about this time the history of Great Britain takes a turning.

If the middle or late sixties was a turning-point in the political history of England it was also a turning-point in intellectual development, although such movements are usually less abrupt. Dickens died in 1870 and Mill in 1873. Browning, Carlyle, and Tennyson were still living, but had produced their greatest work. Darwin had also completed his significant contribution by the publication of *The Descent of Man* in 1871, and Clerk-Maxwell's *Electricity and Magnetism* was published two years later. Macaulay and Hallam had died in 1858, and although Newman lived till 1890 his major work had been accomplished. The second half of the reign was rich in thought and literature and science, but the greatest men were gone or had passed their best. Just as British manufacture and commerce was now being rivalled and in some respects surpassed by other nations, so also in thought it was less a land of giants.

Yet the Englishman growing to maturity in the eighteen-seventies or eighties found himself living in a vital world of thought with many movements and influences stimulating his mind. And these influences were various and divergent. The steady scholar found the universities and schools improving in zeal, skill, and public responsibility. Scholarship was flourishing, and more critical methods were being devoted to the interpretation of Greek and Latin literature and history. It was the age of Jowett and Jebb and Verrall, and in 1889 a very young Oxford scholar, Gilbert Murray, was appointed to the chair of Greek at Glasgow. Classics was still the most obvious and regular *cursus honorum* for the young professional man to follow, and it led to a fine career in academic life, in law, in the Church, or, especially after 1870, in the Civil Service. But the universities were enlarging their curriculum and, in addition to the two ancient disciplines of Classics and mathematics, the newer subjects—law, history, modern languages, and the different branches of the national sciences—were growing in favour.

There were two forces which might draw men away from the

middle of the road in intellectual development. Some, in an age intensely religious and at the same time learned and thoughtful, were drawn to theology and to the Christian ministry as a profession. Others were attracted by the opening vistas of natural science and fell under the influence of such writers as Lyell in geology, Clerk-Maxwell in physics, Pasteur in biology and inorganic chemistry, and, above all, of Darwin. Such men would often be drawn away from the Church, at least from active and apostolic membership of it. They prided themselves on thinking freely, on being objective enquirers into the nature of truth as revealed by observable and calculable phenomena, as opposed to sacred texts, the Revelation proper of the theologians. A brilliant expositor of natural science, T. H. Huxley, came forward as the most gifted mentor of this school. Rarely did they call themselves free-thinkers. That name with all its odious connotations of militant atheism and Continental anti-clericalism was sparingly used, and Leslie Stephen, a Cambridge don who had abandoned his clerical orders, coined the convenient term 'agnostic'. Probably no one act of word-making did so much to ease the strains of social, intellectual, and professional life. For while many were irritated, oppressed, and hampered by the strictures and prejudices of the religious and orthodox, few were in the mood to crusade for anti-religion. The lesson of the French revolutionary period had been learned. It had been seen that the eighteenth-century optimism, which had believed that it was only necessary to remove 'superstition' to effect a vast improvement in human affairs, was a delusion. And however eagerly the Nonconformist might cry 'Disestablish the Church', or the secularist might cry 'Down with the parsons', this was very different from the eighteenth-century philosopher crying *'Écrasez l'infâme'*. England preserved its capacity for quiet social and moral adjustment.

Yet the strain was severe. Men who found it difficult in the light of their knowledge of the physical world to subscribe to the creeds and to accept the literal truth of scripture were frowned upon: their careers might be impeded, especially those of more rigorous mind who could not bring themselves to play the part of the worldly wise conformer. Moreover, there was a social strain as well. The old universities, the most celebrated and patrician schools, admitted science grudgingly, and in general the élite left scientific studies to a lower stratum in the social scale.

This prejudice operated most strongly in Oxford, less in Cambridge, and still less in the Scottish Universities, in London, and in the new colleges, later to be universities, springing up in the larger industrial towns. It was, perhaps, unfortunate that in this utilitarian age the most obvious and popular form of science to be advocated in schools and the easiest to provide and demanded by parents was chemistry, cultivated at the expense of physics and biology. To this day the radical complexion in politics of many of our scientists is not unconnected with the fact that they, or their fathers, heard their studies dismissed as 'stinks' by boys and masters who were wont also to arrogate to themselves other assumptions of superiority.

The world of religious thought was divided into two camps: those who merely defied science and those who strove to reconcile scientific methods with religion and to accept more critical views of scriptural evidence. Such were Temple, Jowett, and others who contributed to the famous volume, published in 1860, called *Essays and Reviews*.

The stricter school were shocked, and this book started one of many controversies that arose as the 'liberalizing' of Christian theology proceeded. The older evangelicals held out against any diminution of the belief in the full literal truth of Scripture. Amongst the Nonconformist sects and the Scottish Presbyterians the same disputes raged, but with the passage of time the liberal view began to prevail, and men and women were no longer driven away from church association by having to accept the Book of Genesis entire.

In addition to this clash between literal inspirationists and liberal theologians, there was another movement in religious life that came to be known by the general term of Anglo-Catholicism. What was first the Tractarian movement and later known as the Oxford movement continued its course. Some of its greatest leaders had entered the Roman communion—Newman and Manning. Others, such as Pusey and Keble, remained constant in their loyalty to the Church of England and unremitting in their endeavour to lead it back to a more Catholic doctrine and ritual. Perhaps because they were concerned to base their beliefs on the tradition of the Church rather than on the Bible alone, they were somewhat less agitated than were the Low and Broad Churchmen by the implications of science. Certainly they leaned to the more conservative views about Scripture, and in their later years such men as the Evangelical Lord Shaftesbury and the Fractarian Pusey could draw closer together as they faced the appalling spectacle of spreading 'infidelity'. But the move towards catholicizing the Church of England went on its way apparently unimpeded by the agonizing problems of 'Darwinism'. A more Catholic view of the Eucharist, the more frequent practice of Communion, the stricter observance of saints' days, the restating of the Anglican position in such a way that the Reformation was no longer to be considered as a necessary break with medieval Christianity, but a grave lapse to be repaired and atoned for, all this could proceed independently of the discussions about the Old Testament. Many of the educated classes in England found rest in the Roman Communion during this period and joined the amalgam of old English families, Irish immigrants, and middle-class converts who make up modern English Catholicism. But the passage of time produced in the end a liberal Anglo-Catholicism, no longer burdened by literal inspirationism. This High Church movement, as it is called, altered the connotation of the older term High Church, which had often meant strong for the rights of the Church but not anti-Protestant. Suspicious congregations watched for signs of unwelcome 'highness' in new incumbents. And by this they meant Puseyism and Ritualism, or Catholicizing or anti-Protestant tendencies of any kind. For this movement was not of the multitude, but of the few; of the clerics rather than of the laity. Bishops and chapters, even a Statute of the Realm tried to stop it, but it crept steadily on. Slowly the mean of Anglican opinion was moved further to Catholicism and the aspect and customs of churches altered. To-day many people may find English cathedrals or parish churches restored with quiet English artistry to something more resembling their medieval condition and uses. So subtle and so delicate are these changes, so well is the peculiar, restrained, English atmosphere preserved, that many are quietly drawn to an appreciation of Catholicism who would be repelled by what they might consider the gaudy and incense-sodden fanes of continental Papistry.

The High Church movement was not of the multitude, but it was conceived as being for the multitude. Towards the end of the century the movement, somewhat offensively called 'slum-

ming', began to influence the High Church clergy. Whereas in
the earlier period the greatest zeal for working in the poorest and
most squalid districts of London and other great cities was shown
by the Evangelicals; now the young Oxford or Cambridge High
Church parson or enthusiastic layman was taught to think meanly
of himself if he had not observed and struggled with the squalor
and misery of the slums. Missions and settlements were maintained by universities and famous schools, and many of those
who worked there were Anglo-Catholics. Not that any sect or
type had a monopoly. The 'cry of outcast London' fell on many
ears. The Salvation Army, inspired by the missionary zeal of
General Booth, its founder, provided a simple doctrine of personal
salvation, more redolent of Wesley than of Newman. The
Secularists also were at work. The Fabians, led by the unrelenting
vigour and acumen of Sidney and Beatrice Webb, were beginning
their labours. Secular settlements were founded, such as Toynbee
Hall. A London docker, starving and miserable in mind and body,
might find himself ready to be 'rescued' by Salvationist or Protestant pastor, by an Anglo- or Roman Catholic priest, or by a
social worker proceeding from rationalist and secular motives.
It is no anomaly, it is scarcely even an accident, that the first head
of a triumphant Socialist majority in Parliament should be Mr.
Attlee, an Oxford graduate who had served a large part of his
adult life in social service in Stepney.

In the period of the eighteen-sixties and seventies the intelligent
reading public of England was much attracted by the writings of
a man who, too urbane to be a prophet and too mild to be a
force, was undoubtedly an influence of much importance. Matthew
Arnold, poet and critic of life and letters, was rising into fame.
His theology was broad, not to say thin. His critical writings
were directed against the average philistine bourgeois of his day
and cannot escape from the imputation of priggishness. Disgusted
by the complacency and crudity of so much of the society in
which he lived, he satirized and censured the drab, mean, and
uncritical ideas of his age. He inculcated high standards of aesthetic
appreciation, and his distinguished verse and his polished prose
entitled him to play the part of a censor. He preached the quest of
'sweetness and light', he sought to lift the pall of philistinism that
hung over Victorian England as the smoke over its cities. He
expressed particular detestation of the smug and self-righteous

439

atmosphere of 'dissenting Protestant tea parties'. His literary and cultural influence was great, but there was another side to his activities. He was an educationist; he was by profession an inspector of schools, and he laboured hard not only at his regular task, but at the task of rousing England to appreciate the grave defects of her educational system and so of her entire culture. Efficiency in work, grace in living, humanity in judgment—all these depended on a more thorough and a wider view of education. In many ways the educational system that we now see, the splendid network of secondary schools, the development of university extension lectures, the growth of new centres of learning, the liberalizing of the old, the eager interest of modern England in music, drama, and other arts, all these are foreshadowed in Matthew Arnold's teaching. He taught us how to cultivate and enjoy the fruits of civilization. But on personal salvation in the spiritual sense he had no coherent message nor on national preservation in the political sense. It may be well for England that much of the hard core of evangelical morality and faith remained. The trials of the twentieth century have been too severe to be met merely by a philosophy of culture. The might of Hohenzollern and of Nazi Germany required to be confronted by some more resistant material than sweetness and light.

On Palmerston's death the Queen sent for Lord John Russell, the veteran Whig statesman. Shortly afterwards he was created an Earl and entered the House of Lords, leaving Gladstone to lead the Commons. Now if Russell had little of the Radical in him, he was of the purest Whig descent and he had a conscious bias in favour of liberal or reforming measures. In 1851 he had made an attempt to alter the Parliamentary franchise, and from that moment the finality of the Act of 1832 was disavowed. In 1859 Disraeli had alarmed his more conservative colleagues by presenting a Reform Bill which, in spite of its attempt to balance increased popular voting with additional votes, once again aroused the hopes of the Radicals. His extra votes for persons of property were ridiculed with the name of 'fancy franchises', and the Bill, satisfying to no one, was dropped. The reform problem came up again, and now there was deeper demand for it. The artisans were growing restless. In 1866 Russell brought forward another Reform Bill, but after long debates it foundered. The Liberal party was by no means united on the question, and some members, notably the able Robert Lowe, who had imbibed a distaste for real, rough democracy in Australia, led a secession against the Bill. Owing to a famous gibe of Bright's, his group were known as the Cave of Adullam, thus bringing into use the term 'cave' for a dissident group within a party. Russell indeed had the bulk of his party with him, for Gladstone in May 1865 had enunciated the famous doctrine that 'every man who is not presumably incapacitated by some consideration of unfitness or of political danger is morally entitled to come within the pale of the constitution'.

Whatever legal construction was to be put on this typically Gladstonian phrase, strong in its essence, cautious in its form, it opened a gate to a wide change in the franchise.

But the Russell Ministry, defeated in the House, had to resign, and the Queen turned once again to the Derby-Disraeli connection. Back they all came, Disraeli again at the Exchequer, Lord Malmesbury, Lord Chelmsford, Lord John Manners, Mr. Spencer Walpole, General Peel, Sir J. Pakington, some to their former offices, others to new offices. Five dukes served in this Ministry: Buckingham, Marlborough, Abercorn, Richmond, and Montrose. It would seem as if the prayer of an early poem of Lord John Manners had been answered 'But give us back our old nobility'. It is common cant in history to speak of England coming under the rule of the new middle classes, a period which can be placed at any time from the reign of Edward III to that of Edward VII. But if a date is wanted to denote the end of the rule of the nobility, the resignation of this Ministry in 1868 would suffice. There were new men in this Cabinet, too. The Earl of Carnarvon was a statesman who appreciated the need for more effective devolution of power on the self-governing colonies and later was to dabble in ideas of Irish autonomy. Sir Stafford Northcote, who entered the Ministry later, was known for his work in administrative, especially civil service, reform, and was to be Chancellor of the Exchequer and Foreign Secretary. Most important of all was Viscount Cranborne, heir of the Earl of Salisbury, a formidable figure, a trenchant speaker. He was to be three times Prime Minister, his periods of office totalling fourteen years.

The Conservative party, it would seem, either lacked talent or it preferred titles. There is truth in both notions. Many of their best men had gone in the Peelite schism, and younger men in political life were often imbued with the general liberalism of the age. The more eminent of the educated classes found it difficult to be good Conservatives. By educated classes is meant the products of the great schools and universities. The term *intelligentsia* was not yet in vogue, and lacking the name we also lacked the thing. In general, the Victorians were less canting and prudish in their social terminology than we are to-day; phrases such as the educated classes, the labouring poor, the superior artisans, persons of property, and so on, are more frank and accurate than modern words such as workers, capitalists, the underprivileged. The Conservatives did not attract or seek talent very anxiously. So many seats had to go to men of influence and quality that there was no considerable residue for young professional men. The present House of Commons is no doubt superior by the formal standards of education which make up so much of modern life, by the test of competitive scholarships and diplomas and degrees. Yet the men who made up a House in the sixties and later, especially on the Tory side, had many admirable qualities. A few were men of high intellectual power and the rest had a kind of ease and confidence, a natural knowledge of men and affairs and a quality which, in a phrase applied both to Parnell and Lord Hartington, has been described as 'you-be-damnedness'. In politics it may go a long way.

One great Act in Imperial History was carried out by this Ministry, the British North America Act of 1867, which brought into a federative government the Colony of Canada proper with the maritime provinces, with provision for the eventual accession of British Columbia and the provinces which were to arise in the prairies of the west. Canada as a Dominion was set on the way to its present greatness. This was not a controversial question and, indeed, was moved primarily from Canada. Other matters also occupied the attention of Ministers without great dispute. An Act made Parliament independent of a demise of the Crown. Until then it had had to be dissolved within six months of the late sovereign's death. A concession was made to the Nonconformists by the abolition of compulsory church rates. There was a successful expedition to Abyssinia, and the Fourth Maori War had begun in New Zealand. But the main problem of politics remained the vital question of Parliamentary Reform. Some change would have to be made. Russell and Gladstone had tried and failed. Disraeli could not remain inactive. He saw that some broad measure was necessary and took as his basis the expedient of making the franchise depend on the payment of poor rates, a simple test of whether a man was or was not contributing to the upkeep of the social system. But this wide extension, for such it was, he proposed to counterweight by giving additional votes to those who paid direct taxation or in other ways gave evidence of their stability or stake in the country. In his Cabinet and party there was much dispute, and the public was both bewildered and amused by the complicated discussion of the franchise problems and the recriminations between Ministers, three of whom, Cranborne, Carnarvon, and General Peel, eventually resigned. In the end the Bill was passed in what must be considered a radical form. The rating franchise gave the vote to settled householders in the towns, and the qualification for an occupier's vote in the counties was lowered to twelve pounds. There was also a considerable redistribution of seats. Some of the smaller boroughs were deprived of one of their members, and forty-five seats thus saved were given to the more populous towns and counties. A peculiar provision was made for the greatest cities, Glasgow, Liverpool, Manchester, Birmingham, and Leeds. These were to return three members, but to prevent one party sweeping all three seats by a block vote, there was to be a limited vote. Each elector was to cast two votes, so that if the larger party put up three candidates and the smaller two, the larger party might not obtain all three seats. It was a crude device for minority representation and has since been superseded by many efficient forms of proportional representation. It did not survive for long, for in 1885 Britain returned to simple majority voting in all constituencies. But the limited vote had important effects. It encouraged parties in the great cities to canvass and organize their voters more carefully than ever before. Especially in Birmingham, the Liberals under Joseph Chamberlain and Schnadhorst in their famous caucus brought political organization to a new degree of efficiency.

The Act of 1867 is said to have added just short of a million new voters and almost doubled the electorate. Political historians usually regard this extension of the franchise as more important than the later Acts of 1885 and 1918. It did make the government of the country potentially a democracy, by Aristotle's definition, a government by the many and the poor. From now on, parties, more strictly organized, were more careful to consult the opinions of the electors, especially those floating voters most easily swayed. At the time no one had any illusions as to the gravity of the step. 'Shooting Niagara', said Carlyle. 'A leap in the dark', was Derby's description; and the Liberal Lowe drew the moral, 'We must educate our masters'.

The Government continued in office, although still in a minority, until the new Act was in force and the new voters registered and seats redistributed. Then the dissolution came. Just before Parliament rose the Government had sustained a defeat on resolutions proposing the disestablishment of the Irish Church which Gladstone now supported. It was this issue which took prominence in the speeches of political leaders at the time of the election. It might seem strange that the million of newly enfranchised working-class voters should care so much about the condition of the Established Church of Ireland. There is little reason to suppose that they did. Election issues are made more by the inner set of politicians than by the public at large. The older voters, those million who had the franchise before, contained many whose primary concern was religious and church affairs. The proposal to deal with the Church in Ireland was, however, a symbol which most radical working men could understand. It was a privileged body. Containing perhaps one-eighth of the Irish people and little more than one-half of the Protestants of Ireland, it was a magnificent target. In a broad sense the Radical voters were aware of the domination of privileged persons and institutions over them. They were against it. Gladstone, supported by their votes, found himself with a majority of over 120 in the new House. It was the largest majority a party had obtained since just after the Reform Bill of 1832, and it was accepted as a portent.

There now began Gladstone's first and most successful ministry. Morley, in his *Life of Gladstone*, calls it 'the day's work of a giant'. Gladstone in his old age told Morley that the golden age of administrative reform was the period between the two Reform Bills. He might have been excused if he had named his own ministry as the golden age. His Cabinet was impressive. Lowe at the

Exchequer, Bruce at the Home Office, Goschen at the Poor Law Board (after 1871 Local Government Board). The great Bright took office at the Board of Trade, to retire, because of ill-health, in 1871. Cardwell, one of the surviving Peelites and, like Gladstone, an old 'double first' of Oxford, was at the War Office. Nor was the Ministry without a respectable patrician element in the Lords. Lord Clarendon, a veteran Whig, was at the Foreign Office, succeeded by Lord Granville in 1870. The Duke of Argyll, one of the orators of the day, Lord Ripon, and Lord Kimberley were also members.

The list of the reforms of this Government is long and can only be summarized. In Ireland the Church was disestablished and partially disendowed in 1869. In 1870 an elaborate measure to make more equitable the law of Irish land tenure was passed. In 1870, by an order in Council, the higher posts in the Home Civil Service were thrown open to competition by examination, and this was the culmination of various forward steps since the report of a Royal Commission in 1853 which had led to the appointment of a permanent Civil Service Commission in 1855. The Army, a subject in which Liberals were not supposed to be much interested, was given probably the most important single overhaul in its history. Cardwell, profiting from much previous study by himself and others, placed the War Office on a more logical footing. All branches were to be under the Secretary of State. Recruitment was to be on a shorter-term basis with six years with the colours and six with the reserve. The regiments were to be allocated to counties or districts and placed on a double battalion footing, which enabled frequent exchange between service at home or abroad. But the step which aroused most controversy was the Government's decision to abolish the practice of permitting commissions to be purchased. This practice, dating from Anne's time and originally a humane measure to permit officers to compensate themselves against the neglect of a parsimonious Parliament, was, in spite of careful rules for its application, discouraging to talent and faithful service. Yet it had hot defenders, and the Lords rejected it only to find that Gladstone could abolish it by prerogative power. The Army was made more competitive and its officers more professionally efficient. But it remained an eminently aristocratic force by custom and by the heavy expenses of an officer's life. If the middle-class

Liberals of the day had cared about things military as they cared about things civilian, they would have insisted on higher pay for officers and severe restriction of extravagance, a chance for the keen professional soldier. But they cared little for these things. The Army, thus reformed, proved itself efficient for all the burdens laid upon it until the end of the century.

In the realm of pure politics the Ballot Act, passed in 1872, was a major step in political democracy. Long and fierce had the argument been waged over this question. Gladstone's Act was a masterpiece of careful forethought and accuracy and it stands to-day complete. It is not easy to estimate its effects. It reduced bribery but did not check it, for a severe Corrupt Practices Act in 1883 was required. It reduced direct and obvious intimidation, but intimidation can never be absent from political life. It made the counting of votes simpler and more accurate, an important matter with the largely increasing electorates. But it settled a question once and for all. Men may agitate for secret ballot. They do not agitate for open ballot once it has been made secret. Elaborate precautions are taken in the Ballot Act for recording the votes of those who are illiterate. The Education Act had been passed earlier in the life of the Ministry to make the first whole-hearted attempt to eliminate illiteracy in England. All the efforts of all the voluntary agencies for education, and they form a magnificent record of missionary and philanthropic zeal, had now failed to provide schools for the mass of English children.

The rock on which English education had foundered was the absence of religious uniformity. The Anglicans naturally felt that the Established Church should take the lead, and it did indeed provide more voluntary schools than any other agency. But the Nonconformists could not endure an Anglican monopoly. The grants which the Government had begun to pay to voluntary schools which accepted inspection had risen from a pittance of £20,000 in 1833 to £541,000 in 1856. It was still woefully inadequate. Scotland, with its greater religious uniformity and a positive ideal of widely diffused popular education which can be traced back to the great John Knox himself, was better served, and Scotsmen were not shy in alluding to this superiority. The later nineteenth century was the age when Scotsmen were notable as professional and technical elements in British life, although the great Augustan age, when Edinburgh had shone in the forefront of European thought and letters, had long since passed. Even more imposing was the example of Prussia and of North America. The eleventh hour had struck for England. It fell to Gladstone to grasp the nettle.

The result was the Education Act of 1870, which was managed in Parliament by W. E. Forster, a Liberal of Quaker antecedents, who was none the less willing to effect a compromise which was to offend the Nonconformists. The Act provided that in any area which was without adequate elementary schools, school boards were to be set up elected by the ratepayers. These boards were to build and maintain schools out of local rates. These 'board schools' were to give non-sectarian religious instruction of a character which would not offend the susceptibilities of parents. Obviously this was an apple of discord, but a Christian country, not at one with itself in Church matters, could hardly do otherwise.

The year 1870 is thus the cardinal date in which the English State assumed responsibility for educating its children. To complete the work it was necessary to make education compulsory, which was done in 1880, and free, in 1891. One other important step was taken by Gladstone. In 1871 the religious tests, which limited the Universities of Oxford and Cambridge to those who would profess themselves Anglicans, were abolished. The older school of Churchmen who still regarded the Universities as seminaries of the Anglican faith were dismayed. Slowly, gingerly, Nonconformists began to send their sons there. In general, the Church of England did not suffer; the traditional Anglican pull of Oxford was strong, and the influence of Anglicanism permeated Nonconformity rather than weakened before the dissenting infiltration. A future Primate, Lang, was to come to Oxford from a Scottish manse, and the mother of the great Haldane was so suspicious of sinister influences that she preferred to send her son from Edinburgh to Goettingen, rather than subject him to Oxford's pseudo-Catholicism. The abolition of tests, in fact, restored Oxford and Cambridge to the nation in general. With the slow decline of religious asperities the Universities took on a more eclectic outlook until Oxford became in this century a kind of English Benares with temples for all, and Jesuits, Dominicans, Benedictines, Congregationalists, Unitarians, Baptists have set up seminaries there with the benign approval of the University.

The work of Gladstone's first ministry was germinal in the

development of English life. It was both an end and a beginning. Its watchword was liberalism in the literal sense of freedom. Men of parts and industry were to be free to compete for civil service places, for commissions in the army, to enter universities. The electors were to be free to vote without fear of intimidation from their superiors or their fellows. A buoyant revenue and low taxation left men free to spend, save, or invest their earnings. At the end of the ministry in 1873 a great reorganization of the Courts of Justice was carried out by the Judicature Act of Lord Selborne and carried into effect by his successor, the Conservative Chancellor Lord Cairns. This unified the old separate Courts of King's Bench, Chancery, Exchequer, and Common Pleas in one High Court, and by abolishing many anomalies made recourse to justice easier. *Laisser-faire* had reached its climax. It was also beginning to decline. Gladstone and his colleagues were no hidebound doctrinaires. They did not shrink from calling in the power of the State to establish national education. There was another thorny problem that they were not afraid to grapple with, what was called the 'temperance' question, by which was meant the problem of intemperance, the waste and evil in a society where much of the patient efforts at social improvement were brought to nothing by drink. Bruce, the Home Secretary, in 1872 passed an Act which limited the hours during which drink could be sold, and sought to limit and reduce the number of licences given for public houses. It has been regarded by many as a fatal error of the Liberals, for it made an enemy of the brewing and distilling interests and all their allies, what became known as 'the Trade'. Yet what else could the Liberals have done? While many ardent social reformers were on the Tory side, notably the venerable and apostolic Lord Shaftesbury, the strongest impetus came from the Radical side. While all good men preached temperance, the Nonconformist bodies often made not merely temperance but total abstinence an article of faith, an eleventh commandment. And they were, if not the majority of Liberal voters, at any rate the most important clients of the party. Nor was it, as is often absurdly supposed, a hatred of human pleasure, a 'manichaeanism' that made them so zealous for 'temperance'. Who, who had ever seen them at their high teas, would accuse them of indifference to material satisfactions? These men and women of the so-called lower middle classes lived not far from real poverty; they had mostly won their way up from proletarian squalor by hard frugality of which the most important was abstinence from drink. It was an abstinence twice blessed, for it not only enabled them to save, but made them more reliable and efficient in their employment. In the sixties, Bright, in a speech which earned a cartoon in *Punch*, had called for an attack on the drink evil. Now the Bill had to be honoured.

From now on, however, we find the drink question dividing the parties very clearly. The Tories undertook the protection of the Trade and won the good will of the more thoughtless and philistine working men. The Liberals, however generously their wealthier leaders might 'indulge' over their dinner tables, were committed to some form of temperance legislation. In 1895 we find the Liberals plunging for Local Veto on licensed houses, somewhat despondently and with adverse results. The Tories also had their troubles, and the Bishops would testify to the magnitude of the drink evil. The future Archbishop Davidson was to receive the rough edge of Lord Salisbury's tongue for his harping in the Lords on this question.

It did, however, introduce a factor in politics in which many people had a direct material interest. There is nothing so difficult for young people of the present day to realize as the fact that late Victorian politics were for the most part free from material inducements to vote for one party or another. The State was not there to give, but to take and to take as sparingly as possible. If we ask how an elector could vote to improve himself economically, it is hard to find an answer. There were no tariffs to be put on or removed, no subsidies, no social service benefits. Budgets might vary slightly in the amount of income tax or the price of tea and sugar, or there might be some small adjustment of local rating, and while Gladstone would probably do all this better than Stafford-Northcote, he had already set public finance on lines that it would not leave for decades to come. Political allegiance was largely a matter of what Bentham would call sympathy and antipathy, of class feeling more than class interest, of religious affinities, of pure political doctrine or simple political sentiment, and, if nothing in home affairs was pressing, then to the securely girt and well-found England of these days the whole wide world was spread before them to agonize over.

And what, it may be asked, were the people, the workers, the labouring poor, making of it all? In many respects they were agents, not patients. Their superiors debated the 'condition of the people' problem. Only very slowly did they use their power to seek their own ends. In one field, however, a large number of the workers had definite interests, and that was in the organization of trades unions. Their legal status was still doubtful until the Gladstone Ministry in 1871 sponsored an Act which permitted them legally to register themselves and find the protection of the law afforded to duly constituted societies. At the same time a Criminal Law Amendment Act legislated so hard against the picketing of workers in strikes that their power to strike effectively seemed to be nugatory. This turned many of them against the Liberals in the election of 1874.

For, however slow the British working classes may have been to fight for their rights and needs, there was one privilege they did learn to exercise, and that was the privilege of changing their rulers. Since the Reform Bill of 1867 no party has been in office for more than ten years and only thrice, in 1900, in 1910, and in 1935, has a government survived a general election after a spell of office. By 1873 Gladstone was tired. He was defeated over an attempt to establish a unified university in Dublin for Protestants and Catholics, but when he resigned he was compelled to return. Disraeli, the master tactician, put him in again to bat out time. If Gladstone was tired, so were many of his colleagues, and the country was tired of them. A great work had been accomplished, and even those who were grateful and approving had lost their enthusiasm. The dissolution of 1874 brought Disraeli back with a majority nominally of 50, but, owing to the divisions in the Radical ranks, more especially the Irish Home Rule elements, it was a safe and sound majority. Gladstone, who had brought income tax down to 3d., hoped to abolish it, and feverishly, it may even be said unworthily, thrust this boon before the electors. They did not care. Disraeli had made capital out of the alleged weakness of Liberal foreign policy, yielding to America over the *Alabama*, yielding to Russia over the Black Sea forts; even although the Franco-Prussian war had never demanded British intervention and Gladstone's conduct over the danger of a breach of Belgian neutrality had won approval, it left an uneasy feeling that Britain did not count in Europe for as much as formerly. The Ministers were stigmatized as 'exhausted volcanoes', accused of threatening all interests and property. Disraeli did not go forth seeking with a lamp for a policy; the reverse of Gladstone's sufficed.

To very large numbers of Englishmen it was with genuine gratitude and relief that they welcomed Disraeli after the intellectually passionate, indefatigable, unresting Gladstone. Disraeli appointed a Cabinet of considerable ability. Lord Derby, the son of his old chief, had the Foreign Office until he resigned in 1878, to be replaced by Lord Salisbury. Northcote took the Exchequer, and amongst the new men are the names of Sir Michael Hicks-Beach, who was to have an eminent career, W. H. Smith, to lead the House from 1886 to 1892, and R. A. Cross, a solicitor by profession, who took the Home Office. It was to Cross that most of the domestic achievements of the Government were to be credited and therefore to Disraeli for choosing him. This Ministry is remembered and justly praised for important advances in local government and health reform. The Public Health Act of 1875 was a great codifying measure and made new advances in the control by Government in the interests of sanitation. Other measures had an even stronger flavour of what is called social reform—an Agricultural Holdings Bill, an Artisans' Dwellings Bill, and a Friendly Societies Bill. The organized workers were gratified by a restatement of the law in respect of strikes and intimidation, and collective action by workers was made a lawful, and became often a fruitful, measure for raising or maintaining wages. All this redounded to the credit of the Government and to Disraeli personally, for he had never ceased to hold a paternalist philosophy which advocated the care of the people in things material rather than submission to their claims for mere political rights. No doubt the Liberals, if returned to power, might have tackled many of these questions, but the fact remains that they were not in power. And some of them made the fatal error of affecting to despise these modest but fruitful measures as compared with their own sweeping *political* reforms. Disraeli at once pounced on them and with one of his sweeping phrases, *sanitas sanitatum*, acquired all the credit and put all the odium of opposition on his opponents. Fewer insanitary houses, better drains, cleaner rivers, slightly, very slightly less smoky cities, these were tangible and obvious benefits, whereas all the grand labours of the Liberal Ministry had done little to make urban England any less brown and unpleasant a land. Psychologically, this was of immense importance to the morale of the Conservative party, and enabled them for a generation to feel themselves true friends of the people.

There was another vacuum left by Gladstone which Disraeli proceeded to fill. The nation had suffered loss of pride. Here, Disraeli, with his imaginative power, was able to make good the loss. He could now do what Palmerston had done so well and make Englishmen feel confident before the world. But now the emphasis was laid not on the word nation but Empire. There had always been much talk of the British Empire, meaning in general the *imperium* or rule of the British State. But now Empire is spelled more often with a capital, and it refers less to the totality than to the circumference of our dominion. Two sudden steps roused the public. In November 1875 Disraeli secretly purchased from the Khedive of Egypt shares in the Suez canal and thus joined Britain with France in its control. He had to seek approval *ex post facto* from Parliament, but it was easily given. This was of high strategic importance and also, as it turned out, profitable. In 1876 he secured statutory authority for a proposal to make the Queen Empress of India. At first the notion did not greatly please the public though it pleased the Queen, but soon it was accepted and was seen to have a great effect on India, where the people were traditionally impressed by princely magnificence. So far, Disraeli, now consciously pressing Imperialism as desirable policy and sentiment, had succeeded well. In the later part of his ministry he fell into a more chequered period. The two factors were imperial and also foreign policy, the terrible Eastern question. In South Africa and in Afghanistan two energetic proconsuls, Bartle Frere and the Viceroy, Lord Lytton, came upon dangerous resistance. In Africa a war with the Zulus led to a defeat at Isandlhwana, and in Afghanistan an expedition, after early success, was turned into disaster by the murder of the British Resident, Cavagnari. Both these defeats were speedily redressed, and victory came to British arms. But the wars were costly, the defeats humiliating, for it is one of the difficulties of imperialism that it should always be successful. Superior civilization backed by invincible power: that is the vision of the imperialist; there should be no exceptions to this rule. The strong Power is disgraced by any defeat, the weak Power need not be. Scotland can think of

Flodden with pride; the English cannot think thus of Bannock-burn. The forces, always alert, of anti-imperialism began to rise in their wrath whether their grievance was a penny on the income tax or a stain on their conscience. And the Government, like all responsible rulers, had to explain why they had taken strong measures without adequate security for success.

But the failures in Africa and India only completed the filling of the cup which had begun with the Turkish question. In 1875 a revolt had begun against the Turks in Bosnia and it was aided by the compatriots in independent Serbia. The European Powers became anxious and began to concert measures to restore peace by bringing influence to bear on the Turkish Government. In May 1876 proposals for intervention made by Russia, Germany, and Austria were rejected by Disraeli. This meant that Britain was to take her own course, that she would watch Russia and trust neither of the two Germanic Empires. It committed Britain to supporting Turkey and possibly to war with Russia. Liberals denounced this severance from the concert of Europe and, immediately afterwards, popular opinion was inflamed by news of the famous Bulgarian atrocities, horrible massacres carried out by the Turks against what was admittedly a dangerous Bulgarian rebellion.

There followed a long struggle in Britain between Liberals stirred by humanitarian passions and Conservatives holding fast to diplomatic traditions and imperial and strategic necessities. Gladstone, who had retired from the leadership of the Liberal party, came back into public life with a pamphlet of furious and magnificent rhetoric against the Turks. At first he carried all before him, and most of the famous men of letters and leaders of thought were with him. The Turkish Government, however, drew encouragement from official British policy and resisted the reforms demanded by the European Powers, and in April 1877 war broke out between Russia and Turkey. In fierce fighting the Russians were successful enough to alarm opinion in England and the Turks skilful and gallant enough to inspire sympathy. The mood of the country changed, and a wave of anti-Russian sentiment brought Gladstone into temporary odium. The Russians advanced close to Constantinople, and in January 1878 the Government ordered the British Fleet to the Sea of Marmora. The war fever rose higher in England, especially in London.

But there was not a firm and general will for war. In the Cabinet itself there were doubts, and first Carnarvon and then Derby, the Foreign Secretary, resigned. The Treaty of San Stephano, negotiated between Russia and Turkey, confirmed Disraeli's worst suspicions of Russian designs for destroying Turkey in Europe by creating a large, independent, and presumably servile Bulgarian State. In March 1878 reservists were called up and Indian troops sent to Malta. Salisbury, who now for the first time held the Foreign Office, showed his steady and skilful hand, and a Conference was arranged to meet at Berlin. As a result of this Conference, over which Bismarck presided, the inroads into Turkish territory were reduced, Bulgaria was diminished and divided, Britain obtained possession of Cyprus, and Austria was permitted to occupy but not fully to annex Bosnia.

This was the high-water mark of Disraeli's career. He claimed to have won peace with honour, and the public applauded a peace which was the result of resolute and independent action by the Government. Very different views have been held about the Berlin settlement, but it lasted for nearly thirty-five years. There have been others less successful. Versailles, drawn up in the extreme of victory, lasted twenty years; Munich, in the excess of submission, lasted for eleven months. Disraeli, who had now become Earl of Beaconsfield, was apparently secure in his power. But the Parliament was not due for dissolution until, at the latest, 1881, and misfortunes now pursued them—the colonial wars, already noticed, and a slower, but perhaps more deadly, process, decline of trade and growing depression in British agriculture. The Liberals, silenced for a time, returned vigorously to the attack. Gladstone, still an unofficial leader, threw down a challenge by accepting nomination for the usually Tory seat of Midlothian (its miners were not enfranchised until 1884) and sped about the country speaking more frequently, more sporadically, and more passionately than was then thought decorous in elder statesmen. The country was polled in the spring of 1880 and the Liberals won a greater victory than in 1868, claiming a majority of nearly 140. Disraeli at once resigned. A year later he died. No slick and easy verdict can be passed on this remarkable man. He was himself the author of many romances, but his own life was a greater romance than any of his novels. Born outside the social, and even the Christian pale, he had risen to the head of the gentlemen of England whom he so admired and whose admiration he at last by talent and hard service extracted. He has been accused of being a snob, in the sense of cultivating the patricians and the nobles, but by the end of his life he needed no longer to cultivate them, he was one himself. Born D'Israeli, he died an Earl. He claimed to have educated his party to march with the times if only for the sake of expediency. Fundamentally, his greatest service to his party was to teach them not to despair, to understand that in the seemingly radical and utilitarian England of his day the springs of tradition and loyalty and natural deferential sentiments were not drying up, but only waiting to be uncovered. A master of the art of government he was not. Neither his education nor his temperament nor his early life disposed him for that. But he was in a supreme degree a master of the art of politics.

By the time of his death there had come about a change in the attitude of Queen Victoria towards Ministers and parties. To an extent that few of her subjects knew she favoured the Conservatives against the Liberals and favoured Disraeli against Gladstone. With all the arts of a courtier, he won the Queen's regard and affection, he espoused the causes which she most naturally admired, and there was in addition a personal bond between them at the last, the sympathy of a lonely widow to a lonely widower.

When we consider the Conservative defeat in 1880, it must be remembered that there were more than misadventures abroad to distress the English people at this time; there were more material anxieties to brood upon than the harm wrought by 'prancing proconsuls' and 'satanic' pro-Turkish imperialist statesmen. The 'seventies were an anxious period for English industry and the beginning of a long and disastrous spell for English agriculture. A slump in trade in 1873-4 was thought to play a part in Gladstone's defeat. The bad harvest of 1878 and 1879 frowned on Disraeli's prospects. It is difficult to know how far these economic factors influenced the electorate in their conduct at elections. For it was not within the power of any government to provide by government action any important alleviation of economic distress. *Laisser-faire* was too securely established to permit of substantial schemes of protection, or of subsidy or of relief by public works. None the less, bad times naturally bear hard on the government that has the misfortune to be in office. Under the English electoral

system of plurality voting in single- or double-member constituencies, a very small movement of votes, then as now,
produced a disproportionate change of seats in the House of
Commons. The military adventures of the Disraeli Government,
although on a small scale, did increase taxation and income tax
rose from 2d. in the pound in 1874 to 5d. in 1789 and 6d. in 1880.
On a public burdened by trade anxieties the increase, however
small, was resented.

In the period after 1870, British trade and industry was facing
more competition. The era of very large profits had passed, and
supply was overtaking demand both at home and abroad. Production still continued to increase and, except for a short period
in the 'seventies, capital was invested abroad from this country.
The railway system was all but complete, and the motor engine
had not yet arrived to supplement and rival transport by steam.
Business organization was taking increasingly the form of joint-
stock companies which usually became also limited companies.
Peel had passed the first joint-stock Companies Act in 1844. In
1855 the principle of limited liability was accepted by statute,
and in 1862 a general consolidating Companies Act permitted
the transformation from the private, personally owned business
to the anonymous company. Banking organization was also
changing. Bagehot in his *Lombard Street*, published in 1873, had
lamented the disappearance of the old private local bank. In 1878
the City of Glasgow Bank failed, with disastrous results to the
West of Scotland business community. Banks then began to form
larger units. In the 'eighties the Midland Bank and also Lloyds
opened London offices, and we see the beginning of the famous
Big Five Banks, which have carried the country through so many
dangerous commercial crises without any catastrophic failures
amongst banks of deposit. There is here a clear and rational
principle at work. Larger units are used as a safeguard against
excessive competition and vicissitudes in trade. The railways
were also becoming more co-operative with each other and many
of the smaller lines became absorbed by the larger, a process
which was to continue until the final unification of all railways
by nationalization. Shipping and shipbuilding remained a para-
mount activity of Great Britain. In the middle of the century the
United States had been keen rivals of the British, but the advent
of the steam engine and the iron ship had given Britain a com-

petitive advantage as well as other factors, such as the westward landward expansion of America and a growing protectionism. Sailing-ships still accounted for half the tonnage on the British register in 1880, but steam soon drew ahead, and by 1900 it was eight times as great. In that year British-owned vessels numbered thirteen million tons out of a total for the world's shipping of twenty-nine million tons. In 1898, British shipyards, led by the Clyde, launched 1,354,000 tons, and in the same year Lloyd's Register reckoned the total production of the rest of the world at 532,000 tons, including both steam and sail. Britain's large share of the carrying trade of the world added to her wealth. Insurance and banking were also services which Britain carried out for other countries, and these operations were to be classed amongst the so-called 'invisible exports' which helped to pay for increasing demands for food and raw material. The population was still expanding steadily. In 1851 it was just under 28 million; by 1891 it had risen to 38 million. Not only grain but meat was freely imported in increasing quantities. The use of refrigeration in the eighteen-eighties began to replace live imported cattle by frozen meat. Textile raw materials were also required, although textile manufacturers were becoming relatively less important in the national economy. Between the eighteen-thirties and the eighteen-eighties textiles had fallen from 72 per cent of the total exports of the country to only 52 per cent, and were to fall still further. The proportion of metals exported increased from 12 per cent in 1836 to 20 per cent in 1880.

But while British industry, with ups and downs and at a decreasing rate, compared to other countries, flourished and expanded, agriculture and especially arable farming for wheat and other grains was disastrously reduced. It was not until after 1870 that the fears of the protectionists for agricultural collapse were verified and, it may be added, the hopes of the Cobdenite free traders for cheap bread fully realized. As the prairies of North America were developed for wheat farming, and as transport by sea and land steadily improved, the English farmer was overwhelmed. From 1877, when the price of wheat averaged fifty-six shillings and ninepence a quarter, it fell to forty-six shillings and fivepence in 1878 and continued to fall until in 1886 it reached thirty-one shillings a quarter. Over the same period the area under wheat decreased by nearly three-tenths. The number of labourers on the land decreased also; rent fell, and farmers became bankrupt or changed to other types of farming. The urbanization of England was steadily intensified. Other nations turned to protection to stay the flood of New World produce. Britain remained wedded to free trade, obstinately or manfully according to the political predilection of the observer.

There is a strange political problem here. Why did this disaster to the largest single national industry not provoke a sharp counter-attack on free trade? French peasants, Prussian junkers, knew how to defend themselves; why were English squires and farmers dumb? So far as the landlord class is concerned, while many suffered severely, many were holders of urban land whose value continued to rise and many also had by marriage or inheritance money incomes which enabled them to bear the strain of reduced rural rents. As for the farmers, they were not a very vocal class. The methods and conventions of English public life made it difficult for farmers to stand for Parliament on their own; they lacked the wealth, the social status; they had not the face to do it. Moreover, there was not a strong enough farmers' vote to sway an election. After 1885 the labourers, at least those who were householders, were enfranchised. The farmers were not too eager to arouse their political spirit, least of all since Joseph Arch had started an agricultural trade union and was fighting hard for higher wages. The Conservative party was a whole—lord, squire, farmer, labourer—and might be kept together on broad national issues, more especially by appeals to pride and patriotism. To raise the flag of protection was to deliver themselves over to the Free Trade Liberals, already by all appearances the more powerful party. It was only by means of the Home Rule schism that the Conservatives were able to win an unexpected ascendancy from 1886 onwards. But by whose aid was this won? By the Liberal Unionists, all of whom had been baptized in the pure free trade faith. The greatest of them all, Joseph Chamberlain, was to turn protectionist, but not till the nineteenth century was out. And even then his conversion to free trade was followed by an unprecedented Conservative defeat. Amelioration for the farmer by means of easier local rating was the only easement which could be provided. This was due to some extent in the Agricultural Rates Act, passed actually by a Unionist Government in 1896. For the rest, the Tories had to sit by the bedside of English agriculture, able only to comfort and to mourn as it slowly sickened of its incurable ailment; they could only say, in an old-fashioned phrase applied to consumptive persons, that it 'had a delicacy'.

The year 1880 dawned very fair for Liberalism and yet Gladstone's second ministry, his last long ministry, was to bring sad disappointment. After the official leader, Lord Hartington, had returned his commission to the Queen and Gladstone was reluctantly sent for, a very fine Cabinet was appointed. It spread from Whig magnates like Lords Granville, Spencer, Hartington, Kimberley, to the ancient Radical, Bright, and the young rising Radical, Chamberlain, and men of eminent capacity like Harcourt, Trevelyan and Dilke. Why then did it not fulfil its promise? Its majority held, its leader did not decline in power or in the awe-inspiring hold he had over the faithful. It failed partly through the sheer vicissitudes and necessities of politics, the storms that beat on all governments. To some extent it was weakened by inherent contradictions in the Liberal philosophy, which had such a strong pacific and conciliatory ethos as to make it weak when action was required. It may also have been said to have failed in not engaging in some wise policy of social improvement. This is more a criticism by posterity than by the contemporary world, but not entirely, for Matthew Arnold was able to tell Liberals that they were lost if they did not attack what Cobbett had called the 'hell-holes' of England, and on the Liberal benches was a figure like Cunningham-Graham the Scottish laird, who seethed with scorn at the middle-class fatuity of his fellow members.

Abroad, the Ministry plunged into difficulties in Africa. The Transvaal had been promised its independence by Gladstone and the Liberals, but, before this could be negotiated, clashes took place between the burghers and British forces, culminating in a small but very sharp defeat at Majuba. Gladstone was in a terrible dilemma; to continue with the policy which he believed right and conciliate the Boers or teach them a hard lesson? He preferred conciliation, and the independence of the Transvaal was recognized, subject to British control of foreign relations. At home this was felt as a terrible humiliation, and the word Majuba pursued Gladstone to the end of his days and his followers for long afterwards.

In 1882 another cloud appears. The internal affairs of Egypt were held to warrant intervention by France and Britain to restore financial order. Alexandria was bombarded, and this step produced the automatic resignation of the Quaker, Bright. Further operations, which the French left to the British, ended in the subjection of Egypt, an occupation loudly declared by the Government to be only temporary. It lasted in one form or another for sixty years. Behind Egypt lay the Sudan, which in 1883 was falling under the control of a fanatical Moslem leader, styled the Mahdi. The British Government was not swift or firm enough in its measures, either to evacuate the Sudan or to hold it. Under pressure from popular agitation, General Gordon, a brilliant but unorthodox leader, was sent with instructions to evacuate the Sudan. Gordon impulsively decided to try to hold Khartoum and was soon besieged there. The Cabinet were now compelled to relieve him and took various measures, always too late, and in January 1885 the Mahdi's forces occupied Khartoum and Gordon was killed. Khartoum was added to Majuba as a name of indelible disgrace.

Gladstone, in the eyes of at least half the nation, had shown himself incompetent to control the Empire at the extremities. Worse still, he seemed unable to control the United Kingdom and scarcely even the House of Commons itself.

What was the adverse spirit that cast so baleful a spell upon this Liberal Parliament, directed by a man of genius and inspired by so much generous enthusiasm? It was Irish Nationalism. In 1868 Gladstone, summoned to the Queen to become First Minister, had said: 'My mission is to pacify Ireland.' In 1873, defending the work of his first Ministry, he had declared to the House of Commons: 'To mete out justice to Ireland . . . has been the work, I will almost say the sacred work, of this Parliament.' Since 1848 when Ireland was settling down after the famine and the futile rising of William Smith O'Brien and the death of O'Connell, British politics had been less disturbed by Irish affairs than in the first half of the century. But in the late 'sixties the Irish problem came to life once more. A militant organization known as the Fenians had attempted armed revolt in Canada and had committed outrages in England of which a bomb plot at Clerkenwell prison was the most notorious. The English public wearily turned their attention to the question. Anger and contempt were high amongst the emotions felt; it was the extraordinary achievement of Gladstone and the Liberal party under his leadership that what might have been merely a trial of strength, a trial to which there could only be one issue, became a question of conscience and of judgment. Nor was the judgment cast against the throwers of bombs and the authors of many cruel and almost senseless crimes, but against the great nation whose majesty had been outraged, because in the light of history and of reason its dominion seemed to be of doubtful legitimacy and its rule deficient in equity. Not thus did Austrians feel about Italians and Slavs, or Germans and Russians about Poles.

It is doubtful whether the Irish Nationalists ever fully appreciated the nature of their appeal to the consideration of Englishmen. It is true that then and since they could show that at every step violence seemed to pay, to produce concessions and reforms. Yet the force which Irish Nationalists could put forth was scarcely adequate to compete with that of the Protestant or 'loyalist' minority in Ireland itself, much less with the military force of Britain, its trained army, its tremendous navy, well adapted to subduing a land where no town of more than twenty thousand inhabitants lies away from the sea. The fact is that the Irish, a name by which it is convenient to designate the Nationalist as opposed to the Orange elements of the nation, were always able most successfully to advertise their grievances by violence. But to advertise is not the same as to compel. Yet they could put English statemen in a dilemma by violent tactics. This forced consideration. Something had to be done. Ireland had either to be governed with stronger laws and more effective power or the complaints of the Nationalists had to be remedied, coercion or conciliation. It had become almost second nature with Liberals to ask whether the rule of Britain was just rather than to ask how it could be securely enforced.

The first step in Gladstone's 'sacred task' had been the disestablishment of the Anglican Church in Ireland. It had been carried out, one of the neatest operations in political surgery, and the scars quickly healed. Next came the land, a less tractable question in which economic, legal, political, and social difficulties abounded. Gladstone's first Irish Land Act of 1870 tried to establish a more equitable relationship between landlord and tenant. The tenant was by the Act entitled to demand compensation for improvements which he had effected during the period of his lease and compensation for disturbance. Some clauses, inserted at the instigation of John Bright, provided for purchase of land by tenants, but remained ineffective although important as the first signs of what was to be the ultimate solution in 1903. For the Bill of 1870, while immensely significant as the recognition that Irish land was a problem clean different from land tenure in England, did little to allay discontent. The problem was utterly intractable. By economic analysis Ireland was suffering from over-population; the curse of Malthus lay upon her. There was a hunger for land-holdings, a supply of tenants which never gave out. The landlords were in most cases separated by religious, political, and social differences from their tenants. Many were absentees leaving the care of their lands to the so-called 'middle-men', a somewhat different race from the agents or factors of England and Scotland. In the late eighteenth century the Irish Parliament had actually considered a proposal to place a special tax on landlords who were absentees. But too much may be made of the absentee landlords. They were often men of great wealth who could afford to be lenient. The small landlord or 'squireen', living sparely on a small rental, might often be a harder master.

In 1881 Gladstone returned to the Irish land problem. This time he had the advantage of an exacting Royal Commission on the subject, and his new Act was more thorough and far-reaching. In the words of one of Gladstone's biographers, Dr. Eyck, 'it lifted the Irish peasant in the course of a generation to a higher level of well-being and personal liberty'. It guaranteed that the tenant would have fixity of tenure, no eviction save on con-ditions laid down in the Act, also free sale of the unexpired portion of his lease. Most important was the attempt to establish fair rents. Land courts were set up to establish fair rents binding on both parties for fifteen years and thus freeing the tenant from the grinding and uneven stress of the demand and supply of land. *Laisser-faire* was cast aside for what was almost a revival of the medieval *justum pretium*. In actual practice the land courts reduced rents on the average by about one-fifth.

Here was a reform, careful and elaborate in its application, revolutionary in its principles. The landed classes in England were startled; two eminent Whig noblemen, the old Argyll and the young Lansdowne, broke their connection with Gladstone at this time; the Irish landlords groaned at their diminishing rents and their threatened authority. Yet the Irish question grew no easier; nor is that surprising, for it was a political problem. The whole principle of British dominion in Ireland was in question; when indeed had the 'native Irish', 'the ancient inhabitants of the country', ever in their starved and bitter hearts accepted it? The Land Act had been passed when agrarian outrages in Ireland, including murder and arson, were being perpetrated and the new method of 'boycott' had been devised to terrorize people from accepting a lease of land from which a tenant had been evicted. In the House of Commons itself business had been reduced to a farce by determined Irish obstruction until Gladstone, with the support of the Opposition, had secured the passing of standing orders to introduce the closure of debate and to increase the power of the chair.

To the Parliament of 1874 there had been returned fifty-six Irish Nationalists or Home Rulers. Until 1878 their leader was Isaac Butt, a Protestant, a graduate of Trinity, Dublin, where he had at an early age been Professor of Political Economy. Slowly he had changed from extreme Unionism to Nationalism. He had been swayed mainly by two forces. One was his examination of Irish economic needs which he saw were different from those of industrial, free-trade Britain; the other, his moving experiences as a barrister in defending Fenian prisoners in the Irish courts. Butt has been underrated by posterity. It is true that his attempts to interest the House of Commons in his annual Bill for Home Rule were unsuccessful, but he founded the Irish Nationalist Party on a broad and liberal basis, accustomed the British public to it, and by his own character and principles redeemed it from the imputation of rebellion and crime. A peaceful mariner, he prepared a well-found ship, which could be used effectively when it fell into pirate hands. This happened in 1878 when Butt gave place to Charles Stewart Parnell, an ignorant and arrogant young Wicklow squire who had resided but never graduated at Cambridge, imbibed a taste for cricket and chemistry, and seemed destined for an obscure and useless life. But American ancestry on his mother's side and some adverse and apostatic acid in his soul drove him from the conventional and loyal paths to become the greatest leader that Irish nationalism has known. His *métier* was leadership, leadership pure and simple, to no very positive end and with no very constructive purpose, but with an animation of spirit and a power of condensed hatred and contempt for England which made him the idol of his resentful countrymen. In the Parliament of 1880 he had sixty-two followers, and he astounded the public by the paralysis he inflicted on House of Commons procedure which had already suffered from the difficulties about admitting the atheist Bradlaugh.

Obstruction in the Commons was not altogether unknown. To use the forms of the House in order to delay business, to waste time in debate as a protest against measures which the majority wanted to carry, these were methods which minorities might employ. Parnell, imposing an inexorable discipline on his devoted followers, brought the work of the House to a standstill. If his aim was permanently to disable parliamentary government, he failed; indeed, the procedure reforms which were carried were such as must sooner or later have been made. But for the purpose of advertising the wrongs of Ireland Parnell's parliamentary methods were splendidly successful and played their part along with the murdered landlord, the boycotted tenant, the burnt rick, and the maimed cattle. All eyes perforce had to turn to Ireland. Not that the agrarian policy was in the main Parnell's work. Michael Davitt had organized his Land-League and obtained funds from Australian and American Irish. Nor is it just to suppose that the worst outrages had the approbation of such gifted leaders as Davitt and Parnell. But the British public tended to see the whole campaign as one united offensive and to confound together perpetrators, abettors, and apologists.

With falling agricultural prices the Irish saw growing misery, evictions increasing from 2,000 in the year 1877 to 10,000 in 1880. They saw a Bill to give compensation to the evicted, presented by the Nationalists in Parliament, adopted without wholehearted support by the Liberal majority and totally rejected in the Lords. It was not till 1881 that Gladstone's great measure was passed. Meanwhile the responsible Ministers of the Crown had to preserve order. Lord Cowper, the Lord-Lieutenant of Ireland, and W. E. Forster, the Chief Secretary, demanded fuller powers, and reluctantly the Cabinet brought in a Coercion Bill. It was against this that Parnell put forward his greatest effort and prolonged a sitting for forty-one hours till Speaker Brand terminated it by putting the question on his own authority. Parnell, who continued to countenance the tenants' right agitation in Ireland, was eventually imprisoned in Kilmainham Jail in Dublin. The imprisonment was not so rigorous as to keep him out of touch with friends. In April 1882 he was temporarily released to visit a dying sister and saw O'Shea, an Irish M.P. who was the husband of the woman who was later to become known to all as Parnell's mistress. Through O'Shea contact was made with the Government, and Gladstone patched up an informal agreement. Parnell was to use his influence to end crime and disorder while the Government were to indemnify some scores of tenants, who were behind with their rents, by an Arrears Bill. In May 1882 Parnell was released with Davitt and other leaders. Lord Cowper and Forster resigned, but it looked as though Liberal leniency had produced conciliation. But the various groups and gangs of extremists in Ireland did not all accept Parnell's writ. The new Chief Secretary, Lord Frederick Cavendish, and his permanent Under-Secretary, Burke, were murdered in Dublin by the agents of a secret ring called the Invincibles. Parnell was horrified and denounced the crime. Gladstone held to the Kilmainham agreement and, while the Parliament of 1880 lasted, the worst of the Irish troubles were over. Parnell was at the height of his fame and, while his countrymen admired him for the way in which he had made the British Government yield to the Nationalists, the public in England, or some large part of it, began to see in Parnell a possible medium for moderate and liberal government in Ireland.

While Gladstone was being vexed to the verge of his endurance by Parnell and the Irish problem, another young man had appeared to sting him like a hornet and in the end become the principal agent in his failure to regain power in 1885. This was Lord Randolph Churchill, the son of the Duke of Marlborough, who had served under Disraeli, and the father of Winston Churchill. Since the Reform Bill of 1832, even perhaps since the Revolution of 1688, English Tories have suffered from a certain political anaemia, a lack of confidence and spirit. They have felt, often enough, that the spirit of the nation was theirs, but the Whigs and Liberals have had one priceless asset, a fundamental doctrine minted in its purity by John Locke and reflected back through the past into Magna Carta, the doctrine of Consent. How could the tradition of aristocratic authority prevail in the end against the ever-growing cancer of popular will? The election of 1880 had deeply discouraged the Conservative Party. Gladstone with his demagogy seemed invincible, and they rightly surmised that before the Parliament was over the scales would be further weighted in its favour by household suffrage in the counties and something like equal electoral districts. This was done by the Reform and Redistribution Acts of 1884. The leaders in the Commons under the unpugnacious Stafford-Northcote seemed to offer no hope of counter-offensive. In the Lords there was Salisbury, a strong and confident statesman, but what the Tories required was a master of politics. Unexpectedly, Lord Randolph Churchill supplied this need. He despised his leaders and formed a little group, styled the Fourth Party. From below the gangway on the Opposition side he began to wage war on Gladstone, cleverly exploiting all his defects, such as his prolixity, and meanly exploiting his merits, such as his courteous sense of what was due to any member of the House who raised any point or traversed any of his arguments. Churchill revived Disraeli's Tory democracy in many ways more effectively, advocating not less but more when social reform was in question. Lukewarm at first about British intervention in Egypt, he attacked Gladstone virulently over the 'desertion' of Gordon at Khartoum. As the Ministry plunged deeper into difficulties, humiliated by Parnell and the Irish, by the Boers in South Africa, by the Russians in Persia and Afghanistan, Churchill led the attack within and without the House, using language which shocked the older school of liberal politicians who accused Churchill of lowering the tone of public life just as Gladstone had been accused of lowering the tone in his Midlothian campaign. Gladstone himself was startled, but with the calm magnanimity of the very old and the very great he was to acknowledge Churchill to be in many ways 'the most courteous man he had ever met', just as he was to describe Parnell as 'the best man to do business with' he had ever come across.

But Joseph Chamberlain, the President of the Board of Trade and Radical reformer from Birmingham, was not old and not magnanimous. He fought his enemies with their own weapons, and, while pressing his colleagues to more radical measures in the council chamber, began to campaign in the countryside against the landlords, who toiled not neither spun, and whose income from rent was no better than 'ransom'. In Chamberlain,

Churchill seemed to have found his match. If Churchill could play the angry demagogue in the English towns, Chamberlain would rouse the sleeping countryside against their natural masters. In June 1885 the Irish vote was cast against the Government on an amendment to the budget, and Gladstone resigned. The Queen called on Lord Salisbury, who at once formed the first and shortest of his three Administrations. He himself took the Foreign Office, the task most congenial to him. Young Churchill was given the India Office, Lord Carnarvon went to Ireland, and Sir Michael Hicks-Beach took the Exchequer. These last three men handled the Irish question with momentous results. They had seen that Parnell was indifferent to the merits and fortunes of either of the British political parties. He could, therefore, be brought to change sides if he thought it would suit the needs of his Ireland. Astoundingly the new Conservative Government abandoned coercion which the Liberal Lord-Lieutenant, Lord Spencer, had enforced with some success. To satisfy the agrarian agitators, a scheme of State-assisted land purchase, Lord Ashbourne's Act, was passed into law. Carnarvon even had secret conversations with Parnell and his lieutenant, Justin McCarthy, on the possibility of some measure of devolution or Home Rule for Ireland. Gladstone also was moving towards Home Rule, partly as the logical conclusion of his general advocacy of self-government (why deny to Ireland what he had demanded for Italy and Bulgaria?), and partly because the revelation that the Conservatives were weakening made him feel that Home Rule was inevitable.

Salisbury's Government was styled the Caretaker Government, for it was only expected to last until the General Election could be held on the new household franchise and the newly distributed constituencies, with few exceptions, single-member areas. The election was held amidst extreme confusion of mind. In the towns, Churchill's spirited offensive against Gladstone and, to an unascertained extent, the votes of Irish immigrants directed by Parnell, turned the scales in the Conservative favour. In the counties, however, Chamberlain, with what was known as his 'unauthorized campaign' of agrarian reform, roused a real class-war spirit, and Liberals made many striking gains. The new Parliament showed a majority of 86 of Liberals over Conservatives, but Parnell, now supported by the full strength of the enfranchised Irish peasantry, had exactly 86 followers, and these were now full-blooded Nationalists and not, like many of the earlier Home Rulers, merely a species of Irish Liberal. Gladstone was negotiating with Parnell through the mysterious Mrs. O'Shea and hoped that the Irish question might be settled by a Conservative proposal supported by all parties and guaranteed a passage through the House of Lords. A dreadful indiscretion by his son Herbert ruined whatever prospects there were of this agreed measure. He revealed to certain editors of newspapers the secret of his father's conversion. Parnell turned away from the Tories towards Gladstone; the Tories stiffened towards unionism, and Lord Carnarvon, the peculiar apostle of self-government, resigned from the Lord-Lieutenancy of Ireland. Now all this might have suited Parnell had he not shocked and infuriated many Liberals by his sudden support of Conservatism in the House and at the polls. Some, like Chamberlain and the Whig magnate Lord Hartington, never forgave. Others, like Spencer and Campbell-Bannerman, overlooked Parnell's treachery and followed Gladstone towards Home Rule.

The question of the Union with Ireland was to shake British politics for forty years to come. Could this storm have been avoided? If the Conservatives had accepted Home Rule bona fide and pressed it, there could have been no serious opposition. But it is difficult to see how the Conservatives could have bent themselves to such a policy in spite of Carnarvon's simple-minded zeal and Salisbury's astute but unconvincing countenancing of the temporary Parnellite alliance. The Ascendancy Class in Ireland, the Protestants of the South, with so much of the land, the wealth, the natural habit of dominion, were inextricably bound up with the social elements that formed the core of English conservatism. The Irish landlord and professional classes had few illusions about the essentially radical and dissident nature of Irish Nationalism. They could teach their English friends. Moreover, in the north-eastern counties were the Protestants of Ulster, organized in the Orange Lodges, the most solid and formidable element in Irish politics. By what means were they to be forced into submission to a government of papist priests and Dublin drifters? The Ulstermen might threaten in their arrogant way that if they were left to fend for themselves they would 'kick the King's crown into the Boyne', but it was scarcely in the nature of loyal English Unionists to deprive the northern Protestants of the protection of the Union Jack. At this period, however, the Ulster question was not fully appreciated, although in 1886 there were bad riots in Belfast against Home Rule, and Churchill, always prompt on a political trail that was both hot and strong, urged Ulster to fight.

When the new Parliament met in January 1886 the Salisbury Government was defeated and resigned, and Gladstone was summoned to office for the third time. His aim was to pass a Bill for Irish Home Rule. He hoped still to retain a united party and he induced Joseph Chamberlain to take office. Chamberlain accepted, but in less than two months resigned as he could not approve of the nature and extent of Gladstone's Irish project. Other eminent Liberals stood aside, horrified at Gladstone's apparently sudden conversion on Home Rule and also offended at the old leader's secretive methods and his private and personal act in committing the Party to so radical and new a course. Old John Bright stood out, the lawyers Selborne and James, the financier and administrator Goschen. Yet in the main the ranks of the party stood surprisingly firm. Unlike Peel, Gladstone never became an emperor without an army and indeed he was always an army in himself. Placing a new young disciple, John Morley, the rising savant and journalist politician, at the Irish Office, Gladstone bent to his task. The Bill which he introduced was to set up an Irish legislature and executive in Dublin with general authority over the whole of Ireland subject to certain reserved matters such as defence, foreign policy, trade, and navigation. Ireland was to return no members to Westminster, a point much objected to until Gladstone, too late, offered to consider amendment. But when the vote came, as many as 93 Liberals opposed the Bill; conciliation and concession to Ireland they wanted by all means, but not what seemed to them an irreversible abdication of British authority and a reversal of the idea of union. Gladstone asked for a dissolution, which the Queen granted, and the country returned a Parliament adverse to Home Rule. Chamberlain's hard-won gains in the counties were mostly lost, for the rural voters cared little for Irish affairs and had been disturbed by a proposal which Gladstone had devised to accompany Home Rule, namely, a generous Land Purchase Bill for Ireland. The simple English labourers had thought that the Liberals were anxious to give *them* land of their own. Many reverted to the older tendency to regard

Liberals as tedious people talking unintelligibly about something that did not matter very much to ordinary English chaps.

Salisbury took office on the meeting of the new Parliament, for Gladstone fully understood his defeat; as he remarked jauntily to his son, 'My word, Herbert, we have had a drubbing and no mistake.' Salisbury had 316 Conservatives proper against 191 Gladstonian Liberals. The Irish Nationalists numbered 85, and the Liberal Unionists 78. Salisbury had a majority of 40 over the combined Liberal and Nationalist forces. He could hold office with safety, provided the Liberal Unionists did not actively join the Opposition. Nor did they. Anger with Parnell, who had doublecrossed them, and with Gladstone, who had tried to dragoon them, kept them aloof from the old Liberals until, slowly, new links were forged which were by 1895 to bring the Liberal Unionists into office and full alliance with Conservatives and even cause the name of Conservative to be almost superseded by that of Unionist. By 1886 the main lines of British politics had been set for the rest of the century. A great accretion of strength had come to the Conservatives, so dispirited in 1880. Not only had many of the wealthier and patrician elements, what was generally called the Whig strain of the party, been carried over, but also there were large numbers of Radicals. John Bright and Joseph Chamberlain were not isolated figures. Birmingham, which had been a frightening bastion of radicalism, jutting out into Southern England, was now solidly 'unionist'. Radical in the general grammatical sense of the word it might remain, as when in 1900 the Birmingham mob nearly captured and lynched the pacifist Lloyd George. It was open to new cries, to imperialism, to protectionism. It became zealous for the armed services, eager to maintain naval supremacy. In no other area than Birmingham was there such a complete swing-over from radicalism to unionism, but in all parts of the country the Liberals lost strength which they could ill afford to lose from the point of view either of numbers or energy.

Lord Salisbury ruled Britain for six full years with a Cabinet of considerable ability. Churchill, who was given the Exchequer, soon resigned and gradually fell out of the centre of public attention as his health declined. Goschen replaced him, the first of the old Liberals to take office. W. H. Smith led the Commons with discretion. At the Irish Office the Prime Minister's nephew,

A. J. Balfour, soon made a name for himself as he set out to provide 'twenty years of firm government' for Ireland. Regarded previously as little more than a dilettante, an unimportant hench- man of Lord Randolph Churchill, the young Irish Secretary was soon known to his enemies as Bloody Balfour. But the odium he aroused in Ireland was compensated by the admiration with which he was regarded by his supporters in Great Britain. It was an inevitable consequence of the Irish policy of drawing attention to their wrongs and extorting concessions by violence that the effect on many Englishmen was to stiffen their backs and to regard with pride and gratitude a Minister who refused to allow the authority of the British Crown to be humiliated and abused.

For Great Britain was now in the full current of proud, imperial enthusiasm. The year 1887 saw the first jubilee of Queen Victoria with its tremendous surge of loyal emotion, national pride, and a sense of imperial destiny. Men felt that the splendid words of Virgil were to be sounded again for the British people:

Tu regere imperio populos, Romane, memento.

Nor, when they compared British rule with that of their rivals in the present or their antetypes in the past, did they feel that we had neglected the poet's injunction to spare the subject and repel the proud. With such broad visions before them people could turn a deaf ear to the mouthings of Irish Nationalists when they groaned 'Remember Mitchelstown', or raked up some other fracas in which the hand of the law had struck with less than its usual lenity against seditious agitators. The unoccupied spaces of the world were rapidly filling up. In 1885 Bechuanaland in South Africa was placed under British protection. At the beginning of the next year Upper Burma was annexed, Socotra was placed under British protection; Eastern New Guinea was partitioned between Germany and Britain; a charter was granted to the Royal Niger Company in West Africa, and the gold rush began in the Transvaal, drawing the attention of the world to that previously unimportant stretch of veldt. In 1887 a Colonial Conference met in London; Zululand was annexed, Pondoland made a Protec- torate, while New Zealand annexed Kerdamec Island. In 1888 the North Borneo Protectorate was formed and a charter granted to the British East Africa Company. The British Chartered Com- pany in South Africa was founded and great mining concessions began to be exploited. In 1890 Cecil Rhodes became Prime Minister of Cape Colony, and his colleague, Dr. Jameson, entered Rhodesia and occupied Mashonaland on behalf of the British South Africa Company. Less than fifty years had elapsed since David Livingstone had begun his first journeys into the interior of Africa and already the European Powers were filling it up. In all these questions there were hard and close negotiations with colonial rivals, above all with Bismarck and Germany. Neither Salisbury at the Foreign Office nor his Liberal predecessor Granville from 1880-5 had shown very hard resistance to German claims. Salisbury was firm for the maintenance of what he called Britain's greatest interest, peace, and there was a general feeling that the great German nation was entitled to its share of African dominion. In the eighteen-nineties the sharpest disputes were to be with France in Siam and the Sudan. Englishmen could afford to be generous. Not only did they possess the Cape and many of the most vital and fertile parts of Africa, but Singapore and the Malayan Peninsula was securely held under protectorate. The Indian Empire was the marvel of the world. Most valuable of all, Britain alone had retained or found lands where people of her own race could settle under their own flag and grow into nations under the Crown. Canada, Australia, and New Zealand, in spite of social and political strains at times acute and even dangerous, were developing their own forms of constitutional democracy. One great concession was made to Germany in return for a settlement of disputed claims on the East African coast; the island of Heligoland, occupied by Britain in the Napoleonic wars, was ceded to Germany. To farseeing strategists it might seem a fatal error, but in 1890 Germany was not yet a naval rival nor did Englishmen feel that a war with our 'cousins', our fellow Teutons, our fellow Protestants, the countrymen of Luther, was a legitimate object of political speculation. Russia still seemed the most likely enemy, France the most insidious rival.

In home affairs the Ministry was usefully active. Its most important political achievement was the Local Government Act of 1888, which set up, for the first time, elected County Councils in England, which took over most of the administrative functions of the Justices of the Peace and also powers exercised by other boards or authorities. The work of this Act was completed by the Local Government Act of 1894 passed by the succeeding, Liberal,

Government. This established Parish Councils and organized the urban and rural districts within the counties. London, always an exception and often an anomaly in government and administration, was placed under a County Council and later, in 1899, divided into subordinate 'Boroughs', which replaced the antique parishes. In Whitehall there was continued growth. The Board of Agriculture was created in 1889, and the Board of Trade was expanding in activity and power. Education required more regulation from the centre, but this was still under the Privy Council Office until 1899. Social reform in this period crept gingerly forward in such matters as the extension of employers' liability and stricter application of factory laws. Yet there could be no radical change in social matters and no major attack on what were recognized to be the greatest social evils of the time (other than drink), unemployment, insecurity for industrial workers, and the dreadful slums of the towns. Before these could be tackled, certain principles had to be accepted, namely, graduated taxation of higher incomes, compulsory contributory and State-assisted insurance, and the subsidizing of house-building from public revenues. All these had to wait until the twentieth century. Yet during the last fifteen years of Queen Victoria's reign there were working some gifted and hard-minded men and women, teaching rather than preaching about the need to make the hand of the State stronger and more generous in its efforts to fight squalor and poverty. These were the so-called Fabian Socialists, whose Society was founded in 1884. They concentrated with ruthless energy on their mission. It was the phenomena of social evil in the towns that mostly engaged their attention; their influence in rural and agricultural life was slight, and they could scarcely raise their heads from their work to consider foreign and imperial questions.

Lord Salisbury is a figure who has not left a deep impress on the national memory for many reasons, of which, perhaps, the most important is that he disdained to impress the public. He was the Queen's first Minister, also her Principal Secretary for Foreign Affairs. His work was to direct the Government rather than to lead a party or to convert the public. Even more than Disraeli he was a foil to Gladstone, for Disraeli and Gladstone were rival types of political artists. Salisbury was a political philistine, and his contempt for anything which savoured of cant or idealism or propaganda could be reckoned as a fault even by those who were normally his supporters. To the public in general and in particular to the upper and middle class public he gave a feeling of comfort and security, of a man who, while provoking no one, would never suffer the dignity and safety of the State to be disparaged or threatened.

The British Empire might roll on in majesty, but it still had to reckon with Charles Stewart Parnell. Balfour was having some success in his firm handling of Ireland and, although Irish, like English, agriculture was suffering from falling prices, the Land Acts were having some good effect and conditions were improving. Two dramatic events brought Parnell personally to the very front of the stage. *The Times* newspaper in 1887, in a series of articles entitled 'Parnellism and Crime', in addition to many grave charges of abetting agrarian outrages, positively accused Parnell of being accessory after the fact to the murder of Burke and Cavendish in 1882. The charge was supported by a facsimile letter alleged to be in Parnell's own hand. Parnell denied the charge, but took no further action, but in 1888, in legal proceedings started by another Irish member, more incriminating documents were produced. Parnell asked the House for a select committee, but the Government appointed instead a special commission of three judges, a device more familiar now than then. The result of a long and painful investigation lasting more than a year was to pile up damaging evidence against the Nationalist politicians. But on the one dramatic charge based on the letters which purported to be in his hand, approving of the murders, he was triumphantly acquitted. The letters were shown to be forgeries and the forger, one Pigott, fled the country and took his own life. Parnell enjoyed wild popularity in Liberal circles, and it seemed as if the next election would bring victory to the Home Rule cause. But in less than two years from his vindication at the inquiry, Parnell was politically ruined by his appearance in the divorce court as co-respondent on the petition of his mistress's husband, Captain O'Shea.

It must be remembered that public exposure in the divorce courts at this time generally excluded a man from the highest places in public life. Five years previously the admirably competent Liberal Minister, Sir Charles Dilke, had been forced out of public life and never afterwards was he admitted to office.

Furthermore, both the Dilke and Parnell cases had in them elements of the odious and the ludicrous; they were no ordinary
affairs. It was difficult for the Liberal party to carry on its campaign
for Home Rule when the Irish leader stood so clearly discredited
in his private life. Gladstone, forced to give judgment, not on a
man's moral conduct, but on a political issue, agreed that Parnell
had to be informed that his retirement was necessary for the sake
of political expediency. The testing moment of Parnell's career
had now arrived. Which would he put first, his avowed aim of
self-government for Ireland or the continued practice of his
unique art of leadership? He did not lack good advice. Friends so
remote and unlikely as Cecil Rhodes and Andrew Carnegie
advised him to retire for the time being. He did not listen. By
his secretive movements he evaded service of a letter which Gladstone had sent to him by Morley and allowed his almost craven
followers to re-elect him leader. Gladstone's letter was then
published and so assumed the appearance of an ultimatum. After
terrible and bitter debates, 44 Nationalist members abjured Parnell
and 26 supported him. The battle was then transferred to Ireland
and waged in every town, in every Catholic and Nationalist
household. The Church declared against Parnell, and although
he put up candidates at by-elections against the orthodox
Nationalists, he was each time defeated. In these contests he wore
himself out and died in October 1891. It is often said that he was
offered as a victim to the Nonconformist conscience of England,
a foolish phrase, as if the English Dissenters had a monopoly of
the Seventh Commandment. It would be truer to say that he
was a victim to canon law, to the unvarying practice of the
Roman Catholic Church exercising its prerogative of sitting in
judgment over mortal sin. Yet Parnell had done for Ireland more
than any man since the great Liberator O'Connell himself. If he
failed at the last moment to achieve his ambition of self-government it was because he was of the stamp of Lucifer; not adultery
but pride was his radical sin, and when the promised land stood
open to him he preferred that his people should not enter it
rather than that they should enter under another commander.
Even his loyal and faithful disciple, John Redmond, a better, a
wiser but less powerful man, was to die the other side of Jordan,
with the Irish Treaty still three years in the future.

The Liberals indeed did come back to office after the General

Election of 1892. But they were in a minority in Great Britain and could only make up a majority from Ireland. With the support of nine Parnellites and 72 anti-Parnellites they had a margin of only 39 over the Unionist Opposition. Gladstone formed his Fourth Administration, which is known in history bracketed with the name of Rosebery, the brilliant young Scottish Peer who served at the Foreign Office in 1886 and again from 1892 to February 1894 when by the Queen's personal choice he succeeded Gladstone. Sir William Harcourt, previously Attorney-General and Home Secretary, was at the Exchequer and led the House of Commons after Gladstone's retirement. Campbell-Bannerman took the War Office, where he had previously served in subordinate office. A Midland lawyer, Fowler, was first of all at the Local Government Board and later at the India Office. Gladstone's disciple Morley went back to the Irish Secretaryship to work for the Second Home Rule Bill. Amongst newer and younger men in the Ministry were Bryce, a learned Oxford lawyer, Sir Edward Grey, a Northumberland baronet, who was given his apprenticeship as Under-Secretary at the Foreign Office, and Asquith, perhaps the most superb product of Balliol College at its prime, who, as Home Secretary, handled all his business with perfect polish and efficiency.

The principal task of this Ministry was to pass a Second Home Rule Bill, similar to the first, but providing this time for Irish Representation at Westminster. During 85 sittings the House of Commons wrestled with this elaborate project, doomed as all men knew to rejection by the Lords, and Gladstone, at the age of 84, dominated the interminable debates. Chamberlain was the most vigorous and dangerous opponent, and John Redmond, with his eloquence, began to establish his ascendancy in the Irish Nationalist ranks. When all was over, the Lords rejected the Bill by the crushing majority of 419 to 41. Gladstone before his retirement pointed the moral, which was that the absolute veto of the House of Lords could not be indefinitely endured and that 'the matter must go forward to its issue'.

For the rest, this Government ruled capably and effectively, showing how a small, well-disciplined majority can hold the reins of government, a conception not easy to grasp by those who have been accustomed to the elephantine landslides of the period after 1918. In foreign and colonial affairs the Ministry maintained a balance between those who were of the Gladstonian school, nicknamed the Little Englanders, and the Imperialists. At the last moment the necessary support was given which led to the acquisition by Britain of Uganda in the face of German ambitions. At home the Local Government Act, already referred to, developed the machinery for more efficient administration and more effective representative control of local affairs. Asquith at the Home Office passed a new and comprehensive Factory Act and only desisted from an Employers' Liability Bill when it was heavily amended in the Lords. In general, the Liberal party was showing signs of quasi-socialist influences which spurred it on towards social reform. The National Liberal Federation, which provided a kind of Annual Parliament for the party, had, in 1891, produced its famous Newcastle programme which foreshadowed, however faintly, the Liberal party's destiny as the pioneer of what was, but was rarely described, by the continental term of social democracy. Harcourt, the Chancellor of the Exchequer, in his budget of 1894 had introduced death duties, that is, graduated duties on the total amount of an estate and not merely legacy duties. Another sign of Liberal sensitiveness to social problems was their advocacy of Local Veto, legislation empowering the electors in local government areas to vote against the issue of licences for the sale of alcohol. Since 1918 Scotland has possessed but made little use of this boon; it had little chance of success in England, and was one of the main causes of the Liberal defeat in the election of 1895 when the Government, defeated over an item in the Army Estimates, rather weakly resigned and allowed Lord Salisbury to face the dissolution of Parliament with all the prestige of office regained. Salisbury's authority stood as high as ever. Conservatism allied with unionism was invincible. The forces that were to threaten it from afar off seemed then inconspicuous. In 1893 the Independent Labour Party had been formed, and a Scotsman of evangelic cast, Keir Hardie, its first chairman, actually sat in Parliament from 1892 to 1895. Of greater significance perhaps was the appearance at a by-election in 1890 of David Lloyd George, a young Welsh lawyer of twenty-six, as Liberal member for Carnarvon Boroughs. It was to be his destiny to be the effective legislator of social reform two decades later. Lloyd George, when he came into the House, found as its 'Father', its senior member, the great Gladstone. These two men overlapped for four years; they knew each other personally, for Lloyd George was once summoned to dinner with Gladstone and has told us since how the old Nestor warned him of the evils and dangers of Bismarck's Germany. It was in 1944 that Lloyd George himself ceased to be the Father of the House. The careers of these two men, both Prime Ministers, cover 112 years, dating from the young Gladstone's election for Newark to the strange 'reformed' Parliament of 1832. Such is the continuity of English political life and institutions. As the last decade of the century ran to its close in the fevers and frights of imperialism, in the gnawing strain of a growing social conscience and shafts of cold fear at the prospect of a hostile Europe, containing in its heart the best organized military force known to history, the English people could pass from year to year confident in the ordered and regular rhythm of a political system made venerable by the traditions of the past and kept active by the pulsations of a generation both intelligent and virile.

Chronological Table

1851–1895

To assist the reader in spanning the gap between Volume IV of Professor Halévy's *History* and the beginning of Volume V, this Table has been appended. It is divided into the arbitrary and always dubious categories of political, social and economic, and cultural events. In addition to the most important events in British political history, some outstanding events in European and world history are noted. Important developments in science and industry are given with the proviso that dates of inventions are always disputable, and some authorities cite the first discovery of a principle, others the completed and marketable invention. In the section headed 'Cultural', notice is taken of important or popular books, but only one or two of the works of the most famous authors are cited. Works by authors or artists outside the United Kingdom are cited sparingly, the intention being to give the reader a general idea of the time at which famous books or works were actually published for the first time. In some cases the influence of such works in England was felt considerably later.

For fuller chronological information readers are referred to the following books, to which the author expresses his obligation:

Arthur Hassall: *British History Chronologically Arranged.*
Gooch, G. P.: *Annals of Culture and Politics.*
Steinberg, S. H.: *Historical Tables.*
Young, G. M.: *Victorian England.* Chronological Appendix.

R. B. McC.

	POLITICAL	SOCIAL AND ECONOMIC	CULTURAL
1851	Ecclesiastical Titles Bill Coup d'état of Louis Napoleon in France (Dec.) Palmerston dismissed Granville Foreign Secretary	Window Tax repealed The Great Exhibition in Hyde Park Gold discoveries in Australia Bunsen Burner invented Perkin discovers aniline purple	Kingsley: Yeast George Borrow: Lavengro Death of Wordsworth University Commission proposes reforms at Oxford Tenniel begins to draw for Punch
1852	Russell Ministry resigns: Derby Prime Minister (Feb.) Dissolution of Parliament Louis Napoleon Emperor Disraeli's budget rejected Derby resigns: Lord Aberdeen forms Coalition Ministry	New Houses of Parliament opened Common Law Procedure Act First Congress of Co-operative Societies in London	Thackeray: Esmond
1853	Indian Civil Service open to competition Gladstone's first budget Russian Army invades Moldavia (July) Turkey declares war on Russia (Oct.) Turkish Fleet destroyed at Sinope Anglo-French Fleet enters Black Sea (Dec.)	Telegraph system in India Brunel constructs Saltash Bridge	Kingsley: Hypatia Charlotte Brontë: Villette Ruskin: Stones of Venice completed Dickens: Bleak House

	POLITICAL	SOCIAL AND ECONOMIC	CULTURAL
1854	Britain and France declare war on Russia (March) Colonial Secretaryship of State separated from Secretaryship of State for War Allied armies land in Crimea (Sept.) Battles of Alma, Balaclava, and Inkerman British Navy operates against Russian Black Sea forts	First railways in India Goebell invents electric bulbs Compound steam engine adapted to marine use	British Medical Association founded Milman: *History of Latin Christianity* Dickens: *Hard Times*
1855	Resignation of Aberdeen's Ministry. Palmerston Prime Minister (Jan.) Fall of Sebastopol (Sept.)	Wood invents hypodermic syringe Paris World Exhibition Merchant Shipping Act Printing telegraph invented	Longfellow: *Hiawatha* First Civil Service Commission appointed
1856	Treaty of Paris ends Crimean War Dispute with China over the *Arrow* Canton bombarded (Nov.) Vice-President of Council appointed to take charge of education	Bessemer invents process of converting iron into steel First production of aniline dyes Matrimonial Causes Act sets up Divorce Court	Pasteur Professor at Paris Froude: *History of England*, first volume Motley: *Rise of Dutch Republic*

	POLITICAL	SOCIAL AND ECONOMIC	CULTURAL
1857	Vote of Censure on Palmerston over *Arrow* affair carried Dissolution of Parliament Majority of 70 for Palmerston Courts of Probate and Divorce created Fenian Brotherhood founded British Navy takes Canton Outbreak of Indian Mutiny (March) Lucknow finally relieved (Nov.) Cawnpore captured (Dec.)	Denmark abolished dues on ships entering the Baltic First Atlantic cable laid Severe commercial crisis	Cambridge University Bill National Portrait Gallery founded Buckle: *History of Civilisation*, Vol. I Flaubert: *Madame Bovary* Trollope: *Barchester Towers*
1858	Princess Royal married to Crown Prince of Prussia Palmerston defeated on Conspiracy to Murder Bill Second Derby Ministry Property qualification for Members of Parliament removed Powers and lands of East India Company transferred to the Crown. Lord Canning first Viceroy (Nov.)	Emancipation of serfs in Russia begun Anglo-Japanese commercial treaty	Carlyle: *Frederick the Great* Dental Hospital founded Oxford and Cambridge Local Examinations instituted
1859	Derby Ministry resigns on defeat of Reform Bill Parliament dissolved War between France and Sardinia with Austria Palmerston Prime Minister (June) Fenian agitators tried, condemned, and later released	Suez Canal begun First electric light plant in New York Spectrum analysis discovered	Darwin: *Origin of Species* Mill: *On Liberty* Meredith: *Richard Feverel* Sinai MS. of New Testament discovered by Tischendorf Smiles: *Self Help* Tennyson: *Idylls of the King*

	POLITICAL	SOCIAL AND ECONOMIC	CULTURAL
1860	Paper Duties Repeal Bill, rejected by Lords Commercial Treaty with France Maori rising in New Zealand Operation by French and British troops in Pekin	Source of Nile discovered	Ruskin: *Unto this Last* G. Eliot: *The Mill on the Floss* *Essays and Reviews*, by Temple, Jowett and others
1861	Outbreak of American Civil War (April) Paper Duties repealed (June) Death of Cavour (June) The *Trent* Affair (Nov.) Death of Prince Albert (Dec.)	First British iron warship Post Office Savings Bank opened Tariff Act in U.S.A. Reiss invents first telephone	Eliot: *Silas Marner* Mrs. Beeton: *Cookery Book* Wagner: *Tannhäuser* Lister Professor of Surgery at Glasgow Tolstoy: *War and Peace* Mill: *Representative Government*
1862	Lincoln proclaims freedom of slaves Bismarck Prime Minister of Prussia	Lancashire Cotton Famine World Exhibition in London Liebig sets up first extract of meat factory in Uruguay Limited Liability Act	Colenso controversy Victor Hugo: *Les Misérables* Turgeniev: *Fathers and Sons*
1863	Prince of Wales marries Alexandra of Denmark Polish rising in Russia Britain cedes Ionian Islands to Greece Confederate defeat at Gettysburg	First international postal congress First underground railway in London	Lyell: *Antiquity of Man* Mill: *Utilitarianism* Death of Thackeray Huxley: *Man's Place in Nature*

	POLITICAL	SOCIAL AND ECONOMIC	CULTURAL
1864	Austro-Prussian Army invades Holstein (Feb.). British Government remains neutral Denmark cedes Schleswig and Holstein (Oct.) Geneva (Red Cross) Convention for protection of wounded	Octavia Hill starts movement for housing reform International Workers' Association founded in London	Swinburne: *Atalanta in Calydon* Newman: *Apologia pro Vita Sua* Pope Pius IX issues syllabus *Quanta Cura* condemning liberalism, socialism, and rationalism
1865	Surrender of Lee ends American Civil War (April) President Lincoln assassinated (April) General Election. Liberal majority 67 Death of Palmerston (Oct.) Russell Prime Minister	Steam tonnage on Lloyd's Register exceeds sailing ships First International Telegraph Congress in Paris Cattle plague in England	Clerk-Maxwell: *Treatise on Electricity and Magnetism* Tolstoy: *War and Peace* Lewis Carroll: *Alice in Wonderland*
1866	Russell resigns on defeat of Reform Bill (June) Derby Prime Minister Defeat of Austrians by Prussia at Sadowa (July) Habeas corpus suspended in Ireland	Siemens invents dynamo Commercial panic Bank Charter Act suspended Cobden Club founded	Huxley: *Elementary Philosophy* Mrs. Eddy founds Christian Science Dostoevsky: *Crime and Punishment*
1867	Disraeli's Reform Act passed Austro-Hungarian Union British North America Act Bismarck forms North German Confederation	Typewriter invented Nobel invents dynamite	Karl Marx: *Das Kapital*, Vol. I Ibsen: *Peer Gynt* Strauss: *Blue Danube Waltz* Bagehot: *English Constitution* University Extension Movement begun

	POLITICAL	SOCIAL AND ECONOMIC	CULTURAL
1868	Disraeli succeeds Derby as Prime Minister (Feb.) Disraeli defeated on Irish Church question (April) General Election. Liberal majority 168 (Nov.) Shogunate abolished in Japan (Feb.) Gladstone Prime Minister (Dec.)		Browning: *Ring and the Book* William Morris: *Earthly Paradise*, Vol. I Brahms: *German Requiem*
1869	Disestablishment of Irish Church Fenian rising in Canada Britain buys territories of Hudson Bay Company	Suez Canal opened Post Office takes over all telegraph lines	Vatican Council meets Matthew Arnold: *Culture and Anarchy* Blackmore: *Lorna Doone*
1870	Franco-Prussian War (July) French defeat at Sedan (Sept.) Republic proclaimed in Paris Italians enter Rome Irish Land Bill passed (Aug.) Education Act Manitoba made Canadian province	Kimberley diamond diggings opened Telegraph with India opened	Dogma of Papal Infallibility proclaimed Schliemann begins to excavate Troy Death of Dickens Open competition for Civil Services

	POLITICAL	SOCIAL AND ECONOMIC	CULTURAL
1871	London Conference abrogates restrictions imposed on Russian Naval Arguments in Black Sea (Jan.) Abolition of purchase of Commissions in the Army Trades Union Act legalizes Unions Criminal Law Amendment Act makes intimidation illegal Local Government Board set up German Empire proclaimed at Versailles (Jan.) Peace between Germany and France; Treaty of Frankfort (May)	Germany adopts gold standard Mont Cenis Tunnel	University Religious Tests abolished Darwin: *Descent of Man* First Impressionist Exhibition at Paris Swinburne: *Songs before Sunrise* Slade School founded Clerk-Maxwell Professor of Physics at Cambridge; Cavendish Laboratory founded
1872	Ballot Act becomes Law *Alabama* arbitration award Responsible Government in Cape Colony	National Union of Agricultural Workers founded Strikes of police, bakers, and gas workers in London Midland Railway puts third-class carriages on all its trains	H. Spencer: *Study of Sociology* Matthew Arnold: *Literature and Dogma* Butler: *Erewhon* Albert Memorial completed
1873	Gladstone resigns on defeat of Irish University Bill, but resumes office Judicature Bill passed	Severe economic crisis in America and Europe Railway Commission	Fitzjames Stephen: *Liberty, Equality and Fraternity* Pater: *Studies in the Renaissance*

	POLITICAL	SOCIAL AND ECONOMIC	CULTURAL
1874	General Election. Conservative majority 50 (Jan.) Disraeli Prime Minister Abolition of Church patronage in Scotland	Factory Act institutes 56-hour week	Green: *History of English People* Stubbs: *Constitutional History* Public Worship Regulation Act
1875	Gladstone resigns leadership of Liberal party. Hartington succeeds him Rising in Bosnia-Herzegovina (July) Republican Constitution established in France	Agricultural Holdings Act Labourers' Dwellings Act Friendly Societies Act Public Health Act	Mason College, Birmingham, founded Theosophical Society founded Mark Twain: *Tom Sawyer*
1876	Britain purchases Suez Canal shares (Feb.) Queen becomes Empress of India (March) Bulgarian Atrocities (May) British Fleet sent into Turkish waters Serbia and Montenegro declare war on Turkey (July) Disraeli Earl of Beaconsfield (Aug.) New Zealand formed into one Colony	Invention of telephone by Bell First Socialist International dissolved Industrial and Provident Societies Act	Bayreuth Opera House opened G. O. Trevelyan: *Life of Macaulay*

	POLITICAL	SOCIAL AND ECONOMIC	CULTURAL
1877	Conference of Powers fails to reach settlement of Turkish question. Warlike feeling in England (Jan.) London Protocol of Powers call on Turks for reforms (March) British annexation of Transvaal (March) Russia declares war on Turkey (April) Russians take Plevna (Dec.)	Edison invents phonograph	Tolstoy: *Anna Karenina* Ibsen: *Pillars of Society* Wimbledon Club standardizes rules of Lawn Tennis
1878	British Fleet ordered to Turkish waters (Jan.) Lord Derby resigns (March) Salisbury Foreign Minister Reserves called out; Indian troops sent to Malta (April) Secret agreement with Turkey secures Cyprus for Britain (June) Congress of Berlin (July) Settlement of Balkan question Invasion of Afghanistan (Sept.) Preliminary Treaty of San Stefano between Russia and Turkey (March)	Mannlicher invents repeating rifle Hughes invents microphone Wheat falls in price from 52 shillings to 46 shillings a quarter	Lecky: *History of England in the XVIIth Century*, Vol. I Stanley: *Through the Dark Continent* Hardy: *Return of the Native* First visit of Australian cricket team to England

	POLITICAL	SOCIAL AND ECONOMIC	CULTURAL
1879	Zulus defeat British at Isandhlwana (Jan.) British defeat Zulus at Ulundi (July) Sir Louis Cavagnari murdered at Kabul (Sept.) Afghan War renewed. General Roberts enters Kabul	Protectionist laws in Germany Edison perfects electric bulb Wet summer a disaster to harvest	Meredith: *The Egoist* Henry George: *Progress and Poverty* St. Thomas Aquinas declared Doctor Ecclesiae
1880	Dissolution of Parliament (March) Liberals 357; Conservatives 265; Nationalists 62 (April) Gladstone Prime Minister End of Afghan War (Sept.) Transvaal declared independent (Oct.) Transvaal Boers attack British garrisons (Dec.)	Relief of Distress Act for Ireland Employers' Liability Bill Boycotting begun in Ireland	Newnes founds *Tit-Bits* Edwin Arnold: *Light of Asia* Shorthouse: *John Inglesant*
1881	Irish Coercion Bill (Jan.) Boers defeat British at Majuba (Feb.) Death of Lord Beaconsfield (April) Boer independence restored subject to British suzerainty (Aug.) Nationalist rising in Egypt (Sept.) Irish Land Act (Aug.)	Canadian Pacific Railway formed Standard Oil Company founded Hyndman founds the Democratic (later Social Democratic) Federation	Revised version of New Testament Ranke: *History of the World* Verdi: *Aida*

	POLITICAL	SOCIAL AND ECONOMIC	CULTURAL
1882	Phoenix Park murders in Dublin Coercion Bill (May) Bombardment of Alexandria (July) Battle of Tel-el-Kebir (Sept.) British occupy Egypt and Sudan	Married Women's Property Act First breech-loading guns fitted on British warships	Seeley: *Natural Religion* Stevenson: *Treasure Island*
1883	Kruger elected President of South African Republic (May) Federal Convention in Sydney British Government decides to evacuate Sudan, after defeat of Hicks Pasha's force	Benz and Daimler factories established Fabian Society founded Maxim gun invented	Seeley: *Expansion of England* Nietzsche: *Zarathustra*
1884	Gordon sent to withdraw British forces from Sudan (Feb.) Convention recognizes the Transvaal as South African Republic subject to veto on foreign treaties British Protectorate over Niger coast and over New Guinea Franchise Bill introduced Gordon relief expedition starts (Sept.)	St. Gotthard Tunnel opened	Victoria University of Manchester, Liverpool, and Leeds *Oxford English Dictionary* begins to appear Toynbee: *Industrial Revolution*

	POLITICAL	SOCIAL AND ECONOMIC	CULTURAL
1885	Death of Gordon and fall of Khartoum (Jan.) Russian occupation of Penjedh in Afghanistan causes danger of war Redistribution of Seats Bill Gladstone defeated on budget. Salisbury Prime Minister (June) Office of Secretary for Scotland created Irish Land Purchase Bill General Election. Liberals 331; Conservatives 247; Nationalists 82	Gold discovered in Transvaal Gottfried Daimler patents the high-speed internal-combustion engine	*Dictionary of National Biography* begun under editorship of Leslie Stephen Rider Haggard: *King Solomon's Mines* Pater: *Marius the Epicurean* Gilbert and Sullivan: *The Mikado* Dicey: *Law of the Constitution*
1886	Salisbury Government resigns. Gladstone Prime Minister Unemployed riots in Trafalgar Square. John Burns and Hyndman arrested Chamberlain resigns from Gladstone's Ministry (March) Orange riots in Belfast (June) Home Rule Bill defeated in Commons (June) General Election (July). Conservatives 316; Liberals 191; Nationalists 85; Liberal Unionists 78	Gold-rush in Transvaal American Federation of Labor founded First safety bicycles manufactured for sale at Coventry First British steel battleship built Wheat falls to 31 shillings a quarter Royal Commission on Depression in Trade	*English Historical Review* founded Anson: *Law and Custom of the Constitution*

	POLITICAL	SOCIAL AND ECONOMIC	CULTURAL
1887	Queen's Jubilee (June) Land League in Ireland proclaimed illegal		Stevenson: *Kidnapped* Conan Doyle: *Study in Scarlet*
1888	Accession of Kaiser Wilhelm II in Germany (March) Local Government Act sets up County Councils Parnell inquiry opened (Oct.)	First railway in China Baghdad railway projected Pasteur Institute established Hertz detects electromagnetic waves Dunlop patents pneumatic tyres	Doughty: *Arabia Deserta* Kipling: *Plain Tales from the Hills* Rodin: *Burghers of Calais* Mrs. Humphrey Ward: *Robert Elles-mere*
1889	Board of Agriculture set up Death of John Bright Naval Defence Act	London dockers' strike led by John Burns	Bernard Shaw: *Fabian Essays* Jerome: *Three Men in a Boat* Booth: *Life and Labour* Ibsen: *Doll's House*, performed in London
1890	Bismarck dismissed (March) Anglo-German Agreement (July) over Zanzibar and Heligoland First Japanese Diet (Nov.) Parnell divorce case	Anti-slavery Congress in Brussels McKinley protectionist tariff in U.S.A. Baring's Bank crisis Forth Bridge completed	Booth: *Darkest England* Stanley: *Darkest Africa* Fraser: *Golden Bough* Mahan: *Influence of Sea Power*, Vol. I
1891	Franco-Russian Alliance (Aug.) Death of Parnell (Oct.) Liberals' Newcastle programme	Trans-Siberian railway begun Fees abolished in elementary schools	Church: *Oxford Movement* Marshall: *Principle of Economics*

	POLITICAL	SOCIAL AND ECONOMIC	CULTURAL
1892	General Election. Liberals 273; Nationalists 81; Conservatives 268; Liberal Unionists 47 (July) Salisbury resigns Gladstone Prime Minister	Small-holdings Act Public Libraries Act	Hardy: *Tess of the D'Urbervilles* Kipling: *Barrack-Room Ballads* Death of Tennyson
1893	Independent Labour Party founded Irish Home Rule Bill rejected by Lords Welsh Church Bill also rejected Dispute with French over Siam	Agricultural Rates Act Second Married Women's Property Act	University of Wales Bradley: *Appearance and Reality* Francis Thompson: *Poems* Tschaikovsky: *Pathetic Symphony*
1894	Gladstone resigns (March) Harcourt's death duties Massacres of Armenians in Turkey War between China and Japan Local Government Act	Manchester Ship Canal completed Panhard motor-car designed	Harmsworth and Kennedy Jones acquire *Evening News* Beardsley: *Yellow Book* Kipling: *Jungle Book* Webb: *History of Trade Unionism* Moore: *Esther Waters*
1895	Rosebery's Government defeated in Commons and resigns (June) Salisbury Prime Minister Chamberlain Colonial Secretary General Election. Unionists 411; Liberals 177; Nationalists 82	Röntgen discovers X-rays Lumière brothers invent cinematograph Marconi invents wireless telegraphy	Yeats: *Poems* Sienkiewicz: *Quo Vadis* Hardy: *Jude the Obscure*

Index

Wilson, James, 276
Window tax, 285, 310
Wiseman, M. P. S., Cardinal, 367–8, 369, 370, 372, 374, 376
Women, employment of in mines forbidden, 27
Wood, Sir Charles, 151, 166, 186n., 192, 199, 210, 280, 285n., 286–8, 310, 316; Secretary for India, 324
Woodstock, 421
Wordsworth, William, 315
Work, hours of, 27, 30, 95–6, 137–8, 171–2

World War I, 426–7
Wortley, James Stuart, *see under* Wharncliffe, James Stuart Wortley

Y

'Young England' Movement, 138, 177, 265, 354, 396

Z

Zolverin, the, 51, 216, 275
Zululand annexed (1887), 471

Printed in Great Britain by offset-lithography
by Jarrold & Sons Ltd, Norwich